INTRODUCTION TO PSYCHOLOGY

WITH THE COLLABORATION OF

Lawrence T. Alexander

H. James Bond

Alphonse Chapanis

James Deese

Ward Edwards

Charles W. Eriksen

Wendell R. Garner

Harold W. Hake

Eckhard H. Hess

Richard S. Lazarus

G. Wilson Shaffer

Robert B. Sleight

Eliot Stellar

Stanley B. Williams

INTRODUCTION

1956 NEW YORK TORONTO LONDON

TO PSYCHOLOGY

Clifford T. Morgan

THE JOHNS HOPKINS UNIVERSITY

McGraw-Hill Book Company, Inc.

Library of Congress Catalog Card Number 55-11931

VI

43100

This book is set in Linotype

Electra. The boldface in the display

headings is Spartan Heavy.

Biological drawings are by Gloria

Hirsch. Graphs and other line

work are by the Illustration

Department of the McGraw-Hill

Book Company.

PREFACE

WE BEGAN THE preparation of this textbook with certain definite aims in mind. We wanted, first of all, to bring to the task more fresh ideas than a single author could generate, and we wanted to have more expert treatment of the different topics than is possible if one person attempts to cover them all. We therefore enlisted the aid of 14 psychologists, each of them reasonably expert in the topics on which he was asked to write. Knowing, however, that a symposium usually lacks the unity and balance desired in an introductory book, the principal author asked his collaborators only to *draft* chapters, not to furnish finished manuscripts. He then edited and rewrote each draft. In this way we have tried to attain a relatively uniform style and organization yet secure the advantages of expert authorship. Although the collaborators have reviewed the revisions of their chapters, and other chapters as well, the principal author is solely responsible for the final product.

A second principal aim in writing was to prepare a book so *flexible* in organization and content that it might serve the needs of rather different beginning courses in psychology. Instructors have their habits and tastes in presenting their courses, and they must adapt to the time available for the course as well as the needs of the students they are teaching. We have tried to organize the book so that each instructor can have considerable freedom in planning the material he will cover and the way in which he wishes to do it. In "Suggestions for Instructors" immediately following this preface, we have outlined three different courses for which this book might be used: *a life-oriented course*, a *science-oriented course*, and a *comprehensive course* that includes all the chapters of the book in a somewhat different order from that in which they appear in the text. These outlines are merely examples, and instructors may delete or add chapters in each of them. In writing the chapters, we have kept these alternative courses and sequences in mind, making sure to cross-reference where necessary and to explain each term as it appears. The glossary at the end of the book is also an aid to using the text in different ways.

In making our decisions about the content of the book, we have kept before us the fact that the overwhelming proportion of students in the introductory course will not become majors in psychology. Rather, they come to the course with a heterogeneous array of vocational ambitions and other motives. If the instructor is fortunate enough to have students of similar purposes grouped together in the same class, his selection can be made rather easily. Most instructors, we believe, will want to assign the chapters of Part One, "Principles of Behavior," although some may feel that the chapter "Psychological Measurement" should be omitted. After Part One, different prescriptions can be made for the premedical student, the prelegal student, majors in social science, home economics, engineering, business, and so on. In most courses we know about, the instructor has students with assorted interests in the same class. In that case, we recommend that the course follow one of our brief outlines, with such changes as the instructor thinks appropriate, but that students be encouraged to read other chapters most relevant to their individual interests and fields of specialization.

Most textbook writers find that they do not have the space between two covers of a book to include all the material they feel should be squeezed in. This problem is most acute in preparing an introductory book. Since a choice must be made, our policy has been to aim for broad coverage of the more important and representative areas of psychology, leaving out the topics that are trivial, controversial, or of interest to relatively specialized groups. On the other hand, we have tried to avoid superficiality and to deal soundly with each topic we have chosen to discuss. Many of the decisions we have had to make were difficult, and other writers would have made them differently. We trust, however, that we have succeeded in presenting a fair and representative picture of psychology for the student who is getting his first serious introduction to it.

Many individuals contributed to the preparation of the manuscript. Helene L. Kuhn typed it in its several revisions and managed many of the details of seeing it through to its final form. During the four years that we have conducted the introductory course at Johns Hopkins along the lines of the book, Dr. Peter D. Bricker and Frederick A. King, assistants in the course, have made many helpful suggestions. Several teachers of the introductory course in other colleges and universities have read the manuscript and given us comments and criticisms: Dan L. Adler, San Francisco State College; Harold W. Coppock, University of Oklahoma; Carl P. Duncan, Northwestern University; Don W. Dysinger, University of Nebraska; Granville C. Fisher, University of Miami; J. T. Freeman, Iowa State College; Elmer D. Hinckley, University of Florida; Sherwood C. McIntyre, Alabama Polytechnic Institute; Fred McKinney, University of Missouri; Philip Nogee, Boston University; William C. H. Prentice, Swarthmore College; Robert G. Ruhl, Los Angeles City College; and Kenneth S.

Wagoner, DePauw University. Although we profited greatly from the careful work of these consultants, they are not to be held responsible in any way for the book in its present form.

We should also like to pay tribute to the inventiveness and technical skill of the artists of the McGraw-Hill Illustration Department who prepared the charts and drawings, and to Gloria Hirsch who produced the biological drawings. For planning and selecting many of the excellent pictures we are especially grateful to Martha Swain. And finally we should like to record our appreciation of the assistance and enthusiasm of the editorial and production staffs of the McGraw-Hill Book Company which have gone beyond what an author could reasonably expect from his publisher. Credit is given in the legends of illustrations to the many individuals and publishers who kindly permitted the use of their material.

Clifford T. Morgan

SUGGESTIONS FOR INSTRUCTORS

THIS BOOK HAS been written and organized with the expectation that instructors may find it necessary to omit some chapters and to assign others in an order different from that in the book. Each instructor must make his selection in the light of the time available to him and the needs of his students. In the hope of simplifying this task, we offer here three possible alternative arrangements. In the first two, some chapters are omitted, while in the third all chapters are included; in each case, the instructor may easily omit chapters that are listed in the outline.

A LIFE-ORIENTED COURSE

The following arrangement is suggested for courses in which the purpose is to present students with an introduction to psychology that emphasizes applications to problems of everyday life:

The Science of Psychology (*Chap. 1*)
Techniques of Study (*at the end of the book*)

Personality (*Chap. 9*)
Maturation and Development (*Chap. 2*)
Intellectual Abilities (*Chap. 15*)

Motivation (*Chap. 3*)
Feeling and Emotion (*Chap. 4*)
Frustration and Conflict (*Chap. 10*)
Mental Health and Psychotherapy (*Chap. 11*)

Attention and Perception (*Chap. 7*)
Learning and Remembering (*Chap. 5*)
Imagination and Thinking (*Chap. 6*)

Social Influences on Behavior (*Chap. 12*)
Attitudes and Beliefs (*Chap. 13*)
Prejudice and Social Conflict (*Chap. 14*)

Aptitudes and Vocational Adjustment (*Chap. 16*)
Work and Efficiency (*Chap. 17*)

A SCIENCE-ORIENTED COURSE

The following arrangement is suggested for courses in which the emphasis is on psychology as a fundamental science:

The Science of Psychology (*Chap. 1*)

Animal Behavior (*Chap. 23*)
The Brain and Nervous System (*Chap. 21*)

Maturation and Development (*Chap. 2*)
Learning and Remembering (*Chap. 5*)
Imagination and Thinking (*Chap. 6*)

Motivation (*Chap. 3*)
Feeling and Emotion (*Chap. 4*)

Frustration and Conflict (*Chap. 10*)

Attention and Perception (*Chap. 7*)
Vision (*Chap. 18*)
Hearing and Lower Senses (*Chap. 19*)
Language and Speech (*Chap. 20*)

Psychological Measurement (*Chap. 8*)
Intellectual Abilities (*Chap. 15*)
Personality (*Chap. 9*)

A COMPREHENSIVE COURSE

The following is an alternative arrangement of chapters that may better suit the organization of some courses in psychology than the one used in the book:

The Science of Psychology (*Chap. 1*)

Maturation and Development (*Chap. 2*)
Learning and Remembering (*Chap. 5*)
Techniques of Study (*at the end of the book*)
Imagination and Thinking (*Chap. 6*)

Motivation (*Chap. 3*)
Feeling and Emotion (*Chap. 4*)
Frustration and Conflict (*Chap. 10*)
Mental Health and Psychotherapy (*Chap. 11*)

Psychological Measurement (*Chap. 8*)
Intellectual Abilities (*Chap. 15*)

Personality (*Chap. 9*)
Attitudes and Beliefs (*Chap. 13*)

Aptitudes and Vocational Adjustment (*Chap. 16*)
Work and Efficiency (*Chap. 17*)
Social Influences on Behavior (*Chap. 12*)
Prejudice and Social Conflict (*Chap. 14*)

Attention and Perception (*Chap. 7*)
Vision (*Chap. 18*)
Hearing and Lower Senses (*Chap. 19*)
Language and Speech (*Chap. 20*)

The Brain and Nervous System (*Chap. 21*)
The Internal Environment (*Chap. 22*)
Animal Behavior (*Chap. 23*)

TO THE STUDENT

IN THE FIRST CHAPTER of the book, we define psychology and indicate what the student may expect to learn in studying it. You may take it for granted, however, that psychology deals with many of the problems of everyday life and thus with many things that you have already experienced. You are therefore in a position to derive some personal benefits from the study of psychology. In a formal college course, however, it is not possible for the instructor to relate your particular case to everything that is taught. Hence, to get the most from your course, you must make many of these applications yourself. To do that, you must continually ask yourself, "How does this apply in my experience?" and "How can I put to use what I am learning?" By taking such an attitude, you will profit much more from the course than if you simply learn by rote what is assigned.

As part of the initial preparation for the course, we suggest that you read "Techniques of Study," which has been written especially to help students improve their study habits. This section is placed at the end of the book because it is not part of the main subject matter of psychology, but the information contained in it has been derived from extensive psychological research, and its precepts have been demonstrated to have practical value. Almost every student, even if he is already doing good college work, can improve the effectiveness of his study if he follows the advice given there.

We have some further suggestions for the reading of each chapter as it is assigned. Probably the first thing you should do is read over the summary. It obviously cannot cover everything that is in the chapter, but it does hit the high spots. Then, after reading the summary, it will usually prove worthwhile to skim through the headings before settling down to a careful reading. In the few minutes that it takes to do this, you can add a few details and get the over-all organization in mind.

Many students try to read textbooks the way they read novels; they sit passively, running their eyes over the words and hoping that information will sink in. This is not the way to read textbooks, however, for they are jam packed with facts and explanations. To assimilate them, you should work at the task, reading every sentence carefully and turning over in your mind what it says and what it means. To make certain that you are really working at the task and also to make reviewing easier, you would be well advised to make a separate outline in your own words. In writing such an outline, your main headings should be approximately the same as those in the book, but under each heading you should write brief sentences that summarize in your own words what you have read.

Many students fail to grasp the subject they are studying because they do not give sufficient attention to illustrations and tables. In this book, the illustrations and tables are fully as important as the corresponding discussions in the text, and when you encounter a reference to one of them, you should turn to it promptly and study it carefully. In some cases, we have used illustrations to teach something not included in the text. At appropriate points in your reading, usually before going on to a new heading, you should scan the illustrations to make certain you have examined them and gleaned all you can from them.

Every technical subject uses terms whose definitions must be learned, and psychology is no exception. Ordinarily, we give a definition in the text whenever a new term is introduced. Also, because chapters will not always be assigned in the order of their arrangement in the book, we have included a glossary in the back part of the book where all important terms are defined. You are especially cautioned not to neglect a definition just because the term is already familiar

to you. Do not, for example, pass over words like "attitude," "personality," "intelligence," and "need" because these are words that you use in everyday speech. In psychology, these and other common terms often have specialized meanings different from those commonly employed. To get the most from your study of psychology, make sure to know the *psychological definitions* of all terms.

Science is the product of scientists who have names, and it is common practice in science to ascribe particular experiments and ideas to the scientists who have contributed them. This practice, however, can be distracting and annoying to the introductory student, and we have tried to avoid it. We have used names only where they are really important or convenient in learning the subject matter. To give credit where credit is due without introducing a profusion of names, we have used superscript references when we cite particular studies or ideas. These superscripts refer to bibliographies in the back of the book to which you can turn to find the name and article or book on which we based our statement.

We have prepared a *Student's Workbook* that you may purchase and use as an aid in study and review. The workbook contains questions and exercises that not only make the study of psychology more interesting but also permit you to assess for yourself how well you have mastered the material.

We suggest, finally, that you look over the "Suggestions for Further Reading" you will find at the end of each chapter. We have selected these with some care to permit the student to learn more about any particular topic that interests him. Each title has a brief descriptive statement under it that is intended to help you decide whether it suits your purpose. We believe that most of the suggested readings will be found in college libraries.

CONTENTS

INTRODUCTION TO PSYCHOLOGY

Chapter 1 THE SCIENCE OF PSYCHOLOGY

NEARLY EVERYONE feels that he would be happier and more successful if he "understood people" a little better. The businessman must manage people, the salesman must sell to people, and the physician contends not only with physical illnesses but with the behavior of the people who have them. Even the man whose work has little to do with people must get along with his wife, his children, his relatives, his fellow workmen, and his friends and neighbors. Indeed, dealing with people effectively is vital in many aspects of vocational success and in many facets of personal happiness.

THE FIELD OF PSYCHOLOGY

This need to understand people leads to an interest in psychology that has both ad-

This chapter was drafted by Clifford T. Morgan of The Johns Hopkins University.

vantages and disadvantages when you begin the formal study of psychology. Such an interest is an advantage to the teacher because it makes his task easier and more enjoyable. Being motivated to learn, as we shall see, is just about the most important condition for learning. Without interest and motivation, a person learns little or nothing; with intense motivation, he can learn a great deal even if he suffers the handicaps of inadequate background, poor ability, or inefficient study habits. And the instructor who teaches interested students has more fun and teaches better than the one who teaches students whose attitude is, "Here I am; teach me."

A ready-made interest in psychology, however, also has its disadvantages. It encourages people to be amateur psychologists who think they know more about the subject than they really do. They can tell you exactly how to bring up your children, how to solve your personal problems, how to tell what another person is thinking, and even when the instructor in psychology is wrong. There is no doubt that a great deal can be learned by practical experience, but the amateur psychologist usually harbors many misconceptions about psychological problems. One of the tasks of a course in psychology is to correct these misconceptions. Perhaps even you will find, as you study this book, that many of your opinions are wrong or inaccurate. We alert you in advance so that you will be prepared to become more expert by mastering some of the scientific facts of psychology.

What to expect. An interest in psychology also leads students to expect both too little and too much from their first course in psychology. They ask for too much when they look for a few patent remedies that they can use to solve their own personal problems and to make their lives immediately more successful and happy. No one learns to be a physician, lawyer, engineer, or other expert in a single course. In every case, long years of training in the subject and in many related subjects are necessary to make a person proficient in its knowledge and techniques. Psychology is no exception. The highly trained psychologist, like the physician or engineer, is able to solve many difficult problems, but it is impossible to master his skills in one course, or even in an undergraduate college major in the field. You will learn much from this book that can be of practical value in understanding people—indeed, the first course in psychology probably is as useful as any beginning college course—but you must expect only to acquire the rudiments of the subject, not to acquire profound knowledge or great skill.

An interest in "understanding people" also can lead a person to underestimate the range of topics covered in psychology. Un-

TABLE 1.1. Test Yourself. Take a piece of paper and write down numbers from 1 to 20. Then read each of the following statements carefully, writing down whether you think it is true or false.

1. Geniuses are usually queerer than people of average intelligence (9).
2. Only human beings, not animals, have the capacity to think (6, 23).
3. Much of human behavior is instinctive (3, 23).
4. Slow learners remember what they learn better than fast learners (5).
5. Intelligent people form most of their opinions by logical reasoning (6).
6. A psychologist is a person who is trained to psychoanalyze people (1, 11).
7. You can size up a person quite well in an interview (9, 16).
8. When one is working for several hours, it is better to take a few long rests than several short ones (17).
9. The study of mathematics exercises the mind so that a person can think more logically in other subjects (5).
10. Grades in college have little to do with success in business careers.
11. Alcohol, taken in small amounts, is a stimulant (17).
12. There is a clear distinction between the normal person and one who is mentally ill (10).
13. Prejudices are mainly due to lack of information (14).
14. Competition among people is characteristic of most human societies (3).
15. The feature of a job that is most important to employees is the pay they get for their work (16).
16. It is possible to classify people fairly well into introverts and extroverts (9).
17. Punishment is an effective way of eliminating undesirable behavior in children (5).
18. By watching closely a person's expression, you can tell quite well the emotion he is experiencing (4).
19. The higher one sets his goals in life, the more he is likely to accomplish and the happier he will be (3).
20. If a person is honest with you, he can usually tell you what his motives are (10).

The footnote on p. 23 gives the correct answers to these questions. The numbers in parentheses following each question refer to chapters in the book that discuss the respective questions. Question 10 is covered in the chapter "Techniques of Study."

derstanding how to deal with people and how to cope with personal problems represents only a small part of the subject matter of psychology. It also considers problems of social groups, of intelligence and abilities, of work and efficiency, of learning and perceiving, of physiological processes, and even of understanding animal behavior. Although all these topics have something to do with understanding people, they are of interest in their own right, and they also have practical significance in many phases of our complex civilization. Students should therefore be prepared to study a subject of considerable breadth—one that touches on a wider variety of problems than they probably anticipated.

Definition of psychology. Now let us see more specifically what the study of psychology involves. If you ask almost any psychologist to define his subject,[1] the chances are that he will say, "*The study of behavior.*" He takes it for granted, of course, that you know he is talking about human and animal behavior, not the behavior of stars or machines or atoms. The person untrained in psychology is usually surprised, however, at the word "behavior." Why not "mind" or "thought" or "feeling"? Why is psychology the study of behavior?

The answer to this question is straightforward. You can study only what you can observe, and behavior is the only aspect of a person that is observable. We know very well that there are events going on within a person—events that can be called "thoughts," "feelings," or more generally, "mental activities." We can and do make fairly trustworthy inferences about these events, but we always make them from the way a person behaves. It is what he says, does, and writes that we as scientists can observe and record. Hence it is only behavior that we can study. A person who cannot talk, write, move a muscle, or be-

have in some way might very well have a "mind," "thoughts," and "feelings," but we could never know what they were, because we would have no access to them. These inner processes are brought to light only through a person's behavior. That is why we say psychology is the study of behavior.[2]

The inclusion of animal behavior in the definition of psychology requires a word of explanation.[3] Much of our economy depends upon animal behavior. Poultrymen, dairymen, hunters, fishermen, pest exterminators, and many others need to understand animal behavior in order to accomplish their purposes. Systematic psychological studies have helped them in the past and promise to do more for them in the future. Even more important is the fact that the study of animal behavior has helped immeasurably in understanding human behavior, because animals have the same rudimentary processes as people do. Many an important experiment that we are unable to do with people because they do not want to be "guinea pigs" can easily be done with animals. Psychologists have therefore frequently used animals as subjects to answer general questions about behavior. For that reason you will find in this book many studies of animal, as well as of human, behavior.

The behavioral sciences. Although behavior is the subject of psychology, it is by no means the exclusive property of psychology. Several other disciplines also make the study of human and animal behavior their business. These include anthropology, sociology, economics, political science, history, and related specialties. Taken together, they have recently come to be called the behavioral sciences. Each of these sciences focuses its attention upon certain aspects of behavior. However, differences among them are not always clear-cut.

Fig. 1.1. The study of animal behavior helps in the understanding of human behavior. The psychologist in this picture is measuring the effects of shock on respiration, blood pressure, and heart rate. (*Three Lions.*)

Sociology and social anthropology are concerned with the behavior of groups of people. They study cultures of various societies or groups of people living together. The sociologist usually deals with the more modern, literate cultures such as our own. The anthropologist studies more primitive, illiterate cultures in an attempt to understand how societies have developed. Each science has devised its own methods and acquired its own fund of information. At the present time, however, the lines between them are becoming fainter as they pool their knowledge and apply each other's methods.

History, of course, is a behavioral science because it attempts to reconstruct and understand the events—mostly events of human behavior—that make history. Economics and political science deal respectively with economic and political behavior, which are simply the aspects of behavior one sees institutionalized in trade and government. To a certain extent both subjects are his-

torical sciences because they make use of records of events that have transpired in the past. To the extent that they have an opportunity to study the effects of different economic and political policies on present-day behavior, they are experimental sciences.

The natural sciences such as physics, chemistry, and biology are not primarily behavioral sciences, yet they sometimes have occasion to study behavior. Some of our most useful knowledge about human perception, for example, has come from physicists and physiologists who ventured to measure human reactions to different kinds of physical stimuli. The biologist and physiologist, who are primarily concerned with structures and functions of the body, have also contributed greatly to our knowledge of behavior by reporting the behavioral effects of damage to the nervous system and to glands of the body. The zoologists, finally, have been interested in the classification of animals and have carried out many studies on the behavior of animals. In this way they have both improved zoological classification and aided the psychologist in his efforts to understand animal behavior.

As science increases its pace and widens its grasp, it becomes harder to find the borders of demarcation among the behavioral sciences. Actually there are no boundary lines, only no man's lands of unexplored territory or overlapping domains in which scientists of different labels work side by side. In the general area of behavioral science, psychology is a kind of meeting ground for the natural sciences such as physics, biology, and physiology and the social sciences such as sociology, economics, and political science. There is a good deal of give-and-take among all these sciences, and as you study this book you will see many ways in which they complement each other.

Psychology as science. So far we have been using the word "science" without defining it. The fact is that it is rather difficult to define. Yet one point on which modern psychologists insist is that their subject is a science—not art, not philosophy, not common sense, but science.[5] What they mean by this insistence requires some explanation.

Psychology is a science, first of all, because it is *empirical*. By "empirical" we mean that it is founded on experiments, surveys, and proven facts as distinguished from argument, reasoning, and opinion. In every science, as in everyday life, there is room for argument and opinion; one scientist may think his results mean one thing while another interprets them quite differently. Scientists must also argue by inference; for example, because $A = B$ and $B = C$ they infer that $A = C$. If the scientist had only his opinions and inferences, however, he would have no science. What makes his science secure as science are the unarguable facts, the observations he

has made, and the instances of $A = B$ and $B = C$ with which no knowledgeable person can argue. Also of crucial importance is his ability to do *research* and through it establish new facts. Without research his science would become static and he would not be able to erase gradually the areas of ignorance and conflicting opinion. Through research, psychology already has acquired a wealth of facts and is continuing to amass new ones. In a later section of this chapter, we shall consider in more detail what we mean by psychological research.

Psychology is also a *systematic* science. Facts, though essential to science, are by themselves of little use. They can be selected to suit one's purpose or acquired without any purpose at all, piling up in a disorderly, meaningless array. What is important in science is that facts "make some sense"—that they yield new laws and principles from which we can understand and predict new facts. This means that we *collect our facts according to some plan, based on the principles we already have established*. We test out our hunches and theories, discarding those that prove wrong and keeping those that are confirmed. In this way principles are continually formulated, modified, and extended in accordance with the facts.

Science has many distinguishing features, but the last that we shall mention here is *measurement*. Almost all of us take it for granted that sciences measure things. We rank highest among the sciences the one that has developed the most precise measurements. For that reason physics is usually credited with being the most "scientific" of the sciences because its measurements are so precise. Actually, measurement is not always essential to science. In a field like zoology, for example, the important facts may consist of a systematic classification of the animal kingdom. Such a classification is not measurement in the strict sense of the word. In psychology, too, you will encounter facts that are matters of classifying different kinds of behavior (see Chapter 23) or perceptions (Chapter 7). On the other hand, most of our problems are questions of "more than" or "less than." We would like to know, for example, whether children of highly intelligent parents are different in intelligence from those of less intelligent parents (see Chapter 15). To answer such questions as this, we need measurements that tell us *how intelligent* both parents and children are. Because most psychological problems are quite complex, the development of methods of measurement has not been easy, but it has been accomplished. In Chapter 8, we shall summarize these methods. Moreover, almost everything discussed in this book has its roots in *measured* facts, though we usually do not delve into the details of such measurements.

ORIGINS OF SCIENTIFIC PSYCHOLOGY

Writing in the early seventeenth century, Francis Bacon, one of the leaders in the development of scientific method, tells the story of the friars who quarreled over the number of teeth in the mouth of a horse.[4] Day after day they searched their ancient writings, and as they found no answer, the dispute became more and more heated. Finally one young friar suggested that they find a horse, open his mouth, and count the teeth. This idea made them so angry that they beat the friar and banished him from their erudite assembly. To them the idea was not only undignified, it was an unholy and unheard-of way of finding truth that only the devil could have put into the young friar's head. Having disposed of the idea and its originator, they returned to

their arguing and searching of literature. Still unsuccessful in finding an answer, they finally declared that the question would forever remain a mystery because historical and theological evidence was lacking.

There is more to scientific method than "looking in a horse's mouth," but settling questions by looking in the right place for the relevant facts is certainly the first and crucial step in science. No science has been well established until a concerted fact-finding effort has gotten under way. Such effort has almost invariably met resistance from groups who feel that their beliefs might be upset or their accepted authorities challenged by new facts. Historically this resistance was first shattered in settling questions about the physical world; hence physics and chemistry were first established as sciences. It took longer to overcome opposition to probing the world of living things and thus to put biology, psychology, and the social sciences on a fact-finding basis. Even today there is often a hue and cry when a scientist brings forth psychological facts that run counter to the established attitudes. Psychology is nevertheless prospering as a fact-finding science.

Natural observation. Although science has its special methods for establishing facts, people have always been able to determine many facts simply by being careful observers of the events transpiring around them. They use what we may call the *method of natural observation.* Merely by being keen observers, the ancients described and classified many animals and plants, explorers charted new seas and lands, and philosophers noted many facts about human behavior.

Before the dawn of modern science, the observation and interpretation of facts was the business of the philosopher. Beginning with the ancient Greeks, philosophers learned all they could about the world

Fig. 1.2. Psychology acquires basic facts through careful research. In this stimulus-response reaction study the blindfolded student was subjected to stimuli such as electric shock and a blank cartridge shot. His responses are indicated on the recorder. (*Frink from Monkmeyer.*)

around them, attempted to arrange their learning in an orderly way, and speculated on its meaning. Thus philosophy became the parent of our modern departments of knowledge. As philosophers increased their knowledge, they developed specialties within the field of philosophy. Natural philosophy dealt with what we now call physics, chemistry, and the natural sciences; mental philosophy concerned what we now call psychology; and moral philosophy considered many of the social problems now encompassed by the social sciences. This parental relation of philosophy to modern academic subjects is still reflected in the fact that a student who has trained in physics, chemistry, or psychology receives the degree of doctor of philosophy as the

mark of his accomplishments rather than doctor of physics, doctor of chemistry, or doctor of psychology.

Experimental psychology. About one hundred years ago, psychology was still a department of philosophy. Philosophers were arguing all sorts of questions about the human mind, much as the friars were arguing the number of teeth in a horse's mouth. By that time, however, physics and chemistry had developed the experimental method. Instead of appealing to authority or waiting for "facts to come along," they had found a way to establish facts. They chose what they wanted to study, set up their experiments, and with scales, test tubes, and other devices discovered one fact after another. Most of the basic principles taught in the introductory physics course and many of the laws of chemistry had been established by this time. The experimental method was paying great dividends in natural science.

Physicists and physiologists were beginning to experiment with some of the problems now encompassed in psychology. They had worked out the laws of color mixture that we describe in Chapter 18, and some of the phenomena of hearing described in Chapter 19. From experiments on the nervous system of animals, others were beginning to learn something of the functions of the brain in behavior (Chapter 21). While these problems on the fringe of psychology were yielding to the experimental method, the philosophers were making little or no progress in their speculations about psychological problems. Many scholars of the time became more and more convinced that the problems of psychology,

like those of natural science, should be brought under the discipline of the scientific method.

Finally, in 1879, Professor Wilhelm Wundt founded the first laboratory of psychology at the University of Leipzig in Germany. Perhaps the first laboratory actually came before that, because William James at Harvard was known to be doing experiments too. In any event, experimental laboratories of psychology mushroomed rapidly, once the movement got under way. In the United States, the first formal laboratory was set up at The Johns Hopkins University in 1883. Within a few more years, laboratories were established at every major university in the country.

A science, like a child, must have time to mature. It takes thousands and thousands of experiments, performed with different methods and under different conditions, to establish a healthy body of sound

Fig. 1.3. Some outstanding leaders in the history of psychology. Wilhelm Wundt founded the first laboratory of psychology in Leipzig in 1879. William James fostered experimentation in his laboratory at Harvard University and wrote influential books. John Dewey was one of the leaders

scientific facts. In the meantime, especially when the facts are sparse and new methods are developing, there is likely to be a period of "isms" characterized by different points of view which are often espoused with considerable zeal. Psychology went through such a period, in which different "schools" of thought occupied the limelight. In the following paragraphs we will discuss some of the most important of these schools.

Introspectionism. When experimental psychology was founded, it was most concerned with the baffling problem of "consciousness." This is still a largely unsolved problem, but we have learned to live with it while we are solving other problems. To the psychologist of the late nineteenth century, this was *the* important problem.[6] The early "thought experiments" described in Chapter 6 were performed at that time. So were many other experiments we have

not seen fit to consider in this book. One particular kind of experiment, however, gained a great deal of support, especially in the United States. This was the introspective experiment, in which a person attempted to make a detailed report of his sensations. A subject was presented with some stimulus—for example, a colored light, a picture, or a block on the table —and then asked to introspect on the sensations this stimulus evoked. By analyzing carefully these sensations, it was hoped that the nature and content of consciousness could be established (see Chapter 6).

Behaviorism. Other psychologists, among them John B. Watson, thought introspective experiments were pointless.[7] To Watson, consciousness seemed to be a pseudo problem or no problem at all. What people did and how they behaved seemed much more important. In fact, he felt that consciousness was no more than a set of "reflex

of functionalism and was an important influence in the development of modern education. Sigmund Freud founded psychoanalysis, which provided a new conception of personality and a new method of treating mental illness. (*Bettmann Archive, FPG, FPG, Bettmann Archive.*)

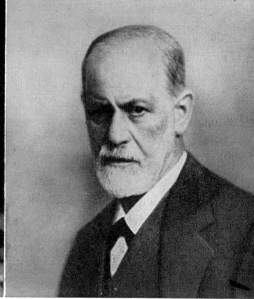

arcs" in which one implicit muscle movement provided the stimulus for another. We shall discuss this problem in Chapter 6 and shall see that Watson was not entirely right; there is more to consciousness, or at least to thinking, than muscle movements. But Watson did have a point, namely, that *we should study the behavior of people rather than their sensations as reported in introspection.* He therefore introduced a new kind of experimental method, the method of experimenting with behavior rather than with introspective reports. His theories went too far, but his method proved to be one of great value. It represents the general method of psychology today.

Gestalt psychology. While behaviorism was displacing introspectionism in the United States, another viewpoint was gaining ground in Germany. Psychologists there felt that introspective and behavioristic psychologists were trying to reduce everything in psychology to a few basic units, much as physicists analyze physical matter into atoms.[8] Such "atomism," they argued, does not correspond to the facts. Consider, for example, the dots in Figure 1.4. In looking at them, a person does not perceive so many isolated dots. Rather he perceives a square and a triangle sitting on a line. The dots are somehow "organized" in perception so that they are seen as a *configuration.* The German word for configuration is

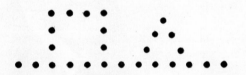

Fig. 1.4. Gestalt psychology emphasized that we perceive configurations. The dots are perceived not as so many isolated elements, but as a square and triangle sitting on a line.

Gestalt; hence the psychologists who emphasized configuration, rather than "elements," were called gestaltists, and their viewpoint was referred to as *gestalt psychology.* We shall discuss and illustrate some of their experiments on perception in Chapter 7. They also investigated problems of thinking and concluded that sudden *insights*—another instance of perceiving the configuration of a situation—characterize the solution of problems by man and higher animals. In Chapter 6, we shall consider some of the gestalt experiments on insight.

Functionalism. The introspectionists, the behaviorists, and the gestaltists were all experimentalists. In each case, they worked assiduously collecting their facts. Each, however, was looking at human behavior through a different window and collecting his facts in a different area. These differences in the aspects of behavior being studied largely accounted for differences in viewpoint. Even while their arguments were going on, there were some who took a compromising point of view. These psychologists, called the *functionalists,* said that we should be interested in everything that a person does, whether this is reporting on a sensation, flexing muscles, or perceiving configurations.

In the end, this moderate point of view prevailed, largely because the experimental facts, acquired at an ever-quickening pace, convinced psychologists that there were merits in all points of view. Gradually the major schools of psychology blended into one. If you ask any psychologist today what school he adheres to, the chances are he will say "None," and then go on to explain that schools are a thing of the past. There are, of course, alternative theories about the explanation of some facts. But these are matters of detail, not of major differences. Although there are many unsolved problems in psychology, just as there are in physics or biology, psychology is today a systematic science with a set of basic principles that leaves very little room for argument.

Psychoanalysis. Any discussion of the development of scientific psychology would be incomplete without some mention of psychoanalysis. In the last section of this chapter, "The Uses of Psychology," we shall consider the difference between psychology and psychoanalysis—and also psychiatry. Suffice it to say here that psychoanalysis is primarily a *method of treating mental illness*. It was developed by a Viennese physician named Sigmund Freud quite apart from the schools of psychology discussed above. In using psychoanalytic methods with patients, however, Freud evolved an elaborate theory of the structure of personality and of the causes of mental illness. This theory is obviously of interest to psychology.[9]

The ideas of Sigmund Freud were long disregarded by psychologists, partly because they were derived from clinical, rather than experimental, observations and partly because they often seemed rather fantastic. In time, however, psychological studies of personality began to make some of Freud's notions somewhat more plausible. Thereupon a more systematic effort was made to test these notions in experiments, and many of them proved to be more or less correct (see Chapters 10 and 11). In recent years, psychoanalytic theories have had a considerable impact on psychology.[10] Psychology does not follow the teachings of Freud because it does not appeal to authority to settle its problems. As a science, it revises its views in accordance with the results of carefully executed research. Psychology and psychoanalysis, however, have found much in common in their interest in understanding human personality.

THE METHODS OF PSYCHOLOGY

In sketching the origins of scientific psychology, we have stressed two features of science: settling problems by looking for facts rather than by speculating; and using experimental methods to establish facts. Although both these features are important to science, they are by no means the only important ones. There is always room in science—in fact, there is always a need—for rigorous speculation. Some facts are important, and some are not. And the experimental method is not the only method for establishing facts. In order to see what else is needed besides facts and experiments, let us consider in somewhat more detail the scientific process as it is particularly pertinent to psychology.

Experimental methods. We have pointed out that the experimental method has been responsible for great advances in the natural sciences and that psychology joined the fold of science when it began to use the experimental method. Throughout this book we shall refer time and time again to experiments that illustrate or support certain principles. It is therefore well to have in mind exactly what an experiment is and why it is such an important aspect of science.

■ *Repetition.* An experiment, first of all, is something we can repeat. In elementary chemistry, for example, we can demonstrate that water is made up of oxygen and hydrogen simply by burning hydrogen (that is, combining it with oxygen) and collecting the water that results. Anyone with the proper equipment can do this experiment, and it has been done over and over again. In psychology, for example, we can demonstrate that recitation is an aid to study by having two groups of students study something, one with recitation and one without, and later measuring differences in learning. This and other experiments can be repeated.

The advantages of repetition are probably obvious. If we are able to repeat an observation over and over again, we can be sure of it beyond all reasonable doubt. So the repetition makes us more certain of our observations. Then too, the same experiment can be done by different people. A scientist in England and one in the United States can do the experiment, and though widely separated in time or place, they can agree on the same observations. Agreement between different observers is an important advantage. Indeed, it is a kind of "check-up-ability"—as one distinguished scientist, J. B. Conant, has called it—that is essential to science. Finally, the repeatability of an experiment makes it convenient. It is something we can do at will without waiting for the next opportunity to make a casual observation. This convenience lets us create such opportunities at our pleasure; it saves a lot of time that otherwise would be wasted waiting for the right observation.

▪ *Control.* The experiment is also important to science because it provides control. One trouble with casual or natural observation is that we cannot be sure of the conditions leading to a particular result. We have to take the conditions as we find them and draw the best conclusions we can. In an experiment, we can *control* the various conditions that might give us misleading results. Suppose, for example, that we try to determine whether caffeine has any effect on intelligence. Many factors might be considered in conducting an experiment on this question, but one important possibility is that a person might be influenced by the knowledge that he received some caffeine. We therefore wish to *control* this possibility. To do that, we select two groups of subjects of comparable intelligence and give

one group pills containing caffeine and the other group pills, called *placebos*, that are identical in appearance but contain no caffeine. The group receiving the placebos is said to be the *control group* because it is like the other group, called the *experimental group*, in every respect except that its pills do not contain caffeine.

We describe many experiments in this book. An important feature of each of them is control. What is controlled varies with the case. If, for example, we want to study the effects of heredity and environment, we try to find twins who have identical heredity to control the factor of heredity; then we put them in different environments and see how they are different psychologically. In another case, we may be interested in some area of the brain. Then our control is to take some animals or human beings who are about alike in most respects, but differ in that some have the brain area removed while others do not. By comparing the behavior of the two groups, we can ascertain what the brain area has to do with behavior.

▪ *Variables.* Another feature of the experiment is the *variable*. To do an experiment, we must have two or more variables. In the example above, caffeine was one variable, and intelligence was the other. The two different variables, moreover, have general names. Caffeine was an *independent variable* because we could vary its amount—which in this case was all-or-none—independently of other factors in the experiment. Intelligence, on the other hand, was a *dependent variable*, because we were interested in whether or not variations in intelligence could depend upon caffeine. In some experiments, it is difficult to tell which is the independent, and which the dependent, variable. In the typical experiment, however, we have at least one independent variable and one or more dependent variables. In the caffeine experiment, for example, we could have had more dependent variables by measuring other things besides intelligence.

When the results of an experiment are presented in a graph, it is customary to let the horizontal axis (also called the abscissa or *x* axis) represent the independent variable and the vertical axis (also called the ordinate or *y* axis) the dependent variable. Figure 1.5, for example, gives the results of an experiment on the effects of high altitude (oxygen lack) on visual sensitivity. The experimenter simulated altitude by varying the amount of oxygen in a sealed chamber. Altitude or oxygen, then, was the independent variable; it is plotted on the horizontal axis. The subjects were tested at different altitudes for the amount of light necessary to see a standard test object. This light, expressed as a percent increase in the amount required at ground level, is the dependent variable and is plotted on the vertical axis of the graph. Thus, the convention for plotting graphs permits us to identify at a glance the independent and dependent variables.

▪ *Limitations.* In many ways the experiment is the best method the scientist has, and he uses it whenever he can. The experimental method, however, has its shortcomings. It is such a good method that scientists often neglect to point out these disadvantages, but knowing them is of some value in appreciating the facts it yields.

Perhaps the most obvious shortcoming is that *it cannot be used in all the instances in which we should like to use it.* Physicists, chemists, and other natural scientists do not face this difficulty often, because the lights, sounds, and chemicals that they work with never raise any objections to their experiments. People and animals are not so docile; they are not always willing to cooperate in our experiments. It is hardly possible, for

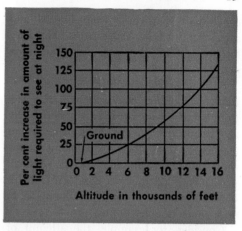

Fig. 1.5. In plotting the results of experiments, the horizontal axis represents the independent variable and the vertical axis the dependent variable.

example, to experiment with what makes a happy marriage, for society's morals and people's own desires are in the way. Nor is it possible to study experimentally (in people) how brain areas are important in intelligence, because a person prefers not to run the chance of losing some intelligence by letting some scientist take away part of his brain. These are just two examples, but it is probably obvious that there are many things in psychology we dare not experiment with.

A second limitation of the experiment is that *it is artificially arranged by the scientist.* In an attempt to uncover important variables, the psychologist must select the ones he wants to control. To do this, he must often be something of a detective and act on hunches or suspicions. In selecting his variables, he may have good fortune and come out with facts that are really important, but if he has bad luck, he may have an experiment that means nothing. Worse yet, he may have an experiment that seems to mean something it really does not. Indeed, the scientist and psychologist must continually stand on guard against false conclusions that come from limited and somewhat artificial experiments. No matter how careful they are, they sometimes make mistakes.

A final limitation of the experiment is that *it sometimes interferes with the very thing we are trying to study.* Physicists long ago discovered, in the field of quantum mechanics, that their experiments sometimes interfered with the behavior of small particles so that their measurements of this behavior were in error. Psychologists have even more trouble of this sort.

Consider, for example, the attempt of the psychologist to find out how people fatigue when they are exposed to loud noises for a long time (Chapter 17). He brings people into the laboratory and subjects them to loud noises (one variable). Then he measures their performance with all sorts of tests (other variables) only to find—he thinks—no fatigue. It turns out that when people know they are in an experiment they are highly motivated to perform well and will not show the fatigue they might exhibit under normal circumstances. Or, to take another example, if a psychologist brings some subjects into an experiment in which they know their personalities are being studied, they usually are not their normal selves but show quite unusual aspects of their personality. Examples of this sort could be multiplied, but the point is that time and time again people or animals do not behave in an experiment as they normally do. This is something we have to consider seriously in psychological experiments.

Survey methods. We have indicated that experimental methods are not always feasible and that science has other methods besides the experimental method. The first of these methods that we shall consider has no generally accepted name, but we shall call it the survey method. Others might call

it the method of controlled observation. Whatever the name, it is similar to the experimental method in that the research worker has variables he measures, but it is different in that he cannot willfully manipulate these variables. He simply makes the most systematic study he can of conditions as he finds them.

Consider the problem of marriage, which we have already mentioned. We cannot study marriage experimentally, but we can study it scientifically with survey techniques. For example, in his famous study of marriage,[11] Professor Terman of Stanford University sought out 792 married couples. He was careful to select them from different income levels (one variable), from different age groups (another variable), from different occupations (another variable), and from different educational groups (still another variable). In fact, he had several more variables that we need not mention here. By using large numbers of subjects, then carefully getting many facts about them, he was able to come to several conclusions about the causes of successful and unsuccessful marriages (see Figure 1.6). Perhaps his conclusions were not as good as if he had done experiments—we shall probably never know—but he was successful in establishing some reliable scientific facts about marriage.

Let us take another example—this time, from political opinions. There is little we can do *experimentally* to find out why people hold the political opinions they do—or to change them. We can, however, survey representative groups of people from time to time, before and after important news or political events. Through surveys we can establish the importance of variables such as income, intelligence, information, and religious background in the molding of public opinion (see Chapter 13).

In its early days, psychology took up the

experimental method largely because it
turned away from philosophy, which has
little scientific method at all, and because it
took its lessons on scientific method from
the natural sciences. It made good progress
with this method, but it was handicapped.
Later, however, it began to adapt survey
methods from the social sciences and to devise some of its own. Today, survey methods are contributing much to our knowledge, especially of personality and of social
problems.

Clinical methods. Some people learn a
good deal about engines and automobiles
not by going to school but by fixing the
machines when they break down. Similarly
physicians through the years have learned
much about health and disease from cases
of illness that have come to them for treatment. The psychologist also learns facts
and laws from working with individual
cases. The methods that he uses in this
work are called clinical methods.*

Such methods ordinarily are used only
when people come to psychologists with
problems. Little Johnny may be doing
badly in school and his parents bring him
to the psychologist to find out why. Little
Mary may be throwing temper tantrums,
not eating her meals, crying all night, and
generally making life miserable for her
parents. Jimmy, an otherwise fine young
boy in high school, may be caught stealing
nickels from the Sunday-school collection
plate. Or young Mr. Doe, married for 5
years, comes in complaining that he and
his wife just cannot get along. These and
other examples could go on endlessly. All
are people with problems who come to the
clinical psychologist for help.

Not all clinical problems require thor-

* Psychiatrists and psychoanalysts, as well as
psychologists, use the clinical method in the
study of behavior. See p. 275 for the distinction
between these specialists.

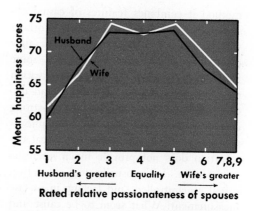

Fig. 1.6. Some results of a survey of factors in marital
happiness. This study illustrates the kinds of results
that may be obtained with survey methods. Marital
happiness was found to depend, in part, on relative
equality of sex drive in the husband and wife. (Based
on L. M. Terman, *Psychological factors in marital
happiness.* New York: McGraw-Hill, 1938, p. 286.)

ough study, but when they do, the psychologist usually begins by getting a detailed account of the person's past history
and of his family relations. He usually
gathers this from interviews with the person and his associates. Very often he may
have an especially trained social worker
delve into the social background and environment of the person.

Then the psychologist will use tests of
various kinds that have been developed
through previous research. He may use intelligence tests, reading tests, interest tests,
tests of emotional maturity and personality,
or any of a large number he has at his
command. From these and the biographical
information, he will try to make a diagnosis
of the problem—see what is wrong—and
then to take steps to remedy it. The tests,
the diagnosis, and the remedy all vary with
the individual case, and we shall see in later
chapters what some of these problems are.

What we are concerned with here is the
clinical method as an aid to science. As a

method it combines features of casual observation, experiment, and survey. Working with individual cases, the clinician may *observe*, or think that he observes, some fact of importance. By casual observation of cases, for example, Sigmund Freud discovered that dreams often reflect strong desires that people have but are unconscious of. In general, however, clinical observation does not provide much scientific information. It is usually too subjective, casual, uncontrolled, and lacking in precise measurement. What seem to be cause and effect in one case may not be in another, and even in a single case it is extremely difficult to separate out with certainty the significant causal factors. Probably the greatest value of clinical observation is to suggest fruitful ideas that may be investigated more rigorously by experimental and survey methods.

Theory in psychology. Having reviewed methods of collecting facts in psychology, we should complete the picture by indicating the role of theory in psychology. We said earlier in this section that speculation by itself is an unscientific way to settle a problem. Yet orderly speculation in the form of scientific theory is not only important to science, it is one of its chief objectives. Indeed science gathers facts not just for the sake of fact finding but to construct theories that summarize and explain facts.

To the layman or businessman, "theory" sometimes has an unsavory connotation. It may mean simply somebody's unsupported and unfounded notion of how things ought to be done. Or it may mean a set of principles obtained from books or highly artificial situations that do not work out very well in practice. Even in science, we have had some pretty bad theories—theories that turned out to be wrong or misleading—but theory nevertheless is essential to science. Indeed, it serves three important functions.

One is as a sort of *scientific shorthand*. A theory can summarize and generalize a lot of facts. In physics, for example, the law of gravitation is a very simple way of

TABLE 1.2. Fields of specialization in psychology. Two different surveys were made of the fields of specialization of members of the American Psychological Association, one in 1948 and the other in 1951. Although the two surveys classify specialties somewhat differently, they present the same general picture of the areas of specialization.

1948		1951	
Field	Per cent	Field	Per cent
Clinical psychology	30	Clinical psychology and personality	43
Advisement and guidance (including school psychologists)	17	Vocational psychology	6
Experimental psychology (including physiological and comparative)	17	General, experimental, and physiological psychology	14
Personnel psychology	14	Industrial psychology	7
Child and educational psychology	12	Developmental and educational psychology	17
Social psychology	5	Social psychology	5
Statistics (including test construction and measurement)	5	Other and unspecified	8

1948 data from Wolfle, *Amer. Psychol.*, 1948, **3**, 503; 1951 data from Sanford, *Amer. Psychol.*, 1952, **7**, 692.

summarizing a host of facts about apples, stones, and feathers falling to the ground, about planets moving in their orbits. Instead of spelling out a great array of physical facts, the law of gravitation very neatly and briefly describes all these facts. In psychology, we have developed a principle—the principle of reinforcement—that people and animals must have some kind of reward or punishment in order to learn. This in a sense is a theory that may not be entirely correct, but it is useful because it gives the essence of literally hundreds of experiments about learning. Hence a theory, to the extent that it states laws or principles, is a useful, shorthand way of summarizing facts.

Theory is also a *predictor*. It lets us tell in advance what will happen—given certain conditions. And, in the end, the object of all science is to predict. If science were just the collection of facts and if one could never predict from one set of facts to another, there would be no point at all in science. It would do us no good to find out anything, because it would never apply to any other situation. A well-developed theory is like a model house or a road map. A map, for example, depicts many of the features of a geographical area, but not all of them. Its main purpose is to tell us how we may travel in the area. Similarly a theory lays out for us in advance many of the important features of an area of knowledge. A good map must be reasonably accurate, but it cannot tell us everything about an area. Likewise, to be useful, a theory must be a rather good approximation of the facts it encompasses, but it need not be perfectly accurate or predict every possible detail.

There is another important use for theory, even if a theory is inaccurate or wrong, and that is to guide us in further *research* and fact finding. It was a theory about the nature of the atom that led atomic scientists to do the experiments that resulted in the atomic bomb. It was a theory that reward and punishment are necessary for learning that led to many experiments that eventually changed considerably modern methods of education. In these and many other cases, theories have been guides for research, and they have been the basis on which scientists decided how to take their next steps in fact collecting. When the theories prove wrong or inadequate, we soon find out in the course of our experiments. When they prove right or largely right, we keep them and use them as a guide for other experiments that add further details to our knowledge.

THE USES OF PSYCHOLOGY

Scientific psychology, like a baby, was of very little practical value when it was born less than a century ago. During its early years, it was busy growing through the assimilation of facts and principles gleaned from basic research. Once it was big enough and knew enough, it could be put to work. Its first large job was the development of intelligence tests during the First World War. Since then it has turned to one practical problem after another. Today a large share of the resources and time of psychologists is devoted to making psychology useful. In this section, we shall explain some of the fields of application of psychology (see Table 1.2).

Clinical psychology. At the present time, clinical psychology is the largest area of specialization within psychology, and it seems to be growing relatively larger by the year. In 1948, approximately 30 per cent of all members of the American Psychological Association, which includes the great majority of psychologists, were employed in the clinical field (see Table 1.2). By 1951, this percentage had increased substantially, and surveys of recent doctorates in psychology indicate that close to 50 per cent are now specializing in this field.

In order to understand better what clinical psychology is, we should first distinguish among three kinds of specialists who do clinical work: the clinical psychologist, the psychiatrist, and the psychoanalyst.

Psychiatry is a branch of medicine; a *psychiatrist* is a person who has trained in medicine, then gone into specialized training in the *diagnosis and treatment of mental disorders*.

A *psychoanalyst* is also a medical man and a psychiatrist—there are a few exceptions—but he is a psychiatrist who *uses the analytic methods of Sigmund Freud* in his treatment of mental disorders. In Chapter 11, we shall consider these methods, and in Chapter 10, we shall go into the theory behind them.

The *clinical psychologist*, on the other hand, has his basic training in *normal psychology* but has gone on to specialize in *psychological testing* and *psychotherapy*. This latter term, which is also applicable to the methods of the psychoanalyst, refers to the *psychological treatment of mental disorder*, as distinguished from shock therapy, drug therapy, and other medical methods of treatment (see Chapter 11).

As we explain later (Chapter 11), the classification and treatment of mental illness has long been the responsibility of psychiatry, a specialty in the medical profession. The psychiatrist, however, first had need of psychologists when he found that intelligence tests helped him estimate what he could accomplish in psychiatric care and treatment. He came to rely on psychologists even more when they brought forth tests for the assessment of personality (see Chapter 9). Today he regularly looks to them for aid in *personality diagnosis*. From their tests and professional opinions, as well as

from his own interviews and knowledge of the case history, he arrives at a diagnosis and a strategy of treatment of mental illness.

For some psychiatrists, aid in diagnosis is all that is expected or accepted from the psychologist. In other cases the psychologist also assists him in psychotherapy. Certainly most *clinical psychologists* of recent vintage are trained and equipped to participate in therapeutic work. In many hospitals, especially those of the Veterans Administration and other public agencies, the need for psychotherapists has been unusually great. In such institutions clinical psychologists frequently undertake considerable psychotherapy. In private practice and private hospitals, this is less often the case, and the matter rests with the preferences of the psychiatrist in charge. It should be pointed out, however, that many psychologists, working both in hospitals and private practice, are currently conducting psychotherapy on their own responsibility. In such cases, they first refer their patients to a physician to determine whether there are any physical complications that require medical care (see Chapter 11).

Although considerable progress has been made in the diagnosis and treatment of mental disorders, we still have a very long way to go before we can feel that the problems are reasonably well in hand. There is, therefore, a pressing need for research in this area. With this everyone concerned will agree. Since the psychiatrist has been trained primarily for *practice* and not for research, whereas the psychologist typically is trained in *research* and its methods, the psychologist has assumed an increasingly responsible role in the field of psychiatric research.

In recent years the idea has been gaining acceptance that psychiatric diagnosis and

Fig. 1.7. Psychologists use tests of various kinds in the diagnosis of personality problems. (*Science Service.*)

care should be in the hands of a psychiatric team consisting of a *psychiatrist*, a *psychologist* and a *social worker*. In such a team, the psychiatrist has final responsibility for care of the patient. The psychologist assumes leadership in research and assists in diagnosis and therapy. The social worker provides information about the family and background of the patient.

Counseling. There is no clear line between the person who has become so badly maladjusted that he needs psychiatric care and the person who has personal problems requiring some professional help (see Chapters 10 and 11). Moreover, if psychiatrists are to confine their efforts to those in direst need of their services, they must have some kind of screen to separate those who need only some wise counseling from those who need intensive psychiatric attention. This role is being filled more and more by the *guidance and counseling psychologist*.

Working in schools, in industry, in colleges, and indeed in private practice, psychologists administer tests of intelligence, aptitudes, interests, and personality and give such guidance as is needed. Often this is a matter of apprising parents of the abilities and limitations of their children, or of helping a student improve his study habits, or of advising him about a vocational choice, or of helping a person work out a minor personal problem. The counseling psychologist may also engage in psychotherapy. When he does, he must always be on the alert for severe emotional problems that should be referred to a physician or psychiatrist for a final judgment.

The employment of counseling psychologists has increased substantially in recent years. Many of the colleges and universities have established psychological clinics or counseling centers. Some of the larger industrial and manufacturing concerns, as we indicate in Chapter 16, have formal counseling programs to render aid in solving personal problems. Many schools, particularly the high schools, are installing counselors whose chief duty is to help students with their vocational and personal problems. At the present rate of growth, this field of psychology will be rapidly expanded in the near future.

Education. In carrying out their training functions, educators encounter many problems that can benefit from psychological knowledge. The study of the development of the child has made us better able to understand how his abilities and personality change in the course of development. Such an understanding, if put to use, enables us better to know what to teach, when to teach it, and how to teach it. Tests of intelligence and personality can, of course, be used to assess how fast the child can progress and in what direction. Psychological research on learning and the effectiveness of different methods of teaching has found application in the writing of textbooks and in classroom methods. In the colleges and universities, methods of selecting students—especially those methods that depend upon tests of aptitudes and special abilities—have required the services of those trained in psychology. In these and other ways psychology is applied in an educational setting.

Industry. Business and industry have been relatively slow to put scientific psychology to work. As Table 1.2 shows, a

Fig. 1.8. Working in schools, clinics, and counseling centers, guidance and counseling psychologists provide assistance to individuals in the solution of personal and vocational problems. (*From the motion picture "Overdependency." Courtesy National Film Board of Canada.*)

relatively small percentage of psychologists are employed in this field. Nevertheless the field is growing, and it may be the next one to undergo the kind of expansion that has been experienced in clinical psychology, counseling, and educational psychology.

The first applications of psychology to industrial problems were in the use of intelligence and aptitude tests. Today many of the larger business firms have well-established programs of selection and placement that make substantial use of psychological tests. In Chapters 16 and 17, we shall describe other applications to problems of training, to supervision of personnel, to improving communications, to counseling employees, and to alleviating industrial strife. Psychologists are seldom in managerial positions enabling them to deal directly with these problems, but they are called upon as consultants. Moreover, an increasing number of businessmen are getting some training in business and industrial psychology.

There are also firms of industrial psychologists, which are growing in number and prestige. They are usually incorporated and sell their services to many different concerns. For one business, they may set up a selection program; for another, they may survey and make recommendations concerning its training program; for another, they may survey the problems of supervision and human relations within the company; for still others, they may survey consumer attitudes toward products or the effectiveness of the company's advertising. This way of utilizing the services of psychologists seems to appeal to many businesses as being more efficient than employing psychologists on a permanent basis. It has advantages for the psychologists too, allowing them to become familiar with similar problems in different enterprises and conserving their time for the solution of practical problems rather than enmeshing them in routine nonpsychological duties that are likely to be involved in regular employment. At any rate, the separate firm of psychologists is becoming an established way of putting psychology to work in industry.

Government. The Federal government is the largest employer in the United States. Add to that the employees of the state and local governments, and you have a force of about nine million people. These employees, moreover, are highly specialized. Whether they be in the postal, diplomatic, forestry, power, law-enforcement, tax-collection, or military services, they have jobs that require special abilities and training. Being for the most part under civil-service or merit systems, government employees are supposed to be selected and promoted according to fair and objective standards. It is no wonder, then, that government has taken the lead in the development and use of scientific methods of selection and placement.

We shall point out at numerous places in the book the way in which intelligence and aptitude tests have been employed in the military services (see especially Chapter 16). By the end of the Second World War, selection tests were available for a long list of specialists such as tank men, gunners, pilots, bombardiers, riflemen, and mechanics. Research on methods of selection continues on a wide scale. Psychologists are needed for this research as well as to administer tests and to adapt them to new uses. Various agencies of the government, including the U.S. Employment Service, have also developed various forms of achievement tests for evaluating and promoting personnel. Many were devised specifically for aiding private employers and jobseekers in their task of fitting the right person to the right job.

Fig. 1.9. Psychologists specializing in the field called human engineering rearrange and simplify levers, knobs, and dials so that the man who uses them has an easier, more efficient, and safer job. (*American Airlines.*)

The Second World War opened up another application of psychology to the government's problems. This is sometimes called *human engineering* or *engineering psychology*. It concerns the *design of equipment* and the tasks of individuals who operate such equipment. Thus psychologists become involved in the design of airplane cockpits, the controls on guns, or the instruments and controls on all sorts of equipment. To these problems they bring their knowledge of perception, of learning, and of experimental methods of measuring human performance under various conditions. Obviously this application is of great concern to the military services, which are charged with getting the most out of very complex equipment. On the other hand, human engineers can assist in the design of "civilian" machines such as automobiles, stoves, lathes, cranes, locomotives, and printing presses—to name just a few. In the next few years we shall probably see more applications in this direction.

Social problems. Last, but not least, of the uses of psychology to be mentioned is the solution of social and economic problems. Many private agencies such as the National Conference of Christians and Jews, the American Jewish Congress, and the National Association for the Advancement of Colored People have become acquainted with the facts and principles that psychologists have uncovered concerning matters of prejudice. In some instances they employ psychologists who have conducted research on prejudice and who advise them concerning strategies for combating it. Municipal and state agencies engaged in dealing with crime and delinquency also make use of psychologists and their skills in waging their battles for healthier communities.

Aside from such social problems as prejudice, crime, and delinquency, our leaders in government are leaning more and more on information collected by polling techniques to find out what people think about important issues, then governing their behavior accordingly (see Chapter 13). During the depression, when the government undertook to help the dire economic plight of farmers, psychologists made careful surveys of what farmers wanted most, what kinds of controls they were willing to accept as necessary for their own betterment, and their attitudes toward numerous policies designed to improve their lot. Often these surveys made it clear that schemes based on sound economic principles would fail solely because people held negative attitudes toward them. In other cases, campaigns were conducted to educate and inform farmers on important problems. Our Treasury Department, in its efforts to increase wartime savings and to combat inflation, often based its decision on how to sell government bonds on information about people's savings habits and attitudes collected through polling techniques. These are just a few ways in which survey methods developed by social psychologists are put to work in the interest of the general welfare and the better solution of social problems.

SUMMARY

1. Although the beginning course in psychology offers much of practical value, the student may expect to acquire from it only the rudiments, not profound knowledge or skill.

2. Psychology covers a wide range of problems: not only those of dealing with people and understanding them, but also the problems of social groups, intelligence and abilities, working efficiently, learning and perceiving, and many others. Psychology, in fact, is the general study of human and animal behavior.

3. Psychology is one of the behavioral sciences. These include certain aspects of history, economics, and social and political sciences and they sometimes overlap the domains of such natural sciences as physiology and physics.

4. Like other natural and social sciences, psychology owes its parentage to philosophy. It made little headway as science, however, until it adopted the experimental method and founded laboratories for psychological research.

5. For many years, psychological research was guided by different "schools" of thought: introspectionism, behaviorism, gestalt psychology, and functionalism. These schools, however, have tended to disappear and merge into one as more and more factual information has accumulated.

6. The experimental method has been a cornerstone in the emergence of modern psychology, because it offers the advantages of (*a*) repetition, (*b*) control of variables, and (*c*) the measurement of variables. It has the limitations, however, of (*a*) not being feasible in every situation, (*b*) artificially restricting situations, and (*c*) sometimes interfering with the variables to be measured.

7. Experimental methods often need to be supplemented by survey methods and clinical methods. Both these may be used when it is possible to measure relevant variables. When experiments are difficult or impossible, they may be the only methods that can be used.

8. Theory is essential in scientific psychology, as it is in every science. It serves (*a*) as a scientific shorthand, (*b*) as a predictor of facts, and (*c*) as a guide to further research.

9. Clinical psychology is currently the largest single field in which psychology is being applied. It deals with research, diagnosis, and therapy in problems of abnormal behavior.

All the statements in Table 1.1 are false.

10. Other important areas in which psychology is being applied are guidance and counseling, education, industry, government, and social problems.

SUGGESTIONS FOR FURTHER READING

Boring, E. G. *A history of experimental psychology* (2d. Ed.). New York: Appleton-Century-Crofts, 1950.
> *An authoritative and well-written history of experimental psychology that is the standard work in its field.*

Brown, C. W., & Ghiselli, E. E. *Scientific method in psychology.* New York: McGraw-Hill, 1955.
> *A unique book that describes the application of scientific method to the problems in many fields of human behavior.*

Chapanis, A., Garner, W. R., & Morgan, C. T. *Applied experimental psychology.* New York: Wiley, 1949.
> *The applications of experimental psychology and its methods to problems of the engineering design of equipment for human use.*

Daniel, R. S., & Louttit, C. M. *Professional problems in psychology.* New York: Prentice-Hall, 1953.
> *An account of the growth of psychology as a profession and a source of information for the preparation of psychological articles and books.*

Gray, J. S. *Psychology applied to human affairs* (2d Ed.). New York: McGraw-Hill, 1954.
> *A textbook covering the different fields of application of psychology.*

Hepner, H. W. *Psychology applied to life and work* (Rev. Ed.). New York: Prentice-Hall, 1950.
> *A textbook covering applications of psychology to personal and vocational problems.*

Rubinstein, E. A., & Lorr, M. (Eds.). *Survey of clinical practice in psychology.* New York: International Universities Press, 1954.
> *An account written by different authorities of the work of clinical psychologists in various settings.*

Wilson, E. B., Jr. *An introduction to scientific research.* New York: McGraw-Hill, 1952.
> *A general, but thorough, description of the steps and principles in scientific research.*

Woodworth, R. S. *Contemporary schools of psychology* (Rev. Ed.). New York: Ronald, 1948.
> *A summary of the various schools of psychology, their historical origins, and their important contributions to psychological theory.*

PART 1

Principles of Behavior

Chapter 2 MATURATION AND DEVELOPMENT

THE BEST PLACE to start the study of behavior is at the beginning, and life begins, as you know, when the sperm of the father fertilizes the egg of the mother. At this instant, a new individual is on his way in life (see Figure 2.1). For about 24 hours, it is nothing more than a tiny speck —a single *cell*, consisting of a dark nucleus surrounded by a light, watery substance, all enclosed in a thin membrane. This cell is alive, and in a short time it reproduces itself by dividing in half. Each half divides again, and the process is repeated until many cells are produced.

While this cell division is going on, the new individual slowly travels down a small tube to the mother's uterus. Usually after

nine days, it has reached the uterus and attaches itself to the wall of the uterus as a tiny cluster of cells about 2/100 inch in diameter. This is the period of the *ovum*. Two weeks after conception, different cells in the cluster become specialized for different functions. Now the new individual, still less than 1/10 inch in diameter, is called an *embryo*. Two months after conception, the specialized cells take the crude form of the human being, and the embryo is then called a *fetus*. At the end of 9 months, the fetus is delivered into the world and becomes an *infant*.

MECHANISMS OF HEREDITY

Much of psychological interest happens between conception and birth, because patterns of behavior as well as the form of the body are maturing during this period. Let us see first, however, what directs this

---

The first part of this chapter was drafted by Eliot Stellar of the University of Pennsylvania and the latter part by Lawrence T. Alexander of the Rand Corporation.

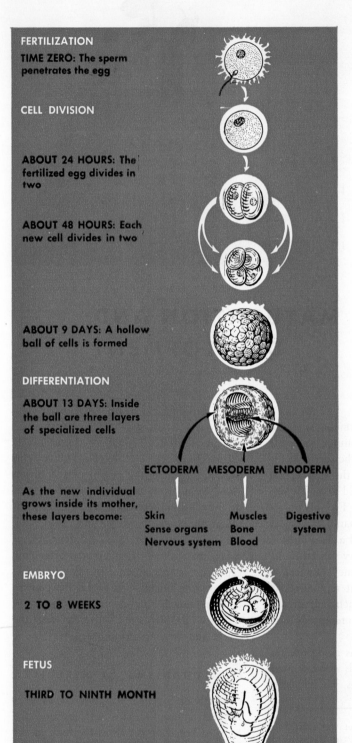

FERTILIZATION

TIME ZERO: The sperm penetrates the egg

CELL DIVISION

ABOUT 24 HOURS: The fertilized egg divides in two

ABOUT 48 HOURS: Each new cell divides in two

ABOUT 9 DAYS: A hollow ball of cells is formed

DIFFERENTIATION

ABOUT 13 DAYS: Inside the ball are three layers of specialized cells

ECTODERM   MESODERM   ENDODERM

As the new individual grows inside its mother, these layers become:

Skin	Muscles	Digestive
Sense organs	Bone	system
Nervous system	Blood	

EMBRYO

2 TO 8 WEEKS

FETUS

THIRD TO NINTH MONTH

Fig. 2.1. Early steps in human development.

growth. To do this we should turn back to the original sperm and egg cells that form the new individual.

Chromosomes. In the nucleus of each of these cells are small threadlike particles, called chromosomes (meaning colored bodies) because they stain darkly when treated with special dyes (Figure 2.2). The sperm or egg of each species of animal has a characteristic number of these chromosomes. In the case of human beings, the number is 24. When the egg and sperm get together, they pool their chromosomes so that the new individual has 48 chromosomes, arranged in 24 pairs. One member of each pair comes from the father through the sperm, and the other member comes from the mother through the egg. As the fertilized egg divides in half, each of the 48 chromosomes also divides. Hence, when cell division is complete, each new cell receives a full set of 48 chromosomes arranged in 24 pairs. The process goes on in each successive division, with the result that each cell of the human body, whether it be in the nervous system, muscle, or any other place, has its complete set of 24 pairs of chromosomes.

We have explained that the egg and sperm have only 24 *single* chromosomes, while the other cells of the body have 24 *pairs* of chromosomes. The reason for the difference is that, in the formation of egg and sperm, there is one stage in which the

Fig. 2.2. Formation of a new individual from the egg of the mother and the sperm of the father.

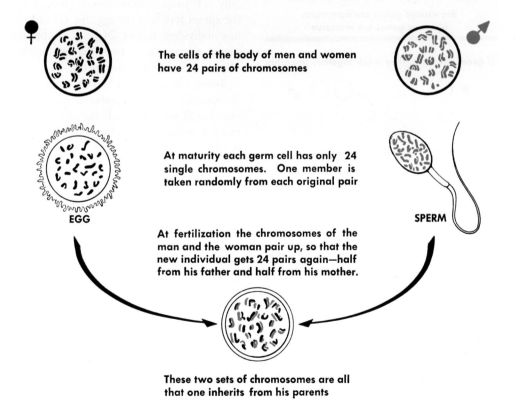

The cells of the body of men and women have 24 pairs of chromosomes

EGG

At maturity each germ cell has only 24 single chromosomes. One member is taken randomly from each original pair

SPERM

At fertilization the chromosomes of the man and the woman pair up, so that the new individual gets 24 pairs again—half from his father and half from his mother.

These two sets of chromosomes are all that one inherits from his parents

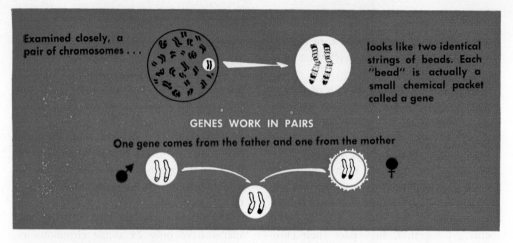

Examined closely, a pair of chromosomes . . .

looks like two identical strings of beads. Each "bead" is actually a small chemical packet called a gene

GENES WORK IN PAIRS

One gene comes from the father and one from the mother

If genes differ, one may dominate the other

Brown-eye gene   Blue-eye gene

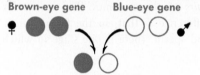

ALL CHILDREN BROWN-EYED
with both brown- and blue-eye genes

Brown-eye genes are dominant.
Blue-eye genes are recessive

If genes are alike, they work together smoothly

ALL CHILDREN BLUE-EYED

with blue-eye genes

Recessive genes carried by the parent may be expressed in the offspring

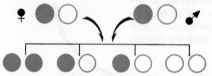

3 CHILDREN BROWN-EYED; 1 BLUE-EYED
Two of the brown-eyed children carry the blue-eye gene

Fig. 2.3. The mechanism of heredity as seen in the inheritance of eye color.

chromosomes do not duplicate themselves in cell division. Instead, the 24 pairs split up into two sets of 24, one set going to one sperm cell or egg cell—as the case may be —and the other set to the other cell. Consequently, the egg and sperm cells possess only 24 single chromosomes. But, when the sperm fertilizes the egg, the cells of the new individual receive 24 *pairs* of chromosomes, one set of 24 from the egg and the other set of 24 from the sperm.

Genes. If you could look at each pair of chromosomes under a powerful microscope, you would see that each one looks like a twisted string of odd-size and odd-shaped beads (see Figure 2.3). These contain *genes*, and it is genes that are the basic units of heredity. They are known to be complex chemical packets that have the unique ability of forming other packets just like themselves or, in some cases, only bearing a similarity to themselves. There is much that we do not know about these genes, but we do know that they direct the formation of every part of the body. In Chapter 22, we discuss the relation between genes and chemical processes in the body.

Genes always work in pairs, one of which came from the mother and the other from the father. A pair of genes working together directs the development of some particular characteristic of the body or of behavior. Sometimes the two genes in a pair are identical even though they come from different parents. In this case there is no doubt about the characteristic they will produce. If, for example, each gene of a pair produces blue eyes, the new individual will certainly have blue eyes (see Figure 2.3). Often, however, the two genes of a pair are not identical; they may govern the same characteristic but in slightly different ways. If, for example, one gene determines brown eyes and the other one blue eyes, what will be the outcome? Usually, in this case, one gene dominates the other so that the *dominant gene*—the gene for brown eyes is dominant—directs the development of the characteristic while the other gene does nothing. The other gene—in this case the one for blue eyes—is called the *recessive gene*.

Sex determination. Because the chromosomes direct the development of all

structures in the body, they determine whether the new individual is male or female (Figure 2.4). One pair of the 24 pairs of chromosomes is especially concerned with this matter. If this pair of chromosomes is identical, in which case both are called X chromosomes, the result will be a female. If one of these chromosomes is not an X chromosome but is a different (and smaller) one called Y, the result is a male.

From these facts it becomes apparent that the sperm of the father, not the egg of the mother, determines the sex of the new individual. Since each of the mother's pair of chromosomes is X, when they split up in the formation of eggs, each egg will have an X chromosome. When the father's pair splits, however, one sperm gets an X chromosome and another sperm gets a Y chromosome. Whichever sperm fertilizes the egg determines the sex of the child. If it has a Y, the child is male; if it has an X, the child is female.

Fig. 2.4. The sex of a child is determined by the chromosomes of the father.

THE SEX OF A PERSON IS DETERMINED BY A SINGLE PAIR OF CHROMOSOMES

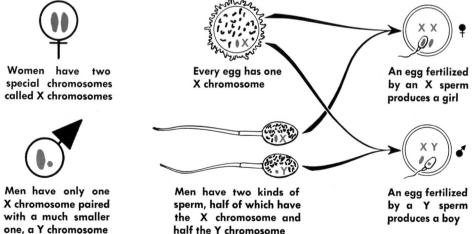

Women have two special chromosomes called X chromosomes

Men have only one X chromosome paired with a much smaller one, a Y chromosome

Every egg has one X chromosome

Men have two kinds of sperm, half of which have the X chromosome and half the Y chromosome

An egg fertilized by an X sperm produces a girl

An egg fertilized by a Y sperm produces a boy

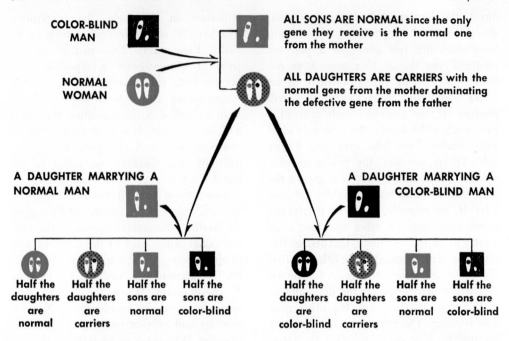

COLOR-BLIND
MAN

ALL SONS ARE NORMAL since the only
gene they receive is the normal one
from the mother

NORMAL
WOMAN

ALL DAUGHTERS ARE CARRIERS with the
normal gene from the mother dominating
the defective gene from the father

A DAUGHTER MARRYING A
NORMAL MAN

A DAUGHTER MARRYING A
COLOR-BLIND MAN

Half the
daughters
are
normal

Half the
daughters
are
carriers

Half the
sons are
normal

Half the
sons are
color-blind

Half the
daughters
are
color-blind

Half the
daughters
are
carriers

Half the
sons are
normal

Half the
sons are
color-blind

Fig. 2.5. The inheritance of color blindness as an example of a sex-linked characteristic.

Sex-linked characteristics. The chromosomes that control sex also direct the development of some other characteristics. For example, if a certain gene carried by the X chromosome is normal, the person has normal vision, but if this gene is defective, the person may be color-blind (see Figure 2.5). We know from genetic studies that the normal gene is dominant. Therefore, for a woman to be color-blind, she must have two defective genes, one in each X chromosome. For a man to be color blind, however, only one defective gene is required, because he has only one X chromosome. Thus color blindness is much more likely in men than in women; it is in fact about sixteen times as frequent. Also, when a mother is color-blind, because both of her X chromosomes carry the defective gene, it is certain that all her sons will be color-blind, because a son receives a de-

fective gene from his mother's X chromosome and only a Y chromosome from his father. On the other hand, a mother with normal color vision may have one defective gene and pass on color blindness to some of her sons—those who by chance get the defective gene.

Color blindness is an example of a sex-linked characteristic. It is called sex-linked because it is determined by a gene carried by the same chromosome that also determines the sex of an individual. Two other examples of such characteristics that may be mentioned are baldness and hemophilia; the latter is a defect in the clotting of blood that may let a person bleed to death from a relatively minor cut.

Differences and similarities in heredity. Because we are all human beings and all have the same general sort of chromosomes and genes, we all resemble each other to some degree. Yet each individual in the world receives his own particular grouping of chromosomes and genes from his parents. Every time a new egg or sperm is formed, it is a matter of chance which member of each pair of chromosomes goes into a particular cell, and each time a sperm and egg unite to make a new individual it is a matter of chance which pair gets together. All combinations are possible, and it turns out that there are an astronomical number of different kinds of fertilized eggs. This means that there is an extremely small chance that two individuals would ever have exactly the same hereditary make-up. Thus we can expect to find wide individual differences among people in their heredity.

There are, on the other hand, grounds for similarities. Brothers and sisters may be alike, because each one gets one-half the chromosomes of each parent. While each brother or sister gets his own particular grouping of chromosomes, many of the particular chromosomes the two get are identical. Of course, children also resemble their parents, because they have some of the same chromosomes. And they bear some resemblance to their grandparents, too. After all, the father and mother each received 24 chromosomes from each of their parents and give 24 out of this grand total of 48 to each child. Some of the chromosomes the child has will be the same ones that one of the grandparents had, and so there will be some resemblance between them in some characteristics.

Although individuals of common parentage have somewhat similar hereditary characteristics, only in the case of *identical twins*, triplets, and so on do they have exactly identical heredity. In these cases, after the sperm penetrates the egg, the new cell divides normally into two cells. Then the two cells split off completely

from each other and develop as two separate individuals. Since the two individuals in this case come from one fertilized egg, they have identical sets of chromosomes.

A more common type of twin is the *fraternal twin*. In this case, the mother produces two eggs at once, and two different sperms from the father fertilize these eggs. These twins are no more alike in heredity than ordinary brothers and sisters. The reason, of course, is that the two eggs and two sperms carry different groupings of chromosomes, just as any two eggs and two sperms produced at different times do. Fraternal twins may not be of the same sex, whereas identical twins always are. They may also differ in size, appearance, and abilities. The only unique thing about fraternal twins is that they are born at the same time. As you will see, the fact that they are born together is important because it means that they will have even more similar environments than ordinary brothers and sisters.

Twins are important in the study of psychology because they give us the chance to separate the roles of heredity and learning on the development of behavior. Since identical twins have exactly the same heredity, any differences between them must be the result of differences in their environment. Fraternal twins, on the other hand, should be no more alike in their heredity than ordinary brothers and sisters. Therefore, any similarities that fraternal twins show and that brothers and sisters do not show can be attributed to the greater similarity of their training.

■ PHYSICAL MATURATION

It is necessary at this point to make a distinction between *heredity* and *maturation*. The term *maturation* refers to *the completion of developmental processes within the body.* Heredity governs these developmental processes, but they must run their course to maturation before each part of the body is fully formed and ready to perform its normal function. Consequently, in order to observe the influences of heredity upon behavior, we must pay especial attention to the schedule of maturation.

In the strict sense of the word, all maturation is a physical phenomenon, because it takes place in the organs of the body. On the other hand, in some instances it is possible to trace simultaneously changes taking place both in behavior and in the internal organs. For convenience, we shall take up such instances in this section under the heading *physical maturation*. It is also possible, however, to observe changes

in behavior, which undoubtedly are due to maturation in internal organs, without knowing precisely the processes involved in maturation. We shall consider such changes in behavior in a subsequent section entitled *maturation of behavior*.

Timing of development. The relation of physical maturation to the development of behavior may be seen in the young fetus several months before birth. Physicians and scientists have sometimes had the opportunity to study such fetuses when it has been necessary, for medical reasons, to remove them prematurely from the mothers. At first, the *nervous system, muscles, sense organs,* and *glands* develop separately and without any connection between them. At this stage of development, one can electrically excite the muscles and get them to contract. At a little later stage, the nervous

Fig. 2.6. The neural mechanisms for responding to stimulation mature relatively early. A fetus, only 14 weeks after conception, reflexly lifts its leg in response to tactual stimulation. The sole of its foot is brushed with a hair. The fetus lifts its leg. The leg is lowered back to normal position. (*Copyright by Davenport Hooker.*)

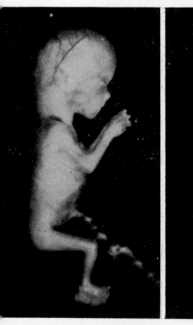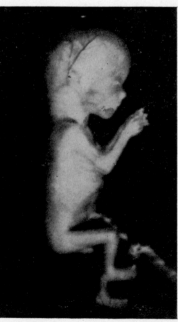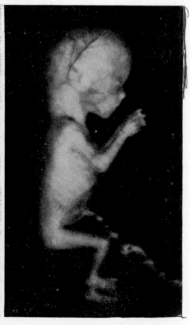

system sends down nerves to the muscles; then one can excite the nervous system electrically and see contractions in the muscles. Finally, the sense organs connect up with the nervous system, thus making a sensory-motor arc. At this stage, one can produce a muscular response by stimulating a sense organ. Such a response is the most rudimentary of all patterns of behavior. (For a fuller discussion of the nervous system and the sensory-motor arc, see Chapter 21.)

The timing of these developments varies somewhat with different parts of the nervous system, different muscles, and different sense organs.[1] Some connections between muscles and sense organs of the skin are established within three months of conception, and thus some reflexes are possible at this time. Connections with the eyes and ears develop more slowly, and reflexes involving these senses do not appear until about the seventh month.

Maturation precedes behavior. One of the interesting and important things about this development is the large "margin of safety" that it provides. Organs mature, and connections are made, well in advance of the time they are needed. The human fetus stands practically no chance of surviving, for example, if it is born before the sixth month, yet it can make breathing movements in the fourth month. The fetus, similarly, makes walking movements with its legs in the fifth month; in the sixth month it will suck if its mouth or cheek is brushed, and it may grasp an object in its palm or even vocalize. The fetus will not need these elements of behavior until it is born, yet they are ready 2, 3, or 4 months ahead of time.

By the time of birth, then, most of the reflexes and elementary forms of behavior are ready for use. Among them are the breathing reactions, sucking reflexes, crying reactions to cold and discomfort, and the other behavior patterns that infants need to get along in the world. Many other patterns, however, that are not needed are not ready; they develop slowly after birth, and in some cases are not fully mature until the child is ten or twelve years old.

The nervous system. Of all the organs of the body, the nervous system and the endocrine glands—we shall define the endocrine glands below—are among the slowest to develop. Although the spinal cord, nerves, and lower parts of the brain are relatively mature at birth, the brain and particularly the cortex go on maturing for some time. Most infants, for example, are unable to follow moving objects with their eyes until several weeks after birth, because the pathways in the brain that are needed for this are not mature.

The cerebral cortex (see Chapter 21), which is important for learning and more complex behavior, is even slower to mature.[2] Scientists have repeatedly observed that removal of the cortex (or lack of it) at birth and for several months afterward makes little difference in behavior; they have concluded, therefore, that it is not functioning at that time.[3] The ability to sit up, to crawl, and to walk all depend on the cortex, and it is not until it matures that infants are able to do these things. Most maturation of the cortex is completed by the age of one to two years, but scientists can tell from electrical records of the brain's activity that some maturation goes on until a person is ten or fifteen years old.[4]

The endocrine glands. The term *endocrine* applies to those glands of the body that empty their secretions, called *hormones*, directly into the blood rather than into cavities of the body. The glands that do the latter are called *exocrine* glands. Examples of endocrine glands are the sex glands (ovaries and testicles), the pancreas which secretes the hormone insulin, and the thyroid glands in the neck. A familiar example of an exocrine gland is the salivary glands which secrete saliva into the mouth. Of the two kinds of glands, the endocrines are the most important in psychology because their hormones, as we shall see (Chapters 3 and 22), affect behavior in a variety of ways. The endocrine glands and their hormones are described in detail in Chapter 22. Here we are interested only in their part in physical maturation.

The endocrine glands, it is important to note, are particularly slow to mature. This fact is probably explained in part by the supply of hormones furnished to the fetus by the mother, making it unnecessary for the fetus to secrete its own. It is also true that many of the hormones of the endocrine glands are not needed until later in life.

The sex glands are perhaps the most interesting example. These do not mature until puberty, at the age of twelve or thirteen, when boys and girls begin taking on the characteristics of men and women. Some of the changes that take place at that time are the growth of the beard and change of voice in boys, and the development of the breasts in girls. These are brought about by sex hormones. So, too, are changes in sexual motivations (see Chapter 3) and the patterns of sexual behavior. Scientists have proved this in experiments with many different animals by injecting sex hormones in infancy and noting the appearance of sexual behavior at a considerably younger age than that at which it would otherwise appear.[5] This is just one kind of evidence that the schedule of maturation of sexual behavior is controlled by the maturation of the sex glands.

■ MATURATION OF BEHAVIOR

We have presented just a few examples of the connection between physical maturation and the emergence of behavior. It is obvious that behavior depends upon the proper functioning of the nervous system. For that reason, we may assume that all instances of the maturation of behavior have a physical basis. We are not always able, however, to state exactly what the underlying factors in behavior are. Moreover, the development of behavior is interesting in its own right. So in this section we shall consider the maturation of behavior quite apart from its physical basis.

There are several kinds of experiments that may be performed to evaluate the role of maturation in behavior. We shall discuss three: (1) the *restriction of practice* so that opportunities to learn are minimized, (2) *special training* that maximizes opportunities to learn, and (3) the comparison of species with *different heredities* and different maturational schedules. A discussion of each of these methods follows.

Restriction of practice.   One of the classical experiments that demonstrates the maturation of behavior was done with salamanders.[6] The psychologist who did the experiment took two groups of salamanders before they had begun to swim. He let one of them grow up in a tank of plain water, but he lightly anesthetized the other group by putting chloretone in their water. This kept them motionless without interfering with their growth. He then waited until the normal salamanders started swimming and had been swimming for five days. Then he transferred the anesthetized tadpoles to plain water. Within a half hour, all of them were swimming normally. To see whether this group learned rapidly in

Fig. 2.7. Maturation of swallowing reactions in chicks. Chicks were kept in the dark from the time of hatching until they were first tested for pecking and swallowing reactions. Thereafter they were allowed 25 trials each day. The graph shows the number of trials in which the chicks successfully seized and swallowed a piece of grain. One group was tested 24 hours after hatching, the second group 5 days afterward. Note that the second group catches up to the first one in 2 days of testing. Both maturation and learning therefore are factors in the development of swallowing reactions. (*Based on data of Cruze, W. W. Maturation and learning in chicks. J. comp. Psychol., 1935, 19, 371–409.*)

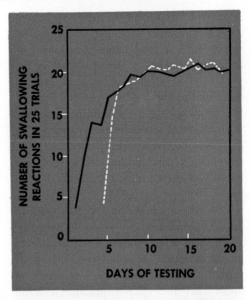

the half hour or simply required a half hour for the anesthetic to wear off, he also anesthetized the control group which was already swimming by this time. When they were returned to plain water, it took them a half hour to swim normally again just as it did the group that had been under prolonged anesthesia. In this way, he demonstrated quite conclusively that maturation was the important factor in the development of the swimming behavior of salamanders.

▪ *Maturation in birds.* Two experiments are of interest here. In one, young birds were forced to wear wooden halters over their wings to prevent them from flying until the time when free birds were flying normally.[7] Just as in the study of salamanders, when the birds were released from the halters they immediately flew in normal fashion. In studying the birds, however, the experimenter made another interesting observation. If he forced the birds to wear the wooden halters too long, they did not fly when he released them. The birds did not appear weakened by this long restriction, but other factors seem to

have prevented their flying (see "Maturation and Learning" below). Perhaps they developed habits of staying on the ground rather than flying.

We may mention briefly a somewhat similar study in chicks.[8] Newly hatched chicks peck fairly accurately but fail to hit the grain about 25 per cent of the time; 5 days later, when they have grown a little stronger, they seldom miss. An experimenter kept a group of chicks in the dark and fed them by hand for 5 days, then let them try pecking for the first time. Like the salamanders and the flying birds, they were practically perfect (see Figure 2.7). So in this case, too, the behavior depended mostly on maturation. The experimenter found, however, that if he kept the chicks in the dark too long, they made more errors in pecking than if he released them sooner. By this time they seemed to learn a preference for hand feeding.

▪ *Maturation of perception.* So far the picture is rather simple. Skills such as swimming, flying, pecking, and walking appear with very little practice when the nervous and muscular mechanisms mature. The development of perception, however, is not quite so simple. The young infant, for example, takes a good many months to use his eyes effectively in seeing objects in the world and in judging their depth. Is this delay due to the need for physical maturation or to the need for learning and practice? Attempts to answer this question have led psychologists to study rats and apes raised in the dark and human beings whose vision has been restored relatively late in life.

Rats who are raised in the dark seem to develop perception as they would normally. With little or no training, they are able to jump accurately to platforms placed at various distances, and this fact seems to mean that their depth perception is all right.[9] If they are required to discriminate a bright from a dark panel, they do that normally, too. If, however, they must discriminate visual patterns, such as an upright and an inverted triangle, they are a little slower than normal animals.[10] All in all, most aspects of visual perception in the rat mature without much practice.

Although this experiment with rats is rather conclusive, it is difficult to say whether it is representative of all species of animals, including man. Apes reared in darkness require considerable training before they are able to discriminate different visual patterns.[11] It is very probable, however, that their eyes are damaged by long periods in the dark and, consequently, that their performance is not directly relevant to the problem of maturation. Similarly, human beings may take a long time to regain normal visual perception after cataracts have been removed.[12] Again it is likely that defects of the eyes, rather than maturational factors, account for the delay. We must therefore wait upon further research before we can state precisely how maturation is concerned in the visual perception

of higher animals. Our best guess at present is that maturation is concerned in the development of perception, but the details need to be worked out.

▪ *Restriction of human infants.* Although psychologists are not yet certain of the exact role of maturation in human visual perception, they know that many other abilities do develop in children through maturation and without practice. They were able to learn this in part from the way in which Hopi Indians treat their infants.[13] These Indians bind their infants tightly to a board so that the infants cannot move for most of the day. Usually the infant is unbound for only an hour or two a day while he is cleaned, and so he does not get the same opportunity to practice sitting, creeping, and walking that normal, unbound infants do. Yet these bound children develop the ability to sit, creep, and walk just as rapidly as children who are never bound. So it takes little or no practice for a human child to develop these capacities.

There are a good many studies in which infants have been restricted in various ways until long after they would normally develop certain kinds of behavior. Most of these studies convince us that very little practice is required for the development of these abilities. A dramatic case is that of a girl whose *deaf-mute* mother hid her from all outside social contact until she was more than six years of age.[14] When neighbors discovered the child, she could not speak; she uttered only incomprehensible sounds. In 2 short months of training, however, she learned many words. By that time, she had started putting sentences together as fast as a child normally does at three years. Of course, she had to learn the vocabulary of English and the rules of constructing sentences, but her progress was rapid. Her case demonstrates strikingly that the *capacity* for learning language is something that gradually matures without practice.

Special training. One way to study maturation is to prevent or restrict training so that only maturation can be at work. That is the method that characterizes the studies we have just described. Exactly the opposite method, however, is also a good one. That is to give children special training to see whether abilities can be made to develop earlier than usual. Psychologists have made studies of this sort. In making them, they have tried to use identical twins as much as possible because such twins should have the same rate and level of maturation.

▪ *Johnny and Jimmy.* One of the most famous studies of this sort turns out to be a bit disappointing because it was later learned that the twins were fraternal, not identical.[15] Nevertheless, it is interesting to see what happened in this case. Johnny was the twin that received the special training. He was given expert guidance in such

activities as sitting, crawling, and walking and had lots of time to practice. He was also given special experience in activities like climbing and roller skating. All the while Jimmy was left to develop on his own, with even less than the normal amount of practice and training. As soon as Johnny had perfected an activity, then Jimmy was tested.

In such basic things as walking, Jimmy caught up with Johnny in very short order. Once given the chance, Jimmy showed that he could equal Johnny with little or no practice. But in special activities where special techniques are helpful, Jimmy was at a disadvantage and sometimes failed to catch up with Johnny at any time. For example, in the task of climbing down from a pedestal, Johnny learned how to hang by his hands and drop to a mattress. Left to his own devices, Jimmy did not learn this feat and, as one might expect, acted afraid when left on the pedestal without guidance.

Fig. 2.8. *Nanook of the North,* Robert Flaherty's 1922 motion picture of Eskimo life, has provided a lasting record of the ways of life in that culture. Since then the work of other famous photographers has contributed to our knowledge of many primitive societies. Here Flaherty's photograph records the practice of baby bundling, common in some Indian and Eskimo groups. Bundling restricts a baby's opportunity to practice reaching, sitting, creeping, and walking, but it does not interfere with motor development. Such babies walk at about the same age as babies who are not restricted. (*Photo by Robert Flaherty, FRGS. Copyright, Revillon Frères.*)

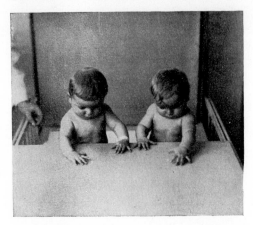

Fig. 2.9. Twins T and C at 38 weeks of age. The behavior of the twins is practically identical. (*Courtesy Dr. Arnold Gesell.*)

■ *Co-twin control study.* A similar study with two girls who were identical twins was less extensive, but perhaps more precise.[16] In this case, the infant receiving the training, twin T, was trained in such activities as climbing stairs. After 6 weeks of intensive training, twin T progressed from the point where she could not climb at all to where she could make five stairs in 26 seconds. At this point, the control, twin C, was allowed to try the stairs. On her first attempt, she climbed all five stairs without help and without practice in 45 seconds. With only 2 weeks of training, twin C could make the stairs in only 10 seconds. The same results were found in other types of basic activity.

The conclusions are that (1) maturation, not learning, is responsible for the development of basic activities; and (2) to the slight extent that special training helps to perfect a basic activity, it develops skill much more rapidly in the more mature individual. Of course, we do not know how fast twin C might have climbed the stairs if the experimenters had waited 2 weeks longer than they did before giving her training. She might still have climbed

them in 10 seconds. It is not easy, however, to find twins on whom to do such extensive studies, and once they are tested, they cannot be considered inexperienced any longer.

Different heredities. We have described experiments in which the influence of maturation has been studied by the *restriction of practice* and by giving *special training.* A third kind of experiment takes advantage of the fact that *maturation is determined by heredity.* As we explained above, maturation is simply the completion of developmental processes that are governed by the genetic make-up of the individual. For that reason, we may expect to find differences in maturation among individuals of *different heredities.* Such differences can be found, obviously, among animals of different species. Apes, for example, have a different heredity from human beings. It is instructive, therefore, to compare the two species in the maturation of comparable kinds of behavior. We shall describe two experiments in which such a comparison was made. It is also possible, of course, to find human beings who have different heredities and different levels of intelligence (see Chapter 15 for the relation between heredity and intelligence). We shall consider in this section studies of the benefits of training for individuals of different intelligence. In each of these cases, the important point is that *heredity sets a limit to maturation;* maturation cannot exceed the limits of development laid down in the genetic make-up of the individual.

■ *Donald and Gua.* The limits set by heredity are brought out clearly in one experiment in which a nine-month-old boy and a seven-month-old female chimpanzee were brought up together like brother and sister.[17] The experimenters made every effort to treat the ape and their child exactly alike. They treated both with the same affection, dressed them alike, and gave them the same chance to practice different kinds of behavior like standing, walking, opening doors, eating with a spoon, and learning to use the toilet. Of course, the difference in heredity between the boy and the chimpanzee is tremendous, so the experiment gives us a chance to see how much this difference can be overcome by training.

As one might expect, Gua, the chimpanzee, developed certain kinds of behavior faster than Donald, the boy. The chimpanzee has about one-third the life span of man and matures much earlier. It is interesting that Gua not only was better in such things as standing and walking in the beginning of the experiment but also learned to use a spoon sooner than Donald and developed faster in the capacity to respond to verbal instructions. But after 9 months, when the study was ended, Donald had caught up on almost everything except strength, and he was beginning to develop capacities like language that Gua showed no signs of learning.

The important point in this experiment is that the ape and the child developed according to their hereditary potentials. Even though the ape's special training allowed it to develop behavior normally seen only in humans, it very soon reached the limits of its hereditary potential and was far outstripped by the child.

▪ *Talking apes.* You have probably seen

Fig. 2.10. Donald and Gua. The chimpanzee and the human infant were reared together and treated alike. In many respects, the chimpanzee, Gua, developed more rapidly than Donald, but Donald caught up to and surpassed Gua, especially in the development of language. (*From Kellogg, W. N. & Kellogg, L. A. The ape and the child. New York: McGraw-Hill, 1933.*)

or heard of talking birds, such as the parrot. Some birds are indeed very good at uttering clear words. They are unable, however, to use the particular word that is appropriate to an object or situation or to combine words in a novel way as human beings can. They do not possess the native ability to learn to use language in a meaningful way.

Several attempts have been made to teach human speech to apes, because they have a brain more nearly like man's than any other animal, and they can utter some articulate sounds. So far none of these attempts has succeeded very well. One experimenter taught an orangutan to say "papa" and "cup" and to use these words with some meaning, but the process was laborious.[18] More recently, a childless couple took a newborn chimpanzee into their home and reared it as a child.[19] Their idea was that an ape might learn to talk if it were treated exactly like a human baby and given all the love and attention possible. After almost 3 years, however, although Viki, the chimpanzee, could occasionally use the words "mama," "papa" and "cup" meaningfully, it had not developed its linguistic skills any more than that.

So far as we know, then, apes can learn to use a few simple words only through painfully slow practice, and there is no evidence that they can ever learn to speak a variety of words or anything like sentences. So the limit of language ability in the ape is very low and can be realized only very gradually and by intensive training. Quite different, of course, is the human infant with his much greater hereditary potential for language behavior.

▪ *Individual differences in ability.* As usual, it is much harder to be certain about hereditary differences in adults than it is in the cases of animals or infants that are easily controlled. We cannot be certain

that some of the limitations people seem to have are always due to hereditary factors. But in some cases of feeble-mindedness, extreme brightness, special skills, talents, and so on, the suggestion is strong that heredity plays an important role. At least we know that when we test people we often find them greatly different in certain abilities. Then if we try to train them all, we find a rather interesting thing. The people who had the superior ability to begin with are even *more* superior to the others at the end of training.[20] In other words, the superior people profit more by training than the inferior people, presumably because they have higher potential ability.

This point is made even more clearly and dramatically in the case of certain types of inherited mental defects. In these individuals, the hereditary limit of intelligence is low. Training may bring them up to a higher level of performance than they had before training, but it will never make them normal in intelligence. Futhermore, the same training given to a normal person will only accentuate the difference between the normal and the feeble-minded, because the normal person has fairly high limits of ability that can be developed by training.

Maturation and learning. Our discussion above has emphasized the importance of maturation in the development of skills and abilities by showing (1) that behavior sometimes appears with little or no opportunity for learning; (2) that, without the prerequisite maturation, training may be of little or no avail; and (3) that differences in heredity establish limits of maturation which cannot be overcome by training. These facts lead to the conclusion that maturation determines the *rate* and the ultimate *limit* of the development of the individual's abilities. A person cannot be taught something before maturation en-

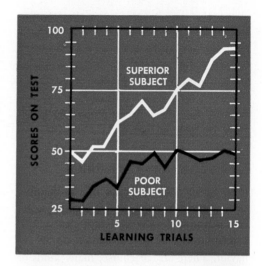

Fig. 2.11. Differences in ability persist after training. Subjects were allowed periods of four minutes to underline all four-letter words in a page of type. They were given 15 such learning periods. The graph depicts the learning of two subjects, one of the best and one of the poorest. Note that, after 15 periods of practice, the difference in their performance was even greater than it was at the start. The conclusion, that training does not erase differences in ability, is typical of many studies. (*After Anastasi, A., & Foley, J. P., Jr. Differential psychology. New York: Macmillan, 1949, p. 210.*)

ables him to learn it, and if maturation does not endow him with the ability to learn it, he cannot acquire the ability. Translated into practical situations, this conclusion means that we waste our time when we try to "push" a child faster than his schedule of maturation permits. He cannot be taught to walk, to talk, or to develop any other skill until maturation makes him ready. It means, too, that we cannot expect training to make a person of poor, or even average, abilities into one of exceptional talents. All that can be done is to exploit to the fullest the abilities that unfold in maturation.

Despite the limits imposed by maturation, it may be taken for granted that the fullest development of the individual depends upon learning—an incalculable amount of learning, day after day and year after year. In the sections below we shall see the importance of learning in the development of motor skills and language. Later, in Chapter 5, we shall consider the learning process in detail. Then, in many different chapters throughout the book, we shall have occasion to show how learning is an important key to the understanding of human behavior.

Before leaving the topic of maturation, however, we should make one additional point: *Sometimes the optimal time to learn a skill is at the time of maturation.* If this opportunity is missed, learning may be more difficult or even impossible.[21] We briefly mentioned two instances of this fact in our discussion above. In the case of the chicks reared in the dark, we said that, if the experimenter "kept the chicks in the dark *too long*, they made more errors in pecking than if he released them sooner." In the case of the birds restrained from flying, if the experimenter "forced the birds to wear the wooden halters *too long*, they did not fly when he released them." In each of these experiments, restriction of practice up to a certain point did not handicap the animals' development. Beyond that point, however, restriction retarded or prevented the acquisition of the skill.

In another chapter of the book (Chapter 23), we discuss in some detail a dramatic case of learning "at the right time." This is the phenomenon of *imprinting* which has been demonstrated in birds.[22] Imprinting is very rapid learning that may take place only at the time maturation makes it possible. In this and the experiments mentioned above, the important point is that the potentialities for learning may fade away if they are not utilized when they appear.[23] Whether this principle is as applicable to human beings as it is to animals, we do not yet know, for we do not have the necessary data. It is, however, an important possibility to keep in mind.

■ MOTOR DEVELOPMENT

So far we have described the mechanism of heredity and the maturation of behavior. It is appropriate now to describe some particular aspects of the development of behavior. There are, of course, many kinds of development—in fact, every topic of psychology can be treated from a developmental point of view—and we shall return often to the theme of development in many of the later chapters. But here we shall cover two aspects that are especially prominent in infancy and early childhood: *motor development* and *language development*.

Psychologists and physiologists use the term *motor* as the adjective referring to the responses people make, including reflexes, general posture, ability to walk, and manual movements. The basic motor abilities develop during a period which extends from before birth to about the age of two years. The skills acquired during this period serve as the foundation for all the vast variety of things that people later learn to do.

Prenatal development. During the prenatal period, the individual exists as an aquatic creature and as a parasite within the body of its mother. Here it is well protected from harmful stimuli, with all its needs supplied. On the whole, the uterine environment is relatively constant, and it is relatively similar from one woman to another.

To the psychologist, the important feature of the fetal period is the unfolding of behavior that takes place. In a few short months—sometimes they seem long to the mother—the nervous system and other parts of the response mechanism almost completely mature. By the seventh month of prenatal life, most reflex patterns are fully developed. Among them are turning movements of the trunk and head, flexing and extending the limbs when touched, grasping objects that touch the palms of the hands, sucking when a nipple or similar object touches the mouth, and crying when in discomfort. Normally the unborn baby does not need all these patterns of behavior so soon, but they are there in case the baby is born before normal term.

Infancy. Most of the features of the prenatal environment—temperature, darkness, quiet, watery environment—are relatively constant and require no adjustment on the part of the fetus. Birth changes all that. It thrusts the infant suddenly into a highly variable environment. In this environment, food is available only at intervals, the temperature changes from time to time, and lights, sounds, and other stimuli impinge intermittently on the infant. The newborn, of course, must now breathe to get his own oxygen. All this requires the infant to make his own adjustments and begin to establish some independence of the environment. He must ingest and digest his own food, and he must regulate the temperature of his own body. It usually takes a few days to make these adjustments well, and in the course of them, he may lose a little of the weight that he had accumulated before birth.

After that, the newborn enters the stage of infancy, which lasts for about two years. The most important events of this period are motor; the infant gains skill in controlling his own body. In contrast to the newborn, for example, the child of two is a miracle of muscular precision. He has good postural control in a wide variety of positions. In fact, he often gets into positions that seem impossible to adults. He can walk forward, backward, and sideways, and he can go up and down a flight of steps. He has developed a good deal of skill with his hands—good enough, in fact, to pick up a small pellet with his thumb and forefinger.

If we chart carefully, as several psychologists have done,[24] the things the infant can do from month to month and year to year, it is easy to see clearly that there is a *pattern* of development. The infant lifts his head before he sits up, he sits before he crawls, and he crawls before he walks. Actually, there are many little—and, to the parent, very important—details in this development. Yet they fit into an orderly sequence; they make a pattern. This pattern is almost exactly the same in every human infant, and each infant passes through the

TABLE 2.1. Stages in motor development. The skills listed here illustrate the progressive development of control over different groups of muscles. This development proceeds in an orderly fashion from the head region down the body and out to the ends of the limbs. For the explanation of Q_1, median, and Q_3, see discussion on p. 47 of the text.

Description of stage	Number of cases	Age, weeks		
		Q_1	Median	Q_3
First-order skills (control of the neck muscles):				
On stomach, chin up	22	2	3	7
On stomach, chest up	22	5	9	10
Held erect, stepping	19	11	13	15
On back, tense for lifting	19	14	15	18
Held erect, knees straight	18	13	15	19
Sit on lap, support at lower ribs and complete head control	22	15	19	20
Second-order skills (control of trunk and upper-limb muscles):				
Sit alone momentarily	22	21	25	26
On stomach, knee push or swim	22	22	25	27
On back, rolling	19	25	29	32
Held erect, stand firmly with help	20	29	30	33
Sit alone one minute	20	27	31	34
Third-order skills (beginning of body-limb coordination in prone position):				
On stomach, some progress	17	33	37	41
On stomach, scoot backward	16	34	40	46
Fourth-order skills (balance in upright position with support; locomotion in prone position):				
Stand holding to furniture	22	41	42	45
Creep	22	41	45	45
Walk when led	21	38	45	46
Pull to stand by furniture	17	42	47	50
Fifth-order skills (unsupported locomotion in upright position):				
Stand alone	21	56	62	66
Walk alone	21	59	64	67

Adapted from Shirley, M. M. *The first two years, a study of twenty-five babies.* Vol. I. *Postural and locomotor development.* Minneapolis: Univ. of Minnesota Press, 1931, p. 99.

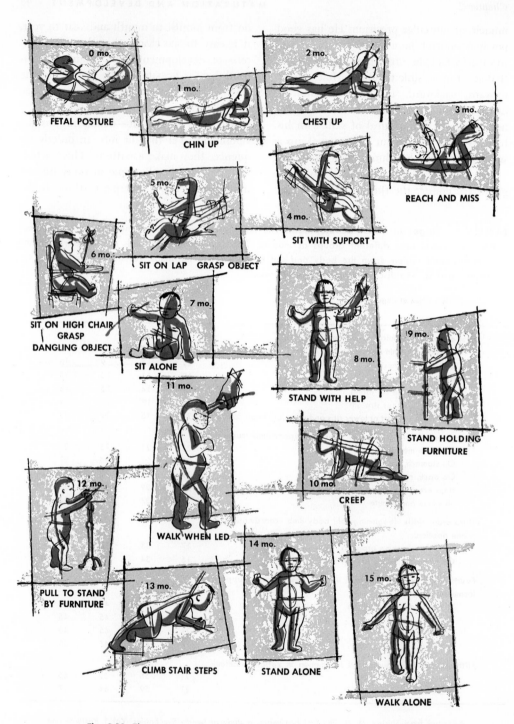

Fig. 2.12. The sequence of motor development.

same steps in the course of his development. As we might suspect, the pattern is so uniform because it is largely the result of maturation of the response mechanism.

Because there is a pattern to development in infancy, it is possible to construct *norms* for development. We may state, for example, that the infant can pick up a pea-sized object at seven months, begins to creep at nine and a half months, etc. These are ages at which the average child displays a particular skill; we call them norms. Many parents buy books that give detailed norms and then watch Junior with bated breath to see whether he progresses on schedule. They should remember, however, that norms are only averages, that some infants will be slower and some faster in acquiring successive stages of skill. They should realize, too, that speed of motor development has very little to do with intelligence,[25] for the child whose motor development is slow (but in the normal range) is as likely to have high or normal intelligence as the one who is rapid (see Chapter 15).

▪ *Orders of skill.* The various stages in the development of motor abilities leading up to and included in walking have been divided into five orders of skills. These have been listed in Table 2.1. By studying the table carefully you can see what they are and when they are reached in slow, average, and fast rates of development.

On the average, by eighteen and a half weeks the child is able to control the muscles which support the head and upper trunk and can move them quite skillfully at will. This is a first-order skill.

Second-order skills include the ability to control the lower trunk muscles and preliminary use of the lower limbs. During this stage the child can support himself in a sitting position, and if he is held, his legs can support the rest of his body. Notice also that he is now able to make the push-ing and pulling movements with his arms and legs (swimming motions) which anticipate the actual movements forward and backward, still on his stomach, which occur in the next stage.

In the next 7 months the child acquires the next three orders of skills: creeping and crawling on all fours; standing and walking with support; and finally, the ability to stand and walk alone. We have selected representative skills from each of the five orders and have drawn pictures to show how the child looks when performing them. You see them in Figure 2.12.

▪ *Norms.* The *age* of appearance of each of these various skills which are preparatory to walking is shown in Table 2.1 in three columns. The *median* age for a skill is the age by which half the children studied showed that skill. The column labeled Q_1 gives the age by which the most advanced 25 per cent showed the skill, and the column labeled Q_3 is the age by which 75 per cent of the children in the group demonstrated the skill. This, of course, is an example of variability in rate of development which we have already mentioned.

Consider, for example, the second-order skill of sitting alone. The median age at which this behavior appears may be thirty-one weeks, but we notice that one-quarter of the children can sit alone by twenty-seven weeks and fully another quarter have not yet reached this stage of development by thirty-four weeks of age. If we were to cite the full range of ages at which children first sit alone, it would be much greater than the seven weeks given here. Consequently, although we may have a good idea of the order in which skills appear and how the attainment of each level sets the stage for the development of succeeding patterns of behavior, it is unwise to try to predict the exact age at which any specific skill will appear for any individual child.

■ *Advanced skills.* Once the child has mastered the art of getting about, he progresses rapidly to more advanced skills like walking up and down stairs, jumping, hopping, skipping, and running. As he develops speed and accuracy he begins to coordinate all these skills into more complex activities. So the little girl who formerly used her doll carriage to steady herself as she took her first halting steps now casually wheels her "baby" to the store on a "shopping" tour. The boy who at first was content merely to balance himself sitting on a tricycle, now hitches on a wagon and goes tearing off down the road playing fire engine.

Prehension.   Prehension is a term denoting the *grasping of objects*. The simplest kind of prehension is palmar grasping; in this, the object is grasped in the palm of the hand, as when a person hangs from the limb of a tree or takes hold of the rungs of a ladder. By using the thumb in apposition to the index finger, a finer prehension is possible, as when a person picks up a pencil or uses a pair of tweezers. This kind of prehension, which is limited to human beings and some of the apes, enables us to manipulate objects with considerable precision. It accounts for many of the feats of skill that only human beings are able to perform.

■ *Order of development.* Prehensile abilities develop rather slowly in the infant. Like locomotion, they grow out of more basic patterns of behavior that must develop beforehand. First the infant must be able to make contact with an object which is some distance in front of him. Then he must learn to grasp it and manipulate it in an efficient manner. When an object is placed before a baby, the earliest kinds of response he makes to it are more or less random arm-waving motions. By about the fourth month, however, the arm movements are directed toward the object, and

he can grasp it after a few misses. The object is grasped with the whole hand, generally in the palm.

These reaching movements follow a definite pattern.[26] At first, as we have noted, they are random movements that involve the whole arm. Later the movements are directed at the object, and the arm is used more or less as a rake—the object is swept in with a roundabout motion. Soon, as the infant gains more control of the various arm muscles, he can use the forearm independently of the upper arm and eventually the wrist separately from the arm. By this time, the reaching movement that was originally a circular pattern has become a straight-line direct approach.

Between the third and fourth months another important ability appears and develops along with the reaching movements. This is the ability to move the thumb in apposition to the other fingers. This is one ability, as we pointed out above, that no other animal except man and some of the apes has. You can see how important it is if you consider the multitude of things you would not be able to do without it.

So we find that as the infant develops the ability to reach out and grasp objects, his ability to manipulate them keeps pace. Figure 2.13 illustrates the development of these basic prehensile skills.

■ *Maturation.* There is a good deal of evidence that maturation, rather than learning, is the important factor in the development of locomotion and prehension.[27] All children develop these skills in the same sequence, and there is relatively little variability in how any particular behavior pattern is expressed. After the child gets the fundamental ability "down pat," we see a great deal of variability in how each child uses it. Here the influences of the environment come into play and learning increases in importance. This, of course, is seen most clearly in the different kinds of toys boys and girls play with and the kinds of games they play.

■ LANGUAGE DEVELOPMENT

There are many kinds of languages, and taken all together, they refer to means of communication. Thus we can say that many other animals use some sort of language, but no other species approaches the extremely complicated but efficient oral language which humans use. What we are going to emphasize particularly is the development of speech—the oral language.

Early Vocalization. Although the infant does not use *words* to communicate to others until after the first year, other means

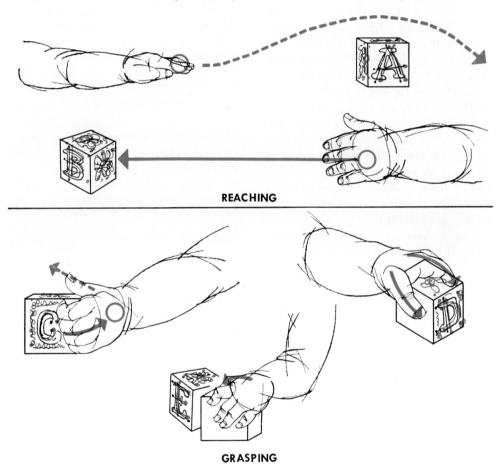

REACHING

GRASPING

Fig. 2.13. Stages in the development of reaching and grasping. (A) sweeping movement at about 22 weeks sometimes misses; (B) direct approach at about 46 weeks; (C) the fingers squeeze the cube against the palm while the thumb remains passive—about 24 weeks; (D) fingers curl over the cube, and the thumb opposes them—about 30 weeks; (E) only the thumb and the tips of the fingers are used—about 52 weeks. (*After Halverson, H. M. An experimental study of prehension in infants by means of systematic cinema records. Genet: Psychol. Monogr., 1931, 10, 107–286.*)

of communication are in evidence as early as the first or second month. At birth the vocalization of the infant is restricted to crying and perhaps some sort of grunting noises. Anyone who has been around a young baby cannot fail to be impressed with such behavior. By the second month, general undifferentiated crying has changed to different types of cries for various states of discomfort. One cannot always tell from the cry just what is wrong, but it does communicate distress of some kind. On the other hand, gurgling and other miscellaneous sounds signify contentment and well-being. Thus, by the end of the first month, the child is using sounds to communicate his needs and feelings to others around him.

As he grows older and the relevant muscles mature, many other sounds appear in the repertoire of the child. In Table 2.2 some of these are listed. In time he enters the so-called babbling stage, when he seems to enjoy just making these sounds over and over again. Many of the sounds the baby makes defy written representation, even with a phonetic alphabet, but babbling is necessary and important because it provides practice with the vocal muscles and lets the child hear its own sounds. Indeed, feeling how sounds are made and at the same time hearing the actual sound helps the infant learn later to associate spoken words with the objects they refer to.[28] By the sixth month the baby can produce practically all the vowel and consonant sounds. These are often combined in simple ways and repeated over and over again. Without understanding the significance of the sounds, the child may say "mama," or "dada," or "re-re-re." By the ninth or tenth month he can imitate sounds made by others. From this point it is easy to see how any of these sounds can be associated with a particular object in the environment, especially if the sound and the object are presented together

TABLE 2.2. The development of language in the infant. This table combines the results of eight major studies of infant development. The average age at which each kind of language behavior appears is given in months. The two numbers represent the range of average ages obtained in the different studies.

Language behavior	Average age, months after birth
Cries, grunts, and makes other respirant sounds	0
Makes different sounds for discomfort, hunger, and pain	1
Makes vowel sounds like *ah, uh, ay*	1–2
Looks toward sound of human voice	2–4
Babbles and coos	3–4
Talks to self, using sounds like *ma, mu, da, na*	4–6
Makes sounds of pleasure and displeasure	5–6
"Sounds off" when he hears a familiar voice	6–7
Puts sounds together and repeats them over and over like *mamamamama, booboo, dadada*	6–9
Imitates sounds made by others	9–10
Understands gestures (can wave bye-bye and often can say it)	9–12
Understands and responds to simple commands ("Hold the spoon," "Look at the doll-baby")	11–15
Imitates syllables and simple words (the first word?)	11–15
Says two different words	12
Says three to five different words	13–18
Understands and responds to the "dont's" ("Don't touch that," "Don't spit it out")	16–20
Names one object or picture in book (cup, ball, doggy, baby, etc.)	17–24
Combines words into phrases ("Go out," "Give me milk," "Where ball")	18–24
Identifies three to five familiar objects or pictures	24
Uses phrases and simple sentences	23–24

Modified from McCarthy, Dorothea. Language development in children. In L. Carmichael (Ed.), *Manual of child psychology*. New York: Wiley, 1946, p. 482.

to the child repeatedly. Figure 2.14 indicates how this may happen.

Comprehension.　　Many studies have shown that the child can respond to sounds long before he can make the sounds himself.[29] By the fourth month he reacts positively to the sound of a human voice by turning his head toward the speaker. At six months he can distinguish between different tones of voice. He responds differently to angry and friendly talking and will stop doing something at the sound of a warning tone.

By ten months he can respond adequately to commands, especially when these are accompanied by gestures. He can wave bye-bye after having his hand waved for him a few times. If his mother says, "Put the spoon in the cup," and points to these objects, he quickly learns to associate the sound of the word with the object to which it refers.

Gestures.　　A baby uses gestures at an early age, and these constitute an important aspect of his prespeech language behavior. By pointing or reaching, the child can con-

Fig. 2.14. Associating a sound with an object. (A) Uttering the sound is associated with hearing it; (B) an adult makes a similar sound which the child imitates; (C) the sound is often accompanied by the object to which it refers; (D) sight of the object is sufficient to produce the sound. (*After Allport, F. H. Social psychology. Boston: Houghton Mifflin, 1924.*)

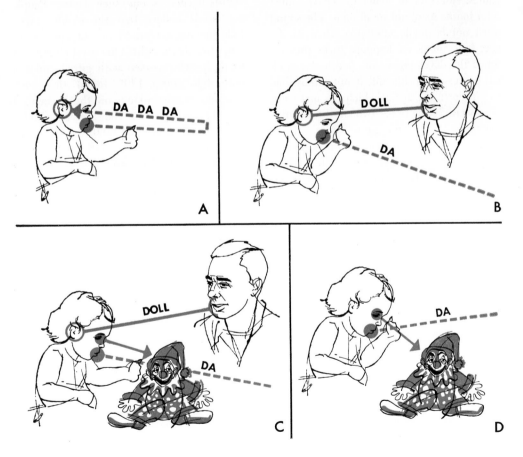

vey information to others and can satisfy his wants. Turning his head or simply pushing the spoon away is a very effective method of demonstrating that he doesn't want any more. In fact, if the child can generally control his environment and get what he wants by using gestures, he may be slow to give them up and to learn to use words instead.

The use of words. Although it may not seem so, it is relatively difficult to determine the age at which the average child utters his first word. What do we mean by the first word? Our criterion is that the sound made must refer to a specific object. That is to say, when the child says "ball" he must mean the spherical object used in games, not toys in general. "Dada" must refer to one man, not to all men. The sound must not be made randomly when his father by coincidence happens to be present. Since the development of speech is a gradual process, it is difficult, if not impossible, to pin down the age at which the first word is spoken. (Sometimes two or three words emerge at about the same time.) If we combine the observations of many child psychologists, however, we can say that on the average the first word is spoken between the tenth and thirteenth months.

Once the first word appears, the vocabulary increases rapidly. Nouns, generally related to things in the immediate environment, come first; then verbs; then adjectives and adverbs; with pronouns appearing last.[29] Children seem to have more difficulty in learning the correct use of pronouns than any other part of speech. Such remarks as "Pick my up" or "Me going outside" are typical.

As the child's vocabulary increases, he begins to combine the words he has learned into sentences. The first type of sentence he uses consists of a single word. He may say, "Eat," to mean "Give me something

to eat," or "Out," meaning "I want to go out." Sometimes people misinterpret this sort of speech, but it is reasonably efficient. Later the infant begins to string two or three words together. By about the age of two we might hear the following sentences, which are incomplete but which contain all the essential words: "Where the doggy go?" "No night-night!" "Meredith going on swing." "When baby wakes up, me give her bottle."

Intelligence and sex. We have traced the main steps in language development in the infant. Maturation plays a part in it; so also does learning. In addition other factors enter the picture, and we ought to say a few words about them.

Intelligence is one such factor. People commonly believe that the children who talk the earliest are the most intelligent. They are partly right. One psychologist, for example, who worked with gifted children with IQs above 140* found that such children began talking, on the average, 4 months earlier than the average child.[30] Children of subnormal intelligence, on the other hand, are several months slower than the average child in beginning to talk. Indeed very feeble-minded children may never learn to talk. There are, however, many reasons why a child may be slow to talk, and he is not necessarily deficient in intelligence if he is slow.[31]

The sex of the child is another factor in learning to talk. Psychological studies of this factor reveal that on the whole girls are slightly ahead of boys in most measures of language skill. In such studies we must control intelligence and socioeconomic background, and we must be careful not to use situations which favor one sex over the

* Less than 2 per cent of the general population are this intelligent. For a more detailed explanation of the IQ and its meaning, see Chap. 15.

other (for example, testing with toys that only boys would be interested in). At all ages studied, girls use more words per sentence than boys, they begin to talk earlier, they articulate better, they are more easily understood, and they have larger vocabularies, especially when they are young.[31] One study even substantiates the popular notion that girls are more talkative than boys and are so from a very early age—the difference, however, is slight.[32]

Social environment. Once the child has matured enough to control his speech mechanism, further progress depends to a great extent upon learning. And, at this early stage, how rapidly he learns depends upon the amount and kind of stimulation he gets from the environment around him. The environment is a complex of many factors and people.

The parents make up one important part of the environment. If the child gets what he wants from his parents by gesturing, he is more reluctant to give up this form of communication in favor of learning to speak. If the child's parents do not bother to point out objects to him and pronounce their names, he will build his vocabulary more slowly. If they consistently use baby talk (because it is cute) or if they are sloppy in their pronunciation and sentence structure, the child will develop bad speech habits which will be extremely difficult to break. It is just as easy for a child to learn to say "thank you" and "train" as it is to learn "ta-ta" or "choo-choo," once he reaches the stage at which he can pronounce the relevant sounds. If he is not ready (able) to pronounce a particular word correctly, no great harm will be done by putting off teaching it to him. There are many other words which he can learn to say correctly at that time.

Many studies have shown that twins are more retarded in speech development than single-birth children. One experimenter reports that five-year-old twins used sentences of about the same length as three-year-old singletons.[33] Another study showed, however, that after twins began school they were not so far behind single children.[34] The likely explanation of these findings is that twins are left alone together in the home more often than single children and consequently they do not have the advantage of stimulation from older, i.e., more skilled, talkers.

Bilingualism is another aspect of the social environment that affects speech development. If two languages are spoken in the home or if the child is forced to learn a foreign language while he is still learning his mother tongue, he gets confused and his skill in both languages is retarded. In one study it was found that it is better for children in a home where two languages are spoken to hear each one from a different adult, each adult using one language exclusively.[35]

One finding which has been consistently reported is the high relationship between the socioeconomic status of the family and the rate of development of language. In one study,[36] the language of poor children was compared with that of well-to-do children by taking records of what they said for 6 hours. The well-to-do children, it turned out, did better than the poor children in every aspect of language that was considered. At all early ages the level of language ability of children of well-educated, well-to-do families is higher than those from poorer, less educated families even when the factor of intelligence is excluded from the picture.

If we consider that learning from a stimulating environment is necessary for rapid development of speech, it is easy to understand the data concerning socioeconomic background. A home with well-educated people in it is more likely to have books, pictures, music, and even a wide variety of the more prosaic articles of household furniture. If the family is well-to-do, also, the number of places to go, activities to engage in, and things available all increase proportionately. In fact, it has been found that the greater the number of toys a child has and the greater amount of travel he experiences, the faster he acquires vocabulary and sentences. Then again, well-to-do parents usually have more time to spend specifically teaching a youngster.

We can say in conclusion that the greater the variety of experiences that are made available to the child and the more time that is spent in teaching him about the world, the greater his mental development in general and his language development in particular.

This concludes our discussion of development in this chapter. We have covered only *motor development* and *language development*. There are, of course, many other aspects of psychological development. These are more appropriately considered, however, in other chapters along with the more general treatment of topics. *Emotional development* is considered in the chapter on emotion (Chapter 4), *perceptual development* in the chapter on perception (Chapter 7), *personality development* in the chapter on personality (Chapter 9), and *intellectual development* in the chapter on intellectual abilities (Chapter 15). Therefore, to obtain a more complete picture of the development of behavior, the student should turn to the developmental sections of these chapters.

SUMMARY

1. Chromosomes are the transmitters of heredity and govern the biological characteristics of each new individual. Through such characteristics, they indirectly control the maturation of the nervous system and sense organs, whose functions are essential in behavior.

2. Because chromosomes from the two parents randomly pair up in the child, each individual is different from every other, except for cases of identical twins and triplets who begin life as a single cell.

3. During the months immediately before and after birth, various organs within the individual are maturing in preparation for their normal functions. Maturation proceeds on a time schedule that is relatively similar for all normal individuals of a species. It so precedes behavior that by the time a function is needed the organs for carrying it out have matured.

4. The development of reflexes and motor abilities, such as sitting, standing, and walking, is almost wholly a matter of maturation.

5. More complex abilities, though capable of considerable training, are limited by the hereditary potential of a person. No amount of training, for example, can make an ape use language as human beings do, nor can differences among people in intellectual ability be erased by special training.

6. Motor skills develop in the infant in a pattern that is similar for all children. This makes it possible to set up norms for the ages at which such abilities as grasping, sitting, and walking should appear. Some individuals are slower than others in their development, but they are not necessarily any less intelligent.

7. Prehension is a particularly important aspect of motor development because it is necessary for the acquisition of other skills that involve the manipulation of objects.

8. Infants begin life with no more language than their cries and grunts. As their language mechanism matures, they make more and more different sounds. Even before they can use these sounds as language, they begin to comprehend the meanings of words that they hear, and they also can communicate some of their wants with gestures and cries.

9. When the first word appears at about one year of age, it is used as a sentence, which usually means, "I want such and such." After that, vocabulary grows by leaps and bounds.

10. Language ability depends in part on maturation, but also on other factors. Those who talk earliest will, on the average, later prove to be the most intelligent.

11. Girls tend to talk a little earlier than boys. Single children also tend to talk earlier than twins. By and large, those with a more stimulating home environment make more rapid progress in language development than those with a poorer environment.

SUGGESTIONS FOR FURTHER READING

Gesell, A. T., & Ilg, F. L. *Infant and child in the culture of today*. New York: Harper, 1942.
> *An interesting and very readable account of the development of the child.*

Hurlock, E. B. *Developmental psychology*. New York: McGraw-Hill, 1953.
> *A text covering each stage of human development from conception to old age.*

Jersild, A. T. *Child psychology* (3d Ed.). New York: Prentice-Hall, 1950.
> *A widely used textbook on child psychology.*

Munn, N. L. *Evolution and growth of human behavior*. Boston: Houghton Mifflin, 1955.
> *A comprehensive text on psychological development which includes chapters on the evolutionary aspects of animal behavior.*

Scheinfeld, A. *The new heredity and you*. Philadelphia: Lippincott, 1950.
> *A fascinating account of the mechanisms of human heredity.*

Zubek, J., & Solberg, P. A. *Human development*. New York: McGraw-Hill, 1954.
> *A text that treats separately each topic in psychological development and in each case gives a brief account of its background in animal behavior.*

Chapter 3 MOTIVATION

ONE MAN WANTS to be a doctor. Another strives for power in the political world. Here is a person who is ravenously hungry and, at the moment, wants to do nothing but eat. A girl is lonely; she wants friends. A man has just committed murder, and we say that his motive was revenge. These are just a few examples of motives and wants that play so large a part in human behavior. They run the gamut from basic wants like hunger and sex to complicated, long-term motives like political ambition and the desire to get married. We never see these wants directly, but we know they exist from how we feel, from what people do and say, and from what they seem to work for.

The first part of this chapter was drafted by Eliot Stellar of the University of Pennsylvania and the latter part by Clifford T. Morgan of The Johns Hopkins University.

■ THE NATURE OF MOTIVATION

Several hundred words in our everyday vocabulary refer to people's motives. Some of the more common ones are wants, striving, desire, need, motive, goal, aspiration, drive, wish, aim, ambition, hunger, thirst, love, and revenge. Each of these many words has its own connotation and is used in a certain context. Many of them can be defined with reasonable precision and prove useful to us in the scientific study of motivation. The problem of terminology is nevertheless difficult, and the student should pay especial attention to the way in which we use terms in this chapter. The general term *motivation* refers to *behavior that is instigated by needs within the individual and is directed toward goals that can satisfy these needs.*

The motivational cycle. Three general aspects of motivation may be distinguished. Each has an effect on the other, and each may be named in several ways. Each may be thought of as a stage in a cycle, for the first leads to the second, the second to the third, and the third to the first (see Figure 3.1).

Any one of three names may be given to the first stage of the motivational cycle: *need*, *drive*, or *motive*. These terms are almost, but not entirely, synonymous. Need refers to a *lack or deficit within the individual*. We customarily distinguish between *physiological needs*, on the one hand, and *derived needs* on the other. A physiological need is some *tissue deficit* in the body, for example, lack of food, air, or water. A derived need may be the lack of something quite subtle such as affection, recognition, or prestige. The term *drive* is often used interchangeably with need, but it has the further implication that a need supplies an impetus to behavior. The animal that is hungry or thirsty, for example, appears to be driven in search of food. *Motive*, similarly, is not used very differently from drive or need, but it implies that a drive has *direction toward some particular goal*. If we speak of prestige motives, we imply that behavior is directed to the goal of achieving prestige. We shall use these terms with their slightly different shades of meaning, throughout.

A second stage in the motivational cycle may be given the general label of *instrumental behavior*. This is any behavior that is instrumental in satisfying a need, drive, or motive. Instrumental behavior may be some general activity or restlessness as, for example, the flouncing and crying of the hungry infant. It may be some reflexive or instinctive activity such as suckling at the mother's breast. Or it may be some highly complex learned behavior such as the campaign activities of a politician seeking election to office or the work of a carpenter in building a house. There are special terms that apply to each kind of instrumental behavior, and we shall consider them a little later in the chapter. It should also be noted that instrumental behavior is an important concept in understanding the subject of learning and is discussed further in Chapter 5.

A third stage in motivation is called the *goal* or *incentive*. Instrumental behavior is directed toward this goal, and when the goal is achieved, the need, drive, or motive is satisfied. If a person is hungry, his goal is to eat; if his need is sex, his goal is sexual satisfaction; if it is affection or companionship, his goal may be marriage, joining a club, or going to the local poolroom. Incentives are the same thing as goals except that they imply a certain *control over motivated behavior*. If, for example, an experimenter wishes to have a rat learn a maze, he may use food as the incentive to induce the rat to run the maze. If an employer wishes to increase his production, he may use bonuses as an incentive to spur additional effort.

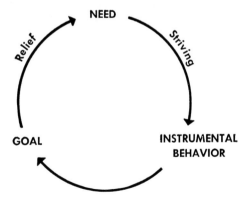

Fig. 3.1. Stages in the motivational cycle. Motivation begins with a need. This gives rise to instrumental behavior which, if successful, leads to a goal. This, in turn, relieves the need.

In the case of the basic physiological needs, goals are relatively fixed and unchangeable. If one is thirsty, for example, water is about the only goal that will do, although there are many forms in which the water may be consumed; if he is hungry, nothing but food will do. For more complex derived needs, however, several alternative goals may satisfy the same need. A need for recognition, for example, may be satisfied by becoming a pillar of the church, rising to eminence in politics, or becoming the best golf player in town. So, though goals must be appropriate to one's needs, the study of goals is itself a complex aspect of the study of motivation (see Chapter 10).

Physiological motivation. Before going on, let us illustrate these three stages in motivation by considering an incident in physiological motivation that occurred in a hospital a few years ago.[1] A three-year-old boy was brought into the hospital for observation because he showed certain abnormalities of physical development. After seven days on regular hospital diet, the boy suddenly died. Autopsy showed that the adrenal glands on the top of his kidneys were abnormal. Normally the adrenal glands keep the salt of the body from flowing out in the urine. But in this abnormal case, the boy had lost salt faster than he could replace it on the standard hospital diet. It seemed clear that the boy died of a salt deficiency.

After the boy's death, his parents reported that from birth he had never eaten "properly." Unlike most children, he hated anything sweet, but he seemed to crave salty things. He eagerly licked the salt off bacon and crackers, and although he would not eat them, he would always ask for more. One day when he was about eighteen months old, he got the salt shaker off the table, and his mother found him eating

salt voraciously. From then on, whenever he came into the kitchen, he would scream and point to the cupboard where the salt shaker was kept. The only thing that would quiet him was to let him have the salt shaker again. By this time his parents had discovered that he would eat fairly well if they put three or four times the normal amount of salt on his food, and in addition, let him eat about a teaspoonful of plain table salt a day.

This unfortunate case illustrates well the stages of motivation as they apply to physiological needs: (1) the boy's body had a physiological need for salt; (2) this need brought out a variety of instrumental behavior, including his attempts to get the salt shaker from the table and the cupboard; (3) the goal was salt, and once he got it, his need was relieved and the craving temporarily disappeared. All motivation, of course, does not have an immediate physiological basis, and many needs, especially complex social needs, can go unsatisfied without resulting in death. Nevertheless, these three stages make a typical pattern of motivated behavior, both simple and complex.

The study of motivation. Now we shall consider motivation in some detail. We shall begin with a study of physiological drives and then examine the ways in which behavior can be instrumental in satisfying needs. After that, we shall explain the acquisition of new motives through learning and present some of the more common social motives. Finally, we shall consider a few concepts that are important in understanding a person's individual motives.

■ PHYSIOLOGICAL DRIVES

We shall begin the detailed study of motivation by considering the physiological drives. Because these drives stem from tissue needs of the body, the principal problem that arises is one of understanding, if possible, the physiological basis of these needs. Much of this section therefore deals with this problem.

Homeostasis. To understand physiological needs, we should have in mind a concept known as *homeostasis. This is the tendency of the body to maintain a balance among internal physiological conditions.* Such a balance is essential for the individual's survival. Body temperature must not get too high or too low. Blood pressure must not rise or fall beyond certain limits. The blood must not get too acidic or alkaline; it must not contain too much carbon dioxide; it must not become too concentrated; it must have a certain amount of sugar in it. If these limits are exceeded, the individual becomes sick and he may die.

Physiologists have discovered a long list of *homeostatic mechanisms* to be involved in maintaining conditions within normal limits.[2] Consider, for example, the case of temperature control. Typical body temperature in man is 98.6°F. It normally stays near that point because the body can cool or heat itself. If one's body temperature tends to get too high, he sweats and thereby evaporates liquid which cools the body. If temperature threatens to fall, he shivers and steps up his metabolism (see Chapter 22 for a discussion of metabolism). Shivering burns the body's fuels faster and thus generates extra heat. In addition, many animals can insulate themselves against heat loss by fluffing their fur and creating a dead-air space around their skin. All that is left of this mechanism in human beings, however, is the goose-pimples one gets when he is too cold.

Physiological mechanisms take care of many of the problems of maintaining a homeostatic balance, but in many cases the body also makes use of *regulatory behavior*[3] —behavior that has the effect of regulating internal physiological conditions—to maintain or restore the balance. Such regulatory behavior is behavior that is *instrumental in satisfying physiological needs.* When the body becomes depleted of water or food, for example, it cannot maintain a balance by calling on its physiological mechanisms. Rather it must obtain more water and food from the outside. It does this through motivated behavior that normally succeeds in procuring more water and food; after that, the homeostatic balance is restored. The important point, then, is that physiological drives are part of a more general physiological mechanism for maintaining homeostatic balance within the body.

Now let us consider each of the principal physiological drives.

Warmth, cold, and pain. Warmth, cold, and pain are senses that take part in our perception of the world, and they are treated as such in Chapter 19. They may also be regarded as drives, for they can serve as powerful motives that keep a person striving to restore them to a satisfactory level. First we shall consider warmth and cold, then pain.

Warmth and cold, as we indicated above, are regulated within limits by the physiological mechanisms of homeostasis. When the body is too hot, it sweats and does other things to reduce the production of heat; when it is too cold, it burns more fuel and keeps to a minimum its loss of heat. In addition, however, the individual may behave in such a way as to achieve a comfortable temperature. When too hot, he takes off clothes; when too cold, he puts them on. He turns the room temperature up or down, opens or closes windows, and so on. In extreme conditions of hot or cold, he may spend most of his efforts in trying to obtain relief. Instances of this sort are so familiar that they need not be dwelt on. The important point is to keep in mind that warmth and cold are among the physiological drives.

In a part of the brain known as the *hypothalamus* (see Figure 21.8 in Chapter 21), there is a center for the regulation of body temperature. This center probably responds directly to the temperature of blood circulating through it. In addition, however, there are receptors for warmth and cold (described in Chapter 19) distributed generously over the surfaces of the body. These are so adapted to the temperature of the body that they are quiescent under ordinary, comfortable circumstances. When the temperature around them becomes either too hot or too cold, however, the warmth or cold receptors—there are two different kinds—are activated. Impulses from the receptors are conveyed to the brain, which instigates efforts to relieve the discomfort.

The physiological mechanism of *pain* as a drive is similar to that for warmth and cold except that there are much more specific reactions to pain. Sense organs for pain, known as free nerve endings (again see Chapter 19), are widely distributed throughout the skin, blood vessels, and internal organs. These sense organs are usually stimulated by some injury to the tissues of the body. The individual then strives to remove the injurious stimulus. If that cannot be done or does not help, he looks for some way to relieve the pain.

Our bodies are equipped with certain automatic mechanisms for avoiding pain. A sudden pain in a limb, for example, makes us *reflexly* withdraw that limb from the source of stimulation (see Chapter 21). We do not have to think about it; we just withdraw, immediately and quickly. Sometimes when the source of pain is deep within our bodies, there is no way to with-

draw from the source of injury. In such cases, we try many techniques to reduce the pain. Modern pain-killing drugs are, of course, the most effective ways of helping such pain. But they can fail, and often they are not available. Then the individual may writhe, tear at his tissues, lie down, try to sleep, try not to move, or try to distract himself. Since none of these techniques is very effective, the individual may become preoccupied with his pain and continue endlessly his efforts to reduce it. Such pain constitutes a powerful drive that channels tremendous efforts toward one goal, the relief of pain.

Now let us turn to such drives as thirst, hunger, sleep, and sex. These drives, unlike those of warmth, cold, and pain, are mainly dependent upon tissue needs *within* the body.

Thirst.   We constantly need water because we are constantly losing it by evaporation from the skin and mouth and in the formation of urine. But what is it about the need for water that makes us thirsty and therefore motivated to drink? A long time ago, some physiologists declared that the throat and mouth get dry when an individual needs water, and therefore he drinks to relieve unpleasant sensations in his throat.[4] Actually the problem is not as simple as that.

Certainly people will report that they drink to wet the mouth, but apparently a dry mouth and thirst are two different things. For example, there was the case of a man once who had no salivary glands.[5] His mouth was always dry, and he would often sip water just to wet his mouth. Despite the fact that his dry mouth was never a good sign of how much he needed water, he would feel thirsty from time to time. Furthermore, he was always able to drink the right amount of water to meet his biological needs. Of course dryness of the

mouth can be a good sign of thirst in normal people, but it is obvious that other
factors must also operate to produce thirst
and permit the individual to regulate his
drinking in accordance with his needs.

This point has been made clear by studies done on dogs.[6] By careful surgery, the
esophagus—the tube from the throat to
the stomach—of each dog in these experiments was brought out through the skin of
the neck. Then it was opened in such a way
that everything the dog drank ran out of
the upper part of the opening. But still the
dog could be maintained by putting food
and water directly into the stomach through
the lower part of the opening. When the
dog was offered water, it drank just about
what it needed, and then stopped, even
though none of the water got into its body.
Of course, after a while it drank again, and
kept repeating the process until water was
put into its stomach. But the important
point is that the dog has some way of
metering the water it passes through its
mouth without depending upon actual relief of its biological need.

The next step in the experiment was to
put enough water directly into the dog's
stomach to satisfy its biological needs and
then let it drink. When the dog drank right
after its stomach was filled, it drank just
about the amount it needed—as judged by
the amount of water that had been lost
through deprivation (see Figure 3.2). But
if it had to wait 15 to 30 minutes after its
stomach was loaded, then it did not drink
at all. So after water had been in the
stomach for a short time, thirst was satisfied.

What happens that makes thirst go away
when water is put into the stomach or
when the animal fills itself by drinking? We
do not know for certain, but the best guess
is this: Lack of water makes all the cells in
the body give up water. Within a center

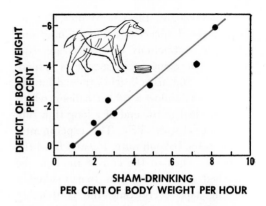

Fig. 3.2. Sham drinking and water deficit. In experiments with fistulated dogs, which can drink water
without any of it getting into the stomach, the
amount of water ingested in a standard experimental
period is directly proportional to the amount of water
that has been lost from the body through water deprivation. (After Adolph, E. F. *The internal environment and behavior: water content. Amer. J. Psychiat.,
1941, 97, 1365–1373.*)

in the hypothalamus, mentioned above, are
some cells that are especially sensitive to
loss of water.[7] Through their connections
with other parts of the brain, they can regulate drinking behavior according to the relative amount of water in the body.

Hunger. The need for food is as obvious
as the need for water. The body is always
using up materials in growth, in the repair
of tissues, and in the storage of reserve supplies. But most important is the fact that
every function of our bodies from heartbeat
to thinking requires energy, and this energy
must ultimately come from the metabolism
of food.

When people need food, they usually report that they are hungry. For some, hunger
means a feeling of strong contractions in
the stomach. But for others, there may be
no particular sensation of stomach contractions, just a general ill feeling of weakness
and lightheadedness. Some people have
both kinds of feeling at once.

A physiologist, the late Walter B. Cannon, showed objectively that hunger and stomach contractions very often are associated.[2] In some very ingenious experiments, he and his colleagues trained human subjects to swallow a rubber balloon which was attached to the end of a long thin rubber tube (Figure 3.3). The experimenter blew up the balloon until it gently filled the stomach. Then to the end of the tube he attached a recording pen that marked a moving tape every time the contracting stomach compressed the air in the balloon. The subject could also make a second pen mark on the paper by pressing a telegraph key every time he felt a pang of hunger. So it was easy to tell whether stomach contractions and hunger sensations occurred at the same time or not. They did. Not only that, the strength of the stomach contractions and the degree of hunger both increased as time elapsed after the last meal.

But stomach contractions are not the whole story. First of all, some people claim they never feel stomach contractions, but still they report the experience of hunger. Second, and perhaps more convincing, are facts obtained from people who have had their entire stomachs removed.[8] They have no stomach contractions, of course, but they still get hungry. The same thing shows up in rats whose stomachs are removed.[9] These animals eat food eagerly, they get

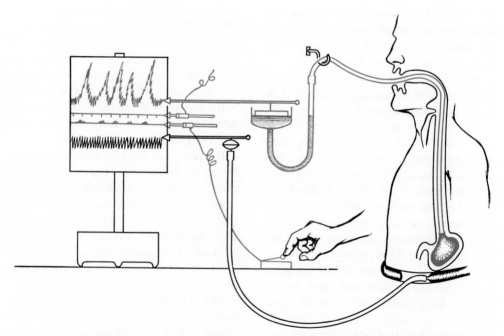

Fig. 3.3. Hunger pangs and contractions of the stomach. The subject swallows a balloon connected with a marker so that a record is made of stomach contractions. He also presses a key whenever he feels a hunger pang. The record shows that spasms of the stomach are correlated with the subject's experience of hunger. (After Cannon, W. B. Hunger and thirst. In Murchison, C. (Ed.) *Handbook of general experimental psychology.* Worcester, Mass.: Clark Univ. Press, 1934, p. 250.)

restless when it is time to eat, and they learn mazes for food rewards just like normal rats. Hunger therefore exists without the stomach or stomach contractions, so we must look to other factors for the explanation of hunger. Unfortunately the exact nature of the other factors is not known. Many kinds of chemical changes take place in the body when an individual is in need of food. Some of them undoubtedly are very important in hunger, too. At the present time, we have only the barest idea of what these chemical changes might be and how they might do their work.

Specific hungers. There is one important aspect of hunger which we have not mentioned yet. This is the fact that organisms not only regulate when and how much they eat, but they also select what they eat. Given a chance, animals and men balance their diets and eat approximately what they need of proteins, fats, carbohydrates, vitamins, and minerals. Organisms therefore are not just motivated by a lack of food, but rather they may be very specifically motivated for many particular foods they might need. As a matter of fact, it has been questioned whether there is any such thing as general hunger apart from the sum total of specific hungers for the various food substances. But we are still far enough from answering this question to warrant treating hunger and specific hungers separately.

▪ *Cafeteria feeding.* The best way to explain specific hungers is to describe some experiments in which human infants were allowed to select their own diets.[10] The experimenter took infants from six to twelve months of age and allowed them to eat all their food from large trays containing from 12 to 20 different foods in separate containers. As you can imagine, the babies made quite a mess of things, but the important point is that they did manage to eat balanced diets. At any given meal, a

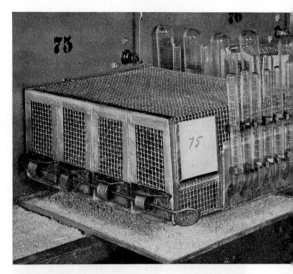

Fig. 3.4. Apparatus used for the study of specific hungers in rats. Each tube contains a solution of a dietary component. The amount of each component selected by the rat in any particular period can be read from the graduated markings on the tubes. (*Courtesy Dr. C. P. Richter.*)

baby might eat all vegetable or all butter. Sometimes, he would eat the same food for days. But over a period of time, the infants balanced out their diets by going from one food to another so that they grew as well as, or better than, infants fed according to a dietitian's formula.

The same sort of results came out of experiments with rats[11] in which they received each component of the diet in a separate container (see Figure 3.4). Many of the rats were able to select diets that permitted them to grow as well as, or better than, rats fed on stock diets. But about one-third of the rats failed to select beneficially. In most of these cases, however, the failure was due to the fact that the rats would not eat the particular protein offered to them. Often if that protein were replaced with another one, the animals would eat balanced diets and grow normally.

The important point for our purposes is

that these experiments show that *animals and human beings have mechanisms which enable them to select the kinds of foods they need.*

▪ *Need and food preference.* You saw an excellent example of how need produces food preference in the case of the boy who suffered from salt deficiency. The same sort of condition can be produced experimentally in rats by surgical removal of the adrenal glands on the top of the kidneys.[12] (These glands are described in Chapter 22.) When these glands are taken out, the rats lose salt constantly, and therefore they

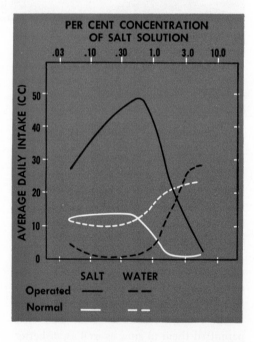

Fig. 3.5. Preferences and aversions for salt and water. Normal rats drink appreciable quantities of weak salt solutions, but when the concentration exceeds 1 per cent, they prefer water. Rats whose adrenal glands have been removed strongly prefer salt solutions until the concentration exceeds 2 per cent; above that point, they prefer water. (Modified from Bare, J. K. *The specific hunger for sodium chloride in normal and adrenalectomized white rats. J. comp. physiol. Psychol.,* 1949, **42**, 242–253.)

must eat extra amounts in their diets if they are to live. This they do, and it can be shown that rats deprived of their adrenal glands will maintain themselves by drinking large amounts of salt water in preference to plain tap water. Increasing their need for salt increased their motivation for salt, and as a result, they ingested much more of it than normal, unmotivated rats (Figure 3.5).

Other specific hungers can be developed in this way by putting the individual into a state of need.[13] For example, if all vitamin B is left out of the diet, the individual will develop a strong hunger for B vitamins. In pregnancy, the need for fats, proteins, and certain minerals is increased, and the individual becomes strongly motivated to eat these foods. Sometimes the motivation becomes so strong that it assumes the character of a pathological craving, and there have been extraordinary cases of pregnant women who ate plaster off the walls or ate mud, presumably to get some of the minerals they needed but could not obtain in their ordinary diets.

In addition to specific hungers for particular foods, needs can produce *specific food aversions.* For example, the parathyroid glands situated on the thyroid gland in the neck (see Chapter 22) secrete a hormone that controls the level of calcium and phosphorus in the body. When the gland is removed, calcium levels fall and phosphorus accumulates, so that more calcium and less phosphorus are needed.[3] It is interesting that animals from whom the parathyroid glands have been removed avidly eat calcium but avoid phosphorus with equal fervor.

As one might also expect, organisms also avoid foods on which they have just been satiated.[14] If an animal's need for protein is satisfied, it will avoid protein, although it may still be quite hungry and highly motivated to eat a fat or carbohydrate (sugar). There are therefore *specific* satiations, as well as specific hungers.

▪ *Habit and food preference.* Since we know that organisms tend to select foods that alleviate their needs, why do people often eat inappropriate foods? We can all think of cases in which this happens. A diabetic patient, whose blood sugar may be dangerously high, may aggravate his condition by eating large amounts of sugar. Other people have been known to eat sweets avidly, neglecting proteins and fats, to the detriment of their health.

There appear to be two reasons for such harmful food preferences. One is that dietary self-selection in animals and infants is not always perfect. You will recall that, in the experiments with rats, many animals did not select foods well enough to maintain normal health and growth. The other reason is that bad habits may be learned, and these habits can distort or override natural food preferences. This fact has been demonstrated in several experiments with animals. In one such experiment,[13] rats were deprived of vitamin B₁, then given their choice between food containing the vitamin and food deficient in it. As one might expect, they chose the food containing the vitamin. The experimenter, however, had mixed some licorice with this food. Licorice is not ordinarily preferred by rats, but it has a strong flavor. After considerable training in this situation, the rats were presented with a choice between the *vitamin-deficient food with licorice* and the vitamin-rich food without licorice. In other words, the licorice was switched from one food to the other. The switch fooled the rats. Now they preferred the food without the vitamin, even though they desperately needed the vitamin. The rats had learned to associate the strong flavor of licorice with the kind of food they needed, and

when the licorice was in the inappropriate food they were misled. In this particular experiment, the rats eventually learned that a switch had been made and changed their preferences back to the vitamin-containing food. The important point, however, is that for a time they were victims of a habit that ran counter to their natural food preferences. Situations in daily living are seldom so simple as they were in this experiment, and there are many opportunities for people to acquire habitual preferences for food.

Sleep. Sleep is typical of physiological drives in about every way except that it involves passive resting of the body rather than an active striving. We therefore consider the need for sleep to be a physiological need comparable to those for water and for food. Occasionally there is a person who does not believe sleep is a need and tries to get along without it. One young man, for example, was convinced that sleep was only a bad habit, and resolved to prove he could stay awake indefinitely.[17] He sat by a time clock, punching it every 10 minutes for 7 days, when his vigil had to be terminated because he appeared on the verge of insanity. Actually, he slept quite a bit the last few days in the 10-minute intervals and often, toward the end, right through some of them. At this point he had lost enough of his sensibilities that he would not believe he had slept and was convinced that his clock was being tampered with in some mysterious way.

The need for sleep is real. Yet we cannot put our finger on any accumulation of waste products or special chemicals in the body that helps bring on sleep.[18] Scientists have transfused blood from sleepy to waking dogs, but this did not make them sleepy. Siamese twins with joint circulation do not always sleep at the same time. And a report of a two-headed baby that lived for a few months says that one head slept while the other was awake (Figure 3.7). Since, in these cases, sleep occurred independently of the condition of the blood, we are led to believe that sleep is regulated by centers in the brain. Such centers are known to exist and are discussed later in Chapter 21. For the present, all we can say is that the physiological conditions that constitute the need for sleep are poorly understood.

Sex.   Sexual motivation is unique in biological motivation. It is a powerful motive, yet the survival of the individual does not depend upon it in any sense. Sexual motivation is also unique because we know more about its physiological basis than we do about the basis of other kinds of biological motivation. There is still much to be learned, particularly about sexual behavior in our own society, but as matters stand now, we have excellent information on the sexual behavior of a wide variety of different animals and in a wide variety of human societies. Sexual behavior can be understood in terms of two main factors: the *sex hormones*, and *habits* acquired through learning.

▪ *The sex hormones.* The testis of the male and the ovary of the female secrete special chemicals that are responsible for the development of the secondary sex characteristics of the body as well as for much of the sexual behavior of the two sexes. When the sex glands mature at puberty, with them develop the masculine and feminine body forms, hair distribution, vocal characteristics, and adult sex organs. At the same time, in animals as well as in human beings, interest in the opposite sex typically develops in a sharp spurt. If the sex glands fail to develop properly or are removed in experimental animals, very few of the characteristics that are typical of each sex will show up in the individual.

One point should be clear. There is no magic about the sex hormones, especially in the case of human beings. They are not solely responsible for sexual behavior—they only help. When sexual motivation is low, extra sex hormones are not likely to help. Neither is it true, as some have thought, that homosexuality occurs because an individual has the wrong sex hormones. Giving a homosexual an extra amount of hormone appropriate to his or her own biological sex will more likely increase the homosexuality than reverse it, if it does anything at all.[19]

Among lower animals like the rat, the sex hormones actually are more crucially

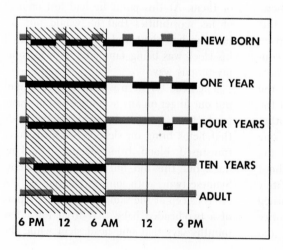

Fig. 3.6. The development of cycles of sleep and waking. The newborn infant alternates sleep and waking five or six times a day. Later on, he sleeps the night through and takes two daily naps. These naps gradually decrease, until only one nightly period of sleep is left. The length and depth of this period become less as the individual grows to adulthood. (*After Kleitman, N. Sleep and wakefulness. Chicago: Univer. Chicago Press, 1939, p. 515.*)

NEW BORN
ONE YEAR
FOUR YEARS
TEN YEARS
ADULT

6 PM   12   6 AM   12   6 PM

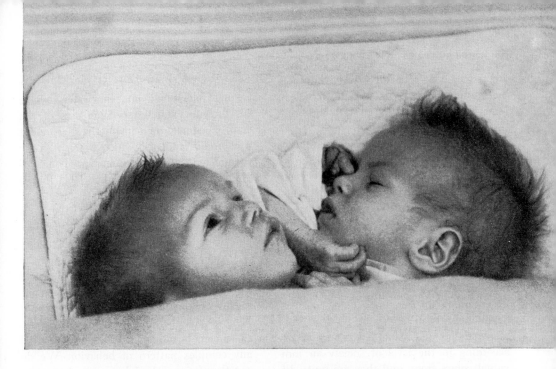

Fig. 3.7. A two-headed baby. One head sleeps while the other is awake, indicating that sleep is controlled by the brain rather than by factors in the blood or the body. (*Courtesy Life Magazine,* © *Time, Inc.*)

important than among the higher animals like the chimpanzee and the human.[20] The spayed female rat will never mate again unless given hormones artificially. The male may continue to mate for a short while after castration but then becomes incapable of sexual motivation, unless restored with sex hormones. The comparable story for human beings is not so clear. There are cases among both sexes in which removal of the sex glands makes sexual motivation disappear, but there are equal numbers of cases in which sexual motivation is unaffected by castration or ovariectomy. The picture is all the more complicated by the fact that there are men and women who are sexually impotent or frigid but who still have perfectly normal supplies of sex hormones. The information we have on monkeys and chimpanzees, however, indicates that the higher animals really do not depend crucially on sex hormones. The males in these

species can be castrated without noticeable effect on sexual motivation. And it is clear that female monkeys and chimpanzees show sexual motivation at times when their hormonal supply is very low. This is not true among the lower female animals, but it is true of women.

So the sex hormones are important in the development of physical sexual characteristics and sexual motivation. But while their importance in sexual behavior is very great among the lower animals, it becomes less and less in the higher animals.

▪ *Habit and sexual motivation.* In the sexual behavior of higher animals, such as monkeys and human beings, the sex hormones are relatively less important and habit and experience relatively more important than they are in lower animals.[21] This may be illustrated by comparing the rat and the monkey. Rats reared in isolation, for example, mate normally the first time they are tested. The male rat may be inhibited by emotional situations, but the female is remarkably resistant to all but the most disturbing situations.

In monkeys and chimpanzees the story is quite different. The male has to learn to mate, usually at the hands of an experienced female. The female chimpanzee, on the other hand, learns to use sexual behavior for nonsexual purposes. For example, she will often win out against a much larger male in competition for food by presenting herself sexually to the male and then making off with the food as the male focuses his attention on her.

Among human beings it is clear from many studies that sexual habits vary widely according to the level of society an individual comes from, and they are quite different in widely differing societies. Kinsey has shown, for example, that premarital intercourse is practiced more by the lower socioeconomic classes than by the higher ones.[23] The reverse is true of masturbation. Also studies of different cultures have shown that some societies strongly encourage homosexual practices among adolescents, whereas other cultures are much more severe than we are in their restriction of homosexuality.[24]

Habit, then, is much more important in the sexual behavior of man and higher animals than it is among the lower animals. Habits can cause sexuality to persist even when sex hormones are absent. And, of course, habit frequently determines the way in which human beings express their sexual motivation and what kinds of sexual outlets they prefer.

Instincts and drives. At this point we should consider a problem that has puzzled scientists for years—the problem of instinct. In everyday speech, we use this term liberally. We say that a mother instinctively cares for her young, that a man

has an instinct to fight, or that a father instinctively leaped into the water to save his drowning youngster. Such uses of the term "instinct" or "instinctive" represent a common tendency, which is scientifically incorrect, to explain summarily all sorts of complex behavior with a mere label that is not defined or explained.

To the modern psychologist, the term *instinct,* or preferably *instinctive,* is acceptable if it is used in a well-defined sense. The definition must include two essential elements: the presence of a *physiological drive,* and the satisfaction of the drive by means of *complex, unlearned patterns of behavior.* Hunger and thirst are physiological drives, but they usually do not entail any complex pattern of behavior. We do not therefore speak of hunger and thirst as instincts. Sexual behavior, however, presents a more complicated problem. Neither in human beings nor in rats are there very complex, unlearned patterns of sexual behavior. In many other animals, however, especially the birds, there are intricate patterns of reflex behavior that are unlearned and serve in the satisfaction of the sexual drive. The initial part of the pattern may be a series of songs and calls; after that, there may be a pattern of pursuit; then a period of courtship characterized by billing and cooing, strutting, spreading of feathers, charging, and other intricate sequences; and finally the acts of copulation. In cases such as this, sexual behavior may properly be called *instinctive.*

The comparative study of animals and human beings makes it clear that man is not nearly so well endowed with instinctive patterns as are many of the lower animals. We have just seen an instance of this point in the matter of sexual behavior. In certain lower animals, sexual satisfaction depends to a great extent on reflexes and instinctive patterns, and these, in turn, depend upon hormones. In human beings, however, instinctive patterns, and the hormones that activate them, are less important and are supplanted by learned mechanisms.

In Chapter 23, we shall consider instinctive patterns in some detail, describing several instances of them among the lower animals. Here, in connection with drives, we shall consider only the example of *maternal behavior*. In both human beings and animals, maternal behavior is almost universal among the females of the species. It appears during the course of pregnancy and persists until the young have been born and reared to weaning. Because maternal behavior has all the earmarks of motivated behavior and has a physiological basis, which is partly known, we regard it as an expression of a *maternal drive*. This drive has its basis in a combination of hormones secreted during pregnancy and shortly thereafter. One of the important hormones in the combination is *prolactin*, a product of the pituitary gland (see page 560). Prolactin stimulates the mammary glands, which supply milk for nursing the young, but it is also important in maternal behavior. It has been injected into virgin female rats that have been given the young of a mother rat. The result is that the injected rat retrieves young and cares for them in much the same way as the natural mother does.[25]

Other elements in the complex pattern of maternal activities are illustrated in Figure 3.8. The pattern is so consistent from mother to mother in the absence of any opportunities for learning it that we are justified in labeling it *instinctive behavior*. Before the young are born, the mother builds a nest. At birth, she cleans them and sees to it that they are safely in the nest. When they wriggle out, she retrieves them. For many long hours each day, she keeps them warm and nurses them. Although the details of the maternal pattern vary from one species to another, it is relatively consistent within a species.

Fig. 3.8. Maternal behavior in the rat. At top the rat is shown in a stretching reaction preparatory to delivery. After the pups are born, the mother cleans them and eats the placenta. In the picture at the bottom, the mother has placed the pups together in a nest. (*From Farris, E. J., & Griffiths, J. Q., Jr. (Eds.) The rat in laboratory investigation. (Rev. Ed.). Philadelphia: Lippincott, 1949.*)

Fig. 3.9. Instinctive maternal behavior includes protecting the young from possible harm. Here a newborn gaur, an East Indian species of wild cattle, is being carefully protected by its mother. (*Science Service.*)

INSTRUMENTAL BEHAVIOR

We have outlined the essentials of what is now known about the basic physiological drives. There are other more complex, non-physiological drives and needs, but before discussing them we should give our attention briefly to *instrumental behavior*, the second stage of the motivational cycle. This is an essential link in our understanding of the way in which complex needs are derived from physiological drives. We shall consider several kinds of instrumental behavior: *general activity, reflexes, instinctive behavior,* and *instrumental learning.* Any of these may be involved in the satisfaction of needs.

Activity. The most general sort of behavior that is instrumental in need satisfaction is simply activity or restlessness. When the human infant is hungry, he cries, wriggles, waves his arms, and thrashes about. When a human adult attempts to solve some problem, he may appear agitated and restless, pace the floor, and generally display excess activity. The cat, dog, or rat that is hungry or in a state of need increases its activity level by running, sniffing, and exploring its environment.

These changes in activity level that accompany physiological needs have been extensively studied.[26] One technique is to put an animal in a revolving cage that is so constructed that when the animal walks the cage revolves. A counter mounted on the side of the cage counts the number of revolutions made in any particular period of time. In the accompanying figure (Figure 3.10), you see a record of the running activity of the rat under various conditions. A female rat at the peak of sexual need runs hundreds or even thousands of revolutions a day, but it cuts down its running activity when its sexual need is low. As animals get hungry or thirsty, too, their running activity increases up to the point of weakness from lack of food or water. So activity is a kind of behavior that is instigated by needs.

We say that such running activity is instrumental because it ordinarily leads to the satisfaction of a need. If one is hungry, he will probably stay hungry if he does not have enough drive to get up and go after food. On the other hand, if he starts foraging about, the chances are that he will hit upon food. Even if the activity seems random and purposeless, it greatly increases the chances of discovering the goal and satisfaction. Thus *activity is instrumental in need satisfaction.*

Reflexes. In addition to general activity, reflexes are instrumental in relieving needs. The human infant and many animals are born with sucking reflexes that come into play when the mouth is near the mother's breast—or the nursing bottle. The reflex withdrawal of one's hand when it touches a hot object is instrumental in avoiding too much pain. The nesting reflexes of the bird or mouse satisfy part of the parental needs. There are a whole variety of sexual reflexes that are brought into play when sexually excited organisms receive the appropriate

stimulation. One could cite such examples endlessly, for human beings and animals have a large repertoire of reflexes that are instrumental in satisfying needs.

Instinctive behavior. As has been explained above, there are even more complex and sometimes elaborately organized sequences of behavior that are evoked by needs and are instrumental in relieving them. These are instinctive reactions. Many birds, we have already noted, engage in very elaborate courtship behavior that leads up to the sexual act. Among both fish and birds, many species migrate thousands of miles to their ancestral breeding grounds, then later retrace their paths to live their adult lives. In each case, a long sequence of instinctive acts is instrumental in leading to the satisfaction of the sexual needs.

Instrumental learning. When you study the subject of learning you will discover

Fig. 3.10. Activity reflects level of motivation. General activity, measured by the number of revolutions run in an activity wheel, usually increases and decreases with fluctuations in drive. The normal female rat shows peaks of activity on days of sexual heat. After the sex glands are removed by spaying, activity drops to a low level. (*Data from Richter, C. P. Animal behavior and internal drives. Quar. Rev. Biol., 1927, 2, 307–343.*)

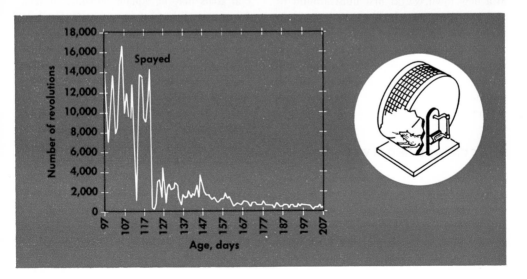

that there are several types of learning and that one of them is called instrumental learning. Such learning is the outcome of motivated behavior, for it depends upon a need and upon some instrumental activity. A common example is the Skinner box (see Chapter 5), so called because it was devised by B. F. Skinner. This has a lever in it which is connected with a feeding machine in such a way that when a rat pushes the lever a pellet of food falls down into a food cup. When a hungry rat is placed in the box, because its general level of activity is high, it wanders around the box and usually pushes the lever quite accidentally. After one such accident, or perhaps three or four, the rat *learns that lever pushing leads to food.* Thereafter it pushes the lever as an instrumental response to acquire food.

Hardly any motivated behavior occurs very many times without undergoing such learning. A hungry baby at first cries as part of his unlearned pattern of activity. Because the mother usually comes when he cries, the baby learns after a while that crying brings the mother and food. Then crying becomes a learned instrumental response to secure food. When we go to live in a new town, we at first hunt around to find the stores at which we may find our needs met. In time we learn which stores we like best and the shortest or most convenient route to these stores. Instrumental learning takes place so universally in the satisfaction of needs that it is hard to think of any case in which it does not occur.

■ ACQUIRED MOTIVES

At the beginning of this chapter, we stated that the term *motive* is to be used when we wish to indicate that behavior arising from a need is directed toward some goal. We say, for example, that a rat has a motive to obtain food, or a person has a

motive to earn money. In each case, we imply both a need and the goal that is necessary to satisfy the need.

Now it is important to realize that motives are not fixed and unchangeable; rather they are altered in the course of instrumental learning. The goal aspect of a motive may be altered in either of two ways: (1) the specific nature of the goal that satisfies a need may change, and (2) new goals, called secondary goals, may be added to the primary goals of physiological needs.

Learning goals. Let us first consider ways in which the specific nature of a goal may be changed through learning. Food is our general goal when we are hungry, yet there are many varieties of food that can satisfy hunger. If a rat, for example, is fed for a long time on pellets, it usually does not change easily to powder, even though the powder is exactly the same food in a slightly different form. Those who have been brought up on vegetable plates usually do not care for hamburger, while some of us have learned exactly the reverse preference. Examples of this kind can be found in our preferences for mates, for weather, for entertainment, for housing, and so on. Several goals may be equally valuable in satisfying a need, but because certain ones have been attained most frequently in the past, we come to prefer them over the others. Thus we see that we may learn to prefer certain goals and in this way our motives may be altered.

This learning of goals goes a step further —and this is a very important step—to the learning of new, *secondary goals*. If there is some condition that regularly precedes a primary goal, this condition may itself become a goal. If, for example, a mother picks her baby up each time he cries (because of hunger) in order to feed him, the baby in time acquires the goal of being picked up and may cry to be picked up even when he

is not hungry. We shall come to other examples in a moment. The general rule for
learning such secondary goals is that some
stimulus or situation be regularly connected
with a primary goal. Eventually the stimulus or situation connected with the primary
goal becomes a learned goal.[27]

This is an extremely important point,
because it is in this way that many complex
social needs are learned in the course of
satisfying physiological needs. For that reason, we shall take time to present two examples in detail.

▪ *The "value" of a white box.* An experimenter put some hungry rats in an alley
that led to a box.[28] Because hungry rats are
active, they eventually wandered into the
box. The experimenter repeated this procedure for several trials. On half the trials, the
inside of the box was white; on the other
half of the trials, the inside was black.
When it was white, there was food in it;
when it was black, there was no food in it.
In this way, the white box was constantly
associated with food; the black box never
was.

The experimenter then went on to test
the effects of this procedure. Specifically
what he wanted to know was whether
"white" had come to be a learned goal for
the rats. Now he put them in a simple maze
in which they could turn to the right to
get to a white box and to the left to get to a
black box. In this case, however, the rats
were never fed in either box. Their only
reward or goal was the color of the box. He
found, in fact, that rats did learn to go to
the white box and to avoid the black box.
Quite obviously the white box was now a
learned goal. Because it had been associated
with food in prior experience, it now was
sufficient to motivate the animal to solve a
new problem. The white box had acquired
goal value through learning.

▪ *The "value" of a poker chip.* The same

Fig. 3.11. A chimpanzee using tokens to obtain food.
The chimpanzee has learned to place poker chips in
the machine to obtain food—in this case, some fruit.
Once the chips have acquired "value," the animal
will learn to do other things to obtain chips. (*Courtesy Dr. Henry W. Nissen.*)

sort of process has been demonstrated even
more dramatically in some experiments on
chimpanzees.[29] These animals were taught
how to get a grape or a raisin by putting a
poker chip in a small vending machine,
called a Chimpomat (Figure 3.11). The experimenter simply showed a hungry chimpanzee how to insert the chip into the slot
of the Chimpomat and collect his reward
at the bottom. The chimpanzees learned
this operation very quickly. What is more
important for our purposes is the fact that
after this initial learning, the chimpanzees
clearly came to *value* the chips. For example, they would work as hard for the chips
as they would for grapes. In one part of
the study, the experimenter had the chimpanzees pull a heavily weighted box into

their cages in order to get a poker chip hidden in it. As a matter of fact, the chimpanzees would pull in the weighted boxes to get chips even when they could not spend them immediately. They simply hoarded large numbers of chips and waited patiently for the chance to spend their hoard.

Later in this same study, the experimenter complicated the lives of his chimpanzees even more by teaching them to use a red chip to get food, a blue one to get water, and a white one to get out of their cages and have the freedom to run around —all with a fine disregard for the rules of poker. Then the chimpanzees would work hardest for the particular colored chip that would satisfy their dominant need at the moment. Here again we see a case of neutral objects acquiring goal value because of their association with the relief of biological needs.

Acquiring fears.   Just as an object may acquire positive value, so may an object acquire negative value and become something to be avoided, hated, or feared because of its association with some biologically painful or emotional situation.[30] For example, one psychologist put rats into a white box and gave them an electric shock through the floor of the box. After ten such trials, the white box was rigged with a lever which could be pushed to make a door open so the rats could escape the box. Then they were put back into the box, this time without any shock. In the first place, they showed fear in the situation very much like what they showed when they were actually shocked. They crouched, tensed, urinated, and defecated. Secondly, after a few experiences in this harmless white box, they learned to push the lever and thus open the door and escape. In other words, the learned fear of the white box itself was sufficient to motivate the

animals to learn to push the lever to escape the box. We shall take up the topic of emotional motivation in the chapter on emotion (Chapter 4). Here we wish only to point out that *fears may be learned.*

Development of social values.   We have now seen that learning takes place in all three stages of motivation. An individual learns new instrumental behavior when it is rewarded by the satisfaction of needs. Then, when certain objects or events are consistently encountered on the way to a goal, these are learned as new goals or values.

Some of the values acquired in this way involve other people and some do not. Those that do involve others are called social values. The chimpanzee, in the experiment described, learned to value poker chips. A carpenter comes to value his tools, a sailor his ship and the sea, a child its toys, a soldier his gun, and a farmer his land. You can undoubtedly multiply this list of *things* people come to value. With little trouble, however, you can also think of many social values: law observance, cleanliness, proper dress, success in school, honesty, courtesy, sexual morality, respect to one's superiors, and so on. Such social values govern relations between people, what they strive for, what they fight for, and many of the complex details of human affairs.

A person tends to acquire social values because from the moment of his birth other people have so much to do with the satisfaction of his needs. The human infant depends upon his mother for the satisfaction of almost all his needs: to eat, to be warm, to be dry, to be in a comfortable position. Thus the mother acquires social value. A little later, when the child no longer needs much physical care, he still must depend upon parents, brothers and sisters, playmates, and others for many of his needs.

They determine where and when he can play, where he can go, what clothes he shall wear, what toys he shall have, when he must sleep, whether he gets a Popsicle, and so on. It is no wonder that he rapidly learns a host of social values and goals.

Besides this more or less inescapable learning of social values, we must also remember that every person is put through a deliberate educational process. By words and acts, parents patiently teach their children what is "right" and what is "wrong," what to aim for in the world, what to value, what to avoid, what to love, what to hate. And each parent imposes his own particular set of values on his child. Added to this are the demands that society also makes. At first, it indirectly dictates to some degree what kinds of values parents instill in their children. Later, when the child lives more with people outside the home, society imposes its values through the school, the church, playmates, clubs, employment, and the myriad of social activities in which we all engage to some extent.

In considering social influences on the development of values, we should also recognize the special role that language plays in the development of social values. Words are stimuli; they can acquire value and pass it on to other words, people, and objects. Thus in the training of a child, the word "don't" acquires some of the negative value that punishment has, and the words "good boy" or "good girl" acquire positive value. These two kinds of words may then serve as the punishments and rewards that parents can use in shaping the attitudes, values, and future behavior of the child. Of course it may be necessary from time to time to strengthen the values attached to these words by further training with biological rewards and punishments, and parents are always doing this too. But the important thing to remember is that when words finally do acquire value, they facilitate the whole process of acquiring new values. Unlike white boxes and poker chips, for example, words are easy to carry around, so they are always available for use as rewards and punishments no matter what the situation.

Enforcement of social values. Even if we were inclined to forget or abandon the social values we have been taught, it would be very difficult to do so. There are countless little ways in which social values get enforced, but they may be divided roughly into four classes: folkways, mores, institutional ways, and taboos (see Table 3.1).

The relatively inconsequential values that people accept mainly out of habit, like a man's tipping his hat to a lady or eating with a knife and fork, are called *folkways*. Not too much pressure is put upon people who disagree with the prevalent social motives of this sort. They are called eccentric, and in most cases are allowed to express their own values.

The more important values like sexual morality are governed by *mores*. Violation of mores brings strong social disapproval. Very often moral matters are not covered by law, or if they are, the law is not readily enforced. Society is always on the watch to see that its members have the desired moral values.

Institutional ways are practices set up under the law. They cover social values that are essential to the way of life in the society and they are enforced by delegated officers of the society or institution.

Finally, *taboos* govern those social values that society regards as the most critical of all. They are the do's and don't's of society that are so deeply inculcated into each of its members that they become part of his conscience. For example, the restrictions against incest or eating human flesh are so strong that no law is needed to enforce them. The average person has no desire to violate these taboos, and should he be tempted to do so, his conscience would probably prevent him from yielding.

As Table 3.1 shows, different societies not only enforce different kinds of social values, but they also may use quite different ways of enforcing the same kind of social values. What is governed by a taboo in one society may be covered by a folkway in another. Most of our society, for example, rears people to be positively motivated to eat meat. Vegetarians are exceptional and are regarded as eccentric. Yet for certain vegetarian societies, meat eating is taboo and their members are as much motivated against it as we are against eating human flesh.

SOCIAL MOTIVES

Our purpose in the last section was to show how new motives may be acquired through instrumental learning which is originally motivated by physiological needs. Many of the new motives that are acquired

in this way, though not all of them, are *social motives*, since they somehow involve other people. In this section, we will consider these social motives in more detail. First we will take up the *social needs* that are implied by the term social motives, and secondly we will deal with the *social techniques* that are used instrumentally to satisfy all sorts of needs.

Social needs. We cannot directly observe social needs, just as we cannot observe physiological needs. They are both hidden from view in the internal processes of the individual. We infer that social needs exist, however, from the fact that individuals are frequently observed to be seeking social goals. By studying such goals, social scientists have attempted to compile, classify, and compare various social needs. The list of social needs is a long one; it is possible to list 20, 30, or even more different social needs. Some of these needs are described and discussed in Chapter 9. For our purposes here, however, social needs may be classified into two general categories, the *affiliative needs* and the *status needs*. These will be the principal topics of this section.

TABLE 3.1. Techniques used by different societies to enforce social values.

Class of social value	Means of enforcement	Name given to violators	Examples	
			In America	In other societies
Folkways	Habit	Eccentric	Inviting an honored guest to stay for dinner	Inviting an honored guest to sleep with one's wife
Mores	Strong social disapproval	Immoral	Premarital chastity	Veiling the face of a woman
Institutional ways	Legal action	Criminal	Respecting private property	Giving up all private property
Taboos	Conscience	Pathological	Refraining from eating human flesh	Refraining from eating any meat

Modified from Katz, D., and Schanck, R. L. *Social psychology.* New York: Wiley, 1938.

• *Affiliative needs.* We are for the most part gregarious people. Most of our waking hours are spent with other individuals— parents, family, friends, neighbors, club members, and so on. Modern society, of course, throws people together in work, entertainment, and living, but most of us seek the company of others even when there is no particular pressure to do so. From this fact we may conclude that *strong needs to affiliate with others are characteristic of most people.*

Affiliative needs have several shapes and forms. One is *dependency.* This is the need to depend upon others, to have someone to look up to and someone to be accepted and loved by—in a word, the need for a parent figure. The source of this need is not hard to find. Individuals come into the world helpless. Then all through the years of infancy, childhood, and adolescence they continue to depend upon parents for the physical needs of life, for decisions about right and wrong, and for control of much of their behavior. When they eventually leave home and parents, they do not easily shed this dependency. They hang on to it, or find someone else to represent their parents. Adults, of course, seldom have the extreme dependency of the child, but few, if any, are able to rid themselves completely of a need to depend upon others. (For a discussion of emotional conflicts about dependency, see Chapter 10.)

Two other examples of affiliative needs are the *need for companionship* and *need for sexual affiliation.* No doubt both needs have much in common with the dependency need, for it is easy to carry over attitudes of dependency on parents and family to our friends and spouses. On the other hand, we must recognize that it is an almost universal tendency among man and animals to seek the companionship of others, and most individuals feel a great lack if they are cut off from such companionship. The need to form a more or less lasting partnership with a member of the opposite sex is not quite so universal, but we see it in most human societies and in some animal societies as well.

• *Status needs.* The status needs form a second general class of needs, which are fairly distinct from the affiliative needs. Since status needs are in a sense antisocial needs, some social scientists prefer to separate them entirely from social needs and to call them *egoistic needs.*[31] Whatever one calls them, they refer to needs to achieve a status that is equal to or better than the status of other members of a group.

Status needs, like the affiliative needs, may take several different forms. One is to achieve a *rank* in the hierarchy of the group. Efforts to achieve such a rank can be observed not only among members of the military profession but also in most human societies, as well as in groups of animals living together. Common barnyard hens, for example, quickly establish a "pecking order" among themselves.[32] One hen, the most dominant, may peck most of the other hens. The least dominant hen, on the other hand, is pecked by all other hens but has no pecking rights of its own. In between, in relatively fixed rank, are other hens who can peck those below them but not those above. Such a pattern of "pecking" and ranking is almost universal in human relationships as well. We see it in groups of children playing together, in the size of offices and desks of businessmen, in the seating of guests at a formal luncheon, and in numerous little details of everyday life.

Other closely related examples of status needs are those for *prestige* and for *power.* The need for prestige is the need to feel better than other persons with whom one

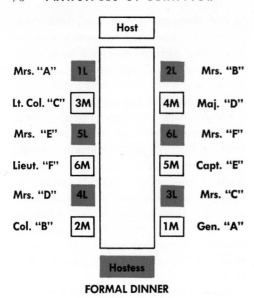

Fig. 3.12. Status needs are represented in formal seating arrangements. The diagram, published in a manual for army officers, gives the proper seating arrangements for formal dinners. It is only one of many evidences of a need to rank the members of social groups. (*Courtesy Fort Benning, Ga., Infantry School.*)

compares himself. We see in daily life many ways in which prestige is sought after and achieved. In children of four or five, a pair of roller skates, a new dress, or a cowboy suit may be a symbol of prestige. A little later, athletic prowess enters the picture as a way of achieving prestige. In adulthood, such symbols as dress, money, automobiles, homes, and the like are regarded as ways of feeling better than the other fellow.

The need for *power* is similar to, but not quite the same thing as, the need for prestige. There are some who shun or ignore prestige, yet aspire to power over their fellow men. Think, for example, of the businessman who quietly and inconspicuously builds up control of an industrial empire, or the professional politician who

holds no public office but "pulls the strings" that move the officeholder. Such individuals are displaying a desire for status but in a different way from those who aspire to achieve prestige.

Still another need, the *need for security*, can be classified with the status needs. This is the need to be secure against the loss of status, friends, loved ones, property, misfortune, income, and so on. We discuss this need rather fully under "Personal Motives" below. It should also be pointed out that Chapter 12 treats at some length the role of prestige and power in the formation and functioning of social groups.

Social techniques. Instrumental behavior frequently involves people, and when it does, it may conveniently be called a *social technique*. To explain social techniques, we shall first describe the *reaction-getting habit* and then consider the general and important problem of *cooperative versus competitive techniques* in the satisfaction of human needs.

▪ *Reaction-getting habits.* One scientist who studied animal behavior for many years tells the story of a pigeon and a horse.[33] The horse had some grain in its nose bag, and the pigeon was hungry. At first, the pigeon was flying around the horse's head and quite by accident frightened the horse so much that it spilled some grain from the nose bag. The pigeon apparently learned very quickly, for as the scientist watched, he saw the bird repeat the trick several times, each time stopping to eat the spilled grain, until it had eaten liberally.

This story illustrates the use of a special sort of instrumental behavior, namely, a social technique, in the satisfaction of needs. The pigeon had established a *reaction-getting habit*, using the horse as another individual, to secure what it wanted. People obviously learn such social techniques, too. A child, for example, who throws temper tantrums when he wants a piece of candy, will, if the tantrum works, quickly learn to throw a tantrum when he wants more candy or anything else. More common is the example of the child crying for his mother to bring food. You can probably think of many others.

In Western society, or any highly organized society, social techniques for gaining one's ends are part and parcel of the pattern of living. The school child takes the proverbial apple to the teacher to win her favor. The workman "butters" the boss to get, he hopes, a raise in wages. The salesman is courteous and deferential to win and keep customers. The advertiser describes the virtues and low cost of his products to make his living. The propagandist shapes the news to win friends and turn them against his enemies. All these, and many more, are techniques that are learned for dealing with other people to satisfy some need, biological or social, of the person using the technique. Every adult in our society should be aware both that he is using such techniques and that others are continually using them on him.

▪ *Cooperation and competition.* Many of the social techniques that are commonly used for satisfying needs may be classified as *cooperative, competitive,* or some mixture of the two. In using cooperative techniques, we attempt to secure the willing assistance of others in gaining our ends. By paying money, rendering a service, winning approval, or appealing to the other fellow's needs, we enlist his help. If we use competitive techniques, we get something from another individual, more or less against his will, because we manage to take it away by brute force or to win in some competition where the spoils go to the winner.

Of course we rarely encounter pure competition or pure cooperation. The student who competes for a grade may also cooperate with his fellow students in preparing notes and studying for examinations. Different manufacturers, though competing in the sales of a product, frequently band together in associations for the promotion of their common interests. Highly organized groups, such as labor and management, compete with each other for their share of the profits, yet organize among themselves to elicit cooperation from their members in their competition with each other. Similarly, nations competing with each other in economic or armed warfare for markets or empire demand a high degree of cooperation from their citizens. So individuals, groups, and nations employ both cooperation and competition in different ways and at different times to pursue their ends.

The problem of cooperation and competition, however, is one of the most important issues of our times. American and Western culture, although highly cooperative in some respects, is also highly competitive. Our games, our schools, our employment opportunities, our sales of merchandise, and indeed our social standing are all highly competitive. So, too, are the affairs of nations.

Is all this competition necessary? There are some who argue that people are instinctively competitive and that for that reason there is little one can do to increase cooperation and reduce competition in human affairs. Psychologists, however, have substantial scientific evidence against this view. They are not in a position to recommend the elimination of all competition, or to prescribe in detail the use of competitive and cooperative techniques. They can, however, assert that competition is not necessarily innate, that cultures do not necessarily have to be competitive, and that cooperative techniques can be learned as replacements for competitive techniques. Their proof comes from studies of animal behavior and of other cultures.

We shall cite two examples from several animal experiments in which cooperation has been studied. In one with rats, *one* pellet was dropped in a cage containing three hungry rats.[34] As might be expected, they at first fought over it. In time, however, they learned that they could not eat and fight at the same time. While two were fighting, the third rat would make

off with the pellet and be eating it without interference. The solution to the problem, which some groups of rats learned, was for them to sit quietly, holding the pellet between them and nibbling off their respective corners of it. In another experiment with chimpanzees, two animals were given the task of pulling in a box baited with food.[35] The box was deliberately made too heavy for one chimp to pull in by itself. In order for either of them to secure food, they had to pull on the rope together. Be-

Fig. 3.13. Cooperation in chimpanzees. Food has been placed on a box too heavy for one chimpanzee to pull in. One chimpanzee solicits the aid of the other and, after much coaxing, succeeds. The two, working together, haul in the box and secure pieces of fruit. (*From Crawford, M. P., The Cooperative solving of problems by young chimpanzees, Comp. Psychol. Monog., 1937, 14, 59.*)

cause they were rewarded with food, they learned to pull together; soon genuine co-operative behavior developed. One chimp, when it wanted food, would make a gesture to the other—the gesture seemed to mean, "Come and help me"—and thus secured its cooperation even when it was not hungry.

Such experiments as these demonstrate that if situations are so arranged that co-operative techniques are rewarded, they will be learned. We have similar, and perhaps more convincing, evidence from the study of cultures other than our own.[36] Some of the more primitive societies are violently competitive, some are extremely cooperative, and some are individualistic. In the last case, individuals in the society have relatively little to do with each other and avoid both competitive and coopera-tive techniques. Such individualism, of course, is largely impossible in a highly organized society. Most interesting, how-ever, is the fact that primitive societies range all the way from extremely competi-tive to extremely cooperative. It means that competitive techniques are not "instinc-tive" and that cooperative techniques may displace them if such techniques prove ef-fective in satisfying the needs of the group.

▌ PERSONAL MOTIVES

In giving the title "Personal Motives" to this section, we do not mean to imply that personal motives are in a different class from physiological and social motives. Actually any motive exists only within an individual, and in the strict sense, all physiological and social motives are really personal motives.

There are certain problems, however, that are best understood by keeping the individual in mind, and it is these we shall consider here.

Functional autonomy. We have ex-plained earlier that motives are acquired because certain conditions are associated with the relief of physiological needs. Rats acquired motives for white boxes and chimpanzees for poker chips because these conditions were associated with securing food. It is an interesting fact that, if animals are no longer rewarded with food in white boxes or in using poker chips, they soon lose their acquired motives. These motives, in order to be maintained in full strength, must be reinforced (see page 112) frequently with food rewards. This is an example of a phenomenon known as *ex-tinction* that we will consider in Chapter 5.

Although acquired motives do sometimes extinguish in human beings, it is more typical of people to retain such motives throughout most of their lives. As G. W. Allport, one of the leading students of personality, has pointed out,[37] acquired motives seem to have a kind of *functional autonomy*. He means by this that motives continue to function autonomously with-out further reinforcement of the physio-logical conditions originally concerned in their acquisition.

Examples of what seems to be functional autonomy of motives abound in everyday life. The poor boy who earned his first pennies to ward off hunger and discomfort continues to work day and night at amass-ing a large fortune long after he has ac-quired enough money to meet his physical needs. A businessman who approaches re-tirement age with ample reserves insists on staying at his job, probably because he finds that it satisfies needs for companionship and activities, even though his original motivation for working was to earn a liv-ing. Even the persistence of sexual interests in middle age, after hormones are no longer of much importance, has been cited as an example of functional autonomy.

You can probably think of other examples of motives that continue to operate long after the original need for them has passed.

Security and frustration. Another important fact of human motivation is that motives are frequently frustrated or threatened with frustration. The topic of frustration is an important one in psychology, and we shall have a great deal more to say about it, especially in Chapters 4 and 10. Here we merely introduce it by pointing to its existence and indicating its relation to feelings of insecurity.

A man may have taken up a business or profession as a way of making a living and thus of satisfying his physiological and social needs. He may have been successful in his work for many years, yet there is always the possibility that he may be thrown out of work—by economic conditions, by failure on his own part, or by ill health. He is frequently reminded of this possibility by what happens to his friends and neighbors, and he can easily envisage the frustration of many of his needs—not just his acquired and somewhat inessential needs, but his physiological needs as well.

Because of this ever-present possibility of frustration, he tries to make sure that the satisfaction of his various physiological and social needs is secure against misfortune, depression, loss of job, and so on. All these fears and desires coalesce in a *need for security*. Such a need can be met only when the individual knows where he stands and what his rights are. If he has status in his community, money in the bank, a steady job, and faith in fair and equitable treatment, then he has a feeling of security. Loss of status, uncertainty of tenure of his job, or capricious laws and government make him insecure.

In a society as highly organized as Western culture, a person depends upon many other people and upon conditions in general for his security. This means, of course, that a person's security is often threatened or even lost through no fault of his own or without any opportunity to regain it. For that reason, the need for security takes on a special importance in people's lives— more so, in many cases, than any of the social needs we discussed in the last section—and it is responsible for much personal unhappiness as well as social unrest. (See Chapter 10 for further discussion of the role of insecurity in the frustration of motives.)

Level of aspiration. We pointed out in an earlier section that goals acquired through learning are not nearly so fixed and unchangeable as are the goals of physiological drives. One of the important and obvious factors affecting such goals is the success a person has in achieving them. A person cannot very well learn the goal of becoming a great athlete, scholar, or musician unless he has had some success along the way. If his success is only modest, he is likely to set a lower goal for himself than if he has been outstandingly successful. The level at which he sets his goal has been given the label *level of aspiration*.

The concept of level of aspiration is a convenient and important one in understanding human motivation in a variety of situations. It will determine whether a person works hard, not so hard, or not at all at any given task. It may determine whether he aspires to a high school, college, or professional education, whether he prepares to be a plumber or doctor, and so on. Consequently, we are all familiar with differences in level of aspiration among the people we know, even if we have not consciously used the term or concept.

Level of aspiration has also been the subject of experimental work.[38] In this work, a variety of situations has been employed. People may be presented with some problem to solve, for example, a puzzle, and asked to indicate how successful they think they will be in solving it. Students may be asked to state the grade they expect in an examination or intelligence test. Thus levels of aspiration may be measured. Then, with such measures, it is possible to determine how previous experience with a task, or performance in successive attempts at the task, can affect level of aspiration.

From studies of this sort we have learned that level of aspiration depends upon many factors. One is the individual characteristics of a person; some people have consistently low levels of aspiration, others quite high levels, and still others intermediate levels. Another factor is ego involvement, or self-esteem; a person's level is usually higher when he compares himself with a group of comparable ability than when his performance has nothing to do with anyone else. Students, for example, often seem as concerned with how many other students in a class received As as with whether they received them. Finally, of course, there is the factor of one's own performance. A person usually does not aspire to a performance far above that which he has been able to reach. If he fails to reach his aspiration, he usually lowers his level. On the other hand, if he achieves one level, he is likely to raise it a little. In general, people keep a level of aspiration that is slightly above their level of performance—at least most normal people do.

Unconscious motivation. Another important fact that must be kept in mind, if we are to understand human motivation, is that many *human motives are unconscious.* That is to say, a person often is not aware of, and cannot report, his own motives. The importance of unconscious motivation will be stressed later in Chapter 10, "Frustration and Conflict." Here we are simply introducing and illustrating the point.

The idea that human motives may be unconscious is a little easier to understand if we remember that many motives are acquired and that such motives are in a sense habits. We all have acquired habits of which we are largely unaware. A person, for example, may bite his nails, pull on his ear, tap on the table, or pace back and forth in front of a class he teaches, all without being aware of any of these things until they are called to his attention. Acquired motives may function in the same way. Moreover, motives are not so easily observed as habits like biting one's nails or pacing in front of a class. Hence, one is less likely to be reminded of them than he is of his habits.

There is still another important reason why motives may be unconscious: they are often acquired under unpleasant circumstances that we like to forget. In other words, we do not want to recognize certain of our motives. Consequently we actively forget them through a process called *repression* which we shall mention again when we deal with "forgetting" in Chapter 5 and shall explain in detail in Chapter 10, "Frustration and Conflict." The essence of the idea of repression is that it lets us fool ourselves about our motives because we frequently do not want to admit to ourselves what they really are. As a result, we disguise them by perceiving them as different from what they really are or by refusing to recognize them at all.

SUMMARY

1. Motivation may be represented as a cycle consisting of three parts: (*a*) a need that arouses (*b*) instrumental behavior, which leads in turn to (*c*) a goal that satisfies the need.

2. Physiological processes within the body tend to maintain a balance called *homeostasis*. When this balance is disturbed, the resulting physiological need arouses regulatory behavior, for example, seeking for a food, water, or a mate, which eventually restores the balance.

3. Such needs as hunger, thirst, and sleep depend upon chemical conditions in the body that are not yet very well understood. These conditions, however, often produce very specific needs or hungers, for infants and animals can select particular kinds of food appropriate to their needs.

4. In lower animals, sexual needs depend on sex hormones, but in human beings these needs can exist in the absence of such hormones.

5. Instinctive behavior is behavior that (*a*) arises from physiological needs and (*b*) consists of unlearned, complex patterns of reactions. Instinctive behavior is almost nonexistent in human beings but is relatively prominent in many of the lower animals.

6. There are several kinds of relatively simple instrumental behavior that may lead to need satisfaction: (*a*) general exploratory activity, (*b*) reflexes, such as the sucking reflex, (*c*) complex instinctive acts, and (*d*) all sorts of learned instrumental acts.

7. Under the influence of a need, an individual quickly learns acts that regularly lead to the appropriate goal. In learning such acts, organisms acquire new goals. Indeed, whatever conditions are usually present in working toward a goal themselves become learned or secondary goals.

8. Through instrumental learning, many new goals or "values" are acquired, for example, money. Fears may also be acquired in this way. Because people, particularly parents, are so intimately a part of human instrumental learning, many of the goals acquired by human beings are "social values."

9. The particular social values that are acquired depend upon one's parents and associates, as well as on the society in which one lives. Once acquired, these social values are enforced by social approval, laws, taboos, and so on.

10. The fact that social values are learned implies that social needs leading to such values are also learned. The many needs acquired by a person may be classified into two general groups: affiliative needs and status needs.

11. Patterns of behavior that involve other people in the satisfaction of a need are called *social techniques*. Animal studies and observations of other cultures indicate that people are not "instinctively" competitive; they learn cooperative techniques if rewarded for using such techniques.

12. Some of the important factors to consider in understanding the motivations of an individual are (*a*) the functional autonomy of motives after the original reasons for acquiring them no longer exist; (*b*) a need for security against possible frustrations of needs; (*c*) a person's level of aspiration as compared with his level of performance; and (*d*) the operation of motives without a person's being aware of their existence or origins.

SUGGESTIONS FOR FURTHER READING

Cannon, W. B. *Bodily changes in pain, hunger, fear and rage* (2d Ed.). New York: Appleton-Century-Crofts, 1929.

> *An account of classical experiments on some of the physiological factors in hunger and thirst.*

Ford, C. S., & Beach, F. A. *Patterns of sexual behavior.* New York: Hoeber, 1951.

> *A good account of sexual motives and practices in both animals and different human societies.*

Klineberg, Otto. *Social psychology* (2d Ed.). New York: Holt, 1953.

> *Contains a critical analysis of the problem of instinctive behavior in man and a summary of the facts of social motivation.*

Langer, W. C. *Psychology and human living.* New York: Appleton-Century-Crofts, 1943.

> *A readable account of the problems of adjustment in modern society with an emphasis on personal and social motives.*

Miller, N. E. Learnable drives and rewards. In S. S. Stevens (Ed.), *Handbook of experimental psychology.* New York: Wiley, 1951.

> *A summary of experiments on the acquisition of motives.*

Miller, N. E., & Dollard, J. *Social learning and imitation.* New Haven, Conn.: Yale Univ. Press, 1941.

> *Contains an analysis of the ways in which social motives develop, especially early in life.*

Morgan, C. T., & Stellar, E. *Physiological psychology* (2d Ed.). New York: McGraw-Hill, 1950. Chaps. 17–20.

> *A textbook summary of the physiological factors in motivation.*

Richter, C. P. Total self-regulatory functions in animals and human beings. *Harvey Lect.*, 1942–1943, **38**, 63–103.

> *A summary of research on specific hungers and other types of regulatory behavior in motivation.*

Young, P. T. *Motivation of behavior.* New York: Wiley, 1936.

> *A textbook covering various aspects of motivation.*

Chapter 4 FEELING AND EMOTION

WE HIGHLY CIVILIZED MEMBERS of Western culture like to think of ourselves as rational beings who go about satisfying our motives in an intelligent way. To a certain extent we do satisfy them that way. But we are also emotional beings—more emotional than we realize. Indeed, most of the affairs of everyday life are tinged with feeling and emotion. Joys and sorrows, excitement and disappointment, love and fear, hope and dismay—all these and many more are feelings we experience in the course of a day or week.

Without such feelings and emotions, living would be pretty dreary. Our feelings add color and spice to living; they are the sauce without which life would be dull fare. We anticipate with pleasure our Saturday-night dates, we remember with a

This chapter was drafted by Clifford T. Morgan of The Johns Hopkins University.

warm glow the satisfaction we got from giving a good speech, and we even recall with amusement the bitter disappointments of childhood. On the other hand, when our emotions are too intense and too easily aroused, they can get us into a good deal of trouble. They can warp our judgment, turn friends into enemies, and make us as miserable as if we were sick with fever.

The study of emotion. Because feelings and emotions are involved in so many aspects of living, it is to be expected that they should occupy an important position in the study of psychology. They are, in fact, considered in many different chapters of this book. Here in this chapter we merely introduce them by tracing their development and explaining what they are. In Chapter 10, "Frustration and Conflict," we show how emotions are aroused by motivational conflicts and how they may lead to inadequate and unhappy personal adjustments to the problems of life. Chapter 11 "Mental Health and Psychotherapy," considers methods of helping individuals establish healthier emotional adjustments. The subject of attitudes, treated in Chapter 13, also bears on the problem of emotions, for attitudes have their roots in the fears, hostilities, and emotional attachments an individual has built up in his past experiences. Chapter 14, "Prejudice and Social Conflict," goes on to show how emotional attitudes victimize minority groups and play a role in industrial and international conflict. In Chapter 16 we shall see that likes, dislikes, and emotionally toned attitudes are important in vocational adjustment. Chapter 21 describes briefly the parts of the brain concerned in emotion, and Chapter 22 considers the effects of chronic emotional stress on the health and well-being of the individual. In view of all these ramifications of the problem of emotion, the student should bear in mind that this chapter is only an introduction and that he can expect to learn considerably more about the emotions in many other parts of the course.

Emotional development. First let us consider the course of emotional development in the infant and the child. Although grown-up people exhibit many different emotions, this is not the case in the newborn infant. About the only emotion we can distinguish in the first few weeks after birth is a diffuse general excitement that is about the same from one occasion to the next.[1] This excitement is not a specific response to any particular stimulus; it shows itself whenever the environment suddenly changes.

It is not long, though, until the diffuse excitement gives way to more specific emotional reactions. The general course of this change is sketched in Figure 4.1, which is based on extensive studies of the emotions displayed at different ages. As the child grows older, he develops an increasing variety of emotional responses. At three months, for example, he responds to unpleasant situations with general signs of distress, but he responds to nursing, fondling, tickling, and rocking with smiling and general signs of delight. After that, emotions rapidly differentiate, and by two years he has a repertory of specific reactions to different situations.

This picture of *emotional development* makes it rather likely that emotion, like

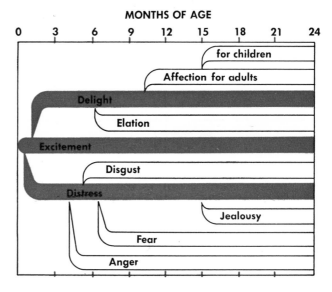

MONTHS OF AGE

Fig. 4.1. Development of emotional expression in the infant. The diagram summarizes studies of the development of emotion. (*Based on Bridges, K. M. B. Emotional development in early infancy. Child Develpm., 1932, 3, 324–341.*)

the motor functions we discussed in Chapter 2, is the product of both maturation and learning. The baby has many opportunities to learn in the first few months, yet he is as slow in acquiring an emotional repertory as he is in walking and talking. It would seem, then, that the nervous system must mature enough to permit the control of muscles of the face, the vocal apparatus, and the body before any diversity of emotional reactions can be fully developed. It is probably also true that there is a maturation of certain centers in the brain that are specifically responsible for patterns of emotion. Thus maturation undoubtedly plays an important role in emotional growth.

Emotional development, on the other hand, undoubtedly depends on learning. This hardly requires proof, but it can be illustrated by a classic experiment.[2] An eleven-month-old boy named Albert was shown a white rat (see Figure 4.2). He was interested in it and tried to play with it. However, on one occasion, when Albert was shown the rat, the experimenter sounded a loud noise. At that, the boy

shrank back. The procedure was repeated several times. In time Albert came to show unmistakable fear reactions to the white rat even when the loud noise was not sounded. He also became fearful in the presence of a rabbit and other white or furry objects, including a white beard. Thus, through learning, white furry objects had become emotionally charged stimuli for Albert.

Emotional reactions, then, are elaborated through both maturation and learning. In this chapter, we shall show in more detail how learning and maturation play roles in the development of emotion.

Aspects of emotion. We have not yet defined emotion. We all know in general what we mean by it, but we find it difficult to say precisely what we mean. That is because emotion has several different aspects. For one, *it is a stirred-up bodily state* in which changes occur in our breathing, heart rate, circulation, and other physiological functions. It is also a pattern of expression—smiling, laughing, crying, cringing, and so on; *it is something we do.* Thirdly, *it is something we feel*—happiness,

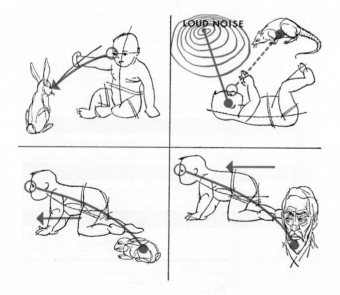

Fig. 4.2. Conditioning of fear in the infant. Before conditioning (1), the child approaches a rabbit without fear. A loud noise (2) startles and scares the child. After the noise has been paired with the presence of a rat, the child appears afraid of the rabbit (3) and of all hairy objects (4). (*After Watson and Rayner*[2] *and Thompson, G. G. Child psychology. Boston: Houghton Mifflin, 1952, p. 144.*)

disappointment, unpleasantness, elation. And finally, *emotion is also a motive*; it keeps us working toward some goals and avoiding others.

Thus it becomes apparent that, in order to understand emotion, we must consider all these aspects of it. The rest of this chapter is therefore divided into four main sections: (1) bodily states in emotion, (2) emotional expression, (3) emotional experience, and (4) emotional motivation.

▇ BODILY STATES IN EMOTION

The stirred-up or upset state that characterizes the more extreme emotions is easy to detect in the internal organs of the body. This may be illustrated by a survey of more than 4,000 airmen who flew in combat in the Second World War and had, at various times, been exposed to great danger.[3] As you can see in the accompanying table (Table 4.1), they were asked to say whether they "often" or "sometimes" experienced certain symptoms while flying combat missions. As you read down the list of symptoms, you will note a wide variety of bodily changes: pounding of the heart, tenseness of the muscles, dryness of the mouth, "cold sweat," need to urinate, and sickness in the stomach. If one were to take the trouble of attaching various measuring instruments to the fliers while they experienced emotion, one could detect an even wider variety of bodily changes and record them in detail.

Autonomic changes. Many of the bodily changes that occur in emotion are initiated by a part of the nervous system called the *autonomic system* (see Figure 4.3), and for that reason such changes are called autonomic changes. The autonomic system consists of many nerves leading from the brain and spinal column (see Chapter 21) out to the various organs of the body, including

TABLE 4.1. Bodily symptoms of fear in combat flying. 1,985 flying officers and 2,519 enlisted fliers of the Second World War were asked how often they experienced different symptoms in combat flying.

Symptom	Percentage answering		
	"Often"	"Some-times"	Total
Pounding heart and rapid pulse	30	56	86
Muscles very tense	30	53	83
Easily irritated, angry, or "sore"	22	58	80
Dryness of the throat or mouth	30	50	80
"Nervous perspiration" or "cold sweat"	26	53	79
"Butterflies" in the stomach	23	53	76
Sense of unreality, that this couldn't be happening	20	49	69
Need to urinate very frequently	25	40	65
Trembling	11	53	64
Confused or rattled	3	50	53
Weak or faint	4	37	41
After mission, not being able to remember details of what happened	5	34	39
Sick to the stomach	5	33	38
Not being able to concentrate	3	32	35

Modified from Shaffer, L. F. Fear and courage in aerial combat. *J. consult. Psychol.*, 1947, **11**, 137–143.

particularly the blood vessels serving both the interior and exterior muscles. The autonomic system has two parts which usually work in opposition to each other. One part, the *sympathetic system*, increases the heart rate and blood pressure and distributes blood to the exterior muscles rather than to the digestive system. It is this part that swings into play when we become emotional—or at least when we become fearful or angry. The other part of the system is called the *parasympathetic* system. It tends to be the more active system of the two when we are calm and relaxed. It does many things that, taken together, build up and conserve the body's stores of energy. Among them is the slowing of the heart, reduction of blood pressure, and diversion of blood to the digestive tract.*

When the sympathetic part of the autonomic system steps up its discharges, as it does in emotion, it produces several symptoms that are worth noting.[4] One set of symptoms concerns the circulation of blood. The blood vessels serving the stomach, intestines, and interior of the body tend to contract in emotion, while those serving the exterior muscles of the trunk and limbs tend to become larger. In this way, blood is diverted from digestive functions to muscular functions, thus preparing the body for action that may involve great muscular activity. At the same time, nervous impulses to the heart make it beat harder and faster, which means that the blood pressure goes up and the pulse rate is quickened. Thus more blood is pumped through the circulatory system to the muscles.

Besides changes in circulation, the autonomic system produces several other bodily changes in emotion. Perhaps, when you have been afraid, you have felt some of them yourself. One is a change in breathing. You may hold your breath briefly, gasp or sigh, and thus interrupt your regular breathing. Another change is in the pupil of the eye, which is ordinarily regulated according to the amount of light entering the eye. In emotion, the pupil gets larger.

* This is an oversimplified statement of the functions of the two systems. They are not always opposed to each other, and there are certain instances in which the parasympathetic system is active in emotion.

Perhaps you have seen this if you have observed a cat or a person in great rage. Another change is drying of the mouth. This occurs because the sympathetic system stops the secretion from the salivary glands, which ordinarily keeps the mouth moist. Still another is the change in the movements of the stomach and intestines. As one can see in X-ray pictures or with the balloon technique (see Figure 3.3), contractions of the stomach and intestines are stopped or reversed in strong emotion. Also the principal sphincters may involuntarily relax, causing a person to defecate or to urinate.

Still another response of the sympathetic system in emotion is the discharge of the hormone *adrenalin*. This is secreted by the adrenal glands, which are located on the top of the kidneys. From this point, the hormone goes into the blood, circulates around the body, and affects many organs of the body. In the liver, it helps mobilize sugar into the blood and thus makes more energy available to the brain and muscles. Adrenalin also stimulates the heart to beat harder and thus aids the impulses of the autonomic system to the heart. (Surgeons use adrenalin to stimulate heart action when the heart has weakened or stopped.) In the skeletal muscles, adrenalin helps mobilize sugar resources so that the muscles can use more of them more rapidly. Thus adrenalin more or less duplicates and reinforces the action of the sympathetic system on various internal organs.

One other bodily change in emotion has recently been used extensively by psychologists in experiments on learning and personality (see pages 110 and 631). This change is the galvanic skin response. It is a change in the electrical resistance of the skin that can be measured by attaching a resistance meter or voltmeter to the skin. The autonomic nervous system indirectly controls the sweat glands of the skin. In strong emotional excitement, the glands increase their secretion, which you can feel as "nervous perspiration" when you are excited. Accompanying this secretion is a drop in electrical resistance of the skin that we call the galvanic skin response, or GSR for short. One can use this galvanic skin response as a fairly sensitive indicator of emotional response.

The "lie" detector. For the past few years, the public has heard a good deal about a "lie" detector that sometimes can be used to detect a person's guilt in crime.[5] This device makes use of several of the autonomic changes we have described above. Although there are several versions of the lie detector, it almost always affords measurements of blood pressure, respiration, and galvanic skin response. The basic assumption underlying the use of the lie detector is this: When one confronts a person with words, questions, or situations connected with a crime, if that person committed the crime, then they constitute a real threat to the person and stir up in him the emotion of fear. This emotion, even if small, can be measured. Actually, this is a fairly valid assumption, for in many cases it has proved true.

Taken by itself, however, the lie detector is not to be trusted completely, because even innocent people are likely to be emotional when subjected to a lie detector test

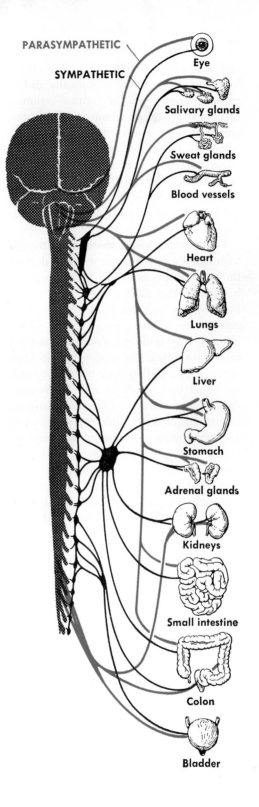

PARASYMPATHETIC

SYMPATHETIC

Eye

Salivary glands

Sweat glands

Blood vessels

Heart

Lungs

Liver

Stomach

Adrenal glands

Kidneys

Small intestine

Colon

Bladder

Fig. 4.3. Schematic diagram of the autonomic nervous system. The autonomic system consists of nerves and ganglia (see Glossary) that serve blood vessels, glands, and other internal organs of the body. It has two main divisions: the parasympathetic system, shown in color, and the sympathetic system.

and accused, by implication, of a crime. Moreover, one often has difficulty distinguishing responses to the "critical" stimuli, that is, the stimuli connected with the crime, from responses to the "neutral" stimuli that have nothing to do with the crime and are presented as a standard of comparison. When used by a skilled operator, the lie detector can be very valuable, but it can easily be misused by people who are not expert in this type of work.[5]

Distinguishing bodily changes. Although we usually can detect an emotional state through changes occurring in the body, it is quite another matter to say *what* state.[6] Psychologists have tried for a good many years to see whether, by measuring bodily changes, they could tell different emotions from each other, for example, fear from anger or joy. If they had been successful, we would more easily be able to measure emotional reactions to different situations, to measure directly differences in mood and temperament among people, and to correlate physiological changes with personality structure. Unfortunately, such work has been for the most part unfruitful. Although we can distinguish mild from severe emotional states, we have so far not been able to distinguish different emotions in this way with any degree of success.

■ EMOTIONAL BEHAVIOR

Rather than measure bodily changes, we can distinguish different emotions much better if we observe emotional behavior. Many of the animals we know have fairly clear-cut patterns of emotional response. We can tell that a cat is angry when it arches its back, raises it tail, bares its fangs, and gives a characteristic hiss. Similarly we can identify anger in a dog when it snarls and takes a characteristic stance. In the same animals, too, we can easily see the difference between fear and friendliness by the pattern of behavior. When a person is very angry, or very much afraid, or very joyous, we usually can tell which it is by the way he behaves. What are the patterns of behavior by which we distinguish one emotion from another? And how accurate are we in telling one emotion from another?

In addressing these questions we shall first consider what is regarded as the most fundamental and universal pattern of emotional response, the *startle pattern.* Then we shall consider *facial and vocal expression,* and after that *postures and gestures* as ways of expressing emotion. In the course of the discussion, it will become clear that it is difficult to judge emotional expression correctly unless we also know the *emotional situations* giving rise to emotion, and this will be our last topic in this section.

The startle response. Perhaps the most primitive of all emotional patterns is the startle response. At least, in very careful studies of many individuals, this response is more consistent from one person to another than any other emotional pattern.[7] You can easily observe it by tiptoeing up to a person who is deep in thought and suddenly yelling "boo" or by shooting off a pistol when he does not expect it. The reaction you get is what psychologists call the startle pattern.

The whole thing takes place very rapidly but in a consistent pattern. The first part of the reaction is a rapid closing of the eyes. The mouth widens in a suggestion of a grin. Then the head and neck are thrust forward, often with the chin tilting up, and the muscles of the neck stand out. The uniformity of this emotional reaction from one person to another makes us believe that it is an inborn reaction that is modified very little by learning and experience.

Fig. 4.4. Differences in emotional expressions in one situation. The children are listening to a radio program. What emotion are they expressing? (*Courtesy Three Lions, Inc., George Pickow, photographer.*)

Facial and vocal expression. Emotional patterns other than the startle pattern are not very consistent among people. They differ from one person to another and from one culture to another. Thus it is clear that each individual develops somewhat unique ways of expressing emotion. Look, for example, at the accompanying picture (Figure 4.4) of some children listening to the radio. Whatever the particular situation was, it was the same for all of them. Yet notice the great differences in facial expression in the different children. If you looked at each of these faces separately, you would find it difficult to say in many cases just what emotion was being expressed.

If, however, emotions are classified into two general groups, those which seem pleasant and those which seem unpleasant, one can observe some consistent differences in the expression of the mouth. In general, in the unpleasant emotions, the mouth turns down; in the pleasant ones, the mouth turns up. The same is true of the eyes; they slant up in mirth, droop down in sadness. Leonardo da Vinci knew this and stated it as a principle to be used in depicting emotional expression.

To study patterns of facial expression, psychologists have presented pictures of faces expressing various spontaneously aroused emotions and have asked people to judge what emotions were represented.[8] In this kind of experiment, where the judge sees only the face, the agreement is far from perfect. There is usually rather good agreement that the emotion is pleasant or unpleasant, but to say whether it is "sorrow," "fear," "anger," "distress," or the like is much more difficult. The same result is true, in general, for *posed* expressions. When professional actors are asked to portray certain emotions and judges rate them on facial expression, agreement as to kind of emotion is not very good.

People ordinarily express a good deal of emotion with their voices. Screams denote fear or surprise; groans, pain or unhappiness; sobs, sorrow; and laughter, enjoyment. A tremor or break in the voice may denote deep sorrow; a loud, sharp, high-pitched voice usually expresses anger. In judging emotions in others, when we can hear their vocal expressions as well as see their faces, we use such cues to help us distinguish one emotion from another.

Posture and gestures. Emotions are expressed with posture and gestures as well as with the face and voice. In fear, a person flees or is "rooted to the spot." In anger, he usually makes aggressive gestures and may even clench his fists and move to attack. In sorrow, a person tends to slump with face downward, and in joy, he holds head high and chest out. Such signs of emotion we all take for granted in this society.

There is some question, however, how consistently emotion is expressed in this way. As in the case of facial expression, there are fairly wide individual differences among people. When judges have only the expressions of the hands and forearms to observe, they agree fairly well only for highly conventional expressions such as worship, but their agreement becomes poorer for the less conventional gestures. If they are permitted both the facial expression and the gesture, however, their agreement improves considerably, though it still is far from perfect.[9]

If one studies emotional expression in different societies, it becomes clear that *such expression is largely learned*. There is, indeed, a "language of emotion" that more or less characterizes each culture. The Chinese may express surprise by sticking out their tongues, disappointment by clapping their hands, and happiness by scratching their ears and cheeks.[10] In our society, sticking out one's tongue is more likely to be a sign of anger, clapping one's hands a sign of happiness, and scratching one's ears a sign of worry. Then, too, cultures vary in the degree of emotional expression. The American Indian, for example, is relatively taciturn and expressionless, while the Frenchman gesticulates for even the mild emotions.

Emotional situations. Any single aspect of emotional expression—facial, vocal, postural, or gestural—is not a very reliable sign of the type of emotion involved. In other words, these components of expression are not very uniform from one person to the next. When judges are given all of them together, however, they agree much better than when considering them singly. Even so, they make a fair number of mistakes and may confuse such different emotions as anger and fear.

What one needs to see in order to judge emotional expression most accurately is not only the pattern of expression, but the situation in which the emotion occurs. Given the situation and the expression, one can do quite well at naming the emotion.[11] This is because all of us know fairly well what our individual emotions are in different situations and thus know what the other person's should be, or is likely to be, in a similar situation. So it is by situations, more than by expression, that we are able to distinguish different emotions. With this in mind, then, let us look at some typical emotions of *fear, anger,* and *pleasure* in terms of the situations that may evoke them.

■ *Fear.* In young children, any kind of situation which comes on suddenly can produce fear. It seems that fear reactions occur when a child is not prepared for what is coming or has not gained sufficient experience to enable him to cope with the situation. Thus during the early months of life the child tends to show fear responses in the presence of any strange, sudden, intense stimulus.[12]

Later on, loud noises, objects that have caused pain, and sudden movements, are fear producing. As the child grows older, he may be afraid of imaginary creatures, of being left alone, of the dark, and of potential bodily harm. Late in childhood, children become especially fearful of social humiliation and ridicule. The kinds of fear-producing situations that are effective at various ages are depicted in the accompanying figure (Figure 4.5). In considering these situations, it is important to realize that the child need not experience fear in a specific situation to come to fear it; he can learn to be afraid simply by being with people who are fearful in such situations.

In adulthood, when a person has acquired a repertoire of social needs, including those for recognition and prestige, fears are most often associated with threats to the satisfaction of a person's needs. College girls, for example, were found in one study to have most of their fears about success in college work and about their social prestige.[13] Most adult fears probably have to do with success and failure in work and social life.

■ *Anger.* In animals there are situations which naturally call forth anger. Witness the typical reaction of a dog and cat to each other. In both young and adult human beings, however, the typical *cause of anger is some kind of frustration.*[12] In the infant, physical restraint is the kind of frustration

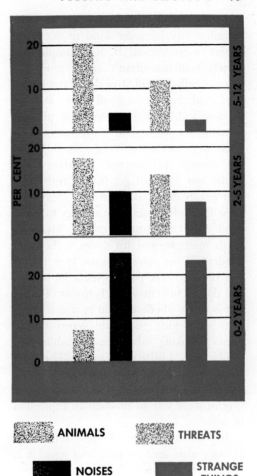

Fig. 4.5. Situations evoking fear in infants and children. Groups of youngsters were exposed to four different kinds of situations: (a) animals, (b) noises or things that made noises; (c) threats of illness, injury, or death; and (d) strange objects or people. The bar graphs show the percentage of each group giving a fear response in these situations. In general, noises and strange things are more effective in young children, while animals and threats are more effective in older children. (Based on data of Jersild, A. T., Markey, F. V., and Jersild, C. L. *Children's fears, dreams, wishes, daydreams, dislikes, pleasant and unpleasant memories. Child Develpm. Monogr.*, 1933, No. 12.)

that evokes anger; later on in life, this stimulus may be some kind of social restraint or frustration. If, for example, you merely hold an infant's arms against his sides, usually he will struggle, beat with his fists, and become red all over. Because dressing and bathing involve some physical restraint, we see a good many instances of anger in this situation. When the child gets old enough to demand attention from adults and does not get it, the frustration that results may make him very angry.

As the child passes from infancy to childhood, his skills improve greatly, his social needs multiply, and his desire to be independent of his parents grows. It is just at this time that the parents use a lot of do's and don't's to control his behavior. The result is anger whenever a do or a don't conflicts with what the child wants to do. Anger-provoking situations in adults are similar, only a little more subtle. Then one needs to interfere with a person's plans, cause him loss of prestige, or thwart his desires in some way to produce an expression of anger.

The particular way of expressing anger changes with age. At preschool ages, it is more likely to take the form of temper tantrums, surliness, bullying, and fighting; in adolescence and adulthood these expressions become more subtle, indirect, and verbal, and they include sarcasm, swearing, gossiping, and plotting. This change in the mode of expression of anger is obviously brought about by social pressures. Such pressures, exerted by parents, friends, associates, and the official agents of society teach the person to repress his natural urges and to express his anger in more socially approved ways.

▪ *Pleasure.* It is often said, by psychologists as well as other people, that there are three basic emotions: fear, anger, and love. The term *love*, however, may be somewhat misleading, for it implies sexual or parental love. Perhaps a better term is *pleasure*, for it indicates a range of pleasant emotions in which we see such behavior as smiling, laughing, hugging, and kissing, or perhaps just a general pattern of contentment.

Early in life, pleasure is observed when the child is physically comfortable. If an infant is well fed, dry, and warm and there are no pins sticking in him, he is usually relaxed, smiling, and cooing. By the second or third month, he shows signs of pleasure when he sees a human face or hears a voice. Still later he expresses pleasure when he exercises a new skill such as reaching out and shaking a rattle or when somebody plays peekaboo with him. In general, as children develop, they find pleasure in situations that are novel but not frightening and that keep them entertained and offer them some success in what they try to do.

Smiling and laughter are specific expressions of pleasure that, like fear and anger, occur in different situations at different ages.[14] Apparently the nervous system of the infant must mature sufficiently before he can smile, for smiling does not occur until about two months of age. After that, for a time, smiling is a response to tickling or stroking the infant. Then, smiling begins to occur when there is an interesting noise or some unusual movement, such as waving one's arms, dancing, standing on one's head, or pulling toys around the floor—as parents who must entertain their children well know.

As children grow to adulthood, they laugh and smile in an increasing variety of situations. What the common elements of all these situations are, is a problem that has puzzled psychologists for a long time. We do not fully understand them yet, but certainly one of the most important elements is *incongruity*.[15] A person laughs when there is some contrast or incongruity between what a situation is perceived to be and what it is supposed to be. If a person falls into the water with his bathing suit on, we do not laugh, for there is nothing incongruous about that. We do laugh, however, if he falls in with his street clothes on, for this is incongruous. Such incongruity usually makes us laugh, however, only if it occurs at someone else's expense; it is funny only when the other fellow falls overboard. There are undoubtedly other common elements in situations which call forth laughter, but incongruity is probably the most important of them.

EMOTIONAL EXPERIENCE

We have described emotions as bodily states that can be measured physiologically and as expressions of behavior that can be directly observed and recorded. Now we consider emotion as a conscious experience —something that we feel and can report upon. We may feel emotion at times when we express it little or not at all. We may feel anger but pen it up inside and hardly show it to our associates. In reading a good story, we may feel delighted or amused, yet make no overt sign. Or in listening to music, looking at a gorgeous view, basking in the sun on the beach, we may experience rich emotions without expressing them overtly, or even without having any noticeable bodily change.

Such emotional experiences may be described by a person and may make a great deal of difference in his enjoyment of life, but they are purely private affairs that cannot come under scientific scrutiny. As we pointed out in the first chapter of this book, psychology is a *science of behavior* and cannot study *experience per se*. Only as experience affects a person's behavior can it become the subject of scientific study. There are, however, two ways in which

emotional experience can make itself felt through behavior. One is in *motivating behavior*; a person tries to avoid unpleasant experiences and to put himself in a position to enjoy pleasant ones. This topic will be treated more fully in the last section of this chapter. The other is in *mild expressions of emotion* through words or other indications of likes and dislikes. A person can report what he is feeling, even when he does not otherwise show it, by telling what annoys him, what he would like to avoid, and what he prefers. These reports or behavioral evidences of emotional experience may be considered under two principal headings: (1) annoyances and aversions, and (2) preferences.

Annoyances and aversions. People have a certain degree of control of their emotional experiences because they can, in many things, choose what they prefer and avoid what they dislike, fear, or hate. They often can choose their food, their music, their movies, their wallpaper, their furniture, and so on. In this way, they can make the experiences aroused by these things as pleasant as possible and avoid those that would make them feel uncomfortable, anxious, or hostile. This of course is not always possible, for in all our lives there are situations which make us feel mildly angry yet which cannot be avoided. These are the annoyances of life. Most of us have so many petty annoyances and irritations that it is interesting to study them in their own right.

One psychologist studied common annoyances and irritations by asking people to list their own annoyances for him.[20] From over 600 people, ranging in age from ten to ninety, he got almost 18,000 annoyances. When account was taken of duplications, these reduced to about 2,600 separate annoyances. Tabulating these into various categories (see Table 4.2), he found

TABLE 4.2. Sources of annoyance. 659 individuals of both sexes ranging from ten to ninety years of age were asked to indicate the things that annoyed them.

Class of annoyance	Per cent of different annoyances
Human behavior	59.0
Things and activities not connected with people (other than clothes)	18.8
Clothes and manner of dress	12.4
Physical characteristics of people that could be altered	5.3
Physical characteristics of people that are unalterable	4.4

Most common annoyances associated with human behavior

A person blowing his nose without a handkerchief

A person coughing in one's face

A person cheating in a game

A woman spitting in public

The odor of dirty feet

A child being treated harshly

Based on Cason, H. Common annoyances: a psychological study of everyday aversions and irritations. *Psychol. Monogr.,* 1930, No. 182.

that more than half the common annoyances are things that other *people* do, such as blowing their noses without handkerchieves, coughing in one's face, smelling dirty, treating others with unkindness. Only a small minority of common annoyances had to do with *things*, such as a streetcar's being late, rather than people. There have been other more specific studies of annoyances, such as the ways in which college professors annoy their students.[21] Such studies of annoyance have a practical value: the person who wishes to "win friends and influence people" can study them and take pains not to arouse unpleasant experiences in other people.

Another somewhat different example of

annoyances was made with tones. Subjects were asked to compare the annoying value of different tones and noises. The results of this study were quite definite. People found very high-pitched noises more annoying than low ones. It is possible, in fact, to say just how loud each of two sounds, of different pitch, must be for them to be equally annoying.[22] Studies such as this have considerable value for the acoustic design of buildings, especially those in which people work.

These are just two examples of the facts one can gather about feelings of annoyance. They illustrate the methods used to ascertain the situations giving rise to these feelings and the measurement of relative annoyance values of different stimuli. Psychologists have conducted many studies like these and are able to conduct others whenever new problems of interest or urgency arise.

Preferences. While some things in life make us feel mildly angry, others make us feel pleasant, amused, delighted, or happy. It is possible to study these pleasant feelings in much the same way as those of annoyance. We can find out what styles and patterns of clothes, what colors, architecture, newspapers, music, weather, and many other things are regarded as pleasant or providing enjoyment. We shall mention here three kinds of methods psychologists use to study such preferences.

One is a *method of rating.* One can ask people to assign to each object or situation a number or letter that represents how much they prefer or do not prefer it. The number 1, for example, may indicate that a person likes it very much; the number 5 may be used to mean that he does not like it at all. Another way of studying preferences is the *method of order of merit.* In this case, a person is presented with several objects—perhaps a group of paintings, selections of poetry, samples of wallpaper, pictures of people—and asked to rank-order them. In this way, it is possible to conclude which of the objects is most preferred and which is least preferred. Another somewhat more laborious, but more precise, method is the *method of paired comparisons*. In this case, a person is presented with only two objects at a time and asked to say which he likes more. Then he is presented with two other objects and makes the judgment again. He continues this until he has compared each object with every other object at least once. By counting the number of times any one object is preferred to each of the others, and doing this for every object in turn, one can construct a quantitative index of aesthetic preference for each of the objects.

Using methods such as these,[23] it has been possible to measure aesthetic preferences of individuals, or groups of persons, for a wide variety of things that are used or consumed in everyday life: colors, perfumes, flavors, musical tunes, clothes, and so on. So even though emotional experience is a very private sort of affair and difficult to describe, it is possible to subject it to scientific study and to come out with some rather precise information, which often proves highly profitable to manufacturers and advertisers of whisky, soap, or other products.

■ EMOTIONAL MOTIVATION

In this last section of the chapter, we turn to the problem of emotional motivation. In discussing motivation in Chapter 3, we pointed out that *motives imply goals*— something the organism attempts to attain. This being the case, it is quite clear that the basic emotions of fear, anger, and pleasure all qualify as motives. In the case of fear, the motive is to *avoid* the situation that

evokes it. In anger, the motive is to *aggress* against the source of provocation. In pleasure, the motive is to *seek or attain* whatever it is that gives pleasure.

At this point, however, there is very little to say about pleasure. We have already described earlier in this chapter the conditions that usually elicit pleasure in the infant. Speaking more generally, pleasure is derived from the *satisfaction of any of a person's motives*, whether they be *physiological motives* for such things as warmth, food, or sexual objects or *social motives* for such ends as affection, dependency, prestige, or power. The subject of pleasure has therefore been adequately covered, at least for our present purposes, in the earlier discussion of motivation.

Anger and fear, however, have a special significance in emotional life that we have not yet explained. Through learning, they are modified into more general emotional states, called *anxiety* and *aggression*. Both states come to have a close relationship to *frustration*, and threats of frustration, of other motives. It is important that we understand these terms and the processes that they represent in order to be ready to deal with the problems of personality and adjustment discussed in later chapters (Chapters 9, 10, and 11).

Fear, phobias, and anxiety. The fact that fear serves as a motive hardly needs any proof, for there is ample evidence of this in daily life. Both parents and society make liberal use of the fear of punishment to enforce their will. Our government uses the threat of fine or imprisonment to enforce its laws. People usually behave in the way that society and their friends expect them to because they fear the loss of friends, privileges, and social prestige. Fear of the loss of freedom is the most potent motive for getting nations to fight. Indeed, everywhere we look, we see fear profoundly in-

Fig. 4.6. Society frequently uses threat of punishment to motivate people. (*Courtesy Jeffrey Norton.*)

fluencing what people do and what they work for.

Fears become important motives in life because we have so many opportunities to acquire them. At first in childhood there are physical hazards like falling down the steps and getting burned in the fire, and the child comes to fear those situations in which he has been harmed. Soon the parent starts using fear deliberately. By punishing and at the same time saying "no," a parent soon teaches an infant to fear punishment and the signal for evoking this fear is the word "no." Later on, teaching of fear gets more complicated. To motivate the child, the parent may put him to bed without his supper, deny him his ice cream or Popsicle, or not allow him to go out and play. Thus he is taught to fear loss or denial of the things he wants.

▪ *Acquiring fears.* In situations of this kind, whether simple or complex, all that is necessary for the person to acquire fear is to experience some signal, word, or situation that is associated with punishment. If the signal is followed by punishment enough times—sometimes only once, sometimes more often—it comes to be a *threat* that arouses fear of the punishment. We have already presented an experimental illustration of this point in the chapter on

motivation (Chapter 3).[16] There, you will recall, we described an experiment in which rats were put into a white box which was so constructed that the experimenter could administer electric shocks through the floor of the box. After they had been shocked in the box a few times, they showed fear—an acquired fear—as soon as they were put in the box and before they were actually shocked. They crouched, tensed, urinated, and defecated. In time, they accidentally hit a lever which was in the box and thus opened an escape door. It took only a few experiences of this sort in the now harmless box for them to learn to push the lever quickly and escape. Thus the fear of the box, acquired in the original shocks the rats received, became a motive for learning to escape from the box.

In just this way, people acquire many different sorts of fears. If a person once had a bad fall from a height, he may go through life fearing high places. Another person who, as a child, was lost and terrified in a crowd of people, may thereafter fear being in a crowd. If locked up in a dark closet some time, he may thereafter be afraid of being in a room with all the doors closed. Because people may have varied experiences of this kind, there are a very large number of specific fears that may be found in one person or another. Some, however, are more common than others, and psychologists have given them names.

▪ *Phobias.* The technical name for a strong *irrational* fear of a certain thing or situation is *phobia*. By irrational, we mean that the situation in which the person displays fear does not justify it. Although most of us have specific fears, they usually are not intense enough to deserve to be called phobias. Some people, on the other hand, who are otherwise normal and healthy may have phobias that do not disrupt their lives. In other cases, however, a phobia may be so powerful and of such a sort that it alters the whole course of a person's life. One outstanding example of this sort was that of William Ellery Leonard, who was a poet and professor of literature at the University of Wisconsin. Leonard had a phobia of going more than a few blocks away from home and university. For years this phobia kept him a virtual prisoner in this small geographical area. Although he knew of his fear, he did not know its underlying cause. During the course of psychoanalysis (see page 11), he was able to remember a frightening incident in his childhood. He had wandered away from his home onto the railroad tracks, and a passing train had scalded him with steam. This was the real origin of his fear. His real motive for staying near home was the fear acquired in this incident. The phobia was so powerful that it dominated his whole life. It was never completely eradicated even though he recognized its source and could be objective enough to write a book about it—*The Locomotive God*.[17]

▪ *Anxiety.* As we shall see in Chapter 5, it is characteristic of learning that a response attached to one situation in the course of learning easily generalizes to other similar situations. This phenomenon, called *generalization*, is just as true of fear

as of any other kind of response. Fears, in fact, are easily generalized to many situations. If, for example, we teach a rat to escape from a shock by responding to the sound of a *low-pitched tone*, we find upon later testing that it has also learned to respond to *high-pitched tones*. It may even show fear when any kind of noise is made or a light flashed on. (Other examples of generalization are given in Chapter 5.) The child, similarly, who is often punished by the parent may come to fear the parent, as well as the act for which he was punished. Fear of the parent may generalize to all adults, to all authority figures, or even to people in general. We see, then, that learned fears may generalize to many situations. Indeed, fear may permeate a person's life so deeply that he is fearful in almost all situations, even when he is alone and there is no one or nothing to threaten him.

This brings us to a distinction psychologists make between fear and anxiety. It is not hard and fast, but it is useful. *Fear is a reaction to things or specific situations; anxiety is a general state of apprehension or uneasiness that occurs in many different situations.* Otherwise said, anxiety is a rather vague fear—an "objectless" fear, it is sometimes called. It is vague because the person usually is not quite sure what he is afraid of, and it may, in fact, be rather difficult for anyone to ascertain. Anxiety is like a mosquito in the dark. You know it is near, but you do not know quite where, and you somehow cannot locate it to make the killing slap and be rid of it. Anxiety is also usually less intense but more persistent than fear, although in some cases individuals can suffer attacks of anxiety that are agonizingly severe.

Frustration and conflict. To summarize what we have just said, *anxiety is a vague fear that is acquired through learning and* *through generalization.* This statement explains how anxieties develop, but it does not tell us what causes them. Actually, there are as many specific causes of anxiety as there are people, for each person has a unique set of experiences that may explain his particular set of anxieties. It is possible, however, to state a general principle that encompasses many of these unique sources of anxiety: *Anxiety results from the frustration of motives or the threat of such frustration.*

▪ *Sources of frustration.* In a later chapter (Chapter 10), we study the problem of frustration at some length. Here we shall merely introduce it in order to fill out the picture of emotion. Sources of frustration may be classified into three general categories:

1. *Environmental obstacles* frustrate the satisfaction of motives by making it difficult for a person to attain his goal.

2. In the case of derived motives, such as those for social affiliation or status, a person may be frustrated because he has *unattainable goals*—unattainable because there is too great a discrepancy between his level of aspiration and his level of performance (see page 82).

3. Probably the most important source of frustration is that due to *motivational conflict.* To illustrate briefly this last source, a person may be in conflict between two motives, for example, motives to eat and to sleep, so that one must give way to the other. Hence one motive must be frustrated, at least for the time being. In Chapter 10, we shall describe different kinds of motivational conflicts. The important point here is that motives can be, and are, frustrated in a variety of ways.

▪ *Threats of frustration.* In our society, a person also experiences many threats of frustration. He may never have gone hungry or been without a home, yet he can imagine that if he loses his job he may suffer such frustrations. He may always have had his share of friends and loved ones, yet he may know of others who have lost these affiliations through accident, separation, or hostile acts. Thus he can feel threatened by the possibility of frustration even if he is not actually frustrated. Of course, if he has been hungry, homeless, and without friends, he is more easily threatened than if he has never known these frustrations. A person who is anxious because he feels the threat of some of his needs being frustrated is said to have a *feeling of insecurity* (see page 82). In our society, it is common for such feelings to concern social needs. As we saw in Chapter 3, we acquire many such needs, yet society does not guarantee their satisfaction, and many people live in anxiety that these needs may be frustrated.

Anger and aggression. Frustration not only produces anxiety, it also evokes anger and aggression. These, as we shall see below, also cause anxiety. Consequently frustration, aggression, and anxiety are linked in a vicious circle. To understand this linkage, recall that the basic cause of anger in the infant is restraint (page 95). Restraint is a kind of frustration because it prevents a person from doing what he wants to do. It is now possible to broaden this statement into the more general principle that *anger results from frustration.* Because the term anger implies a forthright, explosive attack, and reactions to minor frustrations are often less overt, psychologists prefer to use such terms as *hostility* and *aggression.* For many practical purposes, it makes little difference which of these terms we use, though a fine distinction may be made between aggression as a visible display of anger and hostility as a smoldering more generalized anger that may be expressed in more subtle ways. Restated now, our general principle is that *aggression results from frustration.*

Three relatively common phobias are dramatized in these photographs: claustrophobia, or the fear of small places (*left*); acrophobia, or the fear of high places (*middle*); and ochlophobia, or the fear of crowds (*bottom*). (All photos by Alfred Gescheidt.)

▪ *Frustration and aggression.* One can find support for this principle in many familiar situations. Try to take a bone away from a dog, or a toy from a child, and you will ordinarily see a display of aggression. Cut an employee's wages, borrow a person's property without his consent, embarrass a person in public, assign him too much work to do—these and a thousand other restraints and frustrations almost invariably provoke aggression. Similar conclusions have been drawn from systematic research with animals, children, and adults who have suffered extreme frustrations.[18] On the other hand, if a person is thoroughly cowed and has no way of fighting back when he is frustrated, he may not show his anger, though he may harbor strong feelings of aggression. It is even possible, as we shall see in Chapter 10, for a person to have strong aggressive tendencies without his knowing about it. This happens when admitting his hostility may be cause for guilt or shame and thus for considerable anxiety. Consequently, he may hurt the person he loves without knowing why.

Aggressive tendencies may be acquired in much the same way as anxiety is acquired from fear-producing situations. If a child is frequently frustrated, is treated harshly, and lives in an aggressive environment, he may generalize his aggression so that he goes around the world with a chip on his shoulder. In the course of becoming socialized, he may learn that society does not countenance aggression, and he may acquire a reasonably pleasant demeanor, yet all the time feel intensely hostile underneath. Thus both aggression and anxiety may be acquired through learning and generalize to many different situations.

▪ *Aggression and anxiety.* In opening this section, we said that frustration, hostility, and anxiety are linked in a vicious circle. We have explained how frustrations result in anxiety and hostility. It remains only to show that hostility is an important source of anxiety. When I take a bone away from my dog, he growls and makes signs of attacking me. If I were another dog, he undoubtedly would, but I am his master and he doesn't dare. In fact, as I watch him, it is evident that he is afraid to attack me, for he knows very well from past experience that he would get punished if he did.

This is a good illustration of the connection in everyday behavior between aggression and anxiety. People, like dogs, have had many years of punishment for expressing aggression; hence they have learned to become anxious about the consequences of aggressive behavior. This situation has occurred so often that the association between aggression and anxiety is well learned. Whenever a person feels an impulse to aggress, this elicits anxiety. Aggression and anxiety are thus inextricably linked in human behavior. And as a postscript to this point, we may add that failure to express aggression is itself a *frustration of aggressive motives.* Since frustration leads in turn to anxiety and aggression, we do, indeed, have a vicious circle.

This section is only an introduction to the subject of emotional motivation. We have merely outlined its general features. Later on, in Chapter 10, we devote more attention to it. In several other chapters, too, the subject comes up again, because emotions as motives are involved in many aspects of human behavior.

SUMMARY

1. There are many shades of emotion ranging from very intense fear or anger to immense pleasure. These develop in each individual from an initial undifferentiated emotion called excitement.

2. Emotions develop partly through maturation, which is necessary before the basic emotions can be expressed, and partly through learning, which elaborates the varieties of emotion expressed in many different situations.

3. For convenience in study, we distinguish four different aspects of emotion: (*a*) bodily states, (*b*) emotional expression, (*c*) emotional experience, and (*d*) emotional motivation.

4. In rather intense emotion, there are numerous changes that occur within the body. These changes are the result of impulses from the autonomic nervous system and particularly the sympathetic division of this system. In addition, the hormone adrenalin is secreted; this, by itself, can cause many of these changes.

5. Bodily changes in emotional situations can be measured with appropriate instruments and have practical applications in the "lie" detector. It is not possible, however, to tell from such measurements what kind of emotion is involved.

6. Attempts to judge the kind of emotion portrayed by expressions of the face, voice, and hands meet with only moderate success. Best results are obtained when the observer can see not only the entire emotional pattern but also the situations giving rise to emotion.

7. The basic situations giving rise to typical emotions may be summarized as follows: (*a*) fear is aroused in situations that are strange, sudden, or threatening; (*b*) anger is the response to restraint or frustration of what one wants to do; and (*c*) pleasure is the result of the satisfaction of needs in the absence of threats and frustration.

8. Emotional experience, though a personal and private affair, may be studied by (*a*) asking people to indicate the circumstances that annoy them, and (*b*) having them indicate their preferences or aversions in some sort of ranking system.

9. Emotional motives, particularly those stemming from fear and anger, are powerful forces in human behavior. Many fears and hostilities are learned in the course of living by experience with situations in which fear or anger has been provoked.

10. An intense, irrational fear of some specific situation is a phobia. A

vague, "objectless" fear, expressed in many situations without a particular object, is an anxiety.

11. Anxiety is generated by frustration, or threat of frustration, of other motives. Such frustration occurs when (*a*) a person encounters environmental obstacles to need satisfaction, (*b*) he has goals set beyond his ability to attain them, and (*c*) he is caught in motivational conflict.

12. Frustration also leads to aggression. Because aggression is socially disapproved and leads to fear of punishment, aggressive impulses are frequently accompanied by anxiety.

SUGGESTIONS FOR FURTHER READING

Cannon, W. B. *Bodily changes in pain, hunger, fear and rage* (2d Ed.). New York: Appleton-Century-Crofts, 1929.
> *A classical description of the physiological changes in emotion.*

Dollard, J., Doob, L. W., Miller, N. E., Mowrer, O. H., Sears, R. R., Ford, C. S., Hovland, C. I., & Sollenberger, R. T. *Frustration and aggression.* New Haven, Conn.: Yale Univ. Press, 1939.
> *An experimental and theoretical analysis of the relation between frustration and aggression.*

Dunbar, F. *Mind and body: psychosomatic medicine.* New York: Random House, 1947.
> *A popular account, written by a physician, of the role of emotions in health and disease.*

Inbau, F. E. *Lie detection and criminal investigation.* Baltimore: Williams & Wilkins, 1942.
> *An authoritative source on the practical use of lie-detection methods.*

Lund, F. H. *Emotions.* New York: Ronald, 1939.
> *A text on emotions emphasizing the physiological factors in emotion.*

Rappaport, D. *Emotions and memory.* New York: International Universities Press, 1950.
> *An analysis of the effects of emotion and emotional conflicts on memory.*

Reymert, M. L. (Ed.). *Feelings and emotion.* New York: McGraw-Hill, 1950.
> *A symposium of authorities summarizing modern knowledge of emotion.*

Ruckmick, C. A. *The psychology of feeling and emotion.* New York: McGraw-Hill, 1936.
> *A good account of the history of experiments and concepts in the field of emotion.*

Young, P. T. *Emotion in man and animal.* New York: Wiley, 1943.
> *A text and general source of information on emotion.*

Chapter 5 LEARNING AND REMEMBERING

How do organisms learn? Why do we learn some things easily and others only with the greatest of difficulty? How does the infant first learn? Why do some of us learn to adjust to our world and its demands, while others fail so badly at adjustment that they must be put in mental hospitals? What is the easiest way to learn the German irregular verbs?

Questions like these have probably occurred to you from time to time. Answers to them come, in part, from what psychologists know about the psychology of learning. If you have been curious about such questions, keep them in the back of your mind as you read this chapter. We shall introduce you to the general principles of learning and leave it to you to translate them into situations that interest you.

This chapter was drafted by James Deese of The Johns Hopkins University.

The study of learning. Learning may be defined as any *relatively permanent change in behavior that is the result of past experience.* Some of the behavioral changes we observe in individuals as they develop from infancy to adulthood are the result of maturation, which we discussed in Chapter 2. Some are due to disease or physiological changes in the body, which we shall consider in Chapters 21 and 22. All the rest are a matter of learning.

It is difficult to grasp the full import of this statement because we have *learned* to take for granted an incalculable number of things that have been learned. Almost everything one does from the time he awakes until he goes to bed has been learned. As was indicated in Chapter 3, most of our motives are learned. All our social values and traditions are learned. And, of course, all that is taught in and out of school, including the knowledge in this and other textbooks, was learned by somebody sometime, somewhere.

For this reason, psychologists consider learning to be *the* fundamental process in understanding human behavior. This book, in fact, is almost entirely about learning, or characteristics that result from learning. Even in our discussion of development (Chapter 2), motivation (Chapter 3), and emotions (Chapter 4), learning received considerable emphasis. The chapters that follow this one will be even more preoccupied with learning processes. After we have presented the principles of learning in this chapter, we shall have occasion to stress the topic again in several subsequent chapters. Since the line between learning and thinking is rather arbitrary, the next chapter (Chapter 6, "Imagination and Thinking") extends our understanding of the learning process. Many aspects of perception, discussed in Chapter 7, are learned; so are most of the characteristics of personality, considered in Chapter 9. In Chapter 10, we discuss the learning of reactions to frustration and conflict, and later in Chapters 13 and 14 the learning of attitudes and prejudices. In Chapter 21, we consider the physiological basis of learning, and in Chapter 23, the evolution of learning in the animal kingdom. In this chapter, therefore, we only outline the principles of learning; in later chapters these principles are extended and applied to different psychological problems.

Kinds of learning. Probably because learning is such a very large subject, no one way of classifying learning has proved very satisfactory. However, a threefold classification will serve our purposes here: *classical conditioning, instrumental learning,* and *perceptual learning.* Each of the next three major sections will be devoted to one of these classes of learning. There are no sharp lines between them. Indeed, it is often dif-

ficult to decide how any particular instance of learning should be labeled. The distinction, however, will permit us to develop some of the principles of learning in an orderly fashion.

CLASSICAL CONDITIONING

Classical conditioning gets its name because it is the kind that was originally studied, about fifty years ago, by Ivan P. Pavlov (1849–1936), the famous Russian physiologist who introduced the concept of conditioning and established many of its basic principles. Sometimes this type is also called respondent conditioning because it involves a simple reflexlike response to a particular stimulus.

Pavlov's experiments. The best way to introduce classical conditioning is to look at the bare essentials of Pavlov's famous experiments.[1] You have probably had the experience of "watering at the mouth" when you have smelled, seen, or even imagined appealing food. This phenomenon, in brief, is what Pavlov investigated. To study it, he devised an apparatus (Figure 5.1) for measuring the flow of saliva. He then presented food, sights, sounds, and other stimuli in such a way that he could see how these stimuli gradually came to affect the flow of saliva.

Pavlov's first step was to place food in the mouth of a moderately hungry dog. This normally makes saliva flow. Pavlov called this salivary response to food the *unconditioned response,* because it occurs without any learning, and he called the food the *unconditioned stimulus* for the same reason. His next step was to sound a bell immediately before he presented the food. After pairing the sound of the bell and the offer of food a few times, he noticed that the sound of the bell, without the sight of food, now made the dog salivate.

Conditioning had occurred. The bell had become a *conditioned stimulus*, and the flow of saliva had become a *conditioned response* to the bell. In other words, because of the association of food with the sound of the bell, the dog had learned, or become conditioned, to salivate when the bell was sounded. Thus, through conditioning, the bell becomes a stimulus that can evoke a response it never before elicited, namely, salivation.

Next Pavlov changed his procedure, sounding the bell *without* presenting the food. The result, after a few trials of this, was that the dog's salivary response became smaller and smaller and finally stopped altogether. This process, which is essentially the reverse of conditioning, Pavlov called *extinction*. From the facts of conditioning and extinction, he concluded that some reinforcement, in this case the food, must be paired with the conditioning stimulus (bell) for conditioning to occur or to be maintained. For this reason he called the unconditioned stimulus (food) a reinforcement. And from the experiment we can derive a fundamental principle of learning, the *principle of reinforcement*. An animal learns a new conditioned response only if it is reinforced in some way; without reinforcement, the response declines in strength and is extinguished. *Reinforcement may be defined* in this case *as presenting the unconditioned stimulus* (food), which evokes the unconditioned response (salivation), *immediately following the conditioning stimulus* (bell). In considering instrumental learning below, we shall find that reinforcement can also be defined in a somewhat different way.

That, in brief, is Pavlov's basic experiment. There are some additional experiments on conditioning which demonstrate other principles of learning. We shall discuss them in the following paragraphs.

Stimulus generalization. Pavlov discovered very early that if he conditioned an animal to salivate to a bell, it would also salivate to the sound of a buzzer or the beat of a metronome, though to a lesser degree. Thus the animal tended to *generalize* the conditioned response to stimuli that were different from, but somewhat similar to, the one to which it was specifically conditioned. Although Pavlov described generalization of conditioned responses, the best-known ex-

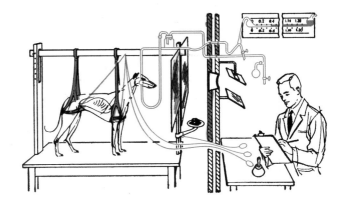

Fig. 5.1. Pavlov's apparatus for studying the conditioned salivary response. Saliva is collected and measured by means of a tube attached to a suction cup placed in the dog's cheek near one of the salivary glands. The apparatus is in a soundproof room with a one-way vision screen between the experimenter and the dog. The experimenter can sound a bell or apply tactual stimuli by remote control. (After Pavlov, I. P. *Lectures on conditioned reflexes.* New York: International Publishers, 1928.)

ample of generalization does not come from Pavlov's laboratory but is a study of the conditioned galvanic skin response in man. You will recall from Chapter 4 that this response, abbreviated GSR, is a reflex of the sweat glands that appears in emotion.

Since the GSR is an emotional response, it may be evoked very easily by giving a subject an unpleasant electric shock. In the particular experiment that we shall use to demonstrate generalization, such a shock was the unconditioned stimulus (reinforcement) for the GSR. The experiment was begun by conditioning the GSR to the sound of a pure tone of a particular frequency.* After the response had been conditioned to this tone, the investigator measured the amount of conditioned GSR given to tones that were of frequencies *different* from that of the original conditioned stimulus.[2] Figure 5.2 is a graph of the results of this experiment. The tone that was used in

---

* Frequency is a physical characteristic of a tone that corresponds roughly with the pitch that a person hears. For the purposes of the present experiment, one can think of frequency as the same thing as pitch. For a discussion of the relation between pitch and frequency, see Chap. 19.

the original conditioning gave the largest GSR, and tones with frequencies closer to it gave larger GSRs than did tones with frequencies more different. Thus the greater *the similarity between stimuli*, the *greater the generalization* between them.

Many responses and characteristics of people seem to be acquired through processes of conditioning and generalization. The experiment with the GSR illustrates these processes. The GSR is a kind of index of emotional disturbance, and this is why it finds its way into lie detection (page 90). In the experiment above, the shock serving as an unconditioned stimulus elicited pain in the subject, and the conditioned stimulus elicited a fear of pain. This simple experiment serves as a model for the development of irrational fears in people. Such fears or phobias (page 99) are irrational because they are acquired through accidental conditioning to some stimulus, then generalized to situations that otherwise have no reason to be frightening. The example of the conditioning of Albert, which we used in Chapter 4, is another case of such generalization. After conditioning to a white animal, he became fearful of all white furry objects.

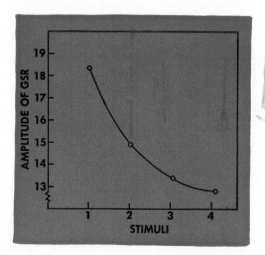

Fig. **5.2.** Generalization of a conditioned galvanic skin response (GSR). Stimulus 1 was the tone to which the GSR was originally conditioned. After conditioning, tests were made with tones of different frequencies, indicated by the numbers 2, 3, and 4. Note that generalization of response is less for stimulus 4, a tone of considerably different frequency, than for stimulus 2, a tone only somewhat different from the one used in conditioning. (*After Hovland, C. I. The generalization of conditioned responses. I. The sensory generalization of conditioned responses with varying frequencies of tone. J. gen. Psychol., 1937, 17, 125–148.*)

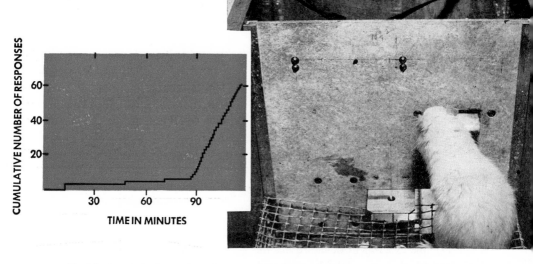

Fig. 5.3. A rat in a Skinner box and a record of its learning. Each time the rat pushes the lever, the line jogs upward a notch. Note that the rat did not make its first response until about 15 minutes after being placed in the box, and its second response about 50 minutes afterward. The effect of food reinforcement becomes apparent, however, at about 90 minutes when the rat begins to press regularly.

INSTRUMENTAL LEARNING

Instrumental learning is much more like the kind of learning we are familiar with in daily life than is classical conditioning. From the preceding chapters it will be remembered that *instrumental behavior* means behavior that accomplishes some result and is not merely a reflex response. Most of the waking behavior of animals and human beings is instrumental. Chickens peck at grain, squirrels dig for nuts, and men open doors. These are all examples of instrumental responses.

The Skinner experiment. To understand the characteristics of instrumental learning,[3] let us consider again (see page 72) the case of the rat's learning to push a lever in a Skinner box (see Figure 5.3). This box, you will remember, contains a device that presents a rat with a pellet of food (or a drop of water) whenever it depresses a lever.

Connected with the box is an apparatus for recording every push.

Sometime before the picture in Figure 5.3 was taken, the rat in the picture had been introduced to the box for the first time. The rat had not eaten in 24 hours and was therefore hungry. After an initial period of timidity, it began to explore the box and eventually depressed the lever. A pellet of food was released, though the rat did not notice it. The rat continued exploring, stopping occasionally to wash as rats do. A second time, somewhat later, it pressed the lever again, and the same thing happened. The third time the rat pressed the lever it still failed to see the pellet of food. On the fourth lever response, however, the rat immediately seized the pellet of food and ate it. Thereafter the rat pressed the lever as rapidly as it could eat food and get back to push the lever again.

This whole procedure was recorded (see Figure 5.3). A device had been connected to the lever in such a way that a recording pen made a jump every time the rat pressed the lever. You can see that the first jump, made about 15 minutes after the rat had been in the box, was followed by a long period during which no response occurred. Another jump in the recording line shows up at about 50 minutes, etc. When the rat had learned to associate the lever with food, the jumps come very close together so that the *rate of responding* appears to be a straight line with a steep slope.

This simple experiment demonstrates the basic features of instrumental learning and, indeed, of much of human learning. The organism, first of all, is *motivated by some need*. The need produces *general exploratory activity*. In the course of such activity, a *response is accidentally made that is instrumental in achieving the appropriate goal*. This response is learned.

Just as in classical conditioning, *reinforcement* is the feature that is essential for instrumental learning to take place. In this case, however, reinforcement must be defined somewhat differently. It is the *attainment of a goal that can satisfy a need*. In the example of the hungry rat in the Skinner box, reinforcement is securing food. If the animal were thirsty, it would be obtaining water. Only because the animal received reinforcement did it learn the appropriate instrumental response.

In both classical conditioning and instrumental learning, it is possible to *extinguish a learned response by withholding reinforcement*. If, for example, the rat no longer gets food when it presses the lever, its rate of responding gradually slows until it stops making any responses at all. Such a procedure is called an extinction procedure, and its result, an *extinction curve*, is illustrated in Figure 5.4.

Secondary reinforcement.   For reasons that will become apparent in a moment,

the kind of reinforcement we have considered so far is called *primary reinforcement*. This is reinforcement of a response by presenting the unconditioned stimulus (in classical conditioning) or the reward of food or water (in instrumental learning). In both types of learning, however, stimuli or circumstances associated with the learning situation also acquire reinforcing value. In classical conditioning, for example, the bell can become a reinforcer, because it comes to elicit the same response, salivation, as the unconditioned stimulus. The name we give to this phenomenon is *secondary reinforcement*. It is an important principle of conditioning and learning. It should be noted in passing that secondary reinforcement is a more general case of the secondary goal discussed in Chapter 3.

To illustrate the way in which secondary reinforcement may be acquired, let us consider again the example of the rat in the Skinner box. The sound of a buzzer, in itself, is not reinforcing to a rat. If, however, the buzzer is paired with a *primary reinforcement* such as the presence of food in the mouth, it does acquire the ability to reinforce. Let us suppose that we sound a buzzer every time a rat is given a pellet of food when it is in its home cage.[4] We then put the rat in the Skinner box and allow it to learn, for the first time, to press the lever. Instead of reinforcing the rat with food, however, we reinforce it with the buzzer that had been paired with eating food in the home cage. We find that the buzzer now works very well as a reinforcer. The rat will learn to press the bar in a way that appears to the casual observer to be simply for the joy of hearing the buzzer. The buzzer in this case is a *secondary reinforcement*. *Any stimulus that acquires reinforcing power because it is paired with a primary or unlearned reinforcement is a secondary reinforcement*.

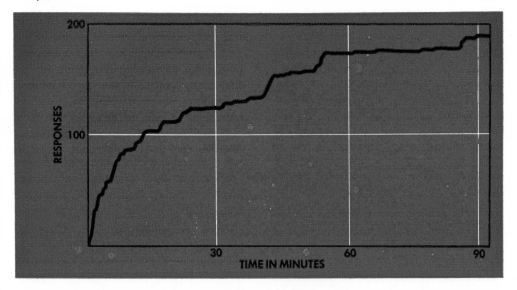

Fig. 5.4. An extinction curve for a rat in a Skinner box. This curve of cumulative responses should read exactly as the curve in Figure 5.3. In this case, however, the curve was obtained after the experimenter stopped giving the rat reinforcement. It, therefore, represents the way the rat continues to respond even when it is receiving no food. Notice that the rat responds rapidly at first, then slows down so that at the end it is giving practically no responses at all. Such a period of extinction practically exhausts the tendency of a rat to press the lever. *(After Skinner, B. F. The behavior of organisms. New York: Appleton-Century-Crofts, 1938.)*

Secondary reinforcement is very important in understanding learning, for it is one of the many mechanisms that bridge the gap between the artificial behavior of the laboratory and behavior in real life. Obviously, much of our learning is the result of secondary reinforcement. Some learning theorists have gone so far as to describe mother love and desire for mother's approval in terms of secondary reinforcement. For example, Keller and Schoenfeld say the following:[5]

Parents, and especially the mother, are among the first secondary reinforcers of a social sort to enter the infant's ken. Their . . . reinforcing potency are quickly established by their continual association with food, warmth, relief from pain, and the like. If, however, the child is reared by a nurse, then she becomes the ever-present second-

ary reinforcement, and it is commonly seen that attachment to the nurse replaces that to the mother.

We cannot prove the truth of this description, but the principle of secondary reinforcement remains a very plausible notion for explaining the way in which attachments develop.

Partial reinforcement. When we described the extinction of conditioned responses, it may have occurred to you that we do not often see extinction in real life. People often forget habits—we shall deal later with forgetting—but they do not seem to stop doing something just because they receive no reinforcement for it. This raises the important question as to why people often persist in their behavior without any visible reinforcement at all. One of the

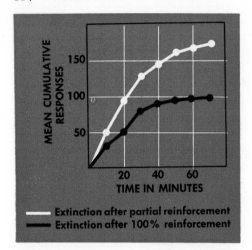

Extinction after partial reinforcement
Extinction after 100% reinforcement

Fig. 5.5. Extinction curves after partial and complete reinforcement. The upper curve was obtained after rats had received partial reinforcement, the lower one after they had been reinforced for every response. Notice that there are more extinction responses following partial reinforcement than following complete reinforcement. Partial reinforcement is, therefore, more effective in "stamping in" responses than reinforcement for every response.

answers is to be found in the facts of *partial reinforcement*. This may be illustrated by turning again to instrumental learning in the Skinner box.

This time let us put two rats into Skinner boxes. We shall reinforce each rat 100 times and then obtain extinction curves. One of the rats will be reinforced with food for every response. The other rat will be reinforced for every fourth response. Thus the first rat will make 100 responses while the second rat makes 400 responses in order to obtain an equivalent amount of food. Such *reinforcement on only some of the responses, rather than all of them, is called partial reinforcement.*

The extinction curves for these two rats will look something like those shown in

Figure 5.5, which were taken from two rats in exactly this way. You will notice the rat that is reinforced only every fourth response gives many more responses during extinction than does the rat that is reinforced every time. Indeed, reinforcing every response favors rapid extinction much more than reinforcing only occasional responses. In brief, *partial reinforcement makes it more difficult to extinguish responses.*

Because it is of very great importance, psychologists have studied partial reinforcement intensively in the past few years.[6] It is a bridge between the relatively permanent behavior of the infant or the animal in nature and the relatively fragile behavior of the laboratory. In nature it seldom happens that an animal gets reinforced for every instance of a particular response. And, as we have seen, it can be demonstrated in the laboratory that partially reinforced behavior is much more resistant to extinction. B. F. Skinner, of Harvard University, who has studied partial reinforcement in the pigeon and rat, has been able to get fantastic numbers of unreinforced responses for just one reinforcement—several thousand in the case of the pigeon.

When young parents first hear of the principles of reinforcement and extinction, they often say, "Ah, here is something we can apply to rearing our child. We will never pick him up when he cries; we will always catch him when he has stopped crying for a few minutes. In this way we can reinforce not-crying and extinguish crying." Unfortunately, this particular application of the basic principles of learning seldom seems to work—and for a good reason. Even the most adamant parents will give in occasionally to the persistent behavior of their children. Thus, just once, or maybe only once every three weeks, mother will pick up the baby while it is crying. This undoes the whole carefully planned program of the parents.[5]

"Well," you will probably say, "the moral is, don't pick up the baby, even once." That is quite correct. However, since we want the baby to have other things such as plenty of love and affection, the moral should be, "don't try to eliminate such behavior once it starts. Try to avoid getting it started, but once it starts you are probably stuck with it." A child who finds that once or twice he is able to postpone his bedtime by fractious behavior is a difficult child at bedtime for many evenings afterward.

Punishment. Before we leave the topic of instrumental learning, we should examine another important problem, namely, that of punishment, because punishment is widely used with the intent of eliminating undesirable behavior. We punish children for running out in the street, and we punish dogs for chewing on rugs. Society pun-

ishes people for driving too fast or for holding up banks. Punishment—or the threat of punishment—is all around us; it is one of the most important factors in controlling behavior. In psychological language, *punishment is the application of an unpleasant or undesirable stimulus in order to eliminate some kind of behavior.* What happens when behavior is punished? Does punishment change behavior or not? If so, when and how? These questions about punishment have been studied in controlled experiments, and we have some answers to them. It turns out that the effects of punishment depend upon two important factors: (1) *the degree to which the punished behavior is motivated,* and (2) *whether or not there is some alternative response to the one being punished.*

Since we have been discussing instrumental learning, we might ask, What is the effect of punishment on a learned in-

Fig. 5.6. The effect of punishment on extinction. The lower extinction curve was obtained after rats had been punished (slapped) for pressing the lever—a response they had just learned. The upper curve was obtained without punishment. The effect of punishment at first is to depress the extinction curve. In the long run, however, the punished rats make just as many responses as the unpunished rats. (*After Skinner, B. F. The behavior of organisms. New York: Appleton-Century-Crofts, 1938.*)

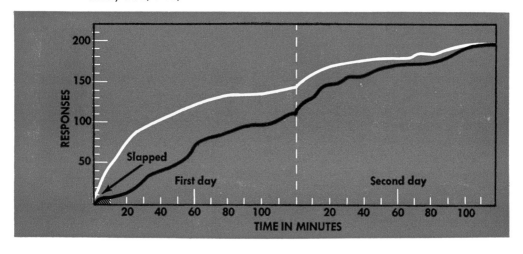

strumental response? Again we can set up the appropriate experiment in a Skinner box. In this particular experiment, two rats were trained as usual to press the lever by reinforcing them with food when they were hungry. One of the rats, however, was slapped for the first few responses made during extinction by a device connected to the lever. The other rat was extinguished in the usual way. The results of such an experiment are shown in Figure 5.6. The two curves in this figure are extinction curves obtained in two rats after an equal amount of conditioning. By comparing the two curves you can see that the initial effect of punishment (slapping) was to reduce the rate of response. The punished rat responded much more slowly after the slapping than did the rat not punished. The amazing fact is, however, that the punished rat had completely caught up with the unpunished rat by the time extinction was over. *The punishment had no effect upon the total number of responses made during extinction.*

This experiment has been repeated many times, using different kinds of punishment administered in different ways, but results are nearly always the same. Punishment has a negligible effect upon the *total reserve* of responses emitted during extinction. It does temporarily reduce the rate of responding. Sometimes, if the punishment is given intermittently over a period of time, rate of responding is greatly reduced and the total reserve may be slightly diminished. In general, however, the permanent effects of punishment are very much smaller than we should have expected.[7]

The experiment outlined above has two important features: (1) the rats were highly motivated to press the lever; and (2) pressing the lever was the *only* means immediately available for them to satisfy their hunger. Therefore, this experiment may be taken as indicative of what happens when a *highly motivated response* that is the *only means available to satisfy the drive* is punished. The punishment reduces the tendency to respond for a time, but it cannot entirely eliminate the response.

For responses that are not highly motivated and for responses that admit alternative ways of satisfying current motivation, the story is somewhat different. Numerous experiments have been performed upon problems related to this situation with the use of human beings as subjects. The results of these experiments are not completely consistent, but the following things seem to be true:[8,9] (1) responses can be eliminated by mild punishment if they are not highly motivated responses; (2) likewise, highly motivated responses can be eliminated by mild punishment if they are not the only responses that can satisfy some drive; (3) the effect of punishment in such cases is usually to make behavior more variable. Animals and people will try to find other ways to satisfy their drives when punished for some particular response.

In any case, the effects of punishment are not always simple or predictable. Furthermore, punishment is complicated by the possibility that it may lead to disturbances of behavior. A child, when he is punished for trying to get something he wants, is frustrated, and this may lead to a tantrum or to aggressive behavior. Because punishment is a frustration, it has the serious consequences of frustration that we mentioned in Chapter 4 and shall consider in detail in Chapter 10.

There are two circumstances in which punishment, or the threat of punishment, usually proves effective in controlling human behavior.

1. Mild punishment may be used as a cue that provides information about what should or should not be done. The punish-

ment of being burned by a fire or getting shocked while playing with an electric circuit teaches the child to stay away from fires and "hot" wires. A low grade in an hour examination is a kind of punishment that tells a student where he stands in his mastery of the subject. Critical remarks made about a person's clothes or behavior may induce him to change his ways. In these and similar cases, a person has alternative things he can do, when punishment tells him what not to do, and thus punishment can be helpful.

2. The threat of punishment also serves well in our society to eliminate undesirable behavior. The threat of going to prison for stealing, the threat of being fined for speeding, the threat of failing a course if one does not study—these and similar threats continually restrain us from doing many things that we might otherwise do. Actual punishment for infractions often does not seem effective—if one can judge by the number of "repeaters" in prisons or even by the number of F's some students manage to accumulate—but in most instances, the threat of punishment serves its purpose well without having harmful effects.

The net effect of what we know about punishment is to lead us to be cautious about its use. Punishment is impossible to avoid; as we say above, punishment or threat of punishment is one of society's most widely used devices for keeping order. Every child must be punished at some time or another, if not by the parents, then by someone else. Punishment, however, should be used discerningly, with an eye to its possible undesirable consequences.

■ PERCEPTUAL LEARNING

In both classical conditioning and instrumental learning, an important element in the learning is some *response* made to a stimulus or situation. In many learning situations, the important element is not so much a response as it is a *stimulus* to which the organism learns to respond in different ways. What we mean by this statement will become clear as the discussion proceeds. It can be illustrated by referring to certain arrangements of conditioning and instrumental-learning situations.

Discriminative learning. In classical conditioning, a dog can be conditioned to salivate in response to a bell. Let us suppose, however, that when the dog is conditioned, we intersperse *reinforced presentations* of the bell with *unreinforced presentations* of a metronome. That is to say, the bell is sometimes sounded and followed by food, but a metronome is also sounded some of the time without ever being followed by food. Because of stimulus generalization, the dog at first responds to the metronome with salivation. On the other hand, these responses are extinguished because they are not reinforced, while those to the bell are maintained by food reinforcement. Hence, after many training trials, the dog learns to respond to the bell and not to the metronome. In this way, we have managed to teach the dog a *conditioned discrimination*. Note that such a discrimination depends upon *differential reinforcement*—the reinforcement of one stimulus and the extinction of another.

Instrumental learning, as well as conditioning, affords opportunities for acquiring such discriminations. A Skinner box, for example, may be arranged with two levers placed under two panels in which lights may be presented.[29] The experimenter can so arrange things that the rat is reinforced when it pushes the lever beneath the lighted panel and is not reinforced when it pushes the lever under the dark panel. In this case, the rat learns to discriminate light from darkness by selecting the appropriate lever to push. There are many other ways in which this basic procedure may be used to teach discriminations.[30] Instead of levers, the experimenter may use doors, alleys, or any means of getting the animal to choose between two alternatives. Instead of lights, he may present cards of a different color or different shapes (see Chapter 23). These are incidental variations on the general principle that a *discrimination may be learned by reinforcing one stimulus and not reinforcing the other one.*

In learning to make discriminations, it is also possible to learn *concepts.* The term concept refers to a *class of objects or some property that objects have in common.* There are many ways, for example, to make a triangle: with three lines, with three dots, with dashed lines, with the triangle's interior completely black and its background white, and so on. There are similarly many ways to make a square. If an animal is repeatedly reinforced for choosing any of these triangular objects and not reinforced for selecting square objects, it can develop a concept of "triangularity." It then consistently discriminates any kind of triangular object from any kind of square object.[31] The learning of concepts is therefore a special case of discriminative learning. Concepts are closely related to a number of problems involved in imagination and thinking; we have therefore deferred a fuller discussion of them until the next chapter (Chapter 6).

Incidental learning. It may have occurred to you that there is much that we may learn about stimulus situations without making any responses to them. If, for example, you are a passenger in an automobile without any responsibility for finding the way to your destination, you nevertheless learn something about the route you travel. You will notice some of the turns that are made, some of the houses you see, and

other landmarks along the way. If later you must drive the route, you will find it familiar to you. In all probability, you will find your way more easily than you could have done if you had not traveled the road before.

This kind of learning has been called *incidental learning,* because it occurs quite incidentally, without the individual's being motivated or required to make a response. It is also called *latent learning,* because it is latent until the occasion for its use arises. Some learning theorists have questioned whether such learning is truly incidental.[33] There is always the possibility of motives and responses that are not evident to the observer. On the other hand, the evidence is reasonably strong for accepting incidental learning at face value.[8]

Incidental learning has been demonstrated in a number of experiments with animals. In one classical experiment,[32] three groups of rats were run daily in a maze. One group was given food reinforcement at the end of each trial. As might be expected, they made steady progress in learning the correct path through the maze. A second group was run without any reinforcement; they simply wandered around the maze for a given period each trial. A third group was treated the same as the second group for the first 10 days. After that, however, the experimenter began rewarding them when they reached the end of the maze.

The results of this experiment are shown in Figure 5.7. All groups of rats evidently learned something, because they made fewer errors as they ran more and more trials. The unreinforced groups, however, did not improve as much as the first, reinforced group. But when the experimenter began to reinforce the third group, their error scores suddenly dropped to about the same level as the first, reinforced group. Apparently the unreinforced rats had learned a great deal about the maze in the early trials. They merely did not give evidence of their learning—it was latent— until they were reinforced for performing well.

This and similar experiments have led psychologists to conclude that incidental learning may take place in the absence of reinforcement. However, *reinforcement is important for performance*. What we have called instrumental learning is learning to perform a response; this learning requires reinforcement. Without such reinforcement, an individual may notice many aspects of his environment and learn relations between objects in his environment. But until he is motivated and rewarded to perform, we have no way of knowing that learning actually took place.

Insightful learning.   Just to fill out the picture, we shall mention briefly another aspect of learning to be considered at length in Chapter 6. This is *learning by insight*. All the instances of learning we have considered so far might be regarded as "stupid" learning. It is a more or less blind trial-and-error process or a robotlike conditioning. Even incidental learning may be regarded as a random, purposeless sort of learning.

In marked contrast to such "stupid" learning is the fact that much of human learning involves reasoning and insight. Instead of being conditioned or trying to solve problems hit or miss, people frequently attempt to size up a situation and reason out the solution. They do not do things blindly; they think. Often the solution comes suddenly by *insight*, when they have correctly perceived the elements of the problem in their proper relationship. In most cases, such insightful solutions depend upon habits that the individual has previously acquired through conditioning and instrumental learning. Nevertheless, a problem

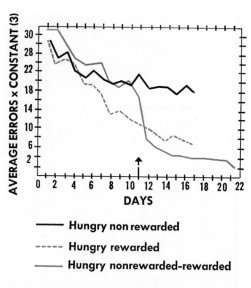

Fig. 5.7. Latent learning of a maze. The unreinforced group of rats makes very little progress in maze learning until reinforcement is introduced. Then it quickly catches up to the group run throughout on reinforcement. For further explanation, see text. (*After Tolman, E. C., and Honzik, C. H. Introduction and removal of reward and maze performance in rats. Univ. Calif. Publ. Psychol., 1930, 4, 257–275.*)

solved in this way is something learned. The individual then can use his knowledge to solve similar problems without resorting to trial-and-error learning. The fullest understanding of learning by insight obviously involves the subject of thinking. For that reason, we discuss insight in Chapter 6 and shall say no more about it here.

ACQUIRING SKILLS

In the preceding sections, we have introduced concepts that are fundamental to all sorts of learning. Now we shall consider some of the more practical, and more complex, problems of human learning. In this section, we shall discuss the *learning of skills*. Learning to talk, to read French, to drive an automobile, to type—all these are

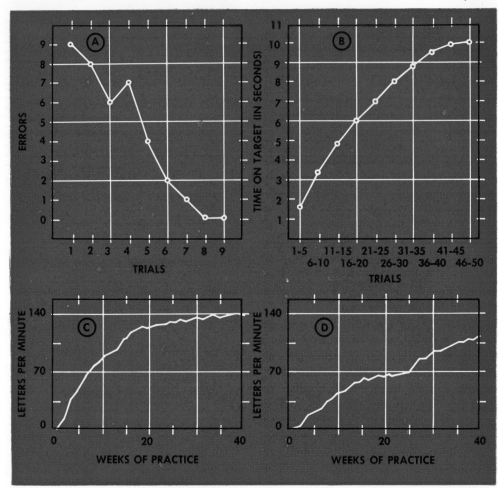

Fig. 5.8. Four examples of learning curves. Curve A represents the learning of a finger maze; it shows how errors are reduced with practice. Curve B measures progress in learning a pursuit meter; it shows that learners improve their accuracy with practice. The score in this case is the amount of time in each 15-second trial that a subject can keep the stylus on the target. Curves C and D are for telegraphy; curve C is for sending and curve D for receiving. Notice that in curve D (receiving), but not in curve C (sending) there is a flat place, called a plateau.

examples of the numerous skills people must acquire in this day and age. In the section that follows this one, we shall take up *transfer of training*—the question of how learning to solve one problem can help or hinder in the solution of other problems. In the last two sections, we shall consider some of the facts of *remembering* and *forgetting*.

Learning curves. If you were to study carefully the way in which a person learned such a skill as driving a car, probably one

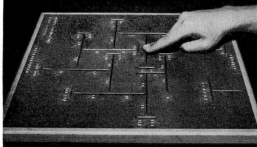

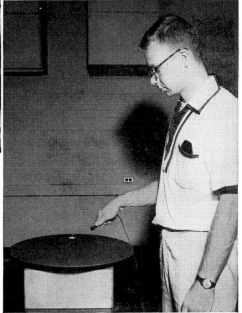

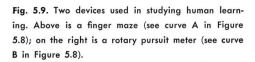

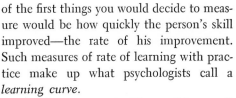

Fig. 5.9. Two devices used in studying human learning. Above is a finger maze (see curve A in Figure 5.8); on the right is a rotary pursuit meter (see curve B in Figure 5.8).

of the first things you would decide to measure would be how quickly the person's skill improved—the rate of his improvement. Such measures of rate of learning with practice make up what psychologists call a *learning curve*.

The four curves in Figure 5.8 are all learning curves. In the first one (A), errors or mistakes are the measure of learning, and improvement is indicated by the *elimination of errors*. The curve happens to be one of college students learning a maze. In Figure 5.9 (left) you see a student, blindfolded, tracing his way through such a maze. The student's task is to learn to find his way from one end of the maze to the other by following the "true path." A maze is a common device used to study complex learning in both rats and men. Rats, of course, are not blindfolded while running through the maze; rather, we put them into a rat-sized maze that usually has enclosed alleys. It might be remarked in passing that rats, when run under these conditions, do almost as well as blindfolded college stu-

dents. Learning the correct path through a maze is charted either by the number of errors the subject makes or the time that it takes him to get through the maze. Curve A is a chart of the elimination of errors in learning the maze.

Another way to measure the rate of learning is to plot the *accuracy* or *correctness* of performance as a function of practice. There are many ways to do this. Curve B in Figure 5.8 shows the percentage of time a learner is able to keep a small metal stylus in contact with a moving disk. A subject working at this problem is shown in Figure 5.9 (right). This apparatus is what is known as a rotary pursuitmeter. It is used in studies of motor learning. The curve of learning for the rotary pursuitmeter is, of course, an increasing-score curve.

Curves C and D in Figure 5.8 are curves of learning for verbal material. These curves are taken from a famous study[10]—one of the earliest experimental studies of human learning—in which the ability to send and receive telegraphic code was measured as a function of practice. These two curves look much like the curve for learning the rotary pursuitmeter; that is, they are increasing-score curves. There is something special, though, about curve D that demands particular attention. You will notice that about halfway through the curve there is a level place where, for a period of time, there does not seem to be much improvement. This period of little or no improvement is known as a *plateau*, and it requires a word of explanation.

Plateaus. Plateaus do not always occur in learning curves, but when they do there are special reasons for them. One reason may be that there are several distinct stages in acquiring the skill. In Figure 5.8, for example, the plateau appears in curve D for receiving code, and not in curve C for sending code. To account for this plateau, Bryan and Harter, who did the experiment, reasoned that the learner hit the plateau because he had reached the limit of his ability to receive *letter by letter* and had not yet begun to learn to receive *word by word* or *phrase by phrase*. In other words, there may be several different habits or several stages of habit involved in acquiring any particular skill; *when one stage of learning is completed before the next begins, a plateau appears in the learning curve.*

This description of the stages in acquiring habits is likely to be familiar to anyone who has tried to learn to play some musical instrument. When one begins the piano, for example, there is an early period during which one learns very rapidly; the fundamentals are easily acquired. But then there comes a long period during which improvement is maddeningly slow or nonexistent. Most people become discouraged at this point and quit. Others who persevere, however, find that they eventually get over the plateau and enter a new stage of learning,

such as integrating the separate movements of the hands and fingers.

There are also other causes of plateaus. Loss of motivation is a factor that has been frequently suggested as a cause of plateaus.[12] After taking piano lessons for some time, for example, a child may lose all interest in learning. Then, even if he is forced to practice regularly, his learning curve is likely to show a plateau. Plateaus do not always occur in learning, but when they do, changing the mode of practice, or completely resting from practice for a period of time helps materially to eliminate them.

Distribution of practice. One of the most important factors in learning is the rate at which a person practices a task. For an amazingly wide variety of situations, short periods of practice interspersed with brief periods of rest permit more efficient learning than continuous practice.[11] This is true for simple instrumental conditioning, and it is true for such complex skills as learning to type. A possible exception to this rule concerns tasks involving problem solving or inductive thinking,[13] but even so, the rule of distributed practice is one of the most general in all learning.

In Figure 5.10 you can see the effect of distributed practice upon some curves of learning.[14] Notice that there is a large and consistent difference between the learning curves for continuous practice and those for distributed practice. The task in which the subjects of this experiment were engaged was learning to follow a complex pattern with a pencil by looking in a mirror. For more complicated tasks the difference between massed and distributed practice is not so great as it is in this experiment.

In most tasks there is some optimal way in which to intersperse practice and rest to obtain the most rapid learning. In trying to find the optimum for a specific task, there are three factors that can be varied:

(1) the length of the practice period, (2) the length of the rest period, and (3) the location of the rest periods in the course of learning.

Practice periods should, in general, be short, for within certain limits, the longer they are the more they tend toward continuous practice and thus the slower the rate of learning.[15] On the other hand, practice periods should not be so short as to break up the task into artificial or meaningless units.

In general, the longer the rest period, the more rapid the learning; improvement tends to increase with the length of the rest period. Very long rest periods, however, do not make learning any more rapid.[14] In other words, the optimal length of a rest period is probably quite short for most tasks, and increasing it beyond a relatively brief optimal time will not increase materially the rate of learning.

We can make no clear-cut recommendations about the location of rest periods, for experiments with different kinds of tasks give different results.[16] The best general summary we can make concerning distribution of practice is this: It is much more important to have short practice periods interspersed with frequent, short rest periods than to have only one or two long rest periods and one or two long practice periods.

This guiding principle for the distribution of practice has applications both to college study and to work in business or industry. Hence, in the last chapter of this book, "Techniques of Study," you will find this problem discussed again as it concerns effective college study. It is also considered in Chapter 17, "Work and Efficiency." Although learning a task and working at a task we know well how to do are not comparable in every respect, the same general advice we have given here is also applicable

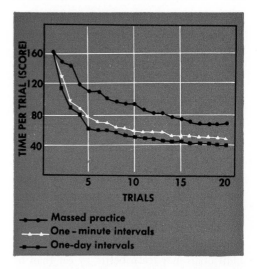

Fig. 5.10. A comparison of massed practice and distributed practice. The curves represent learning under three conditions: massed practice with no rest between trials, practice with one-minute intervals between trials, and practice with one-day intervals between trials. Note that even a one-minute interval makes learning proceed more rapidly than no interval at all. One-day intervals are best of all. (*After Lorge, I. Influence of regularly interpolated time intervals upon subsequent learning. Teach. Coll. Contr. Educ., 1930, No. 438.*)

to the distribution of periods of work and rest in vocational situations.

Reading versus recitation. There are many variations in methods of practice that affect the rate of learning. One variation of particular interest to the student concerns the difference between reading and active recitation in the memorizing of verbal material. We also discuss this problem in the chapter "Techniques of Study." There we point out that simply reading material is vastly inferior to reading plus active recitation of the material to be memorized. In other words, if one only reads something without reciting what he has read, his learning is much less effective than if he reads and also actively recites it. As a matter of fact, if as much as 80 per cent of study time is spent in active recitation, the result is better retention than if all the time is spent reading.[17] This is particularly true for disconnected material, such as foreign-language vocabulary, but it is also true of highly organized, meaningful material.

We cannot make such clear statements about other modes of practice. We cannot, for example, say unequivocally that it is better to learn by reading than by listening. Many investigators have done experiments on this problem, but the results are not clear-cut. The answer probably lies in individual differences between people. Some individuals may learn better by ear than by eye, but for others the reverse is probably true. In any case, the differences are probably small and probably depend upon the particular situation measured.

Meaningfulness of material. As people grow up, they acquire a large repertoire of learned behavior. And as they are presented with new tasks to learn, they find that some are very much like the tasks they have learned before. Or they find that what they have already learned helps in learning the new task. New tasks or materials that are more easily learned because they involve old learning are said to be *meaningful* tasks. It is probably quite obvious that it is easier to learn a meaningful task than to learn a strange one that has little to do with our previous experience.

Memorizing passages of words makes a good example of this factor of *meaningfulness*. If you try to memorize the last paragraph, you will find it much easier than trying to memorize the same number of words taken at random from the dictionary. Also, you would find it easier to memorize the paragraph in its correct order than to do it with the sentences jumbled up. But even memorizing jumbled sentences is easier than memorizing jumbled words.

It is interesting to note that the meaningfulness of paragraphs and sentences as compared with words depends to a very great extent on the statistical structure of language.[18] All through life we learn that certain words are more likely to follow other words. For example, you might expect the sequence of words, "The old brown bear . . ." to be followed by "ran," "climbed," or "growled" but not by "skyscraper," "related," or "pink." This simply illustrates that we learn to distinguish dependent probabilities between words. We learn that certain words are more likely to follow a given word than other words. Such dependent probabilities make up the statistical structure of English and largely explain why we more easily learn meaningful English than non-sense English. There are certain other factors involved in meaningfulness, but this factor of statistical structure is one of the most important in relating language and learning. We consider this factor in some detail in Chapter 20, "Language and Speech."

TRANSFER OF TRAINING

One of the most important problems in the whole of the psychology of learning is that of the transfer of training. The fact that you are engaged in a program of academic study indicates society's implicit faith in transfer of training. The principal value that comes from formal learning in the school situation lies in the application of what we have learned to problems outside the academic world. Because so much of our time is spent in formal learning of things that are useful only outside the classroom, the problem of transfer of training is one of the most important applied problems in learning.

Before looking at some particular instances of the problems of transfer, we shall do well to examine the theory behind transfer of training. A general theory helps us to integrate a lot of separate facts, and this in turn is helpful in applying formal knowledge to problems of daily life. So, as you are reading about the theory of transfer of training, you might consider the ways in which it can apply to real problems.

Principles of transfer. There are two fundamentally different consequences of transfer of training, and these need to be understood clearly. Suppose I have learned that in order to keep the attention of my class in introductory psychology I must tell a joke every 10 minutes or so. This seems like a reasonable device, so I try it in my class in applied psychology, and it works there, too. This is an example of *positive transfer*. What I have learned to do in one situation applies equally well to another situation.

Suppose, however, that I try to carry this one step further and introduce the technique into a talk at the faculty club. Here I discover that my jokes fall flat and the technique fails miserably. This is now an example of *negative transfer*. What worked in one situation is not applicable to another situation.

Therefore, *positive transfer occurs when something previously learned benefits performance or learning in a new situation.* Likewise, *negative transfer occurs when something previously learned hinders performance or learning in a new situation.*

▪ *Similarity of stimuli.* Positive transfer increases with similarity of stimuli. The more similar the stimuli in two situations, the more positive transfer there is from one to the other. This fact is the same one, expressed in different terms, that we learned earlier under the heading of "Stimulus Generalization." In that case, you will recall, a GSR conditioned to a tone of one pitch was also evoked in lesser degree when tones of similar pitch were presented. Such stimulus generalization is a case of positive transfer.

Let us cite two more familiar examples. After one has learned to drive one make and model of car, he usually has little difficulty in transferring to another car. Instruments on the new dashboard may be arranged somewhat differently, the windshield may be a little higher or larger, and many minor features of the two cars are different. In general, however, the stimulus situations presented by the two cars are similar; hence transfer is good. In learning languages, if one has studied Greek, his progress in Latin is faster; if he has studied Latin, his learning of French is made easier; and Latin is also helpful in mastering Italian or Spanish. In each case, the reason is that the two languages have many similarities, and similar stimulus situations produce positive transfer of training.

▪ *Similarity of responses.* The same principle also applies to cases in which there is a similarity of responses. Here, however, there is the possibility of two responses' being so dissimilar that they are opposites, or near opposites, of one another. In that case, the result is negative transfer. To use again the example of driving two cars, positive transfer from one to the other usually occurs, not only because the stimulus situations are similar, but also because similar responses are required. In both cases, one uses his right foot to brake the car, his right foot to accelerate it, and his left foot to operate the clutch, if there is a clutch. To take another example, if a person has learned to play tennis, he finds it easier to learn ping-pong or badminton because similar responses and skills are involved in all three games.

Let us consider cases in which opposite responses are required in two situations with resulting negative transfer. If you are used to steering a sled and then try to pilot a plane, you will have difficulty at first, because extending one's right foot makes a sled go to the left and a plane to the right. Many people have trouble learning to steer with an outboard motor because it requires that one push the stick to the left in order to make the boat turn right, and this seems unnatural.

Negative transfer can be a matter of life and death in airplanes when a pilot has flown one type of plane for a long time and then flies a plane with rather different controls. In the new plane, he may have to do exactly the opposite of what he has been accustomed to do. Airplane accidents are occasionally caused in this way.[34] In one incident, a pilot was undershooting the field in attempting to land. To correct his approach, he pulled back on the throttle and pushed the stick forward. This was the reverse of what he should have done, and it nosed the plane into the ground. The reason he gave afterward—he was fortunate enough to survive to tell the tale—was that he was accustomed to flying planes in which he operated the throttle with his right hand and the stick with his left hand. In this plane, the positions of the controls were different so that he used his left hand on the throttle and his right hand on the stick. In an emergency, he had reverted to his old habits, with almost fatal consequences.

In summary, we may say that *similarity of stimuli and of responses accounts for positive transfer. A dissimilarity of responses, in which opposite or competing responses are required, accounts for negative transfer.*

Transfer of training in formal education. The whole of our formal educational program assumes that there is a certain degree of positive transfer between what is learned in school and what is needed in daily life. It is not surprising, therefore, that psychological studies of transfer of training have had a profound influence upon our contemporary notions of education.

At one time there was a fairly widespread notion that only a limited number of mental faculties needed to be trained, and that once these had been trained, they could be used in a wide variety of situations. Thus schoolboys used to study Greek, Latin, Euclid, and Aristotle, not so much because of their intrinsic value but because they were supposed to train the mind. At one time, too, there was widespread belief in the notion that one could train school children to be neat in their appearance and care of their belongings by teaching them to be neat in the arithmetic and spelling papers they handed in. This general notion has been called the *mental-faculty* theory of transfer or, on occasion, the *formal-discipline* theory of transfer.

This theory has been pretty well buried today, largely because of the results of experimental studies on transfer of training. Some years ago educational psychologists[19] studied the transfer of Latin grammar to English grammer, of Euclidean geometry to the ability to solve reasoning problems, and of classical physics to the ability to understand the mechanical problems of everyday life. The results were rather disappointing. In nearly every case there was some positive transfer, but it was disappointingly small. Educators have gradually relinquished the notion that one could instill an ability through sheer exercise of a faculty or general habit.

Nowadays educators are not concerned with "mental discipline" but with producing the greatest amount of positive transfer from school subjects to everyday life. Part of the technique for accomplishing this is to make school problems as realistic as possible. Hence the modern arithmetic book attempts to cast its problems in a form that makes them like the everyday experience of the child.

At the higher levels of education, positive transfer can best be increased by making it clear to the learner that what he is learning can be transferred to other situations. Even the old subjects of special delight to the adherents of formal discipline can be made useful by bringing this home. A study of Euclidean geometry *can* aid one in improving his ability to reason if he has a good and patient teacher with a flair for pointing out what can be transferred from the formal subject to thinking in our daily experience.

■ RETENTION

One of the most interesting problems to the student of learning is that of retention. How much of what we learn do we retain? Why do we forget? Why do we find it so difficult to remember certain common things? What produces the distortions of memory that are the common experience of everyone? These questions are all basic, and in the next few pages we shall look at some answers to them. Some practical advice for improving retention is given in the chapter, "Techniques of Study."

Forgetting and retention are but opposite sides of the same coin. What we have forgotten is simply the difference between what we have learned and what we have retained. We can measure directly only what has been retained, of course, but sometimes our emphasis is upon "forgetting" rather than "retention."

Measuring retention. There are several different ways of measuring retention. We shall describe three: *recall, recognition,* and *savings.*

The *method of recall* is especially suit-able for the study of retention of verbal material, such as a poem or section of a textbook. For recall, the subject must reproduce, with a minimum of cues, something that has been learned in the past. Of the different methods we shall describe, the method of recall yields the smallest amount of measurable retention, because it is always harder to recall something "cold" than it is to relearn it or to recognize it. The essay examination is an example of a recall method of measuring retention.

A second method, the *method of recognition,* is most frequently used in objective examinations consisting of true-false, multiple-choice, or similar questions. It is inflated by a factor of chance, however, and for this reason is the least useful for experimental purposes. But because it is frequently used in tests of classroom learning, we sometimes find it necessary to evaluate retention in terms of recognition.

The method most frequently used by psychologists in experimental studies of retention is the *method of savings.* In this case the subject learns again a task that he learned some time before. The measure of retention is the difference in time or trials required for original mastery and for the second learning—the saving from the first learning. Suppose, for example, that it took me 20 repetitions to learn a certain poem. After a period of a week it took me only 10 trials to relearn the poem. I would then show a saving of 50 per cent. Such a method has the advantage of being very sensitive and at the same time reliable. Furthermore, it can show negative values. For example, suppose that for some reason or other I had taken 30 trials to relearn the poem; this would represent a negative saving of 50 per cent.

With this brief description of the principal methods of measuring retention, we are now ready to examine the results of scientific studies of retention.

Amount of retention. How much of what we learn stays with us after a period of time? The first attempt to answer this question experimentally was made by the German psychologist Ebbinghaus. Ebbinghaus experimented on many different problems in verbal learning; he always used only himself as subject. The results of his studies were published in 1885 in a monograph, *Über das Gedächtnis*, or *Concerning Memory*.

Ebbinghaus memorized a list of nonsense syllables like *zeb, bep, cex, rab* that have no meaning. Then he allowed a period of rest, varying from a half hour to a month, and then learned them again. In this way he was able to measure the savings for different intervals between original learning and relearning. Ebbinghaus's results are shown in Figure 5.11.

As you can see, the savings are great for short intervals but they decline rapidly during the first day after original learning. Thereafter the decline is much less abrupt. This kind of curve is *negatively accelerated,* which is a way of saying that it declines more rapidly at the beginning than at the end. Such a negatively accelerated curve of

Fig. 5.11. A classical curve of forgetting. This curve was obtained in early experiments by Ebbinghaus (see text).

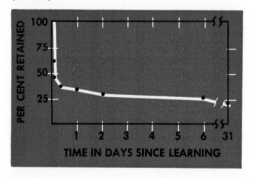

retention is the rule; practically all retention curves are of this sort.

Many investigators have contrasted the retention of *meaningful material* with that for *nonsense material.*[20] Educational psychologists, for example, have studied the ability of students to remember what they have learned in school after periods of rest away from formal instruction. The outcome, in general, has been some sort of negatively accelerated curve like that in Figure 5.11. The curve, however, usually does not fall as fast or as far as the curve for nonsense syllables, which means that meaningful material is more likely to be retained. Such studies make it quite clear that it is relatively hard to remember simple, isolated facts and relatively easy to retain meaningful material or material containing simple ideas.

Sometimes we are discouraged by the fact that we do not seem to recall very well most things that we learn. At least we do not remember a lot that we spend a great deal of time patiently and deliberately learning. After four years, for example, we cannot easily recall the animal phyla that we learned in zoology. We cannot remember the gender of German nouns, so that most Americans who can speak a little German resort to a universal "der" by way of a definite article. Such forgetting, however, should not discourage us too much, for an equally remarkable fact is that we often show extraordinary degrees of *savings.*

One rather dramatic story illustrates the last point rather well.[21] Some years ago a psychologist undertook to read to his son passages in Greek from Sophocles's *Oedipus Tyrannus*. This is not such a remarkable thing for a professor to do, except for the fact that the son was only fifteen months old. Each day for 3 months, the professor read the same three selections of 20 lines each to the boy. When the boy

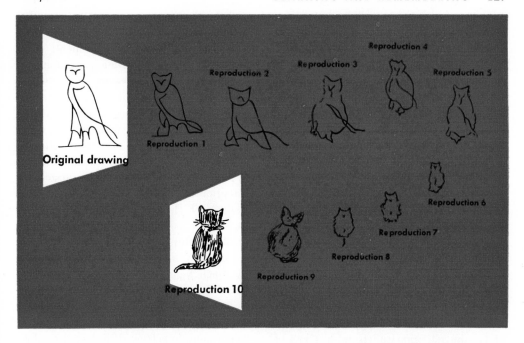

Fig. 5.12. How memory distorts our perception of objects. The original drawing was seen by one subject, and he was asked to reproduce it (first reproduction). Another subject looked at this reproduction and then copied it from memory (second reproduction). This procedure was repeated through the entire series. You can see how drastically the nature of the figure is changed from one reproduction to another. The distortions of memory have changed the figure from the conventionalized Egyptian symbol for an owl to a picture of a cat. (*After Bartlett, F. C. Remembering. Cambridge: Cambridge Univ. Press, 1932, p. 180.*)

was eight years old, he was required to learn by rote these selections plus some others of equal difficulty with which he was not familiar. It took the boy an average of 435 repetitions per selection to learn the new selections, and only 317 repetitions per selection to learn the old ones. Thus, even in infancy, learning of complex nonsense material (since that was surely what it was to the subject of this experiment) results in savings at a later date.

The moral of this story is, Do not be too upset about the precipitous decline in *recall* for the material that you may learn in school; there will probably be some considerable *savings* whenever you have an opportunity to use that material again.

Qualitative changes in retention. You may have played or heard about the game of Gossip. In it, a group of individuals arrange themselves in some order. The first individual then reads a narrative to the second individual, and the second individual passes it on from memory to the third individual, and so on. Then the version at the end is compared with the original narrative. The results are usually astonishing and sometimes amusing. The "message" undergoes many changes. It is usually shortened and distorted in its meaning. This game is of psychological importance because it is a useful model of certain kinds of social communication.[22]

Gossip is also interesting because it parallels the changes in memory that can happen within the same individual.[23] If we ask a single individual to reproduce something after various intervals of time, we get the same losses and distortion of information. A British psychologist, Bartlett, has studied these qualitative changes in great detail. In a verbal narrative, he finds that details are lost and the story loses much of its richness to become a threadbare structure. Certain phrases and words become stereotyped and appear in each repetition.

Similar changes occur in memory for perceptual objects. If subjects are shown some visual forms, and later are asked to reproduce them successively, as in the game of Gossip, retention suffers from a loss of detail. There is a tendency, moreover, for the forms to become more general, more symmetrical, and more similar to familiar objects in successive reproductions. You can see examples of some of these changes in Figure 5.12.

FORGETTING

If you were to ask a reasonably intelligent and well-informed person what caused forgetting, you might get the offhand reply, "Oh, just the passage of time, I guess." If pressed a little harder he might say, "Well, as time passes, the impressions of what we learn just get weaker and finally fade away."

If there is any truth at all in this notion, it cannot be the whole truth. Countless experiments have now demonstrated that it is not just the passage of time that determines how much we forget, but *it is what happens during that time*. What we do in between the time that we learn something

and the time that we attempt to remember it influences how we will remember it. This can be demonstrated in experiments to be described in the following paragraphs.

Retention after sleeping and waking. Perhaps the most striking demonstration comes from a famous experiment[24] in which the ability to remember after a period of sleep was compared with the ability to remember after an equal period of waking. Two subjects were tested for retention of nonsense syllables after various periods of sleep and again after various periods of normal, wakeful activity. The results of this study are depicted in Figure 5.13. Sleep, as you can see, was followed by much higher retention than was wakeful activity. This experiment has been repeated several times, and the results are always about the same.[25] Activity produces much more forgetting than does sleep. Furthermore, after the second hour of sleep, retention hardly declines at all.

Retroactive inhibition. The next question is, What is it about being awake that causes more forgetting than does being asleep? We have many experiments that concern this question. They have been called experiments in *retroactive inhibition* because they show that our activity after we learn something somehow works backward to inhibit memories of what we have learned. Strictly speaking, the experiment on sleep versus waking that we just mentioned is one in retroactive inhibition because it showed that waking activity interfered with retention of something that was learned before the activity.

To understand the notion of retroactive inhibition, it helps to realize that it is just a special case of negative transfer, which we described a few pages back. Actually, retroactive inhibition is the reverse of negative transfer. *It is the harmful effect of learning or activity on the retention of* learning that has gone before. In both negative transfer and retroactive inhibition, practice or experience interferes with the learning or retention of something else. Only the direction is different.

The factors that explain negative transfer are also in large part those that explain retroactive inhibition. The important condition for negative transfer, you will recall, is that a different response to the same stimulus is required in two different situations. This same condition is important for retroactive inhibition. We may illustrate the point by citing an experiment with paired-associate learning.

Paired-associate learning is the name for learning in which a subject must learn to call one word when he is presented with some other word. Suppose, for example, that we ask some subjects to associate the names of states with colors. We may regard the state names as *stimuli* and the color names as *responses*, because the subject must respond with a color ("red," for example) when he is presented with a state name ("Delaware," for example). In such an experiment, we mix up the pairs of color names and state names, so that the subject will not learn that one pair follows another.

Now after the subject has learned this task to a certain criterion of success, our next step in a retroactive-inhibition experiment is to give him a second task in which he must associate the *same* state names with some *new* colors—"Delaware" may now, for example, be associated with "orange." The subject practices the new list of such pairs until he has learned them.

The last part of the experiment, finally, is to have the subject go back to the first list and give the color names he first learned to associate with the state-name stimuli. It should be obvious that the typical subject will find this difficult and that it will take

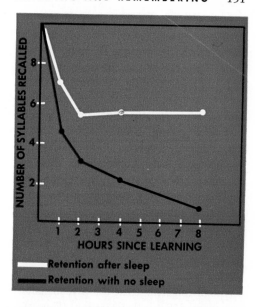

Fig. 5.13. Effect of activity on memory. (*Data from Jenkins, J. G., and Dallenbach, K. M. Oblivescence during sleep and waking. Amer. J. Psychol., 1924, 35, 605–612.*)

a good deal of practice, with many errors, before he relearns perfectly the first list again. In other words, he will display a great deal of retroactive inhibition on his original learning because of the second learning task.

The nature of forgetting. In everyday life, of course, we cannot identify the stimuli and the responses that are involved in retroactive inhibition as we can in the experiment we have just described. In many experiments of this sort, however, psychologists have assured themselves that the principal factor in forgetting is retroactive inhibition. That is to say, forgetting occurs because the stimuli involved in various learning tasks and in various aspects of waking activity are similar and yet different responses must be made to these stimuli in different situations. *We forget because what we do inhibits retroactively what we have learned.*

It is still possible that part of our forgetting is merely a weakening of "memory traces" with the passage of time. Perhaps some of the changes in the brain that must take place in learning are somewhat temporary and simply weaken or fade with time. Certainly there is yet no clear proof that such fading cannot happen. It cannot, however, explain all the facts that psychologists have collected in their experiments. The best and most complete explanation of forgetting is in terms of retroactive inhibition.

Repression and forgetting. Even retroactive inhibition and weakening of memory traces, however, do not account for all forgetting. Quite frequently we see in people a type of forgetting that the psychoanalysts (see page 259) call *repression*. They discovered in their work that people with emotional conflicts tend to *repress* thoughts and memories that are particularly unpleasant or threatening, thereby avoiding, at least consciously, the conflicts that bother them. We shall have more to say about repression in Chapter 10, but we explain it briefly here.

There are many trivial examples of behavior in daily life that are easily interpreted as repression. I frequently forget, for example, that my wife has told me to get liver at the grocery store, because I do not like liver. We have probably all noticed that people tend to forget the names of people they do not like. As we shall see in Chapter 10, however, the more important examples of repression are to be found in people who have powerful motives or strong anxieties that have not been relieved. For example, an individual may forget his early childhood experiences with sex because he has an intense anxiety about them.

As one might expect, it is difficult to produce repression in laboratory experiments because it is difficult—and undesirable—to create anxieties in people that are strong enough to cause repression. Some experimenters, however, have discovered that people tend to forget unpleasant things more rapidly than they do pleasant memories.[26] It is also clear that we tend to remember better what we like and what fits in with our prejudices than we do other events.[27] One investigator, moreover, was able to get people to remember material they had learned and forgotten by removing a source of anxiety connected with the memory.[28] These various findings fit in with the psychoanalytic conception of repression.

Summary

1. Many of the principles of learning can be demonstrated in three basic examples of learning: (*a*) classical conditioning, (*b*) instrumental learning, and (*c*) perceptual learning.

2. In classical conditioning, a neutral stimulus (e.g., a bell) is paired with an unconditioned stimulus (e.g., food) that evokes an unconditioned response (e.g., salivation). After repeated pairings of the two stimuli, the response of salivation becomes conditioned to the bell.

3. Stimulus generalization is one of the phenomena occurring in classical conditioning. That is, a response conditioned to one stimulus may be evoked by all similar stimuli.

4. In instrumental learning, responses that are at first made accidentally are learned as instrumental acts that achieve the satisfaction of some need.

5. In classical conditioning, the term *reinforcement* refers to the presentation of the unconditioned stimulus immediately following the conditioned stimulus (e.g., bell). In instrumental learning, reinforcement refers to the reward or punishment which follows the instrumental act.

6. Extinction is an experimental arrangement in which the conditioning stimulus or instrumental response is no longer reinforced. When, as a result, the unconditioned or instrumental response no longer occurs, the response is said to be extinguished.

7. Any stimulus or situation consistently associated with primary reinforcement acquires the power to reinforce responses. Through this process, called *secondary reinforcement*, secondary goals are acquired.

8. If conditioned or instrumental responses are reinforced only part of the time, the procedure is called *partial reinforcement*. Responses acquired during partial reinforcement are later much more difficult to extinguish than those acquired with regular reinforcement.

9. Punishment, in general, only temporarily eliminates learned responses; it does not reduce the total reserve of responses, as extinction does. There are serious disadvantages to the use of punishment, although there are conditions under which it may be effective.

10. In perceptual learning, the important factor is the stimulus or stimulus situation, rather than the response made to it. Through differential reinforcement of stimuli, the organism learns to respond to one stimulus and not to another. This is called *discriminative learning*.

11. Some learning seems to be incidental. Landmarks, cues, and relationships of objects are learned without any reinforcement. At a later time, when the organism is motivated and rewarded for its performance, this incidental learning may become evident.

12. The solution of problems may also be learned by reasoning and insight, rather than by conditioning or instrumental learning.

13. The learning of a skill may be charted as a curve of decreasing errors or increasing accuracy. Often there are plateaus in such a curve. They usually represent a shift in the kind of learning or a change in motivation.

14. Of the many factors that affect rate of learning, three of the most important are (*a*) whether practice is distributed over a period of time with frequent rests or massed in one period of "cramming," (*b*) whether time is spent in recitation *and* reading or merely reading alone, and (*c*) whether the material to be learned is meaningful or relatively nonsensical.

15. *Transfer of training* refers to the effect of learning one task on the subsequent learning of another. Transfer may be either positive or negative. When both the stimuli and the responses involved in the two tasks are

similar, transfer is positive. When the responses required are competing or opposite to one another, transfer is negative.

16. There are three common methods of measuring retention: recall, recognition, and savings. Of these, recall is the least sensitive and savings (in relearning of the same material) the most sensitive.

17. Forgetting tends to be selective. We remember some things, forget others; details are dropped, and a distortion of the original learning remains.

18. The most important factor in forgetting is retroactive inhibition—a negative transfer or interference—from what we subsequently learn. For this reason, retention is best when a person sleeps or does not attempt to learn anything new immediately after learning a particular task.

SUGGESTIONS FOR FURTHER READING

Deese, J. *The psychology of learning.* New York: McGraw-Hill, 1952.
>   *An introductory textbook on the psychology of learning.*
Hilgard, E. R. *Theories of learning.* New York: Appleton-Century-Crofts, 1948.
>   *A balanced treatment of the major theories of learning and a discussion of experiments related to these theories.*
Hilgard, E. R., & Marquis, D. M. *Conditioning and learning.* New York: Appleton-Century-Crofts, 1940.
>   *A text emphasizing animal experiments in classical conditioning and instrumental learning.*
Hull, C. L. *Principles of behavior.* New York: Appleton-Century-Crofts, 1943.
>   *A rigorous and technical exposition of one of the major theories of learning, which emphasizes the principle of reinforcement.*
Keller, F. S., & Schoenfeld, W. N. *Principles of psychology.* New York: Appleton-Century-Crofts, 1950.
>   *A general introduction to psychology that interprets human behavior in terms of the principles of instrumental learning.*
Kingsley, H. R. *Nature and conditions of learning.* New York: Prentice-Hall, 1944.
>   *A textbook covering the general field of learning.*
McGeoch, J. A., & Irion, A. L. *Psychology of human learning* (Rev. Ed.). New York: Longmans, 1952.
>   *A comprehensive text and reference work on human learning.*
Stephens, J. M. *Educational psychology.* New York: Holt, 1951.
>   *An application of the principles of learning to problems in education.*
Woodworth, R. S., & Schlosberg, H. *Experimental psychology* (Rev. Ed.). New York: Holt, 1954.
>   *A comprehensive text in experimental psychology containing chapters on learning, remembering, and forgetting.*

Chapter 6 IMAGINATION AND THINKING

A WELL-KNOWN SIGN in certain business offices commands us to THINK. What does this mean? What does it tell us to *do?* How differently might we behave if, instead, the sign said FEAR, or ACT, or BELIEVE, or OBEY? Do we really know how thinking differs from other experiences and reactions? An even harder question is, Can we tell when another person is thinking? What is thought? How does it start? When does it stop?

The study of thinking. These questions cannot yet be answered as definitely as all of us would like, because thinking is a process that takes place within a person and is therefore difficult to bring under scientific observation. For 80 years, valiant efforts have been made to experiment with thinking. Some of the experiments have

been informative; others have failed to give us the information we sought; and many are subject to conflicting interpretations. Hence, psychologists are not yet in a position to present the clear picture of thinking that the student might expect. All that we can do in a chapter on thinking is to indicate the progress we have made to date, frankly admitting that there are important gaps in our knowledge.

To give the student a perspective on the problem of thinking, we shall begin by introducing some of the concepts and methods that will be encountered in its study.

▪ *Methods of study.* Thinking, as we have said, is an internal process, not directly available for observation. To study thinking, we must therefore use indirect methods from which we may *infer* the events taking place during thinking. One of these methods has been to ask people to report or

---

This chapter was drafted by Stanley B. Williams of the College of William and Mary.

introspect (see page 9) on the events in thinking of which they are aware. As we shall see below, an individual is not conscious of many of the steps in his own thinking. For that reason the method of introspection has proved to be quite limited. Another method is to use *physiological measures*. By putting electrodes on muscles or on the brain, it has been possible to record some of the activity in thinking, but such methods, like the method of introspection, miss much that transpires in thinking. Our final resort, then, is to use methods in which *subjects are presented with problems that can be solved only by thinking*. These are the methods that have been used most extensively in recent years. By restricting problems to a few, known elements, it is often possible to infer the steps required in solving them. There will be numerous examples of such problems in this chapter.

▪ *The nature of thinking.* If we attempt to make a logical analysis of thinking, probably the first premise that can be accepted is that *thinking consists of representative processes*. By representative processes, we mean processes that represent previous learning and experience. If, for example, you are given a jigsaw puzzle to solve, you will attempt, no doubt, to piece it together partly by trial and error but also partly by thinking. The steps in your thinking will *represent* what you might otherwise do by trial and error. You will *think* of the fragments of the picture spread around you, and *think* of putting the pieces together in a certain way to see whether they fit. Thus you are doing by thinking what you might do by actually putting the pieces in place. Your thinking *represents*, *stands for*, or *takes the place of* observable behavior. This is what we mean when we say that thinking consists of representative processes.

The term representative process is cumbersome, and we frequently prefer to use another term, *symbolic process*, to mean the same thing. The term *symbol*, according to Webster, is "that which suggests something else by reason of relationship, association, convention, etc." This definition covers the representative process in thinking. We therefore regard thinking as a *sequence of symbolic processes*. This terminology enables us to frame the problem of thinking in more specific terms. We may ask, What are the symbols in thinking? How are these symbols assembled in sequences?

The term *symbol* has another more common meaning to refer to things that are observable. The word "house" is a symbol, for it represents the object house. The red light at the intersection is a symbol, for it stands for the instruction "stop." Our world is replete with such *external symbols*. They are not, however, to be confused with the *internal symbols* in thinking. In classical conditioning, the bell becomes an *external symbol* for food, but this in no way implies that the dog uses internal symbols —thinking processes—in responding to the bell. On the other hand, since the symbolic processes of thinking represent the external world and we have learned to respond to many external symbols, thinking is often doubly symbolic. It may consist of internal symbols that represent external symbols. Since language is a system of symbols and thinking often involves language, this is probably the best example of the doubly symbolic character of thinking.

To say that thinking consists of symbolic processes is not to say that we always know what these processes are. On the contrary, our most basic problem in thinking is to identify these symbolic processes. Logically, there are three possibilities: *images, implicit muscle responses*, and other *cen-*

tral processes. An image is some process in the brain that represents past sensory experience. Most people have occasional images and consequently have little difficulty in understanding what is meant by an image. Implicit muscle responses, however, are less familiar. *Implicit*, in this case, means *so small that they cannot be seen by the naked eye.* Implicit muscle responses can be symbolic processes because they can be miniatures of the movements made in explicit, observable trial-and-error behavior. In the muscles are sensory endings (see Chapter 19) that can carry back to the brain impulses that signal contraction of the muscles. Small contractions can, therefore, be symbolic of movements that a person has previously learned. In a paragraph below we shall indicate what is meant by the third possible kind of symbolic process, the central process.

In the history of efforts to study thinking, attention has been focused on first one, then another, of these possibilities. In the early work, when the introspective method was in its heyday (page 9), images were regarded as the main component of thinking. In the first main section of this chapter, we shall consider some of the experiments on the role of images in thinking. From these experiments we learned that images are only a part, and probably a minor part, of thinking. Attention then turned to the study of implicit muscle responses in the hope that they might prove to have an important role in thinking. Our second section below deals with this possibility. The results again gave us only a partial answer; implicit responses only play a part, and probably not a major one, in thinking processes.

Since neither images nor implicit responses seemed to account for thinking, we were left with the third alternative of "other central processes." This is not an unreasonable alternative, even if it does not make the nature of thinking any easier to discern. It simply means that in the brain are processes that are symbolic of learning and past experience yet are not made evident either in images or muscle movements. Physiological methods are not yet available for studying these processes, though cases of injury to the brain do tell us something about them (see Chapter 21), so there is little that we can say about their physiological basis at the present time. However, from indirect methods described in later sections of this chapter, we have been able to come to some conclusions about them.

■ *Learning and thinking.* In embarking on the study of thinking, it should be kept in mind that there is no sharp line between learning and thinking. Animals below man, as we shall see, are capable of thinking, though they do not do so much of it as people do. When a learning problem is presented to either an animal or a person, we are usually unable to prevent the use of thinking in solving the problem. Consequently, many of the learning tasks we described in the last chapter undoubtedly involve thinking. Moreover, most tasks that are designed to require thinking also permit opportunities for instrumental and perceptual learning. And finally, as we pointed out in the last chapter, the result of solving a problem by thinking is to learn something. We therefore have no way of rigorously separating the processes of learning from those of thinking. Our division of the subjects into two chapters is largely one of convenience, not one of rigid classification.

■ THE ROLE OF IMAGES

An image is a purely private affair. We cannot see or study directly the image that another person has. Consequently we can-

Fig. 6.1. A picture test of eidetic imagery. School children were allowed to look at this picture for **35** seconds. After that, they were asked to recall what was in the picture. Those with the best eidetic imagery could recall practically every detail. Some, even though they were unfamiliar with German, could spell the German word backwards. (*Courtesy Dr. G. W. Allport.*)

not define an image in the way that observable things can be defined. Most people, however, report that they have images, so we believe they exist. In some individuals, visual images apparently predominate, while other people report an almost total lack of visual imagery. Auditory imagery occurs frequently, but images of muscular sensations, of pain, hunger, and other organic sensations are relatively rare. Even odors and tastes can be imagined by some individuals.

Granting that images do exist, the logical question is, What is the function of images in the thinking processes? Do they really promote thinking or do they hinder it? One view is that images are *nonfunctional*. The image is like the smoke from a locomotive—a product of the action of the engine but in no way contributing to its

operation. Another view is that images form a crucial *link in the thought processes*, especially during the initial stages of new learning and problem solving. Thus they may act as a guide or controller of our learning efforts, or, in a more modest role, as reporter of current muscular events. A possible third role of the image is as a *reminder of previous experience*. Hence, in problem solving, we may combine a recollective image with a present sensation in order to form a new idea or hypothesis for the solution of a problem.

▪ *Study of images.* Attempts have been made, especially over the last half century, to conduct rigorous experiments on the role of images in thinking. The simplest kind of experiment is to ask a person to report on his experiences.[1] One can instruct him, for example, to recall his breakfast table, and ask "What kind of images do you have?" Most people will give a fairly detailed description, proving that they have images. This kind of experiment, however, only tells us what images and how many relatively a person may have, but it tells us little about the function of images in thinking.

Another kind of experiment is to require a person to solve some sort of manipulative problem, such as tracing his way blindfolded through a maze with his finger or a pencil.[2] After he has done this, he is quizzed about his imagery. Many people in this experiment report truly functional visual imagery; they solve the maze only by building up a "mental map" of it as they go along. Consequently they can draw the maze afterward, sometimes including the blind alleys as well as the true path. Other persons solve the maze by a purely verbal method; they count or name correct turns but do not "see" the maze as a whole in their mind's eye. In either case, use of images seems to promote learning, and the data suggest that images may function effectively in thinking, at least when necessary.

Imageless thought. There are still two other kinds of experiments on the role of images in thinking. One of these has been called the "thought experiment" and was first carried out about 1900. At that time, a group of psychologists at Würzburg, Germany, who were much interested in understanding thought and consciousness, did the experiment many times.[3] They gave their subject some rather simple intellectual problems, such as, "name a fruit," then asked him to describe what images he might have had in arriving at the answer.

The Würzburg psychologists were surprised to discover that very few images are uncovered in this way. Moreover, images do not seem to be necessary to solve this kind of problem. If the problem, say, were to "name a fruit," the subject often could say "apple" immediately but yet be unable to detect any image of a fruit or apple. Apparently the thinking involved in making the appropriate response does not necessarily involve any images. Hence the possibility of *imageless thought* was conceived, a notion that was quite controversial 50 years ago.

Two products of the imageless-thought hypothesis have proved to be of importance. One is the discovery that many of the important events in thinking may not be conscious. We cannot catch and inspect an idea or a thought as we can a bird or a butterfly. This suggests that an idea is more like a process than an object. The other product is that thought often seems to be governed by a *set* that is formed before it occurs. *A set is a readiness to think or respond in a predetermined way.* Given a stimulus word in the experiment we just mentioned, a thought seems to run off automatically, just as if one has already done his thinking before he starts! And

what the thought is, depends on the *set*. You see, for example:

$$\frac{\begin{array}{r}6\\4\end{array}}{}$$

You can give a quick answer, but whether it is 2, 10 or 24 depends on whether you are *set* to subtract, add, or multiply. Of course, with the appropriate instructions, we could have created any one of these sets. *Set*, as a theoretical concept, has become a most important term in the psychologists' vocabulary. We do not see set, yet we must assume it exists in order to explain thinking.

Fig. 6.2. Changes in memory for forms. The forms numbered 1, 2, 3, 4, 5, were presented to subjects and some time afterward they were asked to reproduce the forms they had been shown. The forms numbered in parentheses are some of the reproductions. Note the distortions that have occurred in the original forms. (*From Gibson, J. J. The reproduction of visually perceived forms. J. exper. Psychol., 1929, 12, 1–39.*)

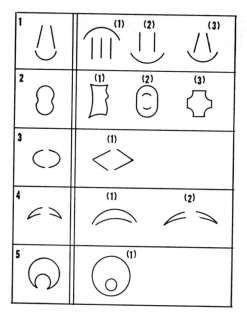

Having gotten this far but no farther, the early experimental psychologists faced a predicament. Their conception of psychology was that it is the science of *conscious experience* (see page 9), yet they established the fact that thinking could take place with no conscious content. The "higher mental processes" had eluded their search. To be sure, images did sometimes accompany thoughts, but the important thing was that images were not essential to thought. The introspective method (see page 9) had come to a blank wall, for one could not very well introspect if there were nothing to introspect about.

Eidetic imagery. There is still another kind of experiment that has been carried out on the role of images in thinking. In such an experiment, a particular stimulus is presented to a subject for a definite period of time and he is asked later to recall it. People vary in their accuracy of recall. A few have nearly perfect recall of visual stimuli; their images we call *eidetic*.

Eidetic imagery is rare, but it is relatively more common among children than adults. For a test example, look at the picture in Figure 6.1 for 35 seconds. Now, without looking at the picture, can you spell the German word in it? Can you spell it backward? In one experiment,[4] 3 out of 30 English school children, unfamiliar with German, could spell it forward and backward; 7 spelled it with only two mistakes. They, and other "eidetikers" often hesitate a moment before recall. During this time they seem to "project" their image on a mental screen, and inspect and read it as if it were an objective stimulus. Some subjects have recalled a page of print so accurately that they could read off any word or line on demand, shifting to different parts of the page as the experimenter requested. This is a rare ability, and ap-

Fig. 6.3. What people dream about. In a study of over 10,000 dreams,[23] the actions performed by the dreamer were classified into categories. Five categories represented in the drawing are: movement (34%), verbal (11%), sedentary (7%), visual (7%), and antagonistic (3%). Other

parently some people have it without knowing it. Edison is said to have had this ability.

Errors of recollection. Most people make errors when faced with a task of recalling the details of a complex picture. The errors themselves are interesting, for they shed light on other psychological processes. Frequently the image is lost with time; frequently it is distorted. Data from one illustrative experiment are abstracted in Figure 6.2. There you see some visual forms that were presented to a group of subjects for a short time and also the different ways in which they later reproduced these forms. Many of the "recollections" bear little resemblance to the original event.

At other places in this book we have discussed the many factors that influence and distort memory (see Chapters 5, 10, 13, and 14). Two of the most important factors are (1) distortions in our original perception of the event, and (2) wishes or other motives that alter our recall of it. Our main point here, however, is simply that *recollections are commonly in error. To the extent that distorted recollections are used in thinking, our thinking will be in error.*

Bizarre images. Many recollective images may be revived and distorted so much from our original experiences that they are truly bizarre. Consider dreams. Sometimes they are accurate recollections of the past; more often not. Commonly they are odd combinations of different recollections. Most of us, for example, have seen lions in cages and have at other times been locked in a room. Nowhere but in a dream, however, does a person ordinarily get locked in a cage with a lion.

Dreams are a kind of thinking, a very bizarre and disconnected kind. So long as we do this kind of thinking when we are

categories of appreciable size in the classification were social (6%), recreational (5%), manual (4%), endeavor (4%), and obtaining something (3%). (*Courtesy of David Stone Martin and Scientific American.*)

asleep, no great harm is done. Even day-dreaming is harmless play, so long as we do not confuse it with reality. Sometimes, though, the barrier between the real world and imagination breaks down, and a person confuses his fantasies with real events. An image regarded as real is a *hallucination*, and repeated hallucinating is a diagnostic symptom of many mental diseases (see Chapter 10).

Function of images. Now, what do these studies show, as far as functional imagery is concerned? They show (1) that images do occur in many people, perhaps in all; (2) that images can help some people solve some problems; (3) that some thought problems get solved without benefit of imagery. Hence it is simply not true, as some evidently very visual-minded writers have claimed, that images are required for thinking. On the other hand, images can be useful, at least to some people.

Does this rule out the view that images are nonfunctional? No, not entirely. Even for people who "think with images," much imagery is apparently useless. Many people report rich imagery completely unconnected with the problem at hand. In the midst of a tense debate, the debater's fantasy may be filled with visions of home, of forest flowers, or of a grade B movie. Our perpetual stream of consciousness overflows with a varied assortment of the trivial and the important, very little of it relatable to the moment.

■ **MUSCLE MOVEMENTS**

We have just seen that images are processes that sometimes take part in thinking but that thinking does not necessarily involve images, nor can thinking be merely a succession of images. We must therefore look for something else to add to the picture if we are to understand the thinking process. When this conclusion had been reached by the early experimental psychologists, it occurred to some of them that the "something else" might be muscle movements. Perhaps, they suggested, *implicit muscle responses*, not seen by the naked eye but sufficient in size to send back impulses to the nervous system, could be essential elements in the flow of thinking processes. This hypothesis was put forth nearly fifty years ago by John B. Watson as the explanation of thought.[5]

Two steps are necessary to test the hypothesis. One is to confirm or deny the existence of implicit responses during thinking. We shall describe two experiments that concern this point. The second step is to demonstrate that implicit responses serve as symbols or cues in the flow of thinking. This is difficult to prove, but it is a more reasonable possibility, as we shall explain below, than it might appear to be on the surface.

Implicit responses. The idea that implicit responses take part in thinking is made plausible by the relationship between thinking and learning (see above). Thinking begins in learning, and a good deal of learning, as we have seen earlier, is acquired by doing. One could suppose that learned responses become smaller and smaller as they are practiced and that thinking consists of these reduced movements, differentiated out of the larger movements of original learning. Several experiments have been carried out to test this supposition. We shall describe two.

One such experiment used persons who already had been taught how to relax their muscles and who were now lying relaxed in a darkened room.[6] On a signal, the subject thought of *bending his right arm*. By means of electrodes attached to the arm and connected to a galvanometer, electrical signs of implicit muscular activity were seen to increase at this time. Control tests showed that the action currents varied consistently with the particular instructions. They died out when the subject was told to relax; they did not occur whenever he was instructed to think of *bending his left arm* or foot or to think of *extending the right arm*. Furthermore, a subject could not simultaneously relax his arm and think of bending it. Similar records were obtained while subjects thought of other activities, such as throwing a ball, turning an ice-cream freezer, and climbing a rope. But, we may say, perhaps the action currents came only from the nerves and not the muscles. Control experiments were run. In these experiments lightweight levers were placed directly on the muscles; when the levers moved, their action was optically magnified eightyfold. The levers told the same story as the electrodes: the muscles actually were shortening.

A similar experiment employed 19 deaf-mutes who "talked" with their hands.[7] Electrodes were placed on their hands during sleep, and the records were especially watched for possible dream activity. Action currents decreased as the subjects went to sleep and stayed at a low level except for occasional bursts of activity. Were these bursts dreams? To find out, the experimenter tried awakening the subjects during bursts and asking them if they had just been dreaming. In 30 out of 33 instances, the 19 subjects answered yes. As a control test, they were awakened 62 times during periods of electrical quiet. In 53 instances there were no dreams, but in 9 there were. In the waking state, 84 per cent of the deaf subjects and 31 per cent of normal hearing subjects showed action currents in the hand while solving problems in arithmetic.

Results such as these convince us that implicit movements do occur in thinking. They help answer the question, which we

raised earlier, of what goes on in imageless thought.

Cue-producing responses. What purpose do such implicit responses serve? Are they just a coincidence or are they a functional part of the thinking process? Some implicit movements are undoubtedly coincidental; they simply represent an "overflow" or "leaking" of activities in the brain. Some of them, however, are probably links in the associative chains of thinking. When they are, their function seems to be one of stimulation, that is, of providing a cue for the next element or response in the chain.

Which way, for example, do you turn your key to unlock your front door at home? The chances are that, when you think out the answer to this question, you imagine yourself putting your key in the lock and turning it. From this you get the cue to answer "right" or "left." In thinking of the event, you probably make some implicit muscle responses so that receptors in the muscles can signal the presence of muscle tension. In this case, the stimulus or cue produced by the implicit response might, because of previous conditioning, give you the answer.

Cue production from implicit responses is undoubtedly especially important in linguistic thinking—the thinking that is done with words. Much of everyday human behavior is talking, reading, or writing and we solve many of our problems in terms of language. Thinking therefore consists in part of *subvocal* talking—talking that is inaudible to others, but sufficiently stimulating (muscularly) to one's self to permit an internal conversation. Words are among the best possible cue-producing responses because each word is usually distinctively different from all others. Except for homonyms, like "pair" and "pear," spoken words can provide many more discriminable cues than movements of arms, legs, fingers, and so on. It is no wonder then, that we have developed language to such a high degree in our thinking processes.

In addition to this argument, there are experiments that seem to indicate that implicit responses can be cue-producing. At least it is difficult to interpret them any other way. We have chosen to present them in the section below, however, because they are germane to the question raised there of symbolic processes in animals. Here let us conclude by saying that the idea of cue-producing responses seems plausible and is now accepted widely among psychologists. We feel justified, moreover, in believing that implicit responses are important in thinking. Some of the early behaviorists, however, overstated their case when they concluded that thinking is nothing but a sequence of implicit responses. The evidence now available does not support such an extreme position. Rather it indicates that both images and implicit responses play a role in thinking. It also leaves room for other central processes to be involved.

■ SYMBOLS AND CONCEPTS

In the introduction to this chapter, we defined thinking as a sequence of symbolic processes. We have been able to identify both images and implicit responses as two specific kinds of symbolic processes. From now on, however, we shall not be concerned with the identification of symbolic processes. Instead we shall turn our attention to questions of when they exist, how they are learned, and when they are used.

Symbolic processes. We have already defined a *symbol* as "that which suggests something else by reason of relationship, association, convention, etc." We pointed out that symbols may be either external events or internal processes. An external symbol comes to be a symbol through con-

ditioning processes in the same way that Pavlov's dog came to react to the dinner bell as a symbol of food. Internal symbols, however, are the ones that interest us most here, because they are the ones that distinguish thinking from conditioning and learning. We have said that it is difficult to study these internal symbols and that we are forced to resort to indirect methods of determining when they exist. Now let us explain some of these methods.

■ *Delayed reaction.* In 1913, W. S. Hunter first used rats in a test for symbolic processes.[8] He called the test "delayed reaction," after his procedure (see Figure 6.4). Hunter's method was first to teach the animal to go to the lighted one of three doorways to get food. After a rat had learned the signal-light cue, Hunter then tested for the ability of the rat to delay its response until some time after the signal had been presented. He put the rat at the starting position but restrained it while he flashed the light briefly at one of the doorways. After a few seconds, the rat was released and permitted to choose the doorway at which to seek food. *The purpose of this delay was to force the rat to use symbolic processes to solve the problem.* Because the choice had to be made some time after the signal was given, there was nothing but a symbolic process available as a cue for the successful solution. Furthermore, the length of time an animal could delay and still solve the problem could be used as a general measure of the effectiveness of such a symbolic process. Rats, Hunter found, could delay for only 1 to 10 seconds. Cats could successfully delay up to 16 to 18 seconds; dogs, 1 to 3 minutes; a two-and-a-half-year-old child, 50 seconds; and a five-year-old child, at least 20 minutes.

These figures have been revised and extended somewhat by later experiments, but the essential point is methodological. By such a test we can prove that an animal can respond to symbolic processes. The test must meet the following criteria: (1) there must be some stimulus which is known to produce a characteristic, differential response; (2) the stimulus must be presented, then withdrawn during the delay interval; and (3) there must be no other stimulus outside the body to indicate the correct response.

In some of Hunter's animals, the symbolic process could be readily identified as a *posture* that oriented the head or body toward the proper box during the delay period. This was not a subtle or high-order symbolism, but it was an effective, cue-producing response. Was it necessary? Tests by other experimenters showed that raccoons, dogs, monkeys, and children could delay successfully *even when their posture was radically disturbed during the delay*. Later tests on rats showed that they too could delay longer, possibly up to 4 minutes, when the stimuli were made more intense or the job of responding a little easier.[9] So these animals, under the proper conditions, can use internal symbolic processes other than postural cues.

▪ *Alternation.* Two other tests having essentially the same purpose as the delayed reaction are tests of *delayed alternation* and of *double alternation*. In simple alternation an animal is required to run a maze by turning first right, then left, then right, then left, etc. In double alternation, the required pattern of turns is RRLL, RRLL, RRLL, etc. Or it may be pushing a lever, picking up inverted cups or some other act in the same RL or RRLL sequence. The important difference between these tests and the delayed-reaction test is that the original stimulus, in addition to the symbol or substitute for it, must be inside, instead of outside, the body. That is to say, in an alternation problem, there is no flash of light to

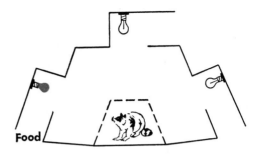

Fig. 6.4. The delayed reaction box. An animal (in this case, a raccoon) is placed in a starting box made of wire mesh. One of three lights is turned on briefly; then after a delay, the wire starting box is lifted so that the animal may go searching for food. (Redrawn from Hunter, W. S. *The delayed reaction in animals and children. Behavior Monogr.,* 1913, **2,** 24.)

indicate the correct response after a delay. All cues for solving the problem must be furnished by the animal itself. Hence the tests are not quite so well controlled as the delayed-reaction tests, because they do not fully meet the first and second criteria above. Yet we can *suppose* that an internal cue for turning left is the result of just having turned right, and so on; and furthermore we can *suppose* that this cue functions the same way as does the light or other external cue in the delayed-reaction test.

If we grant these suppositions, the delayed alternation is a test of symbolic function. Rats have responded correctly in the test even though they were restrained for 15 seconds between each right and left turn; some rats have done this even though their bodies were disoriented or anesthetized during the delay interval.[9] How long monkeys and people can delay has never been measured exactly, but of course we know that people could, with language, delay almost indefinitely.

The double-alternation test is a little different because the second R and the second L response, if successful, must be made to a symbolic cue slightly different from that of the first R or L response. How can the animal "know" to make just two rights and two lefts, instead of several, unless he can count? Hunter and others have found this problem to be very difficult for rats, particularly if the test is in the temporal form and no spatial cues are supplied. The animal is required to run around the block to the right twice and then to the left twice so that *all choice points are identical* with respect to external stimuli.[10] With great difficulty a few rats have learned to do one RRLL sequence but have not been able to extend it. Extending the sequence is possible, though, if the rats, instead of running, simply move a lever with their paws twice to the right, twice to the left, etc. In a *spatial maze*, an animal makes its sequence of turns in order without "running around the block," but the parts of the maze are interchanged and the maze reoriented in the room so that all external cues are continuously disturbed and the animal cannot make use of them to solve the problem. In studies with such a spatial maze, a few rats learned one segment of triple alternation, RRRLLL and of quadruple alternation, RRRRLLLL; at least, they got so they could perform it part of the time, although they never really mastered it.

It is interesting that ability to solve double-alternation problems is correlated with position in the animal kingdom.[10] Raccoons can do double alternation and extend it part of a sequence (two turns), and monkeys can extend it several more turns. Using a special toy form, children above three years of age can do it, but so far no child below three has been successful. Errors are fewer with older children; five-year-olds solve it by counting—by using language—and can, of course, extend the sequences indefinitely.

These are just a few of many experiments with the symbolic aspect of thinking. They demonstrate, first of all, the ways in which it is possible to test and measure symbolic abilities. They tell us also that symbolic abilities, and hence thinking, exist in animals below man. This puts aside the old cliché that man is distinguished from animals by his ability to think. He certainly can and does do a lot more thinking, but animals must be given credit for a little. In the next section we shall have further evidence on this point.

Formation of concepts. Now we shall consider the relation of concepts to the processes of thinking. To do this, however, we must first consider the nature of concepts, for these have so far been introduced only briefly in Chapter 5.

Symbols and concepts are closely related in the way we think, because we use symbols (principally words) to label our concepts. We all know, at least vaguely, what a concept is: it is the response we make, usually in the form of a word, to a *common property of objects or events*. We have a concept of "red" because we can think about red more or less apart from the object it may go with; "red" is the response we make to all objects that reflect light in the "red" part of the visual spectrum. Similarly, we have concepts of "speed," "triangles," "houses," "colleges," and so on, in countless numbers, because we, in each case, have learned to respond to some property that many objects have in common (see Figure 6.5).

There is no limit, theoretically, to the number of classes or concepts we might form. We might, for example, have several thousand color concepts. In practice, however, we use only a small number of the concepts that are possible. A child usually is taught names for red, green, yellow, and blue but seldom is he taught crimson,

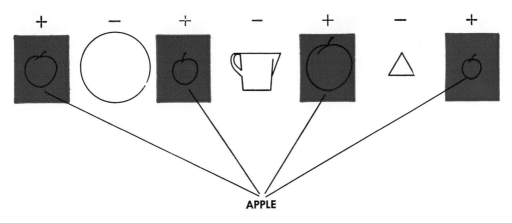

Fig. 6.5. Concept formation. A child hears the word "apple" when he sees some objects, but not others. And he is rewarded if he says "apple" when he sees some objects, but not others. In this way, he generalizes the concept of apple and distinguishes it from other concepts. (Re-drawn from Johnson, D. M. *Essentials of psychology.* New York: McGraw-Hill, 1948, p. 178.)

magenta, scarlet, or shocking pink. "Red" to the child whose experience is limited to one red wagon may be just a name for the wagon object, but later on "red" is the name for a class of colors with similar properties. The end points of the class may not always be certain: he may wonder whether to call an orange-red "red," "yellow," or "orange"; or he may hesitate on purple. Yet the middle points are instantly labeled "red," and the class is named for its most frequent elements.

• *Abstraction.* Before he gets to this stage, however, the child will have had to learn that a red wagon has two names (at least!): red and wagon. Its name is "red" whenever mother is trying to find out whether her infant is color-blind. Its name is "wagon" when it comes to trading it for sister's sled. Obviously the name symbolizes the use of the object and what is done with it. The kind and number of naming words that we know are determined by the frequency of our naming responses, and this in turn is limited both by our sensory capacities and our society's language customs. The fact

that we can learn names for differential responses to objects and that we can discriminate different properties of the same object makes it possible to *abstract*.

When the child abstracts he does a very simple yet subtle thing: he disregards the red-wagon association in responding to the object and responds with either the red-as-a-color relationship or with the wagon-as-a-plaything relationship. In the first case he is simply responding to, say, mother's question by selecting "red" instead of yellow or blue. In the second case he is responding to sister's sled by selecting "wagon" instead of ball or marbles. In either case he is responding to a single property of the object; when people do that they are *abstracting*.

Having learned to abstract, the child can now learn to group properties together. The name for a group of similar properties is a class name, or concept. Thus we say we have a concept of red, of toys, of vehicles, of good and bad. Concepts, like classes, can vary from simple to complex, from having a few members to having many. More importantly, there are classes of classes, and

Fig. 6.6. The abstraction of common elements in Chinese characters. (Selected from Hull, C. L. Quantitative aspects of the evolution of concepts. Psychol. Monogr., 1920, No. 123.)

classes of classes of classes. A concept can name any level of grouping. In the class "dwelling unit" are subclasses of houses, apartments, and caves. In the class "house" are subclasses of mansions and cottages. Cottages include white ones and red ones. Both houses and caves can be big or little, if grouped according to the property of size.

Learning concepts.   As we know, people can learn thousands of concepts and, with the aid of language, give them names. Even without words, animals and man can learn simple concepts. To understand how this comes about, we have to perform discrimination-learning experiments, for concept formation is simply a process of learning to discriminate properties of stimulus objects or, in the case of man, learning to discriminate properties of class names.

Again we can turn to experiments with animals for a simple illustration of the way in which concepts may be formed in discrimination learning. To teach rats the concept of "triangularity," one psychologist[11] began by presenting them with cards bearing triangles, circles, rectangles, etc. He rewarded them, however, when they jumped at the card bearing the triangle and punished them for jumping to other forms. Early in the training, of course, the rats jumped at all the forms. At this point the rats have a concept, perhaps, of "any card in front of me." This was not the concept the experimenter wanted them to learn, however; he had in mind the *abstract* con-

cept of triangularity. It took them many trials with varied stimuli to learn it, but eventually they did. Indeed, they learned to jump at all sorts of triangles and not to any other stimulus. Thus we can say that the rats learned a concept of "triangle," even though they tell us by a jump instead of a word.

▪ *Clues in concept formation.* Needless to say, human beings find triangularity easy to learn. In order to find material difficult enough to challenge college students, one psychologist[12] has used Chinese characters like those in Figure 6.6. The four characters in the top row have one particular part in common; so do the characters in the bottom row. These and other characters were presented to students in a jumbled order without telling them about the common parts. Their task, in fact, was to learn this, thus forming a concept of the common properties of the characters. Each character was presented to the students along with a name. The same name was given to all characters containing the common part. The instruction to the students was simply to learn the names of the characters. What happened was that the students gradually identified the clue and named it by a process similar to discrimination learning.

A number of studies have shown also that children and adults learn differential concepts more easily if the stimulus objects in one class are quite different from those in another class. "Animal" objects, for example, are not at all like mineral ones. Studies have also shown that, for children, *form concepts* are easier to learn than *color concepts*. In other experiments on college students,[13] class names for *concrete objects* were easiest to learn, followed by *spatial forms, colors,* and *numbers* in that order. We might conclude, then, that concrete things are easier to group and classify than are abstract symbols. Yet by using postage stamps and other numerically familiar objects we can make certain number concepts easier than other categories. Hence we can never evaluate concreteness alone; it is only one variable in concept formation and in any given instance might be less influential than stimulus similarity, availability, ease of the naming responses, etc. Still, concreteness may account for the fact that, for most children, arithmetic is harder than reading; for numbers tend to be abstract, that is, they name relations between objects rather than the objects themselves.

Of all the conditions that make for concept formation, the most important is a wide experience with different stimuli and different problems. As one experimenter, Harlow, who has had a great deal of experience in teaching concepts to monkeys and children, puts it, "The studies attest to the fact that broad concepts or principles do not generalize spontaneously from learning or over-learning any specific problem; breadth of concept is obtained from training in a wide variety of situations."[14]

THE SOLUTION OF PROBLEMS

Now we are beginning to get a clearer picture of the stuff of which thinking is made. Its raw material is symbolic processes, which include images and implicit responses. These are chained together in learning so that one becomes a cue that produces still another image or response. Taken together they constitute what the psychologist calls symbolic processes. Such processes represent not only "raw" sensory experiences, but also the words and other symbols that stand for these experiences. In the course of learning, we abstract certain elements that are in common in different situations. Thus we form concepts, and our symbolic processes also represent these concepts.

With this as background, we could say simply that thinking is a flow of symbolic processes. This statement may summarize what thinking is, but it does not tell us what starts it, what guides it, or what brings it to a stop. A river is more than water. It begins somewhere, it flows in first one direction and then another, sometimes swiftly and sometimes slowly, and eventually ends in the ocean. Thinking, too, has beginnings, courses, and ends. What explains them?

Motivation. For one thing, thinking is usually motivated. As Wertheimer,[15] one of the leading investigators in this area, has said, thinking involves "the desire, the craving to face the true issue . . . , to go from an unclear, inadequate relation to a clear, transparent, direct confrontation." Thus he stresses the *directedness* of thought processes. Instead of just "happening" by association, each stage in thinking is controlled by motives.

On the basis of all we now know, we ought to differentiate at least two kinds of motives in thinking: (1) a motive for the behavior immediately preceding the problem, which may be love, greed, curiosity, ambition, etc.; and (2) a motive induced by the problem itself to complete or anticipate the solution of the problem. The former gets thinking started; the latter carries it through to solution. In order to account for great thinkers, such as scientists, artists, writers, and inventors, we might have to postulate even a third kind of motivation: a lifelong interest in creative production or in solving challenging problems. Perhaps this is curiosity. However, there are few topics of which psychology is as ignorant as it is of this one. Apparently the productive thinker is made at least as much as he is born, but exactly how he acquires his special interests is not clear. Our best guess is that there are social influences during childhood which result in a strong ambition or need for achievement. In any case, we cannot attribute creative production to talent or brilliance alone. The difference between a productive and an unproductive scientist is seldom sheer ability; it appears to be due to something like curiosity, ambition, initiative, or pride. These "nonintellective" factors in intellectual performance have only recently come under scientific scrutiny.

Habit and set. Thinking is also guided, and often impeded, by habit and set. Practice in solving problems one way tends to "set" us to solve a new problem in the same way, provided the new problem situation contains stimuli similar to those in the practiced problems. This is the secret of many trick jokes and puzzles. In one trick, you spell words and ask a person how he pronounces them. You use names beginning with Mac, like MacDonald, MacTavish. Then you slip in "machinery" and see whether he pronounces it "MacHinery." With the set for names, he may fall into your trap.

TABLE 6.1.   Practice and test problems used by Luchins. The five practice problems require a roundabout method of solution, but the test problem can be solved easily. Most subjects, however, who acquired a set by solving practice problems first, used the long method of solving the test problem and were blind to the easy method.

Problem number	Given the following empty jars as measures			Obtain this amount of water
	A	B	C	
1. Practice	21	127	3	100
2. Practice	14	163	25	99
3. Practice	18	43	10	5
4. Practice	9	42	6	21
5. Practice	20	59	4	31
6. Test	23	49	3	20

Luchins, A. Mechanization in problem solving: the effect of Einstellung. *Psychol. Monogr.,* 1954, **54,** No. 6.

Set may be produced by immediately preceding experiences, by long-established practices, or by instructions which revive old habits (see "Transfer of Training," Chapter 5). It biases the thinker at the start of his problem and directs him away from certain families of response. It acts as an implied assumption. Like transfer of training, it can be either positive or negative in its effect. If it is helpful, we say, "How clever I am"; if a hindrance, we say, "How blind I was."

Luchins did a systematic experiment on habitual set,[16] using the problems in Table 6.1. In the sixth problem, for example, the subject is required to say how he would measure 20 quarts of water when he has only three jars, holding 23, 49, and 3 quarts, respectively. Subjects do it the easy way by filling the 3-quart jar from the 23-quart jar, provided they have no interfering set. However, if they have just solved the previous problems by a longer method —that is, by filling the middle jar, from it filling the jar to the right twice and the jar to the left once, leaving the required amount in the center jar—they usually use the long method and do not notice the short one. Amazingly enough, 75 per cent of a college group were blind to the easy method after having practiced the long one only five trials! The frequency of habitual, blind solutions is reduced by (1) warning the subject, "Don't be blind!" just before the critical sixth trial, (2) reducing the number of practice trials, and (3) separating the practice and critical trials by several days or weeks. Comparative data show that habit strength and set, as indicated by number of practice trials, can be much stronger factors than any warning against them.

Cooperative problem solving has this possible advantage: that two people may not possess the same hindering set. This is one value of "bull sessions."

Unconscious factors. An autobiographical account of an inventor or mathematician sometimes claims that he solved a problem while he was not even trying to think about it. After persistent labor fails, the thinker turns to other matters, only to have the solution unexpectedly appear. Poincaré[17] and other mathematicians have reported that such unconscious solutions came to them while walking down the street or engaged in some other routine activity but seldom while intensively engaged in another mathematical problem. There is very little of scientific value we can learn from these narratives, because they are rare and occur under uncontrolled conditions. Speculating on them, however, we can guess that a concentrated thinking effort may sometimes get one into a symbolic blind alley, in which case starting over again after a rest may get one into a new path. No doubt many other factors than these we have listed do enter into human thinking. Some of these may be due to "unconscious thinking" in the sense that much of our thought is imageless.

Solution by insight. Let us summarize again. Thinking begins with some kind of problem and a motive to solve that problem. It is guided by some set or determining tendency, and it is helped—or hindered—by previously learned habits. It may go on even when there is no conscious awareness of it. Now we may ask how the problem gets solved.

To this there are at least three answers: by trial and error, by rote, and by insight. In attempting to solve a puzzle you sometimes stumble on the right answer. By trying first one way, then another, you finally hit on one that works. This is very much like instrumental learning that we described in the last chapter—maze learning, for example—except that you use thought processes instead of wandering in the maze.

A second kind of solution may come by rote. If I give you a column of figures to add, you immediately start thinking according to rules you have learned, and in due time you come up with the answer. Or, if you are asked for directions from one place to another or to spell a word, you do a minimum of thinking and a lot of just plain remembering in order to give the answer. You merely reproduce what you have already learned. To understand this way of solving problems, about all one needs to know is how the solutions were learned in the first place.

A third kind of problem solution, however, presents some interesting wrinkles. This is solution by insight, which occurs neither by trial and error nor by rote. It may grow out of blind trial and error or out of rote thinking, but it represents a completely new experience to the thinker. "Aha! I have it," is a characteristic outburst when suddenly he grasps a baffling problem. He has produced a novel solution—novel for him, at least—through thinking. If indeed the solution is truly novel, he has invented or created something that he can pass on to other members of society for them to use in their rote-thinking processes. As we shall see, such insight has something to do with previous learning, but it has taken a good deal of research to tell us exactly how.

■ *The use of insight.* Some problems, of course, are much more easily solved by means of insight than are others. Soldiers, for example, find it hard to get insight into their serial numbers; nothing but simple memorizing will solve this problem. Multiplication tables, however, may be learned either by rote or by insight—learning them by rote may actually interfere with learning them by insight. Other problems, however, may be solved only by insight; or at least insight is much the easier way to solve them.

Fig. 6.7. Problem solving in monkeys. This is the crossed-string problem; food is attached to the chain ending in left foreground, and the animal must perceive which is the correct chain to pull. (*Courtesy Dr. H. F. Harlow.*)

The best experiments on insight probably are those in which the subject must use tools. In some classical experiments by Köhler, for example, a chimpanzee in a cage was given a hoe to procure a banana outside the cage beyond arm's length.[18] Most chimpanzees explored and manipulated the hoe in trial-and-error fashion, but occasionally a chimp would suddenly run toward the hoe, put it out on the *farther* side of the banana and pull it in. This behavior was especially impressive if the chimp, just prior to the successful act, had been on the opposite side of the cage and not even looking at the hoe. Evidently he must have been *thinking* hard. The changed facial expression during solution certainly suggested that the chimp had an "Aha!" experience.

■ *How insights develop.* Many experimenters have repeated Köhler's studies and extended them to children. In general, their results show that insightful manipulation of sticks and hoes does not occur unless the subject has had previous experience in using these instruments in problem solving. In one study,[19] four out of six chimpanzees failed the hoe problem even though the hoe was lying in perfect position to drag the fruit in. However, chimps who were allowed to play with sticks for several days prior to the experiment did very much better, although only one achieved success on the first trial. In an experiment with children,[20] it was found that no child under two and one-half years solved a typical insight problem, that the percentage of successes increased as the age and specific experiences of the children increased, and that insight or understanding often occurred *after* solution instead of with it or preceding it.

The conditions which favor the appearance of sudden solutions certainly deserve much more scientific study than they have received. We need, for example, much more information of the kind Harlow has collected in a truly gigantic series of experiments on discrimination learning in monkeys and children.[14] These researches are novel because, unlike the usual learning experiment which measures habit growth in terms of trials, Harlow measured *transfer from problem to problem*, or from experiment to experiment. Whereas the usual experiment stops after one problem, or at most two or three, Harlow's subjects continued to new ones, finally completing as many as 344 problems. Some of the later problems were similar to earlier ones, but some even required the subject to *reverse* his response to the same cues.

What did the subjects learn here? Only a specific problem? Or did they learn something that transferred to the next problem and then the next? The answer is given in Figure 6.8, which is based on reversal learning. The percentage of correct responses on the *second* trial of each problem is the dependent variable. The first trial, of course, acts as an "instruction" to the subject, telling him that the problem has been changed. What he learns on the first new trial is measured by his performance on the second trial. If he learned nothing, his second trial score would be chance—in this case, 50 per cent. If he learned much, his score would approach 100 per cent. Note that the monkeys initially did very little better than chance but gradually improved to very near perfection. The children start higher, but the trend is the same.

We may conclude that (1) the amount by which a subject can profit by a single experience can gradually increase from nothing to everything, and (2) interproblem improvement is a *transfer effect* from one problem to another. Harlow's name for this is *learning set*, which means *learning to learn*. Since this learning reached near perfection, that is, one-trial learning or complete transfer, it is clear that sudden, insightful solutions were regularly made at the end of the training. Harlow appropri-

ately concluded, "These data clearly show that animals can gradually learn insight."[14] The overwhelming evidence to date, then, is that sudden solutions—with or without the "Aha!" accompaniment—grow out of and are probably due to specific conditioning and learning. In short, in learning to learn, we learn to produce insights.

◼ LOGICAL REASONING

Our sketch of the thought processes is now nearly complete. We have seen what they are made of, that they are motivated and guided by habits and sets, and that they can arrive at solutions to problems in different ways. There is one feature of thinking, however, that we have not discussed. This is reasoning. Perhaps you are accustomed to using "reasoning" and "thinking" as though they were the same. We commonly do that in our unscientific, everyday talk. You can remember, however, many instances of thinking that seem quite lacking in reasoning.

What, then, is reasoning? A little boy was on the right track when he answered, "Putting two and two together." Reasoning certainly is not just any kind of think-

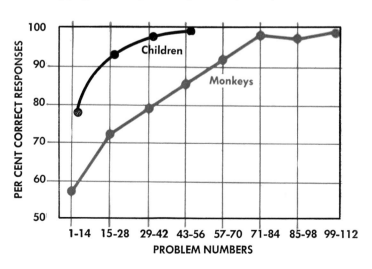

Fig. 6.8. Discrimination learning in monkeys and children. The experiment charted here is discussed in the text. (Adapted from Harlow, H. F. Thinking. In H. Helson, Theoretical foundations of psychology. New York: Van Nostrand, 1951, p. 469.)

ing. It is solving a problem by putting two or more elements of past experience together to make something new.

Simple reasoning. An experiment with rats illustrates a simple form of reasoning. In Figure 6.9, you see a schematic diagram of the experimental setting. The experiment began by allowing the rat to explore a room with a table (A) in it, climbing up to it and down by means of a pole. This is experience I. Next a new table (B) and poles were put into the room and a runway extended from it to a part of the old table which was now blocked off from the rest of the table. The rat learned to run up a pole to the new table and from there to the old table, for food. This is experience II.

What happened when the hungry animal was put at "start" on table A, prevented by the barrier from getting to the food? Typically it first ran back and forth for a while, then climbed down the pole to the floor, ran on the floor to a pole near table B, climbed up, and ran across the elevated path to get the food. In doing this, the animal had to combine two previous experiences, responses I and II, because it had never before run all the way from "start" to "food." Such combining—"putting two and two together"—was regarded as reasoning by the experimenter.

Not all psychologists are satisfied that these experiments demonstrate even rudimentary reasoning in rats, for the line between instrumental learning and simple reasoning is a thin one. Yet there can be no doubt that many animals can carry out this kind of thinking. Certainly man can. The experiment is merely a demonstration of the essential elements of such thinking in a very simple case.

Verbal reasoning. Most human reasoning makes use of symbols—especially verbal symbols. Because we use words so extensively to communicate our thoughts to others, we get in the habit of depending on words to think with. Yet word meanings often are vague or ambiguous, and we can be led astray by them. Also, when reasoning with verbal symbols alone, it may be impossible to test whether our conclusion is correct, for we often lack the opportunity to compare the verbal conclusion with actuality. To help us, society develops standards or norms for checking the results of our reasoning. People come to believe that certain statements are "reasonable" and some are not. Hence, when a person concludes with an "unreasonable" statement, people tell him so immediately and discourage him from making further foolish statements. The trouble with culturally defined standards of reasonableness is that what is reasonable to one group may be completely unreasonable to another. "It stands to reason that . . . ," a college debater argues; but as an American undergraduate, he completely forgets that the conclusion may not be obvious to, say, an Arabian or Chinese opponent.

To make as rigid as possible the standards for reasoning, philosophers and mathematicians, over the centuries, have given us rules for reasoning. These rules are called

Fig. 6.9. An apparatus for testing simple reasoning in rats. For a description of this apparatus and the results obtained with it, see text. (*After Maier, N. R. F. Reasoning in white rats. Comp. Psychol. Monogr., 1929, 6, No. 29.*)

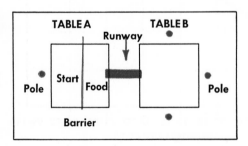

logic, and they prescribe what kinds of implications statements can have and what kinds of conclusions it is permissible to draw from them. Any reasoning that does not conform to these rules is dubbed "illogical" or "fallacious." Since so much in human affairs hangs on the question of how logical we are in our thinking, we should study some of the psychological factors involved in logical and illogical thinking.

Logical thinking. Suppose one conducts a test of reasoning in children and asks them this question: "If all six-year-olds are in school, and if Johnny is six, then where is Johnny?" The psychologist should not be surprised if the answer is, "I hate school," or "He's home sick with a cold," though the logician would be! To the psychologist, the child's answer is "reasonable" because it is a simple association with a stimulus, without regard to logical rules, and this is what people learn long before they learn to reason, let alone reason by the rules of logic.

As children grow older they learn to respond according to certain instructions and rules, to keep their associative responses within certain bounds. Suppose I test a high school student: I instruct him that whenever I say a word I want him to respond with a word that is a class name for objects of the same kind. Now I give him the word "table." He will give me back "furniture" or some comparable word, but he will not say "chair" because that would violate the rule that his response must name a class that includes "table." He has learned to follow a rule.

Now for a more complex case. In college, the student may learn the syllogism, one form of which is:

(1) All A is B.
    (All men are mortal.)
(2) All C is A.
    (All farmers are men.)

(3) Therefore, all C is B.
    (All farmers are mortal.)

This, sure enough, is one of the rules of logic and the student may learn it, perhaps by rote. He will immediately encounter difficulty, however, in applying it to situations in everyday life, because it is not easy to distinguish the syllogism from a fallacy. The form of the syllogism above, for example, *looks* suspiciously like the following:

(1) All A is B.
    (All farmers are men.)
(2) All B is C.
    (All men are mortal.)
(3) Therefore, all C is A.
    (All mortals are farmers.)

wherein the conclusion is unsound because it does not follow from (1) and (2). These are very difficult verbal discriminations even in symbol form. They become harder when put in word form. Many of the statements made in politics, business, or everyday life look like correct syllogisms when they are really fallacies. A political candidate, for example, may say:

Inflation leads to high taxes.
High taxes lead to tax scandals.
So, let's cut taxes!

and we may respond with, "I want lower taxes. Say, he makes good sense."

Illogical thinking. One of the reasons why it is hard to think logically, then, is that it is difficult to tell verbal reasoning that follows the rules of logic from that which does not. Besides that, there are other reasons why we have trouble always being logical. Everyday conversation is not made from a logical mold—and how dull it would be if it were!—but rather from the interplay of personal and motivational factors. With language, we have learned to sell a magazine subscription, to persuade a reluctant parent, to hail a cab, or to stimu-

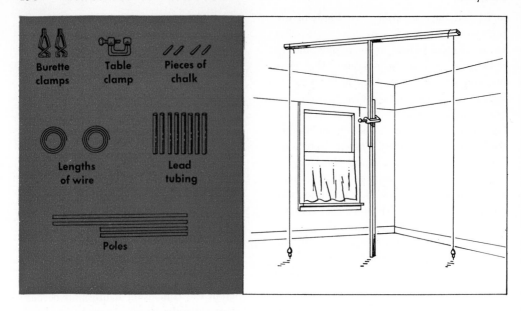

Fig. 6.10. The pendulum problem. This is one of a series of problems used in the study of human reasoning. Subjects were given the materials presented on the left and instructed to form two pendulums that might be swung so as to make chalk marks at particular points on the laboratory floor. On the right is the correct solution. (*Adapted from Maier, N. R. F. Reasoning in humans. J. comp. Psychol., 1930, 10, 115–143.*)

late a mood. Seldom do we use words in order to "think straight." Furthermore we may have received excessive training in logical confusion. A child, for example, is charged by a grownup with, "Give me one good reason why you disobeyed me!" The frightened child cannot do it, so he lies or rationalizes until the adult is satisfied.

Then, too, life itself has a way of confronting us with illogical coincidences, such as the thunderstorm on the only day we play hooky from school. Here an *animistic* reasoning, that our truancy *caused* the thunderstorm, is fostered by nature and often exploited by a moralistic parent. Society's encouragement of such fallacious reasoning is religiously systematic in some cultures and is widespread in our own, especially where cause-and-effect relationships are concerned. It not only can lead to a wrong theory of thunderstorms, it can also lead to wrong habits of reasoning which interfere with the practice of logic.

Distortions in reasoning. Ordinarily, then, we have a strong tendency to respond to "logic" stimuli with free, associative responses, even when we may be trying our level best to be logical. And such responses tend to distort our reasoning. Some circumstances, however, are more likely than others to evoke free associations and thus distortions in reasoning. Since logical thinking is important to all of us, we ought to take a moment to look at some common distortions.

One factor is the complexity of the stimulus situation. If a logical fallacy is presented to people in a complicated way or along with a mass of complex facts and statements, they are less likely to detect it.

Another related source of distortion in reasoning is the language in which premises are expressed. An important factor in such distortion is what has been called the atmosphere effect.[21] This refers to the impression that a statement may make on a person, inclining him to give a yes or no answer quite apart from the logical implications of the statement. If, for example, the premises of a syllogism are presented in the affirmative, "All p's are q's, and all q's are t's," people tend to reject any negative conclusions containing "no" or "are not." With split premises, that is, one stated affirmatively and the other negatively, they tend to accept negative conclusions. Such atmosphere effects are apparently rather common; college students, at least, are amazingly subject to them.

Another important factor is what we may call the *opinion effect* on reasoning. As you might expect, numerous experiments have shown that *emotion*-producing material and words that evoke strong *prejudices, beliefs,* or *opinions* may effectively prevent discriminative, logical deductions. One of the most interesting of these is illustrated by a syllogistic test in two multiple-choice forms.[22] The first form was *symbolic*; it used neutral terms like x, y, and z. The second form was "emotionally toned"; it contained phrases that in 1942 evoked strong personal opinions about air power; for example, "Battleships are not as effective as certain other machines of destruction, since the British battleships *Prince of Wales* and the *Repulse* were sunk by airplanes." Conclusions drawn by subjects in this experiment are in Table 6.2. Conclusion 5 is the only correct answer, for the two premises are so stated as to imply jointly nothing whatever beyond what they say as separate sentences. Yet 90 per cent accepted either conclusions 1 or 2, apparently because they already believed in air power! (Incidentally, note that

when opinions are lacking, as they would be in the symbolic x, y, z form, the students favored conclusions 3 and 4, probably because of atmosphere effect: negative conclusions from split negative-affirmative premises.)

You would be wise to test yourself by some homemade syllogisms. See if you can distinguish the factual truth or falseness of a conclusion from the soundness or unsoundness of its logical dependence on its premises. For example,

(1) All thinking is dreaming.
(2) All reasoning is thinking.
(3) Therefore, all reasoning is dreaming.

The conclusion is false (in terms of this chapter!) but it is a logically sound deduc-

TABLE 6.2. Conclusions accepted by subjects in a test of syllogistic reasoning. One group of subjects was given two premises stated in neutral symbolic terms. Another group was given the same premises stated in emotionally toned sentences. They were then asked to check on a multiple-choice question the conclusions that could be drawn from these premises. See text for correct answer.

Conclusions	Per cent of subjects accepting conclusion	
	Symbolic form	Sentence form
1. Airplanes are more effective than battleships	0	44
2. Airplanes may be more effective than battleships	11	46
3. Airplanes are not more effective than battleships	47	1
4. Airplanes may not be more effective than battleships	32	0
5. None of the above conclusions seems to follow logically	10	9

Modified from Morgan, J. J. B., & Morton, J. T. The distortion of syllogistic reasoning produced by personal convictions. *J. soc. Psychol.,* 1944, **20**, 39–59.

tion from the premises, one of which (1) happens to be factually false.

All too often, belief conquers logic when both contend in the same man. The causes are psychological. We know that they lie in the conditioning history of the individual. People are primarily psychological, not logical, even when they "reason."

SUMMARY

1. Thinking is a sequence of symbolic processes that represent past learning and experience. These processes consist in part of images and implicit muscle responses.

2. Most, if not all, people experience images, and such images often help thinking. Some individuals have such vivid (eidetic) imagery that they use it to recall things almost perfectly. Considerable thinking, however, takes place without the benefit of images.

3. Also involved in thinking are implicit muscle movements that can be recorded with the appropriate instruments. These may be coincidental to thinking, but they may also serve as cue-producing responses that set off the next event in the thinking processes.

4. Both animals and human beings have been demonstrated to use symbolic processes, but language greatly enlarges human capacity to use them.

5. Concepts are learned by abstracting some element, such as shape or color, that is a common property of a number of objects. The name or symbol of a concept subsequently can be used in thinking.

6. Thinking is often directed; it solves, or attempts to solve, problems. Such problem solving requires motivation and especially a goal toward which thinking is directed.

7. Thinking is also guided toward its goal by habits previously formed and by sets toward a particular type of solution.

8. Solutions may be arrived at by trial and error, by rote memory (from solving similar problems in the past), or by insight. Insight is a relatively sudden solution that combines past learning in a new way.

9. Reasoning involves thinking in which elements of previous learning are combined. It has been demonstrated in animals as well as human beings. Most reasoning in people is done with words.

10. Because words are vague, because it is often not possible to check the results of reasoning, and because various groups and societies differ in what they consider "reasonable," reasoning is often fallacious.

11. To avoid such incorrect reasoning, the rules of logic have been developed. These are seldom followed, however, in everyday reasoning, be-

cause (*a*) it is very difficult to discriminate logical from fallacious lines of reasoning, (*b*) our past experiences are often illogical, and (*c*) such factors as "atmosphere effect" and prejudice can easily distort reasoning.

SUGGESTIONS FOR FURTHER READING

Duncker, K. On Problem-solving. *Psychol. Monogr.*, 1945, No. 270.
An account of some interesting and important experiments on problem solving and thinking.

Hayakawa, S. I. *Language in thought and action.* New York: Harcourt, Brace, 1949.
A readable book, intended for the lay reader, that covers some of the problems of thinking and reasoning correctly with words.

Humphrey, G. *Thinking: an introduction to its experimental psychology.* New York: Wiley, 1951.
A text on thinking that emphasizes the classical Würzburg experiments on imageless thought.

Köhler, W. *The mentality of apes.* New York: Harcourt, Brace, 1925.
An account of pioneering studies on thinking and insight in apes.

Leeper, R. Cognitive processes. In S. S. Stevens (Ed.), *Handbook of experimental psychology.* New York: Wiley, 1951. Chap. 19.
A compact summary of current facts and theories in the field of thought processes.

Thouless, R. H. *How to think straight.* New York: Simon and Schuster, 1939.
An interesting little book giving some good advice on how to think straight.

Vinacke, W. E. *The psychology of thinking.* New York: McGraw-Hill, 1952.
A text covering most of the available experimental facts relevant to thinking.

Wertheimer, M. *Productive thinking.* New York: Harper, 1945.
Contains a theoretical analysis of thinking as well as many ideas and experiments on how to solve problems.

Woodworth, R. S., & Schlosberg, H. *Experimental psychology* (Rev. Ed.). New York: Holt, 1954.
A comprehensive text in experimental psychology containing a good summary of experiments on thinking.

Chapter 7 ATTENTION AND PERCEPTION

THE SCIENTIST'S PROBLEM in studying perception is to discover and understand the principles that govern *our awareness of ourselves and of objects, qualities, and relationships in our environment.* Many people may not see that there is really a problem here. So firm is our belief in the objectivity and realness of the world as we perceive it that we seldom question its existence or wonder how we can be aware of it. We all know that we have sense organs such as our eyes and ears. We know further that our ability to see and hear depends upon these organs. We assume that somehow or other copies of the world

This chapter was drafted by Charles W. Eriksen of the University of Illinois. It introduces the student to the basic features of perception. In Part Five, "Knowing the World," are three additional chapters that deal further with the senses and with our perception of the world through language and speech.

get into our sense organs and reach our brain.

The world as a person sees it. Perception, however, is not nearly so simple as that. Indeed, how complex it is becomes apparent when we consider what at first seem to be very obvious questions. Why do we perceive an approaching car as moving and ourselves as stationary? Is a stick half-submerged in the water straight or bent? Is a table really solid as it seems to be?

Consider the perception of the approaching car. It may seem obvious that we perceive it to be moving because the image of it is actually moving across the retinas of our eyes. This answer, however, does not solve the problem, for if a person moves his head, the objects in his visual field also move across his retina, yet in this case he perceives the objects as stationary and his head as doing the moving. So it is not just movement of the image that accounts for the perception of movement. Rather the brain and the sense organs somehow put together a lot of information, and the perception depends on all aspects of this information, not just one.

The question how the stick half-submerged in water is perceived illustrates another problem in perception. Such a stick, viewed by a person looking into the water, looks as though it is bent at the water line. We all know, though, that it is not, for anyone can run his hand along it and feel that it is straight. So in this case, perceptions in two sensory domains do not agree. One is false, and the other is correct. In Figure 7.1, there are several other examples of objects that appear to be different from what they actually are. Such experiences are called *illusions*. An illusion occurs when one of a person's perceptions does not agree with his other perceptions. In the examples shown in Figure 7.1, we can prove that our eyes deceive us by laying down a ruler and measuring the lengths and directions of the lines.

There is also a good deal of the world which is not reflected in perception, often because our sense organs are not acute enough or because the appropriate stimulus cannot get to them. Consider the question of whether a table is really solid. The physicists tell us that the firm stable objects all about us are really collections of small particles revolving around nuclei much as the earth revolves about the sun. Perceptions of objects, however, bear no resemblance to the physicist's description of them, for to the person, things seem to be solid, not to be mere collections of atoms. In this case the reason is that our eyes are not acute enough and it takes highly specialized instruments to reveal objects as they really are.

Stimuli and sense organs. Now let us consider our sense organs and the stimuli that excite them. It is upon these that our awareness of ourselves and the world around us basically depends. As Johannes Müller, an early nineteenth-century physiologist, pointed out, "We do not perceive the world, we only perceive our senses."[1] The objects we see, for example, are the result of radiant energy in the form of waves reaching the retina of the eye. The sounds we hear are again waves of energy striking our eardrums. The movement we feel is the result of fluid stimulating sense organs in the middle ear. So, from the different energies that stimulate various sense organs, we are able to reconstruct the world as we perceive and know it.

Some of our sense organs—those of vision, hearing, smell, taste, touch, warmth, cold, and pain—react to energy changes in our *external environment*. All of us are aware that we have such sense organs. Less familiar, however, is the fact that many sense organs respond to energy changes *inside the body*. The *vestibular* sense organs in the head near the ear respond to the force of gravity and to rotation of the head. The *kinesthetic* receptors in the muscles, tendons, and joints respond to the movement of our limbs and the contraction of our muscles. We shall learn more later (in Chapter 19) about these sense organs and how they work. For the present it is only important to keep in mind the different sense organs through which we perceive the world outside as well as events within our bodies.

Threshold sensitivity. None of our sense organs is infinitely sensitive. Each requires some minimum energy of stimulation for it to respond. There are sounds that are too soft to be heard, light that is too faint to be seen, weights that are too light to be felt, and movements that are too slight to be detected. In a word, every sense has its *absolute threshold*—the minimum of stimulus energy to which it will respond. This

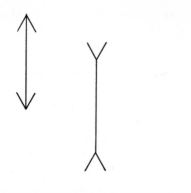

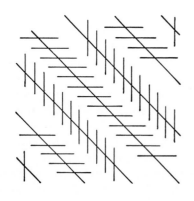

Fig. 7.1. Some examples of illusions. The example at the top is known as the Müller-Lyer illusion; most people see the line on the left as being shorter than the one on the right. In the middle figure, the diagonal lines are really parallel even though they do not seem so. The lower figure is an example of the vertical-horizontal illusion.

absolute threshold varies, of course, with the individual, with the sense involved, and with the kind of stimulus impinging on it. In order for us to perceive anything, the stimulus must be above this threshold.

Even if stimuli were always above the absolute threshold, we would perceive little if they were always exactly the same in intensity and quality. In order for us to perceive, stimuli must somehow be different —one stimulus must be a little more intense than another or of a different color or pitch—so that we can detect differences in them. In a word, there must be differences in stimuli that we can *discriminate*.

Every sense, however, has its limit of discrimination, and this is called its *differential threshold*. That is to say, when differences in stimuli become too small, we can no longer detect them, and the smallest difference that we can just discriminate is the differential threshold. The ear, for example, can detect differences in the pitch of tones, but when the pitch difference becomes very small, there is a point, the differential threshold, at which it is no longer possible to discriminate differences in pitch. Similarly, the eye has a differential threshold for discriminating differences in color or in the brightness of a light. In general, therefore, *there is a limit to the differences we can discriminate.*

The absolute threshold and the differential threshold, taken together, set limits to perception.

■ PRINCIPLES OF PERCEPTION

Perception is so broad a subject that entire books have been written about it. The facts of perception, however, can be summarized in a few general principles. Not only does human perception obey these principles, but the behavior of many animals suggests that their perceptions do too.

Many of the principles are obvious—so obvious that we are apt to overlook them—but some are not. These principles are discussed in the following sections.

Attention. One of the more obvious characteristics of perception is its selective nature. At any given moment our sense organs are bombarded by a multitude of stimuli. Yet only a few of these stimuli are given a clear channel. We perceive clearly only a very few events at one time. Other events are perceived less clearly, and the rest forms a sort of hazy background of which we are partially or completely unaware. This is another way of saying that, of the various events around us, we *attend* to only a very few. So *attention* is a basic factor in perception.

This factor divides our field of experience, so to speak, into a *focus* and a *margin*. In the focus of experience are the events that we perceive clearly. Because we attend to them, they stand out from the background of our experience. Other items in the margin are less clearly perceived. We are aware of their presence but less clearly so. Imperceptibly shading off from the margin are other items which are outside our field of attention and of which, for the moment, we are not consciously aware.

Let us illustrate the nature of attention. While watching a football game, our attention is focused on the ball carrier. We are somewhat dimly aware of the tangle of players at the scrimmage line and of the activity of the blockers, but it is the ball carrier and his movements that most clearly stand out. We are at the same time being bombarded by a number of other stimuli. Our feet may be aching with the cold, unpleasant sensations may be coming from our stomach as a result of the last hot dog we ate, and the fellow in back of us may be carrying on a conversation with his girl. While the play is going on we are not aware of any of these things. Only when the play is finished or time out is called do we perceive how cold our feet are or hear the couple behind us.

Shifting of attention. The fact that we do at some time hear the conversation behind us and do notice the coldness in our feet illustrates another aspect of our field of attention. Attention is constantly shifting. What is at the focus one minute is marginal the next, and still later may have passed completely from conscious awareness. Even when one activity dominates our attention, its dominance usually is not perfectly continuous. Other perceptions come fleetingly into the focus of our awareness and then are replaced again by the dominant item.

What is it that determines what we will attend to? Although attention does shift, it has a certain orderliness to it. It is not completely chaotic, for if it were we should be unable to carry out any extended activity. Actually, as a good advertising man could explain, there are certain principles that determine the direction of our attention—the principles of attention getting. These tell us what will be most clearly perceived and what may be only dimly perceived or not perceived at all. These principles concern two general classes of factors: *external factors* in the environment, and *internal factors* such as motives, set, and expectancy. We shall first consider the external factors under four headings: (1) intensity and size, (2) contrast, (3) repetition, and (4) movement.

Intensity and size. The louder a sound, the more likely a person is to attend to it. The brighter the light, the more likely it is to capture his attention. By the same token he will more likely notice a full-page advertisement than he will a half-column one. This factor of intensity or bigness is most pronounced when he is experiencing something new or unfamiliar; then the items in the environment that are biggest, loudest, or brightest will attract his attention first. In general, if two stimuli are competing for attention, the one that is most intense will be the first to be noticed.

Contrast. As human beings, we tend to adapt or become used to the stimulation around us. The ticking of the clock which may be so noticeable when we enter a room is not noticed after a while. A room may seem hot or cold when we first enter it, but after a few minutes we may hardly be aware of the temperature. On the other hand, if the ticking clock should abruptly stop, we become aware of the sudden silence. As we drive along in a car, we are not aware of the hum of the engine, but let a cylinder misfire and the noise of the engine occupies the center of our attention.

These examples illustrate the role of contrast in determining attention. Any change in the stimulation to which we have become adapted immediately captures our attention. If we are reading in our room and someone turns on the radio in the adjoining room, we are apt to become acutely aware of it. But after a short while it drops from our awareness as we again become absorbed in our reading. Now when the radio is turned off it again receives our ATTENTION for a moment. Both the onset and the termination of a stimulus tend to acquire attention because both contrast with what has preceded them.

The word in capital letters in the above paragraph is another illustration of contrast. Most of you noticed the word as soon as you looked at this part of the page. However, if all the text were in capitals, the word would have gone unnoticed. It attracted attention because it contrasts with the words in lower-case letters.

Repetition. There are times when the repetition of a stimulus is attention-getting.

A misspelled word is more likely to be noticed if it occurs twice in the same paragraph than if it occurs only once. We are more likely to hear a burst of gunfire than a single shot, or to hear our name if it is called twice. Mother, when she calls Junior in for dinner, shouts his name not once but several times.

The advantage of repetition is twofold. A stimulus repeated twice has a better chance of catching us during one of the periodic wanings of attention to a task in which we may be engaged. In addition, repetition increases our sensitivity or alertness to the stimulus.

Movement. Human beings, as well as most animals, are quite sensitive to objects that move in their field of vision. Our eyes are involuntarily attracted to movement in much the same way as the moth is attracted to a flame. Soldiers on a night patrol soon learn this fact and freeze in their tracks when a flare bursts. To fall flat or duck behind shelter is movement that makes their detection more likely than remaining motionless out in the open.

The field of advertising, of course, makes good use of this fact. Some of the most effective advertising signs are those that involve movement, either blinking lights or animated figures.

Motives. The factors of intensity, contrast, repetition, and movement that attract attention are external stimulus factors. Of equal importance are human factors of motives, interests, and other internal states. Our needs and interests govern not only what will attract our attention but also what will hold it. Even the sleepiest student in the class can be made to sit on the edge of his chair by the instructor's announcing that he is going to talk about "Sex Practices of American Females." Appeal to the sex drive is particularly effective in our culture because of the traditional suppression of the drive. Thus advertisements effectively use shapely girls in bathing suits to sell such unrelated items as spark plugs. In a society where food was more scarce than it is in this culture, advertisements showing food objects would probably outnumber those with sex appeal.

Not only are basic motives such as sex and hunger important in directing attention, but any of the great variety of human motives and interests are effective. If a geologist and a bird fancier walk through the same fields, the geologist will notice the detailed features of the terrain, the various kinds of rocks, etc., while the bird lover will notice the number and variety of birds. If you ask the geologist about the birds, he is very apt to say that he did not notice any, much less how many or what kind. And of course the bird lover is not likely to have noted any of the geological features of the terrain.

Set or expectancy. Besides our interests and motives, *set* or expectancy plays a major role in selecting what we will perceive. The geologist would have been able to tell you much more about the bird life in the fields he traversed if he had known beforehand that you were going to ask him. A doctor may hear the phone ring in the night, but not hear the baby's crying. His wife, on the other hand, may sleep through the ringing telephone, but the slightest sound from the child probably will bring her wide awake.

When the drawing in Figure 7.2 is included in a series of two-digit numbers, subjects will report that they have seen the number 13. Another group of subjects who have been exposed to letters of the alphabet will report this drawing to be the letter B. In the one case the subjects have acquired a set or expectancy for numbers, and in the other case the set is for letters.

Of the various factors that determine attention and thus perception, expectancy is

Fig. 7.2. The effect of set on perception. The group of dots and lines can be perceived either as a B or as 13 depending on what a person is expecting.

probably the most important, for our sets and expectancies largely direct and order the succession of our perceptual experiences. Without them, our perceiving would be largely at the mercy of random fluctuations in the environmental stimuli.

■ PERCEPTION OF OBJECTS

One of the most obvious facts of our perceptual experience is that it is filled with objects (see Figure 1.4 in Chapter 1). The stimulation that we are constantly receiving comes into our awareness as shapes and patterns. We do not ordinarily perceive the world about us as patches of colors, variations in brightness, loud or high-pitched sounds. We perceive objects. We see tables, floors, walls, and buildings, and we hear automobile horns, footsteps, and words.

Some of this perception of *objects* is a matter of learning, as we shall see later in this chapter, but much of it is probably an unlearned property of our sense organs and nervous system. These structures tend to organize or modify our perceptions into simple patterns or objects. The measured ticking of a clock, for example, is usually not heard as such. Rather we tend involuntarily to accent the even tick-tick-tick-tick and perceive it as tick-tock, tick-

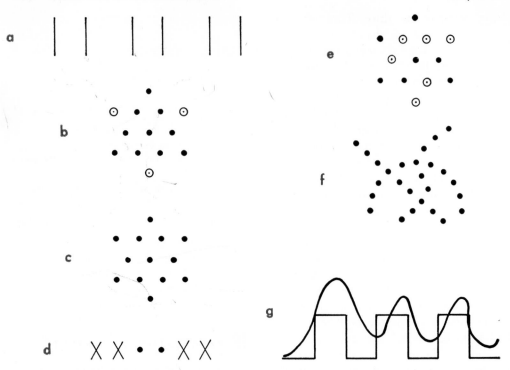

Fig. 7.3. Some examples of perceptual grouping.

tock, etc. Even when we try very hard, it is difficult to overcome such organizing tendencies in perception. They are somehow built into the way the sense organs and nervous system function. Organizing tendencies in perception take several different forms. We shall discuss them under the headings of (1) grouping, (2) figure-ground perception, (3) contour, (4) closure, and (5) apparent movement.

Grouping. One kind of organizing tendency in perception is called *grouping.* Whenever there are several different stimuli, we tend to perceive them as grouped into some pattern. In Figure 7.3, for example, you can see several illustrations of such grouping or patterning. They have been selected to illustrate several different ways in which grouping takes place.

Figure 7.3a illustrates the role of *near-*

ness or *proximity.* Instead of seeing six vertical lines, you see three pairs of parallel lines. Items which are close together in either space or time tend to be perceived as belonging together or constituting a group.

In Figure 7.3b and c we can see the importance of *similarity* in grouping. In Figure 7.3b most of you will see one triangle formed by the dots with its apex at the top and another triangle formed by the circles with its apex at the bottom. You see these triangles because similar items, the dots and the circles respectively, tend to group together. Otherwise you would see Figure 7.3b as a hexagon or six-pointed star, as is the case in Figure 7.3c where the stimuli are all the same. Figure 7.3d is another illustration of grouping according to similarity. If people are shown this figure and then asked to copy it, most of them will unconsciously draw it so that the two Xs are close together and the two circles are close together but so that the circles are farther from the Xs than in the figure. Thus they exhibit grouping due to similarity.

Grouping according to similarity, however, does not always hold. Figure 7.3e is more easily seen as a hexagon than as one figure composed of the dots and another figure composed of the circles. In this case, similarity is competing with the principle of *symmetry* or *good figure*. Neither the circles nor the dots by themselves form a symmetrical organization. In either case certain members must be left out—a fact which most people find disturbing. In general, the tendency to group is a tendency to form a balanced or symmetrical figure that includes all the parts.

Our last principle of grouping is *continuation*. This is illustrated by the tendency of a line that starts out as a curve to be seen as continuing a curved course. Conversely, a straight line is seen as continuing straight or, if it does change direction, as an angle rather than a curve. Figure 7.3**f** and **g** are illustrations of continuation; you see dots in Figure 7.3**f** as several curves and straight lines. Even though the curves and straight lines cross and have dots in common, it is only with effort that you can see a straight line suddenly becoming curved at one of these junction points.

Although all these examples have to do with vision, the same principles of grouping can be observed in the other senses. The rhythm we hear in music also depends upon grouping according to proximity in time and similarity of accents. In the sense of touch, too, there are examples of grouping. Get a friend to help you, ask him to shut his eyes, and mark off three equally

distant points on the back of his hand. Then touch a pencil to the first two points, pausing slightly before you touch the third point. Your friend will report that the first two points were closer together than were the second and third. This illusion illustrates the grouping of stimuli according to nearness or proximity in time.

Figure-ground perception. We have now seen how grouping is important and basic in our perception of objects. Closely related to the grouping tendencies is another fundamental tendency—the tendency to perceive figure and ground. The objects that fill our everyday perceptions are seen as standing out or being separate from the general background of our experience. Pictures hang *on* a wall, words are *on* a page. In this case, the pictures and words are seen as *figure*, while the wall and the page are seen as *ground*. This primitive capacity to distinguish an object from its general sensory background is basic to all object perception.

In glancing at Figure 7.4, you automatically see the black area as being an object. Despite the fact that it may look like no object that you have ever seen, it still is seen as a unitary whole or figure that is distinct from the page. If we examine carefully our general experience of figure-ground relations, we note certain char-

Fig. 7.4. A figure-ground, the simplest kind of perception.

Fig. 7.5. A reversible figure-ground. This drawing may be perceived either as a vase or as two profiles.

acteristics that distinguish the figure from the ground in our perception. The figure seems to have some sort of shape or object quality, while the ground tends to be formless. The ground seems to extend continuously behind the figure, or, in other words, the figure appears to be in front and the ground behind.

In Figure 7.5 is a reversible figure-ground relation. You can see it as either a vase or two profiles. When you see the vase you perceive the white area as the figure against a black ground, and conversely to see the profiles you must perceive the black area as a figure upon a white background. It is difficult to see both vase and profiles simultaneously.

The figure-ground relation is also found in senses other than vision. When we listen to a symphony, the melody or theme is perceived as the figure while the chords are perceived as ground. In boogiewoogie, a figure-ground is used to produce the typical boogiewoogie effect. The pianist uses repetitive chords in the bass as ground

against which to play a varied figure in the treble. In observing a person's movements, we might consider the over-all posture as the ground for, say, the finer movements of the hands and arms.

Contour. We are able to separate objects or things from the general ground in our visual perception only because we can perceive contours. Contours are formed whenever there is a marked change or difference in the degree of brightness or color of the background. If we look at a piece of paper which varies in brightness from white at one border to black at the opposite border, we can perceive no contour, provided the variation in brightness is smooth and gradual. Such a paper appears very uniform to us, and if asked to say where the sheet stops being light and starts to become dark, we can only guess or be arbitrary. On the other hand, if there is a marked change, rather than a gradual change—suppose several shades are skipped—we can perceive the paper as divided into two parts, a light and a dark. The division occurs quite naturally at the place where the brightness gradient abruptly changes.

Contours give shape to the objects in our visual field because they mark off the

Fig. 7.6. Two different faces can be seen although each is shaped by the same contour.

object from other objects or from the general ground. We must be careful not to conclude, however, that contours *are* shapes. The reversible faces in Figure 7.6 show clearly the differences between contour and shape. Here both faces are formed by the same contour, but it is quite clear that both faces do not have the same shape. Contours determine shape, but by themselves are shapeless.

Closure. Our perception of objects is much more complete than the sensory stimulation we receive from the object. Perception tends to "fill in" gaps in stimulation so that we perceive a whole object and not disjointed parts. This "filling in" is termed closure. In Figure 7.7 we have some illustrations of how closure works. Although the lines forming the circle and the square are not complete, nevertheless we still perceive them as a circle and a square. The same is true of the lower figure. Although the stimulation from the contour is not complete, most of you see this as a man on horseback, which is much more than the few lines actually presented to the eye.

Apparent movement. Everyone is familiar with the electric advertising signs in which arrows seem to move back and forth or patterns of lights seem to move across the sign. As you know, in most of these signs nothing really moves in the physical sense. They simply create an illusion of movement by turning lights off and on in sequence. Psychologists call this illusion apparent movement.

We can study apparent movement by having two lights arranged so that they can be turned on and off, one after the other. If the time interval between turning one light off and the other on is too long, what we see is two separate lights, one going on after the other. If we make the time interval shorter, we get apparent movement in

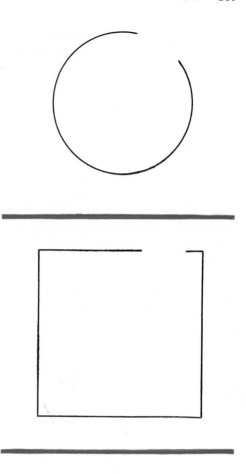

Fig. 7.7. Perceptual closure. The processes of perception fill in gaps so that the figures tend to be perceived as a circle, a square, and a man on horseback.

which a single light is seen as moving back and forth. If the interval is made too short, we again see two separate lights, but this time they seem to be on simultaneously. So the interval of time between the two lights is the important thing in apparent movement. This interval, however, depends a lot upon the particular situation. A shorter time interval is needed, for example, if the lights are close together.

Motion pictures are also examples of apparent movement. When we watch the movies we see the actors as moving about on the screen. In reality, however, there is no movement on the screen at all. What we are seeing is a rapid succession of still pictures. The projector flashes the successive frames in the film on the screen one at a time but at a very rapid rate. We see one still picture in which the objects or people are in one position. Then the light from the projector goes off and when it comes on again we see another picture in which the objects and people are in a slightly different position. If the flashing on and off of the projector is fast enough, we perceive apparent movement in which the objects on the screen appear to move about naturally. If the speed is too slow, we get the impression of jerkiness in the movement.

This concludes our résumé of the *perception of objects*. Closely related to it, however, is the *perception of depth*, which we shall take up in the next section.

■ PERCEPTION OF DEPTH

Depth perception has been a source of puzzlement to scientists and philosophers for hundreds of years. They have been bothered by the problem of how we can see a three-dimensional world with only a two-dimensional retina in each eye. Our retina is able to register images of the world only in terms of right-left or up-down, yet we perceive the world about us as having the extra dimension of depth.

We are a little more sophisticated about the problem today. We realize that the ability to perceive depth is no more amazing than any other perceptual accomplishment. As we have seen, all awareness of ourselves and of the world depends upon physical energy in various forms striking special sense organs. What our brain receives is various patterns of neural impulses, not tiny copies of various objects.

Today we view the problem of depth perception as the question, How do differences or changes in the physical stimulus relate to differences in perceptual experience? And then, How do the differences in the physical stimulus manage to stimulate our sense organs differentially so that our brain is provided with proper cues for depth? For example, when one looks at a near object or at a far object, a flat object or a solid object, his retina receives different patterns of stimulation even though the profile of the objects may be the same. As we shall see below, differences in shadows, in clearness, and in the size of the image in the eye provide cues on the retina as distinctive as if the retina were able to register the third dimension directly.

Perhaps this idea can be made clearer by using an analogy. When a mathematician solves a problem involving speed and weight, he may let x stand for miles per hour and y for weight in pounds. Of course neither x nor y has any physical resemblance to what it is representing, but as long as he is consistent in his operations, his results will correspond with the physical world. His symbols will be adequate substitutes for the real objects.

In the case of perception, different cues such as shadow and clearness are the symbols that represent the physical world. The

Fig. 7.8. Perceiving depth. This picture illustrates three monocular factors in depth perception. The tracks converge in the distance (linear perspective); telephone poles in the distance appear to be behind other poles (interposition); and far objects are more hazy than those nearby (clearness). (*Ewing Galloway.*)

book lying on our desk or the automobile parked across the street form images on the retina. At the same time, senses other than vision are being stimulated too. When we reach for a book or walk to the car, all these sensory cues or symbols are somehow simultaneously perceived so that we judge correctly the distance of the book or car.

Those of you who have watched a baby reach for a rattle have noted how poor his judgment of distance is. Even the two-year-old child who has had an opportunity to move around in the world lacks the clear depth perception of the adult. One two-year-old wanted his father to pick him up so that he could touch the moon. Depth perception obviously improves as children grow older. From Chapter 2 you may recall that there is some uncertainty about the respective roles of maturation and learning in the development of perception. Hence we shall not concern ourselves with that issue here.

Visual cues for depth perception are usually classified into *monocular* and *binocular* cues, that is, those that may be utilized by one eye alone and those that require two eyes. In addition, it is thought that *kinesthetic cues* (see page 505) from

muscles of the eye also contribute to the perception of depth. We shall discuss all these cues in turn.

Monocular cues. Monocular cues, as the name suggests, are cues for depth that operate when only one eye is looking. They were first discovered by the ancient Greeks, then rediscovered by the Renaissance painters who were concerned with the problem of giving depth to their paintings. Their problem of presenting a three-dimensional world on a two-dimensional canvas is essentially the same problem that our retinas are faced with. If the artist is able to paint the scene on his canvas so that it looks essentially as the scene looks when focused on the retina, he succeeds in achieving realistic depth in his pictures. To do that he must paint objects not as they are known to be but as they look when they make an image on the retina of the eye. Let us examine some of the principles the artist uses to accomplish this.

▪ *Linear perspective.* As we shall see illustrated later in the chapter, objects which are farther away project a smaller image on the retina than do near objects. In addition, the distance separating images of far objects is smaller. To understand this point,

Fig. 7.9. Shadows can give an object the appearance of depth. For explanation, see text. (From Gibson, J. J. *The perception of the visual world.* Boston: Houghton Mifflin, 1950, p. 95.)

think of standing between railroad tracks and looking off into the distance. The ties become smaller and the tracks gradually become closer together until they appear to meet at the horizon. Figure 7.8 owes part of its depth effect to such linear perspective.

■ *Clearness.* In general, the more clearly we can see an object, the nearer the object is. The distant mountain seems farther away on a hazy day than on a clear day, because the haze in the atmosphere blurs the fine details so that we see only the grosser features. If we can see the details, we perceive an object as relatively close, but if we

can see only its general outline we perceive it as relatively far away.

■ *Shadows.* The pattern of shadows or of highlights in an object is very important in making the object look solid. In Figure 7.9, for example, the circle on the left looks flat, but the one on the right looks solid like a sphere. Notice that the one on the left is colored a uniform gray while the one on the right is brightest in the center with a gradient of decreasing brightness to the edges. In the latter case, the effect is the same as shining a light on a sphere. The surface closest to the light source receives the most light, and as the surface recedes from the

Fig. 7.10. Shadows and the perception of depth. If the picture is turned upside down, the quonset huts look like towers. For further explanation, see text. (From Gibson, J. J. *The perception of the visual world.* Boston: Houghton Mifflin, 1950, p. 97.)

light less and less light falls on it. Such appearances of lighting and shading are important clues for depth perception.

In Figure 7.10 we see another example of this cue, an aerial photograph of a group of quonset huts. When the picture is turned upside down, the quonset huts look like towers. If you note carefully the differences between the quonset huts and the "towers," you will discover that the shadows are responsible for this effect. The reason, briefly, is that we are accustomed to light coming from above. But when the picture is turned upside down, the light seems to come from below. Since this latter perception in inconsistent with our past experience, we perceive instead the "towers" as being painted black on top.

▪ *Movement.* Whenever you move your head, you can observe that the objects in your visual field appear to move. If you observe closely, you will find that the objects that are nearest you appear to move in the opposite direction while distant objects appear to move in the same direction as your head. This, of course, is an obvious cue to the relative distance of objects, because whether we see real movement or move our heads, the relative amount of movement is less for far objects than for near ones. Although movement is an important cue to depth, it obviously cannot be used by artists as can the other four monocular cues.

Binocular cues. There are some cues to depth perception that depend on the fact that we have two eyes rather than just one. These are called binocular cues. One such cue is *retinal disparity*—the difference in the images falling on the retinas of the two eyes.

▪ *Retinal disparity.* You may understand the factor of retinal disparity by looking at it in either of two ways. One is to think in terms of geometry. This is illustrated in Figure 7.11. In the center of each retina is

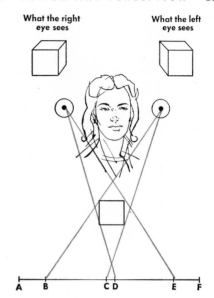

Fig. 7.11. What we see when we look at a cube. Not only does each eye receive a different view of the cube, but together the two eyes see in back of the cube. The right eye can see all the space from A to F except for the distance D to E. The left eye can see all the space from A to F except for the distance B to C. Hence, the two eyes together see the entire space from A to F.

a *fovea* that is much more sensitive than the rest of the retina. When we look at an object we fixate our eyes—point them, so to speak—so that the image of the object falls mostly on the fovea of the retina of each eye. But because the two eyes are separated from each other by about two and a half inches, they get slightly different views of any solid object and the two images of it are not exactly the same. Moreover, the images are more dissimilar when the object is very close, say a few inches, than when it is far away. From these differences we get cues to depth.

With the pictures in Figure 7.12 and a small mirror, you can demonstrate to yourself how retinal disparity contributes to the

Fig. 7.12. Looking into the third dimension. Select a small mirror whose shortest side is at least as long as the height of the pictures. Put the mirror's edge in the space between the two pictures at right angles to the page and with its reflecting side to the right. Put your nose on or near the top edge of the mirror. Close your left eye. Look at the mirror with your right eye and adjust the mirror so that the real picture and its mirror image are aligned in the same plane. Now open the left eye. With both eyes open, focus your attention on the left-hand image. The two pictures should now appear as one three-dimensional picture. (*Stereophotograph by Dorothy S. Gelatt, adapted from Stereo Realist Manual. New York: Morgan & Lester, 1954.*)

solid appearance of objects. Here we have the same scene photographed by a stereoscopic camera, a camera that has two lenses about as far apart as the two eyes. The picture on the left was photographed by the left lens and the one on the right by the right lens. When you look at the mirror reflection of the right-hand scene, according to the directions, the reflection appears to be physically located on top of the left-hand picture. Thus when you open both eyes, one eye sees one picture and the other eye sees the other picture and you achieve the illusion of depth. Although the right-left orientation of the objects in the right-hand scene has been reversed for the demonstration, close scrutiny of the pictures will show that they also differ in other details.

Kinesthetic cues. There are two other possible cues for depth perception: convergence and accommodation. Some scien-

tists have thought that they are cues to depth, and it is plausible that they should be, but it is not yet clearly demonstrated that they are. If so, the cue in each case is kinesthetic, consisting of impulses from muscles of the eye that signal to the brain the position of the muscles and the amount of tension in them.

▪ *Convergence.* For objects farther away than 70 feet, the line of sight of the eyes is essentially parallel. For nearer objects, however, the eyes turn more and more toward each other, that is, they converge. If such convergence aids in depth perception, the cue is probably kinesthetic impulses from sense organs in the muscles that make the eye converge.

▪ *Accommodation.* This is the adjustment of the lens in each eye to the distance of an object, and it is accomplished by the ciliary muscles. There is one ciliary muscle in each eye. It enables the lens to focus the visual image on the retina by relaxing or contracting in varying degrees, thus making the lens thicker or thinner. It is possible that kinesthetic impulses from the ciliary muscle provide a monocular cue to depth. Such a cue, if it is effective, can work only for distances up to about 20 feet, for beyond that distance, further accommodation of the eye is negligible.

Summary. In general, the various cues to depth and distance perception work together and are mutually supporting. In cases where they conflict, one cannot see depth so clearly. When looking at a photograph, for example, most of the monocular depth cues are present, yet you do not perceive all the depth of the real scene. In this case, cues conflict. The monocular cues give the impression of depth, but the binocular cues make the photograph look flat. Your perception, then, is a compromise.

It is possible, however, to see more depth in a photograph by eliminating the conflicting binocular cues. To do that, roll a piece of paper into a tube. Now close one eye, and look with the other eye through the tube at the photograph in Figure 7.8. You will find that the picture seems to have much greater depth. By closing one eye, you have eliminated the conflicting binocular cues, and by using the tube, you avoid seeing the edge or frame of the picture. The frame, of course, is a conflicting cue since real scenes do not have frames around them. You can still further increase the apparent depth by having someone else hold the picture for you. In this case, you have eliminated conflicting cues coming from your arms and body.

◼ PERCEPTUAL CONSTANCY

The world as we perceive it is a stable world. The size of a man does not appear

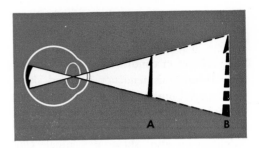

Fig. 7.13. The size of the image on the retina depends upon the size of the object and its distance from the eye. The arrow B, which is twice as far from the eye as arrow A, must be twice as large as arrow A in order to cast the same size image on the retina.

to change as he walks toward us, the dinner plate does not look like a circle when viewed one way and like an ellipse when viewed another, and the location of a sound does not appear to shift when we move our heads. To the layman there is nothing very surprising about this. Why shouldn't the world of objects always look the same or remain constant?

Considered more carefully, however, this question raises some interesting problems, for the physical stimuli from objects often are not constant despite the fact that they appear to be. Indeed, as we move about in the world, the stimulation that we receive continually changes. Even the stimuli coming from the same object change markedly as we change our position with respect to it. When we stand directly in front of the window, for example, the retinal image of the window is a rectangle. But when we move to one side of the window, the image becomes a trapezoid. Despite this change in the shape of the retinal image, we still continue to perceive the window as rectangular. Perceptually, therefore, its shape has not changed, even though its image on the retina has.

The general point is that there is a very strong tendency for the perceived shape of objects to remain the same irrespective of the positions or conditions under which we view them. This tendency is called *shape constancy*. Constancy in perception is not limited to shapes, however. The perceived sizes of objects, their colors, and their brightnesses also show perceptual constancy. Below we shall consider in a little more detail the problems of constancy in size and brightness. They illustrate not only the general problem of constancy but also some of the means by which perceptual constancy is achieved.

Constancy of size.   Since the eye works essentially like a camera, we know that the size of the image on the retina depends upon how far away the object is. The farther the object, the smaller the image. The geometry of this fact is illustrated in Figure 7.13. We can also see from this figure that an image of constant size can be produced on the retina either by a nearby small object or by a larger object at some distance.

Knowing this much about the size of retinal images, we might expect the perceived size of an object to change as we ap-

proach it. At 50 feet, it should appear much larger than it does at 100 feet. But this does not happen. The object instead appears to be about the same size irrespective of its distance. When it is far away, we do not perceive it as smaller; rather, we perceive it as being of the same size—but farther away (see Figure 7.14).

The constancy of object sizes in perception is closely related to our perception of distance. If the cues to depth or distance perception are present, we have good size constancy. Instead of perceiving distant objects as smaller, we perceive them as farther away. If, on the other hand, the cues to depth perception are gradually eliminated, our perception of the size of an unfamiliar object begins to correspond to the retinal image. And with all depth cues gone, constancy is completely eliminated and our perceptions and judgments of size are what one would expect them to be from the geometry of the retinal image.

For a *familiar object,* however, the elimination of depth cues does not completely destroy constancy because we know the approximate true size of the object. This knowledge gives us some degree of size con-

Fig. 7.14. Size constancy. Tall buildings in the background are perceived to be similar in size to tall ones in the foreground even though their images on the retina are greatly different in size. (A. Devaney, Inc., N.Y.)

stancy even in the absence of depth cues. In fact, in this case, we are able to use the size of the retinal image as a cue to the distance of the familiar object. Such a cue, it was pointed out above, is one of the monocular depth cues—linear perspective.

Brightness constancy. Visual objects also appear constant in their degree of whiteness, grayness, or blackness. Such brightness constancy, as we call it, tends to be independent of the illumination under which we view objects. Those objects or surfaces that appear white in a bright light still look white in dim illumination. Similarly what looks black in dim light still looks black in more intense light. Coal looks black even in very bright sunlight, while snow continues to look white even at night. Still another example of brightness constancy is the appearance of the white paper that lies partly in a shadow. We see the paper as being uniformly white; we do not see the shadowed portion as gray, but rather as white-in-the-shadow.

The perception of brightness depends, of course, on how much light gets into the eye. The greater the amount of light, the greater the brightness. However, though this is true for perceiving brightness alone, the brightness constancy of *objects* depends upon what *percentage* of the total light the object reflects. Perhaps we can make this point clearer by briefly reviewing some of the elementary physics of light.

When light falls on a surface or object, some of the light is reflected and some is absorbed. A pure white object reflects practically all the light falling on it, whereas a pure black one absorbs nearly all the incident light. Different shades of gray reflect different percentages of the incident light and absorb the rest. The greater the percentage of light reflected, the lighter the gray. The percentage of the total incident light that a surface reflects is called *albedo*.

With this background, we can now understand brightness constancy a little better. Although the absolute brightness of objects changes as the illumination changes, their albedo does not. A nearly white object that reflects 90 per cent of the incident light in sunlight still reflects 90 per cent of the available light when placed in a poorly lighted room. It is this albedo that we perceive. Since it is constant under different conditions of illumination, our perception of brightness is relatively independent of illumination. Briefly put, *it is our perception of albedo that accounts for brightness constancy.*

Summary. Perceptual constancies are not perfect. Even in the most favorable circumstances, our perceptions are a sort of compromise between what we know the object to be and the sensory image on the retina. Objects do appear to become slightly smaller as they move away from us, and white objects do not look quite as white when they are in shadow. In this sense, then, constancies are only relative. Our perceptions of objects correspond more closely to the true object, however, than to the sizes of images on the retina or to the sensory stimulus in general.

As human beings, we enjoy several advantages from perceptual constancy. It would be exceedingly difficult to move about or operate in a world where sounds changed their location when we moved our heads, and where objects changed their shapes and sizes when we viewed them from different positions and distances. Imagine what it would be like if your friends and associates had a multitude of sizes and shapes that depended upon how far away they were and from what angle you viewed them. Or imagine how difficult it would be to live in our society if the colors of things varied markedly with changes in sunlight and weather. It would be impossible to identify anything by color or whiteness, since the color of an object would depend not only on what time of the day it was but also on such things as cloudiness and shadows.

It is small wonder, then, that our brain uses whatever cues it can to keep our perceptual world as stable as possible.

COOPERATION AMONG THE SENSES

Most of what we have said so far has been about visual perception. That is natural because, for most of us, vision is our most important sense. Perhaps if we were four-legged animals and walked with our heads closer to the ground where the odors are more plentiful, the sense of smell might occupy more of our perceptions. As it is, however, our perceptual world is primarily a visual world. Even so, our perceived visual world owes as much to our other sense organs as it does to vision.

Kinesthetic and static senses. We have already seen how the muscle (kinesthetic) sense may contribute to the perceived depth of the world not only as a direct cue through eye movements but also because walking and moving about in the world provides an *understanding* of distance. The static sense in the inner ear also contributes something. It supplies the brain with information about our head movements and the relation of the head to the earth's gravity. In doing so, it is responsible for the stability of our visual world—for the fact that the world does not move or turn upside down when we move our heads or bend over. An interesting illustration of this contribution of the muscle and static senses to our visual perception is the case of the "moon illusion."

You have all noticed how large the moon looks when it is directly on the horizon. It looks several times larger, at least, than it does when it is overhead. Of course, the moon does not really change size, nor does its distance from us change. The perceived change in size is largely an illusion. Like many of the other illusions, the moon illusion is still not completely understood, but we do know that the muscle and static senses are involved in it. We know this because the moon illusion can be made to disappear by changing the stimulation of our static- and muscle-sense organs. You can demonstrate this for yourself. The next time you see the moon on the horizon, bend over and look at it from between your legs. You will find that the moon has shrunk and now looks about the same size as it does when overhead.

There are other ways of showing how senses other than vision modify perceptions of the visual world. If a person is seated in a dark room and is asked to adjust an illuminated rod to the vertical position, he can do this with considerable accuracy.[2] If now an experimenter stimulates the left side of the subject's neck with an electric current —to excite artificially the kinesthetic sense organs in the neck muscles—while he is adjusting the rod to the vertical, his perception of vertical will be shifted to the left. If the right side of his neck is stimulated, the perceived vertical will shift to the right. The influence of other senses on the visually perceived vertical can be shown in a similar way. If, for example, an experimenter uses earphones to present a sound to only one ear, the subject finds that the perceived vertical shifts toward the side of the sound.

Illusions. Usually the cues that the brain receives from the various senses mutually confirm and support each other. They fit together like the various pieces in a jigsaw puzzle. This sensory information also fits in with the knowledge and assumptions that have been acquired from past experience. All contribute in producing a clear, meaningful, and complete perception.

What happens, however, when our sensory cues do not fit together with each other, or with our knowledge and assumptions about the world—as they sometimes do not? Several things. We may experience an illusion, or we may feel confused and our perceptions may be unclear and unstable. Look, for example, at the picture in Figure 7.15. One young man appears to be twice as tall as the other, yet both seem to be of normal build. Is the small one a midget? He does not look like one. Yet the sensory cues for size make us suspect that he is. What kind of illusion do we have here?

The key to this particular illusion is that the room is not a normal room; it is not like the rectangular rooms with which you have always had experience. Figure 7.16 shows you how this room was constructed. When the door to the room is closed and you view the room with one eye through the small hole in the door, it looks like a normal room to you. The room has been built so as to duplicate the kind of monocu-

lar cues to depth and position you would ordinarily receive from a normal room. Consequently, you perceive it as a rectangular room. The illusion occurs despite your knowledge that the men should be about the same size.

The illusion would tend to disappear if you could step inside the room. Then your muscle and static senses could detect the slant of the floor, and you would perceive the true nature of the situation. The "larger" man would no longer look larger than the other one. Instead you would see him as standing in the slanting corner of the room.

THE ROLE OF LEARNING IN PERCEPTION

One of the things psychologists would like to know about perception is, "How much is the way we perceive the world due to learning and how much to the way our brain and nervous system are put together?" So far in this chapter, we have talked about attention as a factor in perception, the perception of objects and of depth, and the

Fig. 7.15. Why does one man look so much larger than the other? For an explanation, see Fig. 7.16 and text. (*Courtesy Perception Demonstration Center, Princeton Univ.*)

Fig. 7.16. The distorted room. This shows how the room in which the picture in Fig. 7.15 was taken was constructed and how cues from the shape of the room, and the objects in it, have created an illusion of size. (*Courtesy Perception Demonstration Center, Princeton Univ.*)

constancy of perception. In doing so, we have considered some perceptual phenomena that seem to depend upon learning and some that seem to depend on primitive or innate characteristics of the nervous system.

The attention value of an intense stimulus, the figure-ground relation, the grouping of stimuli according to nearness and similarity, the perceiving of certain types of illusions—all these are phenomena that seem to depend upon the way our nervous system is structured. Although we cannot prove conclusively that these phenomena do not depend upon learning, the best evidence that we can gather suggests that they do not. Small children, people in primitive cultures, and even many of the lower animals give every evidence that their perceptions are similar to ours in this respect.

It would be easy to believe that all perception is innate. The objective world somehow seems naturally so stable that it is difficult to believe that we learn our perception of it. For example, we perceive the depth and solidity of the objects about us so clearly and immediately that we are hardly aware that such unconscious cues as perspective and shadows are important. Shapes also are so obvious that most of you would be willing to bet that you never had to learn how to perceive a square or a triangle. Yet despite our subjective feeling that perception is immediate and natural, psychologists have considerable evidence that learning is important in most of our perceptual behavior.

Getting used to distortion. Some of the evidence for the role of learning in perception is so commonplace that we tend to overlook it. Perhaps you have sometime had the misfortune of arriving late at the movies and having to take a seat far down in front and to one side. If so, you have noticed then that the people on the screen appear distorted; their heads are elongated and flat. But if you recall your experience under these circumstances, you remember your discomfort was short-lived. After you had watched the picture for a little while, the distortion disappeared. The geometry of the situation did not change, of course, but you came to perceive these distorted images in keeping with your past experience. This kind of change in perception is much the same as that which occurs in size and shape constancy.

We are also aware of distortions when we view television for the first time. By the time we have become confirmed television addicts, however, we no longer perceive them. In fact, we frequently are unable to notice them even when we try.

Perceiving the world right side up. Psychologists have some interesting experiments that show the importance of learning in perception. One of them concerns our perception of the world as right side up. *The images on our retina are upside down.* (For a fuller discussion of this point, see Chapter 18.) Knowing this, we might ask what would happen to our perception of the world if these images were inverted so that they were now right side up. By using a system of lenses in front of the eye, it is possible to invert the retinal image and see what happens. In experiments in which this has been done, the effect at first is quite bewildering.[3] Every time the subject moves his head the entire world appears to swim around him. Since inverting the images also reverses the right-left positions, walking and moving about prove very difficult. When the subject tries to avoid walking into a chair that to him appears on his left, he steps to the right and thus bumps directly into the chair. To pick up an object that appears to be on his left, he has to learn to reach to his right. Sounds seem to come from the wrong direction.

The interesting feature of this sort of experiment is that, after the subject has worn the lenses for a period of time, his world begins to stabilize itself. Walking about and locating objects in the upside-down world become easier and more automatic. His head can be turned without the world seeming to move. Sounds now seem to come from the place where the object is seen to be and not from the opposite direction. While the subject learns to adjust his behavior to the upside-down world, we should note that the world never comes to look normal to him.

Auditory perception. Similar experiments in auditory perception are performed with a device called a *pseudophone*. This is a pair of tubes that carry sounds from one side of the head to the ear of the opposite side, and vice versa. Subjects who wear a pseudophone report experiences like those of wearing inverted lenses. At first there is a period of confusion. The wearer hears on his left the voice of the person that he sees standing on his right. As he watches a fire blazing on the hearth, he hears the crackle and snapping of the wood coming from the other side of the room. But with the pseudophone, as with the inverted lenses, things begin to straighten out after a few days. Sounds become easy to locate and to identify with the visual objects to which they belong.

Development of perception. The facts that we have been reviewing suggest that we must do a great deal of perceptual learning during our first few years of life. Indeed it would be interesting if we could remember how the world did look to us when we were very small children. This, of course, is not possible, but from what we do know about perceptual learning and development we can hazard a few guesses. Figure 7.17 is an attempt to portray the visual world of a nine-month-old child. The picture shows that vision is most developed in the center of the field and that shape or form perception is still rather amorphous in the periphery. There is also little or no depth perception, and considerable amount of distortion is present.

The effects of learning in perception seem to be almost irreversible. What has been learned permanently alters and influences all our subsequent perceptual behavior. Most of you have had the experience of suddenly looking at an object and failing to recognize or identify it immediately. In the fraction of a second before you recognized it, the object looked quite different from what it did after you recognized it. Yet after the moment of recognition had passed, it was impossible to visualize just what your perception had been like during that fleeting moment of uncertainty. In the same way, the trained bacteriologist can no longer perceive the slide in his microscope as he did when he was first a student. Then the slide was just so much confusion, a hodgepodge of colors and odd forms. What he now sees has been completely changed by the increased knowledge and the fine discriminations he has learned subsequently. No longer is the perception indefinite. He notes all sorts of variations in form and color and knows their meaning.

To see how markedly knowledge of a stimulus affects perception of it, there is a simple experiment that you can perform. Have a friend cut out a series of newspaper headlines that are unfamiliar to you. Make sure, however, that the various headlines are all the same size. Now have your friend stand at a distance from you and hold up one of the headlines for you to see. If you can read it, have him move farther away and try it with another headline. Keep repeating this, each time using a new headline, until he is just far enough away so that you can no longer read the headline. Keeping this distance, have your friend read the headline to you, then look at it again. You will find that you can now read the headline for yourself. Your knowledge of what it says has changed your perception of it. What was perceived before as just an un-intelligible blur of letters is now perceived as meaningful words.

Meaning. Learning affects perception in still other ways. The meaning that objects and things have acquired through our past experience with them is an inseparable part of the way we now perceive them. To a person who has lost a loved one in a hunting accident, a gun has a much different meaning from what it has to a child who is infatuated with cowboys. To the child the perception of the gun is tied up with pleasurable excitement, with fantasies of range wars and galloping horses. To the bereaved person the perception of the gun is one of sadness and fear; it makes him want to put it out of his mind.

The meaningfulness of the things we perceive greatly enriches our perceptual world. In everyday life, objects are not perceived as barren isolated units. The sound I hear is not just a sound; it is the creaking of the stairway which signals my wife's return from the movies. The apple pie in the bakery window is not just seen; one can almost smell the aroma and one's mouth begins to water in anticipation. The sight recalls memories of childhood days in grandma's kitchen and perhaps of various other experiences with apples and pies. Even unfamiliar things have meaning because they are similar to or remind us of other objects. This meaningfulness of objects in terms of use and personal experience is an important factor in our clear perception of them. It aids us immeasurably in discriminating between different objects and in identifying and remembering them.

SOCIAL AND CULTURAL INFLUENCES IN PERCEPTION

The society and culture in which we live, our socioeconomic status, our occupation, and even our own personality have a lot to

do with our perception. These social forces shape perception by determining the kinds of discriminations we make among the objects of the external world. They also influence attention and thus determine in part what we hear and what we see.

There are numerous examples of these social and cultural influences on perception. If we were to visit a tribe of savages, we should be amazed at their ability to read tracks and signs in the forest and to penetrate the protective camouflage of game animals. They would easily detect slight disturbances of the earth and underbrush that we should not even see. The babble of sounds from the jungle would be just so much noise to us, but to the natives they would be meaningful sounds—the call of a bird, the rustle of a monkey in a tree, the padded footfall of a big cat creeping through the brush.

Prejudice. Even within our own society differences in social and environmental influences lead to differences in the way we perceive. The strongly anti-Semitic person is much better able to detect Jewish people from a heterogeneous group of photographs than the less prejudiced person.[6] His prejudice has taught him to notice very small differences or clues that the less prejudiced person overlooks. Here we have a case where a social prejudice acts to sharpen or accentuate the perception of racial differences.

Prejudice may also act to dull the perception of differences between people within a racial group. The person who is strongly anti-Negro fails to perceive the differences between individual Negroes.[7] To him they all look alike. He may be very adept at recognizing light-skinned Negroes or spotting a Negro in a crowd of white people, but he is very poor at distinguishing one Negro from another.

The unprejudiced person realizes that Negroes differ from each other just the same as other people do. He notices their individuality just as clearly as he notices the differences in appearance of white people. His perceptual discriminations in this case are not blunted by socially learned values.

Culture influences our perception in more extensive ways than just through the discriminations it teaches us to make. It is extremely important in forming our values and our point of view, which are constantly involved in our perception and interpretation of the workaday world. Consider the industrialist and the labor leader, and think how different their perceptions are of each other and of their joint problems. The industrialist may perceive the labor leader as a harebrained Communist or at least an unrealistic Socialist who is out to ruin him. The labor leader in turn may perceive the industrialist as a man without social conscience who is out to exploit the workingman for every bit of profit he can. Though both may be in possession of the same facts, the way they perceive their company and almost everything connected with it is quite different, and the perceptions of neither of them would correspond with those of a neutral observer. In Chapters 13 and 14, we shall consider in more detail the relationship of perception to attitudes and prejudice.

Perception and motivation. It is common knowledge that we seldom convince people in an argument. Where people are emotionally involved they tend to see what they want to see, hear what they want to hear, and believe what they want to believe. Love is blind, and the man in love is notoriously poor in perceiving the faults in his loved one. On the other hand, these faults are only too painfully evident to more neutral observers such as his parents. His parents "for the life of them can't understand what he sees in that bleached blonde." Such examples are simply more cases of personal motives and values influencing perception.

Throughout this book we have learned to accept with caution many of the things the layman considers as obvious. In this case, however, the layman's "common knowledge" is substantially correct. Our own wants and acquired values can influence our perception. In one experiment,[9] for example, nursery school children, ages three to five, were presented with a machine which had a crank on it. They received a poker chip for turning the crank 18 turns. By putting this poker chip into a slot, they could obtain candy. Before the experiment began, however, each child estimated the size of the poker chip by comparing it with a white disk whose size could be varied by the experimenter until the child said the two objects matched. Again, after the children had been rewarded with candy for cranking out poker chips, estimates of size were made. The poker chips now seemed significantly larger to the children. The experimenters then instituted an extinction procedure (p. 112) during which the children got no candy for their efforts in cranking. Estimates of size were again made. The chips had shrunk back to their former size. After that, the children were again rewarded with candy, and the chips increased again in apparent size.

This experiment, which is only one of several that might be described, indicates that as the poker chip acquired value—represented something the child wanted—it was perceived as larger than when it had no value. It supports the general conclusion that a person's motivation affects his perception of even such simple physical characteristics as size.

Generally speaking, however, it is in the perceiving of such complex things as social and interpersonal relationships that our own internal needs and biases have their greatest effect. The concrete objects in our world do not allow us much freedom in perception. Everyone perceives them in much the same way. The table, the chair, the bookcase—everyone sees them as such. The occasional atypical individual who does not winds up in a psychiatrist's office. On the other hand, such social situations as parties, conversations, and contacts with friends or associates are often indefinite and ambiguous. Our perceptions of them are less stable and definite than are our perceptions of physical objects. How many times, for example, have you pondered over just what your friend "meant by that remark"? We all remember cases in which a remark was perceived as an insult or slight by one person but was seen as a compliment by another. Most of us have been victims, at one time or another, of having our remarks and behavior misperceived or misinterpreted by others.

SUMMARY

1. There are several basic principles of perception. One is that we perceive best what we attend to. Attention divides the field of experience into a focus that is clearly perceived and a margin of which we are only dimly aware.

2. In general, the larger a stimulus and the more intense it is, the more it commands attention and the better it is perceived.

3. Any contrast between what we are accustomed to and a new situation enhances our perception of the situation.

4. The repetition of a stimulus or its movement is more effective than a stationary stimulus presented only once.

5. Motivation and set affect perception. We tend to perceive what we want to perceive and what we expect to perceive.

6. Perceptual processes organize the world around a person into objects and groups of objects. Thus he tends to perceive as a group (*a*) those objects that are close together, (*b*) those that are similar to each other, (*c*) those that are symmetrically arranged, and (*d*) those that form some continuous line or pattern.

7. Objects are usually seen as figures on a ground. It is, in fact, almost impossible to "see" them any other way. Such figure-ground perception depends, in turn, on the perception of contours marking off an object from its background.

8. Perception also tends to fill in gaps, so that a person sees a whole object even when some of its parts are missing.

9. Apparent movement is a special example of such "filling in," for it is a perception of movement when there is no movement merely because different still objects are presented in close succession.

10. Even though the retina of the eye is flat and receives a two-dimensional picture, a person usually perceives three-dimensional depth because he makes use of several cues for depth. Most of these cues are monocular, some are binocular, and some may be kinesthetic.

11. The principal monocular cues are (*a*) linear perspective, (*b*) clearness, (*c*) shadows, and (*d*) movement.

12. The chief binocular cue to depth is retinal disparity, which is a slight difference in the images projected on the two eyes when they view the same situation.

13. Perhaps kinesthetic cues from muscles of the eyes involved in their focusing and converging also aid depth perception, but we are not certain of this.

14. One of the puzzling facts of perception is that it tends to be relatively constant despite a considerable change in the stimulation of the sense organs. For example, (*a*) shapes usually appear the same whether we view them from an angle or head on; (*b*) sizes tend to appear constant, whether objects are near or far away; and (*c*) brightness similarly remains constant even under rather different illuminations.

15. Perceptions frequently involve the cooperation of different senses. What one hears, for example, affects what one sees, and impulses from the muscle sense can alter one's visual perception.

16. Perceptions are also modified greatly by learning. A person can learn to adjust fairly well to wearing glasses that reverse right and left and turn the world upside down.

17. As objects take on new meanings in experience, these meanings affect perception. Society and culture indirectly affect perception by fashioning our motives, prejudices, and social values.

SUGGESTIONS FOR FURTHER READING

Blake, R. R., & Ramsey, G. V. (Eds.). *Perception: an approach to personality.* New York: Ronald, 1951.

> *A symposium containing discussions of various aspects of perception, especially those influenced by social and cultural factors.*

Boring, E. G. *Sensation and perception in the history of experimental psychology.* New York: Appleton-Century-Crofts, 1942.

> *An authoritative history of concepts, problems, and experiments in the field of perception.*

Carr, H. A. *An introduction to space perception.* New York: Longmans, 1935.

> *A text summarizing the older work on depth perception.*

Chapanis, A., Garner, W. R., & Morgan, C. T. *Applied experimental psychology.* New York: Wiley, 1949. Chaps. 4–9.

> *A text that presents applications of the principles of perception to problems of engineering design.*

Gibson, J. J. *The perception of the visual world.* Boston: Houghton Mifflin, 1950.

> *An account with many illustrations of recent experiments in visual perception.*

Köhler, W. *Gestalt psychology* (2d Ed.). New York: Liveright, 1947. Chaps. 4–6.

    Contains chapters on the classical work of gestalt psychologists on organizing tendencies in perception.

Lawrence, M. *Studies in human behavior.* Princeton, N.J.: Princeton Univ. Press, 1949.

    A laboratory manual that includes experiments, as well as a discussion, on perception.

Osgood, C. E. *Method and theory in experimental psychology.* New York: Oxford Univ. Press, 1953.

    An advanced text covering theory and experiments in the field of perception.

Woodworth, R. S., & Schlosberg, H. *Experimental psychology* (Rev. Ed.). New York: Holt, 1954.

    A text in experimental psychology containing chapters on perception and attention.

Chapter 8 PSYCHOLOGICAL MEASUREMENT

PROGRESS IN SCIENCE often depends upon the development of quantitative methods. Without such methods, science is limited to crude observation and classification. With them, it can greatly extend and refine the conclusions it can draw from its data. To take a simple example, people knew for a long time that stones fall when they are dropped, but physics made little progress as a science until its early scientists began to measure how fast stones fall, how far they fall in a period of time, and whether stones fall as fast as apples. The situation is much the same in psychology. Even the ancients recognized that some people are slow-witted and others nimble-witted; some courageous and others timid. Psychology, however, only began to be a science when it could measure such differences, attach

meaningful numbers to them, and then make useful predictions about them.

Although the problems of measurement are much the same in all sciences, psychologists are probably more concerned about the logic of measurement than are most other scientists. The reason for this is that many of the things they want to measure are rather complex. Courage, for example, is not the same sort of thing as the length of a table; there is no simple yardstick you can stand up beside a man to measure his courage. Although, fortunately, not everything psychological is as difficult to measure as courage, much of it is of this order of complexity. Psychologists have had to devise roundabout ways of getting at what they want to measure. In so doing, they have tried to make sure that their methods of measurement are sound.

To understand psychological measurements, we should begin with some basic

This chapter was drafted by Alphonse Chapanis of The Johns Hopkins University.

questions: What do numbers mean? How do we assign them to the observations we make? What can we do with them, once we have them, to arrive at trustworthy conclusions? These are questions we shall try to answer in this chapter.

SCALES OF MEASUREMENT

Offhand, one might think that we are asking a simple question when we say, "What do numbers mean?" Actually this is a difficult question and one for which philosophers of science have only recently provided a satisfactory answer.

Part of their answer is that numbers may mean many different things depending upon the mathematical rules one wishes to follow.[1] Mathematics is a kind of game, or set of games, in which the rules—sometimes rather complicated rules—tell you what you can and cannot do with the things you play with (the numbers). One rule of ordinary arithmetic, which is only one of the "games" of mathematics, is that $1 + 2 = 2 + 1$. This, however, is not a necessary rule, and mathematicians sometimes handle numbers according to rules in which this is not true.

A second part of the answer to the question, "What do numbers mean?" is that numbers acquire scientific meaning only when they are assigned to real objects or events according to definite rules. Or, to put it another way, *only when we have a set of rules for pairing numbers with objects or events do we have numbers that can be used in measurement.* There are several sets of such rules, and each yields its own particular *scale of measurement.*[2] Four basic scales of measurement are discussed in the following paragraphs: (1) nominal scales, (2) ordinal scales, (3) interval scales, and (4) ratio scales.

Nominal scales. The simplest way to assign numbers to objects is to use them as substitutes for names. Whenever we do that—and we do it quite often in everyday life—we are constructing a nominal scale. Postal-zone numbers, for example, are nothing more than names for certain sections of large cities. The numbers that football and basketball players wear, social-security numbers, army serial numbers, model numbers assigned to automobiles, refrigerators, and television sets—all these are illustrations of numbers used for purposes of identification. *The only rule that must hold in making such nominal scales is that we assign the same number to identical things and different numbers to things that are different.*

Since this is the only rule for nominal scales, it is obvious that they are of limited use. You could, if you wanted, subtract, multiply, and divide the numbers in nominal scales, but the results of such arithmetic would be meaningless. It makes no sense to add the postal-zone numbers 13 and 5 for two street addresses in New York City, for the result, 18, is of no use whatsoever. Nor is there any use in adding army serial numbers or the numbers of football players. Such arithmetic is meaningless because it makes no sense to add, subtract, or multiply the things (street addresses, soldiers, or players) that have only nominal numbers.

Nevertheless, there are two important uses of nominal scales. In psychology, as in other sciences, you find numbers used to *label* subjects, animals, and traits. This helps us to identify and then to keep straight what we are talking about, but we must be careful to recognize the numbers for what they are and not to assign them more refined properties of measurement. Another use we can make of nominal scales is to *count* whatever it is we label. Once we have identified an event, we count how many times it happens, even if we cannot measure its size, weight, or any other property of it. One may not, for example, be able to measure the intensity of support for a political candidate, but one can count the votes for one candidate and those for his opponent. Such counting often proves to be a very useful kind of measurement in psychology.

Ordinal scales. If, in pairing numbers with things, we can also assign some sort of order, such as relative size, position, or magnitude to the things, we can construct a somewhat more useful scale, an ordinal scale. There are two simple rules to follow in making up such a scale. As in the nominal scale, the first rule is that the numbers must tell you about equality or inequality (identity or nonidentity). If two men have the same intelligence, they get assigned the same number; if they have different amounts of intelligence, they get different numbers. The second rule is that the numbers must also tell you about "less than" or "greater than." If one man is more intelligent than another, he gets the higher number. It is also possible to assign him a lower number if a less intelligent person is given a higher number. It makes no difference in ordinal scales whether numbers run from high to low or low to high. All that is necessary is that we be able to tell, not only when two things are alike and when they differ, but also the *direction* in which they differ.

▪ *Examples.* One of the most common examples of an ordinal scale is the street address, for in general the numbers on houses along any block form such a scale. If you are walking along a street and see the number 136 and then the number 140, you are sure that you must continue walking in the same direction if you want to find the number 150. Sometimes, the number 150 is five houses beyond 140, but occasionally it is next door to 140. So the distances between numbers do not correspond exactly to the distances between houses; only the direction is completely trustworthy. There are many other examples of ordinal scales in everyday life—hardness of minerals, the grading of lumber or wool, and (very often) grades in courses.

Most scales in psychology are ordinal scales, because although it is easy to find out that individual A has more of a certain trait than individual B, it is difficult to find out exactly how much more. As a result, *most rating scales, personality tests, intelligence tests, and aptitude tests yield numbers that form ordinal scales.* By no means all psychological measurements are ordinal scales, but so many are that it is important to keep in mind just what they do and do not measure.

▪ *Meaning.* All that one can really trust in ordinal measurements is the order of numbers, not the differences between them. Suppose, for example, that a group of students rates three professors on teaching ability. Suppose too that all the students agree that Professor A is a better lecturer than B, and that C is the poorest lecturer of the three. In this case, we can assign any set of three numbers to the three professors so long as the numbers are in the same order as the ratings. We might assign the number 3 to A, 2 to B, and 1 to C; or we might assign them the numbers 30, 29, 1; or even 2.1, 2, and 1. Any of these sets of numbers will do because we have agreement only that A is better than B and B better than C. Whatever numbers are used it is important to remember that *only the order of the numbers, not the differences between them, is meaningful.*

Interval scales. Whenever possible, of course, it is desirable to assign numbers so that the differences between them, as well as their order, can be meaningful. If we can do this, we have an interval scale, for such a scale carries the guarantee that differences

—the intervals—are meaningful. As a consequence it becomes permissible to add and subtract the numbers on a scale and thus to say that a difference between two numbers is so much more, equal to, or so much less than a difference between two other numbers.

■ *Temperature scales.* Thermometers are good examples of interval scales (see Figure 8.1). The common thermometer uses the Fahrenheit scale, which is marked off so that 32°F represents freezing and 212°F represents boiling. The numbers in between these points were set up to correspond to a definite physical event—the expansion and contraction of a liquid or solid. Thus, you may find on a particular thermometer that a rise of ½ millimeter in a column of mercury means an increase in temperature of 1°F. The important point, however, is that a ½-millimeter change in the height of the mercury *always* means a 1° change in temperature, no matter whether you are talking about the difference between 0° and 1°, between 53° and 54°, or between 153° and 154°. It is this equality up and down the thermometer that is the essential characteristic of an interval scale.

It is important to note, though, what you cannot do with interval scales. You cannot say that one number means twice, or so many times, as much of something as another number. In the Fahrenheit scale, for example, 100°F is not twice as much heat as 50°F. If you are tempted to think so, note the inconsistency as soon as you convert into the centigrade scale. This scale is found on thermometers which scientists commonly use, and in it 0°C is assigned to freezing, 100°C to boiling. Since 100°F equals 38°C, and 50°F equals 10°C, you can see that 38°C is not twice 10°C. Remember that the temperatures have not changed—only the scale and numbers have changed. This is a way of illustrating that

the ratios of numbers on an interval scale are not meaningful; only the relative differences between them are.

■ *Interval scales in psychology.* With a little ingenuity, the psychologist frequently can devise interval scales for the measurement of human characteristics. To do this he must have some way of measuring *differences* among people having various amounts of these characteristics. Although we now have several ways of measuring such differences, one will serve as an illustration.

Suppose that we ask 100 students to rate Professors A, B, and C on their teaching ability. And suppose that 75 per cent of the students agree that A is better than B. If 60 per cent of them rate B better than C, the psychologist says that the difference be-

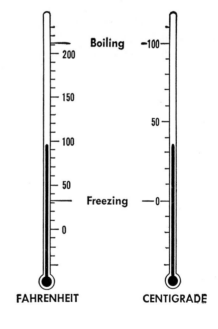

Fig. 8.1. The Fahrenheit and centigrade temperature scales as examples of interval scales. On these scales, equal differences between numbers represent equal differences in temperature, but one cannot say that 60° is twice as hot as 30°.

tween A and B is greater than the difference between B and C. If 75 per cent of the students rate B better than C, he says that the difference between A and B is exactly the same as the difference between B and C. Or if 90 per cent should rate B better than C, he would say that the difference between B and C is greater than the difference between A and B. In drawing such a conclusion, we are relying on a theorem known as the *law of comparative judgment*, which states that *equally noticed differences are equal*.[3]

In practice we need to rate more than three people in order to construct an interval scale, and there are several detailed statistical steps in the procedure that involve a certain amount of theory.[4] The important point, though, is that, if we have some way of measuring differences in ratings or characteristics, we can construct an interval scale in which differences between numbers have some meaning.

Ratio scales.   The most refined of all scales of measurement is the ratio scale. It is constructed according to the three rules governing the other three scales, but in addition the *ratio scale obeys the rule that equal numerical ratios represent equal ratios of the event being measured*. This means that we can do with a ratio scale what we cannot do with any other scale: we can divide one number on the scale into another and the resulting ratio is meaningful.

There are not so many ratio scales as you might think, even in the physical sciences. Some good illustrations, however, are the scales of length, weight, and electrical resistance. The numbers on such scales have an absolute zero, and that lets us make statements about both differences and the number of times that one thing exceeds another. An object, for example, that weighs 6 pounds is twice as heavy as one of 3, and three times as heavy as one of 2 pounds.

The same is true of length and electrical resistance. Note that the reason the ratio scale permits such statements is that the zero really means something. Zero pounds mean no weight at all—nobody can find anything that weighs less. The interval scale, in contrast, has an arbitrary zero.

Psychologists hope someday to make ratio scales for many of the characteristics they wish to measure, but they are far from that ideal at the present time. They can, however, utilize a few scales which have ratio properties. Most of them are in the area of perception. One way to set up ratio measurements in this area is to have subjects make judgments of "twice as much" or "half as much." We can, for instance, show a subject a patch of light that has a fixed brightness, then give him a control which enables him to vary the brightness of another patch of light. His instructions are: "Adjust this patch until it is half [or twice, or three-quarters] as bright as that one." You might think that this would be hard to do, but actual experiments show that subjects can do it without complaint and with remarkable consistency. In this way we can make extensive measurements and construct scales of apparent brightness, pitch, loudness, and other magnitudes that are quite as useful for psychology as scales in the physical sciences (see Chapter 19).

Meaning of numbers.   This brief description of scales of measurement brings out the fact that numbers can mean many different things. What they mean depends on the rules one uses to assign numbers to characteristics that are measured. Only by understanding these rules can we tell what numbers do and do not mean. Because psychologists attempt to measure complex things and their scales are sometimes crude, it is especially important that we take great care in the interpretation of numerical measurements. *We cannot take numbers for*

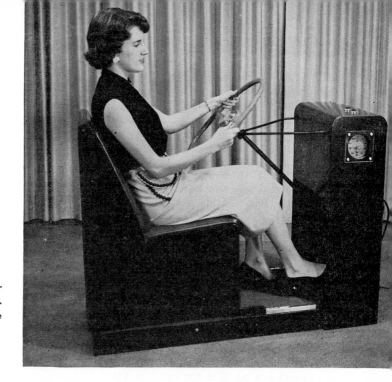

Fig. 8.2. An apparatus for measuring braking reaction time. *(Courtesy American Automobile Association.)*

granted; we must first be sure how they were attached to the things we talk about.

DISTRIBUTIONS OF MEASUREMENTS

Once we have a scale for measuring some human characteristic, our next problem is to know what to say about the measurements we make. This is an especially difficult problem because people differ. They differ in height, weight, intelligence, reaction time, visual acuity, learning ability, honesty, attractiveness, and in all the hundreds of ways in which people can be measured. Sometimes the psychologist is most interested in differences between people, but in other cases his purpose is to make statements which are true for all people. How does he go about making such statements?

It turns out, fortunately, that differences among people are not completely random. In fact, if one looks at the differences in the right way, he can find regularity and consistency even in the way people differ from

each other. This "right way" of looking at the data is a special kind of mathematics called statistics. In the remaining sections of this chapter, we shall describe some of the statistics that we use in looking at psychological measurements. Our purpose in doing this is (1) to provide a common basis for understanding some of the statistical terms that appear in later chapters, and (2) to outline a way of thinking about psychological characteristics that should prove helpful in understanding the world we live in.

An example. A psychologist once wanted to find out how long it takes automobile drivers to react to a red light by putting their feet on a brake pedal. To do this, he built a mock-up of an automobile, consisting of a seat, a steering wheel, an accelerator, and a brake pedal. In front of the driver he showed a moving panorama and a red light to simulate a real driving situation. He arranged the red light in an electrical circuit with a clock so that he could turn the red light on whenever he wanted to and at the

TABLE 8.1. Braking reaction times (in seconds) of 200 normal young men on a test of automobile driving.

0.65	0.42	0.66	0.77	0.61	0.82	0.44	0.68	0.48	0.60
0.61	0.48	0.64	0.58	0.43	0.55	0.71	0.62	0.54	0.62
0.75	0.67	0.46	0.66	0.57	0.54	0.72	0.43	0.76	0.53
0.70	0.77	0.58	0.51	0.55	0.73	0.41	0.56	0.53	0.48
0.74	0.46	0.57	0.48	0.90	0.60	0.63	0.64	0.75	0.55
0.69	0.62	0.64	0.57	0.73	0.56	0.49	0.66	0.70	0.59
0.72	0.62	0.66	0.56	0.59	0.60	0.57	0.49	0.64	0.66
0.45	0.83	0.69	0.78	0.51	0.58	0.66	0.61	0.64	0.56
0.53	0.60	0.62	0.65	0.62	0.44	0.61	0.60	0.74	0.64
0.85	0.49	0.51	0.39	0.58	0.64	0.69	0.68	0.52	0.74
0.55	0.68	0.61	0.40	0.56	0.59	0.45	0.59	0.65	0.62
0.46	0.64	0.36	0.72	0.41	0.74	0.51	0.58	0.69	0.55
0.50	0.55	0.56	0.49	0.65	0.51	0.62	0.67	0.48	0.48
0.60	0.63	0.61	0.64	0.58	0.60	0.73	0.95	0.69	0.52
0.78	0.70	0.54	0.58	0.65	0.51	0.72	0.63	0.54	0.45
0.42	0.47	0.55	0.65	0.56	0.74	0.54	0.66	0.58	0.70
0.59	0.57	0.49	0.63	0.66	0.46	0.57	0.88	0.61	0.46
0.47	0.62	0.55	0.66	0.51	0.53	0.52	0.59	0.53	0.56
0.70	0.47	0.68	0.57	0.54	0.67	0.48	0.57	0.68	0.58
0.63	0.72	0.62	0.39	0.63	0.67	0.57	0.68	0.61	0.52

same instant start counting the time. He also arranged the circuit so that the driver stopped the clock whenever he moved the brake pedal 1 centimeter. In this way, it was possible to measure exactly the brake-reaction time of the driver.

He made at least one brake-reaction-time measurement on each of 200 men, and the 200 measurements are listed in Table 8.1. If you look them over for a moment, you will see that they tend to average around 0.50 to 0.60 second and that they seem to vary from about 0.45 to 0.75 second. Looking them over is not a very satisfactory way to find out what they really are like. If we want to understand them in detail, we must do something that is a little more precise.

Frequency distributions. The first thing a statistician usually does with measurements like these is to arrange and group them numerically in a way that we can most easily understand. He constructs a *frequency*

distribution (Table 8.2). Since individual scores, in this case, are not important by themselves, he makes them more compact by squeezing them into *classes*. Each class includes all scores between certain limits. In Table 8.2, for example, the seventh class from the top shows how many men had scores between 0.75 and 0.77 second, inclusive. Each other class has similar limits set the same distance apart, and there are as many classes as are necessary to include all the scores. This grouping of scores into classes is called a frequency distribution because it permits us to count the *frequency* of scores in each of the classes and then to see how the frequencies are *distributed* among the various classes.

In making such a frequency distribution,

TABLE 8.2. Frequency distribution of the data in Table 8.1. A large number of scores may be summarized by grouping them into classes, then counting the frequency f of scores falling in each class.

Class limits, seconds		Frequency f
From	To	(numbers of men)
0.93	0.95	1
0.90	0.92	1
0.87	0.89	1
0.84	0.86	1
0.81	0.83	2
0.78	0.80	2
0.75	0.77	5
0.72	0.74	13
0.69	0.71	11
0.66	0.68	19
0.63	0.65	21
0.60	0.62	25
0.57	0.59	24
0.54	0.56	22
0.51	0.53	16
0.48	0.50	13
0.45	0.47	11
0.42	0.44	6
0.39	0.41	5
0.36	0.38	1

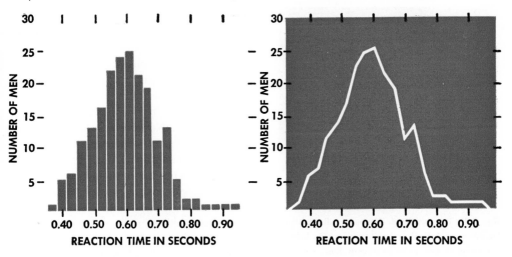

Fig. 8.3. Histogram (left) and frequency polygon (right) of the data in Tables 8.1 and 8.2.

something is lost and something is gained. What is lost is (1) the identity of individual measurements—we cannot, for example, any longer tell from Table 8.2 what the score is for the twenty-seventh man; and (2) the precise value of any individual measurement—we cannot tell, for example, what the five measurements were like in the seventh class. However, the losses are more than offset by what is gained.

The most immediate gain is an increase in the information conveyed by the frequency distribution about the groups as a whole. We can see at a glance that most of the men had scores between 0.60 and 0.62. With only scattered exceptions, the rest had scores between 0.39 and 0.83. Then, by doing a little counting, we can see that nearly half (46 per cent) had scores between 0.54 and 0.65. Thus the construction of a frequency distribution has helped us to appreciate quickly the general nature of our measurements.

Normal curve. From the frequency distribution it is only a short step to the *histogram* and *frequency polygon* (see Figure 8.3). To construct a histogram, one

merely draws a graph of a frequency distribution so that the classes are arranged along the base line (abscissa) and a vertical line or bar represents the frequency of scores in each class. The histogram then is simply an outline or silhouette of a frequency distribution. The frequency polygon shows the same thing in a somewhat different way. To construct a frequency polygon, one first plots the frequency *f* for each class (see Table 8.2) as a point placed at the middle score of the class. Then he connects all the points representing the various *f*s together with a series of lines. The resulting polygon presents the same information as the histogram but in a slightly different way.

From either the histogram or the frequency polygon you can learn something that might not have been obvious in the frequency distribution. Most of the measurements are found near the middle of the distribution. The rest of them tail off from the center toward the two ends of the distribution. In the ideal distribution, all the measures are symmetrically distributed; that is to say, *there are as many on one side of the distribution as on the other side.*

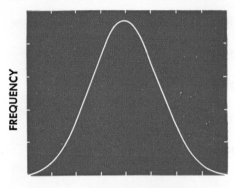

SCALE OF MEASUREMENT

Fig. 8.4. The idealized frequency distribution is known as the normal probability curve. The height of the curve at any point represents the relative frequency of measurements having the particular value indicated on the horizontal axis.

One idealized form of this kind of distribution is called the *normal probability curve* (see Figure 8.4) and is typical of many biological, psychological, and physical measurements. It occurs, in fact, wherever there is a large element of chance entering into a measurement and when each chance event has about a 50-50 probability of occurring. One of the best ways, for example, to obtain such a distribution is to toss pennies. You could put 20 pennies in a jar, shake them up, toss them on the table and count the number of heads from 0 to 20 that appear on each toss. The measurement in this case is the number of heads that turn up. If you repeat this time after time, for say, 100 tosses, and each time tabulate the number of heads, the distribution you get approaches the normal probability curve such as is shown in Figure 8.4.

Many psychological characteristics are much like jars of pennies. Each one is made up of many individual factors combined in chance fashion so that a set of measurements very frequently gives a normal probability curve. The braking-reaction-time ex-

periment above was one example of such a distribution. In Figure 8.5 is another example taken from measurements of intelligence.[5] It depicts the scores of 2,970 children, aged two and one-half to eighteen, measured on one form (Form L) of the Stanford-Binet test of intelligence (see Chapter 15). Notice the bell-shaped symmetry of the measurements. Many other human characteristics—height, weight, strength of grip, learning ability, mechanical ability, cooperativeness, social dominance—yield normally distributed measurements like these. Indeed, we now tend to assume that biological and psychological measurements will be normally distributed—that is, will approximate the normal probability curve—in a large population unless we have good grounds for believing otherwise.

Skewness. Although the measurements of many human characteristics approximate normal curves, those of many others do not. In fact, one kind of distribution the psychologist finds fairly frequently is the *skewed distribution*. Like the normal dis-

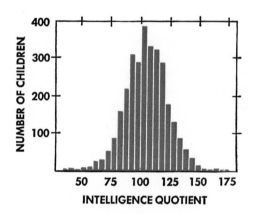

Fig. 8.5. A frequency distribution of the intelligence quotients of 2,970 school children, which approximates the bell-shaped normal curve shown in Fig. 8.4. (Data from McNemar, Q. *The revision of the Stanford-Binet Scale.* Boston: Houghton Mifflin, 1942.)

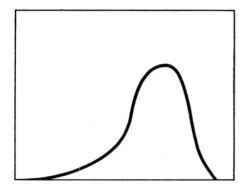
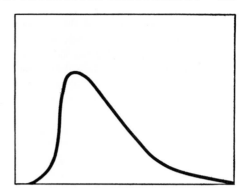

Fig. 8.6. Examples of skewness. A skewed curve has a longer "tail" to one side than to the other. The curve on the left is skewed to the left; that on the right is skewed to the right.

tribution, many skewed distributions have their highest frequencies toward the middle and the lowest frequencies toward the ends of the distribution. The big difference between them, however, is that the highest frequencies are not exactly in the middle of a skewed distribution, as they are in the normal distribution, but rather more to one side or the other. In Figure 8.6 you see two examples of skewed distributions. In some distributions, the skewness is so marked that the highest frequencies occur at one or the other end of the distribution. Many attitude and social measurements yield data of this form.

MEASURES OF CENTRAL TENDENCY

We have now explained the general way in which psychological measurements may yield normal distributions, or occasionally skewed distributions. It is time to turn to some of the specific measures we use to describe such distributions. The first of these are the *measures of central tendency*. Several such measures are available for different purposes, but we will describe the two that are most commonly used: the *mean* and the *median*.

Arithmetic mean. The common *average* is a measure of central tendency. The average is, in fact, so common in our everyday thinking that few people realize that it is one of the important first steps in statistical analysis. It is a single number near the center of the distribution that represents the whole set of measurements. All one needs to do to find an average is to add up all his measurements and divide by the number of measurements he has. Stated in terms of algebra, the formula is

$$M = \frac{\Sigma X}{N}$$

in which Σ is the Greek letter sigma, which we use to mean "sum of," X represents any individual measurement (and thus ΣX means the sum of all individual measurements), N is the number of such measurements, and M is the average or mean. To be strictly correct, we must call this kind of average the *arithmetic mean*, because there are several kinds of averages and this mean is just one of them.

To provide an example of the arithmetic mean and other measures we shall describe, refer to the fifteen scores given in Table 8.3. In most psychological work, it is advisable to have a large number of measurements,

TABLE 8.3.   Computation of the arithmetic mean and standard deviation. The computation proceeds by getting first the sum of X and from that the mean. Then the column of xs can be filled in and the x^2 values computed. From the sum of x^2 one can then obtain the standard deviation σ.

X	X − M = x	(X − M)² = x²
40	22.5	506.25
35	17.5	306.25
33	15.5	240.25
20	2.5	6.25
19	1.5	2.25
19	1.5	2.25
19	1.5	2.25
16	−1.5	2.25
14	−3.5	12.25
11	−6.5	42.25
10	−7.5	56.25
9	−8.5	72.25
7	−10.5	110.25
7	−10.5	110.25
4	−13.5	182.25

$$\Sigma X = 263 \qquad\qquad \Sigma x^2 = 1{,}653.75$$

$$N = 15$$

$$M = \frac{263}{15} = 17.5$$

$$\sigma = \sqrt{\frac{1653.75}{15}} = \sqrt{110.25} = 10.5$$

but for the purposes of this example we have kept the number to fifteen. Also for your convenience we have arranged the scores in order from highest to lowest. Note that the addition of the scores is 263, so ΣX is 263. We have fifteen measurements, so N is 15. The mean, therefore, is 17.5. (The two right-hand columns in Table 8.3, as well as the calculation of Σx^2 and σ, will be explained below.)

Before leaving the arithmetic mean, think back for a moment to what we said about scales of measurement. Nominal and ordinal scales of measurement, you will remember, do not permit one to add or subtract the numbers on the scale, because only the or-

der of the numbers is meaningful. The interval and ratio scales, on the other hand, do permit addition and subtraction because the differences between numbers on these scales, as well as their order, is also meaningful. Now then, in calculating the arithmetic mean, notice that we must add the various scores in order to arrive at the answer, and this implies that we can trust the differences between scores. *An important restriction on the mean, then, is that we use it only with interval and ratio scales,* that is, for measurements in which we can trust *differences.* When used with ordinal or nominal scales, the mean cannot be interpreted, or, if it is, it gives a false description of the data.

The Median. Because the arithmetic mean is calculated by adding all the scores in a distribution, it is usually not very much influenced by the value of any particular score—unless, of course, there are only two or three scores. For that reason we regard the arithmetic mean as a very *stable* measure of central tendency, and we prefer it for most situations in which it is legitimate to use it. As we have just said, however, we cannot trust the mean when the scale of measurement is ordinal, and in that case we must employ a more appropriate measure of central tendency. Furthermore, the mean of skewed distributions is not representative or typical because it is weighted too heavily by extreme values.

In these two cases or in any case that is in doubt, we frequently use the *median* as our measure of central tendency. This is simply the score that ranks exactly in the middle of a distribution of scores. It is therefore an ordinal measurement that does not depend on whether differences along the scale can be trusted. All that it does is give the score that divides the distribution into two parts, an upper half and a lower half. The most direct way to find the median is to arrange all the scores in a distribution in order from lowest to highest, as we have done in Table 8.3, and then count down through one-half of the scores to find the middle score. In the example in Table 8.3, since there are fifteen scores, the middle one is the eighth score. This is 16, so the median is 16. If there is an even number of scores, one obtains the median by taking the score value halfway between the two middle scores.

MEASURES OF VARIABILITY

Measures of central tendency give us only part of the description of the frequency distribution. Such distributions differ from one another not only in central tendency but in their variability. In Figure 8.7, for example, you see two distributions that have exactly the same means, medians, and numbers of cases. One is very slender and the other is quite robust; one has scores grouped near the mean and the other has scores scattering some distance from the mean. To complete our description of a normal distribution, we need some measure of this variability—the degree to which scores spread out from the center of the distribution.

Range. Of several possible measures we might use, the simplest (but not the best) is the *range*. This is the difference between the highest and the lowest scores. In Table 8.3, for example, the data varied from 40 to 4—a range of 36. You can quickly compute that from the scores in Table 8.3. Although it is easy to get, however, the range is a very crude and unstable measure, because it is based on only two measures, the very extreme ones. These, it happens, are rather erratic and only a small change in them will change the size of the range. So statisticians use the range only when all that is needed is a very quick and crude estimate of variability of measurements.

Standard deviation. This is the most precise and most generally useful of the measures of variability. To denote it, we use the small Greek letter sigma (σ). You can see at a glance how it is computed by inspecting its formula

$$\sigma = \sqrt{\frac{\Sigma(X - M)^2}{N}} \quad \text{or} \quad \sqrt{\frac{\Sigma x^2}{N}}$$

in which the symbols, except for x, are used as they have been in previous formulas. Note first that the initial step in computing the standard deviation is to subtract the mean from each score of the distribution. This is $X - M$. (Statisticians commonly use the small letter x to stand for the difference $X - M$.) It is because we must rely on the meaningfulness of differences to make this step that the scales with which the standard deviation is used must be interval or ratio scales. In this way we convert all scores into *deviations* from the arithmetic mean. The next step is to take the square of each of these deviation scores, and the reason for that is to give somewhat more weight to the extreme scores than to those near the

Fig. 8.7. Distributions differing in variability. Both distributions have the same central tendency, but one is narrow and the other is robust. Consequently, they have different variabilities (standard deviations).

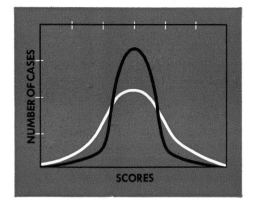

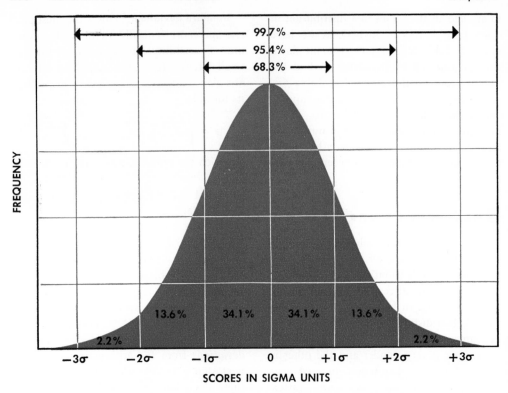

Fig. 8.8. The distribution of scores in a normal curve. Because the normal curve has a known shape, it is possible to state the per cent of scores that lie between plus and minus one standard deviation, or between any other two points expressed in terms of σ units.

center. (Squaring large deviation scores gives proportionately larger numbers than squaring small deviation scores.) The last steps, in quick succession are (1) summing all the squares of the deviations, (2) dividing the sum by N and thus getting an average or mean of the squared deviations, and finally (3) taking the square root of this mean-square deviation. Just to make sure you understand these steps, run through the example in Table 8.3. (When there are large numbers of measurements, we have statistical formulas for computing the standard deviation more efficiently.)

Using measures of variability. Having described some measures of variability, we are now in a position to ask, What good are they? One obvious answer is that they tell us how widely scattered our measurements are. The smaller the measure of variability, the more closely are the scores grouped around the mean. In addition, however, measures of variability often tell us rather precisely how scores are distributed. They do that because the normal curve is of a particular shape, and once we know the mean or median and the measure of variability all we have to do is look at tables of the normal curve and we can then reconstruct the whole distribution of measurements. It is only proper, however, to reconstruct a normal curve from the mean and sigma when we are fully justified in assuming that the original measurements are, in fact, normally distributed.

This point is illustrated in Figure 8.8. There you can see that, knowing the mean and the standard deviation, we can completely describe the normal distribution and say exactly how many scores fall between any two points on the sigma scale. To be more specific, the statistician knows that 68.3 per cent of all cases in a normal distribution lie in the range between 1σ above and 1σ below the mean. About 95 per cent lie in the range between 2σ above and 2σ below the mean. And 99.7 per cent fall between 3σ above and 3σ below the mean. Thus, assuming that the distribution is reasonably normal, the mean and the standard deviation, taken together, give an almost complete description of a frequency distribution.

▪ *Standard scores.* One especially valuable use of the standard deviation merits special mention. We have already mentioned the deviation score $(X - M)$ in the course of explaining the standard deviation. If, after the standard deviation is computed, we divide any such deviation score by the standard deviation, we have a new expression that is called the *standard score* or z score. This may be calculated for every score in a distribution so that we obtain a complete distribution of standard scores. The great advantages of such standard scores are that we can interpret them quite precisely in relation to other scores and that we can compare two or more measures for one individual that have different means and standard deviations. From the curve in Figure 8.9, or better yet from tables that are readily available giving such information in greater detail, we can tell exactly how many cases lie above and below any particular standard score. In this way, we obtain a relative score that takes account of both the

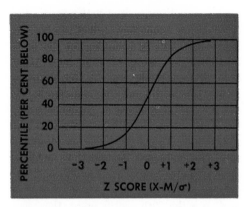

Fig. 8.9. The use of the standard deviation to find standard scores and percentile scores. Any individual's score (X) on a test may be subtracted from the mean (M) to obtain a deviation score (x). Dividing this by the standard deviation (σ) yields a standard score (z score). Such scores may be compared with each other even when they have been derived from quite different tests. By referring to the curve above or to a table of the probability integral, one can determine the per cent of cases falling below any particular z score. This is often called the percentile score.

mean and standard deviation of a distribution. To interpret it we no longer have to know what either the mean or the standard deviation actually was.*

▪ *Centile scores.* There are occasions on which one cannot use, or does not wish to use, the standard score. If one's measurements are not on interval or ratio scales so that the differences between them cannot be trusted, the standard score cannot be used. At other times, one may have to present his measurements to people who do not understand the standard score or standard deviation and who do not have time to

---

* Sometimes the z score and the mean are multiplied arbitrarily by some constant just to make numbers more convenient to handle. The resulting scores may also be called standard scores (see Chap. 15).

learn. In such cases, it is better to use the centile score (sometimes called the percentile score). This is a ranking on the basis of 100 cases—irrespective of how many cases there actually are. If, for example, 32 per cent of the measurements are below and 68 per cent above a particular score, the centile score is 32. In this way we can state simply where a particular measurement stands in a distribution and thus make as exact a comparison as we can with a standard score. Notice, incidentally, that the median is the 50th centile point, the lower quartile is the 25th centile point, and the upper quartile is the 75th centile point.

◼ CORRELATION

We have now come about two-thirds of the way in describing statistical measures of frequency distributions. Central tendency was our first main theme; variability was our second. The remaining topic is correlation.

To make clear what we mean by correlation, let us turn to the common example of heights and weights. We know from casual observation that people differ a lot in both height and weight. If we wish, we can take any particular group of people and find their average heights and their average weights. We can also measure the variability of their heights and the variability of their weights. But we know also that there is a connection or *correlation* between height and weight. In general, people who are taller weigh more than those who are short. Obviously, however, the correlation is not perfect, for some people only 5 feet tall weigh more than some 6 feet tall. So the correlation is one of degree—a statistical matter—and we therefore need some measure that expresses that degree.

Correlation Coefficient. The statistical answer to this question can be given by the single number that we call the *correlation*

coefficient. Its symbol is *r*, and the formula for obtaining it is

$$r = \frac{\Sigma xy}{N \sigma_x \sigma_y}$$

when $x = X - M$, $y = Y - M$. You have already encountered x, X, and M. You will remember that x is the deviation score obtained by subtracting a person's score X from the mean M. In this case, x is the deviation score for one type of measurement, and σ_x is the standard deviation of the distribution of all such measurements. Similarly, y is the deviation score for another type of measurement, and σ_y is the standard deviation of the corresponding distribution. If you study the formula a moment, you can see that, since x/σ_x is a standard score for one measurement and y/σ_y is the corresponding standard score for the other measurement, the formula is nothing more than the mean or average of the products of standard scores for each pair of measurements, that is, $r = \Sigma z_x z_y / N$. In practice, there are more rapid ways of calculating the coefficient r than by this formula, but it tells you what the coefficient is.

Some students may understand the nature of correlation better by visualizing it than by trying to understand the formula. For this purpose let us take an example from the measurement of intelligence (Chapter 15). There are two forms of the Stanford-Binet test of intelligence, Form L and Form M. The scores we examined back in Figure 8.5 were scores for children taking Form L of the test. It happens that upon another occasion these same children were also given Form M of the test. So we have two scores for each child, one on Form L and one on Form M. With the formula above we can calculate the correlation coefficient r, and it turns out to be about .90. But let us also look at the data pictorially

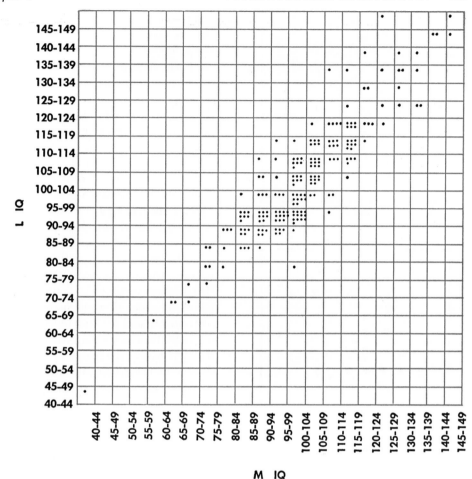

Fig. 8.10. A scattergram of IQs obtained on Form L and Form M of the Stanford-Binet test at chronological age 7. Such a scattergram illustrates the use of correlation to express the reliability of a test, which in this case is quite high. (*Based on Terman, L. M., & Merrill, M. A. Measuring intelligence. Boston: Houghton Mifflin, 1937, p. 45.*)

in the so-called *scatter diagram* (or scattergram) in Figure 8.10. There a pair of scores is represented by one point. Form L scores are shown on the vertical axis; those for the Form M test are shown on the horizontal axis. To locate any child on the diagram we take his score on Form M, find where it belongs on the horizontal axis, then run up vertically until we come to the place where his score on Form L falls.

There we place the point that represents his score on both forms of the intelligence test.

It happens that the scales for the two forms of the test were so constructed that the same person should, ideally, make the same score on each form. If it turned out this way, the correlation between the two forms would be perfect and the correlation coefficient would be 1.00. Moreover, on the

r=0.00

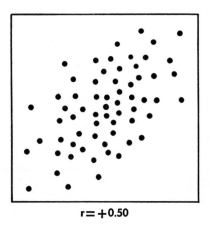

r= +0.50

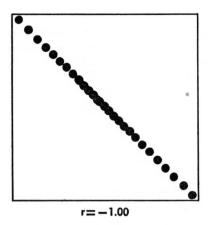

r= −1.00

Fig. 8.11. Scattergrams depicting different amounts of positive and negative correlation.

scatter diagram one would see a perfectly straight line of points running from the lower left-hand corner toward the upper right-hand corner. In Figure 8.10 the scores fall around the straight line but tend to stray in one direction or another a little off the diagonal. What this means is that a person making a score on one test tends to make a somewhat different score on the other form. Thus the correlation is not quite perfect but is, in fact, about .90.

Degrees of correlation. In Figure 8.11 we have used this pictorial method of representing other degrees of correlation. Consider the case of zero correlation when $r = .00$. This means that there is no correlation between the two distributions and that a person making a certain score on one test is no more likely to make that same score on a second test than any other person is. There then is no diagonal on the scattergram; instead, the points fill a circle, most densely in the center and more thinly toward its edge, as one might predict from the normal curve. Between the circle (which represents no correlation) and the diagonal straight line (which represents a perfect correlation) scattergrams can make a variety of ellipses. The more the ellipse approaches a straight line, the higher the correlation.

Before closing this account of correlation, we should note that correlations can be negative as well as positive. When a low score on one measurement corresponds to a high score on another type of measurement and vice versa, the correlation is negative. There is a negative correlation, for example, between the number of errors a student makes on an objective test and his letter grade in the course; the more errors, the lower the grade. A correlation coefficient of − 1.00 is the number representing perfect negative correlation. And, of course, there can be all degrees of negative correlation just as there can of positive correlation.

Minus signs and plus signs in front of correlation coefficients may represent equally close relationships; the sign merely tells us the direction of the relationship.

Causation and correlation. Finally, a word about the interpretation of correlations. Many people think that a high correlation between two sets of measurements means that one of the factors measured *causes* the other. This is usually not so. When there is a high correlation, both sets of individual differences are usually caused by some common factors. In the case of height and weight, for example, we cannot say that a person's height causes his weight, for both height and weight are caused by individual differences in genetic inheritance, nutrition, diseases, etc. A correlation, in short, simply tells us that individual differences in two sets of measurements tend to vary together, not necessarily that one causes the other.

THE INTERPRETATION OF MEASUREMENTS

The measures we have just described may be called *descriptive statistics* because they serve to describe accurately the characteristics of a set of measurements. When we make measurements, however, we are interested not only in describing them but also in *interpreting* them. We want to make inferences from them about people in general or about the basic principles of behavior. To make such interpretations requires some additional statistics.

Representative sampling. The first concept that is essential to interpreting statistical descriptions is that all measurement implies *sampling*. We usually cannot measure all cases of anything, whether it be of animal learning, of perception, of intelligence, of attitudes, of public opinions, or of anything else. There are always too many

animals or people in the world and too many events to allow us to measure all cases in which we might be interested. So when we measure, whether we realize it or not, we are selecting a sample of the total possible measurements we might make.

Ordinarily we try to select a sample that is large enough and representative enough to tell us about a much larger set of measurements we were unable to make. When, for example, psychologists try to measure public opinion regarding presidential candidates, they try to get a representative sample or cross section of the population and then to take enough measurements to represent this population. From their measurements, they predict or infer the opinions of the electorate at large. In our example of intelligence-test scores, those who made the measurements were interested in getting a sample of school children representative enough to reflect the frequency distribution of intelligence at large.

▪ *Biases of samples.* It is not always an easy task to get representative samples. In fact, the most frequent fault with a set of measurements is that it is not representative[6] and that we therefore cannot properly make the inferences from it that we would like. We run into this difficulty because there are always so many "biasing" factors at work. It may happen that, because of factors we are not aware of, the school children in one geographical area may be brighter or duller than school children in general. If we try to sample political opinion by calling people on the telephone, it may happen that people who own telephones are more often of one political opinion than another. If, as many psychologists are forced to do, we use college students for a set of measurements, it may be that they are not representative of the population in general. So various kinds of biases make it difficult to get a representative sample.

■ *Methods of sampling.* We have developed a number of different methods to try to ensure representative sampling, and some of these methods will be described in detail in later chapters (see Chapter 13). In general, they take two different forms. One we may call *random sampling.* We use this when we know little or nothing about biasing factors in our measurement. To sample randomly, we try to see that only chance determines what is included in our sample. In making surveys of radio listening, for example, we select every two-hundredth name in the telephone directory. Or to measure intelligence, we may draw at random two out of every 100 names of children in each of the schools of a state. Or to study learning in rats, we select one out of every ten rats in the laboratory.

The other general method of obtaining a representative sample is to do *controlled sampling.* In this case we select certain factors such as age, sex, economic status, educational level, type of employment, etc., and deliberately counterbalance these factors in making up our sample. In sampling public opinion, for example, we may try to see that people are selected from small towns and large towns, from poor people and rich people, from the West and East, from labor and from management—all in proportion to their numbers in the population at large. This kind of sampling, if it is done correctly, makes reasonably certain that biasing factors are controlled. Thus it is the most economical sampling, because it is usually possible to make correct inferences from a smaller number of cases by controlled sampling than by random sampling.

Reliability of measurements. Another problem that frequently arises in interpreting statistics is the question of reliability of measurements. What we have just been saying assumes that our measuring stick is all right and that we are concerned only with errors in the sample to which we apply that measuring stick. Quite aside from the sample, however, we can have errors in the measuring stick or method of measurement. It is these that we consider under the heading of reliability of measurement.

This problem can be illustrated by considering an example that, we hope, is quite unrealistic. A professor has given his class an examination, and now his somewhat odious task is to grade it. In this case he has no sampling problems because he has obtained papers from all members of the class. All he has to do is choose a measuring stick, that is, a method of scoring them. One possible method is to throw them down the stairs and, assigning a number to each step, grade each paper according to the step it falls on. If he does this, the chances are he will get a frequency distribution (which might even be a normal curve) from which he could obtain a mean and a standard deviation.

There are two obvious faults in this method of grading: it is invalid, and it is unreliable. We shall come to validity later, so let us think now only about reliability. This method would be unreliable simply because it would not give the same answer twice. It would not check itself. If the professor gathered up the papers and threw them down the stairs a second time, he would not get the same score for the same paper. Assuming that the papers landed randomly on the steps, the score a person got on the second grading would bear no relation to the score on the first grading. That is why we say this method is *unreliable.*

There is a statistical method for inferring quite precisely the relative reliability or unreliability of a set of measurements, and it is the correlational method we have already described. By correlating one set of scores with another set obtained by the same method, we have a number describing the reliability of the measurements. This, indeed, was the primary purpose of having two forms of intelligence test, Form L and Form M, in the example we have used. Using two forms to test intelligence is like grading papers independently on two separate occasions. If the results correlate well, as they do in the case of intelligence, then we can assume that our measuring instrument is measuring something reliably. If they do not, our measurements are unreliable—we might as well be throwing papers down the stairs.

Reliability is a *sine qua non* of psychological measurement. If measurement is not reliable, it cannot be much of anything else. If, in other words, we cannot get the same set of scores, or almost the same set of scores, for people on two successive, independent measurements, we are not really measuring. Flipping pennies, playing dice, or spinning roulette wheels would be just about as good. To put the matter another way, if some measuring instrument cannot be correlated rather well with itself, it certainly cannot correlate well with anything else, and thus it is useless for making inferences about anything.

Validity of measurements. A good measurement must not only be reliable, it must also be valid. That is to say, it must measure what it is intended to measure. Another example of examination grading may make this clear. An essay examination is generally supposed to provide a measurement of a person's knowledge and grasp of his subject, not of how many words he can write. Counting words, however, is highly reliable measurement, and if a professor should take to counting he could arrive at some highly reliable grades. In fact such a method of grading would undoubtedly be the most *reliable* of all methods and would give a correlation coefficient between two different counts of each person's words of almost 1.00. Although highly reliable, this method would not be valid, simply because it would not measure what it is supposed to measure.

This problem of validity of measurement is a very serious one for psychologists. It is relatively easy, although not so easy as one might suppose, to devise measuring instruments that are reliable. It is much harder to devise *valid* measures. To determine the validity of measurements, once their reliability has been established, we again use the correlational method. In this case, however, we must have some *criterion* that represents what we want to measure with which to correlate our measurements. One of the major criteria of intelligence, for example, is ability to learn and to solve problems, or to put it more generally, the ability to profit by education. The criterion, then, of an intelligence test *might* be success in school. To assess the validity of an intelligence test, we might therefore correlate a person's scores on intelligence tests with his educational progress—his grades or how far he has progressed for his age. If the correlation is high, we may say that the intelligence test is valid; if it is low, it is not so valid. To take another example, if our purpose is to select pilots, our criterion would be whether they succeed or fail in their training for flying. When we have tests that correlate well with such success or failure, we say they are valid. If they do not correlate with the criterion, no matter how reliable they may be—no matter how well they correlate with themselves—they are invalid. Validity, then, is a merit index of measuring what we want to measure, and we obtain it in statistical terms by correlating measurements with some criterion that represents what we want to measure

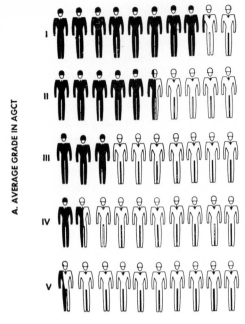

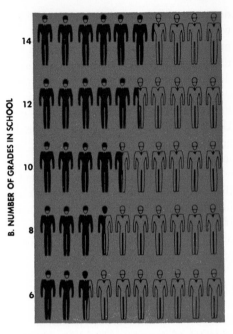

TANK MECHANICS

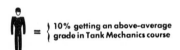 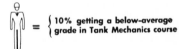

= { 10% getting an above-average grade in Tank Mechanics course

= { 10% getting a below-average grade in Tank Mechanics course

Fig. 8.12. Predicting success in tank driver's school from number of grades completed in school and from scores on the AGCT test. A valid test predicts what it is supposed to predict. In this case, the AGCT predicts success in tank driver's school better than number of grades of education completed. (*After Boring, E. G. (Ed.). Psychology for the armed services. Washington, D.C.: Combat Forces Press, 1945, p. 251.*)

Prediction from correlations. You have now learned that both reliability and validity are necessary characteristics of measurements. Without reliability we cannot hope to make a useful interpretation of measurements, but with it we must also have validity in order to say anything about what measurements represent. Once we have reliable and valid measurements, there are many possible interpretations of them, depending on our purpose, and we shall see many examples throughout the book. One of the most practical benefits of valid

measurements, however, is the *prediction* of events.

To illustrate this point, let us take an example from some measurements made during the Second World War. The Army was faced with the general problem of selecting men for specialized training—in this particular case, training in a tank-mechanics course. Naturally it wanted to pick men who were most likely to succeed in such training. As you see in Figure 8.12, there is some correlation between the number of grades a man has completed in school and his success in the tank-mechanics course. Those who had completed fourteen grades of school had 6 chances in 10 of doing above-average work in the course. Those, however, who had only six grades of school had less than 3 chances in 10 of doing this well. Consequently, the correlation between grades completed and success in the course provided some basis for prediction.

But there was a somewhat higher correlation between the Army General Classification Test[7] and success in the tank-mechanics course. This test, which we shall discuss at more length in Chapters 15 and 16, is a test of intelligence especially designed for the purposes of the Armed Forces. The upper part of Figure 8.12 shows that men in the highest-scoring group (I) on this test had 8 chances in 10 of doing above average work in the course. Those in the lowest-scoring group (V) had hardly any

chance at all of doing this well. This is considerably better prediction than that afforded by number of grades completed.

This example illustrates pictorially the predictions one can make from reliable and valid measurements. Give a statistician a correlation coefficient between a test and a criterion, and he can make up a diagram like that in Figure 8.12 which predicts a person's chances of success from any particular score on the test. He can do this because he has the appropriate formulas that have been proved both mathematically and in practical experience to predict from one set of measurements to another.[9] The use one makes of such predictions depends upon many practical considerations, such as the cost of training people with a low chance of success, or how much choice one has in selecting people. The important point is that valid measurements lead to useful predictions.

S U M M A R Y

1. Psychology, like other sciences, is quantitative. It assigns numbers to objects and events, and thus it makes use of scales of measurement.

2. Four kinds of scales can be distinguished: (*a*) nominal scales, in which numbers are used to identify or label traits, abilities, etc.; (*b*) ordinal scales, in which numbers are used to rank people on some psychological variable; (*c*) interval scales, in which numbers represent differences between people that are meaningful; and (*d*) ratio scales, in which numbers represent the relative amounts by which one person excels another.

3. In order to describe fully any set of measurements, it is helpful to arrange them into class intervals and to count the frequency of cases in each class interval. The result is a frequency distribution.

4. Many distributions of psychological measurements have a particular shape that, in the ideal case, is the normal probability curve.

5. To describe accurately a frequency distribution, two sets of measures are required: measures of central tendency and measures of variability.

6. Of many possible measures of central tendency, the two most often used are (*a*) the mean or average, which is the sum of all the measurements divided by the number of measurements, and (*b*) the median, which is the middle case of all the measurements.

7. Of the possible measures of variability, one that is quickest to compute but the least accurate is the range. A better measure is the standard deviation, which is the root-mean-square of deviations of scores from the average.

8. If a distribution is normal, one can state accurately the shape of the distribution and the percentage of cases lying above or below any particular score merely by knowing the average and the standard deviation.

9. The correlation coefficient states quantitatively the degree to which pairs of scores in two distributions are related. If the correlation is perfect, which it seldom is, the coefficient is ± 1.00. If there is no relation between the scores of two distributions, the coefficient is .00.

10. The measures above are descriptive statistics; they describe distributions. To make inferences from them, we must know that they constitute a representative sample of all the possible measurements of the same kind that we could make.

11. We must also know (*a*) that they are reliable, that is, that repeated measurements would give essentially the same results; and (*b*) that they are valid, which is to say that they measure what they are supposed to measure.

SUGGESTIONS FOR FURTHER READING

Chapanis, A., Garner, W. R., & Morgan, C. T. *Applied experimental psychology.* New York: Wiley, 1949. Chaps. 2 and 3.
> *A two-chapter summary of statistical methods, with especial emphasis on applications to human engineering.*

Guilford, J. P. *Fundamental statistics in psychology and education* (2d Ed.). New York: McGraw-Hill, 1950.
> *A thorough text treating in detail most of the statistical methods used in psychology.*

Lindquist, E. F. *A first course in statistics* (Rev. Ed.). Boston: Houghton Mifflin, 1942.
> *A standard text in psychological statistics.*

Stevens, S. S. Mathematics, measurement, and psychophysics. In S. S. Stevens, *Handbook of experimental psychology.* New York: Wiley, 1951.
> *A chapter on the theory of measurement as it relates to the science of psychology.*

Underwood, B. J., Duncan, C. P., Taylor, J. A., & Cotton, J. W. *Elementary statistics.* New York: Appleton-Century-Crofts, 1954.
> *An elementary and readable presentation of basic statistical methods.*

PART 2

Personality and Adjustment

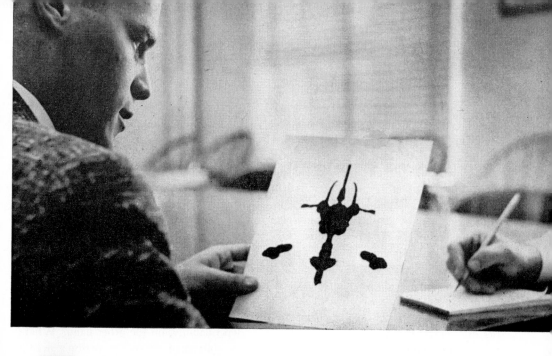

Chapter 9 PERSONALITY

To UNDERSTAND PEOPLE better is one of the desires of almost everyone and especially of the student of psychology. The chapters in Part One should contribute to such an understanding, because a knowledge of the development of the individual, his motives and emotions, and his abilities to learn, think, and perceive is important in comprehending how a person gets to be the kind of individual he is. It is also possible and practicable *to consider the individual as a whole and to describe the interplay between him and other individuals with whom he associates in his daily affairs*. The field of psychology that attempts to do this is called the study of personality.

This chapter was drafted by Charles W. Eriksen of the University of Illinois.

PERSONALITY CHARACTERISTICS

When we attempt to study an individual in a real-life setting, we are immediately struck with the tremendous number of things we might observe. Every moment in the day he is doing something—sleeping, eating, writing, working, playing, talking, walking, and so on. Any attempt to describe and understand every single thing he does would involve us in a tremendously complicated and, in the end, impossible task. Only recently, for example, a group of psychologists attempted to record in detail the activities of one seven-year-old boy for just one day.[1] It took them a book of some 435 pages to do it! Think how voluminous the report would be if we attempted to do

213

this for many individuals over some period of time.

To cope with such a problem, we obviously must make some choices of what to study in attempting to understand personalities. To a certain extent, these choices are rather arbitrary and are made according to what we are most interested in knowing about a person. In some circumstances, we may be satisfied with only general traits of behavior. In others we may want most to characterize a person's attitudes, in others his motives, and in still others his way of dealing with personal problems.

No matter what personality characteristics are chosen for study, there are always two requirements that must be met in order to select those that are meaningful and useful. In the first place, a personality characteristic must really be *characteristic*. It does us little good, for example, to know that Mr. A was angry on a certain Tuesday morning. Anyone might have been angry in the situation he faced that particular morning, and he may not have been angry at any other time for a month. Rather what we would like to know about Mr. A is whether he is characteristically an angry or hostile person or whether he is usually of a serene, sunny disposition which is provoked to anger only occasionally or in the most exasperating of situations. If he is usually serene, and only occasionally angry, we characterize him as a serene person.

Secondly, the aspects of personality that we choose for study should be *distinctive* ones. Almost all adult males in the United States work for a living and almost all go to barbershops to get their hair cut. It does us little good to note, therefore, that a person works for a living or gets his hair cut, for these are not characteristics that distinguish him from most other people. On the other hand, some people work harder

than others or have their hair cut more often than others, so these differences do distinguish people from one another. Then we might regard "industriousness" or "well-kempt appearance" as distinguishing personality characteristics.

Confining ourselves to those aspects of personality that are characteristic and distinctive simplifies considerably the problem of studying personality. Even so, there are an enormous number of distinctive characteristics. Moreover, these characteristics are not always easily separated from each other. Is there a clear-cut distinction, for example, between honesty, on the one hand, and conscientiousness, integrity, or dependability, on the other hand? What is the difference between a person's need to depend on others and his need for affection? In these and many other instances we find that personality characteristics often overlap and are highly correlated with each other. Hence we have several possible sets of characteristics that may not be clearly different from one another. Each set, however, may serve some particular purpose in describing personality. In this section, we shall consider several sets of characteristics under the following headings: (1) traits; (2) types; (3) abilities, interests, and attitudes; (4) motives; and (5) modes of adjustment.

Traits. *A trait is any aspect of personality that is reasonably characteristic and distinctive.* The trait probably constitutes our most comprehensive means of characterizing a person. The problem, however, of deciding which traits are useful and which are not is a difficult one. The unabridged dictionary contains approximately 18,000 adjectives that are used in our language to describe how people act, think, perceive, feel, and behave.[2] It also contains about 4,000 words that might be accepted as traits—such words as humility, sociability, honesty, and forthrightness. Of course many of these terms are synonyms or near synonyms, and others are so rare and unusual as to be of little value. When these synonyms and rare words are carefully edited out, we are left with about 170 words. This is still an unwieldy number to use for scientific purposes. Thus it is apparent that some method of reducing this large number of possible traits to a few most common and relatively

different traits would be most advantageous.

Just such a method is available in the statistical technique known as *factor analysis*.[3] The details of this technique involve mathematics beyond the scope of this book, but the principle of it can be explained by considering a hypothetical example. Suppose that we administer six different tests to a group of people. Let us call the tests

Fig. 9.1. The clustering of traits. Each circle represents a possible trait on which individuals were rated. After the ratings were completed, they were correlated with each other. The number along the line joining two circles is the correlation obtained. In this case, impulsiveness, gregariousness, proneness to witticisms, and facts vs. principles are highly correlated and can be considered to be essentially one trait. (*After Cattell, R. B. Personality. New York: McGraw-Hill, 1950, p. 11.*)

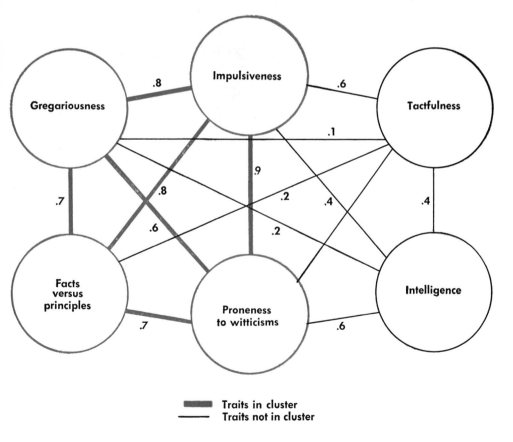

A, B, C, D, E, and F. When the tests have been scored we can calculate correlation coefficients (page 202) between every possible pair of tests. There are fifteen such pairs. From Chapter 8, you will recall that a coefficient of 1.00 is a perfect correlation and a coefficient of .00 is no correlation at all. Let us assume that all correlations in this case are either 1.00 or .00 and that they are as follows:

Tests	A	B	C	D	E
B	1.00				
C	1.00	1.00			
D	.00	.00	.00		
E	.00	.00	.00	1.00	
F	.00	.00	.00	1.00	1.00

In actual practice we seldom obtain correlations of exactly 1.00 or .00, but taking the extremes of high and low correlation illustrates the ideal case.

What does such a set of correlations mean? Notice that there are two clusters of correlations. One cluster is formed by tests A, B, and C; the other by tests D, E, and F. The tests in each cluster correlate perfectly with each other but not at all with tests in the other cluster. Consequently we have isolated *two factors* in the tests. Because there are only two factors, there is no need in the future to use six tests. Tests B and C measure exactly the same thing as test A, and tests E and F measure exactly the same thing as D. We can select any one test in each cluster and measure a factor. What at the outset seemed to be six characteristics can be reduced to merely two.

In actual practice, correlations in a cluster would be high but not perfect, and correlations between clusters would be low but probably not zero. Moreover, some correlations within a cluster would be higher than others. Consequently, we usually cannot test a factor simply by selecting one test within a cluster. Hence more work is necessary to construct a new test that combines features of the tests within a cluster. Nevertheless, our hypothetical example illustrates the principle of factor analysis. In such an analysis, *a few common factors in a large number of tests (or other measurements) may be isolated by discovering those tests that correlate* highly with each other but not with other clusters of tests. A practical illustration of the technique is given in Figure 9.1, which concerns ratings of personality traits.

What happens when factor analysis is used to reduce the number of personality traits? In one study it was found that the 170-odd trait names resulting from our dictionary search could be reduced to only 12 factors.[4] As a first step in this study 171 traits were reduced by combining under one trait all the traits that correlated highly with one another but not very highly with another set of traits. By following this procedure, 35 broad traits or trait clusters were obtained. Then a small group of experienced judges rated a large group of adult men whom they knew reasonably well on each of these 35 broad traits. When all the ratings were made, they were put through a factor analysis. The result was a reduction of the 35 traits to only 12 basic traits or factors (see Table 9.1). In other words, 12 basic traits proved to be about as good as 35 in describing personality because a person's rating on each of the 35 traits could be predicted from his ratings on the 12 basic traits or factors.

One should not jump to the conclusion that there are just twelve basic personality traits. The study we cited is just one of many studies. The number of traits one obtains in such a study depends on several conditions, including the kinds of people observed, the settings or walks of life in which they are studied, the people doing the rating, and the number of possible traits

TABLE 9.1. **One set of primary traits of personality obtained by the method of factor analysis.** A group of experienced judges rated adult men on thirty-five broad traits. Factor analysis was used on the results to identify the traits that for all practical purposes were duplicates, and the long list of traits was consolidated into twelve primary traits.

	versus	
I. Cyclothymia		**Schizothymia**
	Emotionally expressive, frank, placid	Reserved, close-mouthed, anxious
II. General mental capacity		**Mental defect**
	Intelligent, smart, assertive	Unintelligent, dull, submissive
III. Emotionally stable		**Neurotic emotionality**
	Free of neurotic symptoms, realistic about life	Variety of neurotic symptoms, evasive, immature
IV. Dominance		**Submissiveness**
	Self-assertive, confident, aggressive	Submissive, unsure, complaisant
V. Surgency		**Desurgency**
	Cheerful, joyous, humorous, witty	Depressed, pessimistic, dull, phlegmatic
VI. Positive character		**Dependent character**
	Persevering, attentive to people	Fickle, neglectful of social chores
VII. Adventurous cyclothymia		**Withdrawn schizothymia**
	Likes meeting people, strong interest in opposite sex	Shy, little interest in opposite sex
VIII. Sensitive, infantile emotionality		**Mature, tough poise**
	Dependent, immature, gregarious, attention-seeking	Independent-minded, self-sufficient
IX. Socialized, cultured mind		**Boorishness**
	Polished, poised, composed, introspective, sensitive	Awkward, socially clumsy, crude
X. Trustful cyclothymia		**Paranoia**
	Trustful, understanding	Suspicious, jealous
XI. Bohemian unconcernedness		**Conventional practicality**
	Unconventional, eccentric, fitful hysterical upsets	Conventional, unemotional
XII. Sophistication		**Simplicity**
	Logical mind, cool, aloof	Sentimental mind, attentive to people

Modified from Cattell, R. B. *Description and measurement of personality.* Yonkers, N.Y.: World, 1946.

the judges use in making their ratings. Despite these limitations, research in this area is continuing, and there is reason to believe that someday psychologists will have a small manageable number of traits which will adequately describe the more important ways in which personalities can differ.

Types. Before describing other sets of personality characteristics, we should point out a fairly common error in describing personalities. This is to classify people according to types. This error is often made in such statements as, "John is the submissive type," "Harry is the extroverted type," or "Dick is a Don Juan [type]." Such statements may serve to convey more or less correctly one of a person's rather distinctive traits, but they overstep the mark in classifying him as a type.

Such notions of *types* of personality stem from a few dramatic instances of somebody's behavior, from contact with relatively rare personalities, or from fictional characters who have purposely been overdrawn to make them interesting and dra-

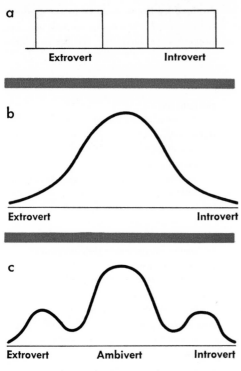

a

Extrovert   Introvert

b

Extrovert   Introvert

c

Extrovert   Ambivert   Introvert

Fig. 9.2. Conceptions of types. It is common, but incorrect, to (**a**) classify people into either one type or another or to (**c**) classify most of them into three types. It is more correct (**b**) to think of people as distributed along a continuum with most people in the middle between two extremes. [*After Stagner, R. The psychology of personality (2d Ed.). New York: McGraw-Hill, 1948, p. 242.*]

matic. We then unthinkingly use these rare instances as models for people in everyday life. The big bully who beats up all the kids in the community becomes a model for an "aggressive type." The relatively rare person who is the "life of the party" may be the model for the "extroverted type." And such fictional characters as Don Juan, Pollyanna, or Scrooge are presented as such distinctive personalities that they serve as models for their respective types. Actually we meet such models so rarely in everyday

life that they can hardly be valid ways of describing characteristic differences among people.

Another objection to "typing" people is that it lumps together a number of different personality traits. The "introverted type" is supposed to be withdrawn, sensitive to criticism, and inhibited in emotional expression; the "extroverted type" is supposed to be thick-skinned, spontaneous in emotional expression, and little affected by personal failures. It more often happens, though, that one person may be as sensitive as the introvert, yet as sociable as the extrovert, and another person may be as thick-skinned as the extrovert but as ill-humored and unfriendly as the introvert. Personality, therefore, is not simple enough to be dumped into a single basket—the type. People are characterized by a number of traits. Some of these may be introvertive and some extrovertive; seldom do they all fit the pattern of any one type. Even in the rare cases where they may, it is very unlikely that the traits will be extreme enough to be accurately described in one type. Most people are not extreme types or extreme in traits but fall somewhere between the extremes. It is therefore quite inaccurate to characterize people by type.

Abilities, attitudes, and interests. Any description of personality characteristics is incomplete if it does not include such things as *abilities*, *attitudes*, and *interests*. It may, for example, be characteristic of a person that he is "intelligent," "conservative," and "sports-loving." Such characteristics, in fact, are usually included in the list of traits used for rating personality. In Table 9.1, you will notice that some of the trait names apply to these characteristics.

Abilities, attitudes, and interests, however, are different from most other traits in two important respects. First of all, *they can be accurately measured by objective tests.* We have dozens of well-validated tests for the measurement of *intellectual abilities* and of specific *aptitudes.* In Chapters 15 and 16, we shall describe some of these tests. We also have available some *attitude scales* for the measurement of attitudes, and we shall discuss these in Chapter 13. We also have, finally, objective tests for the measurement of *interests.* These are described in Chapter 16.

Abilities, attitudes, and interests are unlike other traits in a second important respect. They are more often *measured for such special purposes as the selection of employees, the selection of students, vocational counseling, and public-opinion polling.* Tests of abilities, for example, are used at all educational levels, from first grade to professional school, to assess an individual's fitness for further training. Tests of abilities and interests are widely used in the selection of employees and in vocational counseling. We shall consider such uses of tests of abilities and interests in Chapter 16. In addition, attitudes of people are daily being measured in public-opinion polls and market-research surveys to assess reactions to political issues and to programs of merchandising products. We shall consider the measurement of attitudes for such purposes in Chapter 13.

Because abilities, attitudes, and interests are specialized topics that are considered elsewhere in the book, we shall discuss them no more here. The student should recognize, however, that these are included in the characteristics that are used to describe personality.

Motives. In addition to the personality characteristics we have mentioned so far, it is also possible to describe a person in terms of his motives and goals—why he does what he does. George, for example, may be quite friendly and attentive, thereby exhibiting desirable traits, but his reason

may be that he wants to sell me a sizable insurance policy. Dave, on the other hand, may have the same traits simply because he likes my company. There is a world of difference. John may want very much to be friends but seems reserved and aloof because he does not have the social skills to show his friendship. Consequently I may mistake his motive entirely if I go only by his superficial traits. We therefore need to have concepts of personality that are cast in terms of motives as well as traits. To say this is not to imply that motives and traits are mutually exclusive characteristics. On the contrary, many traits directly or indirectly describe motives. If we consider a person honest, efficient, and industrious we certainly are saying or implying something about his motives. On the other hand, it is possible to focus attention more directly on motives, leaving aside for the moment how these motives may be related to other personality characteristics.

▪ *Basic Motives.* In Chapter 3 we have already explained how individuals start life with a few innate motives and how these soon become elaborated into many diverse acquired motives. The child that at first is fearful only when hurt or losing support later becomes afraid of many things—hitting his little sister, knives, absence of mama, hot stoves, and arousing daddy's anger. Where once there were only one or two fears, there are now dozens of them. In the adult, motives become even more elaborated. Where once there were a few motives, such as for food, water, and warmth, there are now motives for houses, money, cars, clothes, swimming pools, and dozens more. This elaboration of motives in the adult makes it somewhat difficult to describe personality in terms of motives.

Adding to this difficulty is the fact that people must satisfy their motives in different ways. An "old maid" may satisfy her maternal motives by keeping a houseful of cats, while the mother satisfies the same motive by having children. One man who gets angry at his boss may vent his anger by cursing his wife, beating his children, and kicking the dog, while another man may find direct satisfaction—perhaps to his later sorrow—by telling his boss off. Through training and experience, people learn to satisfy their motives in different ways. How can we ascertain the motives that characterize different personalities?

In the next chapter, we shall consider characteristic motives in some detail when we study the adjustment of people to their environments and problems. One set of motives, however, that has proved useful in describing personality is given in Table 9.2. There you see a lengthy list of motives.

These were arrived at in an extensive investigation of personality conducted at the Harvard Psychological Clinic.[5] There a number of young men were intensively studied by a group of clinical psychologists. These psychologists found such a set of motives gave them a satisfactory way of classifying the motives of the young men they were studying. Those skilled in the study of personality, given appropriate information about a person, can rate the strength of each of these motives in a person. Thus they can be used fairly accurately in the description of personality.

▪ *Conflict of motives.* It is obvious, perhaps, that many motives may be present at one time, that a person may not be able to satisfy all of them at once, and that he will have to choose which of them he will

TABLE 9.2. A classification of major personal motives.

Motive	Goal and effects
Abasement	To submit passively to others. To seek and accept injury, blame, and criticism.
Achievement	To accomplish difficult tasks. To rival and surpass others.
Affiliation	To seek and enjoy cooperation with others. To make friends.
Aggression	To overcome opposition forcefully. To fight and revenge injury. To belittle, curse, or ridicule others.
Autonomy	To be free of restraints and obligations. To be independent and free to act according to impulse.
Counteraction	To master or make up for failure by renewed efforts. To overcome weakness and maintain pride and self-respect on a high level.
Deference	To admire and support a superior person. To yield eagerly to other people.
Defendence	To defend oneself against attack, criticism, or blame. To justify and vindicate oneself.
Dominance	To control and influence the behavior of others. To be a leader.
Exhibition	To make an impression. To be seen and heard by others. To show off.
Harmavoidance	To avoid pain, physical injury, illness, and death.
Infavoidance	To avoid humiliation. To refrain from action because of fear of failure.
Nurturance	To help and take care of sick or defenseless people. To assist others who are in trouble.
Order	To put things in order. To achieve cleanliness, arrangement, and organization.
Play	To devote one's free time to sports, games, and parties. To laugh and make a joke of everything. To be lighthearted and gay.
Rejection	To remain aloof and indifferent to an inferior person. To jilt or snub others.
Sentience	To seek and enjoy sensuous impressions and sensations. To genuinely enjoy the arts.

After Murray, H. A. *Explorations in personality.* New York: Oxford Univ. Press, 1938.

satisfy and which he will deny. A college student may, for example, want to go to the movies, have a sandwich, and chat with his friend—all at the same time. He may also want to make good grades that term and may need a good deal of studying to get them. Obviously he cannot satisfy all of these motives at once. Furthermore, his desire for good grades may derive in turn from motives to please his parents, to get a scholarship, or to improve his job opportunities so that ultimately he will have a better income with all the satisfactions that will bring. Some college students in this situation will postpone the short-range motives for the movies and a sandwich in favor of the long-range motives of success in college and later life. Some will not.

Modes of adjustment. Thus we come to the conclusion that it is not enough, even though it is important, to know a person's motives. If we are going to understand personality and describe it adequately, we also need to know how people satisfy their motives and even whether they satisfy them or remain frustrated. We must therefore think in terms of a person's *adjustment* to his environment. In many respects, adjustment is the most inclusive concept of personality that we have, for it includes traits of behavior and motives for behavior as well as the adjustments made with these traits and motives.

The concept of adjustment makes it possible to develop a rather complete understanding of personality. Using a great variety of *methods* for studying personality, which we shall consider in the next section of this chapter, psychologists and psychiatrists have been able to classify typical *modes of adjustment* that are used by different people and in various ways to satisfy their motives. In the next chapter, which is concerned entirely with the problem of

personal adjustment, we describe these modes in considerable detail, so we shall not go into the matter here.

METHODS OF MEASURING PERSONALITY

In order to apply to any practical situations the facts we have learned about personality characteristics, it is necessary to have ways of measuring the characteristics of any particular personality. Indeed, methods of measurement are important tools for increasing our knowledge of personality and for applying what we already know. So we shall now devote our attention to these methods.

We are not always interested, of course, in having complete measures of personality, for often we need only the measures that suit a particular purpose. Personnel psychologists, for example, may want to select people whose personality characteristics make them good salesmen. A military psychologist may want to measure neurotic tendencies that make people unfit for hazardous duty. Experimental psychologists may want to measure anxiety in order to control its influence in their experiments on perception or learning. Consequently a variety of methods of measuring personality have been devised to suit these various specific purposes.

Pencil-and-paper tests. The most convenient type of measure to use for almost any psychological purpose is a pencil-and-paper test that may be given cheaply and quickly to large groups of people at the same time. Such a test of personality is therefore rather popular. During the last 20 years, psychologists have constructed scores of them.[6]

▪ *Questionnaires.* Almost always, they are in the form of questionnaires, in which the persons being tested must answer questions or say "yes" or "no" to simple statements. Samples of statements are as follows:

I generally prefer to attend movies alone.
I occasionally cross the street to avoid meeting someone I know.
I seldom or never go out on double dates.

The person taking the test must say "yes" or "no," or "true" or "false," to each such statement, thus indicating whether he thinks it applies to him. In some questionnaires a person may also be allowed to check "doubtful" or "uncertain."

This sort of test of personality first gained widespread use in the First World War. It was used then to weed out emotionally unstable draftees. The statements in the test were chosen to reflect psychiatric symptoms that might predict future emotional breakdown. They included such items as the following:

I consider myself a very nervous person.
I frequently feel moody and depressed.

Since the First World War, personality questionnaires of this type have grown without bounds. They are mostly designed to measure emotional maladjustment or such general traits as extroversion-introversion. In the popular magazines these days you will even find such questionnaires designed to tell you whether you have a good chance of getting married or what kind of person you ought to marry. When well designed and carefully evaluated by scientific methods, questionnaires may provide reliable advice concerning such problems. The questionnaires offered in popular magazines, however, seldom meet very rigorous scientific requirements, and their use is therefore highly questionable.

▪ *Disadvantages.* Personality questionnaires, in fact, are not particularly good measures of personality. They have two main defects. First of all, they often *lack*

validity. That is to say, no one has found out whether they actually measure what they are supposed to measure. Somebody simply makes them up and puts them on the market without assessing their true worth. In the second place, they are *easy to fake.* In most cases a reasonably intelligent person can tell what each item is driving at, and if he wishes he can slant his answers in either direction he chooses. A person, for example, who knows that a high score on emotional maladjustment might keep him out of the Army can deliberately get a high score. Conversely, a person even though quite maladjusted usually can make a low score if that is necessary to get the job he is after. In the First World War, for example, a group of draftees who made abnormal scores on a personality test at the time of induction were able to make quite normal scores on the same test after the armistice was signed and the war was over.

▪ *Minnesota Multiphasic Personality Inventory.* Not all personality questionnaires are subject to these criticisms. Some have been made as valid as possible and have been constructed either so that they are hard to fake or so that faking can be detected. An example of such a questionnaire is the Minnesota Multiphasic Personality Inventory (MMPI).[7] This test is designed to measure different types of disturbances of personality. It was constructed by taking a very large number of items, such as "I tire easily" and "One should never trust even his friends too much," and giving these items to both normal and mentally ill people. Those items that were answered one way by normal people and the opposite way, say, by depressive patients in hospitals were used to make up a "depression scale." This procedure for selecting items is a way of constructing a *valid* test. Because depressive patients were used as the criterion group (see Chapter 8), a scale can be ob-

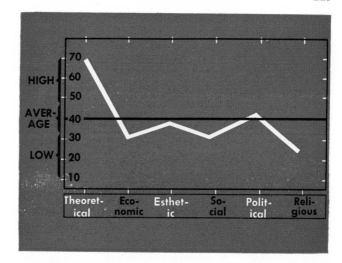

Fig. 9.3. An example of a profile of scores on the Allport-Vernon Study of Values.

tained that measures what it is intended to measure. Other scales were constructed in the same manner for the following:

1. Hypochondriasis—exaggerated anxiety about one's health, and pessimistic interpretation and exaggeration of minor symptoms.

2. Hysteria—various ailments such as headaches and paralyses which have no physical basis.

3. Psychopathic deviation—antisocial and amoral conduct.

4. Paranoia—extreme suspiciousness of others' motives, frequently resulting in elaborate beliefs that certain people are plotting against one.

5. Psychasthenia—irrational thoughts that recur and/or strong compulsions to repeat seemingly meaningless acts.

6. Schizophrenia—withdrawal into a private world of one's own, often accompanied by hallucinations and bizarre behavior.

7. Hypomania—mild elation and excitement without any clear reason.

In addition, scales were constructed for masculinity-femininity from the items that were answered differently by men and women. Finally, there were scales constructed to detect lying and the tendency to place oneself in an overly favorable light.

Although all the items of the MMPI are contained in one test, one can obtain scores for each person on each scale by scoring separately the different items that make up each scale. From a set of scores one can construct a profile, showing an individual's rating on each scale.

▪ *Allport-Vernon Scale.* The Allport-Vernon Study of Values is another pencil-and-paper questionnaire to test personality.[8] It measures a person's major areas of *interest*: theoretical, economic, aesthetic, social, political, and religious. In the first part of the test, the subject must give a yes or no answer to a series of statements such as

The main object of scientific research should be the discovery of pure truth rather than its practical applications.

A "yes" answer to this question would help make up a high score on theoretical interests; a "no" answer would count toward high economic interests. In the second part of the test, the subject must rank four alternatives in the order of his agreement with them. He would, for example, express his agreement with the following statements by indicating a rank order for them:

Do you think that a good government should aim chiefly at _____

a) more aid for the poor, sick, and old?

b) the development of manufacturing and trade?

c) introducing more ethical principles into its policies and diplomacy?

d) establishing a position of prestige and respect among nations?

As in the case of the MMPI, it is possible to construct a profile of the results. In this case, the profile is for the six major areas of interest. You can see an example of such a profile in Figure 9.3.

▪ *Cattell-Luborsky Test.* Sense of humor, as we all realize, is an important characteristic of personality, and it can be used as a test of personality.[4] One test of sense of humor is the Cattell-Luborsky Humor Test of Personality. It is made up of jokes arranged in pairs, and subjects are asked to check which one of each pair they consider funnier. Such preferences for jokes tell something about the subject's repressed motives. A person who is repressing motives to aggress against other people is likely to appreciate jokes that dwell on the mistakes or minor misfortunes of others. On the other hand, a person who is repressing sexual motives tends to rate sexual jokes as funnier.

Situational tests. At best pencil-and-paper questionnaires are somewhat artificial. They attempt to measure personality by asking questions about it. The ideal measure of personality would be something that samples personality itself, that observes people behaving in a fair sample of real-life situations. Situation tests have been devised to meet this purpose. In these the tester or experimenter constructs some type of play situation and observes personality in it.

One classical example of this kind of measure is a study of honesty and dishonesty in children.[9] Children were put in a number of situations affording an opportunity to cheat without their knowing that the experimenters could catch them at it. In one situation, children were given a large number of coins to arrange in patterns. When they completed this task, they were asked to put the coins in a cupboard. An inconspicuous code on the coins, however, permitted the experimenters to tell which coins were returned and which were "stolen." Another situation presented the child with a problem so difficult—a complicated finger maze to be traced with the eyes closed—that a child had to peek or "cheat" to obtain a high score on it. With many situations like these, the investigators exhaustively studied honesty as a personality trait in children. What they found is that *honesty is not a unitary trait. Children who are honest in one situation may be dishonest in another,* and vice versa.

Another example of the use of miniature situations to study personality is to be found in the Office of Strategic Services.[10] During the Second World War, this organization had the task of selecting people to work as agents behind enemy lines. Psychologists in this agency developed a wide variety of situations designed to measure important personality traits for this kind of work. Candidates were given such situations as drilling a squad of men, leading a group of candidates in mock-combat conditions, and solving such problems as improvising a bridge to move heavy equipment across a stream. Then, to make the situations as stressful as possible, the psychologists deliberately made the task more difficult. In one case, for example, a candidate was to construct a tower out of heavy logs within a fairly short period of time and was assigned two helpers to do the job. The helpers, however, were stooges who deliberately failed to carry out orders. They would clumsily knock over parts of the completed structure and argue with the candidate or make insulting remarks about his intelligence, appearance, or race. Faced with such frustrations as these, many candidates broke down in tears or sputtered with rage.

Situational tests such as these are sometimes useful, sometimes not. In the example we just described, the candidates were highly motivated to pass the test and tried hard to do it. In many instances, however, it is not possible to motivate people properly, and in these instances, situation tests are not so fruitful. In many cases, too, it is not possible to disguise situations well enough to keep candidates from seeing through them, and then the situation test may not work at all. The candidate considers the whole thing to be a joke. There

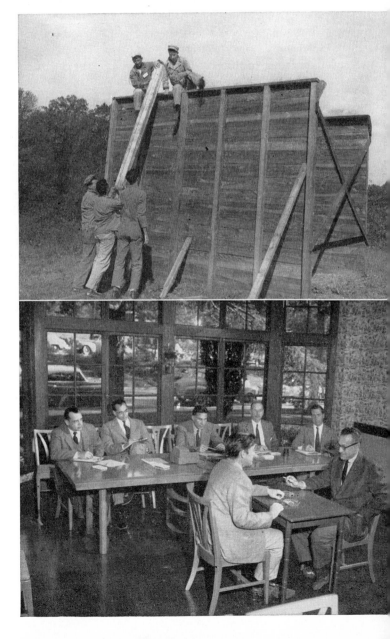

Fig. 9.4. Examples of situational tests. Above is the "wall situation" used by the Office of Strategic Services during the Second World War. A group of men is given the task of climbing and crossing the "canyon," taking their bazooka (log) with them. They have only the materials shown and are not permitted to look around the wall. Pictured below is a situation called "improvisations." The subject (left foreground) interacts with a role player (right) in two psychodramas representing situations of stress and conflict. A trained staff looks on while the conversation is recorded. Afterward the staff rates the subject on a number of aspects of personality. (Courtesy of Dr. Donald MacKinnon, Institute of Personality Assessment and Research, University of California, Berkeley.)

are also grave difficulties in making situational tests both reliable and valid (see Chapter 8 for definitions of these terms). The judgments of observers do not always agree with one another and are therefore not always reliable. The performance of the candidate in the situational test may not correlate at all well with his accomplishment later "on the job," and consequently the test may not be valid. For these reasons the practical usefulness of situational tests largely remains to be demonstrated.

Experimental measurements.   Scientists who are trying to discover basic principles frequently use experimental methods for measurement that would not be practical on a large scale. Research workers in the field of personality have similarly devised experimental measures of personality. Such measures are especially necessary to study in detail the basic processes in personality.

One experiment[11] illustrates the principle that our motives influence our perception (also see page 184). A group of college students first took the Allport-Vernon Study of Values. This test, you will remember, yields scores on six different interest areas. The experimenters then chose a number of words representing each of the interest areas. To represent the economic area, they chose such words as "dollar" and "price"; to represent the religious area, they chose such words as "prayer" and "deity." Then they exposed these words very briefly on a projection screen and measured the length of exposure that was necessary for each college student correctly to identify the word. When they had collected all their measurements, they found that exposure time and interest area were correlated. That is to say, subjects with predominantly economic interests required a shorter exposure to recognize economic words than words representing areas in which they were less interested. Thus, interest or

motive was reflected in speed of recognizing words connected with these interests or motives.

Several experiments of this kind convince us that motives may strongly influence perception. In general if a person has strong motives for aggression, achievement, sex, and the like, these will be reflected in his perception and his more ready recognition of words and objects connected with them. On the other hand, as we shall see in the next chapter, he may have motives that he is unwilling to admit to himself—motives he has repressed so that he is not consciously aware of them. He has, one might say, set up his "defenses" against such motives. These defenses can show up in his perception, however, by producing perceptual blind spots that make him slow to recognize words or stimuli that have to do with them.

Experimental measurements also reveal that personality characteristics, other than motives, affect perception.[12] Consider the patterns in Figure 9.5. In each of these simple patterns is embedded a more complex one. Whether people can see the embedded pattern or not depends somewhat on their personality. Those who are "situation-bound" and unable to assume a detached attitude toward problems have difficulty seeing them. Even some of the perceptual illusions that are described in Chapter 8 reflect personality characteristics.[13] People who are rigid in their personalities, who try to have everything in life fit into a fixed mold, show less susceptibility to apparent movement than do less rigid people. In these and other ways, experimental measurements show a connection between personality and perception.

Let us give, finally, one more example of the experimental measurement of personality.[14] A subject stands blindfolded, with a hook and thread attached to his collar. The other end of the thread is tied to a pen on a *kymograph*, which is a device that moves recording paper around a drum at some constant speed. Thus it will record any moving or swaying of the subject. Now the experimenter tells the subject that he is falling backward. If the subject is suggestible, he will start to sway. Indeed, some people are so suggestible that they would fall over if the experimenter were not prepared to catch them. In any case the degree of suggestibility of the person is measured experimentally by the mark on the kymograph record. This measure of suggestibility can be correlated with suggestibility in other situations. In general these correlations have been small, indicating that "suggestibility," like honesty, is not a unitary trait.

As you can see, most experimental measures of personality require elaborate apparatus and procedures. They are therefore not useful for everyday situations. They are proving helpful, however, in establishing principles of personality and in providing suggestions for designing other, more practicable personality tests.

Personal interview. All the measures of personality that we have been talking about so far may be called *objective measures,* because they give an objective score or number. We may count, for example, the number of times a person prefers "theoretical" over "economic" tasks, the number of inches he sways in a suggestibility test, or the number of times he cheats in a situational honesty test. These are all objective tests that anyone with normal intelligence can count or score.

At the present time, however, there are many features of personality that we cannot measure objectively. It is hard to tell objectively how much a person hates his sister, how strong an attachment he has to his mother, whether he is unhappy because

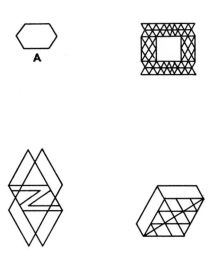

Fig. 9.5. Embedded patterns. An example of patterns used in experimental studies of personality. Can you see pattern A embedded in the other three patterns? Persons who are "situation bound" have difficulty doing this.

he went to the wrong school, or whether he needs more friends and recreation. Even when objective tests yield scores bearing on such problems, someone must evaluate the scores and somehow or other arrive at an interpretation of them. So our objective instruments are not sufficient for measuring all aspects of personality.

Actually, interviewers themselves are reasonably good instruments. Some people, not all of them professional psychologists, are rather good at making judgments of personality. They can listen to a person talk, see him work, and otherwise sample his personality, and then from all the "evidence" they can arrive at a description of his personality. Unfortunately people are not equally good at being measuring instruments. Some have a good deal of skill in evaluating and understanding people, and some have pitifully little. Psychiatrists and clinical psychologists are specialists who have been selected for their skill and in addition have had several years of experience in subjective measurement of personality.

One of the methods on which such specialists rely to a great extent is the personal interview. Although unobjective, it is designed to make the maximum use of the interviewer as a measuring instrument. He tries to sample as wide a range as possible of the person's feelings and attitudes by getting him to talk about his personal experiences. In so doing, the interviewer not only notes what he hears but also observes more intangible behavior: the way the person talks about certain topics—the catch in the voice, for example, whenever mother is mentioned, or the tenseness that appears whenever certain other subjects are brought up—and in many cases what the person is careful *not* to talk about. From these varied observations, the clinician attempts to reconstruct a picture of a person's major motives, his sources of conflict, his modes of adjustment, and the over-all adequacy of the adjustment.

Although the interview is more widely used in the study of personality than any other single method, it has some serious limitations. For one thing, it depends almost entirely on the skill of the interviewer—and skill in interviewing is hard to teach. More serious than that, however, is the difficulty of expressing the results of an interview in quantitative terms. Indeed the understanding one gets through interviewing has little value if it cannot be communicated to someone else. In general such understanding can be communicated only in word descriptions, not in objective scores, and this makes it difficult to compare people by means of the interview.

Rating scales. A partial remedy for this problem is the *rating scale*. It may be used to score impressions of personality obtained in interviews or from informal observation. There are several forms of rating scales. One of the simpler ones lists a number of personality characteristics, such as honesty, reliability, sociability, industriousness, and emotionality, and asks the rater who knows the person being evaluated to give a rating —say, between 1 and 7—on each characteristic. Another method is to provide the rater with a number of alternative descriptions and ask him to check which alternative applies best to the person being rated. From such checks it is usually possible to convert the results into numerical scores on 5- or 7-point scales. In constructing such scales, we usually let 1 stand for one extreme of a characteristic, 7 for the other extreme, and 4 for an average amount of it. An example of such a scale is one for *aggression*, which you see in Table 9.3 (also see Figure 9.6).

Rating scales have the advantage of being adaptable to nearly every situation. Any per-

TABLE 9.3. An example of a rating scale used to measure aggressive behavior toward other persons.

Instructions: Place a check mark after the category that most closely describes the subject's behavior.

A. The degree to which the subject displays hostile or aggressive behavior in his relations with others.

1. Avoids aggression even when it is called for. Never becomes angry or criticizes others.

2. Seldom becomes angry or critical of others. Will do so, however, if strongly prodded or actually attacked.

3. Shows normal amount of aggression when the circumstances seem to call for it. Is neither reluctant nor overready to show hostility.

4. Frequently engages in quarrels or arguments. Is often sarcastic. Tends to be critical of many things.

5. Almost always aggressive. Has trouble getting along with people because he is ready to argue or fight at the drop of a hat.

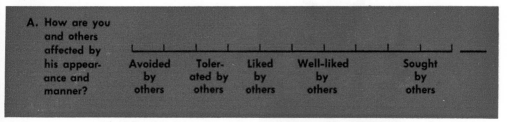

Fig. 9.6. An item on a rating scale. The rater checks a point on the scale to indicate his opinion of the subject. The dash at the end means "no opportunity to observe."

son who knows another person well can rate him on nearly any particular characteristic. We might rate our friends, for example, on such characteristics as cooperativeness, generosity, and thoughtfulness. Similarly the clinician can translate his skilled judgments based on interviews into ratings on such characteristics as feeling of security, anxiousness, and adequacy of personal adjustment. There are, however, many precautions to be observed in constructing and using rating scales, and amateurs cannot ordinarily be expected to use them successfully.

Projective methods. Still other methods, known as projective, are relatively new in the measurement of personality. Their purpose is to get the subject to reveal motives and personality characteristics without knowing that he is doing so. To accomplish this purpose, the person is presented with a vague, undefined task and is asked to do something about it. The basic idea of such a method is that when a subject hardly knows what he is supposed to do but must do something he *projects* his own personality into his performance. That is why the method is called *projective*. (For more about projection, see the next chapter.) One great advantage of the method is that the subject does not know what is being tested or what interpretations the psychologists can make of his results. The test is therefore hard to fake or slant. There are now several different projective tests, but

the Rorschach Test and the Thematic Apperception Test are the two that are most widely known and used.

▪ *The Rorschach Test.* The Rorschach is often called the ink-blot test because it consists of ten ink blots like the one you see in Fig. 9.7. Five of the ten are black and gray, two of them are black and red, and three are entirely in colors. The cards are presented to the subject one at a time with the question, "What might this be?" or "What does this remind you of?" After a subject gives his responses to all the cards, he is then asked to go through them again and describe his responses in detail. In this part of the test, the subject tells what part of the ink blot and what characteristics of it suggested his responses.

All responses of the subject are scored in three main categories:

1. Location—whether the subject used some particular part or the whole blot in making his response

2. Determinant—whether the shading, color, form, or "movement" of the blot suggested the response

3. Content—whether the subject sees animals, human beings, parts of the anatomy, or various other objects in making his responses

From the number of responses a subject makes in these different categories, the clinician infers certain personality traits.[15] A large number of "whole" responses may in

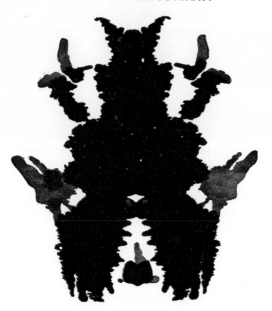

Fig. 9.7. An example of a Rorschach ink blot. Blots similar to this one are shown to a subject with the instruction to indicate what he sees in it. After all his responses are recorded, the examiner inquires more deeply into the subject's responses, finding out what it was about each card that determined his responses.

dicate abstract, theoretical traits, whereas a large number of "small part" responses may indicate a compulsive person occupied with trivialities. If "movement" responses predominate, the person is thought to have introvertive inclinations, but if "color" responses are more numerous, the person is regarded as having warm, free emotional characteristics. All the scoring, however, is not quite this simple, for the clinician can interpret not only the number of different kinds of responses but also their pattern. "Color" responses coupled with "form" responses, for example, indicate free, easy emotional expression, while "color" responses without good form responses indicate an uncontrolled, explosive emotionality. Interpretations also depend upon additional cues such as spontaneous remarks made during the test, signs of emotional upset, and the symbolic meaning of the subject's responses. Seeing a dark scary cave is considered to symbolize sexual fears, or seeing a small child followed by seeing a knife is interpreted as indicating hostility toward a younger sibling.

■ *Thematic Apperception Test.* The second projective test mentioned, the Thematic Apperception Test, is nearly as popular as the Rorschach. Instead of ink blots, it consists of a series of pictures.[5] These are ambiguous enough to permit a variety of interpretations of subjects projecting their motives, feelings, and modes of adjustment. In Figure 9.8 is an example of the kind of picture used in this test. When presented with a picture, the subject is asked to make up a story of what is happening in the picture. In telling the story he is asked to imagine what led up to the scene and what its outcome will be. What makes this a useful projective test is that most people, when they make up stories, identify themselves with one of the characters in the picture, and their stories become thinly disguised biographies. In this way they reveal feelings and desires that they would otherwise hesitate to discuss openly or, in some cases, would be unwilling to admit to themselves.

The Thematic Apperception Test, unlike the Rorschach, has no standardized scoring system. It is interpreted instead by noting recurring themes in the stories: the characteristic needs and frustrations of the hero, the relations of the hero to members of the opposite sex and to parents or authority, and the over-all emotional tone of the stories, whether depressed or overly optimistic. Thus the interpretation of this test is quite subjective.

But no matter how projective tests are scored or interpreted, they yield subjective measures of personality—primarily measures of dominant motives, of conflicts or frustrations, and of modes of adjustment. In a sense, therefore, projective tests are little more than standardized interviews. Like interviews, their value depends on the skill of the person who administers them and interprets them. It is difficult to tell, however, just who has the skill and who does not. Consequently, the validity (see Chapter 8) of projective tests has not yet been firmly established. They are no "open sesame" to the understanding of personality.

HOW PERSONALITY DEVELOPS

We have described different ways of looking at personality and different ways of measuring it. Now it is logical to raise questions about cause and effect. How do biological inheritance, on the one hand, and the social environment, on the other, contribute to personality development? In so far as learning is important, what sorts of influences mold personality? Is what a person learns early in childhood more important than what he learns later on, or vice versa? What accounts for differences in personality? Why do some people develop "good" personalities and others "poor" ones?

There are, of course, general and specific answers to these questions. To understand a particular person, we need to know what particular influences have been at work in his life, and these will be different for each person. On the other hand, we all are subject in varying degrees to many of the same sorts of influences. Thus it is possible to describe the principal influences in personality development. We shall do this in the following paragraphs.

Predispositions. As we shall see, learning is extremely important in molding the personality, but it is not exclusively so. We have good evidence that people are born

Fig. 9.8. An example of the Thematic Apperception Test. Each card is shown to the subject with an instruction to tell a story about its picture. He is asked to explain the situation it represents, discuss events that led up to the situation, indicate the feelings and thoughts of the characters in the picture, and describe the outcome of the situation. [*From Murray, H. A. Thematic Apperception Test. Cambridge, Mass.: Harvard Univ. Press, (copyright) 1943. By permission of the publishers.*]

into the world with certain predispositions to develop along certain lines. These predispositions, of course, are transmitted through the response mechanisms, particularly the nervous system and the glands, and they can emerge only as the response mechanism matures.

Even at birth, when the nervous system is only partly mature, we can see some predispositions unfolding before there has been much chance for any learning to take place. If, for example, you have observed closely several newborn infants, you have noted striking differences between them. Some babies are extremely active, others are quite sluggish. Some cry and fuss most of the time, while others are so placid that their mothers call in the pediatrician to see whether anything is wrong. So far it has been difficult for psychologists to predict from these differences what the infants' adult personalities will be like, partly because there are so many other factors that will later come into play. Certainly there are some innate differences.

We also see such predispositions in some of our statistics about mental diseases. These are discussed in the next chapter and again in detail in Chapter 22, but they are also relevant here. The mental disease *schizophrenia*, one of the most prevalent, tends to run in families.[16] If one or both parents have had schizophrenia, children are more likely to have it. This is only a statistical tendency, for many with a predisposition to schizophrenia develop normal personalities if they grow up in favorable environments. On the other hand, those in unfavorable environments who have no predisposition also may develop it. So such extreme forms of personality development are not entirely hereditary. Rather, they are a product of heredity and environment combined. The important point, however, is that an innate biological predisposition

probably does influence personality development in many ways.

Endocrine glands. Sometimes hereditary and biological influences on personality are obscure, and we cannot see exactly how they work. In other cases we are able to assign the causes directly to the functioning of the endocrine glands. (These are explained in Chapter 22.) The level at which they function probably has something to do with certain features of everyone's personality. In the great majority of instances, however, we are unable to measure (at least at the present time) any direct connection. Only in dramatic cases, when these glands are grossly underdeveloped or overdeveloped, can we see their effects on personality. Then a person's extreme sluggishness or overactivity, his lack or excess of emotionality, his very aggressive or very passive behavior may be blamed primarily on his endocrine glands.

In Chapter 22 we shall deal with the psychological influences of the endocrine glands in some detail. These include other functions in addition to personality. Since these glands are discussed there, and since their influence is only rarely seen in a few extreme cases, we shall not dwell on them here.

Physique and temperament. Still another way in which innate biological factors may influence personality is through body build. It has been a common belief for centuries that body build and personality are correlated. Don't you, for example, think of the big muscular fellow as being dominant and aggressive? Or of the fat person as being jolly and easy going? Or of the frail individual as serious and tense? These are common notions with many people and have been throughout recorded history. In Shakespeare, for example, we find Caesar saying,

Let me have men about me that are fat,
Sleek-headed men, and such as sleep o' nights.

Yond Cassius has a lean and hungry look.
He thinks too much. Such men are dangerous.

Beginning before Aristotle and down through the years, there have been repeated attempts to associate personality and body build. Most of the attempts have been too simple and have put each person into one of two or three types. Thus they have not accounted for all the differences among people in either body build or personality. When subjected to careful scientific test, most of them have proved valueless.

A recent approach to the problem is more sophisticated and more adequate.[17] It provides for three components—not types—of body build. One component is *endomorphy*, which refers to the relative prominence in any person of the abdomen, fat, and deeper tissues. A second component is *mesomorphy*, and this refers to muscles, bones, and connective tissue. A third is *ectomorphy* and refers to relative fragility and "linearity" of body build. Actually it is impossible in a few words to give accurate definitions of these components, but these definitions should serve as rough approximations.

It might help if one thinks of the extreme endomorphic person as appearing round, of the extreme mesomorph as being very square, and of the extreme ectomorph as being very thin. In Figure 9.9, you see some pictures of these extremes. Extremes, however, are very few, and most people are a mixture of the three. Each person can be described quite accurately, however, with numbers. The maximum number a person can have in each component is 7 and the minimum is 1; the average is about 4. A

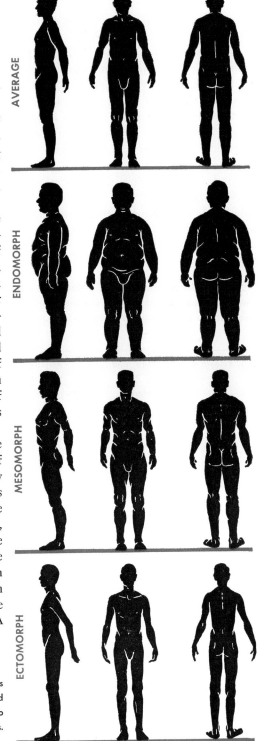

Fig. 9.9. Sheldon's system of body types. The sketches depict extremes in ectomorphy, mesomorphy, and endomorphy, and also the average individual who has about equal proportions of all three components.

person who is skilled in doing the rating can take a standard photograph of a person —undressed, so that clothes will not cover up the shape of the body—and assign numbers for each component. One person, thus, might be given the designation 4–5–2, which would mean a rating of 4 on endomorphy, 5 on mesomorphy, and 2 on ectomorphy. Such a set of ratings is known as a *somatotype.*

This is a modern, scientific, and rather reliable method of stating differences in body build. There remains the corresponding problem, however, of rating personality.

Rather than deal with all aspects of personality, the investigators working on this problem restricted themselves to some simple traits that, taken together, have been called temperament.[18] In this case, they chose three different components of temperament, which they called respectively *viscerotonia, somatotonia,* and *cerebrotonia.* (For some of the traits that characterize each of these components, see Table 9.4.) A person can get a rating on each of these temperamental variables. Such ratings are based on twenty traits in each case, some of which are listed in Table 9.4. Just as was the case for

TABLE 9.4.   Some items from a rating scale for temperament. A rater who is thoroughly familiar with a person rates him on each of the characteristics below. To the highest possible degree of a characteristic, a rater assigns a 7; to the lowest degree, a 1.

Viscerotonia	Somatotonia	Cerebrotonia
___1. Relaxation in posture and movement	___1. Assertiveness of posture and movement	___1. Restraint in posture and movement, tightness
___2. Love of physical comfort	___2. Love of physical adventure	
___3. Slow reaction	___3. The energetic characteristic	___3. Overly fast reactions
	___4. Need and enjoyment of exercise	___4. Love of privacy
		___5. Mental overintensity, hyper-attentionality, apprehensiveness
	___6. Love of risk and chance	___6. Secretiveness of feeling, emotional restraint
___7. Love of polite ceremony	___7. Bold directness of manner	___7. Self-conscious motility of the eyes and face
___8. Love of society, sociophilia	___8. Physical courage for combat	___8. Fear of society, sociophobia
	___9. Competitive aggressiveness	___9. Inhibited social address
___12. Evenness of emotional flow		
___13. Tolerance	___13. The unrestrained voice	___13. Vocal restraint, and general restraint of noise
___14. Complacency		
	___16. Overmaturity of appearance	___16. Youthful intentness of manner and appearance
___17. Smooth, easy communication of feeling, extroversion of viscerotonia		

From Sheldon, W. H., & Stevens, S. S. *The varieties of temperament.* New York: Harper, 1942.

somatotypes, a person gets some number between 1 and 7 on each of these three scales
of temperament.

The investigators who constructed these
scales for body build and temperament report substantial correlations between the
two. That is to say, they find that a high
rating in viscerotonia goes along with a
high rating in endomorphy and that high
ratings similarly tend to be associated for
mesomorphy and somatotonia and for ectomorphy and cerebrotonia. Undoubtedly
there is some relationship, but it is too
early to tell just how good the relationship
is and just how well we can predict temperament or personality from body build.
This is an interesting problem on which
a lot of research needs to be done.

The fact that there is some relationship
has several possible explanations. One is
that there are some common *biological factors* that determine both how the physique
will develop and how the personality will
develop. Another is a purely *social explanation*. A person's physique determines within
limits what he can do. His physique and
abilities also affect other people's reaction
to him. These, in turn, affect his reaction
to himself. In other words, it is quite possible that the relation between body build
and personality is due to a person's reactions to the way others regard his physique.

Abilities.   Each person is endowed with
certain abilities and in the course of growing up acquires more through maturation
and learning. Psychologists divide these into
general and special abilities, and they com-

Fig. 9.10. A cartoonist's picture of the temperamental
characteristics correlated with the extremes of physique. See Fig. 9.9 and text. (*Reproduced by permission of cartoonist, Michael Ramus.*)

monly use the word *intelligence* to refer to general ability to learn, abstract, and solve problems. In addition people have various amounts of special abilities such as musical talent and mechanical aptitude. The abilities, both general and special, are to a certain extent a part of an individual's personality. They also have considerable influence in the development of personality.

There is a fairly common belief, which is incorrect, that extremely intelligent children are frail in physique and somewhat queer or neurotic in personality. There are, of course, some cases of this sort, but as a general rule this idea is wrong. Psychologists have conducted extensive studies of extremely intelligent children—geniuses—and they find that such children on the average are physically stronger, healthier, more stable emotionally, and better adjusted than normal children.[19] This general superiority of the more intelligent, moreover, is not limited to childhood; it is just as true of adults.

There are probably two general reasons for this correlation. One is *biological*, the other *social*. Some individuals are no doubt better all-round biological organisms than are other people. The same biological factors that account for superior strength and health can be expected to produce a better functioning nervous system and, indirectly, better intelligence. On the other hand, superior intelligence helps a person make better social adjustments. Since personality may be regarded as the composite of such adjustments, superior intelligence should be a factor in the development of a "better" personality. The brighter little Johnny is, for example, the sooner he can learn to understand that mother may be cross and grouchy because she has a headache rather than because he is a naughty, unlovable child. And the more intelligent child can learn sooner to see into the future, to delay a satisfac-

tion now for one he may achieve a day or two hence.

Intelligence also influences personality by providing a person with means of recognition. The bright child achieves rewards from parents and teachers for his accomplishments. Another with mechanical ability may become interested in building amateur radio equipment and receive the recognition of adults and friends for his achievements. Thus intelligence and special abilities permit a child or an adult to develop areas of competence from which he acquires confidence and feelings of self-worth and self-esteem. His special abilities are reflected in his personality characteristics.

Abilities also seem to provide their own motivation. A person with a special talent usually has a strong motive to exercise it. The great musician Handel, for example, had a father who strongly opposed his son's interest in music. Nevertheless, even when faced with severe punishment, Handel as a child would sneak to the garret at night to practice the harpsichord. As a consequence of such strong drives to practice, abilities usually show themselves early in childhood.

In considering the effects of abilities on the development of personality, we must realize that many factors, both innate and learned come into play. For example, the personality of a child with subnormal intelligence will develop in one way if he is a member of an intellectual family, and in another way if his parents are also subnormal in intelligence. Similarly a child who is frail in physique may be affected in one way if he is the son of a nonathletic college professor and in another if he is the son of an All-American fullback. The effects of abilities, as well as of other factors, on personality depend very much on the particular environment in which they are found.

Culture.   Whether one is raised in the United States or the jungles of New Guinea, whether he lives in the city or on the farm, and whether he is reared in an upper or lower socioeconomic class makes a great deal of difference in his personality. These circumstances and many others constitute the culture or subculture in which we live. Culture determines to a large extent the experiences a person has, the frustrations and adjustments he must deal with, and the standards of conduct he must meet. Each culture has its distinctive values, morals, and ways of behaving. It dictates the rules for child training and the relationships within a family. Thus in various ways it influences personality.[20]

Such influences are most convincingly demonstrated by the cultures of primitive societies. To study them, cultural anthropologists have lived for periods among the peoples of some of these societies, and they have observed the personality traits, customs, religious beliefs, and methods of child rearing in these societies. The differences are really marked.

The Balinese, for example, have been described as an introverted people who seem emotionally blunted. They do not form warm personal attachments; rather, each member seems to live within himself. The Navajo Indians are passive and forbearing in the face of physical discomfort. The Eskimos are rugged individualists. The Arapesh people of New Guinea seem to be without egotism or competition.

These characteristic differences in personality in various cultures appear to stem from the different experiences presented by each culture. In the Balinese people, for example, the lack of emotional response has been attributed to child-rearing practices. Most of the baby tending is done by little girls, and each child may be cared for by a number of such little "mothers." Such practices prevent intense family relationships from building up. In addition, the Balinese

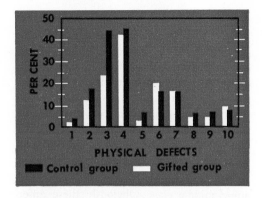

Fig. 9.11. Physical defects of gifted and average children (control group). White bars are for gifted children; black bars are for average children. In all cases, the height of the bar represents the per cent of children having the particular defect or characteristic. 1, frequent headaches; 2, symptoms of general weakness; 3, mouth breathers; 4, occasional or frequent colds; 5, poor or very poor hearing; 6, vision somewhat defective or poor; 7, nervous; 8, speech defects; 9, exceptionally timid; and 10, tendency to worry. (After Terman, L. M. Chap. 17 in Barker, R. G., Kounin, J. S., & Wright, H. F. *Child behavior and development.* New York: McGraw-Hill, 1943, p. 295.)

mother may make things worse by deliberately teasing her child. She will play with him up to the point of evoking love or anger, then lose interest in him or become indifferent. It is small wonder, then, that the Balinese child soon learns to inhibit emotional responses to other people.

Primitive cultures seem to change more slowly and to prescribe ways of behaving more rigidly than do civilized cultures. Our own culture does not "standardize" personality quite so much. Within our culture, however, are many subcultures that do make quite a difference. There is, for example, a marked difference between upper-middle and lower economic classes. Upper-middle-class children are more closely supervised and more likely to be punished for playing in the dirt, for getting into fights, and for showing sexual interests and behavior. Children of the lower socioeconomic groups, on the other hand, learn quite early to be physically aggressive. They fear pain less because they have discovered that bad cuts, suffering injuries, and having one's teeth knocked out, though painful, are generally not serious. In addition, as Kinsey's now famous report shows, children in the lower class have sexual experience earlier, more openly, and more often than those of the upper-middle class. Obviously these differences in training and experience can be expected to produce differences in personality.

Family. The family transmits many of the cultural influences of which we have been speaking, because it largely determines the environment of children during their earlier years and decides how cultural standards are to be imposed and adhered to. The influence of the family, however, is even more far-reaching than that. It gives or withholds affection. It rewards and punishes behavior. Its attitude toward its children may be helpful or discouraging, and it provides models of personalities which the children may or may not try to copy.

Family relationships are important in personality development at all ages, but we have evidence that they are especially important during the first two years.[21] If a baby gets fondling and affection during this period, he is more likely to be emotionally responsive later in life. Conversely, if he lacks fondling then, his emotional responsiveness may be blunted. Children, for example, who are raised from birth in orphan asylums, where they receive every physical care but little personal handling and attention, are less responsive, studies show, than are children who are placed in the orphanage after they are two years of age. Early parental influences are thus important in personality development.

There is even evidence that weaning and toilet training may have a profound influence on personality. Freud believed, from his knowledge of hundreds of adult problems, that weaning a child too early often makes adults who are pessimistic and verbally aggressive, but that late weaning makes for easy-going personalities. He also regarded severe toilet training as likely to produce rigid, compulsive personalities. Clinical experience tends to uphold Freud in these statements. There is some question, however, whether it is the early weaning and toilet training that of themselves influence personality or whether parents who force early weaning and toilet training are the kind of parents whose relations with their children through the years affect their personalities in this way. In other words, early weaning and severe toilet training could just be incidental manifestations of parental attitudes that affect personality in particular ways.

Certainly parental behavior does affect personality development in many ways. Parents are teachers. They administer rewards and punishments to their children, and what children learn, as a result, greatly influences their personalities. Because they reward some behavior and punish other behavior, they help determine the personality traits, goals, and values of the child. One child may discover, for example, that his mother will let him have his own way if he throws a temper tantrum. Another child in another family may find that temper tantrums do not work but feigning illness does. These techniques that a child develops in dealing with his parents naturally carry over into his contacts with other people. The grown man, for example, who sulks because he is angry with his wife probably learned this trait in dealing with his mother.

Probably parents' *attitudes* toward their children are as important as anything else in the way personality develops in the children. Parents who are well adjusted, who love and respect their child as a person, do much to build up within the child a feeling of self-worth and self-confidence. This in turn gives the child a great advantage in facing his problems. Unfortunately, however, many parents reject their children, enmesh the children in the cross fire of their own emotional problems, or take out on the children the ill-treatment that they may have experienced in their own childhood. In fact, studies have shown many mothers and fathers unconsciously relive their own childhood problems through their children.[22] A mother may unconsciously react to her son with the same emotions and feelings that she herself felt as a child toward her older brother. If she resented and disliked her brother, her feelings toward her son conflict. She may find herself competing with him and thus unable to give him encouragement, love, and praise. It is easy for

children in such a situation to feel unwanted and unloved and thus to lack confidence and emotional security that carries over into adulthood.

Parents, finally, influence personality development by being *models*. Much of a child's learning is by imitation. By watching his father, a son learns how to act like a man, and the daughter learns how to assume the role of wife and mother by watching her mother. If the parents are poor models, the chances are that the children will find substitute models in their aunts, uncles, or grandparents, or they may discover models in the comics, movies, or on television. In any case they find models and identify themselves with their models. In so doing, they may copy many of the personality traits of the parents, and even take over their moral and cultural standards. The children, more than they ever realize, take over many of the parents' typical ways of adjusting to problems.

Fig. 9.12. Affection and fondling in the early years are important in personality development. (*From Children's Emotions, a McGraw-Hill Text-Film.*)

To the Good Rev. Smith

To my son Jimmie

To my mother-in-law

Here's how I really am,
but I look like this . . .

IS THIS ME?

by Dave Gerard

To Fido

To my boss

To my wife

To my banker

To Susie — bless her

To my dentist

THE INDIVIDUAL
AND THE SELF

In the preceding sections we have learned how personality is described, how it is measured, and how it is molded by environmental and hereditary influences. Now we come to the problem of understanding the *individual personality as a whole*. This must somehow be done by the clinical psychologist or counselor when he attempts to help an individual with his problems. Each of us tries to do it in dealing with many of the people we know intimately. There is no royal road to understanding the individual, or any set of rules for doing it. There are, however, some important points to consider, and we shall present them under the following headings: (1) individuality, (2) personality syndromes, (3) personality structure, and (4) the self.

Individuality. A person is not simply a profile of characteristics measured by tests or ratings, nor is he a piece of putty molded willy-nilly by environmental circumstances. Personality tests are only samples of behavior (see page 376), and environmental influences combine in different ways to affect personalities quite differently. When we have information about personality characteristics and environmental influences, we must remember that these are merely windows through which we catch brief glimpses of the underlying personality. These glimpses must somehow be synthesized into a coherent picture of an individual.

▪ *Uniqueness of personality.* One of the things we must keep in mind is that *each person is a unique individual*. No two people—not even identical twins reared together—can be exactly alike. Each person has his unique set of abilities and habits and, except for identical twins, his unique hereditary endowment. Two individuals with similar rearing are different because endowment causes them to react differently to environmental influences. Those with similar endowments are different because they have different, or at least slightly different, environmental influences. For this reason, it is not wise in dealing with individuals to generalize glibly from one individual to another. Because Tom and Dick have similar backgrounds and even superficially similar personalities, it does not follow that the two men are to be understood in the same way. An intimate knowledge of their individual motives, traits, and modes of adjustment almost always reveals significant differences between them that make each one a unique personality.

▪ *Continuity of personality.* In understanding any particular person, it should also be borne in mind that personality has a basic continuity. Habits and motives that are learned in years of living are not easily forgotten or supplanted by new ones. Thousands and thousands of learning trials are in the history of any particular individual. Biological factors, of which the individual is partly a product, do not change greatly, at least not in the adult. In addition to learning and endowment, the *roles* a person is called upon to play give continuity to his personality. His family, friends, social class, and economic circumstances all are relatively constant. They continue to make demands on him for certain ways of behaving, which we call roles. These roles do not change, at least not very rapidly. (For a detailed discussion of roles, see Chapter 12.)

Three factors—endowment, learning, and social roles—therefore lead us to expect a certain continuity, consistency, and permanency to personality. For this reason, we cannot expect a person to change very greatly or very quickly. What he will be tomorrow is an extension of what he is today. Moreover, if he seems to be a Dr. Jekyll and Mr. Hyde—a person of changing characteristics—appearances are deceiving. Beneath the exterior is a person whose motives and habits make sense in terms of the individual's past history. In attempting to understand a person, and in knowing what to expect of him, it is therefore best to assume that the future personality will be essentially what it has been in the past.

▪ *Personality changes.* We are not saying, however, that personality never changes. Over a period of time, it usually does. In some, it changes more than it does in others. Nearly everyone gradually acquires some new habits to supplant old ones. Often they discover ways of satisfying motives that were previously frustrated. Sometimes they change their way of life, and this leads to satisfactions they did not know before or to new roles to be played. Marriage, for example, occasionally produces marked personality changes—although marriage is usually no cure for a personality problem— because it affords a new way of life and exposes a person to a different set of influences. Sometimes, too, personality changes take place as a result of intense religious experience, changing jobs, moving to a new community, achieving success in a line of work, etc. In all these cases, however, the change takes place because something has happened to change motives, satisfy motives, teach new habits, or, in a word, change a person's fundamental modes of adjustment.

Most personality changes occur gradually and with no conscious intent. Sometimes, however, there is a deliberate attempt to bring about personality changes. A person may change himself, or someone close to him may effect a change, by working at it diligently over a period of time (see page 276). However, psychotherapy and counseling, which we shall discuss in Chapter 11, are organized methods for bringing about such changes. These methods are employed

when a person faces a problem he feels unable to solve, or when he becomes so incapable of making social adjustments that an important personality change is urgently needed. When successful, psychotherapy and counseling techniques effect personality changes by enabling the individual to discard old habits and to learn new ones that reduce his motivational conflicts (see page 293) and provide satisfactions for his needs. Such personality changes may therefore be regarded as cases of relatively rapid learning.

Personality syndromes. Also of aid in understanding individual persons is the concept of *syndrome*. This term comes from medical terminology, where it refers to a pattern of causes and symptoms of disease. In the field of personality it means a *pattern of causes and characteristics of the personality.* Although each individual's personality is unique, a person may display a syndrome which is similar in many respects to the pattern of characteristics found in other individuals.

Several personality syndromes have been described and measured. In fact, one purpose of some personality tests, such as the MMPI, is to detect such syndromes. For example, a hypochondriacal syndrome, which may consist of many specific characteristics, is one of abnormal concern over bodily health. A psychasthenic syndrome is characterized by excessive doubt, compulsions, obsessions, and unreasonable fears. (Both these syndromes are measured on the MMPI.) Another syndrome, called the authoritarian personality, is marked by highly conventional behavior, desire for power, hostility, prejudice, and intolerance. This kind of personality pattern has been extensively studied[23] and appears to have its causes in rejection or excessive domination of a child by his parents. Still another example of a syndrome is the so-called compulsive personality, which tends toward excessive cleanliness, orderliness, obstinacy, and stinginess.[24]

Our use of the concept of syndrome does not imply, as it might seem to, the classification of people into types, which we criticized earlier in this chapter. Not everyone has a personality syndrome, and hence syndromes cannot be used to classify people. The idea of the syndrome is that some personality characteristics tend to be highly correlated and thus to form patterns. Some individuals consequently display syndromes that are similar to those of other individuals. If we are aware of a syndrome, when it exists, we have a better over-all understanding of a person than we would otherwise have.

Personality structure.   We have presented briefly a few features of personality that help us understand an individual case. It is also helpful to consider a conception of *personality structure* contributed by Sigmund Freud from his extensive experience with psychoanalysis (page 282). This conception tends to oversimplify personality, but it has its merits. Indeed, in its general outlines, it encompasses many of the facts of human behavior that we have covered in this and preceding chapters.

Freud considered personality to have a structure consisting of three parts: the *id*, the *ego*, and the *superego*. The *id*, as he conceived of it, is sort of a storehouse of motives and of "instinctual" reactions for satisfying motives. Left to itself, the id would seek immediate satisfaction for motives as they arose without regard to the realities of life or to morals of any kind. It is usually bridled, however, by the *ego*. This consists of the elaborate ways of behaving and thinking that we have learned for dealing effectively with the world. It delays the satisfaction of motives or channels motives into socially acceptable outlets. It keeps a person working for a living, getting along with people, and generally adjust-

ing to the realities of life. Indeed, Freud characterized the ego with the statement that it is "in the service of the reality principle" (see page 290). The *superego*, finally, corresponds closely with what we more commonly call the *conscience*. It consists of restraints, acquired in the course of personality development, on the activity of the ego and the id. The superego may condemn as wrong things that the ego might do in the satisfaction of the id's motives. In addition, the superego keeps a person working toward the ideals he has acquired in childhood.

This conception sums up well three major aspects of personality. In early chapters, particularly Chapter 3, we described these aspects in somewhat different terms. The first aspect, equivalent to the id, consists of unlearned physiological motives and unlearned reactions for satisfying them. The second, corresponding to ego, is made up of learned instrumental acts for satisfying motives and also of the perceived self, which we shall discuss in the next section. The third, represented by the superego, is the set of socially derived motives that may affect, and sometimes conflict with, the activities of the first two factors. Thus, Freud's basic ideas of personality structure, though clothed in somewhat unfamiliar terminology, are in general accord with the conclusions of experimental psychology.[24]

It has been objected that the Freudian view of personality structure divides personality up into three compartments, each seeming to be a separate personality of its own. It is indeed easy to slip into this way of viewing the id, ego, and superego, but this was not intended. The three terms simply represent convenient concepts for summarizing major aspects of personality that have no clear lines among them. They provide a general picture of what, in detail, becomes very complicated.

The self. It was pointed out above that Freud's concept of the ego corresponds in part to what we familiarly call the *self*. For most of us, the self is the real essence of the personality. Unfortunately the self is rather elusive from the point of view of the scientist. While we are all convinced of the existence of our selves, many problems stand in the way of an objective study of them. Nevertheless there are some conclusions that can be drawn about the self, and these are of benefit in understanding personality.

▪ *Origin of the self.* For the psychologist, the self represents the individual's awareness or perception of his own personality. We learn to perceive our own body and behavior in much the same way that we learn to perceive other objects and events in the world about us (see Chapter 7, "Attention and Perception"). The beginnings of the perceived self can be traced to early infancy, when the infant first starts to learn vague distinctions between his own body and other objects in his environment. At birth the infant is most likely aware only of vague feelings of comfort or discomfort, but as his capacity for learning and memory develops and as his experience widens, the child sees that parts of his body are common to all his experiences. Muscular and organic sensations accompany all his activities, and he discovers that pinching objects such as his doll does not cause pain whereas pinching any part of his own body does. By the time the child is two years old, his distinction between his own body and other objects is well established.

▪ *Self-perception.* While the perception of the body as a unit distinct from the changing background is probably the core around which all later self-perception takes place, there are a number of other influences that contribute importantly to the development of self-awareness. Such awareness is fostered by giving the child a name, by

holding him responsible for his behavior, and by distinguishing between possessions that are his and possessions that belong to the parents, brothers, and sisters. By the family and society treating the child as a unit, he comes to perceive himself as one.

The kind of experiences that the child has are important in determining what his self-perception will be like. The child finds that his behavior and appearance elicit kindness or hostility, respect or rebuke, attention or indifference from parents and fellows. He hears himself described by parents and playmates in terms of various personality traits, and when these traits are consistently applied, he often accepts them as descriptions of himself. Praise and love from the parents, respect and attention from playmates, will contribute to the development of a picture of himself as a desirable person. On the other hand, rejection and excessive criticism at home and indifference from others can lead to a derogatory self-picture, with resulting inferiority feelings.

The traits and abilities of a child determine in large part the kinds of experiences he has and the descriptions applied to him. The physically strong child is more apt to receive the admiration of his playmates than is the weaker child. The intelligent child will have a greater opportunity for success experiences and praise in school. Hence we would expect that the individual's perception of his own personality would tend to coincide with the way in which others perceive him. However, this is not always true. Probably in no case do we ever perceive ourselves exactly as others see us, and in some cases there can be marked differences between the perceived self and the real or objective personality.

Although a child may be quite physically capable and intelligent, if raised by indifferent parents and subjected to constant criticism and belittlement, he may learn to per-

Fig. 9.13. Attitudes of parents are important in the child's development of self-perception. (*From Principles of Development, a McGraw-Hill Text-Film.*)

ceive himself as an inadequate, undesirable person. Most of us have known people who constantly underrate their own performance. By the same token we have also known people with a grossly exaggerated view of their accomplishments and capabilities. Children surrounded by an admiring and doting family who excessively praise even poor performance are frequently found to have excessive self-evaluations.

▪ *The self and emotional adjustment.* There are many instances where knowing the self-picture is a big help in understanding the person's behavior. This is particularly true in those cases where there is a marked discrepancy between the way the person sees himself and the way others see him. Behavior is largely determined by how the person perceives a situation with reference to himself. From our vantage point we may think that John should be a popular fellow with the girls—after all, he has good looks and a ready wit—but if John does not

perceive himself as having these attributes, he may be just another shy wallflower.

If the person's self-picture is too different from the true or objective personality, serious adjustment problems may arise. The person is constantly called upon to explain away or ignore evidence which is incompatible with his view of himself. The mediocre student who pictures himself as an intellectual giant is faced with the objective evidence of his poor grades and failures. Often, instead of changing his self-evaluation, he will use rationalizations (bright people are not interested in getting grades, they have broader interests) to explain the evidence away, or he may completely ignore it by forcing it out of his mind. When such devices are used to maintain a distorted self-perception, they are called *defense mechanisms*, which are described in the next chapter. People are quite adept at fooling themselves, and there is a wide variety of defense mechanisms, as we shall see.

SUMMARY

1. In order to study personality, we must discover characteristics that distinguish different individuals from one another. We may choose one set of characteristics to serve one particular purpose, and another set to serve another purpose.

2. Traits are probably the most comprehensive means of characterizing personalities. Abilities, attitudes, and interests are also useful characteristics. A person's typical motives are still another. We may also describe his typical modes of adjustment to problems in life.

3. Measurements of personality have been devised both to study personality and to use in practical situations. There are several pencil-and-paper tests of personality.

4. Situation tests can also be used. In such tests, a person is placed in a problem situation with other people, and his way of dealing with the problem is observed.

5. For research purposes, one can make experimental measurements of reactions to different stimuli, and these can serve as measures of personality.

6. Interviews, although often used, are not highly reliable or valid measures of personality.

7. Somewhat more objective and valid are rating scales, which require the rating of the presence or degree of particular characteristics.

8. In recent years, projective tests such as the Rorschach and Thematic Apperception Test have come into widespread use.

9. There is considerable evidence that inheritance and biological predispositions are important in personality development.

10. Abilities affect personality development, because they aid or hinder the solution of problems and influence the reactions of other people to a person.

11. A person's culture continually bombards him with pressures, frustrations, and rewards that influence his personality development.

12. A person's family helps mold his personality by training him to behave in certain ways, transmitting to him many of the attitudes he adopts, and presenting him with models of behavior that he often copies.

13. To understand better the individual personality, the following points should be kept in mind: (*a*) each personality is unique; (*b*) personality is continuous and consistent; (*c*) personality changes usually occur very slowly; and (*d*) some individuals display patterns of characteristics called syndromes.

14. Freud conceived of three major aspects of personality structure: (*a*) the id as a storehouse of motives and "instinctual" reactions, (*b*) the ego as the conscious self that attempts to cope realistically with the world, and (*c*) the superego as a conscience that restrains the ego and id and keeps a person working toward ideals acquired in childhood.

15. The self develops through awareness of one's body and through the treatment of a child as a unit. A person's perception of his self has an important bearing on his relations with others and on his emotional adjustment.

SUGGESTIONS FOR FURTHER READING

Allport, G. W. *Personality*. New York: Holt, 1937.

   An original treatment of personality, contributing new concepts of personality, still widely used as a text.

Cattell, R. B. *Personality*. New York: McGraw-Hill, 1950.

   A text on personality emphasizing particularly the measurement of personality characteristics.

Eysenck, H. J. *Dimensions of personality*. London: Routledge, 1947.

   A text on personality with special emphasis on the measurement of basic factors in personality.

Kluckhohn, C., and Murray, H. A. *Personality: in nature, society and culture*. New York: Knopf, 1948.

   A treatment of personality from the standpoint of a social anthropologist and a psychologist.

McClelland, D. C. *Personality*. New York: Sloane, 1951.

   A text that offers new theoretical approaches to some of the problems of personality.

Murphy, G. *Personality*. New York: Harper, 1947.

   A comprehensive text on personality.

Sheldon, W. H., and Stevens, S. S. *The varieties of temperament*. New York: Harper, 1942.

   An account of research on temperament and its constitutional basis.

Stagner, R. *Psychology of personality* (2d Ed.). New York: McGraw-Hill, 1948.

   A widely used text on personality.

Symonds, P. M. *The ego and the self*. New York: Appleton-Century-Crofts, 1951.

   An extended treatment of the concepts of the ego and self.

White, R. W. *Lives in progress: a study of the natural growth of personality*. New York: Dryden, 1952.

   An intensive and interesting study of three healthy young adults, conducted in two phases, first while the subjects were in college and again five to ten years later.

Chapter 10　FRUSTRATION AND CONFLICT

In chapters 3 and 4, we presented principles of *motivation* and *emotion*. In Chapter 9, we covered the topic of *personality*. The student should have the contents of these chapters in mind as he undertakes the reading of the present chapter. In particular, he should review the concepts of *frustration*, *anxiety*, and *aggression*, presented in Chapter 4, and the description of *motives* and of *modes of adjustment* included in Chapter 9.

It is a central fact of human existence that *motives are often frustrated*. It is important to understand how and why such frustration occurs. We shall therefore begin this chapter with a section on the *frustration of motives*. In the course of the discussion, it will become clear that frustration

This chapter was drafted by Richard S. Lazarus of Clark University.

produces anxiety and that people adopt *reactions to frustration* that serve as defenses against such anxiety. The description of these reactions will be the subject of our second section. Then we shall come to the problem of abnormal behavior, which is the result of a person's relying too heavily on defensive reactions to frustration and anxiety. Patterns of abnormal behavior are usually classified into the *neuroses* and *psychoses*, and these therefore will be the headings of the last two sections in the chapter.

◼ FRUSTRATION OF MOTIVES

As we explained in Chapter 3, every motive has a goal. For physiological motives, the goals are relatively fixed; the hungry organism must have food, and the thirsty one must have water, if its motive is to be satisfied. For the more complex social and personal motives, the goals are more flexible. Status, for example, may be achieved by social eminence, by professional success, or by athletic prowess. Nevertheless, whatever the goals may be, they must be achieved or else the motive goes unsatisfied. A motive not satisfied within a reasonable time is a frustrated motive.

Whenever a motive is frustrated, the underlying reason for the frustration can be found—some object, person, or other motives within the person—if we only look carefully enough for it. This reason, whatever it may be, is called the *source of frustration,* and it is possible to distinguish three general sources of frustration: (1) environmental obstacles that prevent the attainment of the goal; (2) personal inadequacies or handicaps that make the goal unattainable; and (3) motivational conflicts within the individual that deny him satisfaction of one motive when he attempts to satisfy another. We shall consider each of these sources of frustration.

Environmental obstacles. The most elementary kind of frustration occurs when the environment presents a *barrier or obstacle* to the attainment of a goal. Of the various kinds of barriers we can imagine, the most obvious is the lack of a goal object in the immediate environment of a person. A man who is hungry but miles away from food, a driver who runs out of gasoline some distance from a filling station, and a man with sexual motives stranded on a desert island by himself are examples of this kind of frustration. In each case, it is some aspect of the environment—physical distance, lack of a suitable conveyance, or simply the perversity of nature—that constitutes an obstacle to the satisfaction of the motive.

There are also more subtle and complex situations that function as environmental obstacles. We usually remain quiet in a library even when we might like to chat because noise is disapproved. We drive at moderate or slow speeds on city streets because it is illegal and dangerous to violate the traffic regulations. It is often impossible to visit our families when we should like to because they live too far away. We may be unable to go swimming on a summer Sunday because it is too cold or there is no place to swim. And our desire to be appreciated or loved may be thwarted because the girl or boy we are courting does not seem to respond. All these are obstacles, presented by people or things in our environment, to the satisfaction of our motives. They are *environmental* sources of frustration.

In early childhood, most frustrations arise from environmental obstacles. You can be sure of this if you simply observe a three- or four-year-old child for a few hours. He will be frustrated, for example, because he cannot get a toy, an ice cream cone, or his lunch; because he falls, cannot get on the swing, or cannot reach what he wants; or because his mother will not let him play, go to the zoo, or stay up late. The child's problem of satisfying wants is therefore almost entirely one of dealing with environmental obstacles. Adults have their fair share of such obstacles too, and we have mentioned a few examples above, but their most serious problems of frustration, as we shall see, have other sources.

At this point, we should call the student's attention to the diagram in Figure 10.1. This is one of a series of diagrams that we shall use to represent different types of frustration of motives. In such diagrams, the ellipse is used to denote the total *environment* of the person, the dot stands for the person, and the vertical line represents a barrier or obstacle. Goals are depicted by either a + or − sign, called a *valence.*

When the sign is positive, it indicates that the goal is something to which a person is attracted; when its sign is negative, it represents punishment or threat—something the person fears or has learned to avoid. The arrow is used like a *vector* in physics to indicate the direction of forces acting on the individual under the influence of various motives. This particular method of depicting frustrating situations was devised by Lewin and helps us visualize the sources and effects of frustration.[1] Figure 10.1 describes the case of frustration by environmental obstacles.

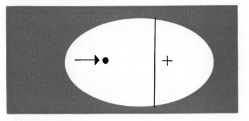

Fig. 10.1. Frustration by environmental obstacles. Some barrier (vertical line) stands between the person (dot) and his goal (+).

Unattainable goals. In Chapter 3, we introduced the concepts of *level of aspiration* and *level of performance*. One's level of aspiration is determined by the goals he has acquired through learning; his level of performance is set by his own abilities and by the skills he has acquired for achieving his goals. When there is a disparity between these two levels, the person suffers a frustration of motives due to his inability to achieve his goals. This situation is basically the same as that diagramed in Figure 10.1 for environmental obstacles, except that in this case the obstacle is the discrepancy between the levels of aspiration and performance.

Looking about at ourselves and other people, we have no difficulty in finding examples of this source of frustration. One of

the most common instances concerns vocational ambitions, which we consider in Chapter 16. Because of social or parental pressure, many young men and women aspire to a profession, such as medicine or engineering, for which they are not fitted by ability, interests, or work habits. Often these goals have been taught so thoroughly by parents and associates that people are unwilling or unable to give them up. The result: frustration. Other examples are the desire for more money than one knows how to earn, the desire of the unattractive girl for suitors, and the desire for social status beyond one's reach. No doubt you can think of others. In each case, *a person is frustrated by his own inability to reach the goals he has set for himself.*

Motivational conflict. Although environmental obstacles and unattainable goals account for many of life's frustrations, the most deep-seated source of frustration—the one that causes people the most unhappiness—is a *conflict of motives* within the person. In a moment, we shall see how some of these conflicts arise, but first we must see what is meant by such motivational conflict. Lewin, the author of the diagram in Figure 10.1, has distinguished three basic types of conflict situation: *approach-approach* conflict, *avoidance-avoidance* conflict, and *approach-avoidance* conflict.

Approach-approach conflict, as the label implies, is a conflict between two positive goals—goals that are equally attractive at the same time (see Figure 10.2). A physiological example of such conflict is that of being both hungry and sleepy at the same time. A social example is that of wanting to go to a dance and a swimming party when both are scheduled for the same night. The proverbial donkey is supposed to have starved to death because he stood halfway between two piles of hay and could

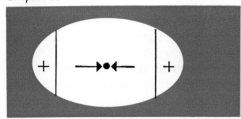

Fig. 10.2. Approach-approach conflict. The individual is attracted by two positive goals that are incompatible with each other.

not decide which to choose. Actually, neither donkeys nor people often "starve themselves to death" merely because they are in conflict between two positive goals. People usually resolve such a conflict by satisfying first one goal, then the other—eating, then going to bed, if one is both hungry and sleepy—or by choosing one of the goals and giving up the other.

A second type of conflict, *avoidance-avoidance conflict*, is diagrammed in Figure 10.3. This involves two negative goals, and it is fairly common. Little Johnny must do his arithmetic or get a spanking. A student may be forced to spend the next two days studying for an examination or face the possibility of failure. A man may be forced to work at a job he intensely dislikes or take the chance of losing his income. Such conflicts are capsuled in the common saying, "caught between the devil and the deep blue sea." You can probably think of many examples in your own experience of things you do not want to do but must either do or face even less desirable alternatives.

Two kinds of behavior are likely to be especially conspicuous in such avoidance-avoidance conflicts. One is *vacillation*. As we shall see below, *the strength of a goal is greater, the closer one is to the goal*. As a person approaches a negative goal, he finds it increasingly repelling. Consequently, he tends to retreat in the other direction.

When he does this, he comes closer to the other negative goal and finds it, in turn, to increase in negative valence. He is like a baseball player caught in a "run down" between first and second base. He runs first one way, then the other. As he runs toward second base, he comes closer to being tagged out, but when he turns and runs back toward first base, he faces the same danger. Such *vacillation is characteristic of avoidance-avoidance conflicts*.

A second important feature of this kind of conflict is *an attempt to leave the conflict situation*. Theoretically, a person might escape avoidance-avoidance conflict by running away altogether from the conflict situation. People do, indeed, try to do this. In practice, however, there are additional negative goals in the periphery of the field, and these ordinarily keep a person from taking this alternative. A child, for example, who does not want either to do arithmetic or to take a spanking may think of slipping away from home. This, however, has even more serious consequences than staying in the situation and "facing the music," so he is wiser not to try it. The adult in avoidance-avoidance conflict, however, may try a quite different way of running away. This is to

Fig. 10.3. Avoidance-avoidance conflict. The individual is caught between two threats or fears. In addition to the goals shown, there are usually other barriers or negative goals to restrain the individual. Otherwise, in this type of conflict, he is inclined to "leave the field" (dotted line) to escape conflict.

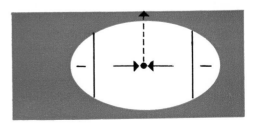

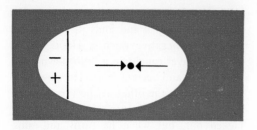

Fig. 10.4. Approach-avoidance conflict. The individual is attracted toward a positive goal, but this goal also has a fear or threat (negative goal) associated with it. Such conflict is difficult to resolve and tends to evoke more anxiety than the approach-approach or avoidance-avoidance conflict.

let his *thoughts and imagination take him away from the uncomfortable situation.* He may spend his time, for example, in daydreaming, instead of facing up to his problem. As a student, you have no doubt found yourself doing this at times when you were supposed to be studying. In extreme cases, a person may conjure up an imaginary world, or re-create in his mind's eye the carefree world of childhood, in which there is no such thing as unpleasant tasks that have to be performed. Carried to such an extreme, this way of leaving the conflict situation is called *fantasy* or *regression*, depending on the form it takes. We shall discuss these in later sections of this chapter.

The third type of conflict, *approach-avoidance conflict*, is the most important of the three because it is the most difficult to resolve. In approach-avoidance conflict, a person is both repelled and attracted by the same goal object. A young bride, for example, may have been brought up in an atmosphere that treated sexual activities as ugly and sinful. As a consequence, sexual matters have for her a negative sign (see Figure 10.4). At the same time, her normal sexual drive, as well as other social values

involved in marriage, have led her into marriage, thus providing the marital situation with a positive sign. Now, as she enters marriage, she is caught between her sexual motives and the attitudes of her parents, which have become her own values. There is no way out of this situation without altering her motives, which in the diagram means erasing or weakening one of the signs.

The example of the bride in conflict gives us a hint about the way in which approach-avoidance conflicts can develop. Note that the bride's conflict arose because of the social values acquired in her early training. These values serve as obstacles to the satisfaction of motives. Since they are within the person, the process of acquiring them (which we considered in Chapter 3) is regarded as one of *internalizing obstacles.* Such obstacles frustrate a person in the same way that the environmental obstacles of childhood do. The fact, however, that they are *internal*, rather than external, makes them much more difficult for the person to deal with. He may find ways of circumventing environmental obstacles, but he can hardly circumvent that which is within himself.

This analysis of frustration, depicted in Figures 10.1 to 10.4, permits us to reduce frustrating situations to their simplest ele-

Fig. 10.5. Double approach-avoidance conflict. Many conflicts that appear to be approach-approach or avoidance-avoidance conflicts are really double approach-avoidance conflicts. For an example, see text.

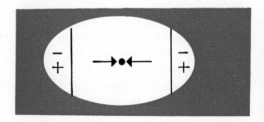

ments. In everyday life, however, things are seldom this simple. More typical are conflicts in which there are many different goals, especially negative ones, surrounding a person with pressures he wishes to avoid. There are also some complex combinations of the kinds of situations we have described. One is the *double approach-avoidance conflict,* diagramed in Figure 10.5. In this, two or more goals may have both positive and negative signs. Consider, for example, the student who is in conflict between making good grades and making the college football team. Superficially, this conflict appears to be a simple case of approach-approach conflict—conflict between two positive goals. The student, however, may have considerable social pressure from family and associates to achieve both goals. He may incur the disapproval of his parents if he fails to make good grades, and he may lose the esteem of his comrades if he does not make the football team. Thus failure at either one carries with it a threat. Each goal, therefore, has a negative value as well as a positive one; hence, the student finds himself in a double approach-avoidance conflict.

In concluding this analysis of conflict, there is one additional point that needs to be emphasized. As we indicated above, *the strength of positive and negative goals varies with psychological distance.* That is, the strength of a goal—the amount that it attracts or repels—is stronger the nearer one is to it. This fact is represented by the gradients in Figure 10.6. However, as this figure also illustrates, there is a difference between the *approach gradient* and the *avoidance gradient:* the avoidance gradient is the steeper of the two.[2] This means, other things being equal, that when a person is some distance from a goal having both positive and negative valences, the positive valence seems stronger. On the other hand,

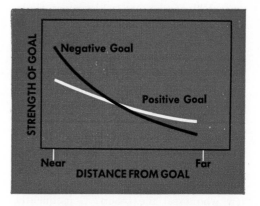

Fig. 10.6. Gradients of goal-strength for positive and negative goals. Other things being equal, goals are "stronger" the closer one is to them. However, negative goals are somewhat stronger than positive ones when a person is near the goal, and positive goals are stronger when he is far from the goal. This fact accounts for a person being trapped in approach-avoidance conflict; he approaches the goal, then stops and is afraid to come any closer.

when one is near such a goal, the negative valence seems stronger. Where the two gradients cross, some distance from the goal, the valences are equal. In other terms, the figure indicates that a person in an approach-avoidance conflict will tend to approach the goal but then, as the tendency to avoid becomes stronger, will come to a stop some distance from the goal.

Common motivational conflicts. All sorts of conflicts and frustrations are possible, depending upon the situations a person faces and the goals he has acquired in the course of his life. The only way one can say what particular frustrations a person may be suffering is to have a very detailed knowledge of the person and his problems. There are certain conflicts, however, that are more common than others in our particular society. In other societies, the list might be somewhat different. The ones that we shall consider are achievement, independence, sex, and hostility.

▪ *Achievement.* In attaining many of our goals, we often are required to compete with our associates. If we succeed in our jobs, the result may be to frustrate other persons who dearly want the promotions we receive. In making good grades, we must compete with fellow students for the limited number of good grades assigned by the instructor. Not everyone can "win," and many of life's rewards are limited to the few who excel the others. Consequently, in achieving success, we often do it at the expense of the other fellow, and he frequently does not look kindly at the person who carries off his coveted prize. Many a friendship has been dissolved for this reason, and many a person incurs animosity because of his success. When a person achieves success, thus satisfying one set of motives, he may risk the frustration of his social motives for companionship, affection, status, and so on (see Chapter 3).

▪ *Independence.* In describing social motives in Chapter 3, we named *dependence* as one of the affiliative needs. Dependence, however, tends to engender an approach-avoidance conflict. We may find it very satisfying to depend on a person, as the child does on the parent, for meeting many of our needs. However, the person on whom we depend usually exercises a good deal of power over us, often denying us the things we want. It is nice to be able to depend on someone, but it is also nice to be so independent that he cannot dictate our behavior or deny us our desires. For just this reason, young people develop a desire to be independent, thus avoiding some of the obstacles presented by the people they depend on.

Independence, on the other hand, has its disadvantages. A person who is on his own may be able to do what he wants, but he also runs the risk of not being able to stand on his own feet. If he cannot earn his own money, keep a job, and fend for himself, he suffers a new set of frustrations. Considerable conflict about dependence and independence then follows. One sees this conflict most conspicuously in the adolescent, who is in transition from the extreme dependence of childhood to the independence of adulthood. Parents themselves may be in conflict about the matter—criticizing the adolescent one moment for being a "baby" and resenting his efforts at independence a moment later—and they may aggravate the adolescent's problems. Such a conflict is normal in adolescents, even if it is somewhat painful, but many individuals never outgrow the conflict and carry it with them through the rest of their lives.

▪ *Sex.* A third common conflict involves sex and is ordinarily a simple case of approach-avoidance conflict between sexual drives and the sexual mores. The strength of sexual drive, of course, varies from one person to another, but most people have enough drive to require frequent satisfaction. Yet many children learn early in life that sex is a subject about which there is much emotion and prohibition. They reach sexual maturity at about twelve years of age, and have well-developed sexual drives in adolescence, yet modern society has made no provision for satisfying them at that age. Among many people, sexual desires are considered to be immoral and indecent, and almost all sexual outlets are frowned upon before marriage. The moral code concerning sex becomes internalized and produces a motivational conflict between positive sexual motives and the negative goals of the moral code.

▪ *Hostility.* Another common motivational conflict is between aggression and social motives. Many situations arise from day to day in which our impulses are to

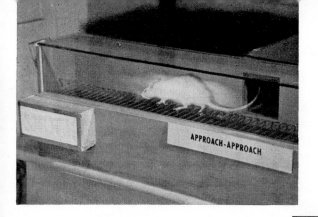

Approach-approach conflict. Emerging from the center doorway, the thirsty rat can find water at either end of the runway.

Avoidance-avoidance conflict. The rat attempts to avoid shock administered at both ends of the runway, but finds the center doorway closed.

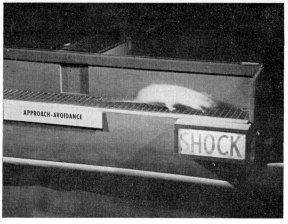

Approach-avoidance conflict. The thirsty rat receives both shock and water at the end of the runway.

Double approach-avoidance conflict. At both ends of the runway the rat receives both shock and water. (*All photos from McGraw-Hill Text-Film, Conflict.*)

fight back. When a person makes a slighting or insulting remark to me, when I get a lower mark on an examination than I think I deserve, when a person keeps me waiting at an appointment—in these and many more situations, I tend to become angry and to do something that may be regarded as aggressive or hostile. Most of us have learned relatively early in life not to engage in physical combat, because we may get hurt and because parents and society do not approve. Consequently, our tendency to aggress is usually not expressed in physical terms. It is more likely to take the form of telling a person off, arguing with him, or cooking up some scheme to get the best of him. In any event, one can say that aggressive or hostile motives have been aroused.

Aggression and hostility, however, are usually not condoned socially—except in strictly limited situations such as athletic events and wars. So aggressive impulses (motives) run headlong into conflict with the satisfaction of various social motives. If one shows hostility, he may lose social approval and social status or may run the risk of retaliation; yet if he does not, his aggressive impulses go unsatisfied. Hence a conflict arises that is difficult, if not impossible, to resolve.

Effects of frustration. We have described and analyzed several kinds of frustration. In the next major section, we shall consider the ways in which people react to frustration. In the meantime, we should consider some of the effects of frustration on the individual in order that we can better understand the mechanisms people use to cope with it. Effects we shall consider are (1) anxiety and aggression, (2) emotional misery and psychosomatic illness, and (3) stupidity and rigidity in solving problems.

▪ *Anxiety and aggression.* In the chapter on emotion, we explained that the two chief effects of frustration are *anxiety* and *aggression.* Anxiety is a vague fear that is acquired in experiences with many emotional and frustrating situations. Through learning, anxiety is evoked whenever a person even feels the *threat* of frustration, as well as frustration itself.

We also explained in Chapter 4 that aggression is a typical reaction to frustration. And since aggression is frequently punished in our society, the individual learns to become anxious about possible punishment when he merely feels aggressive, even though he may not express his aggression. Thus aggressive impulses lead to anxiety.

Because aggression is a motive, it is frustrated when it is restrained. Such frustration also leads to anxiety, which adds to the anxiety already elicited by frustration and aggression. As a result, frustration, aggression, and anxiety make a vicious circle, one leading inevitably to the other. For a fuller account of these points, the student is referred to Chapter 4.

▪ *Emotional misery and psychosomatic illness.* It should be plain from this discussion that *anxiety* is the basic effect of frustration. No matter how a person is frustrated and no matter how he reacts to frustration, he is quite certain to experience considerable anxiety. The effects of anxiety and a person's efforts to deal with it thus become the important theme in the life of a frustrated person.

A most conspicuous feature of anxiety is the *discomfort,* or even extreme *misery,* that it causes a person. Anxious people, by definition, are unhappy people. At best, they are slightly uncomfortable; at worst, they may experience a misery comparable to the pain suffered in severe injury or physical illness. The person who is anxious may not be aware of the frustration and conflict that make him miserable; he may not be conscious of the peculiarities in his behavior resulting from anxiety; but he is most certainly aware of the discomfort and pain caused by anxiety. Very frequently, for example, people come to psychologists or psychiatrists solely to find relief from their misery without being aware of what causes it.

As you may recall from Chapter 4, emotion—and this includes anxiety—is a bodily state in which many of the organs of the body are stirred up. A person suffering mild anxiety for a brief period exhibits and experiences many of the symptoms we described on page 89, but no permanent harm is done. On the other hand, if anxiety is severe and chronic, the constant disturbance of bodily functions can produce or aggravate physical illness. Such an illness is called a *psychosomatic disorder* because it is a disorder in the body caused by psychological difficulties.

The list of disorders that *may* be psychosomatic in origin is a long one and includes intestinal ulcers, high blood pressure, chronic headaches, asthma, hives, and diarrhea.[3] In many cases, such disorders are mainly caused by infection or malfunction of organs, but in others they are either caused or aggravated by excessive anxiety. It is not always easy, even for the trained physician, to distinguish between simple infections or malfunctions and those that are psychosomatic. The problem of psychosomatic disorder is one that has been recognized clearly only in recent years, and much more research is needed before we fully understand it. The important point to recognize here is that anxiety, as well as viruses and bacteria, makes people physically ill. On the other hand, it is not advisable to label all sorts of disorders as psychosomatic just because the person who has them seems to have more than his normal share of anxiety.

▪ *Stupidity and rigidity.* Another important effect of anxiety is to limit a person's ability to learn adequate ways of adjusting to his conflicts.[4] One of the basic effects of anxiety is to reduce trial-and-error behavior (see page 151) in the learning process and to fixate a person's responses. Instead of trying first one thing, then another, to solve his problem, he keeps using the same response over and over again. If such a fixated response does not happen to be the correct one for relieving a frustration, as it usually is not, he is prevented from discovering the most effective way of solving his problems. Hence the anxious person has less chance of hitting on a response that may eliminate his frustration.

Because anxiety fixates responses and prevents a person (or animal) from hitting upon the correct response, the frustrated person, ridden with anxiety, often seems stupid to the innocent observer. To such an observer, the solution to the person's problem seems ridiculously simple. "All he has to do is . . . ," the observer may say —and he may be right. But it is the person's anxiety that blinds him so that he cannot see or try methods that might eliminate his frustration. Thus the anxiety connected with frustration creates a vicious circle: *Frustration makes him anxious; his anxiety keeps him from finding a response that reduces frustration; therefore, he remains frustrated.*

REACTIONS TO FRUSTRATION AND ANXIETY

Now let us consider what people do, and learn to do, to cope with frustration and the anxiety it produces. In considering this problem, you should remember that anxiety is a motive—a powerful motive. From the chapters on motivation and learning, you will recall that any behavior that is instru-

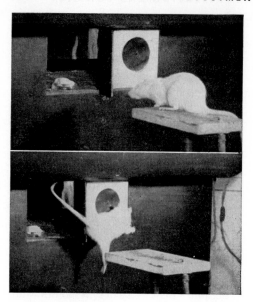

Fig. 10.7. Fixation caused by conflict. The rat above has been given an insoluble problem in which it developed the habit of jumping to the right window. In the top picture, it stares at food in the open window, yet (see bottom picture) jumps compulsively to the right window, which is locked, and is punished by dropping to the floor below. This illustrates how a person who has developed a habit when frustrated may stick to the habit even when a more adequate solution is "obvious." (From Maier, N. R. F. *Frustration*. New York: McGraw-Hill, 1949, Fig. 5 and 5b.)

mental in satisfying a motive tends to be learned. We may therefore expect to find that anxiety accounts for much of human learning and that such learning, in turn, accounts for the ways people react to anxiety. We shall begin by (1) illustrating the role of instrumental learning in reactions to anxiety, and then (2) introducing a special kind of learning, called repression, that figures prominently in reactions to anxiety. After that, we shall consider in turn several typical reactions to anxiety.

Instrumental learning. As we have already seen (Chapter 5), a person or animal

that is motivated usually varies his behavior, trying first one response, then another. Eventually he may hit upon a response that is *reinforced*, that is to say, one that leads to the satisfaction of the motive. If the same response is repeatedly reinforced, it is learned and becomes his regular mode of adjustment whenever he is motivated and in a similar situation. This principle of learning applies just as well to anxiety motives as it does to the motives discussed in Chapter 3. It accounts for the habits that are acquired as means of reducing frustration.[5]

Let us illustrate this principle by taking the example of a frustrated child at an amusement park. The child wants a stick of candy and asks his mother for one. The mother says, "No," explaining that it is too close to suppertime. "Aw, Mom," he pleads, "can't I have one?" She continues to say "No." He pleads some more. Then he accuses his mother of being mean, thus attempting to browbeat her into saying "Yes." Still the answer is "No." At this point, the youngster throws what is commonly called a temper tantrum. He rolls on the ground screaming, beats his head against the wall, or begins to hold his breath—something that often scares mothers but shouldn't. At this point, from mental exhaustion, fear, embarrassment at the scene, or just the desire to be left alone, the mother relents and gives the child the money to buy the candy.

Thus ends one trial of a learning situation which, in less extreme form perhaps, is typical of many in life. The motive for candy made the youngster try first one approach and then another to get the candy. All of them failed until he hit upon the temper tantrum. Since this succeeded, it was reinforced, and the chances are that he has learned to use the temper tantrum the next time he is similarly frustrated. If not, it will take only one or two more repetitions for him to learn this particular mode of adjustment. Then a habitual method of dealing with frustration will have been learned. In all probability the child will hold on to this method of adjustment until it fails. If it does, he may later find some other mode of adjustment. Of course, as he matures, social pressures may make him vary this mode. Even then, it may be only slightly modified, and he may use some form of temper tantrum throughout life as a learned reaction to certain kinds of frustration.

There are many kinds of frustration and many opportunities to learn habitual methods of dealing with them. The opportunities, the frustrations, and the modes adopted will vary with individuals, their families, social groups, and circumstances. The important point is that through learning people *tend to adopt typical, habitual responses to frustrations and that these modes of adjustment are learned* according to the principles of learning that we have described earlier.

Repression. In reacting to anxiety, people employ a mechanism called *repression*. Discovered by Freud in his work with neurotic patients,* repression is a reaction in which a person *rejects from consciousness impulses or thoughts that provoke anxiety.* In more familiar terms, it means that a person refuses to recognize or admit to himself the motives or memories that make him anxious. By this means, he effectively avoids or reduces anxiety.

Repression is, in part, a kind of "forgetting" (see page 132), for a person conveniently represses the things that might make him anxious or uncomfortable. I can easily "forget" to pay a bill, because paying it might bring me uncomfortably close to insolvency. I can forget my dentist's appointment, because I am anxious about dentists' drills. Such forgetting, however, is not true forgetting, for the memories can be recovered when the anxiety connected with them has been reduced or eliminated —when I get my next pay check or after the date with the dentist is past. Hence, although repression often takes the form of forgetting, it goes deeper than that. It applies not only to memories but also to any thoughts or motives that arouse anxiety. A girl, for example, who is caught between rigid moral standards and strong sexual impulses, may deny to herself that she has any sexual inclinations. In this case, it is not a memory that is repressed but rather a physiological motive. Thus, *repression eliminates a conflict or frustration from conscious awareness and thereby reduces anxiety.*

The concept of repression may be clarified by referring once again to the diagrams in Figures 10.1 to 10.5. Ordinary instrumental learning, illustrated by the child's learning the temper tantrum, is most effective in simple frustration (Figure 10.1) when there is merely a barrier to a positive goal. By varying his behavior, a person finds some means of penetrating or circumventing the barrier. Such learning, however, is not so effective in an approach-avoidance conflict involving both positive and negative goals. In this case, the conflict is most easily resolved by altering one of the motives, and repression may be used to accomplish this result. The case of the girl caught in a conflict between moral standards (negative goal) and sexual drive (positive goal) is an illustration. By denying her sexual impulses, she rids herself of the posi-

* Freud discovered the phenomenon of repression while attempting to treat hysterical patients—patients who have symptoms such as blindness or paralysis without any physical basis for them. These patients, he observed, appeared unable to remember certain traumatic experiences, yet were able to recall these experiences after undergoing psychotherapy (see Chapter 11).

tive goal (motive) and thus reduces the problem to one of simple avoidance, which is easily solved. Needless to say, by merely denying her sexual drive, she does not eliminate it, and it remains to frustrate her. Through repression, however, she does eliminate the anxiety connected with sexual impulses and partly solves her problem— for the time being. *Repression, then, is a means of altering conscious goals or motives.* In the majority of cases, it seems to affect motives with positive goals, but it sometimes eliminates from consciousness negative goals or even both types of goals.

In the following paragraphs we list and describe some typical reactions to frustration. These reactions are sometimes called *defense mechanisms* because they are devices that defend a person against anxiety by reducing or eliminating it. In most of these reactions, you will see the repression of motives at work, as well as instances of ordinary instrumental learning.

Reaction formation. It is possible to disguise a motive so completely that it is *expressed in a form that is directly opposite to its original intent.* This defense mechanism is called *reaction formation.* We may see it in the case of the daughter who unconsciously hates her mother but who appears oversolicitous of her mother's health and comfort. To admit to herself that she hates her mother may be so abhorrent and may create so many anxieties that she tries to overcome the anxiety with excessive affection. The common quotation from Shakespeare, "The lady doth protest too much, methinks," refers to this disguise. For when a person is too solicitous or too modest or too affectionate, there is a good chance he harbors aggression or other impulses that are being repressed and disguised by the opposite kind of behavior.

Projection. Still another common disguise that protects a person against anxiety-producing impulses is *projection.* It is a device that *disguises the source of conflict by ascribing motives to someone else.* If a student, for example, has a strong desire to cheat on an examination but is unwilling to admit it to himself because of his moral code, he may become unduly suspicious of others and accuse them of cheating when they are innocent. Or if he has a tendency to be unkind to other people yet knows that this tendency is "wrong," he may accuse other people of being unkind to him when in fact they are not.

Projection is well illustrated in a study of the attitudes of 97 fraternity members toward each other.[6] The students were asked to rate certain of their fraternity brothers on four undesirable traits: stinginess, obstinacy, disorderliness, and bashfulness. After rating others, each student was asked to rate himself. In this way it was possible to compare a student's rating of himself with other members' ratings of him. Some members seemed quite aware of their own traits, for their self-ratings agreed well with the ratings made by other members. From the ratings of the group, however, it appeared that certain students had one or more traits in an undesirable degree. It is interesting that these students assigned a higher degree of their own undesirable traits to other students than they did to themselves. Thus they failed to acknowledge undesirable traits in themselves and assigned them—projected them —to their fraternity brothers.

Other examples of projection abound in human behavior. When a person believes incorrectly that other people are out to do him wrong, one can suspect that he is harboring strong aggressive impulses that he is projecting to other people. The unattractive spinster who will not leave her house because she is sure that men are waiting to attack her must be suspected of

Fig. 10.8. The displacement of aggression. In the experiment depicted here, a rat was rewarded for striking another rat by turning off shock on the grill in the floor. When the second rat was no longer present, the first rat turned to the "innocent bystander," the rubber doll, and struck the doll. Thus aggression was displaced from the unavailable object to an available object. (*Courtesy Dr. Neal E. Miller.*)

projecting her own thwarted sex desires. To recognize such desires in herself would make her anxious, so she defends herself by projecting the desires to someone else. In the extreme form, such projection is the mark of the mental disease called paranoia.

Displacement. Displacement is still another kind of defense against anxiety-producing motives.[7] In displacement, *the object or goal of a motive is disguised by substituting another one in place of it.* An example is the man who gets angry at his boss but is afraid to tell him off, then comes home and bawls out his wife. As another example, consider the little child who finds her newborn brother the new center of attention. Her jealousy makes her want to harm the baby. The family, however, forbids that and teaches her that hurting the baby is naughty. Unable to express her aggression against the baby, she substitutes

a safer object, a doll, and may succeed in totally destroying it. Thus she displaces the baby with the doll and finds an acceptable outlet for her aggression (see Figure 10.8).

Rationalization. Another kind of defense against the anxiety aroused by conflicting motives is *rationalization*. In employing this mode of adjustment, an individual so explains his own behavior as to *conceal the motive it expresses and assign it to some other motive.* There are many examples of this mechanism in everyday affairs. It is among the most common and socially accepted ways of reducing anxiety. A student who is motivated to have a good time may rationalize his school failures as due to inadequate teaching, unfairness of the teacher, or too little time to study. A mother whose real motive is to hold on to her son as long as possible may not permit him to go out on dates, with the rationali-

Fig. 10.9. Rationalization. (Copyright 1944, United Feature Syndicate, Inc., reprinted by permission of Bill Mauldin.)

"Yer lucky. Yer learnin' a trade."

zation that his schoolwork will be hampered or that he will fall into unwholesome company. A father may beat a child because—he rationalizes—the child deserves or needs it, but his real motive may be aggression. By rationalizing his behavior, he can gratify his needs without having to take the blame for them.

Sublimation and compensation. Two similar forms of defense have been given special names by Freud and others who have observed them to be frequently used as modes of adjustment. One is *sublimation.* This is *the use of a substitute activity to gratify a motive.* For example, when a sexual motive cannot be directly satisfied because of external obstacles or internal conflict, the motive is sometimes said to be

satisfied by finding some other outlet which seems to reduce tension. The unattractive girl with normal sexual urges may be unable to find a mate, or an attractive one may be unable to accept sexual activity. Freud believed that the frustrated urge could be partially gratified by channeling it into art, religion, music, or some aesthetic activity that is socially acceptable. Because of the passionate way in which some people embrace their aesthetic activities, Freud argued that the substitute activity is a means of satisfying sexual drives. This interpretation of sublimation is open to question, for it is doubtful that physiological motives can be relieved by substitute activities, and it is more likely that the motives involved, say, in aesthetic activities are not sexual. On the other hand, the general idea that motives may be gratified by substituting one set of activities for other, more typical activities, seems to be sound and acceptable.

Compensation is also a method of adjustment which usually involves a substitute activity for a frustrated motive. However, in compensation, there is usually the implication of failure or loss of self-esteem in one activity which is compensated for by efforts in some other realm of endeavor. The concept of compensation does not carry with it the implication of an outlet for sexual frustration. The unattractive girl may become a bookworm and achieve high scholarship, thereby commanding the respect and prestige that she was unable to win with good looks. The man who is short may develop his skill in boxing to secure the recognition as a "man" that his small stature denied him. An uneducated parent may derive a great deal of substitute satisfaction by having his son well educated. Life is full of such compensations through which a person achieves satisfaction that he otherwise could not obtain.

Fantasy. Sometimes it is possible to gratify a frustrated motive, at least in part, by resorting to fantasy or daydreaming. Fantasy is common among most people and is particularly prominent during adolescence. As a form of adjustment, it rarely leads to constructive action and thus may leave a person's basic conflicts unsolved. On the other hand, in small amounts, daydreaming about success, sexual conquests, and the like can produce a certain amount of satisfaction. A person who has been embarrassed in a social situation feels somewhat better if he indulges a little fantasy about all the things he could have said or would say in the situation. If a girl does not get invited to the junior prom, she can

at least have some fun dreaming about what it would have been like. It has been estimated that more than 95 per cent of college students spend some time daydreaming. Their most frequent subjects for daydreaming are academic honors, success with the opposite sex, and a future of fame and fortune.

Fantasy is rarely serious in its consequences unless it is continuously used as a way of dealing with frustrated needs. The schizophrenic form of mental illness, which we shall describe a little later in this chapter, is an example of fantasy carried too far, for in this illness the patient withdraws so deeply into fantasy that he can no longer get along in the world. *In most people, however, fantasy is a harmless device for satisfying some needs that might otherwise be frustrated.*

Regression. Closely related to fantasy is a reaction called *regression*. This is a *retreat to early or primitive forms of behavior*. We say "early or primitive" because there is some question whether regression is one or both of these. On the one hand, regression seems to be a relapse to habits and ways of behaving that the person learned in childhood; on the other, it seems merely to represent a simpler, more primitive, and less intellectual approach to solving a problem. Whatever its interpretation, regression takes the form of a childish, rather than an adult, reaction to frustration.

Regression is frequently encountered in children of four or five years of age who are beginning to face an increasing variety of complex frustrations.[8] Perhaps the particular occasion that evokes regressive behavior is the birth of another child or the beginning of school adjustments. In any event, the child at this stage frequently reverts to baby talk and acts like a baby of two rather than a child of five.

Regression is by no means limited to

children, for adults often regress too. Childish fits of anger, or pouting when one fails to get his way, may constitute regression to reactions acquired in childhood. A person who goes to bed with the slightest cold or who seems to enjoy being sick may be regressing to behavior which, in childhood, brought him affection and attention. A more extreme form of regression is sometimes seen in schizophrenic illness (see page 270). In this disorder, the adult may talk like a child, act like a child, and "live" almost completely in the world of a child. Along with such behavior there is usually considerable regression in fantasy; the person lives in an imaginary world of childhood. Schizophrenia of this type will be discussed more fully in the last section of this chapter.

Alcohol. In many people's lives today, the drinking of alcohol is a reaction to frustration and anxiety. From everyday experience, it is fairly obvious that alcohol has a soothing effect on anxiety. People who drink only moderately want a drink most after a frustrating day. They are likely to drink when they want to "drown their sorrows," and their behavior under the influence of alcohol is usually more relaxed and free of anxiety. True, some people become boisterous and aggressive when drunk, but this only indicates that alcohol permits them to express their aggression without the usual accompaniment of anxiety. All this is common sense and fairly common knowledge.

Experiments in recent years, however, have given us further understanding of the craving for alcohol and its effects on anxiety. In one experiment with cats,[9] the subjects were taught to open a box to obtain food. After that, they were conditioned to fear the box by receiving blasts of air when they attempted to open it. In this way, an approach-avoidance conflict (see

Figure 10.4) was set up. Next, however, the cats were forcibly fed some alcohol. Thereupon, their fear of the box disappeared; they went to it and opened it— though their drunkenness made them rather awkward about it. Even more significant was the fact that some of the "neurotic" cats, when offered plain milk together with milk containing 5 per cent alcohol, preferred alcoholic milk. Thus, as a result of approach-avoidance conflict and experience with the soothing effects of alcohol, they had developed a "craving" for alcohol. Later in the experiment, fear of the box was extinguished by appropriate training procedures (see page 109). Thereupon, the cats' craving for alcohol disappeared, and they chose to drink only pure milk.

This, and similar experiments, have given us a fairly clear picture of the role of alcohol in motivational conflicts. *Alcohol reduces the painfulness of anxiety without detracting from the value of positive goals.* To put it another way, *alcohol diminishes the anxiety connected with negative goals in an approach-avoidance conflict.* Consequently, the conflict is temporarily resolved. It is understandable, then, that people who are afflicted with conflicts and accompanying anxieties sometimes resort to alcohol. As we shall see in Chapter 22, physiological factors are also involved in alcoholism. Drinking is nevertheless a habit that can serve to relieve the anxiety caused by conflict.

Inadequate adjustments. Up to now we have spoken as though the various ways in which people adjust to motivational conflict were usually successful in solving their problems. Since repression, displacement, reaction formation, projection, etc., are ways of eliminating painful anxiety, the reader may have the impression that these defense mechanisms solve the problem.

Actually that is not so. They solve only part of the problem, and they may even create new and worse difficulties for the individual. Let us see how and why.

▪ *Inadequacies of defense mechanisms.* One of the underlying weaknesses of defense mechanisms is that they are *directed at anxiety, not at the motivational conflicts* that give rise to it. All that they do is conceal or disguise the real problem, and so they leave the original problem ever present and ready to produce anxiety again and again. A person harboring homosexual tendencies, for example, may avoid anxiety by repressing such tendencies, yet they may be reawakened by a wide variety of stimuli. Whenever such an individual is confronted with a situation which excites the homosexual tendencies, the latent conflict is reinstated. For that reason, during the Second World War, many men with latent homosexual impulses developed severe anxieties when thrust into the intimate company of other men, although they could get along in civilian life by avoiding such contact. Many other examples could be cited to show that defense mechanisms, though they temporarily allay anxieties, leave the individual prey to situations that rearouse the conflicts and anxieties.

A second major inadequacy of the defense mechanisms is that they may get the individual into other difficulties with society which in turn frustrate still other important motives. While allaying anxiety from one cause, defense mechanisms can increase anxiety from other causes. The individual with excessive hostility, for example, may project this hostility to others as a mode of defense. To the people who see him, however, his projections seem queer, and when his associates show their disapproval of this behavior, another motive may be frustrated which aggravates his anxieties even further. In the extreme form, projections become a

system of delusions such as are found in the paranoid patient who must be hospitalized because he can no longer appraise reality and has become a menace to himself and others. The hysterical patient has difficulty because the anxiety-reducing symptom may prevent him from being gainfully employed. In these and other instances, defense mechanisms fail because they get the individual into more trouble than he had in the first place.

▪ *Failures in adjustment.* With this thought, we are led to consider the fact that many individuals fail to make adequate adjustments to their conflicts and anxieties. Some people use defensive reactions *too much* and leave unresolved *too many* conflicts that are *too strong*. As a result, they get themselves into trouble from which they are unable to extricate themselves. Unfortunately, there are a good many such people. Consider the astounding fact that there are as many individuals in mental hospitals in the United States as in all other types of hospitals combined. Of every 1,000 people born, approximately fifty will spend some part of their lives in a mental hospital.[10] In addition, there are large numbers of individuals who seek psychiatric advice and treatment each year. There are still others who badly need such help but who, for one reason or another, do not get it. All these people certainly must be regarded as adjustive failures.

People who fail to resolve their conflicts are so numerous and so different from one another that it is difficult to classify them. Psychiatrists, however, have adopted a twofold classification which divides their illnesses into the *psychoneuroses* (or sometimes just neuroses) and *psychoses*. The difference between these forms of mental illness is not always clear-cut. In general, the psychoneurotic is able to hold some form of employment and to live with his family and friends. A person with a psychosis, on the other hand, appears to the lay observer as much more "peculiar," and he is more likely to be so severely handicapped or dangerous that he must be kept at home or in an institution. One can better understand these general classes of illness, however, by considering in detail some of the personality patterns that appear in each class.

Before doing this, there is an important comment to make. When students first read about abnormal behavior, they sometimes become alarmed because they can see in themselves or their friends some of the symptoms that are described. Actually, normal people do sometimes have in mild degree or in times of stress some of the symptoms of the neurotic and psychotic. That fact, however, does not make them abnormal. Before they can properly be called abnormal, the symptoms must form a syndrome (see page 242), they must be severe, and they must be so chronic that they seriously handicap adjustment. The student should keep this in mind in reading the following sections on the psychoneuroses and psychoses.

■ PSYCHONEUROSES

There is no sharp line between normal people—successes in adjustment—and those who must be considered failures in adjustment. Hence the person suffering a neurosis is not different in kind, but only in degree, from the normal person. He has simply used defense mechanisms to such a degree and has fooled himself so thoroughly with them that his functioning is impaired. He has become too anxious or too miserable or too troublesome or too incapacitated in his work and relationships with people.

Classification of neuroses. Neuroses have usually been classified into three basic

Fig. 10.10. The extent of mental illness. One out of twenty is admitted to a mental hospital sometime in his life, and two out of twenty are incapacitated by emotional disorders. (After Bernard, H. W. Toward better personal adjustment. New York: McGraw-Hill, 1951, p. 3.)

kinds: the *hysterias*, the *psychasthenias*, and the *anxiety reactions*. Each of these involves a typical set of symptoms that will be described below. The student must recognize, however, that the classification of neuroses by groups is rather arbitrary. Seldom does a person fall entirely into one category. More often, he has symptoms of more than one kind, and any attempt to label his illness simply identifies his most prominent symptoms.

Hysteria. The character of a hysterical neurosis may be explained by citing the example of a woman who developed a paralysis in which her legs were held together like two stiff pillars. Neurological examination indicated no physical disorder, so physicians looked into other aspects of her case. They discovered that she was the mother of several children, that she had reason to fear having any more, that her husband desired frequent intercourse, and that she had strong prohibitions against both birth control and denying her husband's sexual demands. Here were all the elements of a complex conflict situation. After interviewing the woman at length and investigating the case thoroughly, physicians concluded that her paralysis was an unconscious device for eliminating conflict.

This case illustrates the essential elements of hysteria: the *conversion of motivational conflict into physical symptoms*. The particular symptom that appears in hysteria varies with the individual, his conflict, and his habits. It may be the paralysis of almost any part of the body, loss of feeling in the hand, a blindness or deafness, or any other sort of incapacity. We emphasize, however, that hysterical symptoms have no biological basis, as a physician can usually determine in a physical examination. The symptoms are simply devices for coping with conflict and anxiety.

Hysterical reactions illustrate well the process of *repression*, for in no other neurotic reaction is repression so complete. In most such reactions—displacement, reaction formation, projection, and so on—some, but not all, aspects of a conflict are repressed; one goal is altered, leaving others intact. In hysteria, however, the entire conflict is repressed. The individual completely rejects all thoughts and motives that may be involved and does this so effectively by resorting to physical symptoms that dispose of them all. The woman with the paralyzed legs, for example, no longer had to worry about birth control, resisting her husband's sexual demands, or having more children. With her hysterical symptom, she had completely eliminated the conflict.

The particular symptom that the hysteric employs may first occur by accident or by real physical illness. A person, for example, may be in an automobile accident that causes a real, temporary paralysis. Although the injury is obviously a handicap, it may also prove to be a boon in satisfying other wants. It may make the person's wife, husband or parent become very attentive, thus giving to the person love and care he has lacked. Or the ailment may punish those who have the work and expense of taking care of him; in this way the ailment in-

directly expresses aggression. In still other instances, the ailment may protect the individual from anxiety-producing situations, such as a job, school, or social relations.

An experienced doctor usually can recognize the hysterical personality, even if there are yet no full-blown physical symptoms. One of the signs is unusual naïveté. The individual is naïve because the anxiety he feels in many situations makes him avoid them and thus he either misses or represses experiences that are normal for other people. Another sign of the hysterical personality is that he is easily disturbed emotionally. When confronted with an unpleasant situation, his thoughts are blocked and confused, and he may become so disturbed that he grows ill, becomes dizzy, or faints. This is a sign because, on a small scale, it is the kind of ailment that protects the hysteric against anxiety.

Psychasthenia. Psychasthenia is a general class that includes a variety of neurotic symptoms, of which the most common are *obsessions* and *compulsions*. An obsession is an *idea that constantly intrudes into a person's thoughts*. It is usually foolish and groundless. The person may be obsessed with the notion that he has cancer or syphilis or with the fear that he will kill himself or someone else. Senseless phrases or ideas may run through his mind over and over again. Obsessions are thought to represent a defense against some motive or anxiety, but it is not always easy to tell which one. Many concern sex, and many concern aggression, but they may represent any situation or experience that makes the person very anxious.

Compulsions are *acts*, rather than ideas, *that repeatedly intrude into a person's behavior*. One compulsive person may wash his hands every few minutes; another must count all the steps he goes up; another assiduously avoids stepping on cracks in the sidewalk. Some people do not have such conspicuous compulsions but are compulsive in a more general way. They find ambiguity and uncertainty extremely uncomfortable, and they strive for orderliness of thought, of dress, or of work. Indeed any unusual emphasis on "doing things the right way" may be regarded as compulsive.

Obsessions and compulsions are means of reducing anxieties while repressing the motives that arouse them. If someone, for example, has an obsession about cancer, it may be because he has anxieties over some past act of misconduct for which he may fear punishment. Similarly the compulsive who washes his hands every few minutes may have anxieties over a sexual transgression, and the hand washing is an unconscious attempt to cleanse himself of guilt. In this way obsessive and compulsive individuals find some measure of relief from anxiety. But it is not complete. In fact a cycle is set up in which mounting anxiety evokes the obsession or compulsion, and this in turn temporarily relieves the anxiety until, in the course of time or circumstances, it returns again. The mechanism, however, is a defense that keeps anxiety from reaching unbearable proportions.

It is often hard to tell what the connection is between the obsession or compulsion and the original experience which it represents. Occasionally the person may have some "insight" and know the connection. More often he rationalizes his obsessions and compulsions to make them appear reasonable and appropriate, and thus he disguises to himself their real basis. In such circumstances, it probably will take an experienced doctor to find—usually after extensive probing—the source of the anxiety.

Anxiety reactions.   Not all psychoneuroses have such specific symptoms as one sees in conversion hysteria or psychasthenia. Some are characterized only by general anxiety; the person is chronically anxious without any apparent reason. When such anxiety is severe enough to handicap a person —keep him from working at his job or make him physically ill—we call it an anxiety reaction. This can make him thoroughly miserable, keep him in a state bordering on panic, and upset his health with gastric disturbances and chronic diarrhea.

It is unusually difficult to assign anxiety reactions to any specific cause. They become serious when a person is put under stress or must cope with difficult problems, but they tend to exist most of the time and in most situations. They apparently represent generally frustrated impulses, such as sex, aggression, or desire for social approval, for which the individual has found no good disguised outlets. He apparently has not learned to any considerable extent how to use defense mechanisms to allay anxiety. Or sometimes the panic ensues when the ordinary defenses are not working effectively or when the original problem threatens, in certain situations, to come into awareness.

Those who suffer chronic anxiety reactions, however, do sometimes find a little relief from their anxiety by adopting, as the hysteric does, certain physical symptoms. One such form of relief is *hypochondriasis*, in which the person is excessively concerned with his physical welfare or constantly complaining of minor ailments. Another is *neurasthenia*, and in this the patient complains of general nervousness, fatigue, and insomnia. He may also feel depressed and inadequate and never seem to be able to do anything about his troubles. Because he feels so fatigued and worn out all the time, the neurasthenic may claim that he is unable to work. These symptoms, although they may incapacitate the person, represent some gain to him, for they provide an excuse and a disguise for his real problems—whatever those are. He may go on through his lifetime without insight into what his real problems are and in a chronic state of tension.

▌ PSYCHOSES

In general, we use the term psychosis when a person becomes dangerous to others and himself or when he becomes so incompetent and mentally disordered that society must take care of him in one way or another. We have already discussed the problem of distinguishing between the psychoses and neuroses. Psychoses that are accompanied by no known disease of the brain are called *functional* psychoses. Those that are known to be caused by damage or disease in the brain are called *organic* psychoses. We shall first discuss the functional psychoses, then the organic psychoses.

Functional psychoses. Under this heading we shall consider three kinds of psychoses that are the most frequent of the functional psychoses.

▪ *Manic-depressive psychoses.* The major characteristic of one class of functional psychosis is that the individual has extreme ups or downs in mood. One individual is up more than he is down, and then we say that he is *manic*. Another may be mostly down; he is called *depressive*. Still another may alternate over a period of time between manic phases and depressive phases.

In the manic state, the individual is very active. He may sing, dance, run, talk a lot, and generally release more energy than one would think humanly possible. He may also exhibit some obsessions and various sorts of delusions. Frequently he is aggressive and obstreperous, breaking chairs, attacking people, using vile lan-

guage, and generally putting life and property in jeopardy; or he even tries to be so helpful that he is a terrible nuisance. When a manic attack reaches such proportions, it is often necessary to lock the person up in a room without any furniture that can be broken or used as a weapon.

The same patient who has such manic attacks may be found at other times in a state of severe depression. Depressive patients feel melancholy, worthless, guilty, and hopeless. Some cry a good deal of the time, some keep talking about the terrible sins they imagine they have committed, and some are so depressed that they will take no food or water, have to be forcibly fed through a tube, and may refuse to dress or take care of their toilet needs. The extremely depressed patient is often on the verge of suicide and must be watched closely to see that he does not try suicide or otherwise harm himself.

▪ *Paranoia.* This is a psychosis that is marked with *delusions* and *hallucinations*.

Fig. 10.11. Suicide and insanity rates at various ages. (After Gray, J. S. Psychology applied to human affairs. New York: McGraw-Hill, 1954, p. 174.)

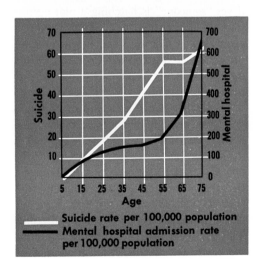

Suicide rate per 100,000 population
Mental hospital admission rate per 100,000 population

The person's hallucinations are imagined voices, music, and other sights and sounds that do not really exist. If you watch such a patient, you will frequently see him acting as though he were talking to someone you cannot see. He will claim to be seeing people and hearing things you know are not there. His delusions are thoughts of grandeur or persecution. He may tell you that he is Napoleon or George Washington and spin quite a tale to prove it. He also may have the delusion that someone is persecuting him, that someone has invented a machine that is slowly destroying him by some kind of wave, or that someone is hatching a nefarious plot to deprive him of his rights as Napoleon or the king of England.

Two factors seem to be most important in the paranoid's mode of adjustment. One is *aggression*. In general, his attitudes, acts, and thoughts are full of aggression, and we may surmise that he has failed to adjust because he has been unable to give vent in normal ways to strong aggressive impulses. The other factor is *projection*. His hallucinations and delusions usually represent a projection of his aggressive or sexual impulses to others, and that is why he believes "someone" is hatching a plot against him or persecuting him. The paranoid's aggression is so strong and he believes his projection of it so firmly that he is often dangerous. If not kept in custody, he may do someone harm.

▪ *Schizophrenia.* The name of this psychosis means, literally, "splitting of the mind," and this is a general description of it. A little better name perhaps would be one that meant "splitting from reality," for the person suffering from it cuts himself off from the outside world and lives in one of his own making a good part of the time. This psychosis used to be called *dementia praecox*, which means "youthful insanity,"

because it tends to develop early in life. Although people may develop it at all ages, the highest rate of admissions to mental hospitals for this disease is for people in the middle twenties.

There are several varieties of schizophrenia that are different shades and forms of the same general kind of failure of adjustment. One is *paranoid schizophrenia* because, like the pure paranoid, the victim has delusions of grandeur and persecution. More often than not the delusions are of persecution. Unlike the pure paranoid, the paranoid schizophrenic has unsystematized delusions—delusions that are not too coherent and are not defended with such elaborate rationalizations. He may shift with little apparent reason from one delusion to another and show bizarre attitudes and behavior.

Another form of this disease, *simple schizophrenia*, is perhaps its purest form. A person so classified has little apparent interest in the world, is generally apathetic to almost all situations, is irresponsible, and withdraws from almost all social contact. He has simply withdrawn into his shell and makes no attempt to adjust to the world. He may exist for years as a vagrant, wandering from place to place or as the family's or town's dependent, or he may get into social difficulty and be jailed or hospitalized.

Perhaps the extreme form of schizophrenia is *catatonic schizophrenia*. It is not so common as the other forms, but when it does occur, it presents a dramatic picture. The catatonic is extremely negativistic, often doing exactly the opposite of what he is asked to do. He may completely ignore people around him and refuse to say anything under any circumstances. Perhaps the most interesting thing about him, though, is his *catatonia*, which is a state of muscular rigidity. For many minutes or even hours, he may stay fixed in some absurd position—in a crouch or with arms outstretched. In fact, it is hard to see how catatonic positions can be maintained for so long, since the normal person could not hold such postures for even a short while.

Last of the schizophrenias to be mentioned is the *hebephrenic* form. In this type, the individual seems to regress to childish levels of behavior. He may giggle incessantly; in fact, everything may seem funny or foolish to him. Typically, his mood seems to bear no relation to the situation. He may talk about the death of his mother and laugh in a silly way. Or he may, for no apparent reason, begin to cry. Sometimes, as he is crying, he may report that he has no real feeling of sadness. He may talk like a child, using the sentences and words of a child. His habits of eating and perhaps of toilet may be as sloppy as those of a small child.

Organic psychoses. As far as we know, the functional psychoses that we have just described are not caused by any physical illness. There is evidence that there may be some inherited predisposition to some of them (see Chapter 22), but we have not yet established their physiological basis. Besides the functional psychoses, however, there are several organic psychoses—so called because they stem directly or indirectly from physical disease or physical changes in the body. We shall mention some of them briefly.

▪ *Involutional melancholia.* This psychosis may make its onset in the middle of life, when men and women undergo a change in their sexual functions and often decline in physical condition. Because of this association with menopause, it has been thought to have some organic basis. It is more frequent in women than in men. Most often melancholia is transitory, lasting only a few months or years. Its chief symptoms may be a frivolous regression to the clothes and manners of younger days, somewhat paranoid accusations against one's friends or even against oneself, and (most characteristic of all) depression.

▪ *Senile and alcoholic psychoses.* These have different origins but symptoms that are somewhat alike. People who grow old may develop psychotic behavior that is characterized by delusions, defects of memory, and general disorientation. The person may imagine that he was just talking to someone who you know was not there, or he may imagine that people are boring holes in his head. As his memory grows worse, he may forget what he has just said but at the same time insist that he remembers things that never happened. Very frequently in senile psychosis the person has a hard time knowing where he is, where he has been, or what is going on —he is generally disoriented.

Chronic alcoholism can gradually destroy mental processes in somewhat the same way as advancing age. Although there are features of alcoholic psychosis that are rather unique, the general picture is still similar to that of the senile psychosis. The common factor in both is probably the destruction of brain tissue. In the alcoholic, the destruction is caused by excessive alcohol. In the aged person, damage may be done by ruptured blood vessels or by loss of blood supply due to hardening of the arteries.

▪ *General paresis.* This organic psychosis has been common, especially before modern methods for the control of syphilis became available. It develops when the syphilis germ lodges in the brain and gradually destroys some brain tissue. The person suffering from it becomes irresponsible and unpredictable and frequently has the most extreme delusions of grandeur. He may think he is worth billions of dollars—and spend money as though he were—claim he built the Empire State building with his own hands, or believe he is the son of royalty. It is fortunate that only a small percentage of people who contract syphilis develop this disease and that modern medical science is now doing an effective job of curing the disease in its early stages.

Summary

1. Every individual sometimes experiences frustration of his needs because (*a*) several needs are present at the same time and (*b*) the environment presents obstacles to the satisfaction of needs.

2. In the infant and child, most frustration is caused by environmental obstacles. The adult, however, is also frustrated by unattainable goals and by motivational conflicts within the individual.

3. Motivational conflicts are of three basic types: (*a*) approach-approach, (*b*) avoidance-avoidance, and (*c*) approach-avoidance. Of these, the approach-avoidance conflict creates the most insoluble problems.

4. Each individual learns his particular modes of adjustment to such conflicts. To the extent that he is unsuccessful in solving them, his frustrations give rise to anxiety.

5. Anxiety makes a person miserable and itself constitutes a frustration. In addition, anxiety fixates a person's behavior, making him less able to learn a satisfactory adjustment.

6. To cope with anxiety, people may acquire a combination of reactions to frustration, called *defense mechanisms*. These mechanisms are ways of disguising one's motives so that they do not cause so much anxiety.

7. In total repression, a person so completely disguises certain motives that he is unaware of them. In this case, the motivational conflict may reveal itself in the form of hysterical blindness or paralysis.

8. Other defensive reactions in which some aspect of one's motives is disguised are (*a*) reaction formation, (*b*) projection, (*c*) displacement, (*d*) rationalization, (*e*) sublimation and compensation, (*f*) fantasy, (*g*) regression, and (*h*) the use of alcohol.

9. Although everyone uses defense mechanisms to some extent, relying on them too much and too often makes for an inadequate adjustment. They may alleviate anxiety, but they do not solve the basic conflicts; they are regarded as queer by other people; and they get the individual into more trouble.

10. Serious failures in adjustment may be classified in two categories: (*a*) the psychoneuroses, and (*b*) the psychoses.

11. The psychoneuroses may be divided into three main groups: (*a*) hysteria, (*b*) psychasthenia, and (*c*) anxiety reactions.

12. The psychoses may be classified as (*a*) functional, or (*b*) organic, depending on whether the psychosis is known to have an organic basis in physical disease.

13. The principal functional psychoses are (*a*) manic-depressive psychosis, (*b*) paranoia, and (*c*) schizophrenia. Some of the common organic psychoses are (*a*) involutional melancholia, (*b*) senile and alcoholic psychoses, and (*c*) general paresis.

SUGGESTIONS FOR FURTHER READING

Cameron, N. A. *Psychology of the behavior disorders.* Boston: Houghton Mifflin, 1947.

> *A text emphasizing both biological and social factors in abnormal behavior.*

Dorcus, R. M., and Shaffer, G. W. *Textbook of abnormal psychology* (4th Ed.). Baltimore: Williams & Wilkins, 1950.

> *A standard text on abnormal psychology, including descriptions of the neuroses and psychoses.*

Hall, C. S. *A primer of Freudian psychology.* Yonkers, N.Y.: World, 1954.

> *A readable introductory book on the Freudian theory of personality.*

Klein, D. B. *Mental hygiene.* New York: Holt, 1944.

> *A text emphasizing the prevention of mental disease.*

Lewin, K. *Dynamic theory of personality.* New York: McGraw-Hill, 1935. Chap. 3.

> *A description of types of conflict.*

Maier, N. R. F. *Frustration.* New York: McGraw-Hill, 1949.

> *An account of research on frustration and a theory of its nature and consequences.*

Page, J. D. *Abnormal psychology.* New York: McGraw-Hill, 1947.

> *An introductory text on abnormal psychology containing a good description of the neuroses and psychoses.*

Shaffer, L. F. *The psychology of adjustment.* Boston: Houghton Mifflin, 1935.

> *Includes a good summary of the defense mechanisms.*

Symonds, P. M. *Dynamic psychology.* New York: Appleton-Century-Crofts, 1949.

> *A book containing detailed descriptions of the defense mechanisms.*

White, R. W. *The abnormal personality.* New York: Ronald, 1948.

> *A widely used text on abnormal psychology.*

Chapter 11 MENTAL HEALTH AND PSYCHOTHERAPY

MENTAL HEALTH is a problem that concerns everyone. The millions who become neurotic or psychotic need help, both to relieve their own misery and maladjustment and to lighten the burden they impose on others. Normal individuals need to know and practice the ways of living that are most satisfying and that guard against the development of maladjustments. Consequently, there are two general aspects of the problem of promoting mental health. One is to give aid to the maladjusted; the other is to help normal individuals improve their individual personal adjustments. In this chapter, we shall cover both topics.

Psychotherapy. *Therapy is the general name given to methods of treating illness.* Mental illness, as we have seen, is often the consequence of emotional maladjust-

This chapter was drafted by G. Wilson Shaffer of The Johns Hopkins University.

ment, but it may also be due to physical diseases of the nervous system, such as syphilis or brain tumors. Different kinds of therapy must therefore be used to treat mental illness. Some therapies aim at eradicating the underlying physical disease. Others involve surgery of the brain (see page 554), subjecting a patient to convulsive electrical shocks, or using drugs that restore him to a more normal state. Because such therapies are strictly in the hands of medical specialists, not psychologists, we shall not discuss them here. On the other hand, for many maladjusted individuals, the appropriate therapy is psychological and hence is called *psychotherapy*. We shall describe several kinds of psychotherapy in this chapter.

Psychotherapy is used not only for those who are seriously ill with psychoses or psychoneuroses but also for those with personality problems that are less serious. Delinquents and maladjusted children, and people with marital, religious, scholastic, or occupational problems may need and benefit from psychotherapy. Indeed, a wide variety of failures in interpersonal and social adjustments may require some form of psychotherapy. We must think of psychotherapy, therefore, as *the treatment of the whole range of problems of adjustment,* from difficulties that may be minor and rather temporary to those that are severe and chronic.

▪ *Trends in psychotherapy.* Early attempts to use psychotherapy were focused on the more severe psychotic disorders that required hospitalization. As our understanding of maladjustment grew, treatment was extended to the severe neuroses and to individuals outside of hospitals. More recently, it has been used more and more with mild neuroses and with those who are just beginning to develop problems in adjustment.

There are some very good reasons for this trend in psychotherapy: (1) the severely and chronically ill cost more to treat, with less chance of benefit, than those who are only mildly maladjusted; (2) the developing shortage of psychotherapists has required their employment where they can do the most good in the shortest time; (3) treatment of mild psychoneurotics offers the greatest benefits to society, for such individuals are still active in social, economic, and political affairs, and any improvement in their adjustment is immediately reflected in their influence on their associates and in everyday affairs; (4) successful treatment of mild maladjustments *prevents* more serious disorders from developing.

▪ *Types of psychotherapists.* Until recently, psychotherapy was carried out by medical practitioners. Once mental illness was recognized as illness, it was logical that those trained to treat other kinds of sickness should also treat the mentally ill. As the research of psychologists came to contribute to our understanding of personality and to the measurement of intelligence, aptitudes, interests, and personality characteristics, the psychologist has played an increasing role in psychotherapy. Today both those who have trained in medicine and those who have trained in psychology are doing psychotherapy.

As we explained in Chapter 1, *psychiatrists* are those who have medical training and specialize in the diagnosis and treatment of mental disorders. *Clinical psychologists,* on the other hand, are those with advanced training in psychology who also specialize in this general field. Because mental illness may sometimes be due to physical disease, both psychiatrists and psychologists must see to it that their patients are given proper medical examinations and, if necessary, medical treatment. The psychiatrist, being medically trained, may sometimes do this himself, but the clinical psychologist must refer the patient to a physician. For that reason clinical psychologists usually work in close cooperation with, or under the supervision of, medically trained psychiatrists. (For further details about the training of clinical psychologists, see page 18.

THE GOALS OF PSYCHO-THERAPY

The person who comes to psychotherapy is faced with problems he has not been able to solve for himself. Some of his problems may lie in his environment; he may be living and working with people who make it difficult for him to adjust. Usually, however, *the major source of the problem is within himself.* Through repression, he may have deceived himself about his real motives, thus leaving his motives in conflict. He has resorted to defense mechanisms to allay the anxieties caused by conflict and these mechanisms have not been successful.

Ideally, the therapist would like the patient to get to the root of his problems and to eliminate them. To accomplish this, the therapist and the patient must work diligently together to uncover repressed motives, find the sources of anxieties, and attain a complete understanding of motives and resources for adjustment. The process, however, may be very long and expensive. The patient may not have the time, money, or capacity to see it to completion. In some cases, too, he may be so unintelligent or so deeply ensnared in his mechanisms that there is little hope of success. Or in many instances his problem may be mild enough so that it is not worth the trouble to try to achieve complete insight and self-understanding. In all these cases, the therapist may set a goal for therapy that falls short of the ideal of complete insight.

The psychotherapist must decide early in the course of treatment what his goal will be, because his over-all strategy, the length of the treatment, and the details of it will depend on this goal. To make this decision he uses several sources of information. One is a *life history* of the person as given by the person himself and by his friends and relatives. Another is *physical and psychological examinations* of the person, including tests of intelligence, personality, and vocational abilities. Another, of course, is the *picture the therapist forms of the person's problems* in the course of the first few interviews.

Having gathered all the information he can, the therapist then sets a goal for the therapy and maps his strategy accordingly.

Although there are a variety of goals on which he may decide, they fall fairly well into three main alternatives: (1) changing the patient's environmental situation, (2) giving the patient emotional support, and (3) enabling the patient to achieve insight and self-understanding. These alternatives are not mutually exclusive. The therapist may decide on some combination of them, proceeding in stages from one to the other.

Changing the situation. This is the simplest goal of treatment. It is not an attempt to bring about any major change in the patient, but rather *to manipulate his situation so as to relieve the stress on him.* A patient may be advised to take a vacation, change his occupation, divorce his wife, renounce his relatives, change his educational goals, etc. While this may be the only treatment possible in some instances, it is not likely to be satisfactory for most persons. Major changes in the environment are frequently difficult or impossible to attain, and when attained they sometimes make matters even worse for the patient. Of greater importance is the fact that most of the difficulty probably lies within the individual, and the manipulation of the environment is apt to bring only minor relief.

This does not imply that situational changes are not important, but rather that they are secondary to the treatment of the individual. In the treatment of children it is frequently necessary to make situational changes, and in solving simple adjustment problems in adults such changes may be adequate to make the patient secure. However, for the great majority of those who come for treatment a good deal more is necessary, and to begin by treating the situation may completely block progress toward other goals of therapy.

Providing support. If the treatment is arranged to give support to the patient but

Fig. 11.1. The psychotherapeutic situation. The patient talks with the psychotherapist. They work together to understand important facts leading up to the illness and to develop ways of working out the underlying problems in a constructive, healthy way. (*Courtesy National Institute of Mental Health, Public Health Service, in cooperation with St. Elizabeths Hospital, Washington, D.C.*)

not to bring about permanent personality changes, it is called supportive. The aim here is to help the individual through some crisis by the use of reassurance and related techniques. Much of what is called *counseling* is supportive psychotherapy.[1] It is usually employed with relatively normal people who face some specific problems of adjustment. The counselor gives information, listens to the person's problems, suggests courses of action, and reassures him about what he has done or proposes to do. In this way the counselor may support the person sufficiently to enable him to make a satisfactory adjustment.

Giving support and reassurance, however, requires an expertness that is not easily acquired. The counselor must do it subtly or he will increase rather than decrease the person's anxiety. It is usually wise to use support therapy only in certain special cases. One type is the chronic case in which illness is of such long standing, the resources for health so poor, and the environmental blocks so great that the chances are small of effecting a permanent change in the person. In such cases, supportive therapy may strengthen the person's ability to deal with some problems and thus permit a somewhat better adjustment. Another kind of case is the person who has been well adjusted most of his life and develops a neurotic disturbance only temporarily because of some crisis in his life. In this instance, supportive therapy may be all that is necessary to reestablish healthy modes of adjustment.

Achieving insight.   The objectives of insight therapy are *to uncover the deep causes of a person's difficulty, to rid the patient of his neurotic defenses,* and thereby to free him for flexible adaptive behavior. Such therapy is called *insight or uncovering therapy.* The development of insight is not obtained through simple intellectual discovery. It is a longer and more painstaking procedure whereby the patient exposes himself to various emotional attitudes and situations.[2] He must bring to the fore the emotional situations he has been unable to face, those which he has repressed and around which he has developed his neurotic defenses.

As a matter of actual practice, almost all psychotherapy includes some support and some insight and eventually even some situational change. However, when the primary effort is that of developing insight and gaining continuous emotional growth, the therapy is called insight therapy. When the effort to support the ego is greater than the effort to obtain insight, the treatment is called supportive.

TECHNIQUES IN PSYCHOTHERAPY

Now let us turn to the specific techniques that therapists use in their efforts to help the maladjusted. There are a variety of such techniques. Some are rather specialized and are used only occasionally when the situation seems to demand them. Some techniques are used more by some therapists than by others because of differences of opinion about their relative effectiveness.

Many of the techniques are difficult to distinguish clearly from one another and represent differences in emphasis rather than radical differences in method.

Directive therapies.   In the early days of psychotherapy, techniques were primarily *directive.* The therapist was an authoritative prescriber. Since the medical practitioner prescribed medicine for physical ailments, he tended to follow the same practice of prescribing for the alleviation of mental suffering. Since the patient developed his difficulties in a particular environment, the therapist was likely to prescribe a change of environment. He often considered the patient unable to plan his own life and took charge of such planning. He prescribed exercise, rest, the development of a hobby, or the joining of a particular kind of community group. In many cases the therapist tried to direct the patient's thinking and emotional life. Thus, in this kind of treatment, the therapist was dominant and the patient depended upon his reactions.

▪ *Reeducation.* Much of the early directive therapy was called reeducation. Austin Riggs was one of the leading therapists who emphasized techniques of reeducation.[4] His therapy was practiced with the psychoneurotic, for whom he usually prescribed temporary environmental change. He believed the patient should be removed from his home and his social and his vocational environments, because it was in these situations that the neurotic disturbance had developed. Then, in another, neutral environment, the patient was sent to school, so to speak, *to learn the principles of satisfactory life adjustment.* He attended lectures and group discussions on the psychology of adjustment. He lived on a regimented schedule of activities that were designed to distract and divert him and to help him develop habits of social cooperation.

Such strictly organized reeducation therapy of the type sponsored by Riggs is seldom practiced today, but reeducation of a less directive type is frequently used. In fact, some kind of reeducation is involved in practically all techniques. Nowadays the reeducation takes place more by developing new insights and habits of thought and is guided informally by the therapist in his handling of therapeutic interviews.

▪ *Desensitization.* Closely related to reeducation is the technique of desensitization. This is designed *to enable the patient to be comfortable in situations in which he has previously been highly anxious.* For many patients there are situations which have been associated with pain, shame, or insecurity that cannot be approached objectively. Even patients with very good insight into their problems often have been unable to change their emotional reactions to these situations. The therapy in such instances is to have the patient, under special conditions, face the anxiety-arousing situation and thus have an opportunity gradually to extinguish his emotional responses to it. If, for example, a person has a great fear of parties, therapy might consist in getting him to parties so arranged that he suffers no embarrassment and finds out that "parties aren't so bad after all." This technique of desensitization is similar in principle to the method of extinction described in Chapter 5.

In some instances desensitization may result from the process of the patient's repeating again and again the circumstances of his anxieties in the presence of the therapist. Reliving these experiences in the secure relationship with the therapist may enable the patient to reduce his emotional response and meet the situations more objectively. Practically all therapeutic techniques make some use of this principle of desensitization but present-day, less direc-

tive methods make it somewhat secondary to the development of a basic understanding of one's problems.

▪ *Suggestion and hypnosis. Suggestion is the uncritical acceptance of an idea or attitude.* It enters into almost all situations in which one person attempts to influence another (see Chapter 13), but people are most responsive to suggestions from people of authority and prestige. Thus the therapist is in a good position to use suggestion. He may suggest that the patient has made enough progress in psychotherapy to be relieved of his "nervous headaches," his "nervous indigestion," or his fear of examinations, and the suggestion may be effective. In more extreme cases, such as hysterical blindness or paralysis, it may be necessary for the patient to go to some trouble —for example, undergoing surgery, taking bad-tasting medicines, or suffering other discomfort—to alleviate the symptoms of paralysis or blindness. In such cases the medical treatment, though of no value in itself, has the power of suggesting the removal of the symptom.

People are most suggestible when they are in a hypnotic state. For that reason early psychotherapists used hypnosis as a therapeutic technique. They would hypnotize the patient, then give him *posthypnotic suggestions* to be effective after he awakened from the hypnotic sleep. A person suffering from hysterical paralysis of the right arm, for example, might be told under hypnosis, "When you wake up, you will be able to use your right arm. It will be completely normal again." In a good many instances, such suggestions as this would work; the individual would not be paralyzed when he awoke.

One drawback of suggestion and hypnosis as aids in therapy is that many patients are difficult to hypnotize. Another important shortcoming is that the techniques remove the symptom but not its cause. Suggestion does not produce insight, nor does it remove the anxiety which underlies the symptom, and thus it does not solve the patient's basic problem. As a consequence, *if symptoms are removed through suggestion, they usually appear again in somewhat different form.* If neurotic headaches, for example, are alleviated through suggestion, the person is likely to develop some other symptom such as indigestion or backaches. For this reason, suggestive techniques are useful only in certain situations where it is important to give the patient temporary relief. If a mother has an intense fear of childbirth, for

example, it may be possible through suggestion to get her through the experience without any serious disturbance.

Hypnosis has some diagnostic value in psychotherapy quite apart from the power of suggestion. A person in a hypnotic state is usually better able to remember events that he has repressed and cannot recall in the normal state. The therapist may, indeed, be able to get the patient, under hypnosis, to relive terrifying situations of the past that are now causing the patient trouble. In this way the therapist obtains necessary information to use in other phases of the treatment. Through posthypnotic

Fig. 11.2. Drugs are sometimes used to aid psychotherapy. This patient is receiving an injection of sodium amytal, a sleep-producing drug. For several minutes before falling into deep sleep, the patient is in a twilight state. During this period, he can re-enact traumatic experiences and discuss unpleasant subjects. In this way, the therapist can uncover deep-seated problems and the patient can achieve some relief of tensions. (*Courtesy Life Magazine* © *Time, Inc.*)

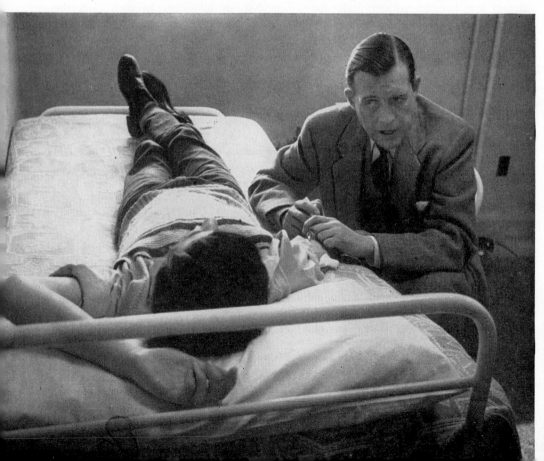

suggestion, he may also be able to have the memories that have been revived under hypnosis carry over into the normal state. Thus hypnosis is a valuable technique in therapy, even though it usually does not itself provide any basic cure of the patient's maladjustment.

Nondirective techniques. The techniques we have just described are directive techniques. They involve explanation, direction, and control of the patient's life. They are, as we have explained, very useful in certain situations. Psychotherapists, however, have come gradually to realize that patients cannot make fundamental changes in their adjustment merely by being told to do so or by external manipulation of their environment. Rather, *for psychotherapy to be of deep and lasting benefit, the patient must learn how to solve his own problems.*

Modern therapies have therefore tended to become *nondirective.* They establish a permissive situation in which the patient is dominant and is given the greatest possible freedom to express his attitudes. There are several varieties of nondirective techniques. One is found in Freud's techniques of *psychoanalysis,* which we shall describe below. Another is a therapy devised by Rogers which is called *client-centered therapy.*[5]

▪ *Client-centered therapy.* Like most modern therapy, this *is designed* not to solve any particular problem of the patient but *to provide an opportunity* for him *to develop* his own *improved methods of adjustment.* The therapist's role in the treatment is to respond to the patient's feelings and to ignore for the most part the particular words or content that he reveals in the therapeutic sessions. In general, client-centered therapy may be described as a therapy in which (1) the individual, not the problem, is the focus; (2) feelings rather than intellect are attended to; (3) the present is given greater attention than

the past; and (4) emotional growth takes place in the therapeutic relationship.

The method begins with some explanation of the roles of the counselor and the client and indicates that they will work out the difficulties together. The therapist takes pains to establish a relationship that is warm and permissive, that is, without pressure to follow any prescribed course and without criticism or judgment of what the patient says. The counselor's main aim is to help the person express his feelings freely. In this process, the client gains the ability to accept his feelings without fear and gradually finds it possible to express feelings that were formerly repressed. He then begins to see new relationships in his emotional attitudes and to react positively to situations to which he formerly responded negatively.

Interviews are usually for 1 hour and are scheduled once or twice a week. The client is made to realize at the outset that there are definite limitations upon the demands that may be made on the counselor. Every effort is made to prevent the development of a dependent relationship. The client is made to understand that the interview is not to be extended beyond the time agreed upon and that he is not expected to drop in casually for extra interviews. When the client is late, no effort is made to make up for the lost time. The time scheduled for the interview is, however, given over entirely to the desires of the client, and the counselor does not allow himself to be interrupted for messages or telephone calls. Throughout the treatment, the counselor does not allow himself to become involved in manipulations of the patient's environment.

Client-centered therapy has been effective in the counseling of college students and in the treatment of normal people with problems of adjustment (such as marital

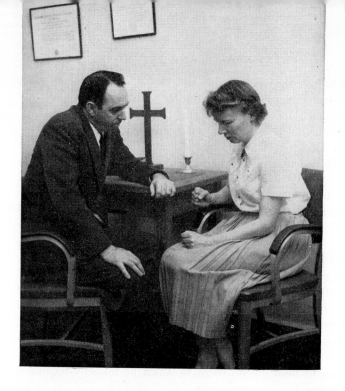

and vocational problems) and with the mild neuroses. It has not been so successful with dependent people and those with extreme emotional difficulties.

Psychoanalysis. Psychoanalysis is a system of therapy that is nondirective but not quite so nondirective as client-centered counseling. Its main objective is *to help the patient achieve a deep understanding of his own mechanisms of adjustment and thereby to help him solve his own basic problems.*[3] It is designed primarily for the treatment of neuroses but has been used with a great variety of disorders. It is usually a long, time-consuming therapy that requires 1 hour a day for 6 months to 3 years.[2] For that reason it usually is worthwhile only for patients with the more extreme, deep-seated problems who can afford the time and expense of long treatment.

In recent years the general public has become acquainted with psychoanalytic therapy more than with other forms of therapy, partly because many prominent persons have undergone "analysis" and partly because it has been popularized through novels, lectures, books, and motion pictures. As a result laymen today frequently confuse the psychoanalyst with the psychologist. Actually the term psychoanalyst should be reserved for a particular group of psychotherapists who follow certain teachings of Sigmund Freud. Such teachings include emphasis on *free association* as the basic technique of therapy and the use of the phenomenon of *transference* to analyze the source of a patient's problems. (We shall define these terms below.)

▪ *Free Association.* Psychoanalysis begins with the therapist's explaining the general procedure, aims, and purposes of the therapy. The patient is told that he should not expect recovery in a specific period of time, that his behavior and attitudes may depend upon emotional factors of which he is unaware, and that these must be traced back to their unconscious motivations chiefly through free association. *He is required to say whatever comes to his mind regardless of how irrelevant or objectionable it may be.* Since letting the mind go is quite different from the ordinary type of thinking, patients frequently take some time to be able to carry on in free association.

In the course of the free associations there are many times when the patient shows *resistance, which is an inability to remember important events in his past or to talk about certain anxiety-charged subjects.* A great part of the analyst's task is to deal with these resistances. By continuous free association, however, the patient goes beyond his unknown resistances and overcomes them. The situation cannot be forced, but the analyst may provide some interpretations. These interpretations are considered tentative and are revised as the free associations continue. The interpretations are not offered to provide solutions but rather to clear the path of the associations and to provide for the possibility of free flow for further understanding.

At any time in the course of the analysis the patient may report dreams for analysis and understanding. The dreams are considered to be important because they may provide a short road to the unconscious. They are not, however, directly interpreted but are material for more free associations. In this connection it should be noted that it is not the content of the dream as reported (manifest content) that is important but rather the motivational conflicts symbolized in the dreams (latent content).

▪ *Transference.* The core of psychoanalytic therapy is the transference that develops as the analysis proceeds. *Transference is a reenactment of previous relationships with people and principally of the parent-child relationship.* When the patient and the therapist have established good rapport, the patient begins to express toward the therapist the same emotional attitudes that he has previously expressed toward other people, especially his parents. The therapist

may, for example, become a father figure and be regarded emotionally by the patient much as he regarded his father. This phenomenon is called transference, because it is a transfer of attitudes from one person to another. When the emotions directed toward the therapist are those of affection and dependence, the transference is called positive; however, a hostile attitude may be dominant, and this is referred to as negative transference. The transference develops gradually and results in the substitution of a conflict between the patient and the analyst for the patient's inner conflict.

The strong affective relationship of the patient toward the analyst is considered an aid to the patient in overcoming his resistance. Since he feels protected, he has the courage to seek and find repressed thoughts. The transference is not used immediately for therapy but is itself analyzed so that its true nature may be demonstrated to the patient.

Handling this transference of emotions requires great adroitness on the part of the analyst. He must meet the transference affection boldly but treat it like something unreal. The success of the analysis will depend primarily upon the passive direction of the transference to the understanding of the resistances. Interpretations must be carefully presented, and the patient must be made to recognize that they are tentative and must be criticized, sifted about, and subjected to searching examination.

The approach to the termination of the analysis is indicated in a number of ways. The patient gives evidence of having cleared up the childhood memories that have been used as resistances for important motives. The analysis cannot, however, be terminated until the transference situation has been resolved. This transference must be broken and a normal doctor-patient relationship established. This is sometimes a difficult matter and constitutes a complex problem.

Distributive analysis and synthesis. The psychoanalysts who practice the methods just described constitute one of the major groups of psychotherapists. Another group, whose leader was Adolf Meyer, feels that the method of treatment should be more elastic and less systematic in outline than that of psychoanalysis. They believe that *therapy should consist both of analysis and of synthesis, distributed according to the opportunities that present themselves in the course of treatment.* For that reason they speak of their method as *distributive analysis and synthesis.*

In this kind of therapy, interviews may be directive or nondirective, but they are more frequently directive. The patient and the therapist discuss the problem in an ordinary conversation. Questions are sometimes asked to direct the patient's attention to situations and attitudes which he is urged to study and discuss. In many instances, the patient may be asked to elaborate on what he has said at some time in the interviews. In other instances, especially when it seems that the patient has a long way to go before he can understand his problems, the therapist may encourage free association and use nondirective methods in the manner of psychoanalysis. The techniques of desensitization, suggestion, and reeducation are also used when they seem to be appropriate to the situation.

This therapy is particularly distinguished for its *emphasis on synthesis.* After each interview, or at least at frequent stages in the therapy, the patient is encouraged to review what has happened and to try to determine its meaning. In developing the synthesis less attention is given to having the patient relive early experiences and more attention to having him understand their meaning and influence on his present attitudes. Every effort is made to prevent the patient from becoming too dependent upon the therapist. The important distinction from psychoanalysis is that, although the transference relationship between the patient and the therapist is recognized and attended to, an extreme degree of transference is avoided in most cases.

SPECIAL PSYCHOTHERAPIES

In addition to the methods we have described, psychotherapy includes a large number of special procedures. Among them are three techniques that deserve at least a brief description here: (1) psychodrama, (2) play and release therapy, and (3) group therapy.

Psychodrama. The drama in some form has been used in mental healing since ancient times. Its therapeutic values were mentioned by many philosophers, and there is evidence that, in the ancient theater, plays were sometimes presented for their therapeutic effects. *Psychodrama,* however, is a specialized technique recently developed by Moreno[6] *to permit patients to act out the roles, situations, and fantasies of their lives.* Although greatly influenced by psychoanalytic concepts, Moreno considered most therapeutic situations to be ineffective because the patient is treated alone and is able to express his feelings only in words. Psychodrama, on the other hand, permits the person to express himself in realistic situations by acts, rather than mere words. It also treats the individual in social situations, which in the past have been the source of some of his difficulties.

Usually in psychodrama no limitations are imposed on the patient and he may act out real situations or fantasies freely and spontaneously. A trained staff of therapeutic actors aid the patient in getting started and they take the roles of people close to

Fig. 11.4. Psychodrama. Psychodrama is a relatively new special technique in psychotherapy. Under the guidance of members of the professional staff, patients use psychodrama to work out various problems in human relationships before a small audience of other patients. (*Courtesy National Institute of Mental Health, Public Health Service, in cooperation with St. Elizabeths Hospital, Washington, D.C.*)

him or involved in his problem. The patient may be required to act out, not only those situations he has experienced in life, but those he has feared and evaded. He may at times portray himself and at times take the part of those who are influential in his life. As the therapy proceeds, it may become evident that he avoids certain roles and situations, and it may be necessary to direct him to live through scenes that are painful or undesirable. Psychodrama thus provides some of the same opportunities for free association and reliving of experiences as does psychoanalysis but uses the vehicle of the play to do it. From time to time, the therapist may analyze and interpret the situations that have been acted out.

The therapy may be carried on with or without an audience. In some situations the audience is allowed to participate in the performance and consequently acts as an aid to the therapy. In other instances the audience may be made up of patients who may themselves be the object of the therapy, since many of their own problems will be dramatized. Much of the success of this therapy depends upon a very astute chief therapist and a carefully trained staff of as-

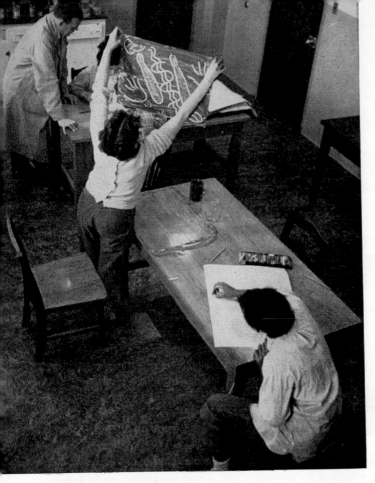

sistants. Even when this is the case, many patients find it impossible to participate in such a dramatic procedure.

Play and release therapy. Recognizing the fact that play provides unusual opportunity for the relief of tension and the development of insight and healthy growth, therapists have presented a variety of techniques known as play or release therapy. This therapy has been developed primarily for the treatment of children, and it utilizes play with toys, puppet shows, drawing, modeling with clay, and a variety of other activities.[7]

The play technique has been most useful as a method of personality study. The child often cannot or will not explain himself in the first person but may reveal much of his inner life if allowed to play freely with toys.

The child who will not tell about his own fears and conflicts may quite easily project these feelings into the toy dolls that he plays with. Feelings of rejection, insecurity, ambivalent attitudes toward parents, repressed hatreds, fears, and aggressions may all be freely revealed in play. Consequently, the play technique, when properly handled, may offer opportunities for personality study that are otherwise difficult to secure.

In addition, the play situation has been found to be useful for personality adjustments. In the security and permissiveness of the play situation the child may release feelings without fear of reprisal and thus may achieve some catharsis. The carefully conducted play situation allows the child to bring his feelings to the surface and to learn to face them, control them, or abandon them. To the extent that these situations are miniatures of real situations, desensitization can take place. The therapist must be alert to what the child says and expresses in his play and must help him gain understanding by reflecting back to him his emotionalized attitudes and by making him realize that he is accepted. He is thus encouraged to reveal more of himself.

The amount of guidance and direction used in the play technique varies within wide limits. One therapist has placed emphasis upon reeducation and habit training. Another has modeled the play technique after nondirective therapy and consequently places the child in command of the situation. In general, those therapies that have avoided much direction have been most successful. The therapist who continually directs and criticizes will certainly not succeed. On the other hand, some limitations on the freedom of the play situation are necessary since the child must develop some appreciation of the rights and privileges of others.

Group therapy. It has been evident for some years now that the number of trained psychotherapists is not sufficient for the care of all those who may profit from treatment. Partly for this reason, methods have been devised for the treatment of groups.[8] Group therapy is, however, important not only for the economy of therapeutic effort but also because it has values of its own. Since the patient's difficulties are frequently those of interpersonal relationships, it is clear that the group may be used as a therapeutic unit through which patients may be reeducated in the techniques of social adjustment.

Wherever the numbers of emotionally disturbed patients have exceeded the facilities for individual treatment, group therapy has been applied with considerable success.

In addition, it has been determined that the group method may be substituted for treatments that were started on an individual basis. In many instances, after a certain degree of success has been attained in individual therapy, it is believed that the patient's further progress will be best obtained in the group situation.

While there are many variations of the method,[9] the more usual type of *group therapy consists of assembling the group under the guidance of a therapist for meetings of about an hour's duration.* The therapist attempts to remain in the background and to allow for a free flow of interpersonal relationships between the members of the group. As the group conversation progresses, certain members of the group may discuss their own problems and symptoms. The perspectives of the other members are presented, and this gradually results in each one interposing some of his own experiences, attitudes, and feelings. Some members of the group will inevitably profit more than others, but most will receive some benefit. The mere recognition of the fact that one's problems are not unique is of some value. The opportunity to view situations and attitudes from a variety of perspectives is also helpful. Such exposure to the problems and experiences of others may help the individual to relieve his feelings of isolation and rejection, overcome his self-consciousness, modify a too strict conscience, give vent to aggressions, and obtain substitute gratifications.

The group method is also valuable because of the kind of support that may be provided. In individual therapy, those patients who find dependence intolerable are unable to accept the therapist's support, while others accept support too readily and react unfavorably when it is withdrawn. In group therapy, the members of the group support and depend upon each other, and there is no obligation to any single person.

Also in individual therapy the situation is somewhat unreal and artificial because the patient experiences emotional expression but is left uncertain as to how others will react to him. The group method has the advantage that the behavior takes place in a situation resembling the social environment, with the members of the group representing many types of people with special meanings for each patient. Thus the situation has all the characteristics of reality, since feelings tend to be expressed more honestly and everyone has an opportunity to participate.

Success will, in part, depend upon the wisdom of the therapist. He must for the most part remain in the background, but he must know when to intervene, not only to provide necessary guidance but also to prevent deleterious verbal attacks by one patient on another. He also needs to be particularly skillful in order not to take over the situation and kill the spontaneity of the group.

The method has been most successful when it is possible to supplement it with some individual therapy or when it is the terminal phase of a treatment that began by individual therapy.

IMPROVING PERSONAL ADJUSTMENTS

From the statistics of mental disease summarized in the preceding chapter, it is apparent that mental health is a widespread problem. Some authorities speak of it as "America's No. 1 health problem." Mental-health problems will undoubtedly touch your life, if they have not already done so. The knowledge you have gained of the underlying causes of such problems and of therapeutic methods for alleviating them should help you to understand better those who have such problems and to be of some

assistance to them. Such knowledge, too, may be of benefit in your own personal adjustments.

In the long run, the best treatment for any problem is to prevent it from arising. This is as true of mental-health problems as it is of others. In recent years, this idea of the prevention of mental-health problems has been recognized by leaders in many walks of life. Research on mental health has been greatly expanded by hospitals, universities, government, and other agencies. Campaigns have been under way to educate the general public concerning the nature and magnitude of mental-health problems. Many states and cities have established clinics to which children and adults can go with their adjustive problems and receive professional aid. Their general purpose is to detect emotional problems in their early stages and thereby prevent their becoming serious. Many colleges have established psychological clinics to aid students. Courses entitled mental hygiene, adjustment, etc., are being offered more widely, both in high schools and colleges and for adults in evening programs. These concerted efforts on many fronts should contribute to a general improvement in mental health.

We have repeatedly emphasized, however, that mental health is an individual problem. *Each person must learn for himself how to achieve and maintain satisfactory adjustments.* In this section we shall outline some of the things a person can do to work toward this goal.[10] Our purpose, however, is not to give any easy rules for solving personal problems. That is not possible. Achieving and maintaining satisfactory adjustments are not easy—at least for many people. One must work diligently at the problem and progress by learning a step at a time. The paragraphs below only offer some general guidance that can assist a person in his efforts.

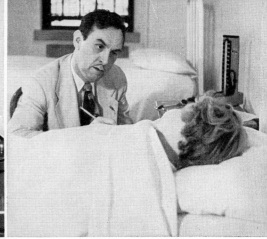

A social worker, trained in sociology and case work, talks with the husband about the patient's problems and life history.

A physician makes a medical examination and prescribes any necessary treatment.

A technician makes an electrical record of "brain waves," from which it is possible to determine whether a tumor, epileptic, or other brain disorder is present.

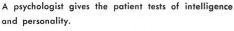

A psychologist gives the patient tests of intelligence and personality.

A patient who comes to a doctor for the treatment of emotional problems is given a comprehensive examination. Before embarking on a course of therapy, the doctor gathers all the information he can about the patient's problem, life history, family background, and physical condition. (All photos courtesy National Institute of Mental Health, Public Health Service in cooperation with St. Elizabeths Hospital, Washington, D.C.)

▪ *Reality principle.* Probably the most general advice to give on the problem of adjustment is, "Be realistic." It does no good for one to fool himself about his real motives, to have goals that are unattainable, or to suffer conflicts that might be avoided. One should try to find out what he can realistically expect to achieve and adjust his efforts and goals accordingly. Personal problems should be addressed objectively, just as one goes about solving a problem in arithmetic, fixing a car, or building a house. In each case, he should acquaint himself with the relevant facts, make sure that he understands what his problem is, then proceed with a plan for solving it. Advice of this sort, however, is more easily given than put into practice. Let us be more specific and trace some of the steps involved in dealing realistically with personal problems.

Achieving self-understanding. We have pointed out in the last chapter and this one that the person who fails to adjust is typically one who has deceived himself about his real motives. He acquires habits of self-deceit because he has tried to avoid the anxiety arising from conflict and frustration. His self-deceiving habits consist of the various defense mechanisms we have described. Such a picture of a maladjusted person contains in it a prescription for adjustment; by avoiding the pitfalls that have gotten others into trouble, a person can take steps to solve or alleviate his own problems.

▪ *Accepting anxiety.* One important step is to accept, rather than avoid, anxiety. Anxiety is a natural outcome of our experiences with fear-provoking situations (see page 101), and it can never be completely eliminated. Though we may avoid it temporarily, we cannot do so successfully for very long. If we face up to it, we "get it over with" and, in the end, have less of it.

We may illustrate this point by considering fairly prevalent attitudes toward dentists. Some people live in mortal fear of getting into a dentist's chair to have a cavity filled. Others do not care for the ordeal, but they accept it philosophically and take it in their stride. Individuals differ, of course, in their sensitivity to pain, but it is doubtful that differences of this kind have much to do with attitudes toward dentists. The important difference is one of accepting or avoiding the discomfort of having one's teeth drilled. Those who accept it find that "it isn't so bad after all." Those who do not are likely to find it "ten times worse than it actually is." These are commonsense conclusions about attitudes toward pain, but they correspond with the psychological facts. There is good evidence that the intensity of experience of pain depends greatly on whether a person accepts it as natural or fears it.[11]

Anxiety is like pain. In fact, it is a kind of pain (see page 256). Trying to avoid anxiety makes it seem worse than it is. Accepting it as natural and inevitable enables a person to build up a tolerance for it that minimizes its importance for him.

▪ *Avoiding the use of defense mechanisms.* When we say that a person should learn to accept anxiety, we are implying that he should also avoid the use of defense mechanisms. We described the various defense mechanisms in Chapter 10 and explained that they are used as ways of defending oneself against anxiety. The excessive use of defense mechanisms, it will be recalled, is the mark of a maladjusted person. Actually, if one accepts and tolerates some anxiety, there is no need to resort to defense mechanisms.

A person can make progress in avoiding defense mechanisms by analyzing his own behavior. Suppose, for example, that a student is inclined to blame the instructor for the poor grade he received in a course. If the student is acquainted with the defense mechanisms, he will recognize that his behavior has all the earmarks of rationalization. Suspecting rationalization, he may be more inclined to face the fact that he failed to attend several lectures, to keep satisfactory notes, or to do much studying. To take another example, if a person feels that his friends are turning against him, he might suspect himself of projecting dislikes or fears that he is unwilling to admit to himself. Or if he finds himself getting very angry over some little incident, perhaps he is displacing aggression from some other person or event that has annoyed him.

The practice of looking for defense mechanisms in oneself, and in others, can be carried too far. One can begin to think that he sees defense mechanisms in completely normal and harmless behavior. On the other hand, nearly everyone sometimes uses them, and a person can improve his adjustment by being on guard against them.

▪ *Understanding motives.* Since defense mechanisms deceive a person about his true motives, the problem of identifying such mechanisms is basically one of understanding one's own motives. In the nature of the case, this is not easy, because it requires him somehow to see through the smoke screen of his own defenses. Moreover, as we explained earlier (Chapters 3 and 9), motives are never easy to put one's finger on. The problem, however, can frequently be clarified by framing it in terms of goals. A person can ask himself, "What do I really want? What are my goals?" If he blamed the instructor, or something else, for a low grade in a course, he may canvass in his own mind the goals he has been trying to attain. One very probable goal—at least it is a common one—is to want a good grade without doing any work. This is human, and there is no need to be ashamed of it or to deceive oneself about it. Unfortu-

nately, it usually cannot be attained, at least by ordinary students in typical courses. Having admitted the real goal, or combination of goals, and seeing that it is unattainable, the person can free himself of the hostility and anxiety that accompany putting the blame on the instructor. At the same time, he can know better what he must do in the future if he wishes to satisfy his desires for grades. Or, of course, he may resolve the problem by deciding that a good grade is not worth the effort. In that case, he can be satisfied, rather than disgruntled, with the lower grade.

In the last two paragraphs, we have used the example of a student rationalizing the cause of a grade because it is a fairly common case in college life. We do not mean to imply that instructors never err in assigning grades. They sometimes do. The important point is that a student may be rationalizing the causes of his disgruntlement, and he may make himself aware of his defenses by asking himself searchingly what his behavior really means. The same principle applies to many other, more personal problems. When a person suspects himself of using defense mechanisms, he should assess for himself what his true goals are.

Altering motives and goals. Achieving an understanding of motives and goals is an important element in mental health. For that reason it is an aim of psychotherapy. It does not, however, guarantee successful adjustment. Patients in psychotherapy often gain insight into their own motives without seeming to improve much in mental health. The trouble in such cases is that they are unwilling or unable to follow up this achievement with other specific changes in their lives. To find mental health, it is also necessary to apply an understanding of oneself to *changing one's motives and goals*. Offhand, this may seem like asking too much of a person. It is not so unreasonable, however, if one remembers that *most motives and goals*, other than the basic physiological motives, *are acquired by training* (see Chapter 3). It is true that the training has taken place over a period of years and that the motives have become deeply ingrained habits. On the other hand, what has been acquired can, with effort and practice, be changed or discarded.

Sometimes the mere recognition of a motive permits a person to discard it with ease. A person, for example, may continually rebel against authority, attempting always to take no directions from superiors and to evade the rules of living. If he comes to understand that he acquired this motive in childhood as a reaction to an overbearing parent and that he is treating all superiors as though they were his father, he may quickly change his attitude toward superiors and get over his rebellion. Another person, when he discovers that strong prestige-seeking motives have been causing him frustration, may decide that the benefits of prestige are not worth the effort. Thereafter his interest in going up the prestige ladder may be greatly abated.

The altering of goals is usually a more laborious and time-consuming process. The person must do it by easy stages and undergo a kind of extinction (page 112) or desensitization (page 279) process. If he rebels against authority, his rebellion is not gone as soon as he understands its source. Rather, each time he feels rebellious, he must remind himself about the nature of the motive and make an effort to be cooperative and reasonable with his superiors. Each time he is successful in his efforts he completes a learning trial (page 258) in which he learns to be more comfortable with superiors. Gradually, his rebellion and its attendant anxiety are extinguished.

Some goals can be changed rather quickly

when a person realizes that he acquired them by taking them over intact from other people. This may be true, for example, of vocational goals, which are often set for the young person by his parents. A boy may come to college with his heart apparently set on being a medical doctor. After a year or two, however, he may find himself frustrated by lack of interest and ability in premedical work. Perhaps his anxiety and frustration develop to an acute stage before he examines closely what his true goals are. By himself, or with the help of a counselor, he may discover that the goal of medicine is not his own goal at all. It was adopted because of the pressures and coaching of an overzealous family. If he discovers this— and some students unfortunately do not— he is in a position to set for himself new goals more in keeping with his interests and abilities. Then his big problem is to convince his parents that he is right, and this is not always easy. College instructors and counselors see many cases of this sort. We shall discuss them further in Chapter 16.

Changes made in goals often do not need to be radical. Some goals present problems of degree rather than of kind. The fact that they are set too high is what makes them unattainable and frustrates a person. We described this situation in Chapters 3 and 10 under the heading of unattainable goals, and emphasized the discrepancy between level of aspiration and level of performance. A person who has no discrepancy between the two but has a low level of both may accomplish so little that he frustrates other motives. One, on the other hand, who sets his level of aspiration so high that he can never reach it is subjecting himself unnecessarily to frustration. The successful adjustment is achieved when a person realistically assesses his own abilities and limitations, then sets goals that are high enough to exact the best from himself but low enough to be attainable and to give him some satisfaction.

Reducing conflict and frustration. Discarding goals so that they no longer demand satisfaction and altering goals so that they are attainable are ways of reducing conflict and frustration. Our society, however, is so complex and our goals so elaborate that there is little chance, even under the best of circumstances, of a person's being completely free of conflict and frustration. All that one can do is reduce them to a minimum. There are still some effective relief measures that we have not mentioned.

■ *Postponing satisfactions.* One such measure is to postpone the satisfaction of a motive to some foreseeable date. An elementary example, which we have used before, is a conflict between hunger and sleepiness. Most people solve this problem by eating first, then sleeping, thereby postponing one goal until the other has been achieved. The principle is also applicable to more complicated conflicts. The student who wants both to have fun and to excel in college can plan to study tonight and go out tomorrow night. If he knows while he studies that he will be going out the next night, he has much less conflict than if he has no such plan. This is one of the reasons why we recommend later, in the chapter "Techniques of Study," that students follow a schedule of work and play. A young married couple who want comforts they cannot yet afford can make their plans for securing these comforts a few years hence. In the meantime, they can work hard, saving their money systematically, until the day arrives when they can see their dreams come true. By having a plan that postpones to a foreseeable time the satisfaction of motives, they reduce the conflict and frustration of the moment.

■ *Frustration tolerance.* To suggest the postponement of satisfactions is to imply that a person should acquire something else that is important in coping with conflicts—*frustration tolerance.* The difference between a normal person and one who fails to adjust is not, as one might think, so much an absence of conflict and frustration as it is an ability to tolerate frustration. The healthy person reacts to frustration as he does to anxiety (see above). He accepts it as normal and as one of the realities of life. He has learned that he cannot always have what he wants when he wants it. He stops fretting about goals that cannot be reached and lets some of his less essential motives go unsatisfied. The effect on him is similar to the effect of accepting anxiety; frustration does not seem to be nearly so frustrating if it is accepted for what it is.

It is not easy to build up a frustration tolerance, but it can be acquired, like other habits, by practice. A person can start with some of the little things—the frustration he feels when he waits too long for a bus, fails to find a parking place, or is turned down for a date. He can try to accept these little frustrations with grace, then attack some of the bigger ones. He will not succeed every time he tries, but trying is half of the battle. If he keeps trying, he will find his successes rewarded by a feeling of being more comfortable and by winning the good will of others. In time he will learn the habit of tolerating frustration.

■ *Expressing emotions.* Some conflicts, especially those involving fear and hostility, cannot be alleviated simply by postponing satisfaction or by acquiring a frustration tolerance. In many cases, the problem is quite different; it is one of venting motives that have been unnecessarily pent up. This, for example, may be the case with repressed hostility (aggression). As we have explained before, a person is caught in conflict when he is afraid to give vent to his feelings.

Perhaps, because of early training, a person is unduly fearful of acting aggressively. In that case, he might express his feelings more openly and still have no reasonable fear of losing friends or alienating people. Normal individuals expect to find others occasionally angry and take it in their stride. Even if a person sometimes makes others angry with an open display of anger, he may be better off than if he is kept uncomfortable by unexpressed emotions. This advice, of course, does not apply to everyone but is intended primarily for the person who is habitually very restrained in emotional expression.

More applicable to people in general is the suggestion *to develop socially acceptable ways of expressing one's feelings.* Without losing his temper, for example, a person may act sternly and state clearly what displeases him. Or by a joking retort he may indicate displeasure but at the same time show good humor about it. One can hardly lose friends worth having or forfeit the respect of others by such mature expressions of emotion. However, knowing how best to express emotion acceptably is a skill that must be varied to suit the situation. Like

other skills, it takes practice. To secure guidance in developing it, one can sometimes pick out another person who seems particularly successful at it and study his way of handling different situations. Learning such a skill is well worth the effort, for it can greatly reduce frustration from pent-up feelings.

▪ *Useful work.* Another way to reduce conflict and frustration is to keep busy at useful work. This idea is an old one, but it is nevertheless sound. Most work that a person does, other than very repetitive activities, is toward some goal. Keeping busy therefore leads to increased satisfaction in things accomplished. Work also occupies a person's thoughts, and while he is working other motives are pushed into the background where they are less able to cause him conflict. Hence work is a double-barreled remedy; it satisfies certain goals while weakening others. By itself, however, work is not a sure cure for conflict; some very maladjusted people work hard. But coupled with other measures we have described, it can contribute to an improved personal adjustment.

SUMMARY

1. Psychotherapy is the psychological treatment of emotional maladjustment. Originally used only with severe disorders, it is now employed more and more with mild disturbances. It is practiced both by psychiatrists (medical specialists) and by clinical psychologists.

2. The goal of psychotherapy may be (*a*) merely changing the patient's situation, (*b*) providing him with emotional support, or (*c*) helping him to achieve insight into his problem. The last is usually necessary and most effective when the patient has been burdened with chronic, deep-seated problems.

3. There are several techniques of psychotherapy that are used according to the theoretical background of the therapist and the severity of the patient's problems. Early therapies were rather directive; they instructed patients in things they should do by attempting to reeducate them, to

desensitize them in emotional situations, or to suggest specific ways of behaving.

4. Modern psychotherapy is more nondirective; it encourages the patient to work out his own problems with the help, but little intervention, of the therapist.

5. Psychoanalytic therapy follows the teachings of Sigmund Freud, emphasizes free association as a technique, and makes use of transference of the patient's attitudes to the therapist.

6. Distributive analysis and synthesis, a method promulgated by Adolf Meyer, is somewhat more directive and places more emphasis on the therapist's periodically synthesizing for the patient what has been learned in the course of therapy.

7. Psychodrama is a special technique that permits a patient to act out roles, situations, and fantasies in his life.

8. Play and release therapy, used principally with children, similarly encourages the patient to exhibit his feelings in a play situation.

9. Group therapy, another special technique, permits troubled people to talk over their problems with each other under the guidance of the therapist.

10. Normal individuals may do much to improve their own personal adjustments by (*a*) attempting to achieve self-understanding, (*b*) altering their goals, and (*c*) learning various measures to reduce conflict and frustration.

11. Self-understanding is aided by (*a*) learning to accept and tolerate anxiety, (*b*) avoiding the use of defense mechanisms, and (*c*) attempting to understand one's own motives.

12. Goals often may be discarded when a person understands what they really are. Goals may also be set at more realistic and attainable levels, thereby eliminating unnecessary frustration.

13. Conflict and frustration may be minimized by (*a*) postponing satisfactions to a foreseeable time, (*b*) acquiring a frustration tolerance, (*c*) finding socially acceptable ways of venting emotions, and (*d*) keeping occupied with useful work.

SUGGESTIONS FOR FURTHER READING

Bernard, H. W. *Toward better personal adjustment.* New York: McGraw-Hill, 1951.

    A text describing methods of making improved personal adjustments.

Dollard, J., Auld, F., and White, A. M. *Steps in psychotherapy.* New York: Macmillan, 1953.

    A case study of the progress of psychotherapy.

Dollard, J., and Miller, N. E. *Personality and psychotherapy*. New York: McGraw-Hill, 1950.

> *An analysis of personality and psychotherapy emphasizing the role of learning in personal adjustments.*

Freud, S. *The basic writings of Sigmund Freud* (Ed. by A. A. Brill). New York: Modern Library, 1938.

> *A source book on the methods and theories of psychoanalysis.*

Ingham, H. V., and Love, L. R. *The process of psychotherapy*. New York: McGraw-Hill, 1954.

> *A general summary of the practice of psychotherapy.*

Lief, A. (Ed.). The commonsense psychiatry of Dr. Adolph Meyer. New York: McGraw-Hill, 1948.

> *Selected papers presenting Meyer's views on psychotherapy and related topics.*

Moreno, J. L. *The theatre of spontaneity: an introduction to psychodrama*. New York: Beacon House, 1947.

> *A description of psychodrama as a technique in psychotherapy.*

McKinney, F. *Psychology of personal adjustment* (Rev. Ed.). New York: Wiley, 1949.

> *A text, written for college students, on problems of improving personal adjustments.*

Richards, T. W. *Modern clinical psychology*. New York: McGraw-Hill, 1946.

> *A college text on the diagnosis and treatment of mental disorders.*

Rogers, C. R. *Client-centered therapy*. Boston: Houghton Mifflin, 1951.

> *A description of the methods and results of nondirective, client-centered therapy.*

Shaffer, G. W., and Lazarus, R. S. *Fundamental concepts in clinical psychology*. New York: McGraw-Hill, 1952.

> *A text on clinical psychology, covering diagnosis and psychotherapy.*

Wolberg, L. R. *Medical hypnosis*. New York: Grune & Stratton, 1948.

> *Contains a description of the uses of hypnosis.*

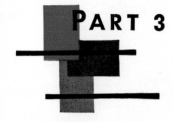

PART 3

Social Processes

$\mathscr{C}hapter$ 12   SOCIAL INFLUENCES
ON BEHAVIOR

DID YOU EVER stop to think how much other people have to say about what you do? Even if you are twenty-one and relatively free of parental control, you still cannot get loose of the control of society. Its pressure is on the whole of your behavior, prescribing everything from the tie to wear with a particular suit to the rules of virtuous living. Ministers and elders exhort you toward moral behavior, employers and neighbors gently force you to give to the Red Cross, and in many subtle ways people dictate how you dress, what you drink, and how you enjoy yourself. Indeed, practically from the moment each of us is born, society pushes, guides, advises, and constrains us in correct and appropriate ways of living. As

Ruth Benedict, the social anthropologist, has put it:[1]

The life history of the individual is first and foremost an accommodation to the patterns and standards traditionally handed down in his community. From the moment of his birth, the customs into which he is born shape his life experience and behavior. By the time he can talk he is a little creature of his culture, and by the time he is grown and able to take part in its activities, its habits are his habits, its beliefs are his beliefs, its impossibilities are his impossibilities. Every child that is born into his group will share them with him, and no child born into one on the opposite side of the globe can ever achieve the thousandth part.

So steady, so insistent, and so pervasive are cultural influences on our behavior that we rarely stop to analyze or perceive their nature. If we were dwellers in the depths of the ocean, probably the last thing we should discover is water. Indeed, it took

The first part of this chapter was drafted by H. James Bond, The Applied Psychology Corporation, and the latter part by Stanley B. Williams, College of William and Mary.

man a long time to "discover" air. Similarly it is difficult to discover and understand the culture that shapes our behavior. Yet it is necessary to do this if we are to understand human behavior at all.

CULTURE

The term *culture,* used in a scientific sense, refers to the *customs and traditions of a people and to the attitudes and beliefs they have about important aspects of their life.* Occasionally culture has been called "social heritage," but this gives the somewhat false impression that culture is inherited unchanged from generation to generation. A more accurate, though more imposing, definition of culture—one provided by the anthropologist Ralph Linton—is "the sum total of behavior patterns, attitudes and values, shared and transmitted by the members of a given society."[2] This definition makes culture an important chapter in psychology.

Social anthropologists have taught us most of what we know about culture. Knowing how difficult it is to get a perspective on our own culture, they have observed and lived in foreign cultures. They have focused their attention on the so-called primitive societies or backward peoples—the Indians, South Sea Islanders, Africans, etc. Thus they have been able to compare different cultures and to draw conclusions about their similarities and differences.

Patterns of culture. The most important, perhaps, of their conclusions is that *each culture has a distinctive pattern of its own.* There are, of course, marked individual differences among people, just as there are in our own Western culture, yet each culture has a characteristic pattern which is reflected in the behavior of all its members. We can illustrate this point by describing briefly three different cultures: the Zuni

Indians in the southwest United States, the Dobu natives of New Guinea in the South Sea Islands, and the Kwakiutl Indians of the Pacific Northwest.[1]

▪ *Zuni culture.* The Zuni Indians live in our own Southwest and are the descendants of the ancient cliff dwellers of New Mexico and Arizona. They are a mild, inoffensive people. What characterizes them most, however, is their *ceremonial life.* According to Benedict, who studied them, ritual and ceremony command their attention as much as any other activity in their life. Zuni men spend the greater part of their waking life in some aspect of ceremony. They must memorize rituals letter-perfect as a condition of their membership in various cults, and some of their performances are truly amazing. Even those who are not permitted to participate in rituals are as concerned as those who are. All the ritual and conventionalism, however, are the outward manifestations of a middle-of-the-road culture. The people apparently want to avoid the disrupting influences of individualism, innovations, and initiative. So they are an epitome of conventionalism. Sobriety, mildness, and moderation in all personal relations are their unspoken rules.

▪ *Dobu culture.* In marked contrast to the Zuni, the Dobu natives of New Guinea have *hostility* as their dominant characteristic. Violence, extreme competition, suspicion, and treachery are the usual order of the day. As Benedict has said in her characterization of this culture:[1]

Life in Dobu fosters extreme forms of animosity and malignance, which most societies have minimized by their institutions. Dobuan institutions on the other hand exalt them to the highest degree. The Dobuan lives without repression man's worst nightmares of the illwill of the universe and according to his view of life virtue consists in selecting a victim upon whom he can vent the malignance he attributes alike to human

Fig. 12.1. Cultural differences in eating behavior. On the left, Americans living in Arabia give a party Arab style. Sitting on the floor barefooted, they eat with their hands only. On the right, natives of Sumatra celebrate the painting of a house. Women and children stand and wait until the men are finished. (*Standard Oil Co., N.J.*)

society and to the powers of nature. All existence appears to him as a cut-throat struggle in which deadly antagonists are pitted against one another in a contest for each one of the goods of life. Suspicion and cruelty are his trusted weapons in the strife and he gives no mercy, as he asks none.

▪ *Kwakiutl culture.* Another society studied by Benedict is that of the Kwakiutl Indians in the northwest United States and western Canada. Its members are also highly individualistic and competitive, as are the Dobu, but in a rather different way. The aim of competition in this group is to increase one's own *social status* and to reduce that of his rivals.

To achieve status, the Kwakiutl observe a custom known as "potlatch"—a feast at which a person distributes or destroys his most valuable property, such as blankets, canoes, copper, or oil. In this feast, he who can distribute the most property achieves honor and prestige, while his rival is put to shame. It is understood, however, that objects of value that are "given" away are later to be repaid at high rates of interest —which reminds one of the phrase "Indian giver"—and the unfortunate recipient who is unable to make repayment at the appointed time suffers heavily in prestige.

Behind this cultural pattern is a way of emotional life. The Kwakiutl seem to know only emotions that swing between victory and shame. Almost every phase of community life—economic exchange, marriages, political life, and religious practices—is conducted in terms of affronts given and received. The greatest affront of all is to be laughed at, and the customary protection against such an insult is, as we have implied, the distribution of property.

We have described these three cultures, the Zuni, the Dobu, and the Kwakiutl, as illustrations of *patterns* of *culture*. The Zuni pattern is one of ceremony and convention, the Dobu is one of unrestrained hostility, and the Kwakiutl is one of competition for status. Not every culture has such distinctive and dramatic patterns, but each has a pattern.

Cultural changes. Although cultures have definite patterns, these patterns are not handed down like heirlooms from one generation to the next. Rather they are constantly changing, sometimes slowly and sometimes fairly rapidly. The medieval era was for Western civilization a period of fairly slow change in culture patterns, while the modern period has been characterized by rapid and dramatic changes. Other cultures, similarly, have had times when changes were rapid and times when they were slow.

The reasons for cultural change are quite complex. In some cases it is because one society overcomes another by force. One culture, through commerce or conquest, may dominate another, as did the ancient Greeks in the Mediterranean and later the Romans in the Mediterranean and in Europe. When cultures mix, even though one people dominates another, each takes on some of the patterns of the other. Sometimes cultural changes are forced by *climatic conditions*, by *exhaustion of natural resources*, or, especially in modern times, by *technological changes*. Today technology is stepping up the pace of cultural change and even the most remote societies have had to yield in some measure to the force of its impact. Finally, some cultural changes are brought about by an *ideology*. Some set of ideas, for which there is some need in the culture, takes hold and brings about major changes in cultural patterns. Christianity and communism are good examples.

On the other hand, it is not correct to assume that cultures change very rapidly or that all aspects of a culture may change, for there is always some continuity of cultural pattern. Some patterns may remain virtually unchanged while others are drastically revamped. Witness the industrialization of Japan growing up alongside emperor worship and its cultural consequences. In cultures, as in music, the arrangement and the tempo may vary, but the underlying melody is often the same.

Awareness of culture. We have already pointed out that few people are aware of the cultural patterns that characterize the society in which they live. Having their behavior molded by the culture from the moment of birth, they take for granted the stereotyped behaviors and attitudes that characterize their culture. *They are therefore unaware of the extent to which culture shapes their habits and values.*

It is also characteristic of cultures that no member of a society ever shares all elements of his culture. Instead, with very rare exceptions, each member knows only his particular subculture. This is because only certain aspects of a culture ordinarily influence a particular person's behavior, and he is not a part of, or greatly influenced by, other major segments of his culture.

As one illustration of this point, let us take the example of class, or cultural, mobility. In the caste and class systems of some societies, it is virtually impossible for a person to move from one class to another higher one. In others, where there are few legal or economic barriers, this may still be true, simply because people in a lower stratum of society are so ignorant of the cultural ways of the "upper" class. Even in a society such as our own, where crossing most class boundaries is more freely done than in most, it is not so easy as it seems. To cross them, a person must discard the habits and attitudes of his childhood or early adult culture and learn the different ones of the cultural class into which he moves. This is sometimes difficult or impossible. Indeed, these hurdles of knowledge and skill within a culture are grounds for such sayings as "You can't make a silk purse out of a sow's ear," and "He's from the wrong side of the tracks."

SOCIAL STRUCTURE

Each culture, we have said, has its distinctive pattern. *Each culture also has its own social structure.* That is to say, it has ranks that are assigned to people, it expects certain people to do one kind of work and others to do other kinds, it expects its families to be constituted in a certain way, and it expects its members to have certain attitudes and beliefs. In some societies, this social structure is rather rigid, in others it is more flexible, but none escapes some degree of structuring.

Much of the structuring arises from differences among people in the goods and services that they produce. One person may make trinkets, another shoes, while a third invents the steam engine. Trinkets may satisfy the rather unessential needs of a few, while the steam engine multiplies a hundredfold many different things that satisfy needs. The dependence of people upon each other is therefore not equally distributed, and some people are much more important to the society than are others.

Of all the ways in which services to a society may be unequal, those arising from sex and age are most common. These differences, therefore, structure all societies in some degree. Infants obviously contribute little and demand much, and mothers on the whole are assigned to take care of them. Children may contribute something but

Fig. 12.2. Some cultural patterns may remain unchanged while others are greatly modified. The Hutterites, a religious sect in the north central United States and Canada, follow their traditional patterns of dress, of weaving, and of goose plucking, while adopting modern methods of farming and using up-to-date commercial products. (*Courtesy Dr. J. W. Eaton, School of Applied Social Sciences, Western Reserve University, and Scientific American.*)

Fig. 12.3. Social structuring arises from differences among people in the goods and services they produce. In the Arab culture, a young man has the job of preparing coffee for his father's guests. (*Standard Oil Co., N.J.*)

still not much, and thus they are expected to treat adults with the respect befitting their different roles. Young men, in nearly all societies, are expected to be warriors in time of danger. Old men are usually the sources of wisdom and leadership. Thus individual differences in ability to meet society's needs have a lot to do with the social structure. So, too, of course, do technological differences in societies. Those societies that are more highly industrialized and have more different work specialties have more elaborate social structures.

Status and role. Age and sex are only two kinds of individual differences contributing to social structure. As we have al-

ready implied, occupation is another. So are position in the family unit, membership in social groups, and many others, depending upon the particular society. What makes social structure is the fact that members of a society categorize people according to differences that are important to their needs. Thus they give to each person in the society what social scientists call a *status*—age status, sex status, occupational status, social status, and so on. *Each status is a position representing differences that are important in the exchange of goods and services and in the satisfaction of needs in the society.*

Different people may occupy a particular

status at different times, and their statuses may change from time to time. Along with status, however, goes a *role*. This is *pattern of behavior that a person is expected to exhibit in a particular status*. A father in the status of "head of a household" has a role of behavior he must play in that status. So does a person in the status of "employer," or of "mother," or of "teacher," etc. So we must make a clear distinction between status and role, one applying to position in the social structure and the other to the behavior that goes along with that position. These concepts of status and role are key concepts in understanding social structure.

■ *Multiple status.* The system of categories of statuses that emerges in a social structure usually permits any particular person to be categorized in many ways, e.g., as "head of a household," "teacher," "employee," or "church member." A person therefore comes to have several statuses in a social structure. For some part of his life, he occupies one status; for another part, another status. In each of these statuses, moreover, he has a role to play that goes along with the particular status. He therefore finds himself in multiple statuses and multiple roles. The following illustration from Linton gives a picture of the multiple statuses a person may occupy:[2]

Let us suppose that a man spends the day working as a clerk in a store. While he is behind the counter, his active status is that of a clerk, established by his position in our society's system of specialized occupations. The role associated with this status provides him with patterns for his relations with customers. These patterns will be well known both to him and to the customers and will enable them to transact business with a minimum of delay or misunderstanding. When he retires to the rest room for a smoke and meets other employees there, his clerk status becomes latent and he assumes another active status based upon his position in the association group composed of the store's employees as a whole. In this status his relations with other employees will be governed by a different set of culture patterns from those employed in his relations with customers. Moreover, since he probably knows most of the other employees, his exercise of these culture patterns will be modified by his personal likes and dislikes of certain individuals and by considerations of their and his own relative positions in the prestige series of the store association's members. When closing time comes, he lays aside both his clerk- and store-association statuses and while on the way home, operates simply in terms of his status with respect to the society's age-sex system. Thus if he is a young man he will at least feel that he ought to get up and give his seat to a lady, while if he is an old one he will be quite comfortable about keeping it. As soon as he arrives at his house, a new set of statuses will be activated. These statuses derive from the kinship ties which relate him to various members of the family group. In pursuance of the roles associated with these family statuses he will try to be cordial to his mother-in-law, affectionate to his wife, and a stern disciplinarian to Junior, whose report card marks a new low. If it happens to be a lodge night, all his familial statuses will become latent at about eight o'clock. As soon as he enters the lodge room and puts on his uniform as Grand Imperial Lizard in the Ancient Order of Dinosaurs he assumes a new status, one which has been latent since the last meeting, and performs in terms of its role until it is time for him to take off his uniform and go home.

Conflicts of roles. Serious trouble can arise when a person is caught in a conflict of roles, and this can easily happen in a society as complex and as mobile as ours. The blustering foreman who drives his men with an iron hand may find his methods quite unsuccessful when he climbs the ladder of executive responsibility. The student leader, accustomed to the role of class president in a small-town high school, may be unhappy when he becomes just another freshman in a large university. The socialite, used to the manners and repartee of cock-tail parties, may find herself offended and uncomfortable in a party of farmers or laborers.

Such changes in status put a person in a conflict of roles. He finds that the role he learned in one status is no longer appropriate in a new status. He becomes uncertain as to what role he should play, and when he is forced to decide on one he may have little confidence in his choice. Thus he may be thrust into motivational conflict of the sort we have previously described (see Chapter 10). The consequences may be disastrous: frustration, anxiety, hostility, and failure of adjustment. If such conflict is widespread in a society—as it may be in times of great economic expansion or depression—it may inspire intergroup and interracial tensions, even international conflicts.

Multiple roles, however, are not always in conflict. In well-organized societies, in fact, conflicts of role are relatively rare. The structure of such societies preserves and isolates statuses so well that conflicts occur only in relatively rare and incongruous situations. There is the story of the Scotsman, for example, who found himself in the role of host to the murderer of his brother. Bound by the conventions of hospitality, he could resolve the conflict of the roles of host and avenger of his brother's death only by conducting the murderer outside the territory of his clan before taking his vengeance. Such conflicts, however, are rather rare.

Multiple roles not only need not conflict, they often complement each other. The roles of parent, craftsman, and friend may each satisfy needs or relieve frustrations that the other roles could not. Or one role may permit a person to relieve frustrations built up in playing another role, as when a parent takes out on his family the aggressions built up during the day as an employee. The various roles we must play therefore run the gamut from producing motivational conflicts to helping in the relief of conflicts.

Social classes. So far we have described social structure in terms of statuses and roles. There is more to social structure, however, than a mere assortment of statuses. In every society, these *statuses are arranged on a scale of prestige.* That is to say, the people in the society regard some statuses more favorably than others or they rank statuses according to their desirability. Then the awards that the community has to distribute, such as wealth, power, respect, and honors, are parceled out according to this prestige scale. Naturally, there is no one-to-one correlation, say, between wealth and prestige, for those of equal prestige may receive somewhat different shares of the wealth. But taken together, the awards of the community correspond fairly well to status on a prestige scale.

Thus the prestige scale becomes the basis for forming social classes or strata. Those high on it are largely in one class; those low on it are mainly in another class. In many societies the class system has become so formalized that it permeates all social organization and behavior. In many ancient kingdoms, for example, the classification of all members into one of three strata—nobility, freemen and slaves—was unequivocal. Each person was one of the three. Frequently his class membership was indicated by his speech, dress, or other symbols clear to any observer. Each class was restricted to certain occupations and indeed to certain kinds of social behavior; freemen, for example, behaved in one way toward nobility, in another toward freemen, and in another toward slaves.

Our own society does not formalize classes so rigidly. It is not so easy to pick out a person's social class, nor are members of a class confined so strictly to that class and its particular occupations as are, say, members of a caste in India. In other words, we have more class mobility. There is nevertheless a definite class structure in American society. An interesting illustration of this point is to be found in a study of the social structure in an actual American community, fictitiously called Jonesville. Mr. Walter Jones, a respected citizen of Jonesville, summarized the feelings of most people in the town in the following way:[20]

Almost everyone in this town is rated in some way, people can rate you in just a few minutes by talking to you. It's remarkable how you can size up people in a hurry—suppose I use a rating scale of zero to 100 and rate people on it. You can be sure this is not a hypothetical thing either. Not to the people of Jonesville. People like the Caldwells and the Volmers [the Lowells and the Cabots of Jonesville] rate 100. The Shaws would be up there too. People like me, oh, a 70 maybe and people like John [a janitor] about 40, no better than that. Remember this is a social rating. If we rated them financially some of them would rank differently.

This quotation only illustrates the point, but it does not prove it. For proof we may go to other studies in which the attitudes of people have been scientifically sampled. One such study[3] was made in a town called "Yankee City," and it revealed a class structure depicted in Figure 12.4. This figure is constructed from a large number of interviews of citizens of Yankee City in which they were asked to rate their fellow townsmen on social status. For the most part, people did not think of social classes by the names used in the illustration. These were furnished by the research workers afterward. Yet it was clear enough that people

distinguished three major classes and within each of them a lower and an upper part. With these they were able to classify almost everyone in the town. The actual percentages you see in Figure 12.4, however, would probably vary from one city or section of the country to another.

Criteria of class. In studies of this sort, the question arises, What criteria do the members of a community use when they rate their fellow members in social classes? The answer is never simple. *Economic criteria* are perhaps the most important, but many other factors enter into the evaluation. In Yankee City, for example, people revealed that they used all the following criteria in making their judgments: *nature of occupation, kind of income* (whether salary, commission, dividend, or the like),

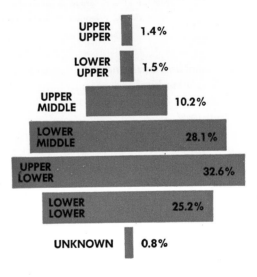

UPPER UPPER   **1.4%**

LOWER UPPER   **1.5%**

UPPER MIDDLE   **10.2%**

LOWER MIDDLE   **28.1%**

UPPER LOWER   **32.6%**

LOWER LOWER   **25.2%**

UNKNOWN   **0.8%**

Fig. 12.4. The class structure of Yankee City. A sample of the citizens of Yankee City, a New England community of about 15,000 people, were classified in six classes on the basis of interviews and other information concerning their socioeconomic status and social activities. (*Data from Warner, W. L., & Lunt, P. S. The social life of a modern community. New Haven: Yale Univ. Press, 1941.*)

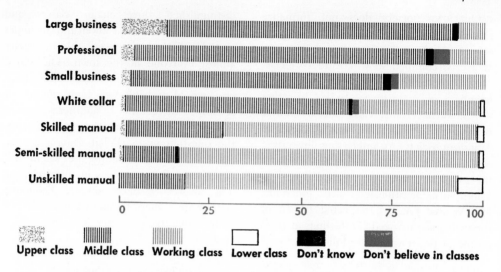

Fig. 12.5. Class identifications according to occupation. Members of the occupational groups named on the left were asked to identify themselves with a social class. The bars show the percentage of each group choosing the respective classes. (*After Centers, R. T. The psychology of social classes. Princeton: Princeton Univ. Press, 1949.*)

moral standing, birth and family geneology, social relationships and organizations, and the *kind of residential area in which the person lived.*

Membership in a class carries with it certain typical attitudes. It is a question whether class membership causes these attitudes, whether occupational status typical of a class engenders these attitudes, or whether people with certain attitudes are more likely to fall in a certain class. At any rate, there seem to be attitudes that characterize American social classes.[3] Most of us are aware of such differences in attitude toward many matters—money, birth, education, comfort, sexual behavior, politics —and they do not need to be detailed here.

Not only are certain attitudes typical of classes in the American social structure, but such attitudes have something to do with the class in which a person feels he belongs. In a national sample of 1,100

adults[4] asked about their attitudes on several issues, including their own social class, people classified themselves as you see in Table 12.1. One of the interesting things about their classification was that so few people (1 per cent) were willing to classify themselves by the unflattering term "lower class." Instead members of the lower class preferred to identify themselves with the "working class." Also revealed by this study was the fact that people judged themselves by their occupations. In Figure 12.5 you see that the higher a person is on the occupational scale, the higher he places himself in social class. Finally, however, the idea that "common attitudes and beliefs are distinctive characteristics of social classes" had something to do with their judgments. Nearly 70 per cent of self-judged members of the middle class, for example, held conservative political opinions, while only 35 per cent of the working class did. Interviews with these people made it clear that they tended to identify themselves with the class that they felt shared their political and social attitudes.

Social classes and behavior. Because attitudes, occupation, morals, and a whole host of things are related to class status, one might be inclined to think that class status greatly influences behavior. Certainly consciousness of class does. In general, however, it is more correct to say that the various statuses and roles that go into a class structure have profound effects on behavior.[5] In any case, it is important to realize that there are many psychological differences associated with class.

The physical and social environment for development of personality is largely a matter of class. Indeed, the kind of home or neighborhood in which one lives, the kind of work, play, and facilities that are available, and even the minimum necessities for satisfying basic needs all go along with social class. Even more important, however, the training and education of a child is largely a matter of class. The manners one learns in eating, the selection of playmates, choice of occupations, and one's educational goal are conditioned by the class in which he lives. Thus many of the influences on development that we have discussed elsewhere (Chapters 2, 7, and 9) depend on the social class of a child's parents.

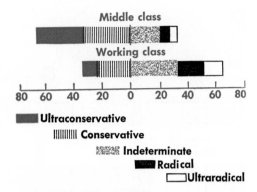

Fig. 12.6. Class differences in attitudes. When asked to indicate their attitudes on six socioeconomic issues, a national sample of members of the middle and working classes gave the results above. In general, members of the working class were more radical than members of the middle class. (*Data from Centers, R. T. Psychological aspects of socioeconomic stratification. Princeton: Princeton Univ. Press, 1948.*)

■ SOCIAL GROUPS

We have now seen that societies have cultures and a social structure. They are also characterized by *social groups*. Each member in a society not only has his status roles and social class, he is also a member of a large number of groups. He always is a member of a family group, at least when he is born, and he usually is a member of a community group, a city, or a town. Besides that he may be in a church group, an industrial group, a political group, a lodge, and many other varieties of groups. These groups affect his behavior, and he

TABLE 12.1. Affiliation with social classes.

A nationwide sample of 1,100 adult men were asked to indicate the social class with which they felt they were affiliated. Below are their replies expressed in per cent of men affiliating with each class or in per cent of those who did not affiliate or had no opinion.

Upper class	3
Middle class	43
Working class	51
Lower class	1
Don't believe in class	1
Don't know	1

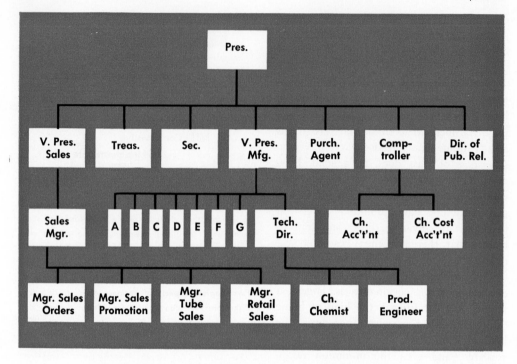

Fig. 12.7. Organization charts to depict the structure of formal organizations. The traditional organization chart (*above*) is vertical, but many of the relationships between individuals are better represented by a concentric organization chart (*right*). Individuals A, B, C, etc., on the traditional chart are coordinate with the Technical Director, and their positions are named on the middle circle of the concentric chart. (*After Browne, C. G. The concentric organization chart. J. appl. Psychol. 1950, 34, 375–377.*)

in turn affects the behavior and structure of the group.

Kinds of groups. There are several ways to classify groups, but we shall mention only a few of them briefly. First we can distinguish between *assembled* groups and *dispersed* groups, that is, between groups consisting of people physically present in the same area at the same time and those made up of people not assembled. People at work, in church, in the classroom, or in the parlor comprise assembled groups. Members of nations, political parties, unions, social classes, etc., make up dis- persed groups. Many groups, of course, are both, because they are sometimes assembled and sometimes dispersed.

We may also distinguish between *formal* and *informal* groups. Formal groups are those with a reasonably permanent organi- zation and structure, such as industrial con- cerns, political parties, church bodies, and armies. Informal groups have no such permanent structure or organization, but appear and disappear, or assemble and dis- perse, depending on the occasion. A lynch- ing mob, a group watching a baseball game, a party at home, and a theater audience

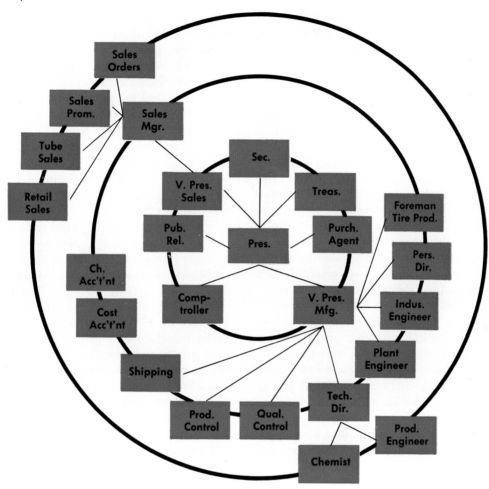

are all good examples of informal groups.

Finally let us distinguish between groups in terms of their primary purposes or functions. The general purpose of a *family group* is probably obvious. *Social* groups such as churches, lodges, clubs, and the like exist to provide social participation and certain facilities for their members. *Power* groups have the purpose of gaining or retaining power over certain segments of a society. Ordinarily a political party may be regarded as a power group. *Ideological* groups, sometimes called *social movements*, are groups constituted with

the primary purpose of effecting some substantial change in the social system.[6] The Nazi party was, and the Communist Party is, an ideological group. We shall have occasion to use some of these distinctions in this and succeeding chapters.

Group structure. To understand the behavior of a group or of individuals in the group, we should have some way of depicting the interpersonal relations within the group. We should like to know who does what to whom and when, for it is the interaction of the behavior of people in a group that for the most part makes the group. In a word, we should like a description of a group's social structure. This is a difficult problem that is far from a satisfactory solution, but we have something to say that bears on it.

▪ *Formal groups.* A formal, organized group is planned, designed, and produced by someone. It is a formal structure of positions, jobs, or roles. It always is based on some division of labor, and it usually consists of subgroups. As a differentiated structure, its parts are labeled, and leaders of the subgroups have titles. It has been customary in formal groups to attempt to depict the group structure by means of an organization chart that stresses the *vertical* relations of authority and command. Such organization charts abound in business, government, and military organizations. They seldom do justice, however, to the many horizontal relations among workers of about equal rank. To correct this, one scientist has suggested a *concentric* organization chart.[7] Both are illustrated in Figure 12.7. Whether or not the concentric chart is the best possible portrait of group structure, it is at least in some ways an improvement over the vertical chart. Probably neither method is the best that can be devised.

One weakness of both charts is their inability to depict (1) numerous minor organizational relationships, and (2) dual or triple roles. Consider, for example, the case of Mr. X, whose duties in a college administration are as follows: In his capacity as member of a committee on student counseling, Mr. X may "advise" the dean of the faculty via a professor who is chairman of the committee. The advice eventually gets back to Mr. X, however, in his capacity of dean of students. This may require consultation with the director of admissions, the same Mr. X, and may even involve the registrar, again Mr. X. As director of admissions, Mr. X's decisions may be restricted by an admissions committee and possibly by a freshman dean Mr. Y, who is in charge of counseling freshmen. Both deans are hired or fired by a college president but are required to "work under the direction" of a faculty committee on plans and policies, which in turn has only veto "power," which may be outvetoed by the president. The president in turn can be overruled or fired by the board of trustees. What is the position of Mr. X on an organization chart?

The foregoing is not an actual case, but it is a "real" case in the sense that structures like it do exist. There is a principle of administration that says every jobholder should know precisely who gives him his orders and to whom he is to give orders. Very few actual group structures are so clearly unambiguous. As a result, a man must play several roles. The actualities of role assignments have run so far ahead of our ability to pictorialize or symbolize them that it is often impossible to understand a working organization by inspecting its organizational chart. In tiny organizations, that doesn't matter; in large ones, it does. It is probably safe to say that no one comprehends the organization of the Federal government today.

▪ *Informal groups.* The informal group is generated out of firsthand experience. Individuals meet or hear about each other, form impressions of each other, and react dominantly, submissively, reverently, admiringly, distastefully, or otherwise. Out of this complex of interactions, leaders emerge with titles, and each person comes to play a more or less definite role in the group. Cliques form. Prestige attitudes are generated. Much of this process—perhaps most—is never verbalized. It results in natural, unguided selection of leaders and followers, roles to play, and thus of a

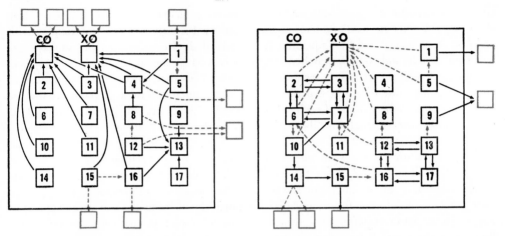

Fig. 12.8. Sociograms of two flight squadrons. Diagram at left represents squadron A; the diagram at right, squadron B. Colored squares represent individuals outside the squadron. Colored, dotted lines are negative choices; solid, black lines are positive choices. For further explanation, see text. (*Data from Jenkins, J. G. Nominating technique as a method of evaluating air group morale. J. Aviat. Med., 1948, 19, 12–19.*)

group structure. The selections—and therefore the structure of the group—may vary from time to time and probably never crystallize completely. How can we picture scientifically the structure of such a group?

One interesting and helpful device is the *sociogram,* which was invented by Moreno.[8] To construct a sociogram, one asks all members of a group, "Which persons would you most like to have for a roommate [or partner, fellow worker, flying partner, leader of your group—whichever is appropriate]?" and "Which persons would you least like to have . . . ? From the answers to these questions one can construct a diagram, the sociogram, representing the interpersonal relations of the group. It has been customary to represent positive choices (likes) with solid lines, and negative choices (dislikes) by broken lines. The sociogram then gives a pictorial idea of the structure of the group.

This technique has been applied to many groups—boys in summer camps, girls in a reformatory, children in classrooms, officer candidates in the Marine Corps, and numerous other groups. To illustrate it we shall use a sociogram of preferences of naval fliers for flying partners, as obtained by Jenkins during the Second World War.[9] This sociogram, illustrated in Figure 12.8, shows an informal group structure within the formal structure of the naval organization. In this particular sociogram, the blocks inside a square represent members of a squadron; those outside the square represent fliers in other squadrons known to one or more members. CO means squadron commander; XO means squadron executive officer. Study the picture closely with two things in mind: (1) the differences between squadrons A and B, and (2) the difference between this picture and the picture of the organized group in Figure 12.7.

What do the differences between squadrons imply? In squadron A, the two leaders are popular, the members have more positive choices than negative choices, all positive choices are in-group and most negative choices are out-group, and there are no cliques. Notice the corresponding features of squadron B. Not so good? As you might easily guess, it turned out that squadron A had high morale and squadron B had low morale. Thus with the sociogram technique, one can get a picture of group structure in terms of what members think of each other and from this infer something about the way the group functions.

▪ *Power structure.* Power is the ability to control. The actual control of the behavior of members of a group does not always correspond to the group's formal organization or to its power structure. We usually think of a group which is controlled from the top as *autocratic* and of a group which is controlled by collective action of most of its membership as *democratic.* This is an oversimplification. Many very democratic societies are strongly controlled from the top, as the United States was during the Second World War, for example. The key to a clear view of this problem lies in the distinction between control and power.

Power is defined as the ability to control, but that ability can be and frequently is delegated. In a democratic society, the members of the society delegate to certain individuals the control of that society. This delegation is revocable, though usually the method of delegation is chosen so that revoking it is not too easy.

The terms *autocratic* and *democratic* can apply to power relationships or to control relationships. Regardless of power considerations, an autocratic control pattern might be pictured as a star with channels of control radiating from the leader; underlings do not communicate with each other. The picture of democratic control is a network, and the leader is merely a traffic center. Figure 12.9 (left) is a symbolic picture of an autocratic control pattern; Figure 12.9 (right) is of a democratic control pattern. The pictures are not completely realistic, but they serve as schematic diagrams, like a radio diagram which illustrates its main components without filling in the details.

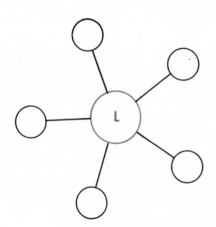

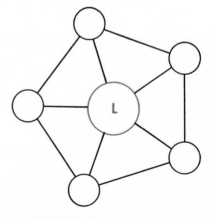

Fig. 12.9. Authoritarian and democratic patterns. For small groups, the structure of authoritarian leadership may be depicted as a star in which individuals depend on the leader for direction. The structure of democratic leadership, on the other hand, may be represented as a wheel in which all members work together and the leader is a "center of traffic." (After Krech, D., & Crutchfield, R. S. Theory and problems of social psychology. New York: McGraw-Hill, 1948, 425–426.)

To give life to the pictures, we must remember the "atmosphere" or "climate" that tends to characterize autocratically and democratically controlled groups. Students of Kurt Lewin have experimentally produced these climates in children's play groups by having the leader, an adult, act democratically with one group and autocratically with another.[10] As a democratic leader, he suggested, persuaded, and refrained from domineering. As an autocrat, he ordered and commanded, permitting no suggestions from the group members (see Figure 12.10). In the democratic group there was less hostility, more enjoyment, and more constructive work, and the group did not fall apart when the leader left it. The experimenters point out, however, that there were some exceptions to this superiority of the democracy.

Social learning. As psychologists we are not so interested in group structure or functions as we are in the behavior of people in groups and in the effects of groups upon their behavior. Let us therefore turn to that general question. There are a good many things that people do in groups and a good many ways in which they are affected by the group.

■ *Socialization.* In this and preceding chapters, we have dwelt several times on the socialization of the individual. This begins in the primary family group, which at first satisfies his needs, then later presents obstacles to this satisfaction—do's and don't's. The family group, therefore, is his first teacher. Through it he learns not only many basic skills but also his characteristic ways of adjusting to frustrations. As the individual makes the transition from his original family group to the other groups of which he is a member as an adult, this process of socialization continues. He depends on groups for the satisfaction of many of his needs, yet these groups approve and

Fig. 12.10. Authoritarian, democratic, and laissez-faire groups. In the authoritarian group (*top*), the leader tells the children exactly what to do. In the democratic group (*middle*), the leader acts as a consultant. In the laissez-faire group (*bottom*), the leader helps only when asked; children are often bored or break into horseplay. (*Courtesy Dr. Ronald Lippitt.*)

disapprove of his behavior and force him continually to learn and to modify his behavior. Thus nearly all that we have said in the last three chapters can be regarded as the effect of groups on a person's behavior. We may, however, be more specific than that and describe in addition the kinds of learning that take place in groups.

■ *Imitation.* If you have ever observed two children in a family of about the ages of two and four, you have noticed how much the child of two imitates everything his older brother or sister does. When the older child starts out the door, so does the younger; when one wants candy, so does the other; and so on. Imitation is particularly striking at the age of two or three, when a child has not yet learned to do many things for himself and learns a short cut to getting what he wants by imitating older children or persons. Though not quite so obvious, perhaps, imitation is a striking feature of the behavior of people in groups. It is a specific kind of social learning that takes place because it is usually rewarded by members of the group.

■ *Opportunity to vary.* Groups also assist in individual learning because they increase the number of opportunities for behavior to vary or, one might say, because they increase trial and error in behavior. In group discussions, new ideas, opposing ideas, or different approaches to a problem are put forward. Some of these "trials" would never have occurred to an individual by himself. When they are proposed by other people, he can profit from their successes and failures. It is this feature of social learning that underlies our use of conferences as ways of solving mutual problems and our insistence on freedom of speech for the public airing of views.

We might illustrate a specific case of such learning with an experiment in which different college classes were given the task of estimating the number of beans in a glass jar.[11] Members of each class made an estimate and later were asked to make another estimate. In between the two estimates, members of one class were not allowed to discuss the problem at all. Another class, however, was encouraged to discuss their estimates with each other between the tests. Both classes showed some improvement in the correctness of their estimates, but the class that was allowed discussion improved much more than did the other. Apparently the comparison of results among individuals in the group permitted them to come closer to the correct answer—before any of them knew it.

■ *Social facilitation.* Still another way in which the group aids learning and performance is through facilitation. One can see the results of such facilitation in rats. In one experiment, rats were allowed to eat individually, with no other rats in sight, until they would eat no more.[12] Then they were brought together in small groups and allowed to eat more if they wished. Most of them began eating again and, on the average, ate 70 per cent more than they did individually.

People behave in a similar manner. In a now classic study, one investigator gave some psychological tests to adults under two sets of conditions: (1) working individually, and (2) working in groups around a common table.[13] When people worked in each other's presence, they speeded up considerably their rate of work. The quality of their work was somewhat worse, but this is understandable, for the tests were such that they could not have speeded up much without suffering some impairment in quality. The important point is that the mere presence of other people facilitated the work of the several individuals.

■ *Cooperation and competition.* When we think about groups and their effect on behavior, we are bound to raise the question of cooperation and competition. If a group is really a group, that is, if there are interpersonal relations that make the group more than a mere collection of individuals, these relations must somehow or other involve cooperation and competition (see Chapter 3). In fact, it may have occurred to you, in reading about the study above on social facilitation, that the explanation of such facilitation might be in a feeling of rivalry or competition that creeps into a person's efforts when he is working in the presence of others. In that particular study, strict instructions were given to the subjects that they were not to compete with each other. Nevertheless there was probably some feeling of competition.

In any event, competitive behavior is something people learn in groups. And this is also the way they learn cooperative behavior. We saw this in Chapter 3, so we do not need to dwell on it here. There you read of animal experiments in which it was possible to teach groups of animals either cooperative or competitive behavior by rewarding them appropriately. If cooperative behavior was rewarded, it was learned; if competitive behavior was rewarded, it was learned. We also pointed out at that time that the cooperative or competitive patterns observed among primitive peoples were perpetuated in their cultures by the kind of training children received in their families and social groups.

◼ LEADERSHIP

One of the most important characteristics of groups is that they have *leaders*. One person may get himself out of a burning building, but 500 school children cannot be evacuated without some coordination. Children can play individually as long as they are climbing ropes or "skinning the cat," but in most games they need a leader. You can play football without a captain, but it is much more fun if you have someone call signals. Anarchists may be efficient individualists when bombing kings and derailing trains, but anarchism applied to a military organization would result in many dead heroes and few victories. Moral: groups need leaders if they are to pull together effectively in a team.

Leaders and social change. Although students of human affairs have long tried to evaluate the role of leaders in group behavior,[14] they have not been able to reach agreement on the matter. Writers from Carlyle to Marx have leaned toward one or another of two extreme opinions about leaders: (1) Leaders are necessary; history hinges on their actions. (2) Leaders are merely the expression of popular needs; they ride the tide of history, but they do not influence it.

The first view may be called the *leader principle* or the "great-man theory" of history. It says that masses of people drift along in aimless confusion until a gifted leader assumes command and tells them what to do. The "man on horseback" is always a dramatic figure. He may accomplish social change (good or bad), but the truth of the matter is that he *appears* to accomplish much more than he actually does. It is said, for example, that Hitler conquered Poland and that Hitler slaughtered millions of people. Literally speaking, Hitler did not do any of these things. Mostly he just talked. But would these things have happened without Hitler? We do not know, for history is an uncontrolled experiment. Yet, by the great-man theory of history, Hitler gets credit for *causing* the events.

The second opinion might be called the *sociological view*. It says that history makes or selects the man, not vice versa. Social and cultural developments are considered to follow their own laws, and the presence of a particular person as leader is purely coincidental. A society is regarded as a sprawling organism, adapting slowly to environmental change. Its habits and customs are its culture. If a social organism finds itself at war, a peace leader will not be tolerated; a nation in defeat demands a quisling type of leader. No leader can be at variance with the needs of the group and remain its leader. According to this view, then, it was not Hitler, but the German people who overran Poland and slaughtered the Jews. Extreme adherents of this view will not even admit the temporary influence of the leader. To them, he may be the people's voice, but never their brain.

There are arguments for and against each of these views of leadership. Neither can be proved or disproved. We have reason to believe that the truth lies somewhere between the two. Social change is probably a function of *leaders, groups,* and *situations,* all of which interact to determine the outcome. Leaders usually make some difference, sometimes great and sometimes small. On the other hand, the needs and attitudes of groups determine whom they will select or follow as their leaders. Of course, the behavior of both leaders and groups depends upon the situations they face.

Psychologists have no business playing the role of historian and explaining history. They can, however, conduct experiments on leadership in different kinds of groups and situations, and they can make systematic surveys of attitudes toward leaders and how leaders function in groups. They can also apply their knowledge of psychological measurement to the measurement of the abilities of leaders. They have done all these things and thus have some information about the functions and characteristics of leaders.

Functions of leaders. Human leadership turns out to be a rather complicated problem. By tabulating what people do in leadership situations or what people say about the groups they are in, it is possible to compile a long list of the things leaders do for members of the group. Human leaders sometimes (1) set up the motivation of their followers, (2) arrange for rewards and punishments of the followers, (3) help the followers when they fail, (4) deal with their anger if they are frustrated, (5) replace them if they drop out, and (6) even provide the "maze paths" or "answers" to their problems. It is interesting to note that all these functions of a leader are carried out when a psychologist trains a rat in an experiment. The list of a leader's functions also includes acting as (1) executive, (2) planner, (3) policy maker, (4) expert, (5) group spokesman, (6) controller or "switchboard" of intragroup relations, (7) arbitrator or mediator, (8) model for copying, (9) symbol for group unity, (10) ideologist, (11) father figure, and (12) scapegoat. Not all of these, of course, are required of every leader, but each applies at some time to some leader in some situation.[15]

All these functions of leaders fall into two broad groups, one of which we might call *inspiration* and the other *execution.* Under "inspiration," we may include all the things the leader does *to* the group, dramatizing its goals, rewarding and punishing members, getting them to work effectively with each other, and so on. Under "execution" we may include what the leader does *for* the group: planning policy, selecting subordinates, dividing up the work, delegating authority, and so on.

It is difficult, if not impossible, for leaders to play these different roles equally well. The inspiring leader, who can make people work together, is likely to neglect his duties as a director and be a person who does not care too much for the routine of executive work. The executive leader, on the other hand, in being concerned with the effectiveness of his organization, is likely to neglect the feelings of his associates and may treat his people harshly. Both kinds of leaders have their place, and each may command loyalty from the group. One makes people feel important and keeps them happy, the other makes them feel secure in the knowledge that the group is being well run.

Personalities of leaders. This brings us to the question of the traits of leadership. Our libraries are filled with well-meaning books on this subject, containing nothing but highly opinionated advice, usually intended for the young males of our society about to be initiated into the glories of adulthood. Opinions unrelated to facts are next to worthless for a science, and that is what most popular writing on leadership is. In recent years, however, scientists have put their efforts to the question, and we are now beginning to get some facts. These have been collected in several kinds of studies which we shall describe. In reading the paragraphs below, one should keep in mind the methods of measuring personality characteristics that we discussed in Chapter 9.

▪ *Questionnaires.* The questionnaires used by research workers are very carefully constructed and pretested for reliability. Respondents are asked not so much for opinions as for observed facts about the behavior of leaders they have seen. Although it is not possible to keep replies wholly free of opinion, it is possible by careful statistical analysis to make some definite conclusions about leadership behavior.

An excellent example of a questionnaire study of leadership is one in which each of 500 different people was asked to give a detailed report on an instance of leadership familiar to him. The report was made on a special form that required 142 separate[16] responses. From the results it was possible to conclude that some of our stereotyped notions of leadership qualities, such as "quickness of decision," are probably not very important. This study showed, on the other hand, that effective leaders are those who advance the goals of the group, have administrative skill, inspire or set the pace for the group, and make members feel secure in their respective places in the group. Good leadership also seemed to be most evident in groups having a great deal of solidarity and pleasant relations among the members.

▪ *Psychological tests and inventories.* In recent years, investigators have applied dozens of tests of ability and of attitudes or interests to persons in positions of leadership.[17] Results show that in American clubs and organizations the leader is likely to be above the average of the group in one or more of the following: intelligence, scholarship, social participation, socioeconomic status, dependability, initiative, persistence, self-confidence, knowing how to get things done, popularity, originality, masculinity, verbal facility, and adaptability. The leader does *not* seem consistently to be above average in introversion-extroversion, self-sufficiency, and emotional control, but he may be very slightly above average in height, weight, appearance, and social dominance. For boys, athletic and physical prowess are important, but for mature men these apparently have lost their charm. Some evidence shows that there is such a thing as too much of a good trait: a child with an IQ of 150 may be a leader of children with IQs of 130 but ineffective with children with IQs of 100. (For the meaning of IQ, see Chapter 15.)

From research to date, however, it appears that the *most promising tests of leadership are those of attitudes and interests* rather than of abilities. We already have a number of such tests, but we have not been too successful yet in devising valid tests of such interests as social climbing, competitiveness for prestige and status, and desire to escape into an authoritarian social structure. A great deal of research is currently being devoted to this topic, and the picture may change radically within a few years.

• *Sociometric tests.* Another approach to the measurement of a leader's characteristics is the sociometric technique that we described earlier in this chapter. The technique, by itself, defines no traits, for members simply state their preferences for persons in the group. Yet certain traits seem to be hidden in the preference ratings and these can sometimes be teased out by special forms of statistical analysis. Although troublesome to make, this kind of analysis frequently yields useful results because sociometric preferences sometimes prove highly valid. From studies made during the Second World War, for example, we have indications that "buddy" ratings can forecast platoon leadership better than can officers' ratings and better than tests of ability.[18] After the war, interest in sociometry and sociograms has increased among research workers. Some of them regard sociometric tests so highly that they assume their validity for leadership; that is to say, they use the sociogram as the final test (the criterion) for all other tests.

• *Work-sample performance tests.* Although all armies have long conducted mock battles for training purposes, the German Army, in the Second World War, seems to have led in using work samples as *tests* of leadership. Later in the war, the American Office of Strategic Services, the British and Australian armies, and the U.S. Army employed similar tests as measures of leadership.[19] The basic idea is to confront a man with a "real-life" or moderately well simulated task: to get troops across a river under enemy fire, to get cooperation in building a bridge, to act like a spy by not letting on to others who he really is, etc. These are rather fascinating tests, but their validity is largely unknown. Many of their advocates, including the Germans, have been content to admire them and trust them without attempting to determine whether they are any good.

• *Leaderless-group tests.* One variation on the work-performance test is a situation in which several persons are confronted with a task, told to do it, and left alone. Since no leader has been designated, the experimenters observe the group to see who emerges as the "natural" leader. Experimenters usually exclude themselves from the group and watch what goes on from the side lines or, in some cases, through peepholes or one-way vision screens. So far the tasks most often given to a group have been (1) discussion of some topic such as college course material, (2) building or assembling some simple structure, (3) sorting and filing and other clerical jobs, and (4) plotting a curve or making up a report on some topic. One of the best of studies of this sort has concluded, after detailed statistical analysis, that there are at least two kinds of leadership ability: (1) "intellectual" leadership, and (2) "doing things with one's hands" leadership. Intellectual leadership correlates somewhat with clerical ability, but neither has much to do with mechanical aptitudes (see Chapter 16).

Of all the methods we have, the leaderless-group test is one of the most promising

Fig. 12.11. Leadership depends on the group and situation, as well as the leader. In Barrie's comedy *The Admirable Crichton*, the roles of master and servant are reversed when the group is stranded on a desert island. (*Sketches by Chamberlain from the New York Herald Tribune.*)

in providing possibilities for genuine experimental analysis, because it lets us see the beginnings of leadership in informal and unstructured groups. This is exactly where we would expect the personality traits of leaders, if any, to be most apparent.

Fitting a leader to a group. Despite difficulties in selecting leaders, there is the fact that some people make pretty good all-round leaders, likely to succeed at leading many kinds of groups in many different situations, in the same way that some athletes excel in many sports. Such all-round leadership, however, is as much due to similarities among situations and among groups as it is to the ability or personality of the leader. This should make clear what we so easily tend to forget: Leadership is an interaction between leader and group and between leader and situation. The breakdown of a bus, for example, may for the moment promote a mechanically apt "Mr. Milquetoast" to a position of command, leaving the politician speechless. And in Barrie's comedy *The Admirable Crichton*, the members of a noble family turn to their butler for leadership when they find themselves stranded on a desert island.

Particularly critical is the interaction between the leader and the group. Somehow the two must fit. The match need not be perfect, but the leader must play a role that the group expects of him. In informal groups, one achieves his role by his own behavior and may even invent his own role. The situation is much like a drama without a script; spontaneous acting is required. In organized, formal groups, one has a brief script to go by. Except for actual plays, however, the script is never filled in completely; there is always some leeway for individualizing the ascribed role. Nevertheless the organization chart, the bylaws, and some unwritten rules tell the player at least the minimum he must do if he is to fill the role. The junior lieutenant operates within well-advertised limits; so does the Queen of England.

■ *Some leader requirements.* Here are some of the things a person must do to play his role of leader:

1. Other things being equal, a leader who favors the efforts of the group will be better than one who does not, unless the latter is a very good actor. A man out of sympathy with war aims will probably be a poor army officer.

2. A leader must accept some responsibility, even when it is unpleasant. Some talented young men have been poor officers simply because they could not accept an authoritarian role, even when necessary. In some cases, their desire to be pals with their subordinates interfered with the requirements of leadership.

3. A leader ought to excel the members of his group in some technical matter of group significance, that is, he must have some kind of "know-how." A ship captain, for example, may need to be a good navigator or a gunner in addition to being a good administrator.

4. A leader needs to excel the members in some other, nontechnical ability. Depending on the group, this may be ability to work hard, ability to judge people, or self-confidence.

These conclusions—and many others that may be reached as research continues—are relative to the group. They have to do with what the group requires of the leader.

■ *General methods of selecting leaders.* There are a good many methods of selecting leaders, but they fall fairly well into three groups or their combinations: (1) election, or some variation of the democratic process such as popular nomination of a panel from which some higher authority selects; (2) outright appointment by superior authority; and (3) psychological or other scientific testing. The method that is used depends on what is permitted by authority or custom. A dictator usually appoints; a democracy elects. Which method is best?

Theoretically, scientific tests should be best. It stands to reason that the best selection can be made by those who know best the aspects of the leadership problem —the group, the situation, and the candidates. Ideally, tests could be made to give all this information in accurate detail; in practice, however, they do not—at least not yet. The same argument could be made for appointment by superior authority, for the superior is more likely to know the demands of a position and a person's ability to fill it than is a large group of people. But who is to select him?

To play safe, what we do in practice is use a combination of all three methods. Americans—and other democrats—believe that top leaders should be elected, not because we can prove that voters know best but because we want the people to be the center of power, even if they make mistakes. We do defer to our elected leaders on the appointment of judges and generals. These, in turn, are making increasing use of psychological tests for the selection of leaders of lower echelons. Some day, we may predict, it will not seem at all strange to see psychological testers and social scientists selecting all but our highest leaders.

SUMMARY

1. The culture of a society influences the attitudes and behavior of its members. Cultures of different societies tend to have characteristic patterns.

2. These patterns are transmitted from one generation to another through the behavior of the people in the culture. Consequently, culture tends to resist change.

3. Changes, however, do come about. Whether such changes are slow or rapid depends upon such factors as commerce, technological developments, and intermingling of peoples.

4. Individuals in a society tend to be unequal in their ability to satisfy the needs of the group. This fact is largely the reason for the development of social structure.

5. Social structures are made up of different statuses. The individuals occupying a particular status are expected to play an appropriate role. A person may have several statuses and roles. Sometimes these conflict and sometimes they supplement each other.

6. Characteristic statuses tend to be arranged on a prestige scale which becomes the basis for a division into social classes. There are several socio-economic criteria for each social class. Members of each class have characteristic attitudes and ways of behaving.

7. Within a particular culture, there are numerous social groups, some informal and some formal, some assembled and some dispersed. We attempt to depict the structure of formal groups with organization charts, but these are not very satisfactory.

8. Informal groups are best represented at present by a sociogram obtained by nomination techniques.

9. Social groups account for much of human learning, because they provide an individual with many different opportunities to learn.

10. Most groups manage to function well only when they have leaders. The leader exerts more influence on the group than do its individual members. To be an effective leader, however, he must represent the needs of the group and help to satisfy these needs.

11. Many different characteristics are found in leaders. At one particular time and in one group, one set of characteristics may be most effective for leadership; at other times, different characteristics.

12. Several methods have been used in the study of leadership: questionnaires, personality inventories, sociometric tests, work-sample tests, and group tests. Although some of these methods show promise, none is at present especially valuable in the selection of leaders.

SUGGESTIONS FOR FURTHER READING

Barnett, H. G. *Innovation: the basis of cultural change.* New York: McGraw-Hill, 1953.

> *A general treatment of the factors involved in cultural change.*

Benedict, R. *Patterns of culture.* Boston: Houghton Mifflin, 1934.

> *A classical description and analysis, written by a social anthropologist, of patterns of culture in primitive societies.*

Centers, R. *The psychology of social classes.* Princeton, N.J.: Princeton Univ. Press, 1949.

> *An account of a national survey of class attitudes and their relation to socioeconomic structure.*

Gouldner, A. W. (Ed.). *Studies in leadership.* New York: Harper, 1950.

> *A discussion of the problems of leadership by authors from different fields.*

Guetzkow, H. (Ed.). *Groups, leadership and men.* Pittsburgh: Carnegie Press, 1951.

> *The transcript of a conference on problems of research on leadership and human relations.*

Heberle, R. *Social movements.* New York: Appleton-Century-Crofts, 1951.

> *A sociological text on the nature and structure of social (ideological) movements.*

Krech, D., and Crutchfield, R. S. *Theory and problems of social psychology.* New York: McGraw-Hill, 1948. Chaps. 10 and 11.

> *A text on social psychology containing chapters on social groups and leadership.*

Newcomb, T. M. *Social psychology.* New York: Dryden, 1950. Chaps. 12–15.

> *A text on social psychology containing chapters on culture and social groups.*

Office of Strategic Services, Assessment Staff. *Assessment of men.* New York: Rinehart, 1948.

> *An account of methods used in the Second World War for the selection of leaders and others assigned to special roles in the Office of Strategic Services.*

Warner, W. L., and Lunt, P. S. *The social life of a modern community.* New Haven, Conn.: Yale Univ. Press, 1941.

> *An intensive study of class structure and attitudes in a New England city.*

Chapter 13 ATTITUDES AND BELIEFS

Although the attitudes of other people are never seen or felt—they are only inferred—they make considerable difference in almost everyone's life. To the person in business or politics they may make the difference between success or failure. The businessman depends upon favorable attitudes of his customers toward his products and services to keep his business going. The politician must have favorable attitudes toward his personality, abilities, and political behavior in order to count on his reelection. Each of us similarly strives to create favorable attitudes and to eliminate unfavorable attitudes on the part of friends, associates, employers, and others. There are, indeed, very few acts or decisions in everyday affairs that do not somehow take account of the way in which attitudes may be affected.

THE NATURE OF ATTITUDES

It is not hard to understand why attitudes are so important in social adjustments if we consider what they are and how they are acquired. Psychologists define attitudes as *tendencies to respond either positively or negatively toward persons, objects, or situations.* A child who has been bitten by a dog has learned to be afraid of dogs, and unless something is done to counteract the experience he will probably have an unfavorable attitude toward dogs for a long time. After putting his hand on a hot stove, a child develops an unfavorable attitude toward hot stoves. On the other hand, when parents give their children toys and lollipops, the children tend to develop a

---

This chapter was drafted by Clifford T. Morgan of The Johns Hopkins University.

positive or favorable attitude toward parents. In these and other examples which might occur to you, the important point is that people *learn to avoid whatever has proved unpleasant and to approach whatever has been rewarding in their previous learning experiences* (see Chapters 3 and 5). When we use the term attitude we are simply referring to the probability that they will react negatively or positively to similar situations when they occur in the future. Many attitudes, as we shall see, are acquired from others, rather than from direct experience. In any case, they are learned, and from them we can predict future behavior.

Social attitudes.   Through a lifetime of learning, individuals develop innumerable attitudes toward various objects, persons, and situations. Some of these attitudes are shared with a large number of other individuals and are called *social attitudes.* Some of them, on the other hand, are not held in common with other persons but rather are private affairs; we call these *personal attitudes.* For example, a person may have attitudes toward his mother, his dog, his violin, his motorboat, his church, and his alma mater. Most individuals have attitudes toward mothers, dogs, etc., but few of them have attitudes toward a particular person's mother or dog, because they do not know his mother and dog. Such personal attitudes may be quite important in an individual's adjustment and may have much to do with his frustrations and personal adjustment—subjects we considered in earlier chapters.

Social attitudes, on the other hand, *concern objects, persons, and issues known to the members of a group and to the society in which they live.* Most Americans have attitudes toward Republicans, tariffs, taxes, labor, wars, prices, automobiles, religion, education, and a long list of people and things that concern many people in one way or another. Such social attitudes are the ones with which leaders in business, politics, and public life are most concerned. It is also these attitudes, as distinguished from personal attitudes, that we can most conveniently study scientifically because they can be measured and compared in large groups of people.

For rather practical reasons, we cannot be interested in all kinds of social attitudes. In the United States, nearly everyone has a favorable attitude toward democracy, virtue, honesty, and peace. Our fund of knowledge is not significantly increased by any detailed demonstration that most people have these attitudes. Much more interesting are the cases in which attitudes are divided pro and con, some being for and some against an idea, person, or possible course of action. Moreover, it is of considerable practical value to know these attitudes pro and con about issues of political or financial importance. The color of the wrapper on a can of beans, for example, may not seem very important, but if it is known that people have a more favorable attitude toward one color than another and that the food packer can sell more beans by using the favored color, he is especially interested in attitudes toward color. For such reasons as this, most of our scientific information about attitudes concerns political issues, on the one hand, or advertising and merchandising of products on the other hand.

Beliefs and opinions.   One cannot discuss the subject of attitudes without also considering beliefs and opinions. An attitude, as we have said, is acquired through learning, but it does not necessarily involve any thinking or higher mental processes. In fact, most attitudes, as we shall see, are built up without the benefit of much thinking. Thus, dogs and other animals, as well as people, are endowed with attitudes. A belief, on the other hand, involves some thinking or at least the results of some thinking. A belief is the *acceptance of some proposition or statement.* Most people believe, for example, that the sun will rise tomorrow morning. Many believe that the world is round. Those of the orthodox Jewish faith believe men should worship with their hats on, while those of the Christian faith believe men should worship with hats removed. These and thousands of other propositions that we accept and act on are in the category of belief as distinguished from attitudes. Such beliefs, it should be noted, are in themselves neutral; unlike attitudes, they are neither pro nor con but merely statements that something is true.

A person holding a belief usually feels that he has some good evidence for his belief. At least he thinks he has some facts or some authority to which he can appeal to support his belief. He believes, for example, that the sun will rise tomorrow morning because it has risen every morning of his life. He may believe in worshiping without a hat on because the leaders of

his church proclaim with authority that this is the way to worship. We may not agree with his grounds for belief—his evidence may be faulty or his authority questionable —but from his point of view he can "prove" his belief.

Somewhere in the borderland between beliefs and attitudes are reactions called *opinions.* An opinion is like a belief in that it is an *acceptance of a proposition.* However, the holder of an opinion usually is a little vague about his facts and does not feel so strongly that he can prove his proposition. Rather he accepts it because it seems right or feels right to him. "I don't really know, but my opinion is . . . ," is a phrase that we hear, perhaps all too often. Opinions, however, are also like attitudes in that they often have a flavor of *being pro or con.* "I think Mr. Smith will be a good president," is both a statement of belief and an expression of a favorable attitude toward Mr. Smith. For this reason, many of the polls with which the public has become familiar in recent years are called public-opinion polls. They attempt to measure some *combination of attitude and belief*

Fig. 13.1. An interviewer asking questions in a public opinion poll. (*Courtesy American Institute of Public Opinion, Princeton, N.J.*)

concerning persons and issues of the day.

Although we can make these distinctions among beliefs, opinions, and attitudes, it is evident that they are seldom clearly separated in the behavior of a person. Occasionally, it is possible to observe a person believing, on the one hand, that Negroes should have equal rights, while on the other expressing an unfavorable attitude toward Negroes. More often, attitudes determine beliefs and vice versa. The person, for example, with an unfavorable attitude toward Negroes is much more likely to believe that they are dirty than is the person with a favorable attitude. The person who really resents taxes is much more likely to believe the report that the government is squandering the taxpayers' money than the person with a more tolerant attitude toward taxes. Beliefs, on the other hand, can shape attitudes. Believing that the government is squandering money makes me more resentful of taxes. Believing that smoking is bad for the health makes me less favorable toward smoking, smokers, and the purveyors of tobacco. Consequently beliefs and attitudes go hand in hand; what affects one is very likely to affect the other, and as we shall see later, changing one may be an avenue to changing the other.

Erroneous beliefs. Beliefs may be based on what people consider to be facts, but this is no guarantee that they will be correct. As we saw in Chapter 6, people are not perfect logic machines, and even the best minds have difficulty drawing perfectly logical inferences from "the facts." Moreover, facts are often rather sparse, for no person has an opportunity to acquire all the facts necessary to accept or reject many of his beliefs. Then, too, emotional attitudes play an important part in the formation of beliefs, and these beliefs may therefore be badly distorted by emotion. For these and other reasons, many beliefs are in some degree erroneous—at least to the more objective person or to the expert who has more evidence with which to test a belief. We shall describe four varieties of erroneous beliefs—superstition, delusions, prejudice, and stereotyping.

▪ *Superstition.* One of these, the superstition, is familiar to everyone even though our society is relatively free of it. A *superstition is a belief* (1) *that concerns phenomena which are explicable by natural causes,* (2) *that is widely held by members of a group or society, yet* (3) *can be demonstrated to be at variance with the known facts.* Some familiar examples are the beliefs that walking under a ladder, seeing a black cat cross his path, or having a room on the thirteenth floor of a hotel all bring bad luck. The sophisticated person knows there is nothing to such beliefs, and they have largely disappeared from Western culture. In a primitive society, however, superstitions may govern much of the social relations of its members.

▪ *Delusions.* Delusions are another kind of erroneous belief that one sees in the emotionally maladjusted individual and occasionally in a society. *Delusions are systematic, but false, beliefs,* usually involving the motives and actions of other people and stemming from some of the defense mechanisms we described in Chapter 10. Examples are the beliefs that one is being followed by people out to spy on him, that his brain is gradually being dissolved by radio waves from some hostile person, or that he is the victim of some vicious conspiracy. Fortunately delusions are seldom widely held by the members of a society or group. Occasionally, however, they are. Hitler succeeded in inculcating the German people with beliefs in their superiority, in the persecution by foreigners, and in foreign encirclement to an extent bordering on a mass delusion.

Fig. 13.2. A cartoonist's picture of stereotypes. The average American and Briton have distorted mental pictures of each other that sometimes handicap friendly cooperation between the two nations. (*Reprinted by permission of Time and Tide, London.*)

▪ *Prejudice.* Of considerably more importance in all societies today are the erroneous beliefs and attitudes called prejudices. By derivation, prejudice means "prejudgment" —to believe something in advance of knowledge of the relevant facts. To a certain extent, all belief is prejudice, since we seldom have sufficient facts to warrant a belief. As used by social scientists, however, prejudice refers to *an attitude or belief that places a person or object at a disadvantage*—sometimes at an advantage, but usually not (see page 355). A prejudice also frequently contradicts the relevant facts. We say, for example, that a person is prejudiced against Catholics when his beliefs and attitudes concerning Catholics are unfavorable despite the existence of facts that do not warrant

such a belief. Similarly, in speaking of racial prejudice, we refer to beliefs that are more unfavorable than the facts would justify. However, some prejudices, like the common prejudice against skunks, may be fully justified. In the next chapter we shall discuss prejudice in more detail.

▪ *Stereotyping.* Still another kind of erroneous belief that is of considerable social importance is the stereotype. *Stereotyped beliefs are those that are widely held and that tend to oversimplify or distort the facts.* If, for example, most people believe that blondes are dumber than brunettes— statistical studies show that they are not— this is an example of stereotyped belief. Other examples of stereotyping are beliefs that Jews are shrewd, that college professors are "long-hairs," that fat men are lazy, that politicians smoke cigars, and that geniuses are peculiar. There is little or no truth to these beliefs, yet they are widely held. Even where there might be some shred of truth in the statement, the stereotype is so over-simplified and exaggerated as to be seriously in error.

DEVELOPMENT OF ATTITUDES AND BELIEFS

The study of attitudes and beliefs has three main approaches. The first is to understand *how they develop and become what they are*. The second is *to measure them* and to assess as accurately as possible what attitudes and beliefs people commonly hold concerning particular issues in which we may be interested. The third is to know *how we may change them* when they are erroneous or are standing in the way of social welfare. We shall devote a major section of this chapter to each of these topics.

Culture. We have already seen in the last chapter that culture consists of the customs and traditions of a people and the attitudes and beliefs they have about important aspects of life. These customs, traditions, attitudes, and beliefs influence each individual through many diverse avenues: his social class, his social groups, his schools, his family, and many others (see Chapter 9). Because the individual experiences all these influences simultaneously, or at least in the course of a day or week, it is difficult to separate them one from another. *In toto*, however, they determine the development of attitudes and beliefs.

One of the ways to assess the influence of culture on attitudes is *to correlate attitudes with cultural differences* such as religious faith, socioeconomic status, or level of education. (For an explanation of the method of correlation, see Chapter 8.) If individuals in one cultural category hold a certain attitude substantially more frequently than those in another category, it may be presumed that the culture influences the attitude. An illustration of such a correlation is to be found in a study sponsored by the Social Science Research Council on attitudes toward armed imperialism.[1] About a thousand individuals were asked the question, "Some say we should use our Army and Navy to make other countries do what we think they should. How do you feel about that?" As you see in Table 13.1, people generally disapproved of this point of view, but it is interesting that those with a college education and those in the higher economic brackets disapproved more than those of lesser education and income. There was no substantial difference, however, between those of Protestant and those of Catholic religious affiliation. From such a study, one may conclude that educational and socioeconomic influences probably are important in determining attitudes toward the use of our Armed Forces.

In recent years a very large number of studies correlating attitudes and culture have been conducted.[2] Almost any public opinion poll, when analyzed according to educational status, income level, religious background, etc., yields information about such a relation. And there have been many experimental studies conducted in the colleges. On some questions, such as birth control, war, and political issues, religious influences prove to be important, Catholics usually being more conservative than Jews and those of religious training usually being more conservative than those without religious affiliation. In almost all beliefs and attitudes, socioeconomic status tends to be important, but not always in a predictable way. The upper socioeconomic classes tend to be more "reasonable" regarding war and the use of force, as in the study we cited, but they tend to be more conservative in political views. It is evident, therefore, that *cultural influences to which individuals are exposed play an important role in the attitudes and beliefs that individuals hold.*

We should not jump to the conclusion, however, that individuals simply take over the attitudes characteristic of their culture, for this is not true. We must remember that the correlations are seldom very high; rather they usually indicate only moderate statistical tendencies. Such an imperfect correlation is to be expected because the individual is exposed to numerous cultural influences and to many different attitudes and beliefs. Though a person may be of one religious training, he ordinarily associates with people of other religious backgrounds. Although he may be of one socioeconomic status, he usually has some contact with members of other socioeconomic groups. In these and other ways, his culture is by no means homogeneous. Even if it were,

there are enough differences among members of any particular cultural group to expose him to a variety of attitudes and beliefs.

Parents and teachers. In the melee of cultural forces continuously playing on an individual, there are two that are especially important because they mediate between the individual and his culture. These are the parents and the teachers. A child's parents and his teachers are products of the culture whose attitudes and beliefs have been influenced, and continue to be influenced, by the culture. Because their social contacts, their reading, their entertainment, and their other relations with the culture are considerably wider and more diverse than those of the child, they are more directly influenced by the culture than he is. Yet, considered together, they spend a good many hours of the day in contact with the child, all the while controlling his behavior and attempting to instill in him particular attitudes and beliefs.

TABLE 13.1.   The relationship of education, income, and religion to attitudes toward armed imperialism. Individuals were asked the question: "Some people say we should use our Army and Navy to make other countries do what we think they should. How do you feel about that?"

Respondents	General approval, per cent	General disapproval, per cent	No response, per cent	Number of respondents
Education				
Grade school	19	57	24	500
High school	13	77	10	455
College	8	83	9	213
Income				
Under $2,000	19	58	23	440
$2,000 to $3,999	16	73	11	478
$4,000 and more	8	86	6	216
Religion				
Protestant	14	70	16	855
Catholic	18	68	14	245

From Krech, D., & Crutchfield, R. S. *Theory and problems of social psychology.* New York: McGraw-Hill, 1948. P. 177. Adapted from Social Science Research Council. *Public reaction to the atomic bomb and world affairs.* Ithaca, N.Y.: Cornell University, 1947.

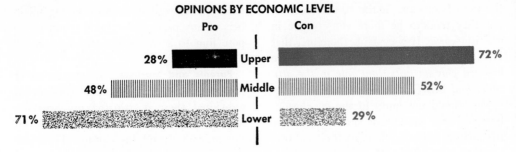

Fig. 13.3. Opinions are frequently related to socioeconomic status. People were asked their opinion about the government control of business in the readjustment period following the Second World War. The majority of upper-class respondents were against such control, but the majority of working-class interviewees were in favor of such control. (*Based on data of National Opinion Research Center.*)

It is not surprising, then, that *the attitudes and beliefs of the child tend to correlate more highly with those of his parents and his teachers than with those of other members of his social groups*. In one study conducted with 200 college students at Northwestern University,[3] for example, the attitudes of the students toward the New Deal administration, toward economic depression, and toward God correlated with the attitudes of the parents to the extent of .29 to .58. In another study,[4] the attitudes of students correlated rather significantly with the attitudes of their teachers.

One could cite many studies illustrating the relation between children's attitudes and those of their parents and teachers. However, the most dramatic illustration is to be found in the analysis of individual attitudes, particularly in the field of racial prejudice, where parental attitudes are especially influential. In a set of interviews with white grammar school children about their attitudes toward Negroes, one investigator[5] got such responses as these:

First-grade girl: "Mamma tells me not to play with black children, keep away from them. Mamma tells me, she told me not to play with them. . . ."

Second-grade girl: "Colored children. Mother doesn't want me to play with colored children. . . . I play with colored children sometimes and Mamma whips me."

Second-grade boy: "Colored children, mother and daddy tell me. They tell me not to play with colored people or colored persons' things."

Third-grade girl: "Mother told me not to play with them because sometimes they have diseases and germs and you get it from them."

As we shall see, a great many prejudicial attitudes and beliefs are transmitted primarily through the family.

Personality. To recognize that the culture molds attitudes and beliefs is not to say that the culture simply gives or transmits them to the inert, passive individual. Though attitudes are in a sense infectious, like bacterial diseases, whether they are formed or not depends upon the personality of the individual. Some individuals at any particular time are relatively immune to some attitudes and beliefs while being particularly susceptible to others. Thus much depends upon the personality of the individual who is exposed to cultural influences. This fact is demonstrated in several studies of the relation between personality, on the one hand, and attitudes and beliefs on the other.

You will remember from the chapter on personality that traits can be rated by persons who know an individual fairly well or by special tests that have been constructed for the purpose. One test measures a person's relative introversion or extroversion, another his relative dominance or submission in social situations, and still others are available to measure other traits. If we give such tests to a group of people and at the same time determine their attitudes on a number of issues, it is possible to correlate attitudes with personality traits. In one study, attitudes on a number of political and social issues were used to divide students into "radical," "conservative," and more moderate groups.[6] Correlating these attitudes with personality traits, the investigator found women students who were radical in attitudes and beliefs to be more introverted, more self-sufficient, and more dominant than other women students in their groups. Such personality traits, it appears, enable a person to adopt more readily beliefs and attitudes that are less conventional. In another study, which we shall consider in Chapter 14, students who held strongly prejudiced attitudes proved to have more repressed needs than students who were less prejudiced.

Unfortunately, however, there are few, if any, general rules that can be applied to personality and attitudes. What may be "radical" attitudes for one cultural group may be the conventional attitudes in another. Thus the personality characteristics which in one group accompany certain attitudes may in another group be correlated with other attitudes. The important point is that, in any given situation, the particular attitudes and beliefs a person adopts are related to his personality characteristics.

Information. A person's beliefs, we have indicated, are based on what he regards as facts. To understand, then, how he acquires his beliefs and related attitudes, we should consider how he acquires his facts.

It goes almost without saying that the typical individual does not have available to him in his own experience all the facts he needs to form an attitude, opinion, or belief about the problem he confronts. In trying to decide whether to vote for Republicans or Democrats, he seldom has seen the candidates in person or knows at first hand how the candidates have behaved or performed in particular situations. In forming an opinion about Negroes, he seldom has had very much contact with Negroes. If he has, he has probably had it in a very restricted situation with a particular small group of Negroes. In considering what car to buy, he has had experience driving only a few cars and probably knows little about the particular model and year of car he is considering buying. In all kinds of decisions or opinions he is called upon to make, there is always a relative scarcity of the facts that he really ought to have to be able to make his choice intelligently.

Not only are the facts scarce, they are frequently misleading. A person who forms an opinion about Negroes may have had contact with a few, atypical Negroes, and may jump to the opinion that all are like the ones he knows. Or he may have picked up the "fact" that Negroes when given intelligence tests tend to score lower than whites. What he may not know is that such Negroes have had inferior schooling and poor socioeconomic circumstances or that they were much less motivated in taking the tests—all very relevant in evaluating the fact that their scores were lower. In a good many circumstances, "a little knowledge is a dangerous thing" because it leads to beliefs that are not justified when all the facts are known. Yet people regularly are called upon to form opinions with only a few of all the relevant facts available. Consequently they acquire erroneous beliefs and opinions, and indirectly prejudiced attitudes, because they know too few of the facts.

▪ *Authorities.* Because we have relatively few firsthand facts upon which to base our beliefs, we find ourselves trusting authorities instead of facts. Indeed, many so-called facts are not facts at all in terms of firsthand experience; they are merely statements of authorities about facts. Only the psychologist who has tested large numbers of Negroes knows for a (firsthand) fact that Negroes score lower on intelligence tests than do whites. We accept his statement as a fact because he says he made the tests and obtained this result. There is nothing wrong with such a reliance on authority, for we could hardly manage otherwise. Not only in politics and art, but also in business and science, we are forced to rely on the statements of experts, authorities, or "eye-witness" reports. Such specialization of knowledge has been essential in the development of our complex civilization, from which we derive so many benefits.

It is well to realize, however, that most of what we believe is not based on firsthand knowledge but rather on what authorities say. Such reliance has both advantages and disadvantages. For one thing *it is difficult for even the most conscientious person to report facts objectively* all the time. The attitudes and beliefs of the authority often affect his perception of the fact and the way he reports it to us (see next chapter). Moreover, his ignorance of other facts, as we have indicated above, may make him unduly impressed with a particular fact and lead him to present it to us in a slanted way or without other facts necessary to form the most correct opinion. Often authorities disagree among themselves on the facts and we must choose between two conflicting authorities.

Adding to our difficulties in forming correct opinions is the tendency of authorities *to acquire prestige and status outside their special fields of competence.* People often regard the successful businessman as the person who is best qualified to manage in government, when actually business and government require rather different knowledge and skills for their successful operation. Beliefs that are appropriate to the purpose of one may be quite in error or inappropriate for the other. The man who has acquired a great reputation as a physicist will be listened to when he pronounces on religion and politics. Yet he is usually no more qualified in these matters than many persons in other fields of endeavor. Scientists often are as guilty of this error as anyone else and make statements outside their field of authority that may be misleading to the person who accepts them. All kinds of authorities, however, make this mistake—and it is an easy one to make—with the result that people unwittingly base their beliefs on statements that authorities have no right to make.

A final obstacle to forming correct beliefs and opinions is the tendency of some authorities *deliberately to distort the facts in order to have us believe what they want us to believe.* The manufacturer may know very well all the facts about his product, but he has his advertiser present us only with certain facts that lead us to form attitudes that are favorable to his product. Our military authorities may know very well the losses we sustain in a particular battle, but they tell us only the losses they believe the enemy sustained in order to deceive both the enemy and ourselves about the real outcome of the battle. The political leader may be intimately aware of corruption among some of his party's members, but he tells only the "good" facts about his administration in order to instill in us a favorable opinion that will reelect him next time. Newspapers often put on the front pages stories that are favorable to their editorial views, while burying on the inside pages, or not publishing at all, those facts not favorable to their views. In this society, the deliberate selection and distortion of facts is practiced in almost every aspect of life as a means of encouraging (erroneous) beliefs that are advantageous to the purveyor of the facts.

■ *Appearances are deceiving.* Our attitudes and beliefs are affected not only by a lack of available facts and by the acceptance of authorities but also by another psychological limitation that may not be so obvious. *Facts are not always what they seem to be.* Some people may seem to be kind and considerate yet may be extremely cruel. Some may seem to be honest on the surface yet be thieves and liars. The communist agent may seem to be taking the side of justice and equality when he fights for Negro rights, when his real purpose is to cause division and dissension among the American people. A husband may seem to become more loving and attentive, only to cover up his infidelity. In each case, the fact is a fact, but it does not mean what it seems to mean.

Scientists and others who become experts in dealing with detailed facts come to learn this lesson rather thoroughly, at least in their own particular fields. Consequently they become cautious about taking facts at their face value. When they observe something that seems to be a fact, they inquire diligently into all available and relevant facts to see whether they get independent facts that agree with each other. Less expert people, however, are not accustomed to be so careful, so they may be more easily deceived. As a consequence, the propagandist often takes them in by presenting facts that are intended to mislead them. The enemy may show a picture of two well-clothed and well-housed prisoners, thereby hoping to convince us that all prisoners are well housed and well clothed. The political candidate kisses one baby, thereby attempting to create the impression that he is friendly, homey, and interested in babies. Or he has his picture taken leaving church, thus advertising the "fact" that he is a churchgoing man. The sophisticated person often sees through such deceiving facts, but they still prove effective in fashioning the beliefs and attitudes of the unsuspecting.

Self-preservation of attitudes and beliefs. So far we have surveyed the role of culture, personality, and information in the *formation* of attitudes and beliefs. We might expect that as a person's culture changes, as his personality matures, and as he becomes better informed, his attitudes and beliefs would change. They do. On the other hand, they do not change as rapidly as one might expect because they have a way of resisting change and preserving themselves once they have been well formed. For this self-preservation of attitudes, there are three principal reasons: (1) selective perceiving and remembering, (2) withdrawal from situations that might change attitudes and beliefs, and (3) social pressures for the preservation of attitudes.

■ *Selective perception and remembering.* Attitudes and beliefs tend to be preserved because they alter *the perception of new experiences, emphasizing those facts that fit in with existing attitudes and beliefs and deemphasizing those that do not.* If I think that Negroes are dirty people and I see a Negro coming home from work in his work clothes, I may notice immediately the fact that his clothes are soiled. A white man in exactly the same state might not be noticed at all, or if so, he would be perceived as a person coming home from a hard day's work. If an individual is strongly opposed to government spending and sees the newspaper heading, "Congress appropriates 20 billion dollars for Armed Forces," he may perceive the 20 billion dollars as an instance of big-government spending while ignoring or forgetting that it is for the defense of the country. If, on the other hand, a person is strongly concerned about adequate defense of the United States, he may perceive this headline as Congress providing for our defense but take no note of the amount of money involved. Thus, of the facts presented to a person, he tends to perceive selectively those that fit in with or are relevant to his attitudes and beliefs and to pay little attention to other facts. In this way, his attitudes and beliefs are reinforced and strengthened, rather than changed, by his perceptions.

Such a selection of facts operates not only in perception but also in memory. We tend to remember those "facts" that fit with our beliefs and to forget those that do not. Perhaps you have noticed that people tend to forget the facts or arguments that they are temporarily forced to face but that do not fit in with their current beliefs. This point was dramatically illustrated in an experiment conducted some years ago with some college students.[7] Some of the students were favorable to communist ideas, some were not. All listened to some passages, part of which were favorable to communism and part of which were not. Some time later they were tested for their memory of these passages. The students who were favorable to communism had remembered much more of the material that was favorable to their point of view than of that which was not. Thus it was shown—and there are many other researches illustrating the same point —that beliefs affect memory selectively, preserving that which fits in with existing beliefs.[8] In the next chapter, we shall show how selective perception and remembering support prejudiced attitudes.

▪ *Withdrawal.* Still another, and perhaps more obvious, way of preserving attitudes and beliefs is *to withdraw from everything that conflicts with what one already believes.* Everyday events supply countless illustrations of this kind of withdrawal from opposing attitudes and beliefs. The person who is a confirmed liberal refuses to read magazines or newspapers that present a conservative point of view. The person who is prejudiced against Jews has nothing to do with them and thus never has a chance to acquire facts about them that might alter his prejudice. The person who dislikes the views of the Hearst press, or Westbrook Pegler, or the *Reader's Digest,* or Walter Winchell refuses to read or listen to these sources. In this way, he withdraws completely from the situations in which attitudes and beliefs contrary to his own are put forth. By reading and listening only to viewpoints that agree with his own, he further strengthens the attitudes and beliefs that he holds.

▪ *Social support.* Still another powerful influence for preserving attitudes and beliefs is the *social approval of associates.* As we have already pointed out above, an individual tends to share his attitudes and beliefs with the members of his particular group or culture. The need for social approval is ordinarily a fairly strong motivation (page 77). So long as a person's attitudes agree with those of his associates he will tend to secure their approval. On the other hand, if he expresses attitudes and beliefs contrary to theirs, he incurs their displeasure and disapproval. Thus he punishes himself and thwarts his desire to be approved. Consequently, he consciously or unconsciously wants to believe the same things his friends do in order to have their approval. Since he already tends to have their attitudes and beliefs by sharing common cultural influences, the need for social approval lends additional support to his attitudes and makes it much more difficult for him to change them.

THE MEASUREMENT OF ATTITUDES AND OPINIONS

Because attitudes, opinions, and beliefs determine so greatly how individuals will react to social situations, it is not strange that there should be considerable interest in the precise measurement of attitudes. Leaders in government and public life are especially sensitive to the wishes of people, either to ensure their survival in office or to render service to the people. Hence it is natural that they should like to know people's attitudes and beliefs. Those who conduct business affairs must similarly know customers' attitudes and beliefs so as not to offend their customers and in order to introduce products to them in the most favorable light. Then, too, leaders and research workers in the field of education, knowing that much of education is a matter of affecting attitudes as well as knowledge, want to know the effects of various educational practices and environments on attitudes and beliefs.

Attitude scales. The educator and research worker have relatively favorable conditions for investigating attitudes, because they usually have access to groups of students who can be studied rather intensively. Their methods, therefore, have been more accurate and detailed than those which, for practical reasons, have been developed for use in the political and commercial fields. Among these methods are some that provide relatively accurate scales for the measurement of attitudes. We shall describe three.

▪ *Thurstone.* One method of measuring attitudes was devised by L. L. Thurstone.

It involves the following steps.[9] First *some issue toward which attitudes might be measured must be defined.* War is an example of such an issue. For the past 20 years, the United States has directly or indirectly been involved in a series of world-wide conflicts, and the issue of the stand we should take, as well as when and where we should become directly involved in one or more of these conflicts, has occupied the thoughts of both the leaders and the people of the United States. Attitudes toward war, therefore, have been one important class of attitudes worthy of study.

Once the issue has been defined, the next step in Thurstone's method is *to collect as many statements as possible that might be relevant to the issue.* In order to be useful in measurement, such statements must be relatively simple and unambiguous; otherwise they do not distinguish one individual from another. "All men are created equal," or "All men desire peace," is likely to be agreed to by most people, and it therefore is not very diagnostic of attitudes. On the other hand such statements as, "When war is declared, we must enlist," or "Wars are justifiable only when waged in defense of weaker nations," are specific enough and clear enough to evoke approval or disapproval and thus to determine attitudes toward different aspects of war.

After statements have been collected that bear on the issue, or are thought to bear on the issue, the next step is *to present them to a large number of judges,* preferably a hundred or more. Each judge is asked to sort these statements into eleven piles, representing a scale from an extremely favorable attitude toward the issue to an extremely unfavorable attitude toward it. In the case of attitudes toward war, a statement which is considered to be very strongly in favor of war "at the drop of a hat" would be put into the first pile, and a statement that is considered to be extremely pacifistic would be sorted into the eleventh pile. Other statements that are judged to be less extreme would be thrown into intervening piles.

This sorting of statements is done in order to establish *scale values* for the different statements. That is to say, the purpose is to assign to each statement a number that indicates to what degree approval or disapproval of the statement represents an attitude that is favorable or unfavorable to the object or issue. To obtain such a number the median value of the judges' ratings is computed (see Chapter 8 for an explanation of median). In Table 13.2, for example, are seven statements that have been rated by judges and given scale values by accepting the median judgment. At one extreme is the statement, "A country cannot amount to much without a national

TABLE 13.2. Some illustrative items from a scale for measuring attitudes toward war. Using a scale from 1 to 11, several judges rate each item for the degree to which it indicates an attitude toward or against a course of action. The median rating (see p. 198) of the judges is the scale value assigned to the item.

Scale value	Item
1.3	1. A country cannot amount to much without a national honor, and war is the only means of preserving it.
2.5	2. When war is declared, we must enlist.
5.2	3. Wars are justifiable only when waged in defense of weaker nations.
5.4	4. Peace and war are both essential to progress.
5.6	5. The most that we can hope to accomplish is the partial elimination of war.
8.4	6. The disrespect for human life and rights involved in a war is a cause of crime waves.
10.6	7. All nations should disarm immediately.

From Droba, D. D. *A scale for measuring attitude toward war.* Chicago: Univ. of Chicago Press, 1930.

honor, and war is the only means of preserving it." The median category for this item is 1.3, meaning that it is considered to represent a strongly prowar attitude. At the other extreme is the statement, "All nations should disarm immediately." A scale value of 10.6 indicates that this is considered to represent a rather strong pacifist attitude.

Judges never agree perfectly on the value to assign a particular statement, but on some items the agreement is better than on others. If judges distribute their responses to an item by putting it in piles 7, 8, and 9, this is good agreement and indicates that the item is mildly unfavorable. On the other hand, judges might have such poor disagreement that the statement might be sorted almost equally among all categories from 1 to 11. In this case, we are forced to conclude that the statement is not a good one to use in attitude measurement, and it must be discarded. In the end, after all the judging is done, a limited number of statements, say, approximately twenty, are selected that (1) show reasonably good agreement among judges, and (2) have scale values that spread out along the continuum from 1 to 11. In this way, a limited number of items that can most reliably be used as a measure of attitudes are chosen.

Once constructed, the attitude scale may be administered to any group one desires. The person taking it is instructed to check the statements with which he agrees. There are many possible ways to score the results, but one is to average the scale values of the items checked by an individual. In any case, one can end up with a number, from 1+ to 11−, that is a measure of the person's attitudes and beliefs concerning the issue in question.

▪ *Likert scale.* There are several other methods of constructing attitude scales. All involve starting with a relatively large number of statements and then selecting from them the statements that prove to be the most reliable indicators of a given attitude. We shall be content with describing one other method, which differs from the Thurstone method in some details and which has been used successfully on a fairly wide scale. This is a method developed by Likert.[10]

Likert's method leaves out the use of judges and the task of sorting statements into categories. It begins instead with statements that can be presented to the subject with the instruction to indicate his reaction to each as: *strongly approve, approve, undecided, disapprove,* or *strongly disapprove.* Statements are given to a pilot group of subjects. Their results are analyzed to see how their responses correlate with each other (see Chapter 8). Items that correlate highly with each other—for example, when an individual strongly approves one statement and also strongly approves another or, vice versa—are considered to be relevant to the attitude being considered. When items do not correlate with other items, they are rejected as not being relevant to the attitude scale. In this way, two things are accomplished: (1) poor statements are discarded, and (2) the statements left in the test are found to consist of certain clusters of items.

We can illustrate these steps by describing Likert's construction of an attitude scale on foreign wars. Starting with a large number of items and giving them to a sample population, he discarded many of them when he found that they did not correlate with the total score. When his analysis was finished, he found he had two clusters of items; one cluster seemed to concern problems of imperialism in foreign affairs and the other internationalism in such affairs. Thus he obtained a scale of attitudes to-

ward foreign affairs that could be broken down into two sets of attitudes, those toward *imperialism* and those toward *internationalism.*

To consider the construction of attitude scales in more detail is beyond the scope of this book. We have presented the more typical, widely used methods, but there are many variations on these methods. The end result of any method is to obtain a "test" which is a reasonably reliable and valid measure (see Chapter 9) of some attitude or attitudes. Once such a scale has been developed, it can then be used for a variety of purposes. Most of the facts that were presented in the first two sections of this chapter concerning the effect on attitudes of culture, socioeconomic status, family, and education were obtained by using such attitude scales. Many of the conclusions drawn about prejudice in the next chapter also are based on the use of such scales.

▪ *Rating methods.* Refined scales for measuring attitudes are desirable in research studies or in other instances where it is possible to use them. All attitude measurement, however, cannot be so precise. Most of us are called upon to weigh a person's attitudes in a variety of situations without the benefit of such scales. In considering a person for employment, we usually try to assess his attitudes about such objects as his employer, his work, the people he works with, and the company he works for. The politician is continually attempting to assess attitudes by talking to the people whom he meets and from the mail he receives from his constituents. Sponsors of radio and television programs similarly make guesses about attitudes toward their programs from the fan mail they receive and by talking casually to people they know who have seen or listened to the program. In all these instances, a "measurement" of attitude is being made by interviewing people, noticing the behavior of a crowd, reading the letters they write, etc. We might call all such methods "rating" methods because they depend upon some person "rating" what other people say or do in terms of the attitudes in which he is interested.

The *rating of attitudes* may vary in precision from rough guesses of "favorable" or "unfavorable" to more accurate estimates of the percentages for and against. By rating each individual on a scale, say, from 1 to 5, and pooling the ratings of a number of individuals, it may even be possible to say how strongly an attitude is held. In many practical situations, however, there is no way of telling how valid or how reliable a rating method may be (see Chapter 8), but no other way of assessing attitudes may be possible. For that reason, such crude methods have long been used in the past and are likely to be used for a long time in the future.

Public opinion and market research. Although relatively few people, other than students of psychology, have heard of attitude scales, most citizens of the United States are now familiar with another kind of attitude measurement, the public-opinion poll. For them such a poll is an attempt to forecast the outcome of political elections. These forecasts, they have learned, may be fairly accurate when the election is not too close. In a close election, however, the polls are often wrong. Because polls are sometimes wrong or do not give good predictions, many are inclined not to trust them.

Unfortunately the public's notion of the public-opinion poll is greatly oversimplified. Predicting elections is only one—and probably the most difficult—of the uses of such a poll. It is being used regularly to assess attitudes on many problems:[11] acreage allotments for farmers, cost of living, programs of road building, the United Nations, buying of U.S. government bonds, profits

of businessmen, inflation and deflation, unemployment, and a host of other problems of concern to people. Such polls are being conducted both by agencies of the government and by groups of psychologists such as the National Opinion Research Center, American Institute of Public Opinion, and the University of Michigan Survey Research Center. These serve various business groups, as well as advertising and manufacturing groups, and in addition conduct research of their own. The results of public-opinion polls are of considerable value to many leaders in all fields who must make decisions affected by attitudes.

▪ *Questions.* Unlike attitude scales, polls must be made with people who represent a fair sample of some particular group, such as those who vote in a particular district, those who farm, those who buy Mouthwash A, or those who smoke. Such people cannot easily be induced to sit down and fill out any complicated attitude scale. They must be interviewed in a face-to-face situation, their interest and cooperation must be secured without imposing too much on their time or their privacy, and they must be asked questions which are rather simple and quickly covered.

To meet these limitations of the poll, it is customary to keep the interview brief, asking eight or ten questions, and to have each question cover some particular attitude. Thus in polling public opinion, a single question must serve as a measure of an attitude, whereas many statements can be used in the attitude scale. This is not always the case, but at best the number of questions or items must be greatly restricted. For this reason, the phrasing of a question is a matter of great importance and one that makes a great difference in the outcome of the poll.

In general the questions developed for use in polls are of two types: the *poll ques-*

tion and the *open-end question. The poll question gives the respondent a fixed number of alternatives.* For example, "Would you like to see more control over labor unions, less control, or about as much as there is now?" *The open-end question allows the respondent to phrase his own answer in his own words.* As you can readily imagine, it is difficult to decide just what the answers to open-end questions mean. In practice, the interviewer already has a number of possible alternatives to the question already coded, and after listening to the respondent, he simply checks one of the possibilities. These alternatives have usually been worked out by having a trial run on a small group of subjects, then classifying their answers into some limited number of categories.

It would seem that the poll question is to be preferred to the open-end question. Certainly it is simpler to use in an interview situation and interviewers need very little training to be able to present it and to record the answers. One difficulty with the poll question, however, is that it greatly restricts the respondent's answer, often forcing him to answer in a way that does not reflect his true opinion. In the example above about control of labor, the respondent might think that in some respects labor ought to be more controlled and in others less so. Such an attitude is not the same as saying that control ought to remain pretty much as it is, yet he has no way of expressing his real attitude. Another difficulty with the poll question is that minor differences in wording can greatly affect the result, often leading to complete misinterpretations of respondents' attitudes. After the Second World War, for example, two leading polling agencies asked the following questions at about the same time:

"After the war would you like to see the United States join some kind of world organization, or would you like to see us stay out?" (Na-

tional Opinion Research Center, January, 1945.)

"Do you think that the United States should join a world organization with police power to maintain world peace?" (American Institute of Public Opinion, April, 1945.)

There is no reason to believe that sentiment changed drastically between January and April, 1945, or that the populations sampled had very different views. However, 64 per cent said "yes" to the first question and 81 per cent to the second question, while 26 per cent said "no" to the first and 11 per cent said "no" to the second. It is quite likely that the phrase "to maintain world peace" greatly increased the affirmative answers, because the pollsters know that inserting any phrase which by itself is generally approved increases the number of approvals of the question as a whole. You can see then why it would be rather difficult to assess public opinion about a particular issue, when only one question is used and when wording is so important.

In practice, the pollsters do a great deal of research to arrive at their questions. Often they run a preliminary poll on small groups using several different phrasings of a question, then study the results to see what difference phrasing makes. From such preliminary studies, they attempt to frame the alternatives that are most likely to give people a chance to express their attitudes. They try to avoid phrasings that are likely to give a spuriously high or spuriously low percentage of answers. They must also try, in so far as time permits, to use different questions either in the same poll or in succeeding polls to be able to interpret the results that they obtain.

■ *Sampling.* Once a public-opinion poll has been prepared, the next question concerns the people to whom it should be given. In most polling, we should like to characterize the attitudes of some particular population. Sometimes this population is all adults in the United States. More often, however, we are interested in some restricted population. Even in political elections we need to know results district by district, because the outcome of elections is determined not by the national result but rather by congressional districts, electoral districts, and states. In other instances, the population may be farmers, retail-store owners, taxpayers, schoolteachers, etc.

Whatever the population, it is almost always impractical to poll the whole group. Whereas the population usually numbers in the thousands or even millions, we can afford to poll only a few hundred or at most a few thousand individuals. We are therefore faced with the problem of sampling some individuals from the total population. Of course, in the end, we wish to draw conclusions about the whole population from the relatively small sample. Statisticians, fortunately, have worked out rather dependable rules for inferring from a sample to a population. Just how accurate such inference is depends upon a number of factors. In general, though, it is possible to use a sample of a few hundred cases and predict with an accuracy of 1 or 2 per cent what the response of the whole population would be if it were polled. To do this, however, it is essential that the sample be so drawn that it is truly representative of the population. Practical people, ignorant of statistical methods, often wonder how one can draw conclusions about a whole population from a small sample. Actually, there is no difficulty at all as long as the sample is truly representative. It is this matter of representative sampling, on which so much hangs or falls, that is the major problem of the pollsters.

There are, in general, three ways of constructing samples so that they are reasonably representative of the population: (1) sampling from lists, (2) area and block sampling, and (3) quota sampling. The method of *sampling from lists* is just what its name implies. If one wanted to sample property owners, for example, he might go to the tax office and secure complete lists of those owning property, then pick every nth name (every tenth, one-hundredth, one-thousandth, etc.) from the list. Or if one wanted to sample telephone users, he could select every nth name from the telephone directory. This method is actually used a great deal in practice where the target population has been recorded on a list. The great danger in this method is that the list may not represent the population. This was the case in the famed *Literary Digest* poll that so badly predicted the election results in 1936.[12] This poll made use of telephone lists, and its results probably represented fairly well how telephone subscribers were going to vote. The trouble was that slightly over half the voters in the United States were at that time telephone subscribers, and that these were the economically favored members of the population who had rather different political attitudes from the rest of the voters. It usually happens that lists of property owners, telephone subscribers, utility users, etc., represent the higher socioeconomic strata of society and cannot be taken as representative of the population as a whole.

A second and superior method of sampling is *area and block sampling*.[11] In this case, the agency conducting the poll selects the people to be polled from large maps showing in detail the addresses of all members of the population. The agency then selects addresses so that they are randomly divided among different geographical areas which represent various socioeconomic strata and other factors in the same proportion that they are presented in the population. The interviewers are then sent to specified addresses. This method assures about the most representative sample one can expect to get and therefore yields very accurate results. However, it is expensive because it means considerable travel for interviewers and often many repeated calls before they find their respondents at home.

A third method is more economical and more widely used than any other, even though its results are less accurate. This is the *quota sampling method*. In this case, the polling agency sets quotas for certain categories such as age, sex, socioeconomic status, and geographical region. Interviewers are then told how many interviews they must conduct with respondents in each category. The interviewers are left some discretion as to how they manage to fill their quota. By establishing quotas in this way, the agency hopes to obtain a fair cross section of the population. Interviewers, however, when given a choice, usually select the person who seems somewhat more cooperative or the house that seems somewhat better kept. Thus biases can creep into the sample. Also biasing it are such factors as whether people are at home when the interviewer calls, for it happens that the people who are not at home may have different attitudes than those who are.[13] Wherever such biases have anything to do with attitudes, the quota sampling method gives inaccurate results. This is one of the reasons why attempts to predict national elections encounter a certain amount of unknown error.

From this brief account of public-opinion polling, one can see that constructing and administering a poll is no simple matter. It requires considerable knowledge and experience with the measurement of attitudes, together with statistical skills, to design and carry out a poll. It is thus not advisable for the inexpert person to try his hand at it. Under the supervision of well-trained persons, public-opinion polls can provide con-siderable information with relatively little error. In the hands of a novice, they are likely to give only misinformation.

■ *Market research*. Closely related to public-opinion polling is a specialized field that has grown greatly in the last 25 years —market research. The principal difference between the two is the kinds of attitudes one is attempting to measure. In market research, the *attitudes concerning specific products or the advertising of products* are measured rather than attitudes toward pub-lic issues. In addition, market research often *elicits specific information* such as what brand of mouthwash a housewife last pur-chased, what advertising she has noticed recently, what magazines she reads regu-larly, or what radio programs she listens to. Such factual information, put together with information about people's likes and dislikes of particular products, enables ad-vertisers to devise more acceptable advertis-ing. It also enables manufacturers to design products that will be more favorably re-ceived. Aside from these differences, how-ever, the methods and the problems of market research are very much like those of public-opinion polling.

Audience measurement. Advertisers, of course, are interested not only in what they advertise and how they advertise but also in the medium through which they adver-tise. This may be the newspaper, magazine, radio, and television. In fact, these enter-prises are wholly or partly financed by the proceeds from advertising. Consequently all parties concerned would like to know the extent of their audiences for their advertis-ing. Hence, in recent years, attempts to measure the size, nature, and attitudes of audiences have increased considerably.

Many of the leading magazines, for ex-ample, continually conduct surveys to de-termine how many people are reading their magazines and what kind of people they are—their buying habits, their educational level, their hobbies, and their reading habits.[14] In addition, they may find out just what parts of a magazine are read most often, what kinds of stories are most popular, and what advertising is most noticed— all so that they may know better the effectiveness of advertising of different types placed in different positions in the magazine.

Radio and television stations have a somewhat different problem. They must first of all find out how many people and what kind of people are tuned in on them at different times of the day and for which type of programs. The most common method of doing this is to call houses by telephone (using the method of lists) and ask such questions as[15]

1. Were you listening to the radio (or watching television) just now?
2. To what program were you listening, please?
3. What station, please?
4. What is advertised?
5. How many men, women, and children in your home were actually listening?

From polls of this sort, one can derive a "Hooper rating," stating what percentage of homes have their sets tuned in to a particular station. Such ratings are quite im-

Fig. 13.4. Propaganda in the cold war. Mrs. Kregzde, translator-announcer, and Mr. Razi, writer-announcer, broadcast to the people of Rumania over the Rumanian Service, Voice of America. (*United States Information Agency.*)

Fig. 13.5. Education or propaganda? A cartoon appearing in a daily newspaper designed to build up a favorable attitude toward increasing teachers' salaries. (*Walt Partymiller cartoon from Gazette and Daily, York, Pa., Apr. 21, 1947.*)

portant in the advertiser's decision whether he is reaching the size and kind of audience he wishes to reach with the program he is offering and the money he is paying for it.

ATTITUDE CHANGE AND PROPAGANDA

It has already been explained that attitudes and beliefs are resistant to change. This fact, however, does not wholly prevent them from being changed by the impact of daily events and by a constant bombardment of propaganda. Indeed propaganda—now a familiar household word—is the deliberate attempt to influence attitudes and beliefs. Because propaganda is so often used by dictators and others who have ulterior and socially questionable purposes, the term has come to have a rather odious reputation. In principle, however, propaganda is not necessarily either good or bad. It can just as well be used to "correct" attitudes and beliefs so that they are nearer to the "facts" as be used to distort them so that

they are further from the facts. Moreover, it is not possible to make any really clearcut distinction between education and propaganda. In education, we try to emphasize the "facts," but these "facts" nevertheless must always be interpreted. In interpreting them, the teacher has a chance to intrude his own biased attitudes and beliefs, with the result that education changes people's attitudes and beliefs. In practice, though, we regard education as a legitimate attempt to change attitudes and beliefs, as well as to inculcate knowledge, in the direction of the "facts," whereas propaganda typically is designed to change them in the direction favorable to the purposes of the propagandist whether these are or are not in accord with the "facts."

Many different devices are used by propagandists to influence attitudes and beliefs. We are less interested here, however, in these particular devices than in the major factors that are involved in attitude change. We shall discuss such factors under the following headings: (1) loaded words, (2) conscious and unconscious propaganda, (3) suggestion, (4) needs, and (5) accomplished facts.

Loaded words. In a later chapter (Chapter 20) we shall see how words serve as symbols to represent objects and experiences. Because we experience directly few of the "facts" necessary to form attitudes and beliefs, most of our information about the world is conveyed through words chosen by someone else to symbolize events. The chooser of words—the advertiser, newspaper reporter, magazine writer, radio commentator, politician—has a very rich language to employ, one which gives him a great deal of latitude in how he may describe any fact or idea to us. There are a multitude of words that are relatively neutral, that accurately describe facts without evoking attitudes one way or the other. On the other hand, there are many words that, through previous attitude formation, can be expected to evoke about the same attitude in most of the people who hear them.

These "loaded" words are the stock in trade of the propagandist. If he wishes to evoke an unfavorable attitude, he may use such words as "czarism," "dictatorship," "regimentation," "agitator," and "brain trust," to which the overwhelming majority of Americans react with strongly negative attitudes. If the propagandist wishes to create a favorable attitude, describing exactly the same set of events, he may use such words as "freedom," "right to work," "taxpayer," "cooperation," and "democracy," all of which are regarded favorably by the great majority of the people.

You are probably familiar with such loaded words in the newspapers, magazines, and broadcasts to which you regularly attend. If you happen to agree with the point of view being expressed, you probably do not notice the "loaded" words and, indeed, may think of them as factually accurate, but

if you disagree with the point of view, you are more likely to notice the "loaded" words as propaganda or distortion of the truth. The person who has no strong attitudes or beliefs on the subject can have his attitudes influenced very easily by the loading of words he reads or listens to.

Let us give one example from a rather careful psychological study.[16] The investigator selected forty terms from the news columns of the *Chicago Tribune*, twenty of which were used by the newspaper in reporting policies it did not support and twenty of which were used in connection with events or policies it did support. To these forty terms, the investigator added ten neutral terms. He presented these terms in a mixed order to several groups of people, including parent-teachers, college students, high school alumni, laborers, and white-collar workers. He asked each person to indicate whether he "liked," "disliked," or "had no feeling about" the word. From these results each word could be assigned a score representing the "feeling tone" for the word, − 100 being extremely unfavorable and + 100 being extremely favorable. Here are some of the feeling-tone values he obtained in this study:

Czarism	−84	Cooperation	+95
Dictatorship	−84	Freedom	+92
Domination	−79	Reemployment	+88

There was no question but that the *Chicago Tribune* was successfully choosing words that evoked very well the strongly unfavorable or favorable attitudes it wished to evoke in support of its own views.

In a follow-up study, the investigator chose twelve loaded terms from the *Chicago Tribune* and twelve terms from the *New York Times* used in reporting exactly the same events in the two newspapers. As before, he determined feeling-tone values for these words. In Table 13.3 are the feeling-tone values for pairs of words used in describing the same events. Again it was clear that the same news was being slanted one way by one newspaper and another way by the other newspaper. Thus in simply reporting the news, "loaded" words were being used to create the desired attitudes toward the events being reported.

Conscious and unconscious propaganda. Those who use loaded words may be doing so quite unconsciously. Often their own attitudes have so distorted their perception of the facts that, when they call someone a "dictator," "Communist," or "agitator," they may believe mistakenly that these words "factually" describe the individual they are talking about. They may believe, for example, that it is a "fact" that Roosevelt was a dictator. Such beliefs, of course, are examples of the way in which attitudes and beliefs distort perception and memory of the "facts." But whether the loaded words are consciously or unconsciously used, the result is the same: *the attitudes of others are influenced in the direction intended by the propagandist.*

Another way to influence attitudes, which may also be unintentional, is more subtle than using loaded words. This is to *provide a particular context for the reporting of information.* For example, several years ago, a leading psychologist wrote an arithmetic book.[17] It was certainly written without any conscious intent to influence economic and political attitudes. In this book, however, were 643 arithmetic problems that emphasized common capitalistic notions. The various problems consistently contained examples involving the employment of workers and the making of a profit thereby, buying and selling at a profit, and lending money at interest rates. Suppose, however, that the author had chosen other examples for the same problems: "If one out of every thousand Southern cotton workers has pellagra because of inadequate wages, how

TABLE 13.3. Feeling-tone values for terms used by the *Chicago Tribune* and the *New York Times* in describing the same events.

Chicago Tribune		New York Times	
Term	Value	Term	Value
Radical	−53	Progressive	+92
Regimentation	−53	Regulation	+32
Government witch-hunting	−38	Senate investigation	+57
The dole	−35	Home relief	+27
Alien	−35	Foreign	0

Based on Sargent, S. S. Emotional stereotypes in The *Chicago Tribune. Sociometry,* 1939, 2, 69–65.

many more cases of pellagra will there be if the cotton-mill owner employs 2,000 more workers at the same wages?" Or, "If $20 a week is required to provide adequate nourishment for a family, what is the degree of undernourishment when relief funds are $5 a week?" The only difference between such problems as these and those actually used is in the context. The consequences, however, are that one set stresses profit-making attitudes, the other attitudes of relieving human distress. In this instance, we have no measure of the effect on children's attitudes, but we can surmise that they were considerable. It is difficult, if not impossible, to write a children's arithmetic book without unconsciously using propaganda that strengthens or changes attitudes.

Suggestion. Psychologists define *suggestion as the uncritical acceptance of a statement.* This is to say that a person may accept a belief, form an attitude, or be incited to action merely by accepting what someone else says and without requiring facts or other proof. The skilled advertiser, propagandist, and political leader know this and employ it to their advantage by changing beliefs and attitudes. They know rather well, moreover, under what circumstances suggestion is likely to work.

▪ *Prestige.* One of these is to make use of prestige. If an advertiser wishes to sell a certain brand of cigarettes, he tries to use the fact that some famous person smokes these cigarettes. Similarly politicians make liberal use of the names of George Washington, Abraham Lincoln, and other respected leaders to attempt to gain acceptance of their ideas. If you watch television for just a few hours or motor down nearly any highway in the United States looking at billboards, you can encounter large numbers of instances in which prestige is used to influence people to buy some product, to vote a political ticket, or to alter their attitudes and behavior in other ways.

To a certain extent, prestige suggestion is merely an instance of our reliance on authorities for the facts behind our beliefs. Since the line between facts and beliefs is often a hazy one, it is natural that we sometimes accept a belief uncritically simply because we are forced to rely on authorities. To a certain extent, prestige suggestion also involves identification with some leader or idol. The girl who would like to be beautiful may have Marlene Grable as her model of beauty, and if Marlene uses Beautiface Cold Cream, the girl is likely to use it too as her way of aspiring to the beauty of the model. Prestige suggestion also plays on already existing attitudes and uses them to form new attitudes. If people have a generally unfavorable attitude toward Communists, the suggestion may be made that such and such a political belief is "communistic" or endorsed by the communist *Daily Worker*. This is a way of taking an existing attitude and turning it toward another—often innocent—victim. Much of the name calling and "smearing" that we see in the political arena deliberately or unconsciously makes use of such suggestion.

Another important aspect of prestige suggestion, however, is that it *alters a person's perception of an object or situation.* By attaching a prestige suggestion to it, he views it in a new light. In one study,[18] for example, students were asked to rank such professions as business, dentistry, journalism, medicine, and politics according to (1) the amount of intelligence they thought the profession required, and (2) the social usefulness of the profession. Some students did this without being given any suggestion. Other groups of students were given suggestion by being told that another group of students had, say, ranked politics highest (or lowest). These suggestions were rather effective. The group that was told that politics had been ranked low by others also ranked it low, and those who were told that others had ranked it high ranked it high. When these groups were later asked specifically what politicians they had in mind when making their rankings, the group ranking politics low said they had in mind politicians such as "Tammany Hall politicians" and the "usual neighborhood politicians." Those ranking politics high had in mind national politics and gave such examples as Roosevelt, Hull, Stimson, Lehman, La Guardia. Thus the effect of the suggestion was to get the students to think of the better or poorer examples of politicians and to express their attitudes accordingly.

▪ *Social suggestion.* "Everybody's doing it," or "More people smoke Nocoff cigarettes than any other cigarette" are examples of another kind of suggestion that is often rather effective. It appeals to the general tendency to conform and also to a person's lack of confidence in his own judgment. In many circumstances, we find ourselves uncertain about what we think or should think, and in these we are inclined to "go along with the crowd" or accept almost any other suggestions made by our peers. Our uncertainty may be due to in-

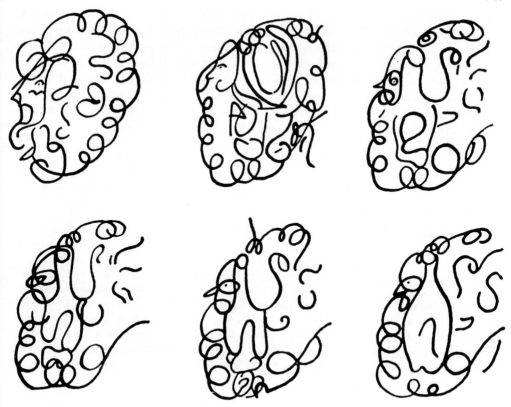

Fig. 13.6. Examples of drawings used in experiment on effects of suggestion. For explanation, see text. (From Luchins, A. S. *Social influence on perception of complex drawings. J. soc. Psychol., 1945, 21, 257–273.*)

experience or merely to our having no prior attitudes and beliefs. On the other hand, it may be due to the *ambiguity* of objects to which we are to react. In many political matters, both candidates or parties stand for virtue, economy, efficiency, etc. How does one tell the difference between the two?

The fact that ambiguity figures in the effects of social suggestion is illustrated in numerous psychological studies. In one of them, subjects viewed a small light in a dark room. Such a light appears to move— a phenomenon called the autokinetic effect. A subject, however, who is told that other people see it move is much more inclined to say it moves, simply as a result of social suggestion. Similarly, if he is told that others see it move in such and such a direction, he is more inclined to say that it moves in that direction.

In another study children were shown ambiguous drawings. Each child had a partner who was a confederate of the experimenter.[19] The confederate was instructed to say the word "face" or "automobile" or "battleship" in advance of the subject's judgment. The subject in these experiments seldom repeated exactly what he heard but would make a response similar to the one he heard. He might report a "nose" or an "ear" when the confederate had said "face." In Figure 13.6 are some of the drawings used in this experiment. Naturally if the drawing had been clearly unequivocal, e.g., an automobile, then calling it a face would not have affected the judgment of it. Only because the drawings were so ambiguous that they might have been almost anything was the social suggestion effective.

Needs. It perhaps goes without saying that suggestion, as well as other methods

of altering attitudes and beliefs, must fit in with a person's needs. Attitudes represent potential instrumental acts, and these, as we have seen (Chapter 3), are learned as ways of satisfying one's needs. It is very difficult to create an attitude about anything in which a person has no interest. A girl who uses no make-up does not care what kind of cold cream Marlene Grable uses. A man who does not smoke is not likely to be influenced by Ronald Gable's choice of cigarettes. So without needs of a

Fig. 13.7. The impact of accomplished facts upon opinions about the course of the Second World War. The chart shows that events of the war brought about marked shifts in public opinion concerning its outcome. Events marked by letters are: A, England and France declare war on Germany; B, Germany invades Norway; C, Germany invades low countries; D, Italy enters war, denounced by Roosevelt; E, mass air raids begin on Britain; F, German-Italian-Japanese pact; G, Roosevelt elected for third term; H, Lend-lease bill proposed in Congress; I, British defeat Italian navy; J, Fall of Athens; K, Germany declares war on Russia; L, Japan seizes bases in French Indo-China; M, Roosevelt orders navy to shoot first; N, *Reuben James* is sunk; O, special Japanese envoy arrives in Washington; P, Pearl Harbor. (*From Cantril, H. Ed. Gauging public opinion. Princeton: Princeton Univ. Press, 1944, p. 221.*)

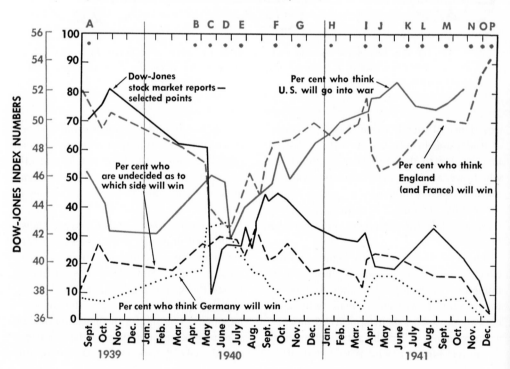

kind that are relevant to the object or situation, it is difficult to form or to alter attitudes toward the object or situation.

For this reason propagandists often go to some trouble to create needs. Advertisers also try to do this in order to enlarge the market for their products. To sell washing machines, they may emphasize how much washday drudgery is saved by the washing machine, then go on to emphasize the advantages of their particular washing machine. Even in matters of labor-management relations, where people feel no need concerning the problem, management may find it necessary to foment labor troubles, to fabricate stories of the dangers of labor uprising, etc., in order to get people to view favorably legislation designed to restrict labor.

Accomplished facts. There are many special techniques and "tricks" for persuading people to alter their attitudes and beliefs, but on the whole they are simply variations of the more general principles of attitude and attitude change that we have described. The attitudes of people are being changed every day by the large-scale use of many of these principles. One should not get the impression, however, that we are wholly at the mercy of the propagandist. He is limited by people's needs, their already existing attitudes, and the efforts of other propagandists who wish to alter attitudes in different directions. Witness the attempts

of advertisers and politicians to compete for our favorable attitudes.

Also important are the "facts" people already have acquired. Advertising and propaganda must face the facts that a man has at his command. If a person knows for himself what is the "truth," he is much less subject to efforts to change his attitudes and beliefs. Education, of course, is in large part a matter of equipping people with the "facts," so education is a powerful immunizer against propaganda that distorts the facts.

The impact of actual events is also a strong antagonist of propaganda, for it tends *to change people's attitudes in accordance with the facts*. In general, people give up unfavorable attitudes toward something if the "facts" force them to. People, for example, who may be very much against the United States becoming involved in war, immediately change their attitudes and back the war effort, once the United States is actually in a war. When political leaders have exhausted other possibilities of persuasion, they often make use of this principle —that accomplished facts change attitudes —and wait for events to take place. Public-opinion surveys conducted throughout the Second World War illustrate this point very well (see Figure 13.7). As the fortunes of war varied, public opinion changed accordingly. Opinions, in fact, correlated fairly well with various events during the war.

SUMMARY

1. Attitudes are tendencies to respond favorably or unfavorably toward some person, object, or situation. Social attitudes, as distinguished from personal attitudes, are those that are shared by several individuals or large groups of people.

2. A belief is the acceptance of some statement or proposition. Attitudes tend to affect beliefs, and vice versa, so that it is difficult in practice to distinguish between them.

3. Four principal types of erroneous beliefs are superstitions, prejudices, delusions, and stereotyped beliefs.

4. Several factors affect the development of attitudes and beliefs. Among the more important factors are a person's culture, family, and educational background.

5. A person bases his beliefs and attitudes on what he regards as "facts." For that reason, his sources of information are important. Most information, unfortunately, comes from "authorities," rather than from firsthand observation, and these "authorities" can select and distort the information he gets.

6. Even the facts a person learns for himself can be grossly misinterpreted, for "appearances are often deceiving."

7. Beliefs and attitudes tend to preserve themselves, because a person selectively perceives and remembers what fits in with his existing attitudes and beliefs.

8. Attitudes are also preserved by the tendency of a person to shut himself off from "facts" that might change his attitudes and beliefs.

9. Attitudes are also preserved by social pressures. A person tends to associate with people who have similar attitudes, and the desire for their social approval tends to keep his own attitudes and beliefs intact.

10. Several methods of measuring attitudes have been developed. One is the attitude scale. This provides a precise measure of the degree of an attitude toward an issue, but it can be used only with people who have the time and interest to take the scale. The rating scale is less refined but easier to use because all that is required is a rough rating of a person's attitude.

11. For many practical purposes, we are limited to the public-opinion poll. This is a series of questions that may be answered briefly in a personal interview. The phrasing of questions, the context in which they are asked, and representative sampling are all extremely important in the results one obtains.

12. Propaganda is a deliberate attempt to influence attitudes and beliefs. Foremost among propaganda techniques is the use of loaded words in the description of facts.

13. Propaganda also makes liberal use of various kinds of suggestion, especially of prestige suggestion and of social suggestion.

14. In order to be effective, propaganda must ordinarily appeal to the needs of people. It must also fit with the facts that people know to be true.

with one another when they come from the same colony, will battle to the death with members of other colonies, and even with members of their own in times of turmoil (e.g., when a new queen is introduced into a beehive). It is probably hopeless to try to eliminate social conflicts from human affairs. However, it is certainly reasonable to try to reduce their frequency, severity, and destructive consequences. If social conflicts were confined to quarrels among individuals from time to time, plus an occasional fist fight, no one would be very much concerned about them. This chapter will be devoted to discussing what psychologists know about social conflicts that might help in minimizing their frequency and destructiveness.

Organization of social conflicts. The most important single way in which social conflicts differ is the degree to which those who participate in them are organized into groups or social institutions. Conflicts may range all the way from a quarrel between two individuals to a war between two halves of the world. Naturally, the notions necessary to understand highly organized conflicts differ from those necessary to understand relatively unorganized ones. In this chapter we shall first examine in detail an example of a relatively unorganized but widespread social conflict—*racial conflict*. Then we shall consider briefly how *social organizations* (groups, institutions) become established and how they operate. Then we shall consider another form of social conflict at a somewhat higher level of organization—*industrial conflict*. Next we shall say a few words about war, and then conclude with a description of two experimental social conflicts. The principles which we discuss under these headings will differ. However, to a large degree this arrangement is for convenience in writing. Most of the principles discussed in this chapter apply

to all social conflicts, regardless of their degree of organization.

■ RACIAL CONFLICTS

The word *race*, in ordinary usage, means *a group of human beings having common and distinctive innate physical characteristics*. It is a much-debated issue, with which we shall not deal here, whether there are any races at all and, if so, what ones and how many there are.[1] However, when we talk of racial conflict we shall refer to social conflict resulting from prejudice against any social group having some distinctive common characteristic, whether that common characteristic be race, religion, national origin, or something else. Most of the illustrations in this section will be drawn from anti-Negro prejudice in the United States, both because this is the kind of prejudice that is most intense in this country and because it has been best studied by psychologists and others. But the same principles which apply to conflict between Negroes and whites also apply to other "racial" conflicts.

Acquiring prejudices. What is a prejudice? In the last chapter we defined it as an unfavorable attitude toward some person, living thing, or inanimate object. As we use it here, however, it refers to *a hostile attitude toward some social group*. Thus any attitude of hostility toward Negroes, Germans, politicians, Communists, or any other group is a prejudice. In other words, it does not matter whether the prejudice has some objective basis or not. If it is hostility toward a group, it is a prejudice.

Prejudices are attitudes, and just like any other attitudes, they obey the principles of attitude formation and maintenance which were discussed in Chapter 13. In particular, *they are learned*. It is very important to ask how prejudices are learned, since one of the best ways of eradicating them is to prevent their being learned in the first place.

Logically, there are two possible ways in which a prejudice could be learned: (1) *from contact with the object of the prejudice* or (2) *from contact with others who have the prejudice.* Prejudices are, in fact, learned in both ways, but various studies indicate that *they are more commonly acquired by contact with people who have them.* One study of rural Tennessee children showed that their parents warned them to avoid Negro children and even objects which have been handled by Negro children, and that the parents sometimes punished their children severely for violating these warnings.[2] A good many studies have shown that there is a high correlation between the attitudes of parents and those of their children, regardless of which attitudes are studied (although some attitudes show higher correlations than others).[3]

Parents are not the only teachers of prejudice. Schoolmates, teachers, and general communication media like newspapers and television are also effective. In addition, most of the people we meet try to influence our attitudes. Hence we are continuously exposed to teachers of prejudice. If all these different sources repeat the same message, then it is no wonder that so many young children accept it. A particularly dramatic demonstration of the fact that prejudice is usually learned from contact with the prejudiced rather than with the people against whom it is directed is the very strong anti-Communist prejudice now held by almost all Americans. Very few Americans have ever met a Communist. What they know about Communists they have learned from newspapers, magazines, and other public information media. If it became desirable— as it was in the Second World War, when the Russians were our allies—to create a more favorable attitude toward Commu-

nists, the public information media woul probably be used effectively for this end.

The first thing that a child learns about prejudice is that the object group is "bad. Later he learns more specific things abou the group. One study showed, for exampl that young Southern white children b lieved Negroes to be lower than whites i many traits, including the "trait" of rel giousness. Older children showed a muc more discriminating pattern of beliefs abou Negroes; for example, they rated Negroes : more religious than whites.[4]

Prejudice may grow out of personal e perience with the group against which it directed, but this source of prejudice probably rare. In fact direct contact wit the group is sometimes a cure for prejudic The Army, for example, tried the exper ment of creating mixed Negro and whi units during the Second World War. Bot before and after the whites saw service i such units, their attitudes toward Negro were measured. In almost all cases th whites were less prejudiced after their e perience in mixed units than they had bee before. And the Negroes in mixed unit incidentally, proved to be quite effective i combat, which the Negroes in segregate units had not been.[5]

Supports for prejudice. Once learne prejudices are not allowed to die ol through forgetting or disuse. Rather the continue to serve the *purpose of gratifyin an individual's needs.* In addition they s alter his perception and memory, as w indicated in the last chapter, that h everyday experiences tend to support h prejudices. Consequently, between h needs and his perceptions, an individu usually maintains his prejudices at fu strength.

■ *Needs.* Probably the need best serve by prejudice is the need for *status.* A preji dice creates a social hierarchy in which th

Fig. 14.1. Children more often learn prejudice from their elders than from one another. (*New York State Commission against Discrimination* photo.)

prejudiced person has a superior status. If one is prejudiced against Negroes, for example, he believes that Negroes are inferior to him and therefore that he is superior to them. Some people need to think well of themselves—to think themselves better than others (see Chapter 3). The poorest, least educated, most unimportant white in a backwoods Southern town has the consolation of "knowing" that he is mentally, morally, and socially superior to most of the residents of his area.

Prejudice also serves the need to express *aggression*. Psychologists have good reason to believe, as we have pointed out in Chapters 4 and 10, that hostility (or aggression) usually originates in the frustration of needs. This notion is certainly consistent with ordinary experience, for we frequently

see people irritated or angry because they have failed to get what they want or because something or somebody has obstructed their efforts. As we have repeatedly pointed out, social motives are frequently frustrated, even in those who are economically fortunate to have all their physiological needs satisfied. It follows, therefore, that most people and particularly the underprivileged are sometimes frustrated and consequently to some extent aggressive.

Aggression resulting from frustration can often be simply vented at whatever is doing the frustrating. When a person of superior status or a situation beyond anyone's control does the frustrating, however, the aggression must be expressed in some other way. The consequence is *displaced aggression* (see Chapter 10). In an experiment[6] in which psychologists deprived students for a prolonged period of sleep, food, smoke, and even permission to talk, one subject of this experiment vented his aggression in hostile drawings. In some other instances, the aggression may be expressed in prejudice against some "inferior" group that cannot aggress back. Such displaced aggression is illustrated by the lieutenant bawling out the sergeant, the sergeant working it out on the private, and the private kicking the dog. It is illustrated more scientifically in an experiment with boys at a summer camp who were frustrated by not being allowed to go to the movies. Before and after the frustration, their attitudes toward Mexicans and Japanese were measured, and these measurements showed that subjects were considerably more prejudiced after frustration than before.[7]

Such displaced aggression is particularly significant in racial conflict. In this case it is called *scapegoating*. The prejudiced person who suffers economic, social, or political frustrations may displace his aggression against some convenient object, and the most convenient object is likely to be the group against whom he already has a prejudice. This is particularly likely if he can so distort the facts that the group seems responsible for his frustrations. A most notable example of this sort of displacement is the German persecution of the Jews in the 1930s. Hitler was able to convince his followers (who were presumably anti-Semitic to begin with) that the Jews were responsible for most of Germany's economic and social woes. Thus he made Jews the scapegoats of displaced aggression.

Further evidence that prejudice serves needs comes from studies of the *personalities of the prejudiced*. In one such study,[8] students were selected who were frankly anti-Semitic. They were found to have more

repressed aggressive and sexual needs—needs that are not permitted free expre sion in ordinary life—than the average stu dent. Apparently anti-Semitism was an ou let for the resulting pent-up aggression. I another study, among children prejudice against Negroes, those who were relativel free of repressed aggression learned muc more easily not to be prejudiced. The on effect of educational procedures on thos with aggressive personality patterns was t make them still more prejudiced, bot against their teachers and against society i general.[8] The value of education as a corre tive for prejudiced attitudes (see Chapt 13 and below) is thus limited by the kin of person who is "educated."

■ *Perception, memory, and judgmen* Prejudice is supported not only by need but also by *changes in perception, memor; and judgment*. We discussed this point i Chapter 13, but it should be reviewe again because it is germane to the preserv; tion of prejudice. Prejudice alters perce; tion so that we tend to see what we war to see or what we believe we are going t see. If we believe that Negroes are dirt and stupid, we take especial note of in stances of dirtiness or stupidity on the pa: of Negroes while paying little attention t similar instances on the part of whites to outstanding examples of cleanliness brilliance on the part of Negroes. Indec with practice, we become quite skilled ; perceiving only that which is consister with our prejudices. Illustrating this poir is an experiment[9] with college students wh were asked to judge whether a series c faces were Jews or non-Jews. The ant Semitic students in the group identific more pictures as Jews and, moreover, we: more often correct in their identification In other words, being prejudiced, thes students had learned to recognize Jew better than the unprejudiced students.

MR. BIGGOTT

"Good heavens! It's not restricted!"

Fig. 14.2. Examples of the Mr. Biggott cartoons used in the study of prejudice. (*Courtesy of American Jewish Committee and Carl Rose.*)

MR. BIGGOTT

Mr. Biggott: "Was it necessary, Reverend, to emphasize the Lord's—er—Jewish background in your sermon?"

MR. BIGGOTT

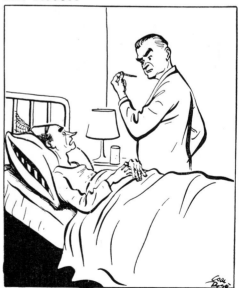

"In case I should need a transfusion, doctor, I want to make certain I don't get anything but blue, sixth-generation American blood!"

The effects of prejudice on *memory* have been less extensively studied than effects on perception, but they have been demonstrated. In an experiment[10] cited in Chapter 13, for example, pro-Communist and anti-Communist students were asked to memorize paragraphs, some of which were "pro" and some "anti." When tested later, pro-Communists remembered pro-Communist paragraphs, and anti-Communists remembered anti-Communist material, better than the paragraphs opposing their prejudices. Such selective memory clearly helps a person maintain his prejudices.

Other experiments illustrate the way in which prejudice can *distort the judgment and interpretation of situations.* In one of these experiments,[11] subjects were shown a series of cartoons involving a character dubbed "Mr. Biggott." Examples of such cartoons are shown in Figure 14.2. Subjects were asked to give their reactions to the cartoons. One subject, known to be prejudiced, interpreted the cartoon in Figure 14.2 as follows: If Mr. Biggott is only a sixth-generation American, he is a newcomer and is not entitled to put on airs.

▪ *Social handicaps.* In the list of conditions that maintain prejudice, last but not least are the social effects of prejudice itself. To the extent that prejudice is permitted to operate in social affairs, to that extent it produces a world that is exactly what the prejudiced person expects it to be. People with anti-Negro prejudices, for example, believe that Negroes are less intelligent than whites. Believing that, they prevent Negroes from getting adequate schooling, library facilities, housing, and other cultural opportunities. The result, of course, is a social handicap for Negroes that prevents them from being as educated and as "intelligent" as whites. Thus the prejudice becomes "true." It creates the social conditions that justify the prejudice. This is obviously a vicious circle in which the effects of prejudice help to maintain

the prejudice by providing an observabl基 basis for it.

One of the psychological factors tha keeps this vicious circle in motion, once : is set up, is the *stereotyping of attitude* that we described in the last chapter. *stereotype is a fixed set of beliefs that ar greatly oversimplified and held generally b members of a group.* Stereotypes are widel held even in the United States where peo ple consider themselves enlightened. Man different studies of college students, fo example, conducted at different times an in different places, show them to agre rather well in the ranking of preferences fo different ethnic groups.[12] The members o one group of college students, moreove agreed with each other surprisingly well i the particular adjectives they used to de scribe different ethnic groups.[13] The stu dents happened to be Princetonians, bu their stereotyped descriptions are no unique with Princeton students or eve with white people in general, for anoth study obtained essentially the same resul with a group of Negro college students. There were some differences in the adje tives used by the two groups—the Negro

Fig. 14.3. One of the effects prejudice is to exclude peop from jobs they are capable holding. (*New York State Comm sion against Discrimination photo*

being somewhat less stereotyped—but the general result was very similar for both groups.

Social effects of prejudice. We have just noted one of the effects of prejudice—the creation of social conditions that confirm the prejudice. But let us look at the social consequences of prejudice in greater detail.

Perhaps the most significant effect of prejudice is that prejudiced people avoid those against whom they bear a prejudice. This fact applied on a scale affecting thousands or millions of people has a very simple result—*segregation*. In the Middle Ages, and also in Eastern Europe in recent times, Jews were required to live in ghettoes. Nowadays we do not have so many ghettoes, but we in America do have large areas in which only Negroes live and much larger ones where Negroes are not permitted to live. But, segregation is not only a matter of where Negroes live. It also prohibits them from shopping in certain white stores, attending white places of entertainment, using white public facilities, including railroad cars and the front seats in buses, and, most important of all, from taking many jobs. Sometimes segregation is carried to ridiculous extremes. Upper-caste Hindus feel defiled if they eat with low-caste Hindus. Probably the most concerted program of segregation of Negroes in the modern world is South Africa's program of *apartheid*.

Segregation with equal facilities is theoretically possible. The United States Supreme Court in 1896 therefore decided that separate, but equal, facilities were permissible. In practice, however, it does not work. Inevitably the segregated minority is forced to use inferior facilities under inconvenient, uncomfortable, or unsanitary conditions, because segregation permits majority groups to "take out" their prejudices on the minority. Becoming convinced

of this fact, the Supreme Court finally ruled in 1954 against segregation in education. This ruling simply gave legal recognition to the social fact that segregated facilities are seldom equal.

Preventing racial conflict. We have seen that racial conflict has its roots in racial prejudice. To prevent or alleviate racial conflict requires, then, that we try to combat racial prejudice. From our analysis of prejudice, it is fairly easy to formulate several rules for coping with it. These rules, however, are easier to state than they are to apply:

1. *Prevent parents and teachers from teaching prejudices to children.* This is difficult to do but has been accomplished more and more in recent years.

2. *Remove the supports for the prejudice and provide prejudiced persons with evidence contrary to the prejudice.* This is not likely to be very effective because of the distorting effects of prejudice on perception, memory, and understanding.

3. *Make prejudice conflict with other strong needs.* The campaigns, extensively used during the Second World War, which attempted to convince people that it is unpatriotic, irreligious, or undemocratic to be prejudiced were quite effective. This technique can backfire, though. If a person is propagandized to believe that prejudice is undemocratic, he may react not by rejecting prejudice, but by rejecting democracy.

4. *Teach people not to be prejudiced.* This works fairly well, but it is difficult to get adults into an educational situation which is aimed at changing their prejudices. Consequently disguised education is likely to be most effective. Television's casual acceptance of Negroes is an excellent example of one way to do this.

5. *Bring potentially conflicting groups together.* The success of the Army's mixed

units indicates that contact helps to reduce prejudice. However, it is important to make sure that the contact is not with the worst specimens of the group against which the prejudice is directed.

If we cannot eliminate prejudice, or if we can do so only slowly, it is still possible to alleviate racial conflict by preventing prejudice from causing conflicts. This approach has been the most effective one in recent years and indirectly helps in reducing prejudices. Here are some of the specific means for carrying it out:

1. *Make and enforce laws against social conflict, segregation, and discrimination.* This can alleviate social conflicts. If social conflicts are illegal and if the law is enforced, they are less likely to occur. The technique has one serious limitation, however. It frustrates the aggressive impulses of the prejudiced. These aggressions may consequently come out in some other way —either by extralegal methods of continuing to oppress the group against which the prejudice is directed (e.g., the Ku Klux Klan) or by displacing the aggressions to some other target.

2. *Reduce economic and other frustrations, both of the prejudiced and of the victims of prejudice.* If everyone is satisfied, then there is less likely to be social conflict.

3. *Place a positive social value on avoiding social conflict.* Teach people that regardless of how they feel it is undesirable to express prejudiced feelings.

4. *Keep potentially conflicting groups apart.* This technique is necessary when conflict otherwise seems inevitable. The best thing a German Jew could do in the 1930s, for example, was to leave Germany.

5. *Remove the identifiability of the group against which prejudice is directed.* Conflict cannot occur unless the potential conflictors recognize one another. Negroes posing as Indian rajahs, for example, have

traveled through the South, using white facilities, without incurring objections. Jews are often not recognized as such unless they call attention to their origin. Probably the most severe prejudice held by modern Americans is that against homosexuals— yet there has never been a homosexual riot and most homosexuals suffer very little from prejudice against them. The reason, of course, is that no one can recognize a homosexual unless he calls attention to his status.

This last technique, potentially the most effective of all, is socially wasteful and hard to apply. It is socially wasteful because it requires those who want to avoid identification to give up their customs, costumes, and other cultural features that distinguish them from other groups. In this way the larger culture loses elements that may be beneficial. The technique is also hard to apply because many people are unable or unwilling to give up the race, religion, or culture into which they were born and in which they believe. When the early Christians were persecuted for being Christians, they could have easily saved themselves from torture and death by abandoning Christianity. No doubt many did, but enough remained Christians to keep the faith alive.

These techniques for avoiding racial conflict are superficial; they treat the symptom of conflict, when the cause is racial prejudice. Such a limited objective is, however reasonable when the elimination of racial prejudice is so difficult to achieve.

SOCIAL ORGANIZATIONS

As we saw at the beginning of this chapter, social conflicts vary in the extent to which the participants are organized. Racial conflict, though widespread, is usually matter between individuals, except in so fa

Fig. 14.4. Teachers can combat prejudice by not teaching it and by ignoring racial differences. (New York State Commission against Discrimination photo.)

as the desires of some of the individuals manage to get built into the institutional structure of the society in which they live (e.g., the Jim Crow or segregation laws). Industrial conflicts and wars, on the other hand, are almost never between individuals. Instead, they involve two or more social institutions, such as nations, companies, or unions. Naturally, such groups are composed of men and led by men who have their individual needs and perceptions. Leaders obviously have much to do with the course of the conflict. However, they only represent their groups (see Chapter 12), and to understand conflicts between groups, we must consider these groups or institutions as a whole.

Social institutions. *A social institution is a collection of objects, customary meth-* *ods of behavior, and techniques of enforcing such behavior on individuals.* These objects, customs, and enforcement techniques (see Chapter 3) are made and changed by people, but the membership in a social institution (e.g., a union) can completely change while the nature of the institution remains essentially the same.

Most social institutions develop because men have common interests and have found that they can promote these interests more effectively by working together. Indeed a group of people with a common goal have considerably more power to promote that goal than the same number of individuals acting singly. Leaders of each side in industrial conflict or war know this and do their best to take advantage of it.

The power of a group stems not only

Fig. 14.5. Bringing different races together in work and play reduces prejudice. (New York State Commission against Discrimination photo.)

from the common interest that joins its members together but also from several factors that make the members think and act alike. For one thing, almost all *social institutions have educational programs designed to ensure unity and agreement.* Many unions and most manufacturers' organizations put out newspapers and other publications. Union halls serve as social meeting places where members informally educate other members. Quite aside from publications and union halls, union members tend to spend their time with one another, thus achieving agreement by simple contact.

Secondly, *people in social institutions tend to act alike because others tend to treat them alike.* I am always polite to policemen, courteous to old ladies, and brusque to beggars. I treat these individuals in a manner which I conceive appropriate to their class memberships. And, in general, most people usually get treated in a manner appropriate to their class and institutional membership. If all members of an institution are treated the same, they will be more apt to respond alike.

Finally, *people tend to identify with those groups or institutions of which they are members.* You probably feel indignant when you hear of a case in which someone

is expelled from college for reasons which seem to you unjust or inadequate. This is largely because you identify with the group of college students. Similarly, most union members and management members seem to feel that their interests are affected by events which happen to any other member of their institutions.

The difficulty with strength in unity is that people are different. The more people there are in an organization, the fewer are the goals on which the members of the organization can agree. Thus we see the members of both political parties coming out against sin, waste, extravagance, bungling, high taxes, and communism; and in favor of virtue, economy, good government and their own candidates. Such meaningless platforms are necessary because any platform which meant anything would generate opposition from some party members.

Organized conflict. The fact that there is weakness as well as strength in unity has made men develop techniques for making the disagreements among members of groups and institutions less important. Foremost among these techniques is that of the *common enemy.* When there is common enemy who seems to threaten members of a group or class, they will often submerge their differences and work for the common good. This technique is often used in international conflict. The worst danger in its use is that it may get out of hand— the leaders may come to believe their own propaganda. A leader who believes that his opponents are liars, murderers, torturers, and Fascists (or Communists) without decency, honor, or morality is not going to find it easy to work out a reasonable compromise of conflicting interests. This is one of the many ways in which disagreements become strikes—or wars.

Two final facts about social institutions need mentioning. First, *the existence of social institutions tends to enlarge social conflicts*, once they start. A dispute which may initially have involved only a few workmen may conceivably result in a strike

of all the steelworkers in the country. Secondly, when a social conflict is being stopped, it is necessary that the *solution be simple enough for the members of the institution to understand it*. It has often happened in labor disputes that a compromise which should have been perfectly satisfactory to both sides was nevertheless rejected because its benefits were too complicated to be understood by the rank and file of union members.

■ INDUSTRIAL CONFLICT

We have just seen that social institutions mobilize their members toward common goals, and sometimes they create a common enemy in order to create such a goal. Once started, a conflict between institutions

Fig. 14.6. Since 1945, New York State has had an anti-discrimination law, enforced by periodic reviews of employers' personnel practices. (*New York State Commission against Discrimination* photo.)

tends to spread and is difficult to stop. These points should be borne in mind as we consider industrial and international conflicts.

Conflict of interests. We have seen that people form social institutions to promote their interests. In the case of industrial conflicts, these institutions are unions and managements (and sometimes associations of unions and associations of managements). Before we can consider how these institutions behave, we must ask what the interests are that their members want to promote. Of course needs for companionship, friendship, leadership, etc., are fulfilled by such institutions, but we shall ignore such needs here. Instead we shall discuss only those needs of management and labor which directly relate to their respective roles in industry.

The basic conflict, of course, is that managements "need" to produce goods for as low a labor cost as possible, while workers "need" to make as much money as possible. It is usually assumed that this conflict of interests underlies most industrial conflict. Certainly it is true that most settlements of industrial conflicts center around wages and hours of work. It seems rather clear, however, that this is too simple a picture of industrial conflict. On the management side, one very important need, which unions frustrate, is the *need for power* (see Chapter 3). To the extent to which unions succeed in enforcing their demands, they prevent management from exercising its power in an unrestricted way. Formerly, when it was respectable for management to attack unions indiscriminately, this motive was openly acknowledged. Today, the power motive is under cover and suspect, but it still operates.

On the employee side, there is a host of evidence which indicates that money is not the most important thing that an employee

gets from his job. We shall summarize this evidence later in Chapter 16, which deals with vocational adjustment. In general, it indicates that psychological factors are usually more important in employee morale than wages. In one study, workers in an electrical plant were singled out as experimental subjects. Various physical conditions of work, incentive plans, and other devices were tried out on them. Every innovation resulted in an increase in output. When conditions were returned to what they had been before the experiment started, once more output went up. The experimenters concluded that the crucial factor in the experiment was that the employees, knowing that they were being experimented on, felt that management was interested in what they did.[15] (This study is described in more detail in Chapter 16.)

Recognition of the importance of non-wage factors in job satisfaction has given rise to an applied science of human relations in industry (see Chapters 1 and 16). Practitioners of this science are concerned not only with the traditional problems of selection, placement, and promotion of personnel but also with worker morale, incentive-pay systems, methods of introducing technological or other changes, suggestion and complaint systems, and so on. The fundamental principle which underlies all work in this field is that the worker is a human being, with a great many needs, and that most of these needs must be satisfied in the job situation if he is to be happy and effective. Effective application of this science has resulted, in many places, in much better industrial relations and a reduction in the number of strikes.

It is now generally recognized that labor and management have many common interests. It is to management's interest to have a stable labor force; it is to labor's interest to have steady jobs. It is to man-

Fig. 14.7. Educational campaigns can teach people not to be prejudiced. (*New York State Commission against Discrimination photo.*)

agement's interest to have a supply of supervisors; it is to labor's interest to have a good promotion and training system. Both sides want a prosperous firm and industry, so high productivity is to the interest of both. Both sides suffer severely from strikes, so industrial peace is to the interest of both. Both sides can profit from a strong, responsible union which can represent and at the same time control the needs and dissatisfactions of its members. Both sides have now come to recognize that wage increases can be passed on to the consumer as higher prices without much danger of loss of sales. Hence higher wages, often producing increased employee satisfaction and more effective work, are to the interest of both sides—though not necessarily to the interests of the consumer.

Avoiding industrial conflict. How can industrial conflict be prevented? One study of social conflicts in a different situation (Japanese relocation centers) came out with a set of recommendations which seems especially pertinent to industrial conflicts.[16]

1. Look for all . . . types of stress, . . . frustration, incompatible desires, and uncertainty.

2. Never dismiss complaints as trivial.

3. Keep in mind that the strength of an administration rests largely on its ability to meet the needs of people; that relief from the various types of stress comprises a major set of needs; and that complaints are clues to needs.

4. Cultivate cooperation, but not extremes of compliance and dependence.

5. Regard extremes of withdrawal, apathy, and indifference as bad signs.

6. Consider aggression as a human reaction to circumstances; not merely as innate cussedness or the work of evil men, or a racial peculiarity.

7. Recognize rumors, suspicions, scapegoat tendencies . . . as symptoms of aggression arising out of stress.

8. Try to guide and control aggression, but do not try to stamp it out.

9. Capitalize on the feelings of relief and cooperativeness that are likely to occur after an outburst of aggression.

Underlying these recommendations is a fundamental principle: workers are people and must be treated as such on the job.

INTERNATIONAL CONFLICTS

Because wars and threats of wars are ever in the news and in our lives, nearly everyone has an opinion about their causes. Undoubtedly there are basic economic conflicts that can easily lead to war, and there are often historical injustices or results of previous wars that lead to more wars. The psychologist, however, should make statements only on the aspects of war that are within his field of study. These mostly concern prejudice—in this case, national prejudice—and the attitudes of people who are the victims of war.

National prejudice. Nationalism is one of the important psychological factors in war. Nationalism is a state of mind, *a set of attitudes held by numbers of people,* which is like any other prejudice we have discussed. In this case it is a prejudice against "foreigners" and other countries and includes a feeling that one's own country is superior in manners, morals, and way of life to those of other countries.

Like other kinds of prejudice, such national prejudice serves the needs of those who hold it. It increases and maintains one's feeling of status, it often has economic utility in favoring our own products over others, and it serves as an outlet for aggression. And nationalistic prejudice has the same deleterious effects as other prejudice. It makes us act in a superior way to other nationals, causing them to resent us. It keeps other nationals out of our country, restricts the entrance of their goods into our markets, and generally makes it more difficult for other countries to make their way in the world. It distorts our perception of events in other countries so that we are incapable of understanding fully the problems or even the behavior of other peoples.

Unfortunately, our leaders, in pursuing what they consider to be our national interests, often find it necessary to inflame prejudice rather than to assuage it. If a country's diplomats are engaged in tense negotiations with a foreign country, they attempt to make it seem to their people that their position is entirely righteous and that the opponent's is quite unjustified. The news releases are deliberately slanted to prejudice people in favor of their own side. In actual war, of course, propaganda is intensified to consolidate a nation behind its warriors fighting the "enemy." Almost invariably the enemy is pictured as a beast, oppressing occupied peoples, slaughtering innocent women and children, and taking people off to labor camps. Both sides use this kind of propaganda, regardless of the truth, and it is usually impossible to tell from listening or reading which, if either, is right. When victory is won and the war is over, the prejudices built up during the war do not always evaporate with the peace. Rather they may smolder on, sometimes for generations, and rise again to contribute to new wars.

Why men fight. We see, then, that from the psychological point of view, war involves the exercise of prejudice and of devices for influencing attitudes that we have already described in this and a previous chapter. We can also ask the question, though, What makes men fight, once their countries have gone to war? Those who are responsible for leading the fighters, and even the civilians, are very much concerned with this question.

The existence of draft laws makes it clear that men do not usually fight only because they believe in the cause for which they are fighting. This is confirmed by attitude studies. One study of combat veterans in the Second World War gave the results shown in Table 14.1. It seems that soldiers fight primarily because they want to get it over with and because they do not want to let their comrades down. Only 5 per cent report ideological motives. The answer seems to be, then, that soldiers fight because their governments are able, by both direct (legal) and indirect (propaganda) means, to make the cost of not fighting more severe than that of fighting. Another study makes it clear that even this kind of incentive evaporates under combat conditions. In a sample of infantry trainees, 50 per cent reported that they had thought at least once that the Second World War was not worth fighting, but this increased to 67 per cent of a sample of combat veterans. A number of other studies show that combat motivation evaporates as experience in combat increases. For example, combat veterans scored consistently lower than nonveterans in willingness for combat and confidence in combat stamina.[19]

EXPERIMENTAL SOCIAL CONFLICTS

We shall close this chapter with a brief discussion of two experiments that illustrate the possibility of bringing social conflicts into laboratory situations for careful study.

The Mintz experiment. One experiment[17] was so designed that subjects had to cooperate in order to do their task properly. A large bottle with a narrow neck was set up in such a way that it could be filled with water from the bottom. From the neck of the bottle protruded fifteen to twenty-one strings, and to each string was attached a cone inside the bottle. The cones were just large enough to pass through the neck of the bottle one by one. Consequently any attempt to pull two or more cones at the same time simply jammed them so that neither one could get through. The task for all subjects was to pull their cones out of the bottle within a given time limit or, in some experiments, before the cones were

TABLE 14.1. Combat incentives named by enlisted infantrymen. A division of infantry veterans who had fought in North Africa and Italy were surveyed in April, 1944, with the question, "Generally, in your combat experience, what was most important to you in making you want to keep going and do as well as you could?" The following is a classification, of the 568 replies.

Incentives	Per cent naming each incentive	
Ending the task	39	
Thoughts of getting the war over.		34
Thoughts of getting relief or rest.		5
Solidarity with the group	14	
Cannot let the other fellows or the outfit down; sticking together; "buddies depending on me"; "my friends around me."		
Sense of duty and self-respect	9	
Personal pride, self-respect.		7
"Doing my part, my duty."		2
Thoughts of home and loved ones	10	
Self-preservation;	6	
"kill or be killed."		
A job to be done;	5	
"somebody has to do the fighting."		
Idealistic reasons	5	
Making a better world; crushing aggressor; "belief in what I'm fighting for."		3
Patriotism, protecting our people and their freedom.		2
Vindictiveness;	2	
anger, revenge, "fighting spirit."		
Lack of any alternative action	2	
"There was nothing else to do"; "easier to keep going."		
Leadership and discipline	1	
Indifference	1	
"Too tired or mad to care"; "don't give a damn any more."		
Miscellaneous	6	

From Smith in Stouffer, S. A., et al. *The American Soldier:* Vol. II. *Combat and its aftermath.* Princeton, N.J.: Princeton Univ. Press., 1949. P. 109.

wetted by water pouring in at the bottom of the bottle.

When subjects were given instructions to cooperate with one another, or when they were just told to get their cones out of the bottle, they succeeded in doing so, with no traffic jams. But when small money rewards and fines were introduced, the subjects almost invariably produced traffic jams. This was true even of groups which had just solved the task under no-reward conditions. The conclusion is that, in situations in which cooperative behavior would be rewarding, it nevertheless is likely not to develop if the stakes are high, even though competitive behavior results in failure for everyone.

The Sherif experiment. A second study[18] comes as close to being an experimental war as anything in the psychological literature. A boy's camp was set up for the experiment. In the initial stage, all the boys were together. Later they were divided into two groups in such a way that all budding groups of friends were separated. In this way each group member initially preferred members of the other group to members of his own. Then the two groups were rela-

tively isolated from each other and encouraged to develop group activities and feelings of group solidarity. The counselors of each group did not suggest or encourage hostility against the other group; they merely permitted it. Next, the two groups were brought together in a series of athletic and other contests. Intense rivalry was developed, and each group accused the other of cheating and bad sportsmanship.

Matters came to a head when the counselors arranged what had been planned as the first of a series of frustrating situations in which each group could blame the other. The winners of the athletic rivalry were brought early to the dining hall, where refreshments were set out. Half the refreshments were in fine shape; the rest were crushed, mangled, and of inferior quality. Naturally, the first group to arrive took the good refreshments. When the second group arrived, it resented being left with poor refreshments. This precipitated a series of hostile acts including malicious destruction of property, raids by each group on the other's cabin, pelting a member of one group with green apples by all the members of the other group, and even the drawing

Fig. 14.8. Enmities overcome. Experiments with animals that are traditional enemies demonstrate that with training they can live together without conflict. (*Science Service.*)

and brandishing of a knife by one boy in a group altercation.

At this point, the experimenters called off the experiment and began using all the methods they could think of to restore peace and friendliness. They succeeded in stopping the more aggressive forms of hostility, but they never did get the two groups to like each other or even to choose willingly to play with each other.

From this lifelike experiment we can draw the same conclusions that we can draw from 100,000 years of human warfare. It is very easy to teach people to hate and to despise one another. People learn particularly easily to hate those who are not members of their own groups—outsiders, "foreigners." With little or no provocation people will fight those whom they hate with any weapons available and at considerable risk to their own welfare. Authority can prevent aggression, or channel it into acceptable kinds of expression, but once men have learned to hate, it is very difficult to teach them to love their enemies. In the light of these conclusions, it is easy to understand why we have not yet learned how to stop or prevent international conflict.

SUMMARY

1. Social conflicts represent an important problem in modern life. Psychologists seek to understand the principles that underlie such conflicts.

2. Research to date is largely concerned with the problem of racial conflicts. The same general principles, however, are also involved in industrial conflicts and international conflicts.

3. Racial conflict has its major roots in prejudice. Prejudice may be acquired either (*a*) by contact with the objects of prejudice or (*b*) by contact with others who have it. The second of these is by far the more important.

4. Once acquired, prejudice has considerable support in (*a*) the needs of an individual to find an outlet for hostility, and (*b*) alterations of perception, memory, and judgment that help preserve prejudice.

5. The principal consequence of prejudice is segregation and the unequal treatment that accompanies it.

6. Certain remedies for prejudice and its resulting racial conflict are suggested. They are, however, difficult to put into practice.

7. Social institutions, such as unions and nations, bind their members together in common interests and goals. Most institutions, in addition, have educational devices for obtaining unity and agreement. People in such institutions tend to think alike for this reason and also because they identify with other members of the group. Hence such institutions tend to increase the power of the group and to organize its energies in a common direction.

8. Leaders of social institutions often manufacture a common enemy to keep the group unified. This and other factors may lead to conflict be-

tween groups. Once started, conflicts between institutions tend to spread and are difficult to halt.

9. Industrial conflicts between union and management are partly caused by a natural conflict of interests. These are aggravated and exaggerated, however, by the organized character of the institutions.

10. On the other hand, there are many interests that labor and management have in common. Emphasizing these interests tends to reduce industrial conflict.

11. International conflicts are caused in part by conflicting national interests, but they are aggravated, as are other conflicts, by prejudice. National prejudice has the same causes, serves the same purposes, and can be alleviated in the same way as other prejudice.

12. Experimental studies of social conflict have been carried out. They demonstrate that it is relatively easy to produce conflict and difficult to eliminate it once it is started.

SUGGESTIONS FOR FURTHER READING

Allport, G. W. *The nature of prejudice.* Cambridge, Mass.: Addison-Wesley, 1954.

  A readable summary and analysis of the literature on group prejudice.

Bettelheim, B., and Janowitz, M. *Dynamics of prejudice: a psychological and sociological study of veterans.* New York: Harper, 1950.

  The report of an extensive study of the sources of prejudice in a group of gentile veterans.

Hartley, E. *Problems in prejudice.* New York: King's Crown, 1946.

  The account of a large-scale study of prejudice in students of six colleges.

Kisker, G. W. (Ed.). *World tension: the psychopathology of international relations.* New York: Prentice-Hall, 1951.

  A symposium on the problem of international tension written by twenty psychologists and psychiatrists representing different nations of the world.

Klineberg, O. *Social psychology* (Rev. Ed.). New York: Holt, 1954.

  A standard text on social psychology treating problems of prejudice.

Kornhauser, A., Dubin, R., and Ross, A. M. (Eds.). *Industrial conflict.* New York: McGraw-Hill, 1954.

  A survey of problems of industrial conflict written by social scientists in different fields.

Krech, D., and Crutchfield, R. S. *Theory and problems of social psychology.* New York: McGraw-Hill, 1948.

  A standard text on social psychology that treats the topics of prejudice and social conflict.

Tolman, E. C. *Drives toward war.* New York: Appleton-Century-Crofts, 1942.

  An analysis of the underlying causes of war as seen by an outstanding learning theorist.

PART 4

Abilities and Performance

Chapter 15   INTELLECTUAL ABILITIES

PEOPLE DIFFER from each other in a great many ways—in interests, abilities, motivations, personality, education, skills, and hobbies. Of all these, one of the most important is *abilities*. Most of us are accustomed to this idea and take it for granted. We know some people who are more intelligent than others; they can learn faster and solve problems more quickly than some of the rest of us. We know still others who are able musicians, carpenters, golfers, mechanics, and so on. Some people have many different abilities in large amounts, some have only one in high degree, and others seem to have been left out entirely when the abilities were passed out.

This chapter was drafted by Lawrence T. Alexander of the Rand Corporation and by Clifford T. Morgan of The Johns Hopkins University.

■ MEASURES OF ABILITIES

In the everyday world, many practical decisions about people are based on some estimate of their abilities. Parents send a child to take music lessons or to college because they think (and hope) that he has the ability to profit from such education. The employer hires the man whom he considers best able to do a job. The public vote for the politician they believe is most able to represent them. So, knowingly or not, we are forever making estimates of people's abilities. These estimates may be crude. They may be based on all too little information about a person. Hence they often turn out to be wrong. But we make them anyway.

Psychologists decided more than fifty years ago to see whether they could provide more accurate measures of human abilities.

375

In this effort, they were prodded first by educators and later by military leaders and businessmen who wanted more accurate measurement of abilities in order to make practical decisions about certain individuals. Today we have literally hundreds of tests of human abilities. Some of them are rather good, some are not so good, but nearly all are useful and better than subjective, everyday estimates of ability.

Tests as samples of tasks. The problem of measuring ability is first of all one of getting a fair *sample* of a person's performance in various tasks. Ability as a carpenter, college student, physician, or executive really consists of ability to do each of many tasks involved in the job. Ideally, then, if we want to measure a person's ability in one of these fields, we should follow him around with a notebook and some measuring equipment in order to determine how well he does each task he is supposed to do. Something like this is done occasionally in industrial situations, but it generally is much too expensive and impractical for large-scale use. Moreover, even if we could carry it out, each person has a somewhat different set of tasks to do, and it would be difficult to compare people on different tasks.

There still remains the problem of how to get a sample of tasks on which we can measure ability. The psychologist's way of solving this problem is *to select a series of tasks that seem to be fairly representative of the abilities to be measured. This sample of tasks makes up his test.* He then gives this test to different people in exactly the same way so that they all do the same tasks, in the same time limits, and under the same instructions. Thus he uses a *standardized test* to measure human abilities. It is important to realize, however, that such a test is really a sample of tasks. If it is a good sample, then it may measure the abilities

we are interested in; if it is not, then it is a poor measure. And no psychological test is a perfect sample; some are good, and some are not so good.

Interpretation of tests. Suppose now that we have a standardized test and give it to a person to measure his ability. We cannot interpret the score he gives us unless we know the score of many other people on the same test, for *in measuring abilities we are only interested in comparing people.** Ability is not like pounds and inches; it is a relative thing. It does us no good to know that John completed 83 questions on an intelligence test unless we are also told that the average number completed by other people is 60 and that fewer than 10 per cent of them completed more than 83 questions. With this information, we have a pretty good picture of how John rates in comparison with other people. Without it, a score of 83 is meaningless.

For this reason, an important step in devising a test is to give it to a large number of people. The group to which it is given is called a *standardization group*, and the various scores made by people in the group are called *test norms*. The test norms tell us what the average score is and also how much variability there is among scores. There are various ways of reporting such norms, and it does not make too much difference which way it is done, because the psychologist can readily convert from one form to another. This can be seen in Figure 15.1, which shows the relationship between different ways of reporting norms.

Figure 15.1 gives a distribution of scores made by a standardization group on a hypothetical test of ability. The scores range from 25 to 70. Below the scores are

---

* See the section on scales of measurement in Chap. 8. Test scores make ordinal scales. For this reason, they must be interpreted by being related to the performance of other people.

three scales. One shows the scores corresponding to 1σ and 2σ above and below the mean. (For a definition of σ, see page 199.) The next scale shows the percentage of persons scoring below any particular score. The last scale shows standard scores. To a person who understands it, the standard score is particularly useful because it indicates directly the relation of the individual score to the standardization group. In this case, the mean has a standard score of 50 and each 10 points in either direction represents a standard deviation.

To illustrate these scales, suppose that a person made a score of 59 on our hypothetical test. By consulting the test norms, we discover that this score is about 1.3σ above the mean, that it is a score as high or higher than 90 per cent of the standardization group made, and that it represents a standard score of 63. Test norms are expressed in any, and sometimes all, of these ways. Age norms are usually given when the test is to be used for people of heterogeneous ages. They are omitted if the test is to be used for a relatively homogeneous group, e.g., young adults. Norms may also be given for grades in school, occupational groups, or any other classification of individuals that may be relevant.

You should now have in mind the basic steps in measuring abilities. *First we must have a standardized test that measures something, then it must be given to a*

Fig. 15.1. Statistical descriptions of a hypothetical distribution of test scores made by a standardization group. At top is the frequency distribution of raw scores that a standardization group might make on a test. The mean of this distribution is 45; the standard deviation, 11. Raw scores may then be expressed in any of three ways: standard deviations, percentiles, or standard scores. In this case, to express them as standard scores, the mean has arbitrarily been set at 50 and the standard deviation at 10.

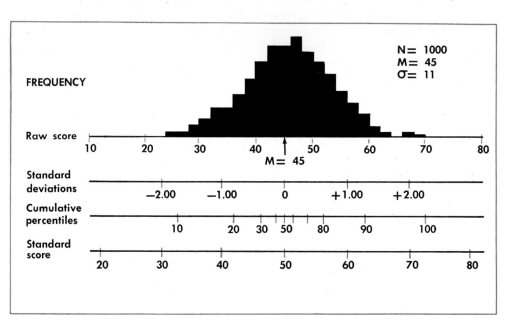

standardization group from which we obtain test norms, and then any person's score is compared with the test norms. One further point, however, is of importance. It concerns the standardization group. If our comparison of a person's score with test norms is to be a fair one, we must be careful to *know the characteristics of the standardization group.* Not any old group will do. If John is ten years old and we give him an intelligence test, it is not fair to use test norms from a standardization group of adults. The group should be boys of John's own age. If we give an intelligence test to a Negro who grew up on a farm in the South, it is not proper to use norms obtained from white people living in Northern cities. So to interpret test results accurately, we must make sure that our test norms represent the kind of people with whom it is proper to compare a person's score.

One should also bear in mind that the standardization group should be reasonably large—at least several hundred and preferably a few thousand. If the group is too small, norms may be too high or too low just as a matter of chance in the selection of people for the group.

Kinds of ability.   Now that it is clear what a test is and how we interpret it, it may occur to you to ask, "What abilities do people have that can be measured?" To this we can answer that there are a very large number of abilities—perhaps as many as there are different tasks that people perform in everyday life. Obviously, however, it is not practicable, nor would it be worthwhile, to try to measure all these specific abilities. Moreover, many tasks require certain common abilities. So psychologists restrict themselves to these relatively few common abilities.

The abilities they attempt to measure fall into two general groups. One is *intellectual ability* or aptitude for intellectual perform-ance. Tests that measure such ability are therefore considered as *intelligence tests.* Actually, intelligence tests measure several abilities, not just one, but these are the abilities that are needed in a wide variety of situations in life, and for convenience we lump them together as "intelligence." Secondly, there are *special abilities* that are required in specific occupations or activities —mechanical, clerical, arithmetic, musical, and artistic abilities, to name just a few. We have come to call tests of such special abilities *aptitude tests,* for we frequently use them to predict aptitude in some particular line of work or type of training. Hence we have two types of tests: intelligence tests and aptitude tests. In this chapter and the next one, we shall describe tests of these two types and summarize conclusions that psychologists have reached from using them.

■ INTELLIGENCE TESTS

There are now many tests of intelligence, and they differ in a number of ways. Some must be given by a trained tester to one person at a time, and these are *individual tests;* some may be given to groups of individuals by almost any person who can follow directions and has a stop watch, and these are *group tests.* Some tests give one overall score for intelligence, whereas others provide separate scores for different abilities. Some are designed for certain age groups, and some for other age groups. Some are designed for the mentally retarded, others for the especially intelligent; some for those who can read and write, others for those who cannot. And so on. Today there are thousands of tests and the testing business is a multimillion dollar industry.

Such a wide variety of tests may be confusing to you, if you have been accustomed to think of intelligence as a single "real" ability, as many people do. Why should we not have just one test of intelligence that "really" measures intelligence? Most tests of intelligence do, in fact, correlate reasonably well with one another, which means that they do tend to measure the same thing. Psychological research has made it clear, on the other hand, that there is more than one kind of intelligence—or that intelligence includes more than one ability. For this reason, what test of intelligence we use depends on what we want to find out. If we want to measure the kind of intelligence involved in going to school, we use one test; if we are interested in the kind involved in military life, we use another; and if it is intelligence useful in general business life, there are other tests to use.

The Stanford-Binet test. The first test of intelligence to be devised was intended for use in school situations and thus stressed the abilities involved in primary education. This test was published by Alfred Binet, a French psychologist, in 1905. Binet designed the test at the request of the Paris school authorities to enable them to pick out children of low intelligence who could not profit from attending school. The test served its purpose and immediately caught the attention of American psychologists. In 1916, Terman of Stanford University brought out a revision of it intended for school children in the United States, and his revision came to be known as the Stanford-Binet test.[1] It became the model for many intelligence tests that have been developed since then. For this reason and because the now familiar IQ, or intelligence quotient, is derived from it, we can learn a good deal about intelligence tests by examining it more closely.

▪ *Mental age.* The Stanford-Binet test, which is an individual test, is used with children from two to sixteen years of age. It consists of a series of subtests arranged according to age levels, that is, according to

Fig. 15.2. Individual intelligence testing. Above, the child is taking a bead-stringing item on the Stanford-Binet test. Her task is to string the beads so that they match the example she is looking at. Below, the boy's task is to place each form in its proper place on the board. This task is used in some nonverbal intelligence tests when a language handicap or unfamiliarity with English indicates that the Stanford-Binet might not be a fair test. (Brooks from Monkmeyer, New York City Board of Education.)

what children of each age can be expected, from test norms, to be able to pass. There are subtests for two-year-olds, others for three-year-olds, and so on. A child being tested is given the subtests in order until he reaches a point where he can pass none of the tests for a particular age level. When the results are tallied, the score he gets tells his *mental age* (MA for short). For example, if a child passed all the tests for age four, half those at age five, and none of those for age six, the child's mental age would be four and a half. Usually the picture is not so simple as that, but this is the principle for computing mental age.

Table 15.1 presents some of the tests from the Stanford-Binet test. Notice what kinds of abilities are tested at various age levels. In the lower age levels, the tests stress *information about objects, pictures, and parts of the body,* as well as *the perception of forms.* In the higher age brackets, the tests stress more *the use of words and numbers in reasoning problems.* At all age levels, there are *tests of vocabulary, correct use of words,* and *the span of memory,* because these represent the more general aspects of intellectual ability.

A child's mental ability obviously increases as he grows older. When we test him at a certain age and obtain a mental-age score, we know merely the level of his ability at that age. On the average, we would expect a child's mental age to increase at the same rate as his chronological age (CA). Indeed, test norms have been

TABLE 15.1. Some illustrative items from the Stanford-Binet test. The sample items below should be passed, on the average, at the ages indicated.

Age	Type of item	Example or description
2	Three-hole form board	Places form (e.g., circle) in correct hole
	Block building	Builds tower from model after demonstration
3	Identifying parts of the body	Points out hair, mouth, etc., on large paper doll
4	Naming objects from memory	One of three objects (e.g., toy dog or shoe) is covered after child has seen them but is not looking; child must then name object from memory.
	Picture identification	Points to correct pictures of objects on a card when asked, "Show me what we cook on," or "What do we carry when it is raining?"
7	Similarities	Answers such questions as, "In what way are coal and wood alike? Ship and automobile?"
	Copying a diamond	Copies a diamond in the record booklet
8	Vocabulary	Defines eight words from a list
	Memory for stories	Listens to a story, then repeats the gist of it.
9	Verbal absurdities	"I saw a well-dressed young man who was walking down the street with his hands in his pockets and twirling a brand new cane. What is foolish about that?"
	Digit reversal	Must repeat five digits backward
Average adult	Vocabulary	Defines twenty words from a list
	Proverbs	Explains in own words the meaning of two or more common proverbs
	Orientation	"Which direction would you have to face so your right hand would be toward the north?"

Selected from Terman, L. M., & Merrill, M. A. *Measuring intelligence.* Boston: Houghton Mifflin, 1937.

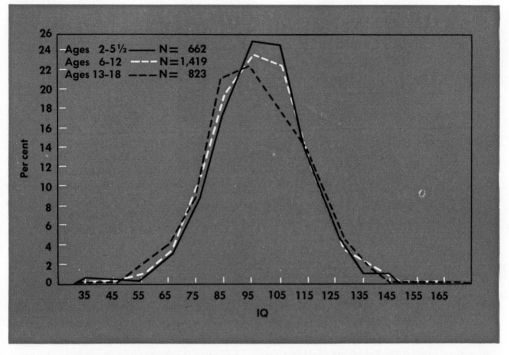

Fig. 15.3. The distribution of IQs for different age groups. Both the means and the variabilities (σ's) of distributions of IQs are approximately the same for different age groups. For this and other reasons, a person's IQ tends to remain constant at different ages. (*After Terman, L. M., & Merrill, M. A. Measuring intelligence. Boston: Houghton Mifflin, 1937, p. 41.*)

established so that it could hardly be otherwise. The bright child, on the other hand, should show a more rapid increase in mental ability, so that his mental age would be greater than his chronological age. The reverse would be true of the dull child.

■ *Intelligence quotient.* This brings us to the idea that relative intelligence is a ratio between mental age and chronological age. If the two children both score an MA of 5 years on the intelligence test, but one is only four years old and the other is five, obviously the younger child is the brighter —in fact, much the brighter—of the two. To express this kind of difference and to do it precisely with numbers, we have the concept of the intelligence quotient (IQ). *The IQ is a ratio of mental age* (MA) *to*

chronological age (CA), *multiplied by 100* to avoid the inconvenience of decimals. The formula is

$$IQ = \frac{\text{mental age}}{\text{chronological age}} \times 100 = \frac{MA}{CA} \times 100$$

Looked at in this way, you can see that the IQ is a rate of mental development. It shows how fast a child's abilities are growing in relation to his chronological age. Applying the IQ formula to the two children mentioned above, we find that the brighter one has an IQ of 125 and the other an IQ of 100.

The IQ is a convenient yardstick of mental ability relative to age, because it enables one to compare children of different ages even though they have different mental ages and pass subtests that are quite differ-

Fig. 15.4. The Wechsler-Bellevue Test for Adults. A veteran (*left*) takes a block-design item and (*right*) an object-assembly item on the Wechsler-Bellevue Test for Adults. (*New York University Testing and Advisement Center.*)

ent in difficulty. Great care had to be taken in selecting subtests and in establishing age norms to make this possible. In fact, *the test was so constructed that the distribution of IQs is substantially the same at all age groups.* Hence it is possible to say that a child of thirteen who has an IQ of 125 and a child of five who has the same IQ are equally bright. Both, in fact, are rather bright, for only about 5 per cent of children have an IQ that high or higher.

The tests of the Stanford-Binet are arranged so that if a person of a certain chronological age passes all the tests at that level he will have an IQ of 100. The distribution of IQs of the group upon which the Binet scale was standardized is also shown in Figure 15.3.

▪ *Limitations of the test.* The Binet test is an excellent instrument for doing what it was designed to do. It has many practical uses, some of which we will examine a little later. However, it also has some limitations. For one, it puts heavy *stress upon verbal ability.* The directions are given orally for the most part, and many of the subtests require the use of words. If the test were

given to a person who for some reason had language difficulties, we should not get an accurate picture of his mental development. Second, the test must be *administered to one individual at a time* and by testers who are highly trained in its use, because, among other things, there are many props that go along with the test. This makes it inconvenient to use when large groups must be tested in a hurry or when trained testers are not available. It gives a score which is indicative of over-all or general mental development, but it does not provide an adequate picture of differential development of various kinds of intellectual abilities. This is an important problem in research on basic mental abilities and is often very important in establishing a diagnosis of mental illness.

Besides these limitations that we have just mentioned, there is the further fact that the Binet is not a good test to use for testing older adolescents or adults. This is because the kind of intellectual performance represented by the concept of mental age does not show any consistent increase beyond the age of sixteen. So far as the Binet

is concerned, mental age reaches a plateau at that point. You can see that this causes trouble in figuring the IQ of a person over sixteen years of age. There is an arithmetic device for getting around this trouble—in Binet scoring you simply assume that any person older than sixteen is only sixteen—but it is much better to use a test specifically designed for adults.

Wechsler-Bellevue Test for Adults. The most widely used test for adults is the Wechsler-Bellevue, developed by Dr. David Wechsler of the Bellevue Psychiatric Hospital, New York.[2] This test, like the Stanford-Binet, is an individual test requiring many props and expert testers for its use. Also, like the Stanford-Binet, it is made up of a wide variety of subtests, many of which are *verbal* and deal with *general information, comprehension, arithmetic, memory for digits,* and *vocabulary.* Many of its other subtests, however, are *performance tests* that do not depend greatly on language or verbal ability. Unlike the

Stanford-Binet, the Wechsler-Bellevue can be scored to separate the verbal and performance tests and give separate IQs on each. This feature is often helpful in testing people of foreign background or of poor education who have not had a fair opportunity to develop their verbal abilities. Such people often do better on performance tests than on verbal tests. It is also helpful in testing the brain-injured or the mentally ill because it sometimes makes clearer just where a person's trouble lies. In general, though, there is good agreement between the Stanford-Binet and the Wechsler-Bellevue. The correlation between the full scales of both tests has been reported as .86; between the Stanford-Binet and the verbal scale, .80; and between the Stanford-Binet and the performance scale, .67. (For the meaning of these coefficients, see Chapter 8.) Since offering the Wechsler-Bellevue Test for Adults, Dr. Wechsler has also developed the Wechsler Intelligence Scale for Children.[3]

Group tests of intelligence. In hospitals and schools, where intelligence testing is usually only part of the handling of an individual's problem, it is convenient to use individual tests of intelligence. In these situations, too, expert personnel, specifically trained in the administration of tests, are frequently available to give the Stanford-Binet, Wechsler-Bellevue, or some other individual test. There are many situations, however, for which a group test is either desirable or absolutely essential. One of these is the military situation in which large groups, adding up to hundreds of thousands each year, need to be tested. Another is the mass testing of students entering colleges or other higher schools. Group tests have been devised to meet such needs.

The First World War furnished the impetus for the first large-scale effort to develop group tests. Hundreds of thousands of young men were being inducted into the service. We needed some quick method for weeding out the mentally unfit and for selecting the most able for officer training. Finally, to utilize manpower effectively, it was desirable to assign people to different battalions and technical training schools according to their abilities.

Psychologists met these needs in the First World War by devising the Army Alpha Test. This yielded scores for classifying men roughly according to intelligence. In the problems in Table 15.2 you see some examples of the materials of this test. Between the two wars, the Army Alpha was frequently revised for use with both servicemen and civilians. Then when the Second World War came along, Army psychologists took advantage of extensive research in mental testing to make a more drastic revision, which they named the Army General Classification Test (AGCT). This was given to several million servicemen upon induction into the armed forces. It was prepared in four different forms, which could be interchanged with one another, each form requiring about an hour to give. In addition, longer forms of the test were devised to break down a person's performance into four different categories: (1) *verbal ability,* (2) *spatial comprehension,* (3) *arithmetic computation,* and (4) *arithmetic reasoning.* The AGCT, like the Stanford-Binet, is so

TABLE 15.2   Some sample items from the Army Alpha Test.

A. If 5½ tons of bark cost $33, what will 3½ cost?   (   )

B. A train is harder to stop than an automobile because
   (   ) it is longer,   (   ) it is heavier,   (   ) the brakes are not so good

C. If the two words of a pair mean the same or nearly the same thing, draw a line under *same*. If they mean the opposite or nearly the opposite, draw a line under *opposite*.

comprehensive	restricted	same	opposite
allure	attract	same	opposite
latent	hidden	same	opposite
deride	ridicule	same	opposite

D. If, when you have arranged the following words to make a sentence, the sentence is true, underline *true*; if it is false, underline *false*.

people enemies arrogant many make	true	false
never who heedless those stumble are	true	false
never man the show the deeds	true	false

E. The pitcher has an important place in—tennis   football   baseball   handball
   Underline which

F. Dismal is to dark as cheerful is to—laugh   bright   house   gloomy
   Underline which

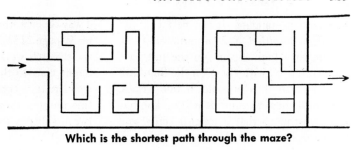

Which is the shortest path through the maze?

Fig. 15.5. Items from the Army Beta Test used during the First World War. The Beta Test was used with illiterates and others for whom the Alpha was an unfair test. (*By permission of the National Academy of Science.*)

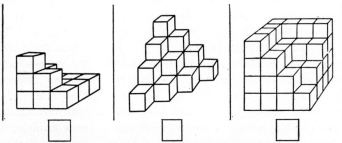

How many cubes in each pile? Write number in appropriate square.

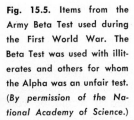

Complete the series.

scored that the average person is assigned 100. For purposes of rough classification, the Army divided people into five groups according to score. In Figure 15.6 you can see the limiting scores for each group and the percentage of testees found in each group. The spread or distribution is much like that on individual tests of intelligence, but the AGCT score and the IQ are not exactly comparable. The Navy developed and used a similar GCT, with this difference: Navy tests have an average of 50.

After the First World War, several group tests were devised for use with civilians—primarily to help in selecting people for jobs in business and industry (see Chapter 16). One of the best known of these tests is the Otis Self-administering Test of Mental Ability (Otis S.A.). This is a short four-page pencil-and-paper test that can be administered simply with a stop watch and under testing conditions that are relatively

Fig. 15.6. On the lower abscissa are scores obtained by multiplying x/σ by a constant (see Chap. 8). On the upper abscissa are equivalent IQs obtained, in this case, by taking .9 of the deviation from 100. In Roman numerals are the five groups used by the Army for rough classification of testees. The percentages indicate the relative numbers falling in each of the groups. Navy (NGCT) scores are exactly half the AGCT scores.

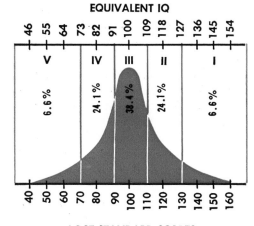

EQUIVALENT IQ

AGCT STANDARD SCORES

easy to keep standard. It can be taken and scored with either a 20-minute or a 30-minute time limit. Scores on the test have been correlated with those on the Stanford-Binet so that it is possible, if one wishes, to convert them to equivalent IQs. The test is so constructed that *it weights verbal and reasoning factors* but does not sample performance factors very well.

There are a number of other tests, used in connection with higher education, that follow the general pattern of the group tests of intelligence. There is one prepared under the sponsorship of the American Council on Education (called the A.C.E. test) which the majority of college students take upon entering college. A similar one is now being used by Selective Service as a basis for the deferment of students in colleges. There are others for use at a more advanced level for students seeking entrance to medical and graduate schools. Since these latter tests are designed for the fairly specific purpose of predicting success in a particular kind of education, they have more of the earmarks of aptitude tests than of general intelligence tests, and we shall consider them in the next chapter under the heading of aptitudes.

The nature of intelligence. It seems natural to think of intelligence as one ability or attribute. We think of Mary as being "bright" and John as being "dumb." These are single labels we apply to a person. Seldom do we think of Mary as being bright in school, but very dumb in other ways—that is, that there are different kinds of intelligence. The fact that most of our tests of intelligence produce one over-all score or IQ further shapes our thinking about intelligence as a unitary thing. Is there a general intelligence as distinguished from specific abilities, or is there just a collection of abilities? What is intelligence actually?

The method of factor analysis furnishes a way of answering this question (see Chapter 9, page 215). To perform a factor analysis, research workers give a good many different tests to the same people to see how well the tests correlate with each other. For this purpose they compute correlations between subtests or individual items on tests, not just the over-all scores, in order to isolate, as best they can, the elements of intelligence. Having a lot of correlations, they then proceed, by statistical analysis, to see which items form clusters and which ones are independent of each other. It may turn out, for example, that all sorts of subtests that have to do with words may correlate with one another but not with other subtests involving numbers. In this way, they isolate *factors* in a number of tests, and in the example just cited it would be concluded that there is a verbal factor that is relatively separate from a numerical factor.

There has been a great amount of research of this kind. Each investigator obtains somewhat different results, depending on the tests he uses and the sample of people he gives them to. Various researches agree, however, in yielding *a number of different factors in intelligence*. The most extensive studies in the United States were carried out by Thurstone.[4] When he had finished an elaborate factor analysis of dozens of tests given to school children, he emerged with seven factors. Each factor represents a cluster of correlations between subtests and thus what is common to them. His seven factors are named and described as follows:

1. *Verbal comprehension* (V)—ability to define and understand words

2. *Word fluency* (W)—ability to think rapidly of words as in extemporaneous speech or solving crossword puzzles

3. *Number* (N)—ability to do arithmetic problems

4. *Space* (S)—ability to draw a design

from memory or to visualize relationships

5. *Memory* (M)—ability to memorize and recall

6. *Perceptual* (P)—ability to grasp visual details and to see differences and similarities among objects

7. *Reasoning* (R)—ability to find rules, principles, or concepts for understanding or solving problems

In the course of discovering these factors, Thurstone could identify the subtests that represented each factor, for he knew which subtests were correlated and which were not. This fact enabled him to devise tests that would measure each factor as independently as possible. To do this, he rearranged his subtests, grouping together those that represented the same factor. Actually, in many instances, he tried to improve on this technique by devising new subtests that seemed to be good measures of the factors he had discovered. Now with a new set of tests, called tests of *primary mental abilities*, he could come to grips with the question whether there is any such thing as general intelligence. Because he had obtained seven factors, he concluded that intelligence is partly made up of separate abilities. The question was whether there is a general factor, apart from the specific ones.

To settle this problem, he obtained scores on each of the tests of primary mental abilities from a large group of children, and intercorrelated these scores with one another. If there were no such thing as general intelligence, each factor measured by a test should be independent of every other, and there should be no correlations among them. The different tests *are*, in fact, *correlated*, some relatively highly and some not so much. But the correlations indicate that there is some general ability that is common to all the tests of primary ability. He therefore came to the conclusion that "each of

the primary factors can be regarded as a composite of an independent primary factor and a general factor which it shares with other primary factors." The answer then to our original question—What is intelligence?—is that *it is both some general ability and a number of specific abilities.*

Interpretation of tests. This conclusion must have considerable bearing on the interpretation of intelligence tests. Though each intelligence test may measure "general intelligence" in some degree and thus measure in part what other intelligence tests are measuring, it also reflects its own particular sample of specific abilities. None of the individual or group tests of intelligence now in common use measures these specific abilities in equal degree. Some weight several abilities more heavily than they weight others. Actually most intelligence tests, particularly the Stanford-Binet and the Otis, are heavily weighted with verbal content. In the case of the Stanford-Binet, this came about because achievement in school, which is a rather verbal matter, was used as a criterion for selecting many of the items on the test. Group tests like the Otis are weighted by verbal and numerical ability partly because it is much easier to make up tests of these abilities than it is of other abilities. In any event, the fact is that such abilities are given greater weight. In making interpretations about individuals' abilities from an intelligence test, this fact must be kept in mind.

Another important thing to remember about intelligence tests is that *they measure present ability, not native capacity.* People have different opportunities to acquire their present abilities. Poor people do not have the same cultural and educational opportunities as those who are financially more fortunate. Moreover, many of the problems used in intelligence tests have a cultural background. If problems concern such

TABLE 15.3. Distribution of intelligence quotients on the revised Stanford-Binet test of intelligence.

IQ	Verbal description	Per cent of children
Above 140	Very superior	1
120–139	Superior	11
110–119	High average	18
90–109	Average	46
80–89	Low average	15
70–79	Borderline	6
Below 70	Mental defective	3
		100

From the data of Merrill, M. A. The significance of IQ's on the revised Stanford-Binet scales. *J. educ. Psychol.*, 1938, 29, 641–651.

things as apples, organs, automobiles, baseball, and trains, then a person who grew up in a culture without these things is certainly going to be handicapped, even if his native capacity is as good or better than average. Growing up in one culture or country thus handicaps a person on intelligence tests devised for the people in some other culture. Those who devise tests try to make their items as free of such influences as possible, but *no one has yet succeeded in making a completely culture-free test of intelligence.* Thus tests assume a relatively common background of culture and education. Whenever a person has not had this background or is deficient in it, it is not sensible to take his results on an intelligence test as comparable to those of other persons who have the common background. Consequently, intelligence tests are usually not suitable instruments for comparing the abilities of different races and cultural groups.

EXTREMES OF INTELLIGENCE

In Figure 15.3 we presented the distribution of Stanford-Binet IQs to be found in the general United States population. In Table 15.3 we have reproduced these data in a slightly different form to show you

more precisely what proportions of children fall within certain limits of IQ. All the scores have been arbitrarily grouped into seven categories: below 70, 70–79, 80–89, 90–109, 110–119, 120–139, and above 140. For convenience, each of these arbitrary categories has been given a characteristic name such as *normal, superior,* etc. As we shall see a little later, there are certain predictions we can make about the educational and occupational successes of each of the groups. The two extreme groups, however —namely, those below 70 and those above 140—represent special problems in our society.

Feeble-mindedness. Those who have Stanford-Binet IQs of less than 70 are regarded as *mentally deficient.* On the basis of intelligence tests, we find that there are approximately 3 per cent of the population in this category. It has been the custom to further subdivide mentally deficient individuals into three groups:

1. *Morons,* IQ 50–70
2. *Imbeciles,* IQ 20–50
3. *Idiots,* IQ below 20

If you remember that the IQ is really a ratio of mental age to chronological age and that mental growth, as measured by the Stanford-Binet test, comes to a stop at about sixteen years of age, you can easily figure out the limits of mental age for these three groups. The moron's ultimate mental age is 8 to 12 years; that of the imbecile, 3 to 7 years; and that of the idiot, below 3 (see Table 15.4).

Knowing these limits of mental growth for the mentally deficient, you can fill in for yourself what we know to be the capacities of the deficient. The *idiot* will, at best, be much like a three-year-old all through life. He will never talk very well. The chances are he will be unable to master some aspects of dressing such as buttoning his clothes or tying his shoes. He can never be trusted to keep himself out of danger. He will not be able to master the simplest tasks at school or at work. The *imbecile*, even as an adult, will be something like the first- or second-grade child, who can talk fairly well, clothe himself, and learn simple skills but is not able to profit much from training in the higher school grades. The *moron* does somewhat better and may eventually finish four to eight school grades. He can learn to read and write with difficulty, and may be able to learn simple occupations and to look after his personal needs.

• *Social maturity*. These descriptions of the intellectual level of the mentally deficient, however, are not a fair account of their abilities. We must remember that the Stanford-Binet IQ tends to weight verbal factors that are especially important in educational success but not always so important in other, more mundane daily affairs. If one studies closely the behavior of high-grade morons with IQs, say, of 65 to 70, one can see rather wide individual differences among them. Some can take care of themselves much better than others. In work and social situations, some seem much more intelligent than others.

For this reason one psychologist has gone to the trouble of devising another scale, the Vineland Social Maturity Scale, which weights *social* and *vocational* intelligence somewhat more than it does *verbal* intelligence.[5] This scale yields a *social age* (SA) which is comparable to the mental age (MA) of the Stanford-Binet test. As its name implies, this scale takes various social abilities as its standard of comparison: *eating with a spoon, washing one's face unaided, being trusted with money, being able to find one's way home*, etc. By checking a child on such items, you can assign a social age to each child in much the same way that a mental age is assigned.

Because the Stanford-Binet and the Vine-

TABLE 15.4. Intelligence and social-maturity levels of the feeble-minded.

	Moron	Imbecile	Idiot
Intelligence quotient	50–70	20–50	Below 20
Maximum mental age	8–12	3–7	Below 3
Age of intellectual maturity	15	10–12	6–8
Maximum social age	10–18	4–9	Below 4
Age of social maturity	20	15	10

Modified from Hilgard, E. R. *Introduction to psychology.* New York: Harcourt, Brace, 1953.

land scales measure different things, it is not surprising that they do not correlate perfectly. In general, the ultimate social age of the mentally deficient is higher than the comparable mental age (see Table 15.4). For the *moron*, it is 10 to 18 years; for the *imbecile*, 4 to 9; and for the *idiot*, something below 4. Moreover, social development usually continues for a somewhat longer period than does mental growth (as tested by the Stanford-Binet).

This difference between social age and mental age has led psychologists to make a distinction between *mental deficiency* and *feeble-mindedness*. Mental deficiency is defined in terms of intelligence-test scores. *Feeble-mindedness*, however, *is a more general term referring to the person's over-all ability to take care of himself and to make an adjustment in the world.* It therefore includes both the mental and social development of the person. In many instances there is a real difference between the two. Moreover, since social development is usually greater than mental development in the feeble-minded, the person's plight is not as bad as it might seem from the IQ score alone.

• *Treatment of feeble-mindedness.* Feeble-mindedness is obviously a problem of some proportions in our society. Hundreds of thousands of feeble-minded children and adults are regularly lodged in special institutions throughout the country. Thousands more are living at home, constituting a burden to their family and friends. All are handicapped in the work they can do and in the kinds of lives they can lead. What can be done about feeble-mindedness?

Well-educated parents who are confronted with the fact that their child is feeble-minded are likely to think that something can be done to raise the child's IQ. Some dramatic stories in the newspapers or magazines sometimes give this impression, because they seem to show that it is possible to do much with a feeble-minded child. This possibility has been carefully investigated in several psychological studies and the evidence unfortunately is against it.[6] Special training produces slight changes in IQ and in social intelligence, but seldom does anything very dramatic occur (for an exception, see the discussion of cretinism in Chapter 22). Feeble-mindedness in most cases is probably a matter of capacity, and there is little one can do to alter the mental and social capacity of the defective child. People usually only deceive themselves if they think otherwise.

There is much that can be done, on the other hand, to make the most of the feeble-minded's limited capacity. Most feeble-minded are high-grade morons (about 60 per cent) and a minority are the low-grade idiots (about 10 per cent). Whatever the grade, the training may be long and tedious, but it is worth the effort if it is relative to the capacity of the child. Gradually he can be taught some of the social skills, such as washing himself, helping with duties around the house, and doing many minor tasks that keep him from being such a burden to others. If his defect is not too severe, he can be taught some vocational skills, such as woodworking, printing, and weaving. The better institutions for the feeble-minded have facilities and teachers for training in

these social and occupational skills, and each year they return to society several thousand individuals who are capable of earning a living and looking after themselves reasonably well.

▪ *Causes of feeble-mindedness.* It may occur to some that we might try to find "cures" for feeble-mindedness. Research workers have indeed expended a great deal of effort in this direction, and the search continues (see Chapter 22). The possibility of finding "cures," of course, depends upon the causes of feeble-mindedness. Although these are now partly understood, we have much more to learn about them.

Just as there are functional and organic psychoses (see Chapter 10), there are two general classes of feeble-mindedness. One corresponds to the functional and is called *primary or familial feeble-mindedness.* In this case, we can find no organic defect, no evidence of injury or disease that might have caused the feeble-mindedness. The person seems quite sound in every respect except for his intellectual deficit. In such cases, we usually find some record of feeble-mindedness occurring in other members of the family, and that is why it is often called familial. Intelligence is probably to some extent inherited (see below), and we should expect that those with low intelligence, both intellectual and social, would tend to have offspring of low intelligence.

Other instances of feeble-mindedness are caused by some kind of biological defect, and these are called *secondary feeble-mindedness.* In some cases the brain of a baby suffers a severe shortage of oxygen during pregnancy, and this may account for feeble-mindedness. In others, the child's brain is injured at birth because of some difficulty in delivery. In still others, something is wrong chemically with the reactions going on in the brain (see Chapter 22). In few of these cases of secondary feeble-mindedness have we yet found any surgery, drugs, or other agents that might be used to cure or alleviate the condition. Research, however, continues to press for answers to this problem, and it is possible, though not very likely, that we shall find, before too many years, methods by which both primary and secondary feeble-mindedness may be helped.

The mentally gifted. At the top end of the distribution of IQs are the superior (120–140) and the very superior (above 140). It is interesting to see what role these play in society and what their problems are —and they do have unique problems. Psychologists have studied the very gifted in three ways: (1) by estimating the intelligence of gifted people who have lived years ago, (2) by following the accomplishments of gifted children into adulthood, and (3) through studying the problems of very bright children in school.

■ *Gifted leaders and writers.* There is enough recorded about the lives of people who have been prominent in history to make fairly reliable estimates of what their IQs would have been if they had lived in a day when they could have taken the Stanford-Binet test.[7] If we know at what age a child began to read, when he used certain words in his vocabulary, when he mastered certain problems in arithmetic, etc., we can match these accomplishments with the standards of the Binet test. This sort of thing has been done for a long list of people. In Table 15.5 are their names and estimated IQs. Not all the great men of history are in this list, for we do not have enough biographical data for them. Still, it is quite plain that men who have contributed much to our literature and to our civilization are also endowed with very high intellectual abilities.

■ *Terman's gifted children.* Even more informative is a monumental study con-

TABLE 15.5. The IQs of some eminent men estimated from biographical data.

John Quincy Adams	165	David Hume	155
Francis Bacon	145	Thomas Jefferson	145
Samuel Taylor Cole-		Gottfried Wilhelm	
ridge	175	Von Leibnitz	185
René Descartes	150	John Stuart Mill	190
Charles Dickens	145	John Milton	145
Benjamin Franklin	145	Wolfgang Amadeus	
Johann Wolfgang		Mozart	150
Von Goethe	185	Alfred Tennyson	155
George Frederick		Daniel Webster	145
Handel	145	William Wordsworth	150

Based on Cox, C. M. *Genetic studies of genius.* Vol. II. Stanford, Calif.: Stanford Univ. Press, 1926.

ducted over a period of 25 years by Terman, the author of the Stanford-Binet test. Terman and his associates, having tested many thousands of children, picked out for further study a group of more than 1,500 who had IQs of 140 or more.[8] These were the highest 1 per cent of the children. He has been able to follow most of these children into their adulthood and many of them are now in middle life. Periodically he sends them questionnaires or otherwise finds out what they are doing, and thus he has built up a very detailed picture of their achievements.

One interesting thing about them is the homes they came from. About a third were the children of professional people, about half came from homes of the higher business classes, and only a small proportion (7 per cent) came from the working classes.

This is quite out of proportion to the numbers of people in each of these classes, and indicates that relatively more gifted children come from the higher socioeconomic classes (see Chapter 12). This fact is undoubtedly accounted for by both heredity and environment. These classes can provide a better environment for the development of intellectual abilities, and be-

Fig. 15.7. Gifted children may be encouraged to participate in special educational projects. In some school systems, children may be relieved of the boredom of regular education and have their talents developed by working on such special projects as typewriting and painting. (New York City Board of Education.)

cause the more successful people tend to be the more gifted, they also pass on their gifts through heredity.

The later success, in fact, of Terman's gifted children is a second striking discovery of his studies. About 700 people of the original study could be contacted 25 years later. Of these, about 150 were very successful as judged by such criteria as (1) being listed in *Who's Who* or *American Men of Science,* (2) holding responsible managerial positions, or (3) receiving recognition for outstanding intellectual or professional achievement. Most of the others were less outstanding but still much more successful than people of average intelligence. On the other hand, there were some who certainly

were not very successful—some who had committed crimes, some who dropped out of school early, and some who were distinctly vocational misfits and had been unsuccessful at a number of jobs. Careful comparisons of those who were very successful with those who were least successful showed that factors in personality made the difference. The least successful were more poorly adjusted emotionally and more poorly motivated to succeed. Despite the exceptions, the most striking fact was that children of superior ability generally made such an outstanding record of social and intellectual achievement.

Contrary to some common misconceptions about the genius, Terman's gifted children were above average in height, weight, and physical appearance. They also were generally better adjusted and more socially adaptable, and they had more capacity for leadership than average children. Thus Terman disproved the notion that the genius is likely to be peculiar, unadjusted, and socially backward. Some geniuses, of course, are like that—and so are some average people—but in general geniuses are less so than those of average intellectual ability.

■ *Problems of the gifted.* What we have said is true despite the many difficulties that a gifted child faces. Because he is brighter, he is more likely to be bored by children of his own age, more likely to seek the company of older children and adults and to pester them with intellectual questions. In public schools, which have been designed for the average child, his problem is acute because his intellectual ability and performance usually far exceed those of other children of the same age and in the same classroom. Moreover, he usually is being taught by a teacher who is far from a genius and often is unable to match either the child's knowledge or his problem-solving ability.

Teachers, faced with a child of extremely high ability, are likely to consider him fresh, smart-alecky, and a show-off and hence often treat him harshly. The very bright child often finds the pace of normal education so slow and easy that he becomes bored and loses interest in the activities of the classroom. Then he may become a personality problem and a real annoyance for the schoolteacher. Public schools, today, are usually somewhat sophisticated about the problems of the gifted child. The better ones find out early what a child's IQ is and try to include an appropriate program for the gifted child. In some instances, the gifted children are put in special classes by themselves in which they can achieve more and be given tasks commensurate with their abilities. In other instances, special additional activities are planned for the gifted child.

GROUP DIFFERENCES IN ABILITIES

Everyday thinking is colored by notions about the abilities of different *groups* of people. Many think that the Negroes and foreigners are not so intelligent as white Americans. We regard older people as much wiser than, if not as quick as, younger people. Employers think women and young people more suitable for certain positions, men and older people for other jobs. We think of people who come from "good families" of the upper socioeconomic strata as being more able than those who come from the working classes.

Psychological research, indeed, indicates that there are differences among various groups of people, but these differences are often not the same ones that the layman imagines or as great as he may think.[9] In other chapters (Chapters 12 and 13), we have described differences in culture and in attitudes. Here let us see what the facts are about differences in intellectual abilities.

Differences between men and women. In our society there is a division of labor between the sexes. Men are expected to earn a living, and women are expected to care for the home—though that pattern has been changing in the last generation. In other cultures, the economic roles of the sexes are sometimes reversed. This fact alone should make us skeptical of large inherited differences in capacities between men and women. On the other hand, there is the fact that most of the leaders in the arts and sciences and in business and industry have been men. The eminent woman is the exception rather than the rule. May we assume from this that men are more intelligent than women? Since psychologists have administered thousands of intelligence tests to both men and women, it is easy to answer this question quantitatively.

▪ *Abilities of women.* Women have a reputation for their ability to talk, and they deserve it. Girls, on the average, learn to talk at an earlier age than boys do. Later, when they can take intelligence tests, they do better on all tests involving the use of language. Thus they are superior to men in verbal abilities. Closely related to this is the fact that they generally do better on items involving social relations.[10]

Girls are also better on two other, related kinds of abilities: perceiving details quickly and accurately and making quick, accurate manual movements. This may account, in part, for the fact that most women employed in business and industry work in clerical and secretarial jobs and also for the good record they made during the Second World War in many kinds of industrial jobs. Women also seem to have better immediate memories than men. You will recall that the Stanford-Binet has a series of tests at all age levels which measure immediate memory for a series of numbers or words. On the average, women are better in these items than are men.

▪ *Abilities of men.* On the Stanford-Binet test, boys surpass girls on the items that involve spatial, numerical, and mechanical tasks. Correlated with this is the fact that they do better on tasks involving the perception of spatial relationships, the comprehension of mechanical tools and machines, and mathematical ability. Boys are better in working with numbers and in numerical reasoning tasks.

▪ *Interpreting sex differences.* We see, then, that men and women differ significantly in certain *specific abilities*. These conclusions, reached from careful analysis of tests of ability, fit in pretty well with popular conceptions of the difference in ability between men and women.

The question then arises, How did these differences come to be—through training, or by constitutional make-up? This is difficult to answer, for it is next to impossible to separate the influences of heredity and of environment on the development of specific abilities. It seems likely, however, that at least some of the differences measured on intelligence tests are due to training and environment, for as we shall see below, these influences can affect the abilities measured on intelligence tests.

There are two other important factors to consider in interpreting sex differences in abilities. One is that all the differences we measure are *average* differences between groups. Average differences, taken by themselves, do not tell us how a particular boy and girl are likely to compare on an ability. There is a great deal of variability in the abilities of either boys or girls, producing considerable overlap between the two distributions. In tests of language ability, for example, the average score of girls is higher than that of boys. Looking at the distribu-

tion of scores for the two groups, however, we discover that as many as 40 per cent of the boys score higher than the girls' average, that is, higher than 50 per cent of the girls. Thus average differences *between* groups are small compared to differences *within* groups. This is an important point to keep in mind in interpreting any differences between any two groups of people.

Finally, in comparing boys and girls in intelligence, one should also remember that in over-all intelligence the two are equal. That is to say, on average IQ of men and of women is the same. Intelligence tests were, in fact, constructed so as to make it so. Thus the abilities in which women exceed men are counterbalanced by those in which men surpass women. So differences between the sexes are restricted to specific abilities, not to the composite of specific and general abilities that we call intelligence.

Age differences in ability. The United States is currently facing population changes which require an accurate evaluation of the abilities of older people. For one thing, we may be heading toward a time in which the population will not continue to increase as it has in the past and may even decrease. This development may tend to aggravate the already developing manpower shortage. Also, we are becoming a nation of older people.[11] In 1830, for example, the median age of the population was 17.2 years. In 1950 the median age had increased to 30.1. The age group over forty-five now includes over 28 per cent of the population. Because of these factors it is necessary to determine what changes occur in the various kinds of abilities as we grow older.

The most general statement we can make about the change in abilities with age is this: as an individual approaches maturity, all his abilities increase to a peak level and then decline. The decline is slow, but it continues on as he grows older. Different abilities reach their peak at different times and begin their decline at different ages and at different rates.

As an example of the change in general intelligence that occurs with age, let us look at the results of a study in which the Army Alpha Test was given to the inhabitants of a group of New England villages.[12] Practically all the people from the ages of ten to sixty were tested. Figure 15.8 shows the changes in score over these ages. The T score on the left ordinate is, as you may recall, a way of expressing the raw scores so that they may be compared from group to group. We see from the figure that *general mental ability rises to a peak somewhere between the ages of sixteen and twenty and then declines* steadily throughout life.

The older people do as well as young people in vocabulary and general information tests, but they do more poorly in tests which require the individual to work quickly or to adapt to situations which are different from those he is used to.

It is necessary to stress again the amount of variability within groups. In practically all the studies on aging there are many individuals in the oldest group who did as well as, or better than, the average performance of the best group. The implications of these findings are important. If we must make social, economic, political, or any other kind of important decisions concerning the abilities of whole groups, then we must rely on group averages. But if the problem is to select a relatively small number of *individuals* then the decision as to who shall be chosen should not be determined by sex, race, nationality, age, or other "group" factors but should rest upon the tested abilities of the individuals.

Occupational level. As you probably would expect, people in some occupations

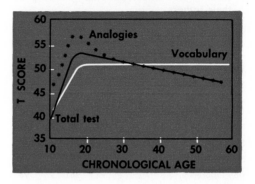

Fig. 15.8. The relation of mental test ability to age. For explanation, see text. (*Based on Jones, H. E., & Conrad, H. S. The growth and decline of intelligence. Genet. Psychol. Monogr., 1933, 13, 223–298.*)

are, on the whole, more intelligent than those in others. We have a good many studies that show this, but the one that is largest in scope comes from data obtained during the Second World War.[13] (See Figure 16.1, in Chapter 16.) Accountants, lawyers, engineers, and teachers head the list with average AGCT scores above 120. At the bottom of the list are farmhands, miners, and teamsters with scores in the neighborhood of 90. The variability, however, is large. There were some people in every occupation who scored over 130, and there were some who scored at 100 or below. Again, though there is an average difference in intelligence between groups, there is a great deal of overlap. You cannot tell too much about a person's intelligence simply by knowing his occupation.

It is not hard to understand how these occupational differences come about. In general, the higher-ranking occupations require considerably more schooling than the lower-ranking ones. The child with low intelligence tends not to finish as many years of school. When he does, he usually

TABLE 15.6. IQs of children averaged according to the occupational grouping of their fathers.

Father's occupation	Age of child			
	2–5½	6–9	10–14	15–18
Professional	115	115	118	116
Semiprofessional and managerial	112	107	112	117
Clerical, skilled, and business	108	105	107	110
Rural owners	98	95	92	94
Semiskilled	104	105	103	107
Slightly skilled	97	100	101	96
Day laborers	94	96	97	98

Data of McNemar, Q. The revision of the Stanford-Binet Scale. Boston: Houghton Mifflin, 1942.

tends to make a poor grade record. This latter fact also partly explains the outcome, because the colleges and professional schools tend to admit those with higher grades and to screen out those with poorer ones. We should consider also the use of special tests of intelligence by these schools for deciding whom they will admit. This introduces a *spurious correlation*; if intelligence is used to admit a person to certain occupations, these occupations will average higher in intelligence, even if there is no necessary relation between occupation and intelligence.

A more interesting and not so easily explained difference in intelligence is among the *children* of parents of different occupational groupings. The children of those in the higher occupational classes tend to have higher IQs than children of parents at lower occupational levels. Illustrating this are the data in Table 15.6, taken from one study of this question.[14] The children of professional people average about 115, while those of day laborers average about 95.

Home environment. The intellectual environment of children of professional parents is naturally rather different from that of children of day laborers. When we find a difference in intelligence between the two groups of children, the age-old question of heredity versus environment comes to mind. Are children of these two groups of parents different in intelligence because they have different inheritance or because they have different intellectual environments? This is an important but very difficult question, and psychologists have carried out extensive studies in an attempt to answer it. Even so, we do not have as conclusive an answer as we should like to have. Here are just a few of the most important facts bearing on the question:

In Table 15.6 are the IQs of children tested in different age groups from two to eighteen and arranged according to seven major occupational groups (of fathers).[14] The differences in the youngest group (two to five and one-half) are just about the same as those in the oldest group (fifteen to eighteen). From these data, we must conclude either that the differences are hereditary or that they are established very early in life.

There is also the fact that, when children are taken from their true parents and placed in foster homes—as many thousands of children are every year—their intelligence seems more closely related to the intelligence and educational level of the true parents than to those of the foster parents. In one study, the correlations of the child's IQ with the intelligence and education of his true parents are of the order of .30 to .40, while those with the education of his foster parents are in the neighborhood of zero.[15] In other studies, correlations of foster children's IQs are substantially higher with IQs of the true parents than they are with those of the foster parents. From this we can conclude that relative differences in intelligence are set principally by inheritance rather than by the intellectual influences of the foster home.

There are many studies on the other hand, in which the intelligence of foster children is considerably higher than one would predict from the IQs of their true parents. In one of the more dramatic studies, made by Iowa University psychologists,[16] children whose true mothers had an IQ of 91 showed an average intelligence of more than 109 when measured at an average age of thirteen, usually 10 years or more after they had been placed in foster homes. Since we are not certain how high their IQs would have been had they been raised by true parents, we cannot be sure how much of a gain this is, but it is probably fair to say that children of subnormal parents may gain as much as 10 IQ points when raised in superior homes.

This fact, unlike the first two we presented, points to the influence of the intellectual environment. Even so, it appears that the gain is not so much as it should be, were it not limited by inheritance. If, for example, one compares the IQs of foster children of subnormal parents with the IQs of true children reared in families of similar status, the foster children tend to be somewhat behind. In one study the foster children averaged 107 while true children averaged 115.[17]

Facts and researches on the influence of the home environment could fill a book, but these that we have cited are typical. What can we make of them? Which is more important, heredity or home environment? About all we can say is that both are important. A good environment can improve intelligence, yet poor inheritance limits how much it can be improved. So, even though no amount of favorable influence can fully overcome poor inheritance, such influences can develop what latent intelligence one has to its fullest potentiali-

ties. An improvement made in this way makes considerable difference in what a person may be able to do.

Cultural environment. If the home of a child makes a difference in his intelligence, we might wonder whether other features of his culture outside the home also contribute to his apparent intelligence. After all, the child lives in other environments outside the home, especially as he grows from infancy into childhood. At two or three, he starts to play with other children, and by the age of seven he begins spending a good part of his day in school. In growing up, he experiences intellectual influences from his playmates, his school, and even the community's library facilities. What effect do these influences have on intelligence?

One way of approaching this question is to compare rural and urban children, because they differ considerably in the richness of intellectual influences in their respective cultures. It is interesting, indeed, that urban children, on the average, score higher on intelligence tests than do rural children; just how much higher depends upon which particular groups are compared, but it is frequently several points.[14] Such differences may be explained in part by the brighter families' migrating to the city, leaving the less intelligent behind. They might also be explained in part by a cultural bias of the intelligence tests; the tests may include items which are more familiar to city children than to farm children.

Undoubtedly there is something to be said for both these points, but our present data are somewhat inconclusive. On the one hand, it seems rather certain that the stimulating environment of the city, like that of a superior home, can raise substandard intelligence. At least we have some striking evidence for this view in a study conducted on Negro city boys of twelve years of age.[18] Over 400 boys who

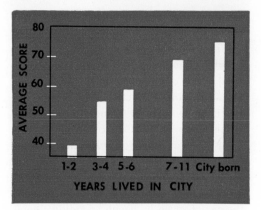

Fig. 15.9. Intelligence scores for Negro boys living in the city for varying numbers of years. (*Based on Kline-berg, O. Negro intelligence and selective migration. New York: Columbia Univ. Press, 1935.*)

had moved to the city were given intelligence tests and compared with another 300-odd boys who had been born and reared in the city. In Figure 15.9, you see that the longer the boys had lived in the city, the higher the intelligence scores. Those who had been in the city only 1 to 2 years averaged only 40 (test score, not IQ), whereas those born in the city averaged 75. This is a sizable difference, and it is hard to see how it could be accounted for by selective migration. Apparently city influences affected measured intelligence.

The problem of cultural influences enters into all attempts to determine whether there are racial differences in intelligence. As you probably realize, it has long been a question whether some "races" are inferior to others in intelligence. When psychologists attempt to settle the question with research—and they have made many studies—they immediately encounter the fact that "races" other than U.S.-born whites have not had the same cultural environments that American whites have had. There is also the fact that different groups migrating to this country come

from varying socioeconomic and cultural groups in their country of birth. So most studies on this question are inconclusive.

The group differences that have been most thoroughly studied are those between American Negroes and American whites. All have the same country of birth and all speak the same language—though the language habits of most Negroes differ considerably from those of most whites. Even so, Negroes on the average have inferior educational advantages and usually inferior intellectual environments. It is not surprising, then, that any large group of Negroes usually averages several points less than groups of whites on intelligence tests.[9] This does not necessarily mean any biologically inherited inferiority in intelligence, and cultural differences certainly explain part or all of the difference.

Our most comprehensive data on these racial differences come from the intelligence tests given in the First World War. In general, Negro draftees did more poorly than the whites. However, Southern draftees were poorer on the average than Northern draftees. And there were Negroes from some Northern states who averaged better than the whites from some Southern states. Moreover, as we saw above, city Negroes and city whites did better than rural Negroes and rural whites. It is therefore very difficult to separate the factors of race, geography, rural-urban origin, and educational advantages. The latter three factors, however, may all be considered cultural influences as distinguished from biological differences in the races. Since cultural influences are of proven importance, it is safest to assume that differences between whites and Negroes are a matter of cultural environment—at least until the cultural advantages of the two groups are equal or until it is possible to get a culture-free test of any racial difference.

SUMMARY

1. A test is a sample of a person's performance on a set of tasks. Only to the extent that it is a fair sample of his performance is it a useful or meaningful measuring device.

2. Test scores cannot be treated as absolute measures like length and weight. Rather, they are interpreted by comparing them with the scores of other people in a comparison group.

3. Tests of ability may be classified into two general kinds: (*a*) those that measure intellectual abilities and are called *intelligence tests,* and (*b*) those that measure special abilities required in particular occupations or schools and are called *aptitude tests.*

4. Intelligence tests are of two general types: individual tests and group tests.

5. The Stanford-Binet is an individual test devised for children of school age. It yields a score called mental age, and from this an IQ may be computed if one knows the chronological age. The Wechsler-Bellevue test is an individual test for adults.

6. There are other group tests of intelligence that may be used for testing large groups of people at the same time. The best-known of these are the Otis and the Army General Classification Test.

7. Intelligence is not a single ability. By factor analysis, it has been demonstrated that about seven abilities are involved in conventional intelligence tests. Some tests weight certain of these abilities more than other tests do.

8. Those individuals who have an IQ of less than 70 are regarded as mentally deficient. They are classified into three groups: morons, imbeciles, and idiots.

9. Tests have been devised for measuring the social intelligence of these groups. In general, the social intelligence of the mentally deficient is higher than their intellectual ability.

10. At the high end of the distribution of IQs are the mentally gifted. Those with IQs between 130 and 140 are considered very superior; those above 140 are regarded as near genius.

11. Many of the outstanding leaders of history have been mentally gifted. In general, the gifted are far more successful, more physically fit, and better adjusted than those of average intelligence, though there are notable exceptions.

12. There are measurable differences in intellectual abilities among various groups in the population. Women excel men in verbal abilities, but

men excel women in certain spatial and mechanical abilities. There are several other differences between men and women in specific abilities.

13. Intelligence tends to decline in old age, but some abilities decline considerably more than others.

14. People in the "higher" occupational groups are, on the average, more intelligent than those in the "lower" occupations.

15. Both the inheritance of a person and the home environment in which he is reared are related to his intelligence.

SUGGESTIONS FOR FURTHER READING

Anastasi, A., and Foley, J. P., Jr. *Differential psychology* (Rev. Ed.). New York: Macmillan, 1949.

   A comprehensive text on psychological differences among groups.

Cronbach, L. J. *Essentials of psychological testing.* New York: Harper, 1949.

   An introduction to the field of psychological tests.

Freeman, F. S. *Theory and practice of psychological testing.* New York: Holt, 1950.

   A text covering the principles of psychological testing.

Goodenough, F. *Mental testing; its history, principles and applications.* New York: Rinehart, 1949.

   Another competent text discussing various aspects of psychological testing.

Klineberg, O. *Race differences.* New York: Harper, 1935.

   An account of extensive psychological testing of different racial groups.

Terman, L. M., and Merrill, M. A. *Measuring intelligence.* Boston: Houghton Mifflin, 1937.

   A book describing the construction, standardization, and use of the revised Stanford-Binet test of intelligence.

Terman, L. M., and Oden, M. H. *The gifted child grows up.* Stanford, Calif.: Stanford Univ. Press, 1947.

   A summary of a 25-year follow-up study of a large group of gifted persons chosen as children.

Thurstone, L. L. Primary mental abilities. *Psychometr. Monogr.,* 1938, No. 1.

   A description of the techniques of factor analysis as used in the development of tests of intelligence.

Tyler, L. E. *The psychology of human differences.* New York: Appleton-Century-Crofts, 1947.

   A text covering psychological differences among various groups.

Wechsler, D. *Measurement of adult intelligence* (3d Ed.). Baltimore: Williams & Wilkins, 1944.

   Information about the Wechsler-Bellevue test.

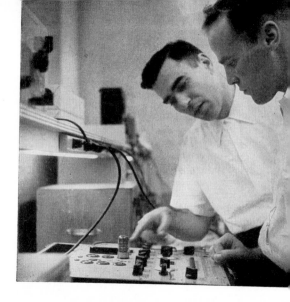

Chapter 16 APTITUDES AND VOCATIONAL ADJUSTMENT

THE PROBLEMS of business, industry, government, and the general world of work are touched upon by many subjects the student has an opportunity to study. Psychology is no exception. Almost every aspect of vocational life, from choosing a vocation to being happy in one's work, has its psychological aspects. In this chapter we have chosen four principal areas to which psychological knowledge can be, and has been, effectively applied. The first is the problem of choosing a vocation, the second is the selection of employees for vocational positions, the third is the supervision of people in their work, and the fourth is

the problem of securing the greatest possible satisfaction in work.

■ VOCATIONAL CHOICES

For many members of our society who are handicapped by ability and education or by limited possibilities of employment, there is little opportunity to choose a vocation. They drift into a job and a line of work without ever discovering what they would most like to do or are best fitted for. Others with greater ability and greater opportunity may fare no better, simply because they do not consider early enough the problem of choosing a vocation or because they do not recognize and cope with the obstacles to a sound choice.

Problems in choosing a vocation. There are, indeed, a number of difficulties to be faced in trying to decide on a vocation.

This chapter was drafted by Clifford T. Morgan of The Johns Hopkins University from material supplied by Lawrence T. Alexander of the Rand Corporation, Robert B. Sleight of the Applied Psychology Corporation, and Wendell R. Garner of The Johns Hopkins University.

TABLE 16.1.   The social status of occupations. When asked to rank different occupations according to social status, most groups give about the same rankings. Below are the rankings by graduate students compared with those by day laborers.

Occupation	Ranking by graduate students	Ranking by day laborers
Physician	1	2½
Banker, stock and loan broker	2	2½
Superintendent of state institution	3	5
Captain in army or navy	4	4
Manager of business	5	1
Hotelkeeper	6	7
Grade school teacher	7	10
Real-estate and insurance agents	8	14
Retail trader	9	9
Commercial traveler	10	8
Bookkeeper, cashier, and accountant	11	11
Foreman	12	6
Farm proprietor	13	16
Clerk and stenographer	14	12
Policeman	15	13
Skilled factory worker	16	15
Salesperson and clerk	17	17
Train, bus, and streetcar drivers	18	18
Waiter and domestic servant	19	20
Janitor	20	19
Laundry worker	21	24
Unskilled factory worker	22	23
Farm laborer	23	21
Casual laborer	24	25
Coal miner	25	22
Unemployed	26	26

From Cattell, R. B. The concept of social status. *J. soc. Psychol.*, 1942, **15**, 293–308.

One is the *romantic idea*. Many lines of work appear very glamorous to the young person. In his dreams he may see himself the white-coated surgeon miraculously saving human lives, the opera star bowing to the applause of the audience, or the tycoon of industry who, like Midas, turns everything he touches into gold. What he may not realize is how few—indeed, how extremely few—people ever reach these pinnacles of success. In fact there are a good many vocations, e.g., acting, music, medicine, and the professions in general, in which the number of aspirants is many times the number who can expect to make the grade, let alone go on to great success.

In some vocations, e.g., medicine, the *nature and cost* of education is such that only the financially privileged have a reasonable chance of completing the training. In other instances, e.g., law, the doors may be open to anyone of ability, but the *training is long and arduous*. Hence when a person considers what he wants to be, he had better consider realistically whether he has the finances, stamina, and other resources for entering his chosen vocation.

Another serious obstacle to making a

sound vocational choice is the *parental and social pressure* to enter some vocation with relatively high social status. Each occupation has a fairly definite social status in the eyes of most people in the United States. As you can see in Table 16.1, it makes very little difference who does the rating; whether they be college students or laborers, this social status is about the same. Physicians, bankers, lawyers, and businessmen rank near the top of the hierarchy; whereas salespeople, clerks, janitors, miners, etc., rank near the bottom. Parents, friends, and associates continually put pressure on us to choose vocations high in social status and discourage us from choosing those that are lower, often quite unmindful of what we are best fitted for and would most enjoy.

Parents and society are not easily persuaded to change their social values, but the young person can try to disengage himself from their pressures long enough to see whether they are pushing him into a poor choice.

There is the question, finally, whether a person has the *intellectual ability* necessary to succeed in an occupation. Not all the people in any occupation are geniuses, nor is there any occupational group that does not include some intelligent people, but there are certain limits of intelligence for each group. These limits have been illustrated in Figure 16.1 for some of the more familiar occupations. Accountants and teachers, for example, have the highest average intelligence in the list, and all who enter these occupations must have well

Fig. 16.1. The ranges of AGCT scores for selected occupations. Each bar shows the range between the 10th and 90th percentiles for a sample of hundreds of men selected randomly from an occupation. Scores below the median are shown in black; those above the median in color. Notice the great overlap. (*After Anastasi, A., & Foley, J. P., Jr. Differential psychology (Rev. Ed.). New York: Macmillan, 1949, p. 798. Data from Stewart.*)

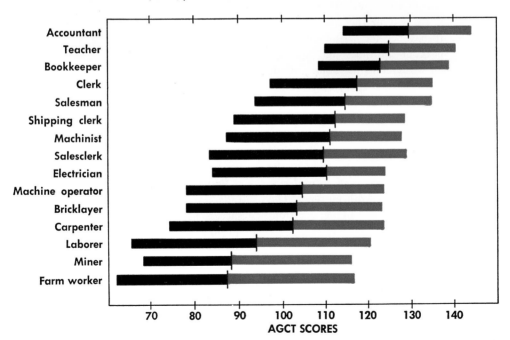

above average intelligence. At the other extreme, farmers may have relatively low intelligence, even though some have as high a score as teachers or accountants. A person is wise to compare his own intelligence level with that of different occupational groups and to choose an occupation in which he is likely to have average or superior intelligence.

Scholastic aptitudes. Most of the occupations that are high in social status, and most of those that the college student is likely to consider, require a rather long period of training. In order to have a chance at succeeding in any chosen occupation, the student must first succeed in training for it. We therefore have the question not only of the intelligence required in the occupation but also of the aptitude required in the training preparatory to it.

Aptitudes are not clearly distinguishable from intelligence. As we pointed out in the last chapter, intelligence includes a number of specific abilities, and certain of these abilities are stressed in the training for a vocation. It has become customary, however, to speak of aptitudes and aptitude testing when we refer to the ability or the ability test that is used specifically for the purpose of predicting success or failure in some specific training or line of work. If we are trying to predict success in training, we speak of *scholastic aptitude;* if it is a vocation we have in mind, we refer to the abilities required as *vocational aptitudes.*

Some tests may serve both purposes. The data in Figure 16.2 for example, are from the Army General Classification Test (AGCT), which is designed as a test of general intelligence. However, this test predicts fairly well whether a person is likely to succeed in officer-candidate school, and it therefore can be used as a scholastic-aptitude test. Figure 16.2, for example, gives

data on this point from the Second World War. If a person scored 140 or over on the AGCT, his chances of succeeding in officer-candidate school were better than 9 in 10. If his score was less than 110, his chances of succeeding were under 5 in 10. This illustrates the kind of predictions it is possible to make from a good scholastic-aptitude test, though such predictions depend also on the population stratum of individuals with whom it is used and on the type of training involved.

A number of scholastic-aptitude tests have been developed for various kinds of training. Probably the most widely used is the American Council on Education Psychological Examination—usually abbreviated A.C.E.—administered to students entering the liberal-arts colleges of the United States. Similar tests are available for schools of medicine, dentistry, nursing, and several other professions. More are being devised each year. Another, called the Graduate Record Examination, has been designed for students who plan to pursue graduate work for the master's or doctor's degree in such specialties as psychology, economics, engineering, and physics. There is an increasing tendency for graduate and professional schools to require the appropriate aptitude test of all students who apply to them. If you are such a student, you should be prepared to take such a test at the time and place announced in your particular school.

Vocational aptitudes. Scholastic-aptitude tests measure a person's aptitude for success in relatively prolonged training requiring 3, 4, or more years. The great majority of jobs in business and industry, however, do not require such training. Success in these jobs or in training for these jobs can be forecast from a knowledge of specific vocational aptitudes without too much regard for intelligence or scholastic

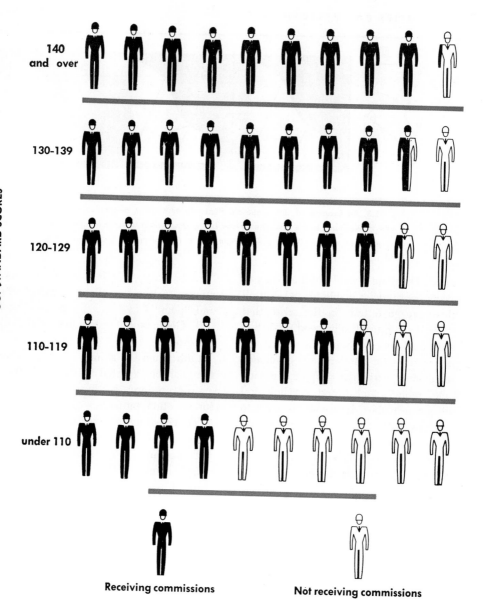

GCT STANDARD SCORES

140 and over

130-139

120-129

110-119

under 110

Receiving commissions   Not receiving commissions

OFFICER CANDIDATES

Fig. 16.2. The prediction of success in officer candidate school from AGCT test scores. The illustration indicates the chances in 100 that an officer candidate making a certain score on the AGCT would receive a commission. Data are for 5,520 men in 14 schools. See Figure 15.6 for the distribution of AGCT scores. (*After Boring, E. G. (Ed.). Psychology for the armed services. Washington: Combat Forces Press, 1945, p. 242.*)

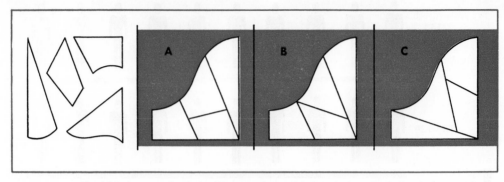

Fig. 16.3. An example of the Minnesota Paper Formboard: A mechanical-aptitude test. The example is like items in the test. The person being tested must indicate whether pieces on the left fit together to make A, B, or C. (After Munn, N. L. Psychology (2d Ed.). Boston: Houghton Mifflin, 1951.)

aptitude. There are several hundred tests of vocational aptitude available today.[1] Not all of them are good tests in the sense that they have been proved to be good predictors of vocational success. Some are. Many are slight variations of another test, developed to serve some particular purpose. In fact, if time, money, and expert psychological talent are available, it usually is wise to modify existing tests to meet the needs of a particular business or industry. We shall describe the steps that are necessary in selecting a valid test, then consider briefly two of the many types of tests that are available.

■ *Validation of tests. To evaluate* the ability of vocational-aptitude tests to predict success on the job, the following steps are necessary:

1. Give the test to *all* applicants for the kind of job in question until a large number of applicants, preferably several hundred, have been tested.

2. Select applicants for employment *without* considering the test results.

3. After those who are employed have been on the job long enough to be evaluated, divide them according to performance into two or more *criterion* groups. The division may be into "satisfactory" and "unsatisfactory," or it may be into several groups, such as "excellent," "good," "fair," and "poor."

4. Compare the tests results of the different groups.

Only when the groups are more different than can be expected by chance is the test a valid one and worthy of subsequent use for selection purposes.

To construct a new test the steps are essentially the same as for evaluating a test, but the analysis must be made for individual items on the test rather than for the test as a whole. Items are selected that discriminate between the criterion groups; other items are discarded. These procedures for evaluating and constructing tests of known validity can be modified somewhat by a person trained in test construction.

■ *Mechanical-ability tests.* Many tests that are intended for mechanics, machine operators, assembly-line workers, repairmen, and similar workers involve mechanical knowledge or ability to manipulate objects. Such tests are called *mechanical-ability tests.* Our experience with such tests indicates that there is a relatively unique mechanical-ability factor common to the tests. People who score high on one mechanical-ability test tend to do so on another. On the other hand, different jobs require different combinations of mechanical abilities; hence there are many different tests. Some examples are given in Figures 16.3 and 16.4.

▪ *Psychomotor Tests.* So far there is little evidence of a general motor ability comparable to perceptual or mechanical ability. Rather a person who has good manual dexterity is not necessarily good at the kind of coordination involved in running a tractor or an airplane. So psychomotor tests must be conceived, developed, and proved for particular jobs and occupations. Such tests involve such psychomotor tasks as manual dexterity, steadiness, muscular strength, speed of response to a signal, and the coordination of many movements into a unified whole. There are many other vocational-aptitude tests for clerical and highly specialized occupations, but these examples will serve to illustrate the kinds of materials used in such tests.

▪ *The Use of Aptitude Tests.* Aptitude tests are used both by the employer to select employees for his jobs and by the vocational counselor in helping a person assess his aptitudes for different types of work. The same tests are usually not suitable for both purposes. The employer, knowing exactly what jobs he has in mind, wants a test that will forecast success in his jobs as accurately as possible. He, therefore, would like a test designed specifically for his purposes, e.g., for butter wrappers, electrical welders, or lathe operators. The counselor, on the other hand, is trying to help a person make a choice—usually a fairly general choice—among different lines of work. For this purpose, the counselor wants fairly general tests that sample many different aspects of specific aptitudes. He has a large number of such general tests to choose from.[2]

Vocational-aptitude tests, as well as the vocational-interest tests we shall describe

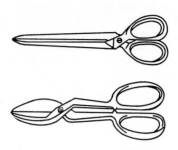

Fig. 16.4. Which would be the better shears for cutting metal? This is an example of an item on the Bennett-Fry Test of Mechanical Comprehension. Those on the test, however, are generally more difficult. (*Courtesy of Psychological Corporation.*)

below, are frequently available in schools and communities. A psychological clinic or student counseling service, in colleges that have one, is usually prepared to administer such tests. The U.S. Employment Service and the Veterans Administration provide testing services for those who qualify for assistance. In the larger cities, there are usually several independent agencies and individuals that offer competent testing facilities for a reasonable fee.

Vocational interests. To succeed at a job, a person must have not only the abilities and aptitudes required by the job but also a set of interests that permit him to like its various aspects. Interests, as well as aptitudes, must therefore be taken into account in making a vocational choice. Psychologists have tried two general approaches in developing tests of interest that might serve in vocational guidance. One, developed by Strong, has been called the *empirical approach*; the other, developed by Kuder, has been called the *theoretical approach*.[3] Each approach has its advantages and its limitations.

▪ *Strong Vocational Interest Test.* To devise a test that might tell whether a person has the proper interests to enter a voca-

TABLE 16.2. Sample items and types of items on the Strong Vocational Interest Test.

Sample occupation items

1. Actor (not movie)	L	I	D
2. Advertiser	L	I	D
3. Architect	L	I	D
4. Army officer	L	I	D
5. Artist	L	I	D
6. Astronomer	L	I	D
7. Athletic director	L	I	D

Types of items	Number
Occupations	100
School subjects	36
Amusements	49
Activities	48
Kinds of people	47
Preference for activities	40
Comparison between items	40
Present abilities	40
Total	400

Reprinted by permission from Strong, E. K., Jr. Vocational interest blank for men (revised), Form M. Stanford: Stanford Univ. Press, 1938.

tion, Professor Strong at Stanford University began by selecting several hundred items that might conceivably distinguish interests in different occupations (see Table 16.2). Items on the test concern *amusements, school subjects, activities, kinds of people*, etc. Most of the items are presented so that a person taking the paper-and-pencil test can indicate whether he *dislikes* (D) *likes* (L), or *is indifferent to* (I) the item.

Strong had several hundred people, chosen to be as representative as possible of a particular occupation or vocation, take the test so he could find out what the interests of successful people actually were. From their responses he was able to discard many items on which there were no substantial differences among occupational

groups and to retain those items that su[c]cessfully discriminated among such group[s]. Some items, of course, discriminated b[e]tween certain groups such as doctors ar[d] lawyers but not between others, such [as] physicians and chemists. They neverth[e]less proved useful. In the end, he was ab[le] to construct a method of scoring his te[st] for each occupation to summarize how w[ell] the testee's interests correspond with tho[se] of people employed in each of several o[c]cupations.

The Strong vocational test, as used [in] recent years, contains 400 discriminati[ng] items. It can be scored for 42 occupation[s] in which men are employed and 24 occup[a]tions open to women. Each way of scori[ng] gives a person's grade as A, B+, B, B−, [or] C. If he receives an A, his interests corr[e]spond quite well with those of the occup[a]tion and the prognosis of success, as far [as] interests go, is excellent. On the other han[d] a grade of C means that his interests d[o] not correspond at all well with those of th[e] occupation and that his chances of succes[s] so far as interests go, are rather poo[r]. Grades of B+, B, and B− are less certai[n] and are interpreted as giving intermedia[te] degrees of correspondence of interest. [A] sample of some of the occupations f[or] which Strong scales are available is liste[d] in Table 16.3.

▪ *Kuder Preference Record.* It is both a[n] advantage and a limitation of the Stron[g] test that it provides scores for specific o[c]cupations. In order for a person to use i[ts] results, he must state the occupations i[n] which he is interested and have the te[st] separately scored for each occupatio[n.] Fortunately machine scoring has been d[e]veloped, so the results on several scales ca[n] be obtained rather quickly and cheapl[y.] Nevertheless the Strong does not give [a] direct general picture of a person's inte[r]ests. For this purpose the Kuder Preferenc[e]

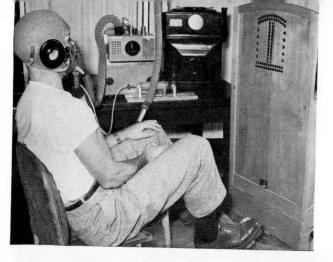

Some vocational aptitude tests in common use.

A psychomotor test used by the Air Force in the selection of pilots. The test simulates some features of piloting a plane. (*Air Force photo, School of Aviation Medicine, Randolph Field, Texas.*)

A tweezer and pinboard test of finger dexterity, used for jobs involving fine work such as watchmaking. (*New York University Testing and Advisement Center.*)

A bimanual nut-and-bolt test, used for jobs involving the assembling of small parts. (*New York University Testing and Advisement Center.*)

A rate of manipulation test for mechanical work involving certain types of machine operation. (*New York University Testing and Advisement Center.*)

Record is more suitable. It simply divides all interests into nine general categories: *Mechanical, Computational, Scientific, Persuasive, Artistic, Literary, Musical, Social,* and *Clerical.*

A person takes the test in much the same way as he does the Strong vocational test. He indicates his *likes* and *dislikes* (see Figure 16.5) and receives a score on each of the nine interest categories. Then in order to see how his interests correspond with those of different occupations the counselor turns to occupational norms which indicate how people in these occupations score in each of the categories. The testee may, for example, be considering the occupation of engineering. By turning to the appropriate table, his counselor can

TABLE 16.3. Some of the occupations for which the Strong Vocational Interest Test may be scored. The test is scored separately for each occupation and for men and women. Of the occupations listed below, those accompanied by an asterisk (*) are scored for women only, those accompanied by a dagger (†) are scored for both men and women, and the rest are scored for men only.

Accountant	Librarian*
Advertising man	Life-insurance sales†
Architect	Mathematician
Artist†	Minister
Author†	Musician
Aviator	Nurse*
Banker	Occupational therapist*
Buyer*	Office worker†
Carpenter	Personnel manager
Chemist	Pharmacist
City school	Physician†
superintendent	Policeman
Coast guard	Printer
Dentist†	Production manager
Dietitian*	Psychologist†
Engineer	Public administrator
Farmer	Social-science teacher
Forest service	Social worker*
Housewife*	Stenographer-secretary*
Laboratory technician	Veterinarian
Lawyer†	YMCA-YWCA secretary†

tell him, for example, that 27 per cent of engineers score as low as he does on "scientific interests," 50 per cent as low as he on "computational interests," and so on. On the other hand, by comparing his scores with those of ministers, teachers, or members of other occupations, he may secure a profile for a different profession. The adviser, by looking at these profiles, may be able to inform the student that his interests correspond more with those in sales, teaching, and social service than they do with those in engineering, science, or medicine.

▪ *The use of interest tests.* Interest tests, like aptitude tests, are not infallible. People sometimes succeed in an occupation with few, if any, of the interests prevalent among others in the occupation. All a counselor can conclude from interest tests is that the odds are strongly favorable, strongly unfavorable, or perhaps about even. On the other hand, follow-up studies of people who have taken interest tests show that many more fail to succeed in a profession when their interest test indicates a poor prognosis than when the interest pattern appears highly favorable. The student, or anyone else, who chooses an occupation after receiving strongly unfavorable advice based on interest tests is taking a considerable chance and may later regret his choice.

▪ EMPLOYEE SELECTION

Just as the employee has the task of choosing the right job or vocation, the employer has the problem of choosing the right employee for his job. The employee runs the risk of unhappiness and failure if he makes a mistake. The employer may waste money in lowered efficiency and may disrupt the organization of his work if he picks the wrong people to fill his jobs. Thus both employee and employer are interested in avoiding mistakes or at least in keeping them down to the minimum.

Job analysis. In order to know who can do his work best, an employer must first know exactly what work it is he wants done. No one can tell who is the best man for a job without knowing what the job is. The process of finding out what a job is has been called *job analysis.* Many people are inclined to think that this is a simple matter, that all one has to do is let a workman or supervisor tell you what the job entails. Experience shows that this is not the case. In one study, for example, secretaries were asked to write down during the course of each day's work exactly everything they did.[4] When their notes were collected and tabulated, it turned out that their jobs consisted of over 800 distinguishable duties. Neither the secretaries nor their supervisors could remember beforehand more than a fraction of these duties.

Having employees note down what they do is only one of several ways of doing a job analysis. Different methods are suitable for different jobs, and some methods are much more expensive than others. Another method is to have an expert job analyst take over the job for a few days and do it himself to see exactly what it entails. A third method, which is especially suitable for repetitive jobs like those on an assembly line, is to take motion pictures of the work and later analyze these in detail. Still another is simply to take the output of production and establish exactly what it is a person has to make. This is particularly useful for machinists and carpenters whose efforts are reflected in finished products.

Most job analyses are made so that a complete list of duties can be compiled. These lists, as in the case of secretarial duties cited above, often get to be rather long. Then the question arises, What duties are the most important? Many duties do

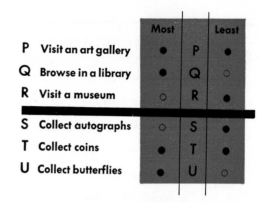

Fig. 16.5. The Kuder Preference Record. Two examples of items in Kuder's interest test. With a pinprick the subject indicates which of the three alternatives he likes most and which he likes least. In this case, he likes Q least and R most of P, Q, and R; and he likes S most and U least of S, T, and U. (*Courtesy Dr. G. F. Kuder and Science Research Associates.*)

not distinguish one job from another, or if they do, they are not important because almost anyone can do them and hence they do not spell success or failure in the job. For this reason, psychologists have recently devised a method called *critical incidents.*[5] In applying this method, the analyst attempts to determine those aspects of the job that are critical for its best performance. The method is especially applicable to jobs where safety is a consideration, such as driving a truck or piloting an airplane. In these jobs, it is not what the person does most of the time that is important but what he does some of the time—in emergencies or especially dangerous situations—that determines whether he is successful, or in fact whether he and his equipment survive. The critical-incidents technique is also proving useful, however, in many other jobs, including industrial, secretarial, and managerial jobs.

Once a job analysis is completed, it can be used to write a *job specification,* which

JOB TITLE *ENGINE LATHE OPERATOR, FIRST CLASS*

Amount O	Amount C	Amount B	Amount A	CHARACTERISTICS REQUIRED
	✓			1. Work rapidly for long periods
	✓			2. Strength of hands
	✓			3. Strength of arms
	✓			4. Strength of back
	✓			5. Strength of legs
	✓			6. Dexterity of fingers
		✓		7. Dexterity of hands and arms
✓				8. Dexterity of foot and leg
		✓		9. Eye-hand coordination
✓				10. Foot-hand-eye coördination
	✓			11. Coordination of both hands
	✓			12. Estimate size of objects
	✓			13. Estimate quantity of objects
		✓		14. Perceive form of objects
	✓			15. Estimate speed of moving objects
	✓			16. Keenness of vision
	✓			17. Keenness of hearing
✓				18. Sense of smell
✓				19. Sense of taste
	✓			20. Touch discrimination
		✓		21. Muscular discrimination
		✓		22. Memory for details (things)
	✓			23. Memory for ideas (abstract)
	✓			24. Memory for oral directions
	✓			25. Memory for written directions
	✓			26. Arithmetic computation
	✓			27. Intelligence
	✓			28. Adaptability
	✓			29. Ability to make decisions
		✓		30. Ability to plan
		✓		31. Initiative
		✓		32. Understanding mechanical devices
	✓			33. Attention to many items
	✓			34. Oral expression
✓				35. Skill in written expression
	✓			36. Tact in dealing with people
	✓			37. Memory of names and persons
	✓			38. Personal appearance
	✓			39. Concentration amidst distractions
	✓			40. Emotional stability
	✓			41. Work under hazardous conditions
	✓			42. Estimate quality of objects
	✓			43. Unpleasant physical conditions
	✓			44. Color discrimination
	✓			45. Ability to meet and deal with public
✓				46. Height
✓				47. Weight
				48. ____
				49. ____
				50. ____

Fig. 16.6. A worker-characteristics form. The letters have the following meanings for satisfactory performance on the job: O, not required; C, a medium or low degree required; B, an above-average degree required; and A, a very high degree required. (*From U.S. Department of Labor, U.S. Employment Service. Training and reference manual for job analysis. Washington: U.S. Government Printing Office, 1944.*)

is a detailed account of all the facts pertinent to a job. Job specifications may then be compared to see which ones are different and which are essentially the same. All jobs having the same specification are considered to be the same job even if they have different names—and they often do, depending upon the locality of the country or the particular business or industry. Jobs that are distinguishably different yet have certain similarities are grouped into *occupations*. Occupations, in turn, can be compared and classified into major occupational families.

The U.S. Employment Service has made studies of over 30,000 occupations in industry, business, and government and has classified them in the *Dictionary of Occupational Titles*.[6] This invaluable dictionary shows how nearly all the jobs in the United States are classified into different occupations and gives the names and job specifications for each. It has served during and since the Second World War as a means of fitting men to particular jobs and also as a way of finding out what and where our major manpower shortages are.

Worker characteristics. Once it is known just what a job entails, the next step is to translate this information into a *job description*. This is a description of both the job and the worker who is needed to fill the job. On the one hand, it gives the kind of work performed, the amount of supervision given and received, the level of difficulty of the work, the standard of work required, the working conditions, and the machines, tools, equipment, and materials that the worker must use. On the other hand, it states the physical and psychological demands of the job, the amount of previous experience considered necessary, the requisite kind and amount of training —in a word, the *worker characteristics* required for a job.

Worker characteristics include a statement of how important each trait and ability is to the job. Each job requires its own particular combination of traits, interests, and abilities. In some of these, little may be required; in others, a great deal. A relatively complete list of the kinds of characteristics that may be included in such a statement are *strength of hands, fingers, legs, and arms; dexterity of various kinds; keenness of the senses, such as depth of vision, color perception; memory for such things as faces, details, and oral and written instructions; arithmetic computation; intelligence; ability to express oneself orally;* and *ability to handle people.* Figure 16.6 shows a standard War Manpower Commission form used during the Second World War and since for rating the kind and degree of these various characteristics.

Selection methods. When an employer knows what worker characteristics are required for the jobs he wishes to fill, his next task is to select those applicants for the job who meet these requirements or who best meet them. This is the process known as *personnel selection*. Since employers have been selecting employees for centuries and scientific methods have been available for only a few decades, it is natural that present-day methods of selection are a mixture of opinions and facts, some of the facts being based on long employment experience and some on modern scientific research.

▪ *Application blanks.* The most generally used source of information about the characteristics of a job applicant is the application blank. This may be made out by the applicant or by someone in an employment office who asks the applicant questions and records the answers on the blank. When used wisely, it is by far the simplest method of obtaining *some* of the desired information about the worker such as age, sex,

TABLE 16.4.   Some information often requested on the application blank.

1. Name	and in what capacity
2. Address	Occupation
3. Birthplace	14. Education
4. Age	Grade school
5. Height	*Name*
6. Weight	*Years*
7. Sex	High school
8. Health	*Major course*
9. Physical defects	Business and evening schools
10. Father's occupation	*Major course*
11. Number of brothers and sisters	College
12. Most recent employment	*Major course*
Employer	*Degree received*
Address	15. Special abilities
Dates of employment	16. Honors received or offices held
Salary	17. Membership in organizations, societies, etc.
Title of your job	
Brief description of work	18. Hobbies
Supervisor	19. Places traveled
(Same for other previous employment)	20. Articles or books written
13. Personal references	21. Reason for wanting a job with company
Name	
Address	22. Date available for work
How long known	

education, and most recent employment. Application blanks, however, are frequently loaded with too many items that actually have no relevancy to the job concerned, such as birthplace, height, weight, and number of brothers and sisters. Application blanks, moreover, do not allow one to appraise accurately the *quality* of such things as education and previous employment. Some applicants may have had considerable education and employment experience but may not have profited from them as much as they should have. So the application blank has its limitations.

Because the application blank is used so widely in selecting employees, it behooves

the student and prospective employee to be prepared to supply the information that it may require. Even the best of memories may not be able to cope with all the questions on such a blank, so it is an excellent idea to make a list in advance of all the items that it may include and to keep available your records of such matters as beginning and ending dates of employment, name of supervisor, name of position held, and salaries received. For the benefit of the student, Table 16.4 includes many of the items frequently called for on application blanks. It is a composite of many typical blanks.

▪ *Interviews.* A second timeworn device used in selection is the employment interview. In 1947 a survey was conducted of personnel-selection practices used in 325 prominent industrial concerns, with the finding that 96 per cent of these concerns used an interview as part of their employment procedure.[7]

Despite its widespread use, the interview is very often not so good a selection device as its users might think (see related discussion in Chapter 9). One classic psychological study,[8] for example, illustrates what can happen under some circumstances. Twelve sales managers interviewed 57 applicants for an actual job under realistic yet controlled conditions. The sales managers were experienced interviewers, because their regular positions required frequent interviewing, but they were not necessarily *trained*. They were allowed to conduct the interview as they saw fit. They were required to rank the applicants in order of desirability for the job, and when the interviewing was completed, their rankings were collected and compared. The results are shown in Table 16.5. They showed very little agreement. Applicant A, for example, was ranked sixth by one interviewer and fifty-sixth by another. Applicant B was ranked as the best man by one interviewer and the worst one by another. These results are fairly typical of many that have been conducted. Where interviews are conducted under "normal" conditions, there very often is little agreement among interviewers. This fact makes it clear that if the interview is to serve effectively as a selection method, certain precautions must be taken.

There are three principal factors that can make the difference between good interviewing and practically worthless interviewing:

1. The interviewer should know well the job about which he is interviewing.

2. He should acquire good technique. This is usually nondirective (see Chapter 11); the interviewer draws out the applicant, rather than asking direct questions. On the other hand, he must be able to keep the interview on the track, and by the time he completes it he must know the answers to a predetermined list of questions.

3. He should be carefully selected for the task. Some people cannot put applicants at ease or establish rapport with them; others are notoriously poor judges of people anyway.

TABLE 16.5. Sample results of a study of the effectiveness of the interview. Twelve sales managers interviewed fifty-seven applicants, then ranked them for suitability for the job. Below are the ranks assigned to three applicants. Agreement among interviewers is clearly not satisfactory.

Applicant	Interviewer											
	1	2	3	4	5	6	7	8	9	10	11	12
A	33	46	6	56	26	32	12	38	23	22	22	9
B	53	10	6	21	16	9	20	2	57	28	1	26
C	43	11	13	11	37	40	36	46	25	15	29	1

Data from Hollingworth, H. L. *Vocational psychology and character analysis.* New York: Appleton-Century-Crofts, 1929.

Many interviews being conducted every day do not meet these important conditions and are therefore untrustworthy. If these conditions are met, however, the interview can be a valuable aid in selection.[9]

▪ *Letters of recommendation.* The letter of recommendation, like the application blank and interview, is widely used as a supplementary device for choosing employees. This is particularly true in selecting students for colleges and professional schools and in selecting clerical, white-collar, and professional personnel. Though widely used, it is subject to the same limitations as those of the application and interview and to a few additional ones. Those who write such letters are usually busy people who toss them off as one of many chores in a day's work. The writer may not know very much about the job for which the applicant is applying or about the standards of performance required in the job. He is inclined also to be lenient in his evaluation of the applicant, since the applicant will be working for *someone else.* Furthermore, because the writer is often chosen for his high rank in supervision, he may not know very much about the applicant. Finally, the words that are used to describe such traits as *honesty, reliability,* and *initiative* are rather vague, meaning different things to different people. It is extremely difficult to use them in a way that discriminates between well-qualified and unqualified applicants.

The users of recommendations have long been aware of their shortcomings and in recent years have taken steps to remedy them. The "letter" now often includes a check list of traits on which the recommender is asked to rate the applicant. This has the advantage of brevity and of giving ratings that may be compared for different applicants. It has the disadvantages, however, of being rather stereotyped, of permitting the recommender to omit important information, and of encouraging leniency in the rating of the applicant. To offset these limitations, recommendation blanks that call for ratings on traits also often ask the recommender to make comments freely as he would in a letter. Even so, the recommendation is seldom a highly reliable source of information for selecting employees.

▪ *Trade tests*. Applications, interviews, and recommendations are the three most common sources of information used in selecting employees, especially for the more remunerative occupations. The benefits of scientific tests are not as widely exploited as they might be, but they are finding more and more use each year for all sorts of occupations from the semiskilled to the executive classes. A variety of tests are being used, but the two kinds that have proved most valid are the trade tests and the aptitude tests.

The trade test is an achievement test; it measures (or attempts to measure) just how good a person is at his trade. It is usually given orally by an employment interviewer, but it may be administered as a paper-and-pencil test. It usually consists of a few well-chosen items that correlate well with degree of knowledge and experience in a particular job. Of the large number of trade tests available today, many were con-

structed by expert job analysts in th U.S. Employment Service as part of a pro gram to provide a relatively complete lis of tests.[10]

Some of the questions on a trade test re quire definitions. A carpenter, for exampl may be asked, "What do you mean by shore?" (Answer: "An upright brace.") Some deal with methods used in the trade A plumber, for example, may be asked "What are the most commonly used meth ods of testing plumbing systems?" (An swer: "Air, water, smoke, peppermint." Other questions deal with use, procedures location, names, purpose and number. An example of number as a basic element in a question is, "How many jaws has a uni versal chuck?" (Answer: "Three.")

Questions and tests of this type hav been prepared, standardized, and validated for most of the common trades. They usually have a high validity in that they dis tinguish well the different levels of ac complishment within the trade. These, fo convenience, are divided into three grades the expert, having long experience in the trade; the apprentice, who is in the process of learning it; and the related worker, who by working with or around experts and apprentices has picked up a limited knowl edge of the trade. In Table 16.6 is evi dence of how well a trade test can distin guish among these three grades of training In this case the trade is painting. In the highest-scoring category we find that 78 per cent are experts, while no related workers make high scores. On the other hand, few experts make low scores, al though nearly all related workers do.

▪ *Aptitude tests*. We have already described aptitude tests in connection with the choice of a vocation. They can be used both to advise a person about his vocational abilities and to help the employer determine who is best suited for his jobs. The

TABLE 16.6. Distribution of scores made on "Trade Questions for Painters" by expert painters, apprentices, and related workers.

Score group	Distribution, per cent		
	Experts	Apprentices	Related workers
9–15	78	17	0
6– 8	14	40	4
0– 5	8	43	96

Data from Stead, W. H., et al. *Occupational counseling techniques.* New York: American Book, 1940.

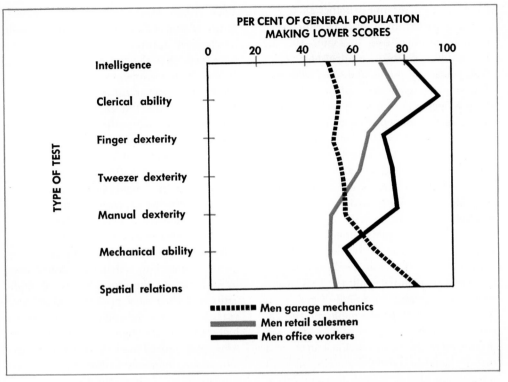

Fig. 16.7. Profiles of abilities for three occupations. Scores along the top of the psychograph are based upon a standard sample of men drawn from all occupational levels. Men office workers, for example, seem to score higher than the average person on tests of intelligence, clerical ability, and manual dexterity, but are about average in mechanical ability. (*After Ghiselli, E. E., & Brown, C. W. Personnel and industrial psychology (2d Ed.). New York: McGraw-Hill, 1955, p. 47.*)

employer is faced, however, with the problem of deciding which of hundreds of possible aptitude tests is most valid for a particular job. To do that he must first consider, as we have previously explained, the worker characteristics essential for that job. This problem has been met by the construction of *psychographs.*[11]

There are two kinds of psychographs, job psychographs and individual psychographs. *Job psychographs*, illustrated in Figure 16.7, show the traits and abilities required in a job or a family of jobs. It is drawn up, as you see in the illustration, in terms of percentages of the population. The amount of

a trait or ability required in a job is defined by the percentage of people in a population who have as much as, or more than, is necessary. To make this kind of representation as simple as possible, the U.S. Employment Service has distinguished three grades of abilities. The A grade is the amount possessed by only the upper 2 per cent of the population; the B grade, the amount possessed by the next 28 per cent; and the C grade, the amount possessed by the remaining 70 per cent. These three grades are close enough for most purposes of weighing the traits or abilities required.

Quite a few occupations have been investigated to determine whether there is a particular pattern of abilities by which each might be distinguished. In Figure 16.7 are the profiles of three occupations: *office clerk, garage mechanic,* and *retail salesman.* The scores along the top and the bottom of the psychograph are based upon a standard sample of men drawn from all occupational levels. Clerks seem to score higher than the average person on tests of intelligence, clerical ability, and manual dexterity but are about average in mechanical ability. Contrast this score with that of the garage mechanic.

To select an employee, one must know whether an applicant's abilities correspond with those stated in the profile, or job psychograph, of required abilities. This means that some way must be found of constructing an *individual psychograph* for the applicant and matching this with the job psychograph. In some circumstances, this may be done by rating the applicant with information obtained from the application blank, interview, and recommendations. Better yet, it may be done by tests selected to measure the required abilities. Very often some of the tests we have already described are chosen because they are supposed to measure the indicated abilities. In the ideal case, however, research is carried out to see what tests best measure the abilities.

Validity of selection. This brings us to a point that cannot be overemphasized. In Chapter 8 we have explained validity as the measurement of what one hopes or thinks he is measuring. In choosing people for jobs by means of the selection procedures we have described, validity means selecting the people who prove to be able to do the job best. Valid selection procedures are those that successfully select the best and eliminate the unfit.

Unfortunately many procedures have *face validity* but do not have true validity. Be-

cause a job seems to require mechanical aptitude and because a particular test of mechanical aptitude may be available, it may seem that the test should be the one to use. It may happen, however, that traits other than mechanical aptitude are important or that the test measures the wrong sort of mechanical aptitudes. In that case, the test may seem to have validity but may be sadly lacking in it.

In the practical world, one cannot always do things as they should be done, and often it may prove too expensive or may require too much research to find out whether one's selection procedures are valid. As we indicated earlier in this chapter, the real validity of a procedure can be established only by carrying out the procedure on all applicants and then showing—some months or years later—that the applicants who scored highest in the selection were the same ones who later proved most successful on the job. If less than this is done, it should be recognized as a short cut that leaves the validity of the procedures in some question.

■ SUPERVISION

The selection of an employee and his acceptance of a job are just the beginning of the problems of vocational adjustment. After that it remains to be seen whether the employee will succeed in his work and the employer will be effective in supervising him. Millions of words—most of them no more than embellished common sense—have been written about "how to succeed." We shall not repeat many of them here. There are, however, certain principles of effective supervision, as well as some scientific information about the satisfactions a person can have in his job, and we shall present these briefly.

■ *Succeeding in Supervision.* If you are a college student, the chances are rather good

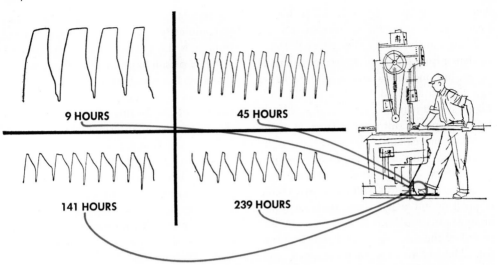

Fig. 16.8. Knowledge of results aids training. The records are of foot-action patterns in the operation of a disk-cutting machine. The person being trained has the record of an experienced operator as a guide and attempts to duplicate the record. Notice the great improvement in the course of 239 hours of supervised training. (Based on Lindahl, L. G. *Movement analysis as an industrial training method. J. appl. Psychol.*, 1945, **29**, 420–436.)

that you will find that your vocation entails the supervision of people. Most college graduates in business and industry are primarily employed in supervisory work. But even doctors, lawyers, teachers, and others in independent work have secretaries, assistants, and students whom they will be called upon to supervise. Despite this fact, relatively few receive any systematic instruction in the art and science of supervision, and many supervisors are consequently poorly prepared for their jobs. The few principles that we sketch here are no substitute for a thorough training in supervision, but if heeded, they may help a good deal.

Training. The supervisor is, first of all, a teacher. He starts teaching by instructing a new employee in his duties, and he continues to teach as new methods are introduced, as the organization undergoes change, and as day-by-day problems are solved. The most important part of the training, of course, is during the first few weeks that an employee is on the job, but it goes on after that, month in and month out. Whether the employee learns his job slowly or rapidly, correctly or incorrectly, and whether he keeps up as the work changes depends very much on the skill of the supervisor as a teacher.

▪ *Knowledge of results.* Perhaps the most important principle a supervisor should keep in mind—and often does not—is that learning proceeds best when a person has knowledge of results. To know what he should be doing and to correct his mistakes, a person should know what he has just done and whether it is right or wrong. This is related to the principle of reinforcement which we stressed in the chapter on learning (Chapter 5). In simple learning situations, reinforcement is reward or punishment for an instrumental act, but in complex situations it is primarily a matter of knowing the outcome of one's work, whether it is good or bad, acceptable or unacceptable, accurate or inaccurate.

Many illustrations of this principle could be drawn from practical experience in supervision, but one should suffice here.[12] In this case the job involved operating a lathe in a highly skilled manner. The operator, in fact, had to learn an intricate pattern of hand and foot movements executed at a certain speed and with a certain form, rhythm, and pattern of pressures. Operators had trouble acquiring this skill until supervision stepped in and analyzed the problem. First an apparatus was built to provide a graphic record of the movements of a *skilled* operator. The record was then analyzed and labeled so that the trainee could see what movements were represented in the record. Then the trainees were asked to operate the machine so that they produced a record as much like that of the expert as possible. You see the results in Figure 16.8. The trainees, once they had knowledge of their own results, learned considerably faster than they had learned before.

Relatively few problems in supervision require the construction of a recording machine to provide knowledge of results. More often the supervisor can supply the necessary knowledge by giving careful directions, pointing out mistakes as a teacher would, and telling the employee as often as possible just what the quality of his work is.

In playing the role of a good teacher, there are several other pointers, drawn from the psychology of learning, that the supervisor should follow. In general, guidance is much more effective early in learning than later; consequently it is better to show somebody how to do things right in the first place than it is to wait until after he has learned bad habits. People also usually master one thing at a time better than they master many things at a time. Therefore, training should be limited to a reasonable

number of tasks and to a reasonable degree of complexity at any one time. Transfer of training is also a powerful ally to be enlisted. When a person has learned one task, then is the time to show him other tasks that are similar to it or other tasks that involve the same principle. In this way one can capitalize on positive transfer and avoid negative transfer (see Chapter 5).

We have run over these points hurriedly because they are all applications of principles presented in detail earlier. The alert supervisor will know well his principles of learning and will continually seek ways to make use of them in helping his employees work effectively.

Communication.   Closely allied to the supervisor's role as a teacher is his responsibility for communication.[13] Almost all instructions and information are transmitted to an employee through language, written or spoken. He learns what he is supposed to do and to know from the supervisor's words. If, therefore, the supervisor is to be effective, he must concern himself with language and with ways to use it effectively in communication. Unfortunately supervisors are all too often unaware of the problem of communication.

The good supervisor, first of all, makes sure to tell his employees what they should know. He does not leave it to them to "read his mind" or to "pick up" what they should know; he sees to it that they are promptly and accurately informed. He should realize, secondly, that they usually are neither so bright nor so well educated as he, and consequently that he should phrase his communications in simple, direct style. In another chapter dealing with communication (Chapter 20), we have given examples of "officialese" and how it must be "translated" into English. The points made there apply here. The supervisor should also communicate in small doses, for most people have a limited capacity to absorb information. Hence long, involved communications are seldom read or listened to, and if they are, they are seldom digested. Only a few important points should be dispensed at a time.

Following the principles of good communication is not only necessary to instruct and inform employees in their work; it also has just as important a bearing on morale. If a supervisor restricts his communications to those dealing with work, rules of work, changes in hours, and so on, he breeds ignorance and misunderstanding. He leaves the employee in the dark about all sorts of things: the problems of management, the methods of evaluating the employee's work, the money paid in wages versus that distributed in dividends or taken in profits, general policies of the management, and its financial problems. In the absence of good information, employees pick up the little bits that leak out and distort them into fantastic misconceptions. Layoffs and wage cuts are rumored; huge profits are imagined; promotions are often perceived as a matter of "connections" rather than of merit, and so on. The remedy for the ill will and disgruntlement engendered by such distortions is to provide information succinctly, promptly, and truthfully about all matters in which the employees have an interest.

Evaluation. Besides being a teacher and a communicator, the supervisor must be an evaluator. He must evaluate the worth of the jobs under his supervision and the worth of the employees holding those jobs.[13]

The first of these evaluations is known as *job evaluation* and is an assessment of the remuneration to be offered and paid for a particular job. The traditional way of deciding what to pay is to accept the general market evaluation of a job. The supervisor finds out, for example, what secretaries or machinists currently "are getting" and offers this when he wishes to employ a person for such a job. This relatively unscientific way of evaluating a job often fails to get employees who have the necessary abilities, and it neglects the question of what is fair compensation for the skills and abilities involved in a job. It is gradually being displaced by more systematic methods of evaluation, sometimes done by people who are specialists in these methods. Their general purpose is to assess the worker characteristics required in a job and then pay according to the relative scarcity or plenty of these characteristics in the general population. If, for example, the job requires a degree of intelligence that is relatively rare, they pay highly for the job, but if, on the other hand, it requires skills or abilities that almost everyone has, they pay a relatively low wage. There are many different systems for arriving at such an evaluation; but in any case their purpose is to assign a fair value to a job that is well done, not to a worker.

The second aspect of evaluation concerns the worker. Is he doing his job satisfactorily or not? Is he doing it unusually well? Could he do another job better than he is doing his present one? Is he worthy of promotion to another job? These are difficult questions that need to be answered fairly in order to reward the worker for his efforts and to make the most of his abilities in an organization. Again there are many methods for making such a worker evaluation.

In industries or businesses where employees produce something that is measurable, the evaluation can be made almost solely in terms of amount and quality of production. In addition, there are a good many fringe criteria that may be employed such as *seniority on the job, number of times a person is tardy for work, number of accidents,* and *amount of time required in*

EMPLOYEE PERFORMANCE AND WORK APPRAISAL FORM

Date... 19

Judge the employee on the basis of the work now being done. Be sure that each characteristic is considered separately, regardless of where the appraisal falls on any of the other characteristics. Place a check (∨) in the box below the group of words which best describes the individual, but only one check for each line. However, it is essential that every line be checked.

NAME.. JOB TITLE.. DEPT..

How long under your supervision?..Date of Employment?..

1. Knowledge of Job: Consider knowledge essential to person's job.	Has an Exceptionally thorough knowledge of work ☐	Has good knowledge of work ☐	Requires Considerable coaching ☐	Has inadequate knowledge of work ☐
2. Quality of Work: Consider the ability to turn out work which meets quality standards.	Highest Quality ☐	Well Done ☐	Passable ☐	Poor ☐
3. Quantity of Work: Consider the volume of work produced under normal conditions.	Large Volume ☐	Good Volume ☐	Slightly Below Average Volume ☐	Unsatisfactory Volume ☐
4. Attendance & Punctuality: Consider frequency of absences as well as latenesses.	Record is Excellent ☐	Occasionally Absent or Late ☐	Frequently Absent or Late ☐	Undependable; Absent or Late Without Notice ☐
5. Attitude: Consider his attitude toward his work, company and associates, and his willingness to work with and for others.	Unusually Fine Attitude ☐	Good Attitude ☐	Passable ☐	Poor Attitude ☐
6. Judgment: Consider his ability to make decisions and to utilize working time to best advantage.	Justifies Utmost Confidence ☐	Applies Himself Well; Needs Little Supervision ☐	Needs Frequent Checking ☐	Cannot be relied upon; Needs constant Supervision ☐
7. Reliability: Consider the ability of the person to get the work out under pressure, and to follow job through to completion.	Can always be counted upon ☐	Generally can be counted on ☐	Unpredictable under Pressure ☐	"Cracks up" under pressure ☐
8. Flexibility — Adaptability: Consider the speed with which he learns and the amount of instruction required to teach him new duties.	Learns Fast ☐	Learns Reasonably Fast ☐	Slow to Learn ☐	Unable to Learn ☐
9. Personal Characteristics: Consider Appearance, Personality, Integrity, "Housekeeping".	Decidedly Favorable ☐	Good ☐	Passable ☐	Generally Unsatisfactory ☐

Appraised by.. Date.........................Reviewed by.. Date........................

(See other side)

Fig. 16.9. An example of the kind of form commonly used to appraise the performance of employees.

training for a job. When such criteria are used, some way must be found of weighting each of them into some composite judgment, and there are systems for doing this.

In many kinds of work, especially in office operations or work requiring initiative and responsibility, none of the production or fringe criteria may be adequate. Then supervisors must turn to some kind of *rating* made by the immediate supervisors or associates of the person. One of the common methods used, for example, in the civil-service system and military establishment is the efficiency report. This is usually a rating of "excellent," "satisfactory," or "unsatisfactory" of several aspects of a person's work and is made out by the immediate supervisor. Because supervisors tend to be lenient, such ratings usually are inflated and therefore yield far too few "unsatisfactories" and far too many "excellents" to be very useful in discriminating the worth of different employees.

To overcome the deficiencies of the simple efficiency report, psychologists have devised other more precise methods. One is the *man-to-man* rating, in which the supervisor must compare each person with several other persons known to him or under his supervision. This method, although it forces a comparative rating of individuals, is handicapped by the fact that the supervisor is usually not equally familiar with the work of all who are compared. A second method is the *forced-choice* rating blank.[14] This presents the supervisor with pairs of adjectives and asks him to check the member of each pair most descriptive of the individual. The members of the pair have been carefully chosen through research so that they appear equally attractive or unattractive to the supervisor but so that one is important and the other unimportant in determining the worth of an individual (see Figure 16.10). A supervisor often objects to this forced-choice technique, because he does not know whether his ratings will turn out to be favorable or unfavorable to the person being rated until they are scored in the front office. Research indicates, however, that the method is a good one *if* supervisors carefully and honestly make out the forced-choice forms.

These are just a sample of the scientific methods available for evaluating a person's worth. The good supervisor accepts the responsibility for evaluating worth, uses the best methods suitable to his problem, and is always on the alert for any better methods that he might use. In this way he can reward fairly people who are deserving and he can also maintain the effectiveness and morale of his group.

Counseling. We should mention briefly a fourth, and often unrecognized, psychological responsibility of the supervisor. This

Fig. 16.10. The forced-choice-rating technique. The examples are some of those formerly used by the U.S. Army on the Job Proficiency section of an Officer Efficiency Report.

INSTRUCTIONS: Read carefully each group of four phrases, then check the one that is most descriptive of the person being rated and also the one that is least descriptive of him.

	Most	Least
A. A go-getter who always does a good job	☐	☐
B. Cool under all circumstances	☐	☐
C. Doesn't listen to suggestions	☐	☐
D. Drives instead of leads	☐	☐
A. Always criticizes, never praises	☐	☐
B. Carries out order by "passing the buck"	☐	☐
C. Knows his job and performs it well	☐	☐
D. Plays no favorites	☐	☐
A. Constantly striving for new knowledge and ideas	☐	☐
B. Businesslike	☐	☐

is counseling. Employees are not mere machines that may be "broken in" and then operated at high speed to produce all they can. Employees are people, and people have problems, as we have emphasized elsewhere in the book (Part Two). These problems affect their work. A man's nagging wife, his personal relations with fellow workmen, his worries about his children's health, and countless other personal problems seriously affect his work and indirectly the work of his associates.

This fact was well demonstrated years ago in the famous Hawthorne study of the Western Electric Company.[15] In this study it was revealed that personal problems had as much to do with factory production as any other single factor. The management discovered, too, after some experimentation, that a counseling system in which they listened to their employees' problems and tried to render psychological help made their employees happier and more productive. So they and many other companies have instituted and maintained regular counseling services.

We have seen elsewhere (Chapter 11) that counseling is an occupation that requires special skills and trained personnel if it is to be done most effectively. Where feasible, therefore, it is desirable to have members of the staff whose principal function is counseling. On the other hand, every supervisor should be aware of the personal problems of his employees. He should realize, for example, that when a workman starts coming in drunk, when a secretary becomes sulky and disgruntled, or when two men "simply do not get along," the problem is one in emotional adjustment. He should try to understand what the problem is and to offer some kind of help that will alleviate it.

■ JOB SATISFACTION

So far this chapter has considered the psychological aspects of vocational choice, employee selection, and supervision. To round out our discussion of vocational adjustment we must also consider job satisfaction. This is important to both the em-

TABLE 16.7. What industrial workers say they want in a job. The table below is a summary of several different surveys. Different language and varying numbers of alternatives were used in the surveys. The factors named at left have been paraphrased but represent approximately the areas covered. The numbers are rankings of the factors considered in each study.

	Women factory workers	Union workers	Nonunion workers	Men	Women	Employees of five factories
Steady work	1	1	1	1	3	1
Type of work				3	1	3
Opportunity for advancement	5	4	4	2	2	4
Good working companions	4			4	5	
High pay	6	2½	2	5½	8	2
Good boss	3	5½	5	5½	4	6
Comfortable working conditions	2	2½	3	8½	6	7
Benefits		5½	6	8½	9	5
Opportunity to learn a job	8					
Good hours	9	7½	7	7	7	
Opportunity to use one's ideas	7	7½	8			
Easy work	10					

Modified from Harrell, T. W. *Industrial Psychology.* New York: Rinehart, 1949.

ployee and his supervisor, because the employee needs to know what satisfactions he can expect in his work and the supervisor must know how to provide these satisfactions

In the chapter "Motivation," we emphasized that people have social and egoistic needs as well as biological ones. We may expect consequently that their efforts both at work and at play will be directed toward the satisfaction of all their needs, not just those for material things such as food, clothing, and housing. This expectation has been confirmed in many psychological studies of the satisfactions people derive (or fail to derive) from their work. In such studies employees have been asked in one way or another what they consider to be most important to them in their jobs. Although the results vary somewhat from one locality to another and from one kind of work to another, we are justified in drawing some conclusions that generally apply to most people who work.

Pay.   For those of us who work for a living, pay or income is what lets us buy the material things we want. Without it, moreover, we could not live. You might think, therefore, that pay would head the list of things people consider important to them in their respective jobs. Such is not the case. When asked to rank pay along with several other features of their jobs, most people rank it relatively low and very few rank it first (see Table 16.7).[16]

Even when they rank pay high, they usually indicate that it is not just high pay that they want. Rather they want to be paid as well as other people doing the same work, or as well as other people in the same industry. Thus most people are more concerned about being paid fairly than about being paid a large amount. Fair treatment is more important than the amount of money received.

The fact that pay is seldom listed as the most important factor in working should not lead us to think that it is unimportant. Probably most people assume that they will be paid enough to take care of their basic necessities. Above that point, then, pay becomes relatively unimportant. If the pay scale were dropped far below its present level for a particular person, then pay would become important again. It is interesting to see, though, how often people decide which job to take or which to keep on grounds other than the amount of pay they receive.

Security.   Probably the factor most often stated as important in work is job security. People want to know that they will have steady work and that the work will continue for many years. They also want security in the personal sense of wanting to work on safe jobs. They do not want to run the risk of losing their earning power because of accidents on the job.

The importance of security in job satisfaction partly explains why high pay is not an extremely important problem. Most people would prefer a low salary which is guaranteed over a long period of time to a high salary which may not last long. Such concerns are typical of the human species. People are able to look well beyond the immediate satisfactions and to anticipate the problem of satisfying their needs at some time in the future. They are more concerned about making a guaranteed minimum salary over a long period of time than they are about making the most money right now.

Good working conditions.   Good working conditions are frequently listed as important considerations in working. People like to work in a clean and neat working area. If they work in an industrial plant, they want it to be one which makes them feel they are working in a pleasant environment and one of which they can be proud. Comfortable jobs are often important, and short hours are frequently preferred over higher pay.

The large class of people called white-collar workers is the best example of people to whom working conditions are more important than high pay. Office workers, clerks, and stenographers often earn much less money than they could if they were doing skilled manual labor, and yet they do not often change their job category. In addition, of course, white-collar workers usually have steadier work and can look forward to long-continued employment.

Opportunity for advancement. Another illustration of the fact that people are frequently more concerned about the future than about the present is that they usually give *opportunity for advancement* a high rating. A man often turns down a higher-paying job, for example, to take one which starts at a lower salary but which ensures early advancement. Sometimes the concern about advancement takes the form of wanting a guaranteed rate of promotion after a fixed period of time. In other instances people simply want to be assured that they will be told about opportunities for advancement and that they can compete for it. In still other cases, a person is most interested in the company's providing training opportunities for employees so that he can learn the skills necessary for advancement.

Regardless of the particular form the concern about advancement takes, it is clear that people are as interested in the future as they are in the present. It is equally clear that concepts of fair play are important when people ask for equal opportunity for advancement or opportunity to learn. In such cases, people are not asking for a guarantee of advancement, but only for a fair chance. Nobody wants to work where the boss's son-in-law gets promoted regardless of his qualifications.

Personnel relations. Probably more important to most people than almost anything else are the personnel relations they have in their jobs. People want to work with companions and coworkers whom they like. They will work for a good boss, and quit when they don't like the boss. They want help from management in their work, and knowledge about how their work is progressing. They want to be sure that they have somebody to whom they can take their grievances and that they will get a fair deal when they have a grievance. For that reason, the organization which provides special means of handling grievances will always have an advantage in attracting workers. Last, but not least, they want recognition of the importance of their work. They want to be told when they are doing a good job and helped when they are doing a poor one, and they want to feel that their work and their efforts to do better work are appreciated.

This factor of wanting appreciation for work has raised a good many problems for psychologists who have tried to do experiments in industry. In the Hawthorne experiments mentioned above, several girls were studied over the course of two years.[15] The girls were put in a separate room where many different working conditions could be controlled. First, the illumination was changed, and production immediately went up. Then other factors were changed: the girls were given rest periods, sometimes for 5 minutes, then sometimes for 10 minutes. They were given free lunches, and at one time were allowed to go home earlier. Every time a change was made, production got better. Then all the rest periods, free lunches, etc., were taken away, *and production went up still higher.*

What had happened here? The answer, it was learned later, was in the *attention* the girls were getting. Every time a change was made, the girls were reminded that other people were concerned with what they were doing, and this appreciation was what really made production go up.

All this points up the fact that people work for many things besides money. They want security, future opportunity, pleasant working conditions, and good relations with their coworkers and their bosses. Basic biologic factors are important, but we should never forget that people are complex organisms with complex motives, and that the satisfaction of these complex motives is important.

SUMMARY

1. Scholastic-aptitude tests have been developed to estimate ability to succeed in college and other advanced training.

2. Vocational-aptitude tests assess the likelihood of success in some particular vocation.

3. Vocational-interest tests serve as additional aids in vocational choice by measuring the degree to which a person's interests coincide with those found most frequently in a vocation.

4. These various tests can be administered and interpreted by vocational counselors, who are often available in high schools, colleges, and employment offices.

5. In choosing a vocation, a person should also consider realistically the competition in a field and whether he has the stamina and financial resources to complete the necessary training.

6. Scientific methods for selecting employees have been greatly improved in recent years. The employer must first make a job analysis to determine accurately the requirements of a job; then he must assess the characteristics that a worker must have to do the job adequately.

7. Traditional methods of selecting employees through application blanks, interviews, and letters of recommendation are relatively unreliable unless precautions are taken to obtain the best results from them.

8. Trade tests may be very helpful in selecting skilled workers. Aptitude tests also can be quite valid in selecting many types of employees if the tests are properly chosen and proved through careful research.

9. The duties of the supervisor of employees have several psychological aspects. One is to be a teacher and trainer, not only in "breaking in" a new employee but also in day-by-day supervision.

10. The supervisor must also be able to communicate his instructions promptly and intelligibly and to keep employees informed on most matters that they feel concern them in their work.

11. He must also evaluate both the job and the worker on the job so that he can make the fullest use of workers' abilities and reward them fairly for their accomplishments.

12. The supervisor, finally, must consider the personal and emotiona problems of an employee, because these seriously affect performance, and must offer counseling or other psychological aid that may alleviate the problems.

13. Employees work not just for pay but for the satisfaction of all their needs. In fact, once pay is reasonable and fair, other factors loom con siderably more important. These are job security, good working conditions, opportunity for advancement, and good personnel relations—to name just a few of the more important ones.

SUGGESTIONS FOR FURTHER READING

Bellows, R. M. *Psychology of personnel in business and industry.* New York: Prentice-Hall, 1949.

A *text on industrial psychology which includes chapters on communication, counseling, and leadership.*

Blum, M. L. *Industrial psychology and its social foundations.* New York: Harper, 1949.

A *book stressing the role of motivation and of social factors in industrial life.*

Ghiselli, E. E., and Brown, C. W. *Personnel and industrial psychology* (2d Ed.). New York: McGraw-Hill, 1955.

A *widely used text covering the general field of industrial psychology.*

Karn, H. W., and Gilmer, B. von H. *Readings in industrial and business psychology.* New York: McGraw-Hill, 1952.

The selected writings of different authors with emphasis on recent developments in the field.

Maier, N. R. F. *Principles of human relations.* New York: Wiley, 1952.

The importance of human relations in industry, and methods for improving them.

Parker, W. E., and Kleemeier, R. W. *Human relations in supervision.* New York: McGraw-Hill, 1951.

A *brief, readable introduction to the field of industrial psychology.*

Shartle, C. L. *Occupational information* (Rev. Ed.). New York: Prentice-Hall, 1952.

A *source book of information about the nature and classification of different occupations.*

Super, D. E. *Appraising vocational fitness by means of psychological tests.* New York: Harper, 1949.

The use of tests in vocational counseling and selection.

Thorndike, R. L. *Personnel selection.* New York: Wiley, 1949.

An authoritative text on methods of constructing and using tests for selection purposes.

Tiffin, J. *Industrial psychology* (3d Ed.). New York: Prentice-Hall, 1952.

A *widely used text covering the general field of industrial psychology.*

Chapter 17   WORK AND EFFICIENCY

MOST PEOPLE spend half or more of their waking hours in some form of work to earn a living. Outside working hours they are also busy in such activities as studying, reading, writing, mowing the lawn, repairing the house, or fixing the car. In most of these activities we have some interest in the question of efficiency: What is the fastest way of getting our work done with the minimum of effort? This question is in part a psychological question, because it concerns the conditions under which we are best able to think and use our learned skills. As students of psychology, we are therefore interested in problems of work, rest, and efficiency.

This chapter was drafted by Wendell R. Garner of The Johns Hopkins University.

THE WORK CURVE

People seldom work at the same pace over a long period of time. Work has its ups and downs. For example, you probably do not study as effectively at the end of a long period of study as you do at the beginning. Indeed, you may not study as well at the beginning as you do after you have been at it for a little while. So you know that the efficiency of work changes during any considerable period of time.

When we have some measure of the efficiency of work and plot our measurements against the minutes or hours of the work period, the graph that results is called a work curve. Work curves are somewhat different for different types of work, but those

429

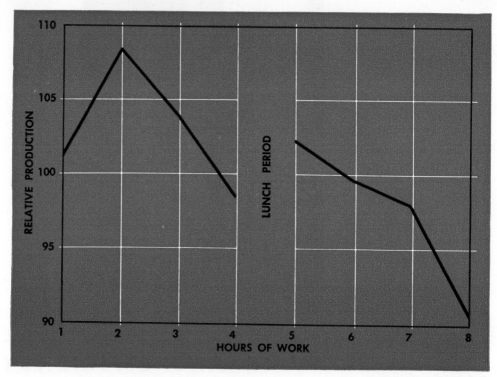

Fig. 17.1. A typical work curve for heavy hand work. The curve is rather characteristic of work curves obtained for heavy work. The figures have been adjusted to let 100 stand for the average rate of production for the eight-hour day.

in Figure 17.1 have been found in many industries and for many tasks. The typical work curve in Figure 17.1 was obtained several years ago for a job involving heavy handwork. Notice that production was slightly better than average for the first hour of the day but it improved during the second hour. During the third hour it was still better than average, but it had dropped considerably from the second hour. And it dropped even more during the fourth hour. After the lunch period, production increased again, but then it dropped steadily for the rest of the afternoon.

Curves of this general description are frequently found in industry and other working situations. The precise shape of the curve, however, depends on a number

of factors which we shall discuss below. By studying the effect of these factors on the work curve, we have been able to analyze the curve into four components, each of which represents a factor in work. These four components are *warming up, beginning spurt, end spurt,* and *fatigue*. We shall consider the first three factors in this section, then devote the next section to a discussion of fatigue.

Warming up. A *warm-up effect* is one of the features that may appear in a work curve. It is illustrated in the top line of Figure 17.2. Most of us are familiar with the idea of warming up and deliberately make use of it. A boxer warms up before a fight by dancing around and shadow boxing. A runner runs back and forth lightly. You have all seen football players running a ball before actually going into a game. In these cases, the warming up is actually done before the athlete enters the game, because he knows that he will not be at his top performance if he does not warm up first.

This same type of warming up takes place in other types of activity, even in intellectual activities such as studying for an examination or writing a term paper. When you first start to work, you are poorly organized; you are not really *set* for the job, and perhaps you fidget or even get up and walk around. The warming-up period may take longer for some people than for others, and it may take longer for some activities than for others. But *warming up is of value in almost every type of activity.*

Referring now to Figure 17.1, one can see that warming up accounts for the fact that production is greater during the second hour than during the first hour. If the warming up is very slow, the work curve may rise throughout the whole morning period. On the other hand, if it is very fast, it may be over in the first few minutes and not have any appreciable effect on the total productivity for the first hour.

Beginning spurt. The middle curve in Figure 17.2 illustrates another factor in work curves, the beginning spurt. This is exactly the opposite of the warming-up effect and can completely cancel it. We may start off a particular job with a great deal of enthusiasm and put our full effort into it. Then the realization that this job is going on for a long time hits us, and we slow down to a steadier pace—a pace more suitable for the long haul. After people have worked on the same job a good many times, they are less likely to show a beginning spurt. It is characteristic of a new job or activity and does not occur in some jobs.

End spurt. When activity is increased at the end of a job, we call it an end spurt.

The end of the day brings with it an increased enthusiasm, and a final burst of energy sends production up. The end spurt commonly occurs in athletic events and probably represents the athlete's willingness to use up all the energy he has left, because he knows he need not save it for any later effort. A long-distance runner, for example, usually manages to put on an extra burst of speed at the end of the run, and a boxer frequently fights more vigorously in the last round than he has in any preceding one.

Occasionally the end spurt at the end of a day is so large that it hits a peak of production for the day. When this happens, it is clear that the worker has not really been working at top effort all along. As we shall

Fig. **17.2.** The components of the work curve. A work curve can be analyzed into the components indicated. The shape of any particular work curve will depend on the relative importance of the various components. (*After Chapanis, A., Garner, W. R., & Morgan, C. T. Applied experimental psychology. New York: Wiley, 1949, p. 380.*)

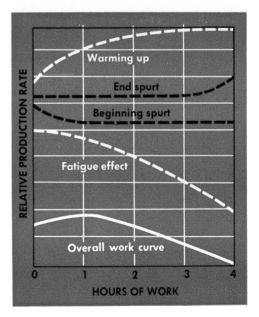

see in the discussion on fatigue, it is important to recognize the difference between what a man can do and what he is willing to do.

■ EFFECTS OF FATIGUE

The most important trend in a work curve usually represents fatigue. This is a general downward trend throughout the whole period of work. It is on this trend that effects of other factors such as warming up, beginning spurt, and end spurt are superimposed. This factor of fatigue makes the efficiency of work fall far short of what one might expect by looking at the peaks of the work curve. For that reason we ought to consider in some detail what fatigue is and how it affects efficiency.

Fatigue is a common word, and we are therefore inclined to think that we know what it means. Certainly we *feel* fatigue, and we have many words to describe this *feeling*—tired, weary, exhausted, spent, worn out, beat, dead. Such subjective reports of fatigue probably make up the best definition of fatigue that can be offered at the present time. *Fatigue is a feeling of being tired.* Although this may not appear to be a satisfactory definition, we are unable to supply a more objective one, because, as we shall see below, there is no completely consistent way of measuring fatigue. Sometimes fatigue is defined as a *decrement in performance*, and this will do for the majority of situations in which fatigue is present, but there are times, as we shall see, when people are fatigued but show no decrement in performance.

Output. Perhaps the first thing we think of in connection with fatigue is that a fatigued person does less of whatever he is doing than he did before he was fatigued. If he is shoveling coal, he shovels less coal when he is fatigued than when he is not.

If he is typing, he usually types fewer words per minute when he is fatigued than when he is rested. In these cases and in similar cases, we are talking about the amount of work accomplished, and it is easy to measure the amount. We can measure weight of the coal shoveled or the number of words typed. When the activity or work is of a kind for which an amount can be measured, our first attempt to measure fatigue is always in terms of the amount of work done.

In almost any type of work *which is primarily physical*, fatigue shows up as a decreased amount done. Typically, the amount at first drops slowly or not at all. Then it drops faster and faster, as shown in Figure 17.2. If the work is kept up long enough, eventually fatigue becomes so great that no work at all can be done. In common language, we say that a person is completely exhausted when he is so fatigued that he can no longer work at all.

Errors. In many types of activity, fatigue is *not* indicated by a decreased amount of work. Sometimes, the work simply cannot be measured in amounts. Studying for an examination is an activity that can hardly be measured as an amount. In other cases, the physical effort involved in the work is so slight that no change in amount occurs. In such cases, however, a measurement of errors frequently reveals fatigue when a measurement of amount does not. In receiving telegraphic code, for example, fatigue is reflected in an increase in the number of errors. In one study, receivers made between three and four times as many errors in the third hour of receiving code as they did in the first hour.[1]

In a study of typing errors, the time required to type successive lines was measured, and although the time required per line (a measure of amount of work) went up at first, it later went back down again.[2] An analysis of the errors made, however, showed that the number of errors per line continued to increase long after the time per line leveled off.

Whether fatigue shows up as increased *time* taken to do a certain amount of work or as increased *errors* depends on the attitude or set of the worker. If he has been instructed to work for perfect accuracy, he can do so over a long period of time. Then as he becomes more and more fatigued, he must slow down in order to keep from making errors. If, on the other hand, the worker has been instructed to work primarily for speed, he may continue to work at the same rate for long periods of time but will make more and more errors.

Thus we see that fatigue can show itself in more ways than one, and *we must be careful, in looking for the effects of fatigue, to examine all possible changes in performance.* If we measure one thing and neglect another, we are apt to find that there is no change in what we are measuring. The change may take place instead in some aspect of performance that we fail to measure. Especially is this true when the worker knows what one is going to measure, for then he strives to keep his performance up in that particular respect. But if he is really fatigued, his work will deteriorate in some other way.

Accidents. Some years ago, when long work days were the rule rather than the exception, accident rates were compiled for many different industries over 6-hour work periods. It was found that over half of all the accidents occurred in the last 2 hours of work and that less than one-fifth of them occurred in the first 2 hours of work.[3] The effects of fatigue were showing up as an increased number of accidents. Thus, another important effect of fatigue is to increase the likelihood of accidents. Later we shall see that a change in motivation is largely responsible for effects of this kind.

Physiological effects. Another effect of fatigue is to change physiological performance. In fact, when we cannot observe fatigue in a person's behavior, we can often detect it in measures of physiological functions. There are several such functions that have been used. One is level of muscle tension. When people are well rested their muscle tension is low, but when they are tired and continue to work their muscle tension increases. Another is *skin resistance*, measured by applying an electrical potential across an area of the skin in much the same way that the GSR (pages 90 and 110) is measured. Rested people have a relatively high resistance, but tired people have a somewhat lower one. Still other kinds of measures that are sometimes used are *heart rate, blood pressure,* or *oxygen consumption.*

Oxygen provides a particularly good measure because it is used up in direct proportion to energy expenditure in the body. In instances in which performance holds up over long periods of time, one can tell that more effort is being expended and that the body is working less efficiently because the person uses up more oxygen from the air he breathes. Oxygen consumption is, in fact, a rather good index of the effort that different tasks require and of the relative efficiency of doing them in different ways. A man walking at the rate of 2 miles per hour, for example, uses about 20,000 cubic centimeters of oxygen per mile, but one walking at the rate of 5 miles per hour uses over 25,000 cubic centimeters per mile. Or to cite quickly another study, more oxygen is consumed in pulling a wheelbarrow a given distance than in pushing it that distance.[4] So oxygen consumption may be used as an index of physiological efficiency as well as of fatigue.

Fatigue as a change in motivation. We have seen that fatigue can be most easily measured and thought of as a change in performance of some kind. The change in performance can be in *amount, errors,* or *accidents.* In other cases, where a change in performance cannot easily be measured, we can show a change in psychomotor ability. These changes in ability are usually measured with such things as laboratory tests of reaction time, hand steadiness, etc. In still other cases we can show that even though the same amount of work is getting done —i.e., there is no change in performance— the work is getting done with less physiological efficiency.

There is still another way in which fatigue can show up. Suppose that you observe men at work over long periods of time and that their production continues to decline. We have clear evidence of fatigue. Suppose that you then stop the men at work

Fig. 17.3. Flagging motivation may decrease performance while ability remains unchanged. Tests may tell us that a worker's ability has not changed, but the fact that actual performance has declined during the course of the working period indicates that motivation has changed. See text for further explanation.

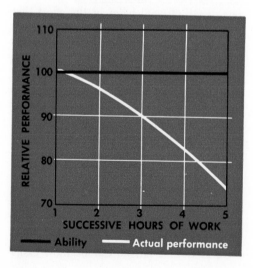

and give them some tests of ability. The chances are that you will find their ability to perform on these tests is as good after many hours of work as it was when they were fresh. You might also find that their work was being done with no loss in physiological efficiency. So the men are still able to work as well after many hours as in the first hour, but they actually do not work as well. What then accounts for the decline in their production? You might be justified in supposing that it is due to a change in *motivation* rather than fatigue—that the men simply are not trying as hard as they might.[5]

This situation is shown schematically in Figure 17.3. This shows that the curve of work output continues to drop but that the curve of ability as measured by laboratory tests does not go down. What has changed is the person's feeling of what is necessary or his willingness to work. This effect of fatigue is very common in our everyday life. If you have been driving an automobile for several hours and are stopped and given a driving test, you probably will do as well as if you had not been driving for a long time. However, while you are actually driving, you probably change your idea of what is necessary. You are less alert, you do not slow down quite as soon when you approach an intersection, and you take more chances when you pass another car—not because you are unable to do the correct thing, but rather because it no longer seems quite as necessary to do so. The term *vigilance* has been used to describe what diminishes in this effect, and it is very apt. You can do as well, but you are less vigilant.

It is the very nature of this effect of fatigue that makes it so important. If you have been digging a ditch for several hours, you are fatigued, and you know it. If you are driving a car, however, you do not realize that you are fatigued because the only effect of the fatigue has been to make you relax your standards of what you consider to be good performance. You do not drive as well because you think you do not have to, and when you have an accident because of carelessness you will be sure that you have done everything just as you should. But when you are tired, what you *think* you should do and what you *really* should do are often two different things.

■ WORK AND REST

We have seen that there are many factors that affect how we work. Fatigue is the most important of these factors. We can show its effects in many different ways. Because fatigue is so important, we are greatly concerned with ways of preventing it and means of overcoming it after it has occurred.

Recovery from fatigue. Perhaps the best way of seeing how we can prevent or overcome fatigue is to see just how fast we recover from it. Figure 17.4 shows the results of one experiment performed with university students.[6] The students were required to lift a weight with their fingers, and the height to which they lifted the weight was measured on each trial. They were required to continue lifting the weight until they could no longer lift it at all. Then they were given rest periods for various lengths of time, after which they were required to lift the weight again. The height to which they could lift the weight on this first trial after rest was a measure of the relative recovery from fatigue. If they still could not lift it at all, they had not recovered at all. If they could lift it as high as they had on the first trial previously, then the recovery was 100 per cent.

Figure 17.4 shows that recovery from fatigue is fairly rapid at first but then slows down considerably. Even after 20 minutes

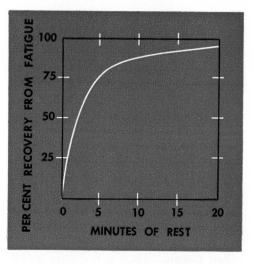

Fig. 17.4. Recovery from fatigue. These are the results of a test for recovery from fatigue. Subjects lifted a weight with their fingers until they could no longer lift it. Then, after various periods of rest, they were required to lift the weight again. The curve shows how high, relative to first lifting, they could lift the weight after rest. (After Manzer, C. W. *An experimental investigation of responses. Arch. Psychol. N.Y., 1927, No. 90.*)

of rest, the students had not completely recovered from the fatigue. In fact, at the rate they were recovering, a total of 40 minutes would be required for them to get back to normal.

If the students were stopped before they had reached complete fatigue, and then given rest periods, recovery was much faster. For example, they might have been stopped when they were lifting the weight only 50 per cent as high as they had on the first trial. In this case recovery would be complete in a much shorter period of time. In fact, recovery from fatigue is so much faster after short periods of work than after long periods that much greater over-all efficiency can be obtained with short work periods than with long work periods. For example, suppose you have a certain amount of snow that has to be shoveled. If you start right in and keep going until you can barely lift the shovel, you will have to stop and take a rest. It will require a long rest, however, for you to recover from your fatigue and get back to work. On the other hand, if you shovel for a little while, then rest for a little while, then shovel, etc., you never need very long rest periods, because recovery from fatigue is so rapid when only a little work has been done. In this way you can shovel steadily for a much longer period of time, and you actually can get the whole job done much sooner than if you keep shoveling until you are completely fatigued.

Rest periods. There is a definite moral to this story: to stave off fatigue and still get work done, one should schedule rest periods often enough to keep from getting very tired. How often they should be and how long they should be depends on the kind of work. Heavy manual labor requires frequent and reasonably long rest periods. For sedentary work, rest periods do not need to be either so often or so long. (See related discussion in Chapter 5 of periods of practice in learning.)

In recent years industry has been applying these principles more and more by providing for regular rest periods throughout the work day. Industrial concerns have learned by experience as well as experiment that such rest periods allay fatigue and increase productivity, that necessary rest is not time lost but rather work gained. They often face the practical decision, however, of how long to make the periods and when to schedule them. Usually they have provided for periods of 10 to 15 minutes. By studying production records carefully it is possible to schedule the periods just before production tends to fall off. In the case of clerical and sedentary workers, one break about midmorning and another about mid-afternoon are usually about right.

One of the things we learn from studies of industrial fatigue is that it is better, usually, to schedule rest periods than to allow people to take them irregularly. In one study, for example, production was greater with scheduled periods than with irregular ones even though the total time taken in rest in the latter instance was slightly greater.[7] The reason for this apparently lies in the *set* of a person for work. Most of us manage to adjust our level of effort to the total amount of work to be accomplished or to the total time we have to work. If, for example, you are starting to run a mile, you do not run as fast as if you are starting to run 100 yards. Likewise, if a person has 10 minutes to work, he is likely to work harder than if he has 2 hours to work. So when a person has a definite time to rest he is likely to pace himself at a little faster rate than if he works until he gets tired and voluntarily stops.

Length of the work day and work week. Another factor in work efficiency is the length of the working day. The facts of this matter are very interesting. Many people assume, rather naturally, that if we want to get more from a particular worker, the thing to do is increase the number of hours per day or per week that he works. In recent years, however, it has become increasingly clear that there is a real limit to the number of hours most people can work in a day or week and still work with reasonable efficiency. Perhaps it is obvious that a man gets less efficient *per hour* if he works 10 hours a day than if he works 8 hours a day. What was not realized for a long time, however, is that he can be so much less efficient that the total work done in the 10-hour day can be less than the total work done in the 8-hour day.

A number of studies demonstrate both points.[8] If maximum production per hour is what we want, then a work week between

36 and 44 hours is best. If, however, we want the maximum production per work week, a work week between 48 and 54 hours is best. The reason for this difference is that the hourly efficiency drops when the work week is increased from 40 to 50 hours, but the drop in efficiency is not great enough to offset the greater number of hours. If, however, the work week is increased beyond this point, then the drop in hourly efficiency is so great that it completely offsets the increased number of hours.

■ ENVIRONMENTAL FACTORS

We have discussed fatigue in considerable detail because it is so important to the efficiency of people at work. Several other factors, however, also affect efficiency. These may be divided roughly into two general classes: the environmental aspects of the work situation, and the physiological conditions of the individual.

Sound. One of the environmental factors is sound. There is usually some kind of sound in almost everybody's work situation, varying from low background noises to the sounds of machinery and voices or even music that has been deliberately introduced into the work situation. Such sounds can be classified as unwanted or wanted. We ordinarily call unwanted sounds *noise*, whether or not they meet the physical definition of noise given in Chapter 19. The most common form of wanted sound in modern work situations is *music*. So our discussion of sounds is mostly about noise and music.

The effects of noise on work has come in for a good deal of scientific research. Sometimes this research seems to show that a lot of noise harms working efficiency. However, such research often has weaknesses in it that make one question its conclusions. The most trustworthy research, on the whole, shows little or no measurable effects of noise on production or other direct measures of efficiency.[9] Too much noise, of course, interferes with communication because it masks people's voices. Noises that are extremely loud and continuous may, over a long period of time, injure a person's hearing.

Most typically, however, noise has much more subtle effects on efficiency. When people work all day in a high noise level, they become more tense and tired. Though their production may not fall off, they do their work at the expense of more effort and discomfort. Besides that, there is the fact that most people do not like very loud noises. Such likes and dislikes, because they affect a person's comfort, need to be considered in making the working environment as pleasant as possible.

As you probably know, a good many people like to have music of some kind while they work. Perhaps your roommate does, and you find it annoying. Studies show that, on the whole, relatively few people really dislike music and that a great many people definitely prefer it as a background for their work. For that reason, many firms in recent years have been deliberately introducing music into industrial work situations. It is hard to be sure whether such music directly increases working efficiency, although several attempts have been made to find out. We do know that, since most people like it, they feel a little better about their work, and that fact probably makes them more efficient.[10]

One has to be somewhat careful about the choice of music. Music with a strong rhythm commands attention and tends to make people adjust their work to the rhythm. If they are working at a task with a different rhythm, such music may interfere with their work. So the type of music needs to be adjusted to the type of work

It also should be suited to the time of day. Lullaby music, if played late in the afternoon, may lull people to sleep.

Illumination. Lighting is another obvious environmental factor in working efficiency. Almost any task we work at requires our eyes and consequently some light. Different tasks require different amounts of light. If all we have to do is move about freely, as in shoveling snow or loading a truck, we do not need much light, but if we must see fine details as in reading, threading needles, or fixing a watch, we need a lot of light. So the illumination required for the best working efficiency varies with the kind of task.

General studies of the effects of lighting in industrial situations, unfortunately, have yielded results that are confounded with other factors such as morale or motivation.

In the Hawthorne study that we mentioned earlier (Chapter 16), increasing the illumination for a group of girls working in a relay-assembly task sent their production up.[11] But their production also went up when, later, illumination was reduced. Here the effect of illumination was confounded with the effect of the girls' feeling better about their work because someone was taking the trouble to pay attention to them and to do something about their working conditions. So, to set standards of illumination for different tasks, it has been necessary to make systematic studies of comfort and fatigue for specific types of tasks.

We have learned that it is better to err on the side of too much illumination than to risk having too little. It is also desirable to have good even illumination of the whole

Fig. 17.5. A well-illuminated plant. Such a plant has enough illumination for the detail of work required and provides a good even illumination throughout the entire working area. (Courtesy of General Electric Co., Lamp Division.)

room or work space, rather than of the small area in which one is working. Thus general lighting, rather than lighting of many individual work places, is desirable. Well-illuminated industrial plants, such as you see in Figure 17.5, employ this principle. For this reason it is better to employ indirect lighting, rather than direct lighting, for in this way we get more even illumination of work spaces and avoid bright, glary regions that fatigue the eyes and prove annoying.

Illumination engineers have worked out in some detail the illuminations required for specific tasks.[12] The unit of measurement that they use is the foot-candle. This is the light falling on a surface at 1 foot distance from a candle that is about as bright as the candles we commonly employ when eating by candlelight. For simply seeing large objects and making our way about in hallways, etc., all that we need is about 5 foot-candles of illumination. Somewhat more is required for general work, such as moving crates, working in warehouses, or loading trucks. On the other hand, for working continuously at severe tasks such as needlework or reading fine print, 40 to 100 foot-candles are necessary. Tasks of intermediate difficulty have illumination requirements that fall in between.

Temperature and humidity. Probably the most important of the environmental factors affecting efficiency are the temperature and the humidity of the air in which we work. A great deal of attention has been paid to these problems, probably because the problems are always with us. More research has concerned high temperatures than low ones, primarily because it is easier to make a room warmer if it is cold than it is to make it colder if it is warm. We may soon see the time, however, when air conditioning is as common as central heating. Certainly in terms of the evidence we

have, air conditioning in hotter climates would greatly increase working efficiency.

Warm surroundings, indeed, have a harmful effect on working efficiency. As an illustration, we shall use an experiment done on the ability of men to receive telegraphic code accurately. Five men were placed in a room especially constructed to allow accurate control of temperature. These men were required to receive telegraphic code for 3 hours at a time, and they were tested at different temperatures. Messages were sent to them at a rapid rate; hence they made a number of errors even at temperatures which would normally not be considered too severe. The results of this experiment are shown in Figure 17.6, where the

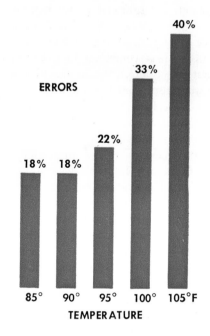

Fig. 17.6. Errors in receiving telegraphic code made at different environmental temperatures. The bars indicate relative number of errors made at different temperatures. See text for description of the experiment. *(Data from Mackworth, N. H. Researches on the measurement of human performance. Medical Research Council, England, 1950, No. 268.)*

percentage of mistakes made at temperatures from 85 to 105°F are shown. The humidity was approximately 65 per cent at each of the different temperatures. The illustration makes it clear that performance deteriorated quite severely, particularly when the temperature became as great as 100°F.

This experiment also led to another very interesting finding. When the operators were separated into three different groups according to their skill at receiving telegraphic code, the poorer operators deteriorated more under the high temperatures than did the better operators. Thus the greater the initial skill, the better performance held up under severe conditions.

We could cite much more evidence on this point, but suffice it to say that high temperatures decrease efficiency. They also reduce comfort, and even though people *can* work under conditions in which they do not feel comfortable, in the long run they work best when they are comfortable. Surveys have been made to determine the temperature ranges which people consider comfortable, and as you might expect, these comfortable ranges depend on several factors.[13] For example, people generally consider higher temperatures more comfortable in the summer than in the winter. At a humidity of 50 per cent, for example, most people feel comfortable in winter with temperatures between 66 and 76°F. In summer they feel comfortable with temperatures between 70 and 81°F.

Another factor in comfort is humidity. Most people feel comfortable with humidities between 30 and 70 per cent. But the humidity also determines the range of comfortable temperatures. Generally speaking, the higher the humidity, the lower the comfortable temperature. Most people, for example, consider a temperature of 95°F intolerable when humidity is 100 per cent,

although they can tolerate and work in temperatures as high as 110°F if the humidity is below 30 per cent. Thus the old saying that "it ain't the heat, it's the humidity" is quite true. Within the ranges of summer temperatures found in the United States, very few places would have really uncomfortable temperatures if the humidity were low enough. But when the temperature is 95 or 100°F, and the humidity rises above 80 per cent, a person's efficiency is greatly lowered.

Ventilation. Ventilating engineers have conducted enough studies to show rather clearly that ventilation, quite aside from temperature, affects efficiency.[13] Of course, if the temperature is high, moving air in a room helps by speeding up the evaporation of perspiration, which has a cooling effect on the skin. In addition, even at normal temperatures, stale or stagnant air decreases efficiency, and moving the air in and out of the room helps offset the effect. In most practical situations, this has nothing to do with the amount of oxygen in the room but is primarily a matter of annoying odors and fumes. The odors that issue forth from machinery, radiators, and people's bodies on the whole do not make people feel comfortable, and getting rid of them, where they tend to be excessive, helps efficiency.

Oxygen lack. Most people under normal circumstances never suffer any appreciable lack of oxygen, for even a relatively large number of people in a room do not deplete the oxygen supply to any significant degree. In an airplane or at high altitudes, however, oxygen becomes sparse enough to impair efficiency.[14] There are several psychological effects of such oxygen deficiency.

At an altitude of 14,000 feet, for example, seeing becomes very difficult. About twice as much light as normal is required. A man has tremors of the head and can no longer make precise movements. Even the

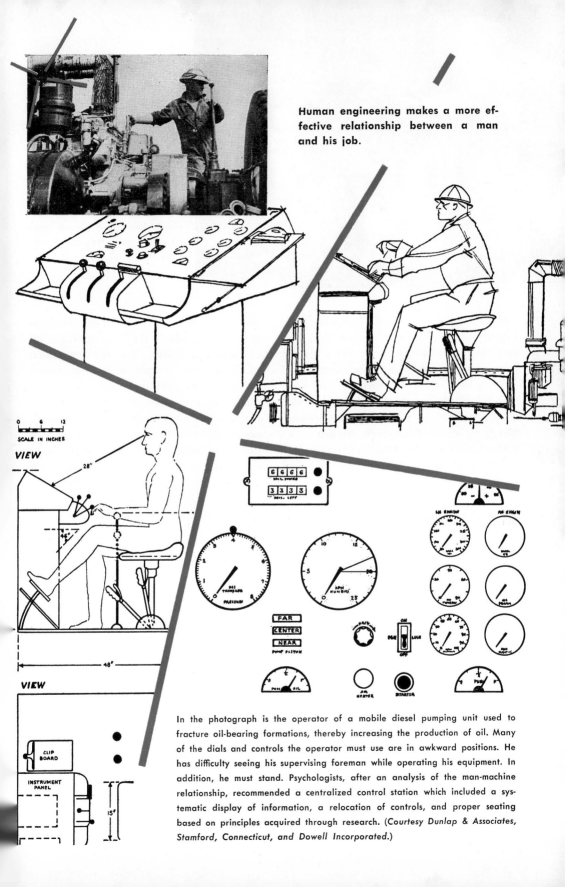

Human engineering makes a more effective relationship between a man and his job.

SCALE IN INCHES

VIEW

VIEW

CLIP BOARD

INSTRUMENT PANEL

In the photograph is the operator of a mobile diesel pumping unit used to fracture oil-bearing formations, thereby increasing the production of oil. Many of the dials and controls the operator must use are in awkward positions. He has difficulty seeing his supervising foreman while operating his equipment. In addition, he must stand. Psychologists, after an analysis of the man-machine relationship, recommended a centralized control station which included a systematic display of information, a relocation of controls, and proper seating based on principles acquired through research. (*Courtesy Dunlap & Associates, Stamford, Connecticut, and Dowell Incorporated.*)

Fig. 17.7. Oxygen for athletes. Tests have shown that oxygen given to athletes during rest periods helps them recover more quickly from fatigue. (*Science Service.*)

slightest amount of exercise leaves him panting for breath. Worse than this, his memory and thinking processes become very poor. Since anoxia produces no pain, however, he does not feel particularly bad and may actually feel quite gay. There are, indeed, examples of pilots who have completely collapsed from such oxygen lack without even realizing that they were going to do so. Mountain climbers have had the same experience.

◼ PHYSIOLOGICAL FACTORS

Oxygen lack is an environmental condition which has its profound effects because it leads to a physiological imbalance in the body. It may have occurred to you that there are other physiological conditions that may affect efficiency. Obviously when people are ill, have brain injuries, lose limbs, or suffer paralyses, efficiency is likely to be impaired. This is not the place to discuss such conditions. Some common questions that we should consider, however, concern the factors of sleep, alcohol, caffeine, and tobacco.

Sleep. Most adults spend about one-third of their lives in sleep. The physiology of sleep is not too well understood, but we do know that it is a state of relative inactivity during which the body makes a lot of metabolic repairs. We also know that people are not completely inactive during sleep, for they shift their position and flex their muscles periodically. We know, too, that the depth of sleep varies; in general, people are in their deepest sleep an hour or two after retiring, but throughout the night the depth of sleep continually varies from relatively light to relatively deep. This variation is depicted in Figure 17.8, which is a summary of many researches on the depth of sleep.

Occasionally a person who thinks he enjoys life so much that he does not want to miss any of it asks the question, Is sleep necessary? And many persons, particularly college students, for one reason or another cut themselves short on sleep (see discussion on page 65). Is this a good idea or not? *Is sleep really necessary?* If so, how much?

There are dozens of research studies on these questions. They have run into the same problems that we have already encountered in other attempts to measure fatigue. If a man goes one night without sleep, it is hard to tell much difference the next day. He may confess that he is a little lightheaded, his attention may wander a little, and he may have an unusual desire to sit down or lie down. His performance, however, is likely to be about the same, for he can do a fair day's work, take examinations, answer letters, and otherwise function normally.

Suppose we keep the man up for still another night, and then another. In several studies, people have been kept from sleeping for three successive nights.[15] On the fourth day, they have been given all sorts of tests—psychomotor, intelligence, arithmetic, etc. The interesting fact is that they can do just about as well on all these objective tests of efficiency as they could when they were rested. Rather prolonged loss of sleep, therefore, does not impair efficiency if we use systematic tests to measure it.

There are, nevertheless, rather profound effects that can be discovered in other ways. People tend to become silly, irritable, and restless. Some may even develop symptoms that resemble mental illness—symptoms such as *delusions of grandeur or persecution,* or *false memories of people and of the passage of time.* Their *judgment* becomes

impaired, and if they drive cars they are more likely to take chances. In general, people who have been deprived of sleep for a long time show all the subtle symptoms of persons who have worked hard for too many hours or who suffer a little oxygen lack. Perhaps the most obvious symptom is that they do not want to work; indeed, all they want to do is lie down and go to sleep. So *loss of sleep,* like other effects of fatigue, *does not change a person's capacity to perform, but it does change his willingness or motivation to perform.*

Alcohol. Because so many people use alcoholic beverages either occasionally or habitually, the influence of alcohol is a question of some importance. Much has been written about the effects of alcohol on personality, morals, and efficiency. In Chapter 10, we discuss emotional factors in the use of alcohol, and in Chapter 22 we mention physiological factors in alcoholism. Here we shall consider only the question of alcohol's effect on efficiency.

Scores of researches have purported to test the effects of alcohol on efficiency.[16] Many of them are worthless, however, because they did not conceal from the subjects whether or not they were receiving alcohol and thus they failed to eliminate the effects of suggestion (see page 347). In the controlled experiments, alcohol was suitably disguised when given to subjects so that they could not tell, except from the effects themselves, how much, if any, alcohol they were given. As you may have observed, there are wide individual differences in the effects of alcohol. Some people have a very high tolerance for it, and others a very low tolerance. Moreover, alcohol affects people in various ways, making some aggressive and active, others depressed and introverted.

We can, however, make the unequivocal statement that *alcohol lowers efficiency.* We can take almost any test of capacity—reflex

Fig. 17.8. Fluctuations in the depth of sleep during the night. This is a schematic way of representing the results of many researches on the depth of sleep. The intensity of sound necessary to awaken the sleeper is a convenient measure of the depth of sleep. Note that depth of sleep fluctuates throughout the night. (*After Kleitman, N. Sleep and wakefulness. Chicago: Univ. of Chicago Press, 1939.*)

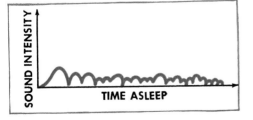

TABLE 17.1. Effects of tobacco smoking on efficiency. Below are the results of one carefully controlled study. Tests were given on days when tobacco was smoked and compared with days on which it was not. Plus (+) indicates a gain in efficiency; minus (—), a loss in efficiency; and zero (O), no decided change. Three separate comparisons were made.

Type of test	Tests on nonsmokers			Tests on smokers		
	1	2	3	1	2	3
Pulse (increased)	+	+	+	+	+	+
Tremor of hand (increased)	—	—	—	—	—	—
Tapping	O	O	O	O	O	O
Muscular fatigue	+	+	+	+	O	O
Canceling As, speed	O	O	O	O	O	O
Canceling As, accuracy	O	O	O	O	+	+
Reading reaction time	+	+?	+	+	+?	+
Learning reaction time	+	+	+	+	+	+
Adding, speed	—	—	—	+	+	+
Adding, accuracy	—?	—	—?	O	O	O
Memory span	—	—	—	—	—	—
Rote learning	—	O	O	—	O	O

From Hull, C. L. The influence of tobacco smoking on mental and motor efficiency. *Psychol. Monogr.*, 1924, **33**, No. 150.

time of the knee jerk, ability to make tapping movements, hand steadiness, adding and subtracting numbers, rate of learning—and alcohol, when it is taken in sufficient quantity to have an effect, impairs performance. Hence we do not have the trouble that we have in cases of sleep loss or fatigue of measuring effects on performance. Alcohol definitely impairs efficiency by any objective index.

Why then do some people feel that they can work a little better with a nip of alcohol? Why is it a common conception that a little alcohol is a stimulant? The impression comes partly from the fact that people often feel a little better, or a little happier, after imbibing a little. Because alcohol dulls capacities, it also dulls some of the worries, inhibitions, or repressions that make us feel unhappy and unmotivated to work. Thus it may give us more pep and more zest for work, but in so doing it also impairs the capacity to work well—an effect that is just about the opposite of fatigue and sleeplessness. Too much alcohol, of course, makes

people unwilling to do much of anything and eventually puts them in a stupor.

Caffeine. Caffeine is a drug that is found in coffee, tea, the cola drinks, and some other common "soft" beverages. Most people in our American culture consume relatively large quantities of it. Because of its practical importance, psychologists have run a large number of experiments to assess its effects on efficiency.[4] The best of these experiments have used "fake" pills along with real pills containing caffeine and have compared efficiency with and without caffeine when the subject did not know whether he had received caffeine or not.

The experiments are not completely consistent with one another, but they justify the general conclusion that caffeine is a stimulant. In mild doses, it usually produces some small increase on such measures of efficiency as tapping, typewriting, adding and subtracting, and simple problem solving. Sometimes, however, large doses of caffeine may slightly impair performance, but the general effect of the drug in mild doses is to help rather than to impair efficiency. It should be added, however, that caffeine is habit-forming, and once the habit is acquired, people may show drowsiness, headaches, dizziness, and other discomforts— factors that impair efficiency—when they are deprived of their regular ration of caffeine.

Tobacco. Finally let us take up another habit that the majority of adult Americans have acquired—the smoking habit. Much has been written about the ills and benefits of this habit, and there has been much research, some of it poor and misleading and some of it good, to find out how smoking affects efficiency. In one of the better experiments, subjects were blindfolded and provided with a stem through which they could draw "smoke" from a pipe.[17] On some days they actually did get smoke, and on others they unknowingly drew in hot air that had been warmed by putting an electric heating coil in the pipe. To keep the subjects fooled, they were allowed to smell tobacco smoke in the room while they sucked in air. Other experiments have used other devices to control the effects of suggestion.

By and large controlled experiments do not yield any conclusive proof that smoking affects efficiency. The results of one study are illustrated in Table 17.1. Seldom are any great changes, one way or the other, brought about by smoking. Some changes go in one direction for nonsmokers and in the other direction for smokers. In general, smoking increases the pulse rate a little and decreases muscular tremor. It makes no difference for tapping or such simple tasks as crossing out all the As in a passage of prose. It may increase reaction time a little, but for more complex functions it does not have consistent effects. We must conclude from studies such as this either that our available techniques are not good enough to detect the impairing effects of smoking or that smoking has little, if any, consistent effects on psychological efficiency.

SUMMARY

1. Work curves that are typical of amount of work done during the course of a day have their ups and downs. They can be analyzed, however, into four principal components: (*a*) a warming-up effect, (*b*) a beginning spurt, (*c*) an end spurt, and (*d*) a fatigue effect.

2. Fatigue can be measured in a number of ways: (*a*) by amount produced, (*b*) by errors or quality of work, (*c*) by accidents, (*d*) by physiological effects, and (*e*) by changes in motivation.

3. Often, when there is a measurable effect of fatigue on production, errors, or accidents, fatigue shows up as a lowered motivation for work or as increased physiological effort for the same amount of work done.

4. Recovery from fatigue generally is faster when the fatigue is mild than when it has become severe. Thus it is better to take short rests frequently than long rests infrequently.

5. If one attempts to lengthen the work day or the work week, there is a point beyond which total production declines. Consequently there is an optimum work day and work week.

6. Such environmental factors as noise, music, lighting, temperature, humidity, and ventilation all have measurable effects on comfort and efficiency.

7. Loss of sleep tends to reduce willingness to work rather than ability to work.

8. Alcohol is usually a depressant even though it may seem like a stimulant.

9. Caffeine, on the other hand, is a stimulant that can increase performance slightly.

10. In general, smoking has little if any effect on ability to perform most tasks.

SUGGESTIONS FOR FURTHER READING

Bartley, S. H., and Chute, E. *Fatigue and impairment in man.* New York: McGraw-Hill, 1947.

    A report of research studies on fatigue, stressing the importance of psychological factors in fatigue.

Berrien, F. K. *Practical psychology* (Rev. Ed.). New York: Macmillan, 1952.

    A text on applied psychology which includes chapters on efficiency.

Bills, A. G. *The psychology of efficiency.* New York: Harper, 1943.

    A comprehensive survey of the field of human efficiency.

Carmichael, L., and Dearborn, W. F. *Reading and visual fatigue.* Boston: Houghton Mifflin, 1947.

    The summary of an extensive research project on visual fatigue during prolonged reading.

Chapanis, A., Garner, W. R., and Morgan, C. T. *Applied experimental psychology.* New York: Wiley, 1949. Chaps. 13 and 14.

    A text that includes chapters on the relation of work and environmental factors to efficiency.

Poffenberger, A. T. *Principles of applied psychology.* New York: Appleton-Century-Crofts, 1942.

    A comprehensive text on applied psychology, covering the topics of work and efficiency.

Roethlisberger, F. J., and Dickson, W. J. *Management and the worker.* Cambridge, Mass.: Harvard Univ. Press, 1939.

    A description of the Hawthorne studies that emphasizes the importance of motivation and morale in industrial efficiency.

Ryan, T. A. *Work and effort.* New York: Ronald, 1947.

    An analysis of theories and experimental work in the field of efficiency.

Vernon, H. M. *Industrial fatigue and efficiency.* New York: Dutton, 1921.

    A summary of experiments on industrial fatigue and efficiency carried out in England during the First World War.

PART 5

Knowing the World

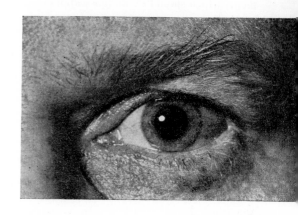

Chapter 18 VISION

MOST OF US grow up so engrossed in studying the gadgets of our mechanized world that we scarcely have time to wonder at the intricacy of our own bodies. Few of us, for example, have stopped to realize what a marvelous instrument we have in the human eye. With this instrument a normal human being, under good conditions, can see a wire $\frac{1}{16}$ inch in diameter at a distance of $\frac{1}{4}$ mile. It is so sensitive that, when it is fully dark-adapted, the average person may see the flare of a match 50 miles away on a clear, dark night. Yet, in contrast, the eye can momentarily look at the sun when it is at its zenith in the sky. If you compute the ratio of these two intensities—the flare of a match 50 miles away and the intensity

of the sun—you will find that the total range of intensities to which the human eye can respond is something of the order of 100,000,000,000,000:1. The average person, moreover, can see several hundred thousand different colors. Truly, then, we have in the eye an extraordinary instrument. Indeed, there are scarcely any physical instruments which approach the total range of sensitivity of the human eye.

The eye also renders remarkable psychological service. It is our major source of contact with the world, and the person who is deprived of his sight has suffered a severe and irreparable loss. Not only do we learn about objects through our eyes, but we also get most of our ideas by way of them. Consider the wealth of information which is contained in your college library, all designed for assimilation through the eyes. So our eyes are instruments of extraordinary

This chapter was drafted by Alphonse Chapanis of The Johns Hopkins University.

delicacy, sensitivity, and usefulness—instruments which should excite our wonder and admiration.

THE STIMULUS FOR VISION

Before we can understand how the eye works and how we sense the visual world, we need to consider the physical stimulus for vision. If you were asked what you see, you would probably say that you see light. This is true—you do see light. But we must distinguish between the physical stimulus that excites the eye and the psychological sensation of light that you actually experience. First we shall consider some of the physical properties of light.

Electromagnetic radiation.   We see objects either because they emit radiant energy or because radiant energy is reflected from them. This energy, which physicists call electromagnetic radiations, consists of electric charges moving through space at approximately 186,000 miles per second. It is difficult to explain just what these charges or electromagnetic radiations are like, but it is conventional and convenient to talk about them as though they traveled in

waves. It is also possible to measure and classify radiant energy in terms of the distance from the peak of one wave to the peak of the next, that is to say, in terms of *wavelength*. Some electromagnetic radiations have wavelengths as short as 10 trillionths of an inch (the cosmic rays), some have wavelengths of many miles (radio waves), and there are all sorts of wavelengths in between (Figure 18.1). The entire range of all possible waves is called the *electromagnetic spectrum*.

Visible radiant energy.   Although all radiant energy—all wavelengths of the electromagnetic spectrum—is very much the same physically, not all of it is visible. Somewhere in the middle of the spectrum, between 16 and 32 millionths of an inch in length (Figure 18.1), are the wavelengths that we can see, and these are known as the visible spectrum. Because the word "light" implies seeing, it is only these wavelengths that are called light or light waves. Scientists use a metric scale rather than inches and feet, however, to express length, so the *visible spectrum of wavelengths is said to extend from about 400 to 800 millimicrons* ($m\mu$). A micron is one millionth

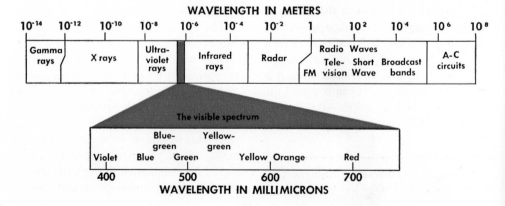

Fig. 18.1. The electromagnetic and visible spectra. Electromagnetic waves have a spectrum from as short as 10^{-14} meters to as long as 10^{8} meters. The part of the spectrum that is visible and is called light is only a tiny fraction in the neighborhood of 10^{-6} meters.

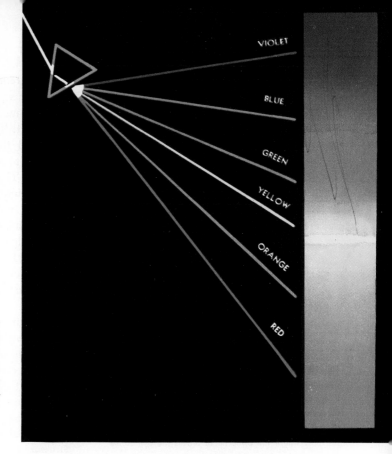

Fig. 18.2. All the colors of the visible spectrum are produced when a prism is used to break up white light into its components. *(From Bustanoby, J. H. Principles of color and color mixing. New York: McGraw-Hill, 1947.)*

of a meter and a millimicron is one thousandth of that.

As Isaac Newton discovered in 1666, it is possible to break the visible spectrum up into its component wavelengths.[1] The trick for doing that is to pass a beam of sunlight through a triangular glass prism (see Figure 18.2), because such a prism bends short wavelengths (which appear violet) more than long wavelengths (which appear red). A prism, in fact, spreads all the wavelengths out in a broad band so that we can see and measure each wavelength in a bundle of light. Each wavelength of the visible spectrum has a characteristic color.

THE EYE AND HOW IT WORKS

In certain respects, the eye looks and behaves like a camera (Figure 18.3). Both the eye and a camera are essentially dark chambers which admit light through an opening in front. Immediately behind the opening in each case is a lens which focuses images of outside objects onto the rear surface. *The surface on which the image is projected in the eye is called the retina;* in the camera, it is the photographic film. Both the camera and the eye can be adjusted to control the amount of light falling on this surface. To control light entering a camera, the photographer adjusts the diaphragm in front of the lens. When he encounters too much light, he "stops down" the camera, and when light is relatively dim, he increases the size of the opening in the diaphragm. The eye, however, has its own automatic (reflex) mechanism for making such an adjustment. Its diaphragm is the *iris,* which is the colored part of the eye; this iris controls the size of the aperture, known as the *pupil*, which admits light to the eye. In dim light, the iris expands the pupil, thus increasing the amount of light passing through it; in bright light, the iris contracts the pupil, thus reducing the amount of light admitted. This adjustment permits a person to see in dimmer and in brighter illuminations than would otherwise be possible. You can easily observe the adjustment by having a person close his eyelids for a while and then open them. The normal pupil has a maximum range of adjustment of 2 to 8 millimeters in diameter —corresponding to a sixteenfold change in area.

Fig. 18.3. The eye likened to a camera. In both the eye and a camera the image is focused by a lens and is upside down and reversed on the photosensitive surface. In the eye this surface is called the retina. The part of the retina where vision is clearest is the fovea; the part where the optic nerve leaves the eye is the blind spot (see Figs. 18.4 and 18.21).

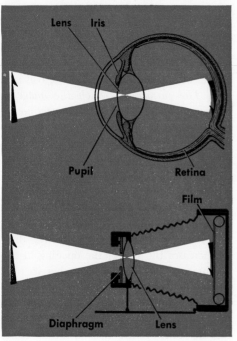

Inverted retinal images. From Chapter 7, you may remember that images on the retina are inverted and turned around from right to left. This is the case in both the camera and the eye, because the rays of light come to a point and cross in the lens of the eye. This fact can be proved by the following simple demonstration: Punch a small hole (not more than ⅛ inch in diameter) in a large piece of paper. Make sure that the edges of the hole are clean and not frayed. Hold the piece of paper about 3 or 4 inches in front of one eye and look through the hole at some distant object. Now take a small card and move it slowly between your eye and the hole in the paper. If you move the card upward very carefully and slowly to intercept the rays of light between your eye and the hole, you will actually see the hole being covered from above. If you move the card from above downward, you will see the hole being covered from below.

Structure of the eye. Although it is helpful and instructive to compare the eye with the camera, this comparison must not be pushed too far. A closer look at the eye reveals an organ of enormous complexity —so complex that the drawing in Figure 18.4, which is complicated enough, shows only its essential features. Unlike the camera, the eye is a roughly spheroidal organ. Its walls consist of three separate layers: the *sclerotic coat*, the *choroid coat*, and the *retina*. The first and outer layer, the sclerotic coat, is a tough fibrous material that protects the eyeball and maintains its shape. In the front of the eye, this sclerotic layer becomes transparent and bulges out to form the *cornea*. Underneath the sclerotic layer is the choroid layer, which corresponds roughly to the opaque backing on a photographic film or to the blackening on the inside of a camera. This dark layer absorbs stray light in the eyeball and prevents light

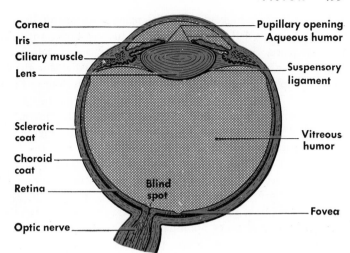

Fig. 18.4. The anatomy of the eye. The principal parts of the eye are shown. For further explanation, see text.

from entering the eye except through the cornea and lens. The retinal layer, the innermost layer of the eyeball, as we have said, is like a photographic film, for it is the sensitive organ that enables us to see. The interior of the eye, finally, is divided into two chambers: a small one in front of the lens, between it and the cornea, and a large one behind the lens, the main chamber of the eye. These chambers are filled with gelatinous fluids sometimes called humors.

Rods and cones. Because the retina is the sensitive organ for seeing, it deserves a closer look than the other structures of the eye. If we examine it with a microscope, we can see that it is made up of extremely tiny cells of two basic types—*rods* and *cones*. Figure 18.5 depicts these two cells. As you can see, rods are cylindrical in shape, but the cones are rather tapered. Our best estimate is that the eye contains between 110,000,000 and 125,000,000 rods, and between 6,300,000 and 6,800,000 cones.[2] This tremendous number of rods and cones, however, does not spread uniformly over the entire retina. Rather the cones are most numerous in a highly specialized region of the retina known as the

fovea, and the rods occur most frequently about 20 degrees away from the fovea.

Connections of the cones and rods. From the rods and cones, tiny nerve fibers stretch into the retina and make connections with still other types of cells: bipolar, horizontal, and ganglion cells. From the ganglion cells come the fibers which make up the optic nerve. The connections of these various cells are so enormously complex that microanatomists have been able to trace out only some of the more obvious ones, and physiologists can only surmise what function these cells serve. From the psychologist's standpoint, this network of connections allows a good many possibilities for explaining some of the curious visual phenomena that we shall discuss later. Figure 18.5 shows a diagram of some of these nervous connections in the retina.

The fovea. The fovea is the part of the retina that we use most in looking at objects, and it therefore deserves special attention. The fovea is the region of most distinct vision. When we want to see something very clearly, we naturally turn our head and eyes so that an image of the object falls on this part of the retina.

Mother Nature took some special pains when she designed this part of the eye. In the first place, the cones in the fovea are much longer and more slender than those in the periphery of the eye. In fact, foveal cones look something like rods. Because they are smaller, many more of them can be packed into the small foveal area. A second interesting feature of the foveal cones is that they have their own individual nervous connections with the optic nerve—they have "private lines" to the brain.[3] Outside the fovea, however, several cones, or several rods and cones, are usually linked together into common nerve pathways. Rods, in fact, never have private connections; there are always groups of them discharging into single nerve pathways.

A curious feature of the retina is that the *receptors point backward*. Consequently, when an image of some object is brought to a focus on the retina, the light must travel through all the nerve fibers and cell layers of the retina before it arrives at the photosensitive cells. These intervening layers are rather transparent, but they undoubtedly blur the image a little. They do less blurring in the fovea than elsewhere in the retina because they are pushed to the side in the fovea.

In Figure 18.4 is a part of the retina labeled the *blind spot*. This is the point at which fibers of ganglion cells leave the retina, forming the optic nerve which connects with the brain. The spot is blind because it lacks both rods and cones. Later in this chapter we shall have more to say about the blind spot.

Accommodation. In most cameras one adjusts the focus for objects at different distances by moving the lens back and forth. The lens of the eye does not work this way; rather *it changes its shape to focus at different distances*. Such changes are termed *accommodation*. They consist of a thickening or thinning of the lens which

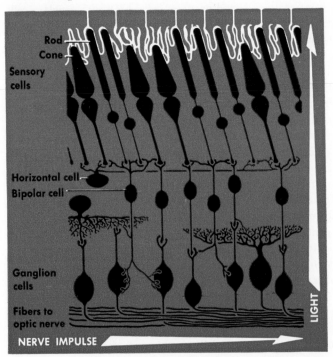

Fig. 18.5. A schematic diagram of the cells of the retina. At the top are the sensory cells, the rods and cones. These connect with bipolar cells, which connect in turn with the ganglion cells. Fibers of the ganglion cells make up the optic nerve. Note the many interconnections, especially those of the horizontal and ganglion cells.

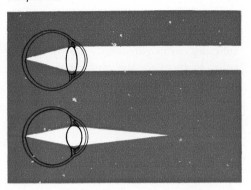

Fig. 18.6. The accommodation of the lens. The lens flattens to focus images of objects far away, and it fattens to focus on nearby objects.

is controlled by a muscle known as the *ciliary muscle.* This muscle, which is attached to ligaments that suspend the lens in place, so contracts and relaxes that the lens becomes thin and flat to focus the eye on far objects and becomes thick and curved to focus it on near objects (Figure 18.6).

Shape of the eye. By looking around at the number of people who wear glasses, one can get a fair notion of the proportion of the population who have ocular defects of one sort or another. Of course, there are several reasons why this is not a good way to collect statistics. Many people who should wear glasses do not, some people wear glasses only part of the time, and some people, like actors and actresses, wear contact lenses, which are hard to spot. At any rate eye doctors estimate that one-quarter to one-third of the adult population either should or does wear glasses to correct ocular defects. These defects are largely a matter of the kinds of eyes people are born with, for eye defects tend to run in families. As inherited characteristics, they are as much a part of a person's physical make-up as his height, hair color, or eye color.

The ocular defects whose effects in vision can be corrected by glasses are of two general varieties: a distortion of the shape of the eyeball, and irregularities in the lens. Although eyes are amazingly constant in shape, it does not take much distortion in shape to make them imperfect optical instruments. In some cases, the over-all length of the eyeball is a little longer or shorter than it should be, and in other cases the curved surface of the cornea is a little too flat or too curved.

Farsightedness. About two-thirds of the people in America can see all right at a distance of 20 feet or more. For that reason it is possible to put blackboards at the front of classrooms in school, signposts at considerable distances along roads, and seats far back in theaters. Some people, however, are pathologically farsighted, that

Fig. 18.7. Farsightedness and nearsightedness. In the normal person (*top*) the image is focused on the retina. The farsighted person (*middle*) has an eyeball that is too short and focuses images on a plane behind the retina. The nearsighted person (*bottom*) has an eyeball that is too long and focuses images in a plane in front of the retina.

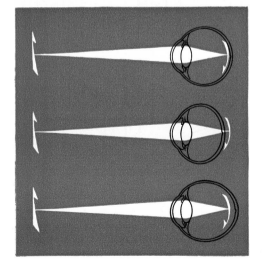

is to say, they cannot see things that are very close (Figure 18.7). Usually their trouble is that the eyeball is too short. Consequently when a farsighted person wants to look at an object that is close by, he must accommodate appreciably more than the normal person in order to bring the object to focus on his retina. If his eyeball is markedly shorter than normal, he may be quite unable to produce enough accommodation to obtain a focus. At best, in such extreme cases, a book 30 inches away always looks fuzzy. If such a person reads for several hours at a time, the prolonged strain of accommodating—that is, of contracting the ciliary muscle—may bring on severe headaches and a variety of other symptoms which are collectively called eyestrain.

Nearsightedness. We encounter a condition that is exactly the reverse in near-

sightedness. Here the difficulty is usually an abnormally long eyeball. For a person suffering nearsightedness, nearby objects come to focus on the retina with little or no accommodation in the lens, but the lens cannot flatten enough to compensate for the long eyeball and bring far objects into focus.

Oldsightedness. This goes by the technical name of *presbyopia*, but it is also called *oldsightedness* because it is characteristic of old people. In short, it is a farsightedness that comes on with advancing age. You can easily observe it in the way older people usually hold a newspaper far out in front of them to read. Such farsightedness is due to a hardening of the lens of the eye. This hardening process begins almost at birth and progresses throughout life. We can, in fact, guess the age of a person with rather good accuracy simply by measuring the maximum accommodation that he can accomplish with his lens. If you would like to check this, have someone you know close one eye and hold this page at arm's length in front of the other eye. Now have him bring it slowly toward his eye and stop when the print begins to blur. Then measure the distance between his eye and the book; this distance is called the near point of vision, and from it you may estimate your subject's age by using Figure 18.8. Unfortunately there were two points we could not get into this figure because they are so far to the right of the other points: the near point for fifty-year-olds averages 15 inches, and for sixty-year-olds it is 39 inches. Figure 18.8, however, works only for people who have normal eyes to start with, and naturally nearsighted or farsighted people give different results.

Astigmatism. Another very common defect of the eye is *astigmatism*. This is usually an irregularity in the surface of the cornea, in which the cornea does not have

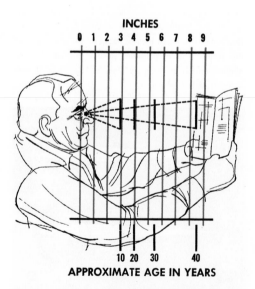

INCHES

0 1 2 3 4 5 6 7 8 9

10 20 30   40

APPROXIMATE AGE IN YEARS

Fig. 18.8. The near point of vision depends on age. The near point of vision is the nearest distance one can hold, say, a printed page and still see it clearly. This point increases with age. At 50 years of age, it averages 15 inches; at 60 years, 39 inches.

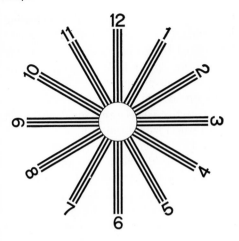

Fig. 18.9. A chart used to test for astigmatism. The astigmatic person usually finds that some of the sets of three lines are clear and sharp, but that others blur and fuse into a single blob. *(American Optical Company.)*

equal curvature in all directions. As a consequence, the astigmatic person sees lines oriented in certain directions as out of focus and others oriented in other directions as in focus. This fact is utilized in test charts that are commonly used to detect astigmatism (Figure 18.9). When an astigmatic person looks at such charts at a proper distance, he reports that some lines are sharp and that others appear to run together and fuse.

Fortunately, all the optical defects that we have just described—farsightedness, nearsightedness, oldsightedness, and astigmatism—are easily corrected with the right kinds of glasses.

■ COLOR AND BRIGHTNESS

Although we need all our visual abilities to cope effectively with our visual world, our ability to see color is probably the one that is most impressive and the one we enjoy most. Color is all around us in our nat-

ural environment, and man has taken the trouble to invent machines and dyes that add an impressive array of colors to almost every feature of daily life—neon signs, paints, fabrics, wallpaper, etc. Without the eye's ability to discriminate many tints and shades, we could not appreciate all this color. So it is interesting to consider how we perceive colors.

Classification of colors. Imagine that you were stranded on a desert island, or some place where you had plenty of time on your hands, and that by some peculiar coincidence you came upon a trunk in which you found thousands of samples of every conceivable color. To while away the time you might decide to sort out all the samples into those that are alike and those that are different and to arrange similar colors next to each other. You would need a lot of time, because you would find that you could discriminate thousands of colors, and it would take a long while to arrange them in any orderly pattern. But you could do it, and you would find, in the end, that it takes only *three* kinds of perceptions to arrange all the color samples. These are the perceptions of *hue*, of *saturation*, and of *brightness*. Because these perceptions are important, we shall explain them in detail and show how they can be used to classify all possible colors.

Hue. This is what most people have in mind when they speak of a color. They mean that the color is blue, yellow, red, green, or some shade in between. On your deserted island, probably the first thing you would do in trying to sort out colors would be to group them into a few piles—one for each of the common colors. You would soon find, though, that some of the blues would shade toward the reds and thus be classified as purple, whereas some would shade toward the greens. Some of the yellows would look reddish or orange, and some would look greenish or chartreuse. So you would discriminate more and more hues. Continuing your sorting, you would end up with many samples of hues in between green and yellow, yellow and red, red and blue, and blue and green. In short, you would have to arrange all your samples in a *circle* in order to have hues that are similar, yet slightly different, sitting side by side. Thus we can classify all colors according to hue, and a circle represents an orderly arrangement of all the hues we can perceive.

Saturation.   Once you had all your samples arranged in a circle, however, you would still notice differences among samples of the same hue. You might, for example, have several samples of red that were perceived as "pure red." Since you would not be able to perceive that one sample was any more yellow or any more blue than the other, you would have to admit to yourself that each had exactly the same hue. Yet you would probably notice that these samples of red differed in *amount of red*. One sample might seem to have a lot of red and another a barely detectable amount. This difference in amount of color, as distinguished from the hue of a color, we call *saturation*.

To arrange samples according to their saturation, you would probably find it convenient to consider the circle of hues as the rim of a wheel. Then you could make spokes of the wheel by taking samples of the same hue and putting samples of low saturation toward the center of the wheel and those of high saturation toward the outside. When all the samples had been arranged in order, you would end up with something like the pattern in Figure 18.10. In the very center would be a sample that had no hue or color of any kind; it would be plain gray. To your left would be the blue hues increasing in saturation, and to

your right the yellow hues also increasing in saturation; similarly on the top would be the red hues, and more or less on the bottom the green hues. If your samples were arranged in equal steps of saturation, that is to say, equally increasing amounts of the respective colors, you would no longer have a wheel with a rim. For, as you see in Figure 18.10, there are many more steps of saturation in the reds and purples than there are in the yellows and greens. You would, at any rate have succeeded in classifying colors according to two kinds of perceptions, one of hue and the other of saturation.

Brightness.   But the job would not be done. Even after arranging all the samples as spokes radiating out from a common center, there would still be differences in samples having the same hue and the same saturation. If you studied these differences closely, you would perceive them to be differences in *brightness* or lightness. One sample would appear to be very dark, even though it had some hue and saturation; another would appear very light, even though it too had hue and saturation; and other samples would fall in between on a scale of grayness or brightness. So you would have a third dimension of your perception of colors.

To represent this, a single surface on the ground would no longer do. You would have to build some shelves, if you could, and lay out circles and spokes on each shelf. The bottom shelf would be for the darkest colors—the ones of very little brightness—and it would have only a few samples on it because it is not possible to have very much saturation with so little brightness. The top shelf would have the lightest colors—the ones of very high brightness—but this too would have only a few samples around it because colors cannot become highly saturated when the

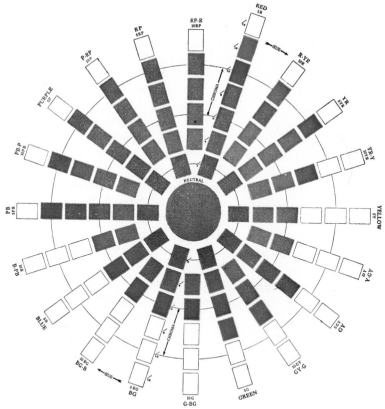

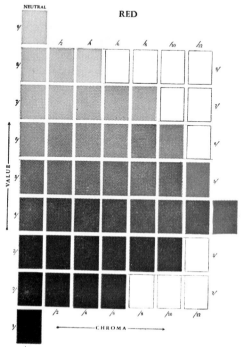

Fig. 18.10. Two pages from the Munsell Book of Color illustrating the hue, saturation, and brightness of colors. The page above shows colored samples all of the same brightness (value 5/ in Munsell terminology). They vary only in hue and saturation (chroma in Munsell terminology). The reddish sample at the top of the vertical column is designated as 10RP 5/10. The page below shows samples that all, except for the first column, have the same hue (5.0 Red in the Munsell system). They differ only in brightness or in saturation (value and chroma respectively in Munsell terminology). A very useful feature of the Munsell system is that it provides a standard nomenclature for all the colors. For example, the red sample on the right of the top row (*at the lower right of the page*) is designated as 5.0 R 8/4.

brightness is too high. The intervening shelves would represent colors whose brightness is in the middle range. These would have more samples on them because the medium brightnesses are the ones that can be most highly saturated. Figure 18.10 illustrates colors which have the same hue, but vary in lightness and saturation.

The color solid. Having classified all your samples in the three dimensions of hue, saturation, and brightness, you would find that you had completed the job. There would be no other kind of differences that you could perceive in your samples, for these three dimensions are sufficient for classifying all colors. In a crude way, you would have built up what color scientists call a *color solid*, which is a way of representing all the colors we can see (Figure 18.11). In this solid, the axis running up and down through the solid represents brightness, the direction of a color in a circle around the axis represents hue, and the distance along the radius away from the upright axis represents saturation.

Munsell system. In our hypothetical example, you might construct a color solid to while away your time, but the scientists who devised it were doing more than that. They gave us, in fact, some scales of measurement that have many practical uses. Because color plays such an important part in our modern society, we are continually faced with problems of specifying and matching various colors. Paint manufacturers and dyemakers, for example, must be able to reproduce their colors quite accurately year after year, even when methods of manufacture and materials change. The color solid gives us a way of accurately specifying any particular color in terms of all three essential dimensions.

To use the color solid in a practical way, Albert H. Munsell many years ago proposed a system of numbers to be assigned to each

of the three dimensions, and his system has been widely adopted and used commercially. To standardize it he prepared the *Munsell Book of Color*, which shows colors arranged in steps like those you selected in the imaginary desert island experiment. In his book, numbers are given for each sample of color, and thus people can use the book to specify accurately any color they desire. So, instead of ordering "a light pinkish-red paint of medium saturation" which means different things to different people, you can order 5.0 R 6/6—if you know how to use the numbers—and the paint manufacturer can look this up in the Munsell book and know exactly what you mean. Photographs of two pages from the *Munsell Book of Color* appear in Figure 18.10 and illustrate the scales of numbers assigned to hue, saturation, and brightness.

Complementary colors. The colors one sees in real life are made up of large numbers of different wavelengths. The average person, in fact, practically never has a chance to see a single wavelength. Perceptions of color, nevertheless, are very simple, and we never have the impression that anything we see is a mixture of three or four or many wavelengths. From this fact we may infer an important characteristic of the human eye: *it is not an instrument that analyzes light, as some physical instruments do, but rather an instrument that integrates and mixes the effects of lights of different wavelengths.*

To study the mixing that goes on in the eye, all we need to do is obtain some instruments for presenting people with different combinations of different wavelengths. Newton did this as early as 1666 and discovered some laws of color mixture that are just about as good today as they were in his time.[1] Newton first mixed many wavelengths from the spectrum in roughly equal proportions, and this mixture, he found, people perceive as *white*. He also found, however, that people see white too when only two wavelengths, selected from the appropriate parts of the spectrum, are mixed together. In this way he discovered the *law of complementary colors*.

The law is very simple. For each hue that we can perceive, there is some other hue that, mixed in the proper proportion with it, will cancel out all hue and give us a perception of white or gray varying only in brightness. Red, for example, is the complementary for blue-green, and greenish-blue is the complementary for yellow. We must, however, be very exact about the matter and select a particular wavelength of red, say, 640 millimicrons, and for that there is a particular complementary wavelength in the blue-green, which happens to be 494 millimicrons. The best way to see all combinations of complementary colors is to refer to the notion of a color circle and to note the wavelengths that produce each of the hues on the circle. When the hues have been correctly arranged on the circle, as in Figure 18.12, any line drawn through the center of the circle will connect complementary wavelengths. Any pair of complementaries, when mixed together, cancel out all hue and saturation, leaving only a neutral gray.

In Figure 18.12, you will note that a great many wavelengths have no complementaries. These are the ones that lie along the edge of the shaded sector. The reason for this is that in making a circle out of the spectrum of wavelengths we encounter a gap between the reds and the blues. The gap, however, is in wavelengths and not in perception, for this portion of the circle represents the purples, which are definite hues and can have high saturations. The purples do not correspond to any set of single wavelengths, and to "make" them we must combine the blue and the red

wavelengths. This region of the color circle, you will notice, is opposite the green and yellow-green region of the spectrum. Thus purple is the hue that is complementary to green, but since it takes red and blue wavelengths mixed to make purple, it takes a similar combination of them to make a complementary of the corresponding green wavelength.

Psychologically pure colors. In Figure 18.12 four "pure" colors are indicated on the circle. Pure green is that green that has no trace of blue or yellow in it. Pure yellow is that yellow that has no trace of red or green in it. And so on. Different experimenters get slightly different values for the pure colors, and the ones shown in Figure 18.12 were measured by Dimmick and Hubbard.[4] Most people think that the spectral colors even at the longest wavelengths are a little too yellowish to be called pure red.

Color mixture. What will happen if, in mixing wavelengths, we do not use wavelengths that are complementaries of each other? This is a question that is rather practical, for in everyday life we seldom have lights that are pure enough in wavelength to make complementary matches, and if we do they will seldom be exactly the right wavelengths to match. The answer is that the mixing of any two hues that are not complementaries results in a hue that lies in an intermediate position on the color circle. We can, in fact, find approximately the resulting hue by drawing a line connecting the two hues that are mixed and then making a point on the line that represents the proportions in which they are mixed. Thus if we mix a yellow and a green, we may draw a line between their respective positions on the circle, and if we have mixed one part of green with two parts of yellow, we mark off one-third of the distance on that line from green to yellow.

Fig. 18.11. The color cone or solid. When all of the colors are arranged in three dimensions, they form a color cone (or sometimes it is called a color solid). At the top are colors of highest brightness, at the bottom those of lowest brightness. Around the circles are colors of different hue. And the distance out from the center axis of the cone represents saturation. (*Reproduced by permission from More Business, copyright 1937 by the American Photoengravers Association.*)

This point now designates the spoke which in turn indicates the resulting hue. If one wants to know what will happen when he mixes any two wavelengths, he can use this procedure to figure it out from the color circle.

It will occur to some students who have had occasion to mix paints that the rules for mixing wavelengths do not seem to be the same as those for mixing paints. That is true. The perception of a mixture of yellow and blue wavelengths, for example, is gray or white, but the perception of a mixture of blue and yellow paints is green. Why?

Paints do not emit light; they reflect it. They never, however, reflect all the light that strikes them. If they are colored, they absorb some wavelengths, and it is the remaining ones that give them their color. For example, yellow paint generally absorbs violet and blue wavelengths; it reflects some green and red, somewhat more yellow-green and orange, and a lot of the yellow wavelengths. Blue paint, on the other

hand, absorbs red, orange, and yellow wavelengths while reflecting the yellow-green, green, blue, and violet ones. When these two paints are mixed, the result is one of subtraction as well as addition. Each of the paints absorbs its part of the spectrum, and what is left to reflect depends upon both the absorption and the reflectance of the two paints. In the case of yellow and blue paints, most of the reflected wavelengths are green. Consequently the rules for the color mixing of paints do not violate the rules of color mixture we gave earlier. When one mixes paints the important thing is to figure out what wavelengths finally reach the eye.

Color sensitivity of the retina. It is the retina, of course, that is sensitive to light, and it is through the functioning of the retina that we perceive color. It is appropriate, therefore, to say something about the retina's role in color perception.

First and foremost is the fact that the cones are the receptors for color. A few scientists have recently voiced the opinion

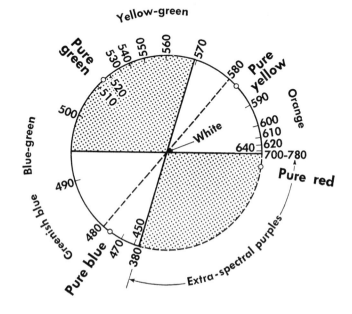

Fig. 18.12. The color circle. This diagram shows the arrangement of various hues and their corresponding wavelengths on a circle. Points opposite each other on the unshaded sectors represent complementary hues. Those on the shaded sectors have no complementary wavelengths in the visible spectrum.

that rods may take part in the process, but the overwhelming weight of evidence and opinion favors cones as the exclusive receptors for color. Since this is not a textbook in physiology, we shall not try to prove this.

We have good reason to believe, moreover, that we are able to see color because there are three or more different kinds of cones, each especially sensitive to certain regions of the visible spectrum. The most famous of the three-receptor theories of color vision is that proposed both by Young and by Helmholtz in the nineteenth century.[5] Their theory was that one receptor is especially sensitive in the red region, another in the green, and another in the blue. Our perception of color, then, would depend on the combination of receptors stimulated by any particular light. Modern physiologists have recently been able to record impulses from cells in the retina during its stimulation by different wavelengths of light. They have provided good proof that individual receptors in the retina do respond to relatively small regions of the visible spectrum. Their data, moreover, make us suspect that there are more than three different kinds of receptors, but they have not yet settled the question of the number of color receptors or the exact way in which receptors work to enable us to see color.

One of the ways of telling that there are different receptors in color perception is to study color perception in different parts of the retina. Such a study yields some rather curious facts. In the fovea, for instance, there is a small region that is blue-yellow–blind. This is only about ½ degree in size—a scant ³⁄₁₀ millimeter—so it is no wonder that people are not aware of its existence. Within this region, people see only reds, greens, or some combination of them. So the receptors for red and green perception are apparently all right but those for yellow and blue are either missing or less numerous than they are outside of the region.

In the region outside the yellow-blue–blind area, color perception is normal in people with normal vision and the principles we have explained apply. If, however, one carefully explores the retina at different distances and in different directions from the fovea, he can see that color perception is not uniform throughout the entire retina. Instead he will be able to construct a map of the *color zones* of the retina (Figure 18.13, page 466). There you will see that the ability to perceive red and green is confined to a relatively small area of the retina. The area in which we can see yellow and blue is appreciably larger and extends well into the periphery of the retina. Beyond this area, however, the retina becomes color-blind, for we can see only white (brightness) and no color in the peripheral regions.

You can check your own color zones by taking some colored pencils and moving them slowly from your direct line of sight out toward the edge of your field of view. If you do this carefully, you will see the colors fade as you move into the "corner" of your eye. The color zones apparently vary greatly from one person to another, and maps of them depend on the kind of stimulus one uses to measure them. The maps in Figure 18.13, however, give a general idea of what they are like.

■ COLOR BLINDNESS

About one person in 25 is color-blind, and this defect is likely to influence his everyday behavior in many small and large ways. Some women, for example, can wear only one particular shade of lipstick, because if they use any other shade they cannot see lipstick smears on their clothes.

A color-blind house painter once ruefully told us that he had to repaint half a house because the color he had used on one side of the house did not match the other. Some color-blind chemists have to rely on their laboratory assistants to identify colors in flame tests of metallic substances, and some electronic technicians cannot match strands of wire by their color codes.

What is color blindness? It is certainly not the inability to identify a color by a particular name, for that is a question of language. Nor is it actually blindness. Most color-blind people are not really blind to color. They can usually see a great many colors, but they confuse certain critical ones.

It was John Dalton, the author of the atomic theory in chemistry, who clearly recognized this fact and presented one of the earliest and best scientific accounts of the defect. Dalton himself was so color-blind that when Oxford University conferred on him the scarlet gown of a doctor of civil laws, the scientist wore the gown everywhere for several days, not realizing that he presented such a conspicuous appearance. This greatly astonished his friends, who knew he was a Quaker and was supposed to wear the somber garb of that sect. In 1794, at the age of twenty-eight, Dalton described to the Manchester Literary and Philosophical Society his sensations of color. This classic description of color blindness caused the defect to become known for more than a century afterward as *Daltonism*. He said:[6]

All crimsons appear to me to consist chiefly of dark blue; but many of them seem to have a tinge of dark brown. I have seen specimens of crimson, claret, and mud which were very nearly alike. . . . The colour of a florid complexion appears to me that of a dull, opake, blackish blue, upon a white ground. . . . Blood appears to me . . . not unlike the colour called bottle green. . . . There is not much difference in

colour between a stick of red sealing wax and green.

Reduced to essentials, color blindness is a defect that makes a person unable to tell the difference between two or more colors that most other people can easily distinguish. It is not, as is commonly supposed, a single type of deficiency. There are, on the contrary, several varieties of color blindness, and for each kind the defect exists in varying degrees.

Total color blindness. Total color blindness, known more technically as *achromatism*, is extremely rare. Only about a hundred cases of it have been described in the whole history of visual science. To the totally color-blind person—who usually has other visual defects as well—the world looks like a black and white photograph. He can distinguish among white, black, and gray of various intensities, but he does not see colors as such.

Two-color vision. By far the most common kind of color blindness is two-color vision, known as *dichromatism*.[7] For people with this defect, color perception is essentially reduced to two hues: the yellows and the blues. Most of them confuse reds, greens, and yellows of certain shades with one another and are unable to distinguish clearly among bluish-greens, blues, and violets. There is also a particular shade of blue-green that dichromats confuse with gray. They never, however, confuse the yellows and blues.

Among the dichromats, visual scientists distinguish two principal varieties. One group has a defect only in color vision, not in brightness vision. This group, known as *deuteranopes*, can make all the brightness discriminations called for in the color solid. Only the ability to distinguish red and green hues is lacking. A second group, called *protanopes*, cannot perceive brightness in the red region as well as normal people do. Show a protanope a red stimulus and he not only does not see it as red, he may confuse it with black.

There is a third group of dichromats, called *tritanopes*, who behave as though they cannot see blue colors. So few tritanopes have been found that we know very little about their vision. But the fact that there seem to be three principal varieties of dichromats is a strong argument for those people who believe in a three-receptor theory of color vision.

Anomalous color defect.   Besides the people who are frank dichromats, there are others who are "color-weak." Their impairment may be so slight that only the most

careful tests can reveal it. Such people have little trouble with bright or vivid colors, but their defect appears when they attempt to distinguish among the very pale or light browns, tans, greens, and pinks. We call such "color weakness" *anomalous color defect*. There are three principal varieties of anomalous trichromats, and they are called *deuteranomalous*, *protanomalous*, or *tritanomalous*, depending on the kind of dichromat they most resemble.

Inheritance of color blindness.   Most kinds of color blindness are inherited, and the defect has been identified as a sex-linked recessive characteristic (see Chapter 2). That means that it is carried on the

Fig. 18.13. The color zones of the retina (see text). (*Data of Sir W. Abney, from Stagner, R., &* *Karwoski, T. F. Psychology. New York: McGraw-Hill, 1952.*)

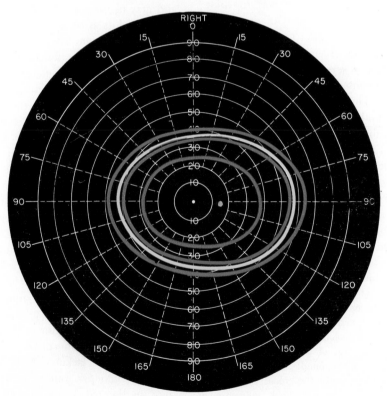

sex chromosomes, of which each man and each woman has a pair. This kind of genetic linkage results in some rather involved pedigrees. A color-blind man who marries a normal woman with no defective genes will have normal children. All his daughters, however, will be carriers of his defective genes and will transmit them to their sons, half of whom (on the average) will be color-blind. Thus the defect carries from father to grandsons through the father's daughters. If a woman who is a carrier marries a color-blind man, all the children—boys and girls alike—stand a 50–50 chance of being color-blind. When a color-blind woman and a normal man mate, their sons will all be color-blind, but their daughters, although all outwardly normal, will be carriers of the defective genes. Consequently while about one man in 15 is color-blind, less than one woman in 100 is so afflicted. Some of these relationships were illustrated in Figure 2.5 of Chapter 2.

Awareness of color defect. During the Second World War, it was a common experience in Air Forces and Navy recruiting centers to have color-blind applicants emphatically deny their color blindness. They often would say, "What do you mean, Doc? I can see colors. I've never had trouble with colors."

To the color-normal person it seems incomprehensible that a man can go through life unaware that he is failing to see the richness and variety of colors as others do. To understand this puzzling situation we must look for the explanation in several directions. In the first place, most color-blind people do see some colors. A second part of the explanation is that you cannot appreciate a sensation if you have never sensed it. A man born without taste buds will never understand the saltiness of the ocean or the sweetness of an apple. What is

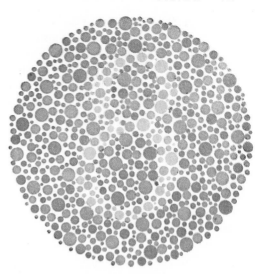

Fig. 18.14. A plate from the Ishihara Test of color blindness. The plate is seen by a normal person as a figure 8, by the red-green blind as a figure 3, and by the totally color-blind as no figure at all. (*By permission of the C. H. Stoelting Co., Chicago, distributors of the Ishihara Test in the United States, Canada, and Mexico.*)

the tone of a 50,000-cycle sound, above the range of human hearing? Or what is the color of infrared light? We cannot give the answers to these questions because they are outside the realm of our experiences. Moreover, since we have never experienced them, we never miss the fact that we *cannot* experience them. Color vision defects, then, do not reveal themselves in a positive manner.

The last part of the explanation is that the color-deviant person has learned to use correct color names for many common objects. He knows that grass is green, lemons are yellow, ripe apples are red, and so on because he has learned these names from infancy. From experience he becomes habituated to follow the names used by everyone else and readily accepts correction. If you correct the mistake of a color-deviant person who calls a light green "pink," he will reply, "Oh, yes, it's green. I see it now." All our color names will satisfy him because this is a matter of learning anyway. The difficulty is that he has fewer color sensations than color names and he is often not sure which names to assign to his sensations.

Detecting color-vision defects. Usually it requires special tests to find out whether a person has defective color vision. If you ask him to name the colors of common objects, the chances are that he will give you the correct names. But his defect will show up if you take him out on a dark night away from all other means of identification and ask him to pick out yellow, green, and red lights at a distance. These principles underlie many lantern tests in use for testing color vision.

Another, and more satisfactory way of testing color vision, is with *pseudoisochromatic* plates (see Figure 18.14). One test, for example, consists of a card with brilliant purplish-red dots which form a numeral against a background of deeply saturated blue-green dots. A normal person can see the number immediately, because its color contrasts so vividly with the background. But individuals with certain types of color deficiency cannot read the number, because to them the dots are all apparently of the same color. Now that you know how these tests work, you should be able to figure out why they are called *pseudoisochromatic*.

■ **SENSITIVITY OF THE EYE**

In the beginning of this chapter, we described the eye as so sensitive that a person can see the flare of a match at a distance of 50 miles. This is true if it is a clear night, if the curvature of the earth does not get in the way, and if the eye is well dark-adapted. The sensitivity of the eye is indeed remarkable. If we measure it carefully under a variety of conditions, we can learn a few more things about vision from it.

Thresholds of sensitivity. There are, in general, two kinds of sensitivity we can measure. One is the least amount of light that a person can see, and this we call the absolute threshold. To measure this threshold, we present a person with a patch of light and vary it up and down in intensity until we find an intensity that he can just barely see. Another kind of sensitivity is *contrast sensitivity*. To measure it, we present a person with two patches of light that are different in brightness and ask him to say which is the brighter. Then we reduce the difference until he can barely tell that one is brighter than the other, and this difference is the *contrast threshold*. Most of what we have to say here will concern the absolute threshold rather than the contrast threshold.

Dark adaptation. Certainly everybody knows that the eye becomes more sensitive in the dark. Simply recall the times you have gone to a movie in the afternoon and found yourself unable to see your way down the aisle or into your seat until you had waited a few minutes for your eyes to get accustomed to the dark. Of course when you come out of the dark and into a bright light again, your eyes light-adapt and lose some of their sensitivity.

We can measure the course of dark adaptation by fully adapting the eye to a bright light, then putting the person in the dark and measuring his absolute threshold over a period of several minutes. The resulting measurements will look something like the curve in Figure 18.15. At first the threshold is quite high—so high that a candle could be burning in a room and he would not know it unless he saw the flame itself. Sensitivity improves, however, at first very rapidly and then more slowly. After a half hour, sensitivity is 1,000 to 100,000 times

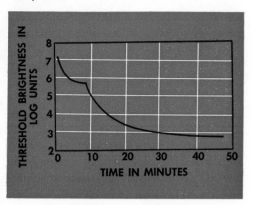

Fig. 18.15. A typical curve of dark adaptation. After a subject has been in normal or bright illumination for some time, he is placed in the dark and asked to indicate the weakest light (threshold brightness) that he can see. Thresholds are taken repeatedly, minute after minute, and the results plotted up in a curve of dark adaptation. Notice the two limbs of the curve.

greater than it had been at the beginning of dark-adaptation. Notice, however, that the dark-adaptation curve has two segments: after an initial drop it levels out for a few minutes; then it drops more rapidly again before leveling out for good. What, do you suppose, is the meaning of these two segments of the curve?

Keep this question in mind as you continue to read, for we shall answer it below.

Luminosity. While we have our subject in the dark room and he has become well adapted to the dark, let us make some more measurements of his absolute threshold. This time, however, let us test him at different *wavelengths* of the visible spectrum. First we find his threshold at one wavelength, then at another wavelength, and at another, until we have enough measurements to draw a curve that shows his sensitivity for the whole spectrum. In making these measurements, however, we must be careful about the part of the retina the subject uses in looking at the patch of light, because this makes a difference.

Suppose that for some reason—which will become clear in a minute—we want him to see the patch with the part of his retina that is about 20 degrees from the fovea. To accomplish that we can provide him with a small light to fixate with his fovea that is 20 degrees from the test patch of light. Then we make the desired measurements.[8] In the *lower curve* of Figure 18.16, you see the kind of results we should obtain. The retina at 20 degrees from the fovea is apparently most sensitive to wavelengths of about 505 millimicrons. For wavelengths that are longer or shorter, it is less sensitive.

Having charted this curve, let us now dispense with the special fixation point and permit the subject to look directly at the patch. Suppose we then make another set of measurements of sensitivity at different wavelengths. This time the curve will represent the sensitivity of the fovea. To see what it looks like, refer again to Figure 18.16 and examine the *upper curve* in that figure. Notice two distinguishing features. Now the best measurement (the lowest part of the curve) is at 555 millimicrons—wavelengths about 50 millimicrons longer than they were in the first set of measurements. Also note that the great bulk of the curve—all but the part in the red region—is much higher than the first curve. This means that the eye under these conditions is generally less sensitive than it was before.

We chose the fovea and a position on the retina 20 degrees from the fovea to make these two sets of measurements, because (1) cones are most numerous in the fovea—indeed, the fovea is free of rods—and (2) rods are most numerous at 20 degrees from the fovea. Hence the first curve we got measures the sensitivity of the rods and the second measures the sensitivity of the cones. Curves of this sort are known as *luminosity functions*. The upper

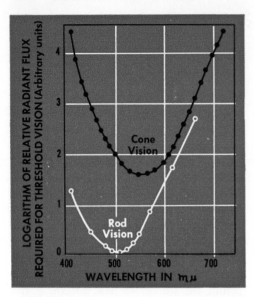

Fig. 18.16. Thresholds for seeing at different wavelengths. The lower curve was obtained while the subject was viewing a patch of light 20 degrees from the fovea where the rods are most numerous. The upper curve was obtained when the subject used his fovea to see with; cones are most numerous in the fovea. For further explanation, see text.

one is called the cone luminosity function, and the lower one is called the rod luminosity function.

From the fact that there are two luminosity curves, one for the cones and one for the rods, you can infer the answer to the question, Why are there two segments of the dark-adaptation curve (see Figure 18.5)? The first segment represents cone function and the second segment rod function. The cones are not very sensitive, and they reach their maximum sensitivity early in dark adaptation, whereas the rods continue to increase in sensitivity about 1,000 times greater than that of the cones.

Color perception. It is appropriate to revert for a moment to the subject of color perception. If, in securing luminosity functions, we ask our subject to report not only whether he sees the test patch of light,

but in addition (if he does) to indicate its color, we discover an important difference between the two curves. In the case of the upper curve when the subject is using his fovea, he can report correctly the color (hue) of the wavelength used in the tests. In making judgments for the lower curve, however, the subject is totally color-blind. Even though he is presented with single wavelengths, he sees them all as gray. This fact is the basis of the ancient saying, "When all candles bee out, all cats bee gray." And for this reason, the interval between the rod and cone curves is called the *photochromatic interval—the interval of intensities in which we can see light but not colors.* This fact is also rather convincing proof that the cones are the receptors for color perception and that the rods are not.

Purkinje effect. The luminosity curve may be plotted in another way (see Figure 18.17). Instead of putting down the absolute thresholds, we may express them in relative terms by taking the best threshold —at 505 in the rod curve and 555 in the cone curve—and expressing all other thresholds of each curve as percentages of the maximum. This turns the curves upside down, and it also fixes the best thresholds at 100 per cent. From this kind of plot we can see that for cone vision (that is, for daylight levels of light adaptation) sensitivity is *relatively* better in the red and poorer in the blue than it is for rod vision (that is, for twilight levels of light adaptation).[9]

This relative difference in the brightnesses of colors was discovered more than a century ago by the Bohemian physiologist Purkinje. He noticed what you may observe for yourself if you are sitting outside on a warm summer night just before the sun sets. When the sun is still shining, the reds seem relatively bright as compared with the greens and the blues. As twilight comes on, however, the reddish colors become much darker, while the blue colors hardly seem to change at all in brightness. This change in the apparent brightness of colors is called the *Purkinje shift*. What accounts for it is the shifting of the eye from cone functions to rod functions in the course of dark adaptation.

■ VISUAL ACUITY

The objects we see in the world always have not only the color and brightness that we have been describing, but also some form. Sometimes it may be hard to discern form, as when we see objects in a fog or at night, but whatever we see almost invariably seems to have some form. Our perception of form, moreover, usually has two aspects, size and shape. These two aspects are more or less independent, for objects of any particular shape may be large or small and objects of any particular size may have any one of a great variety of shapes. In Chapter 7, on perception, we treated size and shape in some detail, for they illustrate well some of the general principles of perception. We shall, therefore, not consider them again. Here, however, we should like to study the visual capacity that enables us to see size and shape. This capacity is *visual acuity, which is the ability of a person to perceive fine differences in the details of the visual environment.* To measure visual acuity, we always try to find some way of stating the smallest object whose shape a person can recognize when presented with it in some standard situation. There are several different ways of measuring visual acuity, but they are of two general types: one that physicians use for diagnostic purposes, and the other that laboratory scientists use in their research work.

Eye charts. All of us, having suffered through at least a few physical examinations, are familiar with the physician's eye chart. This chart compares a person's visual acuity with that of the average individual. It is so designed that letters of different sizes on the chart represent what the average person sees at various distances. On many charts, for example, the biggest letter can be just read at 200 feet, the next biggest letters are half as large and so can be read at 100 feet, and so on. If at 20 feet from the chart an individual can see what the average person can see at 20 feet, he has 20/20 vision. If at 20 feet from the chart he can see only those letters that the average person can see at 100 feet, he has 20/100 vision, which is not so good. If, on the other hand, he can see those letters that the average person can see only at 10 feet, he has 20/10 vision, which is excellent.

Fig. 18.17. Relative luminosity functions. The curves below represent a different way of plotting the same data as those in Fig. 18.16. Instead of being plotted in logarithms, each threshold is divided into the threshold at which the eye is most sensitive. This is done separately, however, for the rod and cone curves so that the peaks of each arbitrarily become 100 per cent.

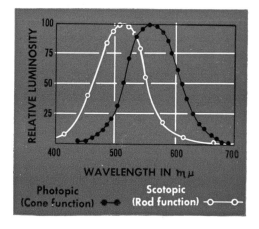

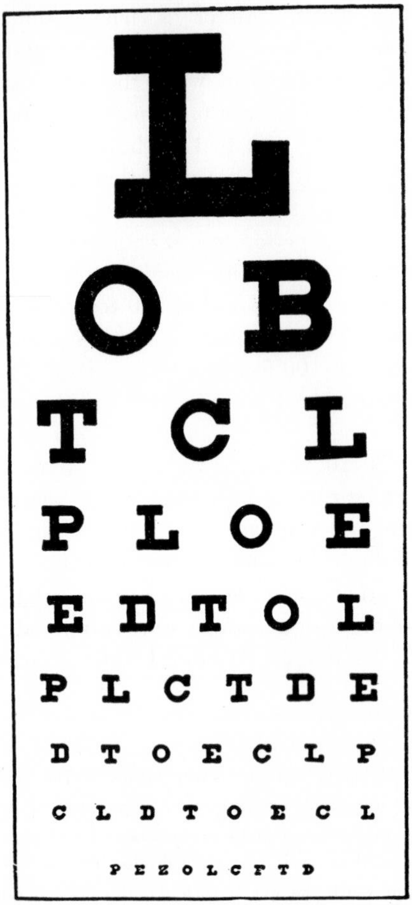

Fig. 18.18. An eye chart for testing visual acuity. This is similar to eye charts used by physicians for testing visual acuity. Look at it from a distance of 20 or 30 feet and see how far down you can read the letters. Then come closer and see how much farther you can read. In this way, you can demonstrate that vision depends upon size of objects and the distance one is from them.

Sometimes physicians prefer to use distance rather than size of letters as an index of visual acuity. For many years this was the case in physical examinations given by the U.S. Navy. In such examinations, the person starts walking toward the eye chart and continues until he can read the letters on it—and there is only one size of letter.

In expressing results of this kind of test, it has been the practice to put down the distance at which a person sees the letters that would be seen by a normal person at 20 feet. In either case, a person's acuity is compared with normal acuity at 20 feet.

It is also possible and, in fact, desirable to use test objects that are not letters. Two such objects are illustrated in Figure 18.19. One is called the Landolt ring and the other the parallel bars. Both can be used with people who cannot read, because all they have to do is tell where the gap is in the Landolt ring or the direction of orientation of the parallel bars. Another advantage of these test objects is that they are always the same in shape, whereas the letters of a test chart differ in size and shape and are not equally hard to recognize. For that reason, visual scientists who are interested in precise laboratory measurements prefer such test objects.

Near and far acuity. In view of what we have already said about nearsightedness and farsightedness, you will not be surprised to learn that visual acuity may vary with different distances. The acuity at 13 inches, for example, may be quite different from visual acuity at 20 feet. Beyond 20 feet, however, acuity appears to be fairly constant. To understand these facts, recall that the lens in the front of the eye has to change shape in order for the eye to focus near and far objects on the retina, and that people differ markedly in their ability to do this. Accommodation remains fairly constant, however, for objects at distances greater than 20 feet.

The fact that people may differ in their near and far acuity is sometimes of practical importance. In some industries and in many military situations, a person's visual acuity may be critical in his ability to his job. Fliers, riflemen, and artillerymen, to mention only a few of the military specialties, must have good visual acuity. Machinists, needleworkers, many machine operators, and inspectors must also have it. To select people for these positions, tests of visual acuity are frequently administered as part of a physical examination. If the job calls for good distance acuity, as in the case of truck drivers, it is important that the test be made at 20 feet or more, but if the job calls for good near acuity (e.g., toolmaking and watch repairing) it should be tested at distances comparable to those important in the job. Otherwise differences between near and far acuity may make the tests invalid.

Retinal position. We all use our eyes so much that we commonly overlook certain peculiarities about our seeing process and should never notice them if they were not pointed out to us. If, for example, you stare steadily at a letter on this page, it is impossible for you to read letters 2 inches away; or if you look at the road straight ahead, while driving, you will not be able to read most signs along the side of the road. From such facts we know that visual acuity is not nearly so good at the side of the retina as it is at the fovea.

In Figure 18.20, you can see more precisely how visual acuity varies with the

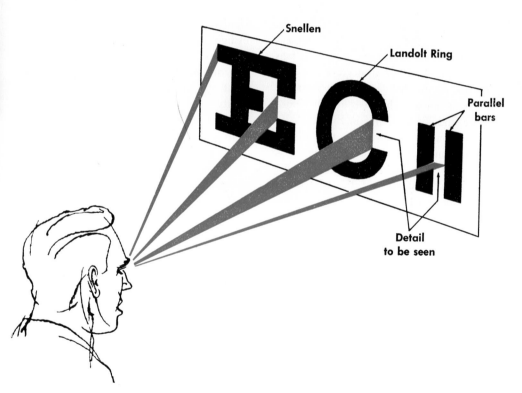

Fig. 18.19. The Landolt ring and parallel bars. Some letters are easier to see than others, and a person may recognize a letter without seeing all of its detail. For that reason, the most careful scientific studies of visual acuity make use of the Landolt ring or parallel bars. Neither requires that a person read. He only needs to indicate the direction in which the white space points, or whether he sees two bars or one.

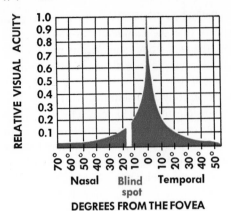

Fig. 18.20. How visual acuity varies with the part of the retina used in viewing.

part of the retina used.[10] Acuity is, of course, best when one looks directly at an object, that is, when the image of the object falls on the fovea. Only 5 degrees off the fovea, visual acuity is only half as good, and at 40, 45, or 50 degrees it is only about one-twentieth as good as it is at the fovea. You can see what it is at other positions by studying the curve in Figure 18.20. This distribution is similar to that of the rods and cones, as described on page 453.

The blind spot. Before we leave Figure 18.20, notice the part of the illustration that has been left uncolored. This is the place in the retina at which blood vessels enter and the optic nerve leaves the eyeball, and it has no rods or cones. It is located about 15 degrees from the fovea, on the side of the retina toward the nose, and it is about 7 by 5 degrees in size. You cannot see anything in this area, and because of that it is called the *blind spot.* Yet if you try to find this spot in your visual field, you probably will have trouble —partly because we see with one eye what the blind spot of the other eye blanks out and also because the blind spot is so far off to the side of the fovea that we do not notice it. It is there, nonetheless, in everybody's eye, and you can prove this to yourself, if you like, by following the instructions under Figure 18.21.

Amount of light. Visual acuity improves with increasing light.[11] We recognize this fact every time we turn on extra lamps to read a book or try to get as much light as we can for visual tasks. In the dark, obviously, visual acuity is zero. As some kind of light is turned on, visual acuity improves very rapidly, but then more and more light has diminishing returns, even though almost any increase in light improves visual acuity somewhat. This means that there is no such thing as the "best amount" of light. Rather the important problem in everyday life is to get as much light as we need to do the kind of visual work we are going to do.

Because light is so important to visual acuity and because visual acuity is required in almost everything anybody does, the subject has been explored very intensively. There is, in fact, a special branch of engineering called *illumination engineering* that handles practical applications of the sub-

Fig. 18.21. Demonstrating the blind spot. Close your left eye, and look at the cross with your right eye. Then move the book toward you or away from you until the sketch of the girl disappears, or largely disappears, from view. At this point, the image of the girl is falling on the blind spot.

ject. Illumination engineers have provided reference handbooks to which we can go for answers to many practical questions. They have given us rules to follow in providing enough light for different visual tasks (see discussion in Chapter 17).

Contrast. By this time, it has probably become apparent that many factors affect visual acuity. Although we shall not be able to mention all these factors, there are two more that are interesting and have practical significance. One is *contrast*. This is the difference in brightness between an object and its immediate background. If, for example, we are viewing dark letters on a white background, visual acuity will be

better when the letters are coal black than when they are a light gray, because the black makes a greater contrast with the white than does the light gray.[12] This means that when we are painting signs or making anything we wish people to see as easily as possible or at as great a distance as possible, we should make the contrast between the dark and the light parts of the object as great as possible. In this way visual acuity is increased.

Surround. A final factor to consider is the *surround* of an object we are viewing. Even though the object itself has high contrast and is illuminated by good light, visual acuity may not be what it could be

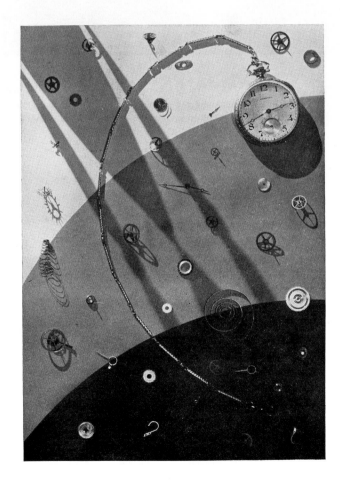

Fig. 18.22. Visual acuity depends upon contrast. It is harder to see the watch parts against the dark background than against the lighter backgrounds. The higher the contrast between an object and its background, the more clearly one can perceive the details of the object. (*From Luckiesh. Light, vision and seeing. Princeton: Van Nostrand, 1944.*)

Fig. 18.23. Seeing is better when the background is uniformly illuminated. In direct lighting, visual acuity is poor because only the book the boy is reading is illuminated. Visual acuity is much better when the entire working area is illuminated. (*Westinghouse.*)

if the general illumination in the room is poor. Indeed, it is relatively easy to demonstrate in the laboratory that, if the general light in a room is either much greater or much less than that on the object we are viewing, visual acuity is impaired. In Figure 18.23, you see examples of poor lighting and good lighting of the surround. The best rule is that the lighting of the surround should be about the same as the lighting of the object.

Another surround condition that markedly affects visual acuity is *glare*. Glare, or *dazzle*, is produced by light sources of relatively high intensity in the visual field. In general, glare sources reduce the sensitivity of the eye and the visual acuity of the observer. Visual scientists have collected many data on glare and have classified glare in a variety of ways. Perhaps the most important conclusion they have reached is this: the closer the glare source is to the direct line of vision, the more distracting and deleterious are its effects. This conclusion is illustrated in Figure 18.24, which indicates that relative acuity increases the farther the glare source is from the direct line of view.[13]

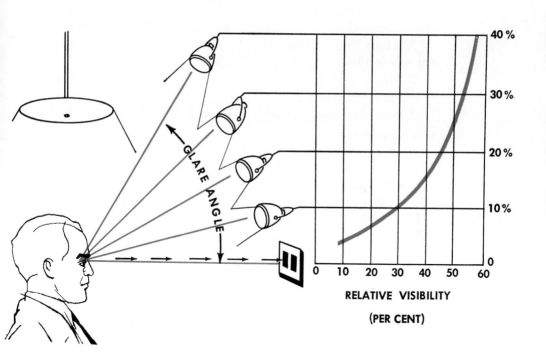

Fig. 18.24. Visual acuity is diminished by glare. The smaller the glare angle, that is, the more the source of glare is in the same direction as the object viewed, the harder it is for a person to see. Visual acuity, which is here called visibility, improves as the glare angle is increased.

SUMMARY

1. Only electromagnetic energy having wavelengths between about 400 and 800 millimicrons is visible to the eye.

2. The eye has a lens that focuses an inverted image on a photosensitive surface, the retina.

3. The sensitive elements in the retina are the rods and cones. These are connected to the brain via an intricate network of cells and nerve fibers. The cones are most concentrated in the fovea of the retina, which is used in looking directly at an object. The rods are relatively most numerous in the periphery of the retina.

4. The lens of the eye changes in shape to accommodate to near or to far objects. If the lens has an irregular surface, it produces the visual defect known as *astigmatism*. If the eyeball is too long or too short, the person may be nearsighted or farsighted. Farsightedness increases with age.

5. Three kinds of perceptions are necessary to classify all colors into one scheme: hue, saturation, and brightness.

6. Hue is what is commonly meant by color: blue, green, yellow, red, or shades in between.

7. Saturation is the relative amount of color, as distinguished from gray, in a stimulus.

8. Brightness refers to the relative lightness or darkness of the stimulus.

9. Hues can be arranged in a circle, saturations as steps on the radii of the circle, and brightnesses as a third dimension. To portray all three, a color solid is used.

10. Certain hues are complementary, e.g., yellow and greenish-blue, and red and bluish-green. Every possible hue has a complementary approximately opposite it on the color circle. When hues that are not complementary are mixed, the result is an intervening hue on the color.

11. The retina of the eye can be mapped for different hues, showing a certain zone for yellow, another for blue, etc.

12. Total color blindness is very rare, but partial color blindness occurs in one out of every 25 people. Such color blindness shows up as a confusion of certain pairs of colors. Three general kinds of confusion have been distinguished.

13. Some individuals are color-weak rather than color-blind. Color blindness is a sex-linked hereditary characteristic that follows rules described in Chapter 2.

14. Many people are unaware that they are color-blind because they have learned the proper color names to use with objects, but their defect can be detected by any one of several tests.

15. The eye can adapt to a wide range of illuminations. In dark adaptation, there is a shift from cone function to rod function. In the course of this shift, the eye's best sensitivity to wavelengths changes from about 555 millimicrons to about 505 millicrons.

16. Visual acuity, measured in eye examinations, is important in a number of occupations. It is better in the fovea than in the periphery of the eye, and nothing at all can be seen at the blind spot.

17. Visual acuity is much better under high illumination than under dim light. It is also better when the contrast between an object and its background is high. Finally, it is better when the surrounding illumination is about the same as that on the object, and not more or less.

SUGGESTIONS FOR FURTHER READING

Bartley, S. H. *Vision: a study of its basis.* New York: Van Nostrand, 1941.
    A book emphasizing physiological processes in vision.
Boring, E. G. *Sensation and perception in the history of experimental psychology.* New York: Appleton-Century-Crofts, 1942.
    An authoritative history of experimental work in vision.
Chapanis, A., Garner, W. R., and Morgan, C. T. *Applied experimental psychology.* New York: Wiley, 1949.
    A text on the applications of experimental psychology to engineering problems, including especially visual problems.
Committee on Undersea Warfare. *Human factors in undersea warfare.* Washington: National Research Council, 1949.
    A study containing several chapters on vision with emphasis on applications to practical problems.
Davson, H. *The physiology of the eye.* New York: Blakiston, 1950.
    A text covering the physiological functions of the eye.
Evans, R. M. *An introduction to color.* New York: Wiley, 1948.
    A readable and well-illustrated book on the fundamentals of color vision and on the use of color in everyday affairs.
Gibson, J. J. *The perception of the visual world.* Boston: Houghton Mifflin, 1950.
    An analysis of the more complex phenomena of visual perception.
Hartridge, H. *Colours and how we see them.* London: G. Bell, 1949.
    An interesting book covering phenomena of color vision.
Morgan, C. T., and Stellar, E. *Physiological psychology* (2d Ed.). New York: McGraw-Hill, 1950.
    A text that includes chapters on the physiological basis of vision.
Pirenne, M. H. *Vision and the eye.* London: Chapman and Hall, 1948.
    The basic facts about vision and the eye, presented in readable fashion.
Weston, H. C. *Sight, light, and efficiency.* London: H. K. Lewis, 1949.
    A book emphasizing the visual aspects of work and efficiency.

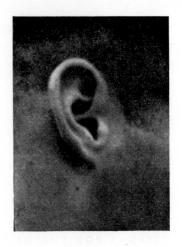

Chapter 19 HEARING AND LOWER SENSES

VISION is probably our most important asset in knowing and learning about our world, but hearing runs it a close second. Through hearing, we can understand speech, and speech is our most common medium for imparting and acquiring knowledge. Through hearing too we receive a great many signals and cues—the warning automobile horn, the chime of the clock, the fire engine's siren, the footsteps of a person approaching from behind, and many other common cues. Through hearing many people also find a great source of enjoyment in music. Thus hearing is an indispensable sense for appreciating our environment. In this chapter we shall

The first part of this chapter was drafted by Wendell R. Garner of The Johns Hopkins University and the latter part by Harold W. Hake of the University of Illinois.

consider the principles that explain how we hear.

We shall also discuss senses other than hearing and vision. Such senses are sometimes called the lower senses, because they are not, in general, so important or so highly developed as hearing and vision. There are several possible ways of classifying the lower senses. The classification we shall use divides them into three main groups: the *chemical senses*, the *skin senses*, and the *deep senses*. The chemical senses include *taste* and *smell*. The skin senses include *pressure*, *warmth*, *cold*, and *pain*. The deep senses include a *muscle sense*, a sense of equilibrium called the *vestibular sense*, and the *organic senses*, which are similar to the skin senses but are located in some of the organs of the body. The first part of the chapter will be concerned with hearing and the latter part with the lower senses.

THE PHYSICAL BASIS FOR HEARING

Before we can understand the sense of hearing we must first understand the physical stimulus for hearing and how it determines what we hear. Of course, if you are asked to say what you hear, you would say that you hear sound. That is true—you do hear sound. To know only that, however, is not enough; you should also be able to distinguish between the physical sound that stimulates the ear and the psychological sound, which is what you actually experience.

Sound waves. The air, as you know, is not a vacuum; it is a collection of molecules. These molecules are always moving about at random, colliding with each other and exerting pressure on each other. The more closely packed together they are, the greater the air pressure; the fewer they are, the less the pressure. When there is no sound or wind, they are evenly distributed in the air around us and thus they have a uniform pressure. When there is a sound, however, they increase and decrease in pressure and the changes in pressure move through the air as waves do along the surface of the water. It is, in fact, such changes in pressure that constitute the physical sound that we hear.

Sound waves are ordinarily generated by the vibration of some physical object in the air. When such an object vibrates, the molecules close to the object are first pushed together more than they usually are and thus are put under *positive pressure*. The molecules that are under positive pressure push against the molecules close to them and these in turn transmit the pressure to neighboring molecules. In this way a wave of positive pressure moves through the air like ripples on the water. Sound-

pressure waves, however, travel much faster than waves of water; at sea level, they travel about 760 miles per hour or 1,100 feet per second.

But most objects, when they are struck, do not move in just one direction. A violin string, for example, vibrates back and forth when it is plucked. As the string moves

Fig. 19.1. Three sine waves with different amplitudes and frequencies. The two upper sine waves have the same amplitude or pressure, but the middle one has a frequency twice that of the upper one. The two lower sine waves have the same frequency, but the bottom one has an amplitude twice that of the middle one.

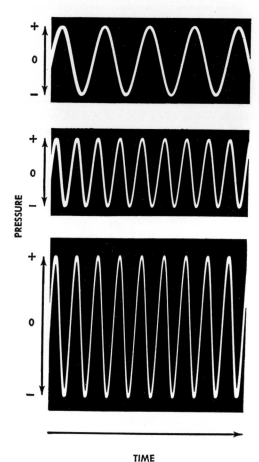

TIME

first in one direction, a positive pressure wave begins to propagate through the air; but when the string swings back to its original position and beyond, a little vacuum (or negative pressure) is created just behind the wave of positive pressure. This vacuum moves along with the speed of sound just as the positive pressure wave does. These alternations in air pressure moving along through the air are called a *sound wave*, and this sound wave is the physical stimulus for everything we hear. Different vibrations produce different sound waves. To understand the physical stimulus for hearing, then, we must understand the characteristics of such a sound wave.

Sine waves. Common observation tells us that there is an infinite variety of possible sound waves. We regard one kind of wave, however, as the simplest, because this

one, called a *sine wave*, can be used in different ways to duplicate or analyze any other kind. In Figure 19.1, you see a diagram of the sine wave, so called because it may be mathematically expressed by the sine function of trigonometry. It is produced when a single vibrating object moves back and forth *freely* and changes the pressure of the air. The sound that we hear when we listen to a sine wave is called a *pure tone*. Because it takes special equipment to make sine waves, people usually hear a pure tone only in the laboratory. Some musical instruments, such as the flute, however, are able to produce notes that are almost pure tones.

If sound waves are changes in the pressure of air, you may wonder how we are able to take pictures of them. There are, in fact, several ways of *seeing*, as well as of hearing, sound waves. The one used most often in the laboratory is a *cathode-ray oscilloscope*, which has a screen very much like a television screen (see Figure 19.2). If we have a microphone with which to convert sound waves into electrical signals, we can lead its wires into the oscilloscope, and on the screen appears a wavy line. The height of these waves represents the amount of change in air pressure, and the distance across the screen represents time.

Pitch and frequency of tones. From such pictures we can make two different kinds of measurements of sine waves. One is to count how often the sine wave alternates between positive and negative pressure—how often it goes up and down—in any given period of time. This measure is called the *frequency*, and we ordinarily state it in *cycles per second*. The sound wave at the top of Figure 19.1 alternates fewer times per second than the two lower sine waves, so it has a lower frequency. To be more specific, if a sine wave goes to positive pressure, then to negative pressure, and back

Fig. 19.2. A laboratory oscilloscope. This instrument can be used to show a picture of a sound wave. The horizontal dimension of the picture is the time scale. The vertical dimension shows the pressure changes of the sound wave. The wave shown in this picture is a sine wave.

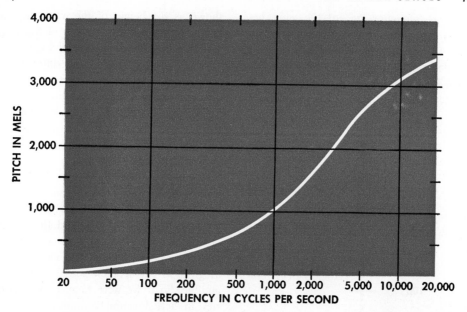

Fig. 19.3. The pitch scale. Units of pitch are called mels. The pitch of a 1,000-cycle tone is arbitrarily assigned a value of 1,000 mels. Tones that sound twice as high in pitch are assigned 2,000 mels; those that sound half as high, 500 mels. In this way, a pitch scale relating pitch to frequency has been constructed. (*After Stevens, S. S., & Volkmann, J. The relation of pitch to frequency: a revised scale. Amer. J. Psychol., 1940, 53, 329–353.*

again 500 times in a second, its frequency is 500 cycles per second, for the sine wave has completed that many cycles in 1 second.

Now it is important to note that frequency and pitch are not the same thing. One is physical, and the other is psychological. *Frequency is the physical measure of a tone, and pitch is a psychological attribute of it.* We say that pitch is a separate attribute, because people can judge pitch without knowing anything about frequency. They can, for example, listen to two tones and can judge that one is higher in pitch than another. They can even say when one tone is twice the pitch, or half the pitch, of another. So pitch can be judged quite independently of frequency.

By having people make pitch judgments in which they select a frequency of sine wave that has twice the pitch of some other frequency it is possible to construct a *pitch scale* (see Figure 19.3). In making such a scale, we can arbitrarily assign a pitch of 1 to a 1,000-cycle tone. Then the tone that is judged to be twice that pitch is assigned the number 2; that which sounds half as loud receives the number ½; and so on. Having constructed a pitch scale in this way, we can see how pitch and frequency are correlated. As you see in Figure 19.3 pitch rises very slowly below 1,000 cycles and above 4,000 cycles. Between 1,000 and 4,000 cycles, it is more nearly proportional to frequency, but a 4,000-cycle tone has little more than twice the pitch of a 1,000-cycle tone. From 4,000 cycles to 20,000 cycles, a five-fold change in frequency, pitch increases by only 50 per cent. This fact demonstrates conclusively that *pitch and frequency are not the same,* because pitch does not increase or decrease in exact proportion to frequency.

Loudness and the intensity of tones. A second kind of measure of a sound wave is its intensity. In Figure 19.1 intensity is

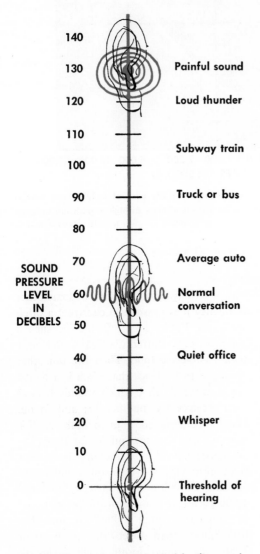

Fig. 19.4. The sound pressure level of familiar sounds. Each of the sounds indicated on the right has a sound pressure level (intensity) of approximately the number of decibels shown on the left.

shown as the height of the wave, and this height represents the pressure of the wave. The two bottom sine waves of Figure 19.1 have the same frequency but different amplitudes or intensities. Thus, while frequency gives us a measure of how often the sound wave changes from positive to negative pressure, intensity gives us a measure of how great the pressure changes are.

Scientists have developed a special scale for measuring the intensities of tones and of sounds of all kinds, partly because the range of sound intensities that we can hear is very great. The loudest sound that people can listen to without experiencing discomfort has a pressure about one million times as great as the weakest sound that is just audible. So if we were to measure intensities in actual sound pressures we should have to deal with a very large scale of numbers. Consequently, we use the *decibel* (db.) as our unit of measurement.

To explain here exactly what the decibel unit is would take us into more detail than would be justified. Our main purposes will be served by understanding two main features of the decibel. First of all, it represents a ratio of two intensities, not a difference between them (see Chapter 8). When two intensities are expressed in decibels, the numbers tell us that one intensity is so many times the other intensity, but they do not say what either intensity is. Secondly, it turns out that 20 decibels represents a ratio of 10 times; 40 decibels, 100 times; and so on up to 100 decibels which represents a ratio of 100,000 times. (A person familiar with logarithms can figure out for himself what any odd number of decibels means if he keeps in mind that the number of decibels is equal to 20 times the logarithm of the ratio of two sound pressures.)

In order for such a scale to be meaningful, there must be some starting point. Scientists have arbitrarily agreed to use a pressure of 0.0002 dyne per square centimeter —a dyne is a unit of pressure—as the starting point for this scale, and when this starting point is used, we talk about the decibel scale as the scale of *sound pressure level* (SPL).

For most practical purposes we can simply regard a decibel scale as a set of numbers like a scale of temperature and then learn that certain numbers mean certain loudnesses. To give you an idea what the numbers mean, Figure 19.4 shows the scale of sound pressure level with different levels illustrated by sounds with which you are familiar. If, when we talk about different sound pressure levels, you are not sure what they mean, reference to this chart will at least give you a rough idea of how loud the sounds are.

Just as frequency corresponds most closely to the pitch of tones, intensity corresponds most closely to the loudness of tones. Once again the two do not correspond perfectly. At high sound pressures, for example, a difference in intensity of 10 decibels sounds like a big difference in loudness. At low sound pressures, this much difference in intensity sounds like only a small difference in loudness. In fact, as we shall see later, decibel differences that cannot even be noticed at low intensities are quite obvious at high intensities.

Timbre and the complexity of tones. So far we have talked about sine waves or pure tones, but we have also pointed out that we do not very often hear them. What we commonly hear are the various kinds of *complex waves*. We have shown oscillographic pictures of three such waves in Figure 19.5. They illustrate the fact that complex waves can have any possible shape. Some of the shapes are *periodic*, which is to say that they repeat themselves. Examples of such shapes are the pictures of the sounds of a

harmonica tone and of an *oh* in Figure 19.5. Some complex tones, however, are *aperiodic*; they do not repeat themselves. The picture of the hissing noise in Figure 19.5 is a good example.

In 1822, a French mathematician named Fourier showed that any periodic function can be expressed as the sum of a number of different sine waves. This fact provides a very simple technique for describing a complex periodic wave. With a sine wave, all we need to know to describe it are the frequency and intensity. For a complex

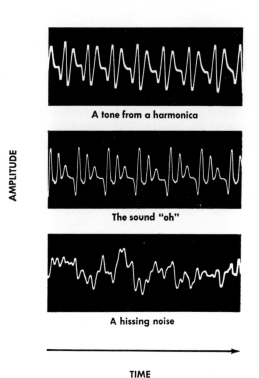

A tone from a harmonica

The sound "oh"

A hissing noise

TIME

Fig. 19.5. Oscillographic pictures of three complex sound waves. The wave at the top is a musical note played on a harmonica. The middle wave is the sustained vowel "oh." Both of these sound waves are *periodic* because the same pattern repeats itself. The sound wave at the bottom is noise; it is an *aperiodic* wave because it is completely irregular.

wave, we simply need to know the´ frequency and intensity of each of the sine-wave components of the complex wave. Thus we might describe the tone of a musical instrument by saying that it has a sound pressure level of 70 decibels at 400 cycles per second, 62 decibels at 800 cycles per second, 43 decibels at 1,200 cycles per second, 29 decibels at 1,600 cycles per second, etc. A description of a complex tone in this way is known as a *Fourier analysis*.

Notice that in this example each of the frequencies involved is some multiple of the lowest frequency. All musical instruments produce tones of this type. The lowest frequency is called the *fundamental*, and all other frequencies are called *harmonics*. The frequency which is twice as great as the fundamental is called the *second harmonic*; that which is three times as great, the *third harmonic*; etc.

The complexity of a tone, then, is a matter of the number and intensities of the different sine waves that make up the complete tone. The psychological counterpart of complexity is *timbre* or *tonal quality*, and it is timbre that lets us distinguish rather easily different musical instruments and different voices from each other. A pure tone, for example, sounds very thin and lacking in tonal quality compared to the complex tone produced by an instrument such as the violin. In contrast, we would describe the violin tone as rich. The difference is that the violin tone has many strong harmonics. It is not just *more or less* timbre, however, that distinguishes different instruments. Rather the timbres of different instruments are *different*, and we learn that each instrument has a characteristic timbre.

There are, of course, other sounds that have little or no tonal quality and these are called *noises*. In Figure 19.5 was a picture of a noise. In that instance the noise was

made by blowing air across a microphone. Notice that the picture of the noise is not periodic; it does not repeat itself in any regular pattern as do the sounds of musical instruments. That is because it is made up of many different frequencies which are not multiples or harmonics of each other; rather, the frequencies are mixed more or less randomly. When the mixture is really random, we speak of *random noise*. In other instances, such as clicks or tapping sounds, the noises are not completely random, for they contain certain dominant frequencies. They are, nevertheless, noises because they contain many frequencies that are not multiples of each other.

■ HOW THE EAR WORKS

So far we have described the physical sounds that impinge on our ears and the psychological attributes of pitch, loudness, and timbre that we perceive from them. Our next step is to bridge the gap between the two by describing the organs of hearing and their workings. In this way we can see how the ear translates physical sounds into nervous impulses, thereby providing the information for auditory experience.

Conduction in the ear. Figure 19.6 shows a cross section of the major features of the ear. It consists of three principal parts: the outer ear, which collects the sound; the middle ear, which transmits the sound; and the inner ear, which transforms the sound into nervous impulses.

The outer ear, or *pinna*, besides being a decoration, collects sounds which then travel through a small air-filled duct, called the *auditory canal*, to the eardrum. The *eardrum* is a thin membrane stretched tightly across the inner end of the canal. Alternations in the pressure of the sound wave move this small membrane back and forth, and it is at this point that the ear's

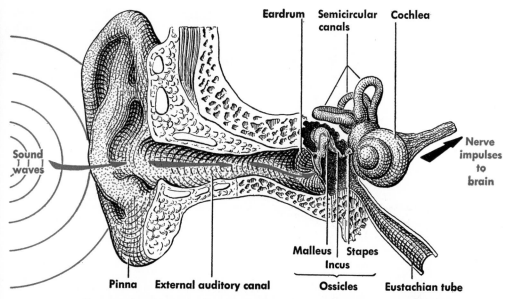

Fig. 19.6. The human ear. The ear consists of three principal parts: an external ear, a middle ear, and an inner ear. The external ear consists of the pinna and a canal that conducts sound waves to the eardrum. The eardrum, marking the division between the external and middle ears, is set into vibration by sound waves. This vibration is transmitted by the bones of the middle ear (malleus, incus, and stapes) to the fluid of the cochlea. Sound waves in this fluid stimulate the sensory cells of the cochlea.

sound system changes from one of air conduction to one of bone conduction.

The eardrum is the boundary separating the outer ear from the beginning of the *middle ear*. The rest of the middle ear consists of three small bones, the *ossicles*, which are so connected that they form a bridge between the eardrum and the *inner ear*. These three bones also act as a series of levers which conduct sounds to the inner ear.

The cochlea. The inner ear is by far the most complicated of the three major parts of the ear. It consists of two kinds of sense organs, one concerned in the sense of balance and the other in hearing. The organs for balance are called the vestibular sense organs and will be discussed later in this chapter. The sense organs for hearing are contained in a bony structure, which is

spiraled like a snail and hence is called the *cochlea,* meaning snail shell. This cochlea has three different ducts or canals spiraling around together, separated from each other by membranes and each filled with fluid. Figure 19.7 shows a cross section of these ducts. The *cochlear canal* is the smallest of the three and is separated from the *vestibular canal* by *Reissner's membrane,* and from the *tympanic canal* by the *basilar membrane*. The basilar membrane is the most important of these membranes, for on it lies the *organ of Corti,* in which sound waves give rise to auditory impulses. These impulses travel along an *auditory nerve* that comes out of the core of the cochlear spiral and leads to the brain.

The *oval window* (see Figure 19.19) receives sound vibrations from one of the bones of the middle ear and transmits them

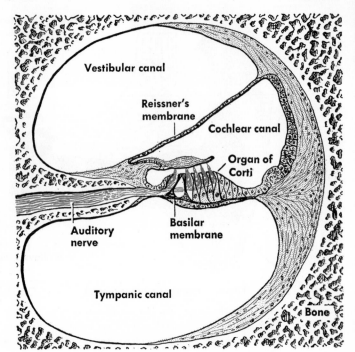

Fig. 19.7. A cross-sectional diagram of the cochlea. Sound waves in the canals of the cochlea deflect the organ of Corti on the basilar membrane and in this way initiate nervous impulses in the fibers of the auditory nerve. For further explanation, see text.

in turn into the vestibular canal. Thus when a sound wave moves the ossicles back and forth, this movement is transmitted to the fluid of the cochlea. This in turn *bends the basilar membrane,* causing it to excite the cells of the organ of Corti, thereby setting off nervous impulses. The basilar membrane, however, changes width from one end to the other. At the end nearest the oval window it is narrowest, and it becomes progressively wider toward the other end. The narrow end, it is important to note, is bent most easily by tones of high frequency, whereas the broader end bends more easily when low-frequency sounds come into the cochlea. Thus the cochlea can analyze sounds into their component frequencies, at least in a crude way, in the same way that a mathematician can do it by Fourier analysis. The cochlea does it, however, by having different places on the basilar membrane respond to different frequencies.

Scientists are not entirely agreed about the accuracy of this analysis in the cochlea, but it now seems fairly certain that it takes place and, moreover, that it is what enables us to perceive pitch.[1] Thus we can see that one pitch sounds different from another because different places on the basilar membrane are stimulated. The brain can appreciate such differences because they are represented by nervous impulses in different sets of nerve fibers coming from various areas of the basilar membrane.

Whereas place of origin of nervous impulses accounts for different pitches, the number of nervous impulses probably governs loudness. When sound pressures are high, the basilar membrane vibrates with greater amplitude. This triggers off more impulses per second in the nerve fibers serving that particular area of the membrane and increases the number of fibers that fire. Thus the total number of impulses goes up with increasing sound pressures, giving rise to the experience of greater loudness.

THE LIMITS OF HEARING

We have now come to understand the stimulus for hearing and have seen how the ear converts a sound wave into a pattern of neural impulses that eventually determines what we hear. The mere fact that a physical sound exists, however, does not ensure that we shall hear anything—even when the hearing mechanism is in good working order—because there are limits to what we can hear. We cannot hear every intensity of a sound wave, nor can we hear all possible frequencies.

Intensity limits. It is probably obvious that intensity limits a person's hearing. If a tone is too weak, we cannot hear it at all, and even though physical measurement might show that a sound wave exists, a sound wave that is too weak cannot be an adequate stimulus. As indicated in Figure 19.4, a sound pressure level of zero decibels is approximately the lowest intensity of

Fig. 19.8. The absolute threshold of hearing for pure tones of different frequency.

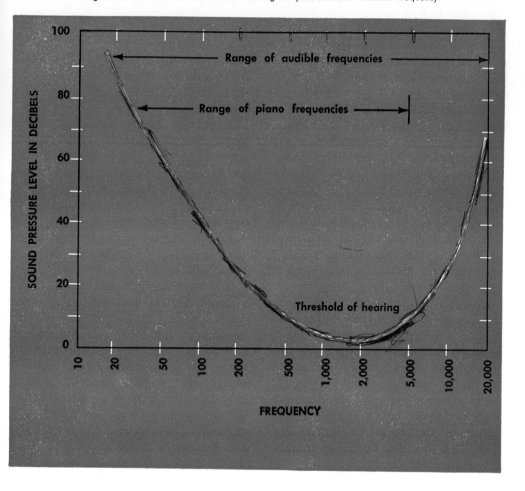

sound that normal human beings ever hear. However, as Figure 19.8 shows, the intensity of many frequencies must be even greater than that to reach the absolute threshold, that is, the just-audible intensity.

The curve of Figure 19.8 depicts absolute thresholds for tones of different frequencies. From it we see that hearing is best for frequencies between 1,000 and 5,000 cycles per second. At a frequency of 50 cycles per second, for example, it requires a sound pressure about 1,000 times as great for a tone to be heard as it does for a frequency of 2,000 cycles per second. Similarly at higher frequencies, greater intensities are required for hearing. Note too that there is an *upper limit* of sound pressure, because sound pressures that are too great arouse pain. If you will turn back to Figure 19.4, you can see that this level is approximately 130 decibels above the absolute threshold of hearing.

Now refer again to the curve of Figure 19.8. It suggests that tones in the middle range of frequencies are much louder than those either higher or lower. At low intensities, this is actually true. But at higher intensities of tones, all tones tend to sound equally loud. For example, at a sound pressure level of 110 or 120 decibels, tones of all frequencies are about equally loud. Thus the differences in absolute thresholds do not carry over into differences of loudness at high sound pressure levels.

Frequency limits. Just as there is a limiting range of the intensities we can hear, so is there a limiting range of frequencies. Generally speaking, we can say that the audible range of frequencies is between 20 and 20,000 cycles per second. As you can see from Figure 19.8, however, this range is not a precisely defined one. Tones over this range of frequencies can be heard only at very high intensities, and at lower intensities the range is considerably smaller.

So that you may have a more realistic idea of the frequency limits of hearing, the tones of a piano are also indicated in Figure 19.8. From this you can see that the range of notes is considerably narrower than the range of frequencies we can actually hear, particularly at the higher frequencies. It is, in fact, generally true that we seldom hear frequencies near the higher limits. Speech, for example, contains very few frequencies above about 7,000 cycles per second. Tones at these very high frequencies hardly sound like tones at all; rather they sound weak, very thin, and almost without a real pitch. Perhaps you have noticed that even the highest notes on a piano have very little tonal character compared to the notes in the middle range of frequencies.

At very low frequencies, one can still hear sounds, but they are not tonal. Instead, we actually hear the individual pressure changes rather than a tone corresponding to the frequency of the note. A tone of 8 or 10 cycles per second, for example, is a throbbing sound. In practice, it is very difficult to produce a pure tone at these very low frequencies, and as a result, it is difficult to measure the frequency at which we no longer hear a tone. Another difficulty is that these very low frequency tones have harmonics, and the harmonics may sound tonal even though the fundamental frequency does not.

Intensity differences.   Our ears not only limit the range of intensities and frequencies we can hear, they also limit the amount of change or difference between two tones that we can detect. To find this limit we sound two tones, one at a time, and ask observers to tell us whether they are the same or different. Then we change either the intensity or the frequency, making the difference smaller or larger, until we have the difference that the observer can just detect. Psychologists have measured this limit with great care for practically all possible intensities and frequencies.

Both the frequency and the intensity of a tone affect the limit for detecting differences in intensity. Detection is poorer for weak tones than it is for loud ones. For most practical purposes, however, a number to remember is one decibel, for *one decibel is a difference in intensity that we can always detect as long as sounds are reasonably loud*. The other point worth noting is that *detection of a difference is poorer for the very low and very high frequencies than it is for the middle ones*.

Frequency differences. Practically the same rules hold for discriminating differences in frequency, though of course the measure is different. In this case we find the smallest difference in frequency (cycles per second) that a person can detect. If we express this in per cent by dividing the difference by the frequency of one of the tones, we have a measure that is relatively constant for all kinds of tones. Actually, as in the case of intensity, the *per cent that can be detected is better for high frequencies than it is for low ones*, and it is *better for the middle range of frequencies than it is for high tones or low tones*. To demonstrate this last point, you might strike some keys on the piano, and then you would realize that it is relatively easy to tell the difference, say, between an E and an F in the middle of the keyboard, but relatively hard to do it in the extreme bass or treble.

One should not confuse the ability to detect differences with the ability to identify a single note or tone—what is sometimes called absolute pitch. A very few fortunate people can identify nearly all the notes of the musical scale when they hear them played singly. Most of us have a hard time telling which octave a note is in and can identify accurately no more than 8 or 10

different tones. For most purposes, however, we do not need this ability because the important task is usually to perceive the difference between two tones rather than the identity of a single one.

Masking. All that we have been saying about the limits of hearing assumes that people are listening in relative quiet. The limits of hearing can be quite different, however, if more than one tone is sounded at a time or if somebody is making a noise when we are trying to listen to a tone. Then it is not so easy to hear a tone or to detect a difference between two tones. Such a change in the limits of hearing because of other tones or noise is known as masking.

You are all familiar with the masking of sounds by other sounds in everyday life. If you are talking on the telephone and there is a noise around you or in the telephone circuit, you cannot hear so well; or if an airplane flies overhead during a lecture, you may not hear what the lecturer is saying. Research workers have measured such effects of masking on the limits of hearing as carefully as they have measured hearing in the quiet, and masking turns out to be a complex subject. The main points, however, are these: First, *tones near together in frequency mask each other well*—that is, each tone makes it hard for the other to be heard—but tones far apart in frequency do not mask very well. Secondly, *low tones mask high tones better than the other way around*. Consequently, if two tones are sounded together, you will be able to hear the tone of lower pitch more easily.

DISSONANCE AND CONSONANCE

Those who are interested in music usually like to know what it is about two or more tones played together that makes them sound consonant (harmonious) or dissonant. When two or more musical notes are played together and produce a pleasing sound, we speak of the notes as being *harmonious* or *consonant*; they seem to go together. If the notes are not pleasing, we speak of *dissonance* or say that the notes are not in harmony. What accounts for consonance and dissonance?

Part of the answer is in the interaction of the harmonics of the two tones. Octave notes always sound harmonious because the harmonics of the two notes fit together. Suppose, for example, that someone plays two notes of 200 and 400 cycles per second. (The 2:1 ratio means that the notes are an octave apart.) The first note has sine-wave frequencies of 200, 400, 600, 800, 1,000, 1,200, etc., cycles per second. The second note has frequencies of 400, 800, 1,200, 1,600, etc., cycles per second. Notice that all the harmonics of the second tone match harmonics of the first tone. The result is that we hear a single merged tone, and the two tones together sound consonant.

As another, more complex, example of *consonant* tones, let us take two notes of 200 and 300 cycles per second. This ratio of 3:2 gives a musical interval known as a perfect *fifth*. The harmonics of the lower-pitched tone are the same as above, while the frequencies of the higher-pitched tone are 300, 600, 900, 1,200, etc. The entire series of frequencies will be 200, 300, 400, 600, 800, 900, 1,000, etc. Notice that here all the frequencies are either 200 or 100 cycles apart, forming a regular pattern. This orderly relation of the harmonics also makes a consonant sound.

To illustrate a *dissonant* pair of notes, suppose we play a note of 100 cycles per second (which has harmonics at every even hundred cycles per second) and a note of 178 cycles per second. These two notes are

a full note less than an octave apart, as a D and the C above it would be. The harmonics of the second note are 356, 534, 712, 890, 1,068, etc., cycles per second. In this case the harmonics of 712 and 890 cycles per second do not correspond with the harmonics of 700 and 900 cycles per second of the lower note. The resulting roughness makes the pair of notes sound dissonant.

We must warn you, however, that dissonance and consonance are not entirely explained merely by presence or absence of particular harmonics. We do not know all the reasons why some combinations of tones sound harmonious and others do not. Undoubtedly learning plays a part. So also does the sequence of sounds, for a certain combination may sound harmonious in some melodies, but not in others. The relations of the harmonics are thus only one important factor in consonance.[2]

AUDITORY SPACE PERCEPTION

Hearing does not provide us with very adequate information about the size or position of objects in space. Nevertheless, we can perceive the *direction of sound* and its *distance* from us fairly well. So we do have some auditory space perception.

Cues to direction. In visual perception (see Chapter 7), the fact that we have *two eyes* usually helps us considerably in judging the *depth* of an object, but *one* does just as well as two for judging the *direction* of an object. In hearing, however, the rules are essentially reversed. To tell *direction* from auditory cues, we must have two ears, although one ear is just about as good as two for judging *depth*.

There are three types of *binaural cues* for perceiving the direction of a sound. (The

Fig. 19.9. How we perceive the direction of a sound. Each arc represents successive crests of the sound wave as it travels from the source, which in this case is a loudspeaker. Notice that when the head is facing the source, the sound wave reaches both ears at the same time, but that it reaches the nearer ear first when the head is turned away from the speaker. In addition, the farther ear receives a less intense sound because of the shadow cast by the head and because it is farther away.

term *binaural* refers to the use of two ears.) The first and most important is *time*. If a click is sounded off to one side of your head, the sound travels through the air at a rate of 1,100 feet per second, and arrives at the nearer ear before it arrives at the farther one. This effect is shown diagrammatically in Figure 19.9. When the source of the sound is directly opposite one ear, the difference in time of arrival at the two ears is at a maximum and is about $\frac{1}{2}$ millisecond (or $\frac{1}{2000}$ second). When the source of sound is directly ahead, then the sound wave reaches both ears at the same time. At positions in between, the difference in time of arrival at the two ears will naturally be more than zero and less than the maximum value. Thus the time difference serves as a cue to the direction of the sound. The time differences are, of course, very small, and it is remarkable that people can use them as such effective cues to the direction of a sound.

A second binaural cue is *intensity*. It works since the head casts a sound shadow, and the ear opposite to any sound source lies in this shadow. As you can see from Figure 19.9, the head makes a shadow because a sound coming from one side must go around the head to get to the other side,

and before it gets there a great deal of it is absorbed. As a consequence, the sound reaching the farther ear is much weaker than that striking the nearer ear. Once again, as in the case of time difference, the amount of this shadow depends on the direction of the sound source. It is greatest when the sound source is off to the side, zero when it is directly in front, and at intermediate values when the sound source lies at other angles.

The third cue is *phase*. The difference in phase of the sine-wave tone at the two ears comes about in the same way as the difference in time of arrival. The sine wave is simply a succession of positive and negative pressures, and the maximum positive pressure of the sine wave reaches one ear sooner than the other if the sound source is to one side of the head (see Figure 19.1). Thus at any one time the tones at the two ears may be out of phase, but the amount by which they will be out of phase once again depends on the exact direction of the sound source. In everyday life, however, the phase cue is useful only at relatively low frequencies because the distance between the ears is so large relative to the wavelength of high-frequency tones that phase differences are unreliable at high frequencies.

Taken together, these three cues enable people to judge the direction of a sound rather well. When both the head and the source of sound are stationary, they usually can tell with an accuracy of at least 20 degrees of the circle around the head where a sound comes from. When either the head or the sound source is allowed to move, they can do quite a bit better, because they then can perceive how the cues change with changes in the relative position of the head and the source. It is for this reason that people learn automatically to move their heads when they are trying to judge where a sound comes from.

Cues to distance.   As we have just seen, the fact that we have two ears makes it possible for us to perceive the direction of a sound. With just one ear we could not perceive direction without moving our heads. For this reason, hard-of-hearing people who use a hearing aid always have trouble in locating the direction of a sound because the hearing aid has just one receiver. Because of this difficulty, it has been suggested that two separate hearing aids, one for each ear, should be used to permit those who are hard of hearing to perceive the direction of sounds.

Only one ear is needed, however, to perceive *distance*, because the cues to distance are *intensity* and *frequency composition* and one ear can use them as well as can two. The first of these cues depends on the fact that distant sounds are usually much weaker than near sounds. If we have not heard a sound before, we usually judge it to be farther away if it is a weak sound than if it is a loud sound. We cannot usually judge the distance on the basis of intensity, however, unless we know what the sound is. To use this cue effectively, therefore, we must be familiar with the sound. A train whistle in the distance may be as loud as the chime of a clock nearby, and yet we know that the train is far away and the clock is close at hand. We know this, however, only because we are familiar with the two sounds and know that a train whistle would be much louder than the chime of the clock if both were at the same distance.

The other cue to distance is *frequency composition* or complexity of a sound. This, as pointed out earlier, refers to the number of frequencies that make up a sound and to the relative sound pressures of each of these frequencies. Fortunately we can use frequency composition or complexity as a cue because the air and objects in the path of a sound absorb high frequencies much more than they do low frequencies. Thus a low-frequency sound can be heard much farther away than can a high-frequency sound. Foghorns, for example, are always low-pitched because they must be heard over many miles of the sea. If a foghorn were high-pitched, it could be heard only by ships very near the horn.

Since the high frequencies in sound are absorbed more than the low frequencies, then the farther away one is from the source of sound, the more the sound will appear low-pitched. When you listen to an orchestra at a distance, you cannot hear the high notes very well. Thus when you hear music being played, but can hear the low notes much better than the high notes, you judge the sound to be far away. At very great distances, even orchestral music will sound very low-pitched and rumbling, because you can hear only the low pitches.

DEAFNESS

We should not end this survey of hearing without saying something about deafness. Deafness is a serious problem in a civilization that depends so much on spoken com-

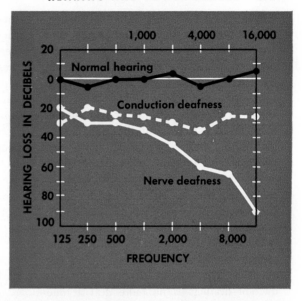

Fig. 19.10. Audiograms for normal hearing and two major kinds of deafness. The average threshold for normal individuals at different frequencies is taken as zero. Any particular individual does not have exactly this threshold but does not depart from it by more than a few decibels. The person with conductive deafness has a rather uniform hearing loss at all frequencies. The person with nerve deafness has a greater hearing loss at high frequencies than at low ones.

munication, for the deaf or hard-of-hearing person has a difficult time communicating. Either everything must be written out for him, or he must "hear" by sign language. Some hard-of-hearing people become quite proficient at reading lips, but this procedure is at best a poor substitute for heard speech.

Deafness is fairly common in our society, and until very recent years any kind of deafness was a serious handicap. It was not until the advent of the modern electronic hearing aid that partially deaf people had a sensory aid as good as that provided by eyeglasses. A totally deaf person cannot be helped with a hearing aid, however, any more than a totally blind person can see with glasses.

Deafness is also a two-way problem; it handicaps a person as a speaker, as well as a listener. Because he can never hear his own voice, a deaf person eventually loses his ability to speak well. That is why many deaf people speak in a peculiar tone—they have no way of knowing whether or not their voices sound like the voices of other people. In addition, deafness can create a serious emotional problem. The deaf person tends to withdraw from society, because he cannot, without great difficulty, communicate with it and because of the irritation other people show when he cannot understand them.

Kinds of deafness. To measure deafness clinically one uses an instrument known as the *audiometer*. This is simply a device for testing the intensity and frequency limits of hearing that we described earlier in this chapter. It produces pure tones at several different frequencies and provides accurate control of the sound pressure at each frequency. The clinician uses it to find the minimum sound pressure (in decibels) that a person can hear at each frequency. The decibels required are then plotted on a chart such as you see in Figure 19.10, a chart that is called an *audiogram*. This shows the sound pressure level required to hear the various tones compared to what an average person can hear. The difference between what the deaf person can hear and what the normal person can hear is the measure of hearing loss.

The top curve in Figure 19.10 is a typical

audiogram for a person with normal hearing. Notice that even the normal person does not hear all tones at exactly the same sound pressure level as the *average* normal person does, for there are always individual variations from the average. The other two curves in Figure 19.10 are for two individuals who are partially deaf, that is, have sizable hearing losses. We have drawn two curves because there are two different kinds of deafness. These two kinds have different causes, and they are characterized by different patterns of hearing loss in their audiograms.

One kind, *conduction deafness*, has roughly the same hearing loss at all frequencies. The person suffering from conduction deafness is no more deaf at one frequency than he is at another. The term *conduction deafness* is used because such an audiogram usually indicates that something is wrong with conduction in the ear. The ear may be stopped up, the eardrum may be broken, or the ossicles of the middle ear may be damaged. The effect of conduction deafness is much the same as that of stuffing cotton in one's ears.

The lowest curve in Figure 19.10 represents the other kind of hearing loss, namely, *nerve deafness*. As its name suggests, in this type of deafness something is wrong with the auditory nervous system. Either the nerves themselves have been damaged, or there has been damage in the cochlea, particularly to the basilar membrane. It is characteristic of nerve deafness that hearing loss is much greater at the high frequencies, which means that the nerve-deaf person can hear low-pitched sounds reasonably well but can hear high-pitched sounds very poorly or not at all. Such a person has a great deal of trouble understanding speech, because, as we shall see in the next chapter, the high frequencies are very important in speech comprehension. He can hear the louder low tones all right, but he is not able to distinguish easily between the word sounds. Because he can hear sound but cannot comprehend speech easily, he is likely to become very annoyed. Also for the same reason, this kind of deafness has sometimes been called *perception deafness*.

Nerve deafness is very common in older people. In fact, nearly all of us can expect to have at least mild nerve deafness by the time we are sixty, just as most of us can expect to be a bit farsighted by that age. But for most people, the deafness will not be serious enough to require a hearing aid.

■ THE CHEMICAL SENSES

So far, in the preceding chapter and this one, we have covered the two senses, vision and hearing, that most people would consider to be our most important ones. It remains for us to describe the others. We can divide them into three main groups: the *chemical senses*, the *skin senses*, and the *deep senses*. Since these senses do not figure as prominently in our lives as do vision and hearing, our descriptions, in general, will be brief. We shall begin with the chemical senses, which consist of *smell* and *taste*.

The smell receptors.   The receptors for smell respond to chemical substances, but only if those substances are volatile. Liquids, for example, do not stimulate the sense of smell. Smell receptors are located high up in the nasal passages leading from the nostrils to the throat (see Figure 19.11). They lie in two small patches, one on the left and one on the right, in the roofs of these passages. They are a little off the main route of air as it moves through the nose in normal breathing, and consequently our sense of smell is relatively dulled when we are breathing quietly. A sudden sniff or vigorous intake of air, however, stirs up the air in the nasal passages and brings it more directly to the receptors. This is why we see animals and people sniffing when they are trying to identify an odor.

Primary odors. Just by recalling the odors that you encounter in everyday life, you can realize that there are many shades and qualities of them. Perhaps, however, there are a few primary odors which, when mixed in different proportions, can match or produce the entire gamut of smells. This possibility, you will recall, worked out very well in the case of vision, for in that sense only three different stimuli (a red, a green, and a blue) are necessary to "make" any of the variety of hues we perceive. Unfortunately, however, this happy solution has not worked for the sense of smell. Although research workers have devoted considerable effort to the problem, we are not yet certain what the primary odors are, or even whether there is a limited number of them.

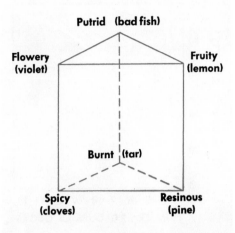

Fig. 19.12. Henning's smell prism. Henning proposed that there are six basic odors and that they might be represented as corners on a prism. Other odors are regarded as mixtures of these primary odors.

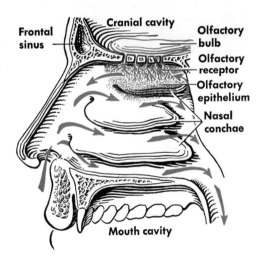

Fig. 19.11. A cross section of the nose. Air currents inhaled through the nostrils are wafted to the upper part of the nasal cavity where they may stimulate the olfactory receptors.

For a tentative list of primary odors, psychologists have generally favored a classification suggested by Henning. This assumes that there are six basic smells which may be mixed to give intermediate ones as shown in the accompanying *smell prism* (see Figure 19.12). Industrial chemists, who are faced with the problem of making artificial perfumes and scents, prefer a simpler fourfold classification of odors, suggested by Crocker.[3] According to this classification, the four primary odors and examples of them are fragrant (musk), acid (vinegar), burnt (roast coffee), and caprylic (goaty or sweaty).

To illustrate the difficulty in accepting this or any other scheme of primary odors, we can turn to an experiment in which 15 subjects were asked to classify 32 different odors.[4] Their instructions were to sniff the samples and to classify in groups all odors that seemed similar. They were allowed to make as many different groups as they considered necessary. In the accompanying

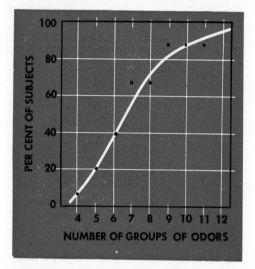

Fig. 19.13. Number of groups required to classify olfactory stimuli. This graph summarizes an experiment in which subjects were asked to classify odors according to their similarities and differences. One subject could classify all odors into four groups, but most subjects required more. (After Ross, S., & Harriman, A. B. A preliminary study of the Crocker-Henderson odor-classification system. Amer. J. Psychol., 1949, *62*, 399–404.)

graph (Figure 19.13) are the number of groups employed by different proportions of subjects. Only one of them could classify all odors into just four groups. About half of them needed five or six groups. Some subjects, however, needed as many as 12 or more groups to classify the stimuli. From this and other experiments, it appears that people cannot agree very well on how many primary odors there are.

Smell sensitivity. In hearing and vision we were able to state precisely how much energy is required for a person to detect or discriminate a stimulus. This is often not the case in smell because we are unable to control accurately how much of a stimulus gets to the smell receptors. Sniffing, we have already pointed out, is the best way to get

odors to the smell receptors, yet sniffs vary from one person to another and from one sniff to the next. So even if we know how much odorous material is introduced into the nose, we cannot say accurately how much arrives at the smell receptors.

Two partial solutions to this problem have been used. One is blast-injection technique. A certain amount of odorous vapor is put into a bottle under pressure and a tube led from the bottle to a person's nose (see Figure 19.14). A clamp on the tube holds the vapor in the bottle until the clamp is released. At that moment, a blast of vapor of known concentration and amount is sent into the nose by the pressure in the bottle. This method has given better measures of smell sensitivity than was possible with cruder techniques. A second method for controlling smell stimuli makes use of the *olfactorium*. This is a sealed glass room that shuts out all unwanted odors and permits the subject to breathe air containing some uniform amount of odorous material.

With methods like these it has been possible to compare the amounts of odorous material needed for a person to detect its presence. Thresholds of detection vary considerably for the different odors, but in general they are rather small. Anesthetic ether, which is one of the less odorous materials, requires only 6 milligrams per liter of air—a milligram is about 40 millionths of an ounce—to be detected. Artificial musk, one of the most odorous of substances, can be sensed in extraordinarily small dilutions. Only 0.00004 milligram of it in a liter of air can be smelled. This is such an enormous amount of dilution that no physical or chemical means can be used to measure it, which means that the nose must be responding to no more than a few chemical molecules per sniff. However, impressive as this may be, the sense of smell in many animals surpasses that in man.

Fig. 19.14. The blast-injection technique for the study of smell. For explanation, see text.

Taste receptors. The receptors for taste are specialized cells which are grouped together in little clusters known as *taste buds* (see Figure 19.15). These buds are located for the most part on the top and sides of the tongue, but a few of them are also at the back of the mouth and in the throat. If you examine the tongue closely—which you may do simply by looking at your own tongue in a mirror—you will notice a number of bumps on it, some large and some small. These bumps, called *papillae*, are richly populated with taste buds. To stimulate the taste receptors, substances must be in solutions which wash around the papillae and penetrate to the taste cells within them.

Primary taste qualities. We have said that we are not yet certain of the primary odors. Fortunately we are clearer about the primary taste qualities. Several lines of evidence point to *four* qualities. These have been named *salty, sour, sweet,* and *bitter*. Part of the evidence for these qualities is the fact that the tongue is not uniformly sensitive to all stimuli. If, for example, we apply minute drops of a bitter solution,

such as quinine, to different parts of the tongue, we find the bitter taste most pronounced when the drops are put at the *back* of the tongue. The taste of sweetness, on the other hand, is most noticeable when sugar solutions are placed on the *tip* of the tongue. The sides of the tongue respond mainly to sour stimuli, and the *tip and part of the sides* respond to salty solutions. This and other evidence support the idea of four primary taste qualities.

Fig. 19.15. A taste bud.

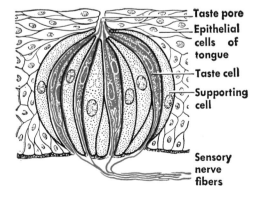

Taste pore

Epithelial cells of tongue

Taste cell

Supporting cell

Sensory nerve fibers

If we now try, however, to state what kinds of solutions give rise to the different qualities, we run into trouble. Sugars such as common table sugar taste sweet, but so do many other chemical compounds, such as saccharine, which have little in common, chemically, with sugar. The taste of bitter presents a similar problem. A class of compounds that the organic chemist calls *alkaloids*, which include quinine and nicotine, taste bitter, but so also do substances like some of the mineral salts that have little in common with the alkaloids. However, all this may prove only that we have not yet discovered which aspects of a chemical substance are the key ones in determining taste quality.

In the cases of sour and of salty tastes, there is a somewhat better correlation between chemical composition and taste. All the stimuli that taste sour are acids. Moreover, the degree of sourness that we taste is fairly proportional to the total number of acid (H^+) ions present. Salty taste, similarly, is usually aroused by what the chemist calls salts (meaning the chemical product of acids and alkalies). Common table salt, however, is about the only salt that has a uniquely salty taste; most other salts also arouse experiences of bitter or sweet in addition to that of salt.

Taste sensitivity. Just as it is difficult to measure accurately a person's threshold for odors, so it is difficult to measure thresholds for taste. All stimuli for taste must be in solution and must reach the taste cells lying beneath the surface of the papillae. For an experimenter to control taste stimuli precisely, he must make sure that all saliva is removed from the surface to be stimulated and also that it is washed free of any solutions which have been used in preceding tests. The temperature of the tongue and the size of the area stimulated must also be carefully controlled.

When an investigator takes all these precautions, he can make measurements of taste sensitivity. From measurements that have been made, it is clear that taste sensitivity is not nearly so good, relatively, as smell sensitivity. It takes, for example, from four parts in 100 to one part in 1,000 to be easily detected. In general, our sensitivity for acids and bitter substances is better than it is for sweet and salty substances.

Adaptation. All, or nearly all, our different sense organs adapt to stimuli. That is to say, they gradually become less sensitive during the course of stimulation, and the stronger the stimulation the greater is such adaptation. Some senses, such as those for hearing and for equilibrium (see below) adapt relatively little. The senses of taste and smell, however, are among those that adapt readily.

We have all noticed such adaptation. Sometimes, upon entering a room, you are almost taken aback by a strong odor. Yet, after you have been in the room for a while, you no longer notice the odor and may be unable to tell whether it is still there. Similarly, you appreciate the full flavor of your favorite food only when you first taste it. Adaptation soon sets in so that you lose some of the strength of the flavor. It is possible to measure such adaptation in the laboratory, and research workers have gathered many curves showing the rate of adaptation for various odors and tastes.[5]

Taste or smell? Although we all believe that we taste with our tongues and smell with our noses, most of us do not realize how commonly we confuse taste and smell. Indeed, we often think we are identifying a flavor by taste when smell is the more important. You can prove this by getting a friend to hold his nose while you place drops of familiar beverages on his tongue. If you place a drop of lemon juice on it, the chances are that he will say merely that it

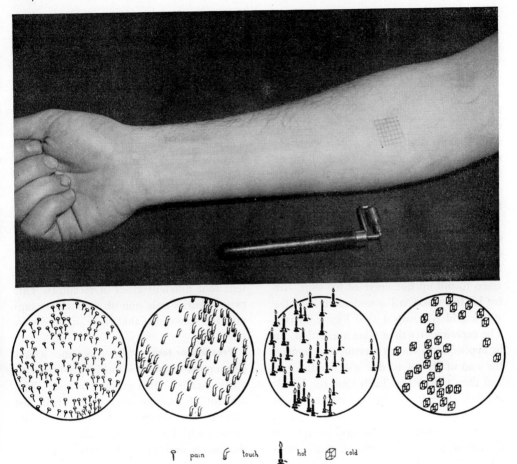

Fig. 19.16. Mapping the sensitivity of the skin. By marking a grid on an area of the skin, then systematically stimulating different spots, one can construct a map of the sensitive spots. This map is usually different for pain, pressure, warm, and cold stimuli, indicating that these are four distinct skin senses. (*Diagram from Gerard, R. W. The body functions. New York: Wiley, 1941, P. 64.*)

is something sour. Or if you drop a little Coca-Cola on it, he may only know that it is something bitter-sweet. (Potato is also indistinguishable from apple.) If now you repeat the experiment without your friend holding his nose, he will immediately be able to identify the lemon juice and Coca-Cola. Some smells, like tobacco smoke, so mask a flavor that gourmets have been known to refuse to eat in smoke-filled restaurants. Even the feel of food to the tongue or the crunchiness (stimulation of jaw muscles) may participate in, and alter, a food's *flavor*. This part played by smell explains why food is so "tasteless" when you have a stuffy head cold.

THE SKIN SENSES

Vision, hearing, and the chemical senses are the sensory channels that we use most in perceiving the world. If these channels are functioning properly, we hardly need any other senses to appreciate what is going on around us. For this reason we tend to ignore what we could do, if we had to, with our skin senses. In general, we rely on our skin senses only for such simple experiences as itches and tinglings, feelings of hot and cold, and painful sensations of injury. Actually the skin senses are capable of telling us much more than that. We could, for example, identify many objects by their touch or even read braille, as the blind have been forced to do.

The four senses. Let us begin our account of these senses with an experiment that has now become a common one in the psychological laboratory. A subject is seated and asked to roll up the sleeve of his shirt, baring his forearm. On the undersurface of the arm a grid is stamped (see Figure 19.16). The experimenter then takes a hair that can be applied with known pressure and touches the end of it first to one spot on the grid and then to another. Each time the hair is applied, the subject reports whether or not he feels pressure. The experimenter keeps a chart corresponding to the grid stamped on the subject's arm and marks on it each position at which the subject reports pressure.

Having plotted all the squares on the grid where pressure is reported, the experimenter now abandons his hair and takes up a rod that has been cooled to a temperature, say, of 28°C and is kept at that temperature throughout the experiment. With this rod, he goes again from square to square and charts the points at which the subject reports "cold." He then does the same thing with a rod that has been maintained at a temperature above normal, say, 35°C, and he maps all the spots for which "warm" is reported. Finally, with a fine, sharp needle applied with a constant, light pressure, he goes over the entire grid again and plots the "pain spots."

Now let us look at the chart on which all these points are plotted (see Figure 19.16). First of all, you can see that not all areas are equally sensitive. In some squares, the subject reports "pressure," in others he does not. Thus you see that the skin has a *punctate sensitivity*—it is sensitive at some points and not others. (Actually detailed analysis shows that the skin is simply *more* sensitive or *less* sensitive from one square to another.) Secondly, you will notice that there are different maps for the different stimulators. The places of greatest sensitivity of pressure, cold, warmth, and pain are, on the whole, different. You now see that there is not one skin sense, but four different ones, and you may infer that they represent four different kinds of receptors. This experiment is only one of several that support the conclusion that there are four skin senses.

Pressure or touch. The experience a subject reports when he is touched lightly with a hair is called either pressure or touch. The amount of pressure required to elicit this experience varies greatly for different parts of the body. The tip of the tongue, the lips, the fingers, and the hand are the most sensitive areas. The arms and legs are less sensitive, while the trunk and calloused areas are the least sensitive of all. We experience pressure, it should also be noted, not only when some object touches the skin but also when hairs on the body are slightly moved.

Psychologists have studied carefully what it is about a stimulus that elicits the experience of pressure. They wanted to know in particular whether it was the weight of an object on the skin or simply a bending of the skin that aroused sensation. They have concluded that it is the latter—the deforming or bending of the skin.[6] If you have handy some mercury, you can demonstrate this yourself. Put some mercury in a small glass to a depth of an inch and a half or more, then dip the tip of your finger in the mercury. Mercury, being rather heavy —thirteen times as heavy as water—will exert pressure over the surface of the immersed skin. You will observe, however, that you do not feel the pressure at the tip of your finger but only at the mercury line. It is here that there is a *gradient of pressure* on your skin—a change from air pressure to the pressure exerted by the mercury. Thus it is a *gradient of pressure, not uniformly distributed pressure, that arouses the experience of pressure.*

Receptors for pressure. For more than fifty years there have been many attempts to determine the receptors for pressure. Seldom have scientists worked so assiduously at a problem with so little success. We think that a fairly complex structure, called the Meissner corpuscle (see Figure 19.17), serves the pressure sense in the hairless regions of the body and that another struc-

ture, the *basket nerve ending*, does it for the roots of hairs. We also have good reason to believe that simple *free nerve endings*— endings not associated with any special structure—also convey touch impulses, because we can feel pressure in some areas of the skin where no receptors other than free nerve endings are to be found. A final answer to this problem, however, awaits further, more definitive research.

Temperature stimulation. In the experiment with which we began this section, the maps of "cold" spots and "warm" spots were different. This fact has been taken to mean that there are two different senses for experiencing warmth and cold. We are in fact rather sure of that, even though research to date has not established with certainty just what the respective receptors are. We do know, however, that the experiences of warmth and cold are elicited by any change in the normal gradient of skin tem-

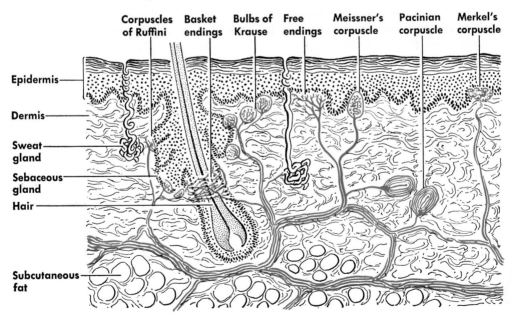

Fig. 19.17. Structures of the human skin. Not all of the structures shown in the diagram are to be found in any one area of the skin. See text for further explanation.

perature. This gradient, in the case of the forearm, for example, is about 5°C and is the difference between the temperature of circulating blood (37.5°C) and that of the surface of the skin (32 or 33°C). A stimulus of 28 to 30°C, which is definitely felt as cold, increases this gradient a little, while a stimulus of 34°C, which can be felt as warm, decreases it a little. Thus it takes a change in skin temperature of only 1 or 2°C to be experienced as warmth or cold.

Pain. A good many very diverse stimuli produce pain—a needle prick, a hard blow to the skin, scalding steam, or strong acid. For that reason, it is impossible to say in physical terms exactly what produces pain. One laboratory method of producing pain, which has proved rather precise, is to use a device that radiates heat to a given area of the skin.[7] As the radiant heat is increased in intensity, a person first reports warmth, as you might expect, and then at a particular intensity he reports pain. Other methods which are not quite so precise make use of pinpricks and chemical solutions.

▪ *Injury to tissues.* The biological utility of pain, of course, is quite clear. It keeps us from incurring a grave injury. This utility is illustrated by those rare individuals who have no pain sensitivity. One such person, a seven-year-old girl, was described who had in her short life accumulated multiple scars, bruises, self-mutilations, fractures, dislocations, and other local deformities.[8] "On several occasions the parents smelled the odor of burning flesh and found her leaning casually on a hot stove."

Because of the close relation between pain and bodily injury, scientists have been inclined to believe for a long time that injury to tissues is the common immediate stimulus for the sensation of pain. Recent evidence makes this view rather plausible.[9] When an observer is asked to report pain while heat is radiated to a patch of skin on his forehead, he will usually report a sensation of pain when the temperature of his skin reaches the point at which tissues begin to break down. The amount of pain felt is not directly related to the amount of tissue damage, however. Rather, it is related to the rate of destruction, and a painful sensation results when stimulation produces a critical state in which destructive forces just begin to exceed the rate of repair.

The receptor for pain is almost certainly the unspecialized free nerve ending that is abundant in most parts of the skin, particularly where sensitivity to pain is greatest.

Adaptation. Like the chemical senses, those of the skin are able to adapt to stimuli within rather wide limits. Pain adapts rather incompletely—if you have ever had a bad toothache, you have discovered how slowly the sensations of pain adapt—but both touch and thermal sensitivity change appreciably during the course of stimulation. Adaptation is especially marked in the senses of warmth and cold. If, for example, one immerses his left hand in warm water and his right hand in cold water, the sensations of warm and cold, respectively, gradually die out. But then, if both hands are immersed in water at a temperature between those to which the hands are adapted, the left hand now feels cold and the right one feels warm.

▪ THE DEEP SENSES

Except when we have a stomach-ache or a headache, we are usually unaware of stimuli inside the body. Yet hidden away in the linings of internal organs, in our muscles, and in our joints is a large variety of sense organs.

▪ *Subcutaneous sensibility.* Some of these sense organs are not far beneath the skin, yet are not a part of our skin senses. This fact can be demonstrated by applying an anesthetic to the skin. After the skin has

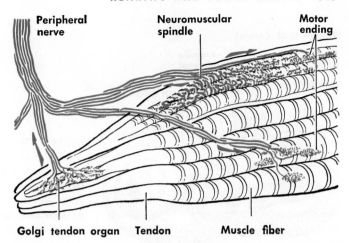

Peripheral nerve **Neuromuscular spindle** **Motor ending**

Golgi tendon organ **Tendon** **Muscle fiber**

Fig. 19.18. Kinesthetic receptors in muscle. The two kinesthetic receptors shown in this diagram are the neuromuscular spindle and the Golgi tendon organ.

become insensitive, we can still feel heavy pressure applied to the skin and some pain if the skin is pinched. There are therefore deep-pressure and pain receptors in the subcutaneous layers below the skin. It is thought that these deep-pressure receptors are the relatively large *Pacinian corpuscles* (see Figure 19.17) that are found in the regions that have deep-pressure sensitivity. As in the case of the skin senses, the receptors for deep pain are almost certainly free nerve endings.

▪ *Organic senses.* We know relatively little about receptors in the internal organs within the body cavity, mainly because these areas are so inaccessible to experimentation. But there must be cold and warm receptors in the esophagus and stomach, for we can experience cold and warmth in these parts. They also have something similar to the deep subcutaneous receptors for pressure and pain, because they yield corresponding experiences when stretched. So far as other internal organs are concerned, it is clear that we can feel pressure and pain when they are irritated or put under pressure, but we do not know to what extent these experiences arise from receptors in the organs themselves and to what extent they may arise from

other tissues and the abdominal wall which are indirectly affected by these organs.

Kinesthetic sense. A bodily sense that physiologists now know a good deal about is one that most laymen have never head of: kinesthesis. In some ways, it is the most important sense we have, because it provides an automatic system for coordinating our muscles in walking and in all our skilled movements. One can see how important it is only by observing a person who has been deprived of it. This sometimes happens in a form of syphilis known as *tabes dorsalis,* which attacks the sensory pathways from the kinesthetic sense organs. A patient with this disease is getting no information from his muscles about their movements. He is able to walk, balance a ball, or carry out other skills only by watching carefully what his arms and legs are doing. If syphilis should invade the brain stem and interrupt kinesthetic impulses from the face and mouth, uncoordinated movements of the face may also occur along with a slurring of speech that may be so severe as to be unintelligible.

The kinesthetic receptors are found in three distinct places. One is in the muscles, where free nerve endings surround small

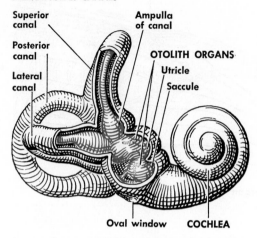

SEMICIRCULAR CANALS

Superior canal

Posterior canal

Lateral canal

Ampulla of canal

OTOLITH ORGANS

Utricle

Saccule

Oval window   COCHLEA

Fig. 19.19. The vestibular sense organs. The three semicircular canals are so arranged that one is in each plane. Organs in the ampullae of these canals respond to rotation or movement of the head. The otolith organs located in the saccule and utricle, on the other hand, are stimulated by gravity and hence by the position of the head.

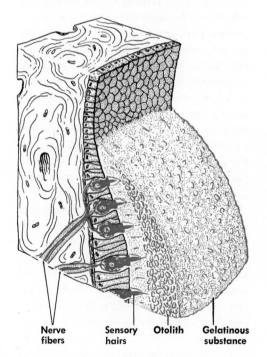

Nerve fibers   Sensory hairs   Otolith   Gelatinous substance

Fig. 19.20. The otolith organs. The sketch shows the microscopic structure of the otolith organs in the saccule and utricle. The otoliths embedded in a gelatinous substance exert pressure on the sensory hairs according to the position of the head. Stimulation of the hairs evokes impulses in sensory nerve fibers which join other fibers from the ear and end in the medulla of the brain.

muscle spindles (see Figure 19.18). These kinesthetic receptors signal the *stretch* of a muscle—and each time one muscle is contracted another one in the neighborhood is usually stretched. A second location of kinesthetic receptors is in the tendons that connect muscles to bones. The receptors here are nerve endings that serve a specialized organ known as the *Golgi tendon organ* (see Figure 19.18). They are stimulated when a muscle contracts and puts tension on the tendon. Finally, some receptors are to be found in the linings of the joints. These are stimulated whenever a limb moves, changing the relative positions of two bones in the joint. We are still not certain about the receptors in the joints, but it is possible that they are *Pacinian corpuscles*—the same receptors that yield deep pressure when regions below the skin are stimulated.

The vestibular sense organs. Like kinesthesis, the vestibular sense is important in balance and movement, but it does not provide experiences of which we are ordinarily aware. The organs of the vestibular sense are well known because they are highly specialized, are reasonably large, and can be studied in detail under the microscope. They are, in fact, part of the inner ear. The inner ear is a series of cavities, only one of which, the cochlea, is concerned with hearing. The rest of the cavities constitute the vestibular organs (see Figures 19.19 and 19.20). They divide into two main groups: the semicircular canals and the otolith organs.

There are three semicircular canals, each roughly perpendicular to both the others, and they are so oriented as to represent three different planes of movements. In an enlarged part of each canal is a set of hair cells somewhat similar in general structure to those in the cochlea. These cells are encompassed by the fluid that fills the canal and are stimulated when some pressure is exerted on this fluid. Such pressure occurs mainly when the head is rotated, and thus the canals are sense organs for rotation. It appears, however, that the receptors do not respond merely to continuous rotation—continuous pressure—but to *changes in rate of rotation*, that is, to acceleration or deceleration of the head. So when a person is rotated, or rotates himself as some stage performers do, it is only while he is increasing speed or slowing down that the semicircular organs are stimulated.

Dancers and acrobats who do a lot of spinning have learned some tricks which help them overcome the effects of this sense during their gyrations. Watch a ballet dancer spinning, and you will see that he keeps his head as motionless as possible by fixating some object in the environment. The head whips around to pick a new fixation point before the body catches up.

There are two other cavities making up the vestibular organ. On the walls of these cavities are thickenings which contain their receptor cells. These protrude into a gelatinous mass that contains small crystals, the otoliths (*oto* means "ear," and *lith* means "stone"). These receptors appear to be positional or static receptors, for they respond merely to the tilt or position of the head and do not require rotation to be stimulated.

■ *Vestibular reactions.* The canals and the otolith organs together provide a sense of balance. Impulses from these organs help a person right himself when he has been thrown off balance. More specifically, they control a number of reflexes that automatically compensate for loss of balance. One such reflex is a movement of the head back to a normal position whenever it has been turned away from it. Another is a reflex twisting of the trunk and body to return the whole body to normal position. Perhaps the best illustration of these effects of the vestibular sense organs is the righting reaction of the cat, an animal famed for its ability to land right side up when dropped from any height or position. A cat, when turned upside down and dropped, first twists its head around to normal position, then its trunk, and then, through some indirect reflexes, brings its four feet around to orient toward the ground. This series of reactions is controlled primarily by the vestibular receptors.

There is a special connection between the vestibular receptors and the eyes. If one turns his head quickly, his eyes ordinarily move simultaneously in the opposite direction so that they continue to fixate the same point. These are compensatory movements of the eyes that are controlled in part by the vestibular receptors. When we have been spinning around and then stop, our eyes continue to move back and forth in a movement that is called *rotation nystagmus*. The eyes drift to one side, then move quickly to the other, then drift, then jump, and so on. Such nystagmus is a reflex evoked by the stimulation that the receptors in the semicircular canals have received.

▪ *Motion sickness.* Motion sickness, which has caused some people so much misery, is an effect of vestibular stimulation. There are several common forms of this discomfort: train sickness, car sickness, sea sickness, and air sickness. We know that the vestibular organs are responsible for such sickness, because the occasional individual whose vestibular system is not functioning does not suffer motion sickness and also because we can produce motion sickness experimentally by stimulating the vestibular organs.[10] The sickness comes about because vestibular impulses evoke reflex reactions in the alimentary tract. Of course, other factors such as anxiety can also augment such reactions, and they therefore contribute to the direct effects of vestibular stimulation. There are now certain well-publicized drugs, e.g., Dramamine, which reduce or prevent motion sickness, but it is not yet known whether they work on the vestibular sense, alimentary tract, or some other part of the nervous system concerned in the reaction.

SUMMARY

1. The stimulus for human hearing is alternations of air pressure called *sound waves*. All sound waves, no matter how complex, may be analyzed into sine waves, each of which has a certain frequency and intensity.

2. Pitch and loudness, though correlated respectively with frequency and intensity, are psychological attributes of sounds.

3. Simple sine waves are called *pure tones*. Noises are sound waves that consist of many frequencies mixed more or less randomly.

4. Sound waves enter the canal of the outer ear and cause the eardrum to vibrate. This vibration is transmitted via some bones to the inner ear, which contains the organ of hearing, the cochlea.

5. In the cochlea, sound waves travel through a fluid to bend the basilar membrane, thereby exciting auditory-nerve impulses. In general, the place at which the basilar membrane is bent determines pitch, and the degree of the bending determines loudness.

6. There is a lower limit of hearing below which we are unable to hear sounds. This limit is less for tones of the middle frequencies than it is for higher or lower ones.

7. On the other hand, there is an upper limit beyond which sounds produce pain but no increase in loudness. This is about the same for all frequencies.

8. There are also limits in the ability to discriminate differences in frequency and in intensity.

9. Hearing is made more difficult if a sound is masked by some other sound.

10. If the harmonics of two tones "fit" together, they are likely to sound consonant; if they do not, they may be experienced as dissonant.

11. The three principal cues to the direction of a sound—time of arrival, intensity, and phase—all depend upon differences in the sound as it arrives at the two ears. The cues to distance, however, largely depend on one ear and are (*a*) intensity and (*b*) frequency composition.

12. Deafness is fairly common in the population. Two types can be distinguished: conductive deafness, which involves some loss in the conduction of sounds to the inner ear, and nerve deafness, which involves some defect in the basilar membrane or the auditory nerve. Nerve deafness tends to be greater for high tones than for low tones, and it is increasingly common in old age.

13. It is not certain how many qualities there are in the sense of smell, although as few as four or six will account for most odors.

14. Taste, on the other hand, seems to have four basic qualities: sweet, salt, sour, and bitter.

15. Smell is much more acute than taste, sometimes requiring only a few molecules per liter of air for detection. Both senses adapt fairly rapidly to continued stimulation.

16. There are four basic senses associated with the skin: warmth, cold, pressure, and pain. Several highly specialized structures in the skin have been suggested as the receptors for these senses.

17. The best-established fact is that free nerve endings can serve as receptors for pain. Pain adapts less rapidly than the other skin senses.

18. The deep senses consist principally of the kinesthetic and vestibular senses.

19. Kinesthetic receptors are found in muscles, tendons, and joints. Impulses from these receptors make posture and coordination almost automatic.

20. The vestibular sense organs are located in the head near the cochlea and in the inner ear. They respond to the rotation of the head or to changes in its position, thus providing a sense of balance.

21. Motion sickness is an autonomic disturbance resulting from stimulation of the vestibular organs.

SUGGESTIONS FOR FURTHER READING

Chapanis, A., Garner, W. R., and Morgan, C. T. *Applied experimental psychology.* New York: Wiley, 1949.

> *A text containing chapters on hearing, with emphasis on practical applications.*

Davis, H. (Ed.). *Hearing and deafness.* New York: Rinehart, 1947.

> *A broad survey of facts and problems of hearing and deafness, written for the intelligent layman.*

Fletcher, H. *Speech and hearing in communication.* New York: Van Nostrand, 1953.

> *An authoritative book on speech and hearing from the standpoint of communication.*

Geldard, F. A. *The human senses.* New York: Wiley, 1953.

> *An introductory text covering all the senses.*

Hirsh, I. J. *The measurement of hearing.* New York: McGraw-Hill, 1952.

> *A text covering the physical and psychological aspects of the measurement of hearing.*

Moncrieff, R. W. *The chemical senses.* New York: Wiley, 1946.

> *A summary and discussion of research on the chemical senses.*

Morgan, C. T., and Stellar, E. *Physiological psychology* (2d Ed.). New York. McGraw-Hill, 1950.

> *A text containing several chapters on the physiological aspects of hearing and the lower senses.*

Osgood, C. E. *Method and theory in experimental psychology.* New York: Oxford Univ. Press, 1953.

> *Theories and experiments on hearing and the lower senses.*

Stevens, S. S., and Davis, H. *Hearing.* New York: Wiley, 1938.

> *A summary of research on the psychology and physiology of hearing.*

Wever, E. G. *Theory of hearing.* New York: Wiley, 1949.

> *An analysis of the physiological basis of hearing.*

Wolff, H. G., and Wolf, S. *Pain.* Springfield, Ill.: Charles C Thomas, 1948.

> *A little book covering various aspects of the topic of pain.*

Woodworth, R. S., and Schlosberg, H. *Experimental psychology* (Rev. Ed.). New York: Holt, 1954.

> *A standard text in experimental psychology containing chapters on the different senses.*

Chapter 20 LANGUAGE AND SPEECH

THE RED LIGHT we encounter at intersections in our cities and towns may be perceived in two entirely different ways: simply as a red light of a certain hue, saturation, and brightness, or as a *signal* not to cross the intersection. Thus we may study the perception of a stimulus in terms either of the experience it produces or of the *meanings* it has acquired in the course of previous learning. In the two preceding chapters, we have done the first; here we shall do the second.

Signals may acquire meaning in at least two rather different ways. One is by the *natural relation of events* in everyday life. We learn, for example, that the growl of a dog may be followed by a bite, that thunder is often a prelude to rain, that where there is

smoke there is fire. In each case, the meaning perceived depends upon our previously having learned that certain stimuli in the world belong together. There are signals, on the other hand, that have developed meanings by *social agreement*. The red light at an intersection, the whistle of a football referee, and the words we speak or write are all examples of such signals. People in a society or locality develop them as conventions for communicating with each other. Such are the signals whose perception we shall study in this chapter.

Perception of language. There are many kinds of social signals that have been and can be used for communication. In some parts of the world, including some American street corners, whistling is a well-understood signal; in others, drumming is used extensively. Almost all societies use *gestures* of the hands and face as communicating

---

This chapter was drafted by Harold W. Hake of the University of Illinois.

devices, and in societies speaking different languages but in close contact with each other—as was the case with the American Indians—hundreds of gestures may be used to surmount the language barrier. The most universal system of communicating with signals, however, is a *language* in which words are spoken and written in different combinations to convey meaning.

Language, of course, may be either written or spoken. Of the two forms of language, the oral is historically the older. Later, by a gradual progression from pictures to such characters as the letters in our alphabet, written language evolved. For this reason, and because written language is usually more carefully regulated by custom and grammarians, there are some important differences between written and spoken language. The basic elements of the two are of course different, one being letters and the other being sounds. Our speaking and writing vocabularies are also different—the written is usually much the larger. Furthermore, our speaking and writing grammars differ; we tend to convey different kinds of information in the two media; and, finally, our written language is not so repetitive and redundant as our oral one.

Despite all these differences, the two obviously have much in common, for they follow many of the same rules, and one form can easily be translated into the other by persons familiar with the language. We shall therefore treat them together in this chapter, first giving more emphasis to speech and then more to written language, pointing out their similarities more than their differences. There are many interesting apparent differences among the languages of different societies, such as German, Russian, Chinese, and American, but to keep the chapter relatively uncomplicated we shall confine our comments to the English language.

The study of language.   There are several groups of students and scientists in our society, besides the psychologists, who make it their business to study speech. Each has its point of view and special interest. Some are interested in the sounds of speech, how they are made, how they are related to written symbols and how speech may be improved; these are the *phoneticians*. Some are interested most in the meaning of words; these are called *semanticists*. Others are concerned with the rules and habits for speaking and writing words; these are the *grammaticists*. Finally, there are specialists who compare different languages with each other and who study the history of words and languages; these are the *philologists*.

Psychologists have a somewhat different interest in language. They are not concerned with its history or grammar but rather with its use as a means of communication—a way in which people behave, and a stimulus that people perceive and respond to.[1]

■ SPEECH AS A STIMULUS

Because we use speech so much for communication, it is probably the most important class of sounds we hear. Speech sounds, however, are very complicated and differ from one speaker to another. Even the sounds made in speaking the same language differ considerably. A Southern accent, for example, is very different from a Brooklyn accent. The fact that the speech of persons with widely dissimilar accents can be understood with a minimum of difficulty by the average listener poses one of the interesting questions studied by persons investigating speech as a stimulus.

The comprehension of speech.   Speech sounds are made by blowing air across the vocal cords, thereby setting the cords to vibrating, then modifying the sound produced in this way with movements of the

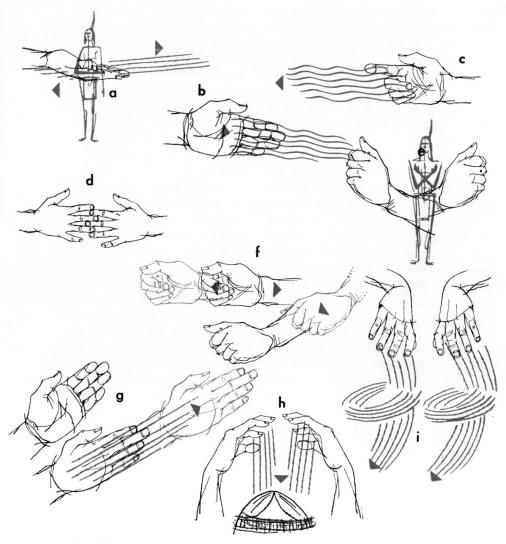

Fig. 20.1. Some manual signs in Indian sign language. See if you can tell which sign is used to represent each of the following: fast, fight, fish, fond, house, hot, hungry, snake, and snow. Correct answers are given in the footnote on p. 516. (*After Tomkins, W. Universal Indian sign language. San Diego: William Tomkins, 1931.*)

tongue, lips, and mouth. This is not the place to discuss how speech sounds are produced. However, in order to understand how they are heard and interpreted, we must understand their physical nature. To do that, we must analyze them into their various sine-wave frequencies in the same way that we have learned to analyze other complex sounds in the last chapter. Obviously, however, the frequencies of the speech sounds change from instant to instant, so that we cannot analyze a steady sound. To cope with this difficulty we can analyze many such sounds to determine the frequencies that are contained in speech *on the average.*

Figure 20.2 shows such an analysis of the frequencies in speech sounds of the English language. This analysis is an average for all speech sounds, and for both male and female voices. The curve shows the relative sound pressure levels at the different frequencies. From this curve you can see that there is *much greater intensity in the low frequencies than in the high ones.* There is, for example, 25 decibels more sound pressure at frequencies between 200 and 500 cycles per second than at 5,000 cycles per second. From this fact you might conclude that the low frequencies are much more important in speech comprehension than the high ones, but you would be wrong.

Studies have shown that the *high frequencies, although much less intense, are much more important in the comprehension of speech.* In such studies, electrical circuits called filters are used to eliminate some of the frequencies while leaving the others intact. When this is done, speech comprehen-

Fig. 20.2. The average intensity of different frequencies in speech. The curve is an average of male and female voices. Notice how much more intense the lower frequencies are compared to the higher frequencies.

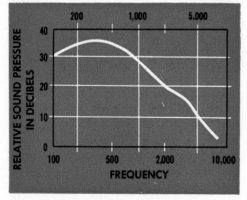

sion turns out to be about as good when all the frequencies above 2,000 cycles per second are eliminated as when all those below 2,000 cycles per second are eliminated. Thus we can conclude that all frequencies above 2,000 cycles per second are as important as all frequencies below that frequency. And yet Figure 20.2 clearly indicates that only a small amount of the total intensity comes from these higher frequencies. Why should this be so?

In order to understand the reason for this, we need to look at the frequency patterns obtained from individual speech sounds. As illustrated in Figure 20.3, a sustained vowel sound like *oh* produces a periodic sound wave. This means that the sound wave can be analyzed into a series of separate sine waves. Figure 20.3 shows an analysis of this type for most of the pure vowel sounds. This analysis is a very simple one, because it shows only the frequencies of the fundamental and the first important harmonic. There are, of course, many other harmonics as well, but these other harmonics are less important. In addition, the analysis in Figure 20.3 shows only the location of the frequencies, not the sound pressure levels, which are less important.

Notice that *each vowel sound has a different frequency pattern.* The *ee* sound has a fairly low fundamental, and its first important harmonic is very high. At the opposite extreme, the *oo* sound has a low fundamental and a very low harmonic. It is the pattern of these frequencies that we hear and that makes the difference in the sounds of the various vowels. When a vowel is sounded, of course, the most intense frequency component is the fundamental. However, if we could hear only the fundamental frequency, we could not discriminate between the words "fool" and "feel," because the vowel sounds in these words both have approximately the same fundamental

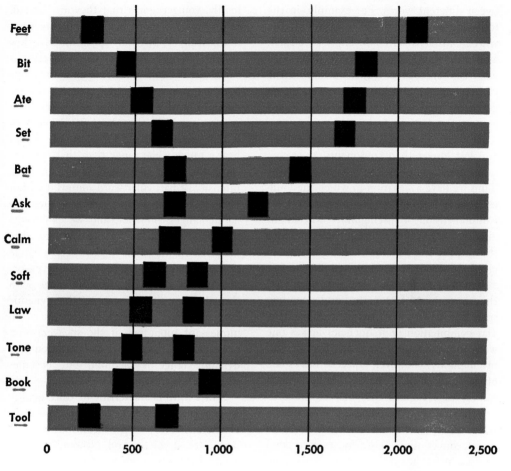

Fig. 20.3. The fundamental and lowest important harmonic frequencies for different vowel sounds. Vowel sounds are indicated by the underlined letters in the words at the left. Notice that each vowel sound has a different spacing of the two frequencies (fundamental and harmonic). (*Data from Potter, R. K., & Peterson, G. E. The representation of vowels and their movements. J. acoust. Soc. Amer., 1948, 20, 528–535.*)

frequency. It is their greatly different harmonics that enable us to tell them apart. Thus the important thing which allows us to discriminate between vowel sounds is the pattern of the harmonics, not the pitch of the fundamental. That is one reason for the higher frequencies' being more important than they would seem at first glance.

Another reason is that the *consonants usually contain many more high frequencies* *than the vowels do.* Hence consonants are much more important than vowels for understanding a word or a sentence. Sounds like *sh*, *t*, and *k* are almost all high-frequency noises. Even the vocalized consonants, like *d* and *g*, have a great many high frequencies in them.

The consonants carry most of the information in language, because they are the sounds which allow us to discriminate between different words. For example, in the following sentence we have taken all the vowels out: *Ths sctn f th chptr s bt spch.* You still would have a pretty good idea what the sentence is. But if we take all the consonants out, and leave the vowels in, we get this unintelligible series: *i eio o e ae i aou ee.*

Because all vowel sounds are vocalized and last longer than consonants, they contain much more of the speech intensity. Thus we have a situation in which the loudest sounds are not the most important for comprehension or intelligibility. We might almost say that the low frequencies produce the most sound but that the high frequencies produce the most intelligibility.

Dynamics of speech. We have seen that the important factor in understanding speech is its pattern of frequencies; a particular combination of frequencies makes one word sound different from another. Besides intelligibility, however, speech has some other interesting aspects. From speech sounds we *recognize* the voice of a friend, or of a stranger. We recognize a voice on a telephone as the same voice we heard in direct conversation yesterday, even though we have never heard this particular voice on the telephone before. And we still recognize that the sound of the voice over the telephone is much different from the sound of the same voice in direct talking. We can also usually tell from the tone of voice when the speaker is angry, or happy, or disappointed. What is it in speech that allows us to recognize all these different qualities— qualities which have nothing to do with the understanding of the particular words used?

There are several factors that are important to the perception of quality. One of these is *intensity.* When people speak

Correct answers for signs in Figure 20.1 are: a, hungry; b, fond; c, fast; d, fight; e, house; f, snake; g, fish; h, hot; and i, snow.

loudly, you recognize that they are excited, or angry, or perhaps having difficulty communicating. When they speak quietly, they are rarely angry. Another factor is what is called the *dynamic range*, which is the range between the loudest and weakest sounds made. The dynamic range of most voices is surprisingly small—about 30 decibels of sound pressure level. We can, of course, hear a much wider range than that, and because the range of a voice is so small the intensity of particular word sounds does not seem important. People differ in their dynamic ranges, however, and we can recognize this difference and use it to identify the voice of a particular person. The situation also makes a difference, and any particular person varies his dynamic range with the situation. In an oration, the dynamic range is usually reduced, sometimes to an unpleasant monotone if the speaker is inexperienced. In normal conversation the dynamic range is medium, but becomes greater when the speaker is excited.

Still a third characteristic of voice quality is *fundamental pitch.* Some people have characteristically deep voices; others have high-pitched voices. And, although there is a lot of difference among the fundamental pitches of people of the same sex, the average female voice is higher-pitched than the average man's. These consistencies help us recognize people by their voices. In singing, the fundamental pitch is purposely changed to match the melody. But the pitch also changes under conditions of excitement or other stress. The voices of most people become higher-pitched when they are excited than when they are calm.

One other characteristic of voice quality is the *rate of talking.* People vary quite a bit in their talking rate. Very slow talkers will speak under 100 words per minute, while the fastest talkers occasionally go well over 200 words per minute. Fast talking is so well recognized as a sign of excitement that many radio and television announcers deliberately learn to talk at a very fast rate to give the impression of excitement. Those of you who have heard a sports announcer describing a horse race are quite familiar with this trick.

You must realize, of course, that we do not consciously analyze different voices in these various ways. What we judge about a speaker's voice is the over-all effect produced by the combination of these aspects of voice quality, and from this over-all effect we form opinions about the speaker himself, or about his emotions and feelings at the time he is talking.

THE STRUCTURE OF LANGUAGE

Now let us see how various sounds are combined to make the words, sentences, and paragraphs that make up everyday language. Let us, in other words, study the structure of language. To do that we shall discuss both written and spoken language and use examples from each.

Phonetics of speech. Long before methods were available for analyzing speech into its component frequencies and intensities, the phoneticians developed a classification of speech sounds based on the way we shape our mouths to produce speech. Their two main classes of sounds, as you already know, are the *vowels* and the *consonants*. Vowels are produced by letting air escape freely through the mouth passage; consonants are produced by interrupting or constricting in some way the stream of air as it passes through the mouth. The phonetician can distinguish particular vowels and consonants according to which part of the tongue acts to modify the sound, the height to which the tongue is raised, the position of the lips, and so on.

With this method of classification, a skilled phonetician can distinguish 42 classes of vowel sounds and 36 consonants. He has a different printed phonetic symbol to represent each of these possible sounds. Thus he is able to list all the sounds that can be reliably distinguished by experts. Speech sounds classified in this way are evidently not the stimuli of speech to which we all respond, however, because the ordinary person cannot distinguish all the sounds defined by the phonetician. Instead of 42 vowels, he can easily distinguish about 8 vowel sounds and with some difficulty no more than 14 or 15. To define the sounds that we distinguish, rather than those we can produce, a different method of classification is necessary.

Phonemes. To make such a classification, the linguist attempts to find out *which sounds are actually distinguished in everyday use*. Such sounds he calls *phonemes*. They differ from one language to another and even among communities that use the same language. To compile a list of phonemes, the linguist starts out with a large sample of speech written down in phonetic symbols. He then notices carefully how often each of the sounds is preceded or followed by each of the other sounds that he has recorded. For example, he lists all the sounds that begin a word and then tabulates the sounds that are combined with them. Whenever he finds sounds that are similar but are never followed by the same sound, he groups them together into one phoneme. The reason he does this is that people do not need to distinguish sounds that are always followed by different sounds.

An example will make this point clear. Consider the sound of *k* in the two words *key* and *cool*. If you say these words to yourself, you will realize that the *k* sound is different in the two words—simply notice the position of your lips when you say them. No confusion results, however, by considering these two sounds to be the same, for the *k* in *key* is never followed by the *oo* and the *k* in *cool* is never followed by the *e*. Consequently, though the phonetician can distinguish these two *k*'s, we do not need to pay any attention to differences between them, for the *oo* and the *e* that follow them are our cues. For that reason, the phonetician considers the two *k*'s to be one and the same phoneme /k/.*

By this kind of analysis, applied to all the spoken language of a community or society, the linguist defines the essential components of speech. He can draw up a list of essential phonemes that are used in any particular spoken language. The resulting classification is much simpler than the phonetic classification. The essential phonemes, of course, vary from one language to another and from one accent to another. In fact, it is with phonemes, as they are used in particular words, that the linguist can state rather precisely what an accent is.

Verbal context. Phonemes are the essential units of spoken language. About 40 are usually required to transcribe accurately any variety of English. Thus all the sentences we speak and the thousands of words we use in making these sentences can be analyzed into 40 units. Conversely these units are combined into syllables, the syllables into words, words into sentences, and so on. Phonemes are the units from which spoken language seems to have been formed and into which it may be analyzed.

▪ *Frequency of units.* If someone were given 40 units and told to construct a new oral language, one of the first decisions he would face is how often to use each of the various units. He could, on the one hand,

* The diagonals indicate that the *phonemic* letter k is meant. *Phonetic* symbols are written in brackets.

make sure to use each unit just as often as any other unit. In this way he could make the greatest use of the available units. He might, on the other hand, throw away all the units except one and use just that one unit. The result would not be a language —even the animals use more units than that—for it could convey one and only one message. Or he might take some middle course and use some units a good many times and other units only a few times.

It is this middle course that characterizes the languages that people use: *some units are used much more frequently than others.* Of the 40 English phonemes, 9 are used to make up more than half the sounds we produce. The most frequent sound (*i* as in *bit*) is used, on the average, more than 100 times as often as the least frequent sound (*z* as in *azure*). And as you probably have observed yourself, consonant sounds occur more often than the vowel sounds. Indeed, only 12 consonant sounds make up about 60 per cent of all sounds produced in speech.

If we study the way in which units are combined into words, we note the same thing. Some units tend to be used more in one part of a word than in another. English words end and begin more often with consonants than with vowels. Moreover, of the consonants that begin words, more than one-half are from a group of five sounds, and of those that end words, more than one-half come from a group of eight different sounds. We use some words much more than others. Although the average college student probably can recognize 250,000 or more different words, he uses relatively few of these words with any regularity. It has been estimated that only 121 words make up about 60 per cent of our speech and about 45 per cent of our writing.

The fact that some units and some combinations of units (words) are used more frequently than others is not simply a statistical matter. It is related to our ability to perceive and comprehend speech. Because we hear or read some units and words much more than others, we expect and anticipate them. Thus we find it easier to perceive them than others.[2,3]

▪ *Sequence of units.* Certain units not only appear more often than others, they are also more likely than others to follow certain units. In other words, *certain sounds tend to follow other sounds, and certain letters tend to follow other letters.* Thus some *sequences* of units are more likely to occur than others. This fact helps us considerably in our perception of language. It can be illustrated by describing an experiment in which subjects were shown words for very brief periods of time.[4] The words were not those of English, but were pseudo words artificially created for the experiment. The experimenter first constructed a list of "words" in which the letters were drawn completely at random, and presented this list to his subjects. He measured the length of visual exposure necessary to identify the words. This list of words was called a "zero-order" list. He also used another list composed of "words" in which the letters were used as frequently as they occur in English. The letter *e*, for example, occurred as often in these words as it does in ordinary prose, and this was true of every other

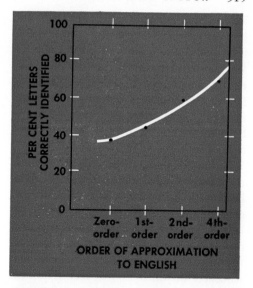

Fig. 20.4. The recognition of pseudo words. These are the results of the experiment described in the text on the recognition of pseudo words when presented to subjects for short exposures. The closer the words approximated English, the more they were correctly identified. (Data from Miller, Bruner, and Postman. See Miller, G. A. Language and communication. New York: McGraw-Hill, 1951. P. 201.)

letter he used. These words were "first-order" words. Another set of "second-order" words was formed in the same way as the "first-order" list, but in addition each letter in these words was preceded by a given letter as often as it is preceded by that letter in English. "Third-order" and "fourth-order" words were formed by the same rules except that each letter was preceded by the combination of two letters and three letters, respectively, as often as it is in English. Examples of these words are given in Table 20.1. As you can see, the words begin to look more and more like English as the words progress from "zero order" to "fourth order." But they are all *nonsense* words.

You can probably guess what the result of the experiment was. As the pseudo words more closely approximated the sequences of

TABLE 20.1. Samples of pseudo words constructed according to the statistical properties of English.

Zero order	First order	Second order	Fourth order
yrulpzoc	stanugop	wallyoff	ricaning
ozhgpmtj	vtyehulo	therares	vernalit
dlegqmnw	eincaase	chevadne	mossiant
gfujxzaq	iydewakn	nermblim	bittlers
wxpaujvb	rpitcqet	onesteva	oneticul

Selected from Miller, G. A. *Language and communication.* New York: McGraw-Hill, 1951. P. 201.

letters found in English, the subjects found it easier to perceive them correctly, and the length of exposure required became shorter and shorter. You can see exactly how the results came out in Figure 20.4. Thus the fact that English uses certain sequences of units more than others and the fact that we learn these over the years *helps us in perceiving language.*

At the beginning of this section, we used the phrase "verbal context" as our main heading. We are now in a position to understand this term. To perceive speech and written language we need to perceive not merely the isolated phonemes or letters of the language but also the frequencies and sequences in which they appear. The fact that one sound or one sequence of sounds is more likely to occur than another gives language a "verbal context" that makes a difference in our perception of the units of the language. Thus the stimuli or signals that make up a language are both the units of the language and the context provided by the way in which these units are combined.

THE USE OF LANGUAGE

People who speak the same language use about the same units and combine these units in about the same ways. Thus they manage to communicate with each other. Even so, among people who speak the same language, there is a considerable variation in the way they use it. Aside from accents and dialects, which represent minor differences in combining language units, some have a larger vocabulary than others, some diversify their language more than others, some are easier to understand, and some are more difficult. Some are relatively fluent and some less fluent. Let us look into a few of these differences in the use of language.

Vocabulary. The English language has well over a half million words in it. There is probably no one who knows all these words, even if we omit the thousands of technical words used only by scholars to denote their materials and concepts. In fact, most people have a surprisingly small vocabulary—considering the large number of words available—and can expand this vocabulary only under special conditions.

The number of words a person knows is usually considered to be his vocabulary; but, to be more accurate, each person has not just one, but rather several vocabularies. First of all there is the vocabulary he can *recognize.* This is almost always considerably larger than the one he can speak or write. In an earlier chapter, when we traced the development of language in the child, we pointed out that children can understand and recognize words before they can use them—at least in a way that others can understand—and this difference continues throughout life. The latest estimates of the number of words that the average college student can recognize, which is ordinarily considered to be his vocabulary, is about 250,000 words. The number of words that he uses, however, is much smaller.

There is also a difference in the vocabulary that a person *can* use and that which he ordinarily uses. What this difference is varies from one person to another, but you can make some estimate of it by comparing the words you use, say, in writing a theme or an examination paper with the words you use in your everyday speech. When we try hard, which we usually do if we want to impress someone with our vocabulary, we use many more words than we do when we are speaking casually.

The size of a person's vocabulary has long been considered a measure of his general knowledge and abilities. In sizing up people in daily affairs, we usually consider the person who uses the "highfalutin" words as being better-educated than those who do not. Psychologists have made use of this relation between education and vocabulary, as we saw in Chapter 15, to construct tests of intelligence. Such tests as the Stanford-Binet, for example, contain sections designed to measure vocabulary size and to give it weight in the over-all index of intelligence. Nearly all forms of aptitude and intelligence tests directly or indirectly give considerable weight to vocabulary. This is not unreasonable, because words are symbols that stand for the things and events we know, and there should be a high correlation between the words we can use and recognize and our other knowledge and abilities.

Verbal diversification. Vocabulary size, then, is one measure of a person's use of language. Another measure is the *diversity* of a person's language, which is to say, how stereotyped or flexible he is in his use of language. Actually there are several measures of verbal diversification.

▪ *Type-token ratio.* One is the type-token ratio.[5] It is obtained by making two counts of the words a person produces in some sample of his speech or writing. One is simply the number of words; this is the number of *tokens* produced. The second is the number of different words he produces; this is the number of *types* produced. Dividing the number of types by the number of tokens gives the type-token ratio.

This ratio tends to go along with vocabulary size, for those of us who have limited vocabularies must use the few words we know more often than do people who have a larger number of words at their command. It also partly describes some of the difference between written and spoken language. Written language usually has higher ratios than spoken language. When we write we choose our words with greater care and

thus use more different words to express shades of meaning. The type-token ratio is, as one might also expect, smaller for children than for adults. The vocabulary of children is limited, and they use short sentences with frequent repetition of words. The type-token ratio, finally, can also be taken as an index of language ability. Children and adults of relatively greater intellectual ability are less likely to reuse words and thus they show a higher ratio in their speech and writing.

▪ *Verb-adjective ratio.* Another index of verbal diversification which has some interesting applications is the *verb-adjective ratio.* As its name implies, it is formed by taking the number of verbs in a sample of speech and dividing it by the number of words which qualify the action of the verb, including both adverbs and adjectives. Consequently, the higher this ratio for a sample of speech, the more "active" it is.

As one might expect, the *verb-adjective ratio varies considerably with different language samples.*[6] Scientific writing makes little use of verbs and has a low ratio of about 1.3. Writing which contains dialogue or has more "human interest" yields a higher ratio. In plays there are about nine verbs per adjective.

The ratio can also be taken as one *measure of personality characteristics.* It correlates, for example, with occupational interests. Persons who are genuinely interested in selling have very low ratios; they use few verbs and a great many descriptive parts of speech. The ratio also correlates with emotional stability. School children who are rated by their teachers as being relatively unstable tend to use more verbs in their speech and to have higher ratios. So too do persons who have been chronically anxious and have come to psychotherapists for help with their problems of adjustment.

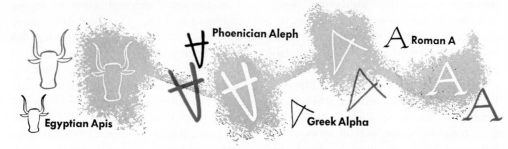

Fig. 20.5. Development of the letter A from the Egyptian Apis. The Egyptian character *apis*, meaning sacred bull, seems to be the forerunner of the Phoenician character *aleph*, which meant ox. The *aleph* became the Greek *alpha* and later our A. Many of the letters in our alphabet evolved in this way from characters that once had very specific meanings.

Comprehension. Although we usually manage to understand people who use the same language we use, some of us succeed in making language relatively easy to understand and others make the task unbearably difficult. Research workers in language and psychology have studied this problem in some detail. The results of one of the more recent studies is described in a book by Rudolf Flesch, called *The Art of Plain Talk.*[7] He has described four elements of language expression that make for ease of reading and comprehension. We have used some of his principles in this book to make it easier for you to understand it.

Flesch's four elements are *number of words in a sentence, number of syllables in a word, number of personal words,* and *number of personal sentences.* In general, the shorter the sentence, the more easily it is comprehended. Also, the shorter the words—as measured by syllables but not necessarily by letters—the easier they are to understand. Finally, the greater the percentage of personal words and of personal sentences, the easier the reading. Flesch has combined these elements into an index which one can compute by following his rules. This index is a fairly good measure, though not a perfect one, of the relative difficulty or ease with which one can comprehend a sample of writing or speech.

An example of how a complicated, almost unintelligible sample of legal prose can be improved has been provided by Flesch.

Ultimate consumer means a person or group of persons, generally constituting a domestic household, who purchase eggs generally at the individual stores of retailers or purchase and receive deliveries of eggs at the place of abode of the individual or domestic household from producers or retail route sellers and who use such eggs for their consumption as food.

Flesch comments,[8]

That's a lot of words; let's try to cut down on them. Let's say just "people" instead of "a person or group of persons"; then let's leave out all those clauses with the word "generally" in them (they don't belong in a definition anyway); then let's say "eat" instead of "use for consumption as food." Now let's see what we have:

Ultimate consumers are people who buy eggs to eat them.

Fluency. We have been discussing vocabulary size, verbal diversification, and ease of comprehension. Another rather obvious way in which people differ is in the amount of language they can produce in a given period of time. This we call fluency. Some persons can go on effortlessly producing words for a long period of time, while others must labor at stating the time of day.

Those who have studied verbal fluency find that there are two factors involved in it. One is the sheer *ability to produce words,* where the only restriction is that all the words must be associated with each other in some way. You can test this factor, for example, by asking a person to name all varieties of dogs, or all species of fruits, or all the members of his family and then clocking the speed with which he produces these words. The second factor is an *ability to express ideas* in terms of words and their meanings. This is more difficult to measure, but some glib individuals are notable for their ability to pick exactly the right word to say what they wish to say and to do it at high speed.

Fluency, like other measures of the use of language, correlates with other knowledge and abilities. Children are not so fluent as adults, and fluency, in general, increases with intelligence. As you might expect, fluency correlates with vocabulary size, because one has to have an extensive vocabulary in order to be fluent. It also goes along with occupational interests. Lawyers, ministers, and salesmen, by everyday observation and by specific tests, are more fluent than people in most other occupations.

■ THE MEANING OF MEANING

So far in this chapter we have considered the perception of language stimuli, the structure of language, and the different ways in which it is used. We have not yet considered how we know what a person means when he makes sounds or writes words to convey some information to us. The primary purpose of language, of course, is to communicate meaning. How is this done?

The meaning of a message seems to be carried in two ways. One is by common experiences with words as they have been used with things and events. The child comes to know the meaning of such words as *chair, doll, food, bed,* and so on because these words are spoken when he is perceiving these objects directly with his senses. In this way, we build up a large number of words whose meaning we think we know and understand when we communicate with each other. This kind of meaning, which can be verified by pointing to objects or events, has been called *extensional meaning.* A second kind of meaning is derived from the first by using dictionaries or verbal equivalents. Most of us have never seen the *platypus* and therefore have no extensional meaning for the word, but if we look it up in the dictionary we shall find it described in terms of words, such as *small aquatic mammal* and *bill like that of a duck,* for which we have had extensional meanings. This kind of derived meaning has been called *intentional meaning.*

Indices of meaning. You probably take it for granted that people have somewhat different meanings in mind when they use words. That is to be expected, because many words do not have precise meanings. You might also guess that the intentional (derived) meanings of words are not so fully agreed upon as are the extensional (demonstrable) meanings. That is also true. You probably would not suspect, however, how much the meaning of a word varies from one person to another even for words which most of us think we understand. Students of language have, nevertheless, demonstrated this in a quantitative way.

Since language was developed for communication between people and since they manage to communicate only when the listener (or reader) has the same meaning for a word as the speaker (or writer), the only practicable way to measure the meaning of a word is through agreement among people. We can devise an index of meaning, then, by determining to what extent people agree. We can let .00 stand for no agreement at all and 1.00 for the maximum agreement. To obtain the index of a particular word we establish *how much agreement there is and divide that number by the maximum agreement.*

One research worker,[9] who devised this kind of index, asked subjects to define words extensionally by accepting or rejecting persons, objects, or phenomena which were offered as examples of the class of things symbolized by a word. Suppose 100 subjects are asked whether they consider Franklin D. Roosevelt as an example of the class of things covered by the word *liberal*. We can then count the number of yes responses and divide by the total possible, 100. If 100 yes responses are given (or 100 no responses), then we have complete agreement among the subjects about this particular extensional definition of *liberal*. If only 50 yes responses are given to the question, then we would have complete disagreement, since as many subjects reject the example as accept it. As a matter of fact, a study conducted in this manner produced an index of agreement of only .24 in the case of Roosevelt. This represents considerable disagreement. About Herbert Hoover there was considerable agreement that he was not an example of the class of liberals. The index for his name was .90.

A different method can be used to obtain indices of intentional meanings. One experimenter[9] established the meanings of certain psychological terms by searching psychological textbooks to obtain representative definitions for each term. Then, after editing the definitions to exclude from them all words except nouns, verbs, adjectives, and adverbs, an agreement index was computed for each term by counting the number of words common to all definitions and dividing by the total number of different words which occurred in all definitions. The index for *learning* was only .024; for *perception*, .006; and for *emotion*, .010. This is not a very high degree of terminological agreement. The indices for biochemical terms was somewhat higher. For example, indices of .080 for *fats*, .150 for *lipids*, and .127 for *enzymes* were obtained. But these are still very low values, and we must conclude that our agreement on the meaning of some words, taken one at a time, is not very high.

Meaning in context. If our understanding of meanings were as poor as these results implied, one might wonder how we ever manage to communicate with each other. Note, however, that they apply to the meanings of individual words, defined separately. We should, indeed, do badly if we were to try to communicate with only one word at a time. Language, however, is not like that. It is spoken and written according to rules. Just as certain sequences of letters, sounds, and words give the structure of language a context, so the fact that words occur in certain sequences more than in others gives their meaning a context. This *context makes the meaning of words much more precise than it would otherwise be.* How often have you heard someone exclaim, "You have quoted me out of context"? In this way, he is trying to say that you cannot tell precisely the meaning of one set of words without knowing the other words with which they are used.

Just as we were able to illustrate verbal context by building up sequences of letters and sounds, we can show the context of meaning by choosing words according to their *order* of context. This has been done in Table 20.2. In that table, the *zero-order* list was constructed by choosing words at random. In the *first-order* sentence, words occur with about the same frequency as we expect them to occur in English. This is also true of sentences of a higher order, but in the *second-order* sentence one word is preceded by another as often as we might expect it to be in English. In the *third-order* sentence, they are preceded by pairs of words as often as we might expect them in sequences in ordinary English, in the *fourth-order* sentence by triplets, and so on up to the seventh order. Then finally a sample of prose is given.

The method used in constructing these sentences is an interesting one, and one which you can try at home or with your friends. To obtain the *second-order* list, a common word, such as *he*, *it*, or *the*, is presented to a person who is asked to use the word in a sentence. The word he uses directly after the one given him is noted and then presented to another person who is asked to use that word in a sentence. This method is repeated, using a different person each time, until a sentence as long as is desired is obtained. The assumption which is made here is that the persons asked to form sentences will use one word following another about as frequently as the two words occur together in the English language.

In the case of the *third-order* sentences, persons are given two words, such as *he is*, *it became*, *the world*, and asked to use them, as presented, in a sentence. Then the word used directly after the sequence is added to the sequence, the first word of the sequence is dropped, and the new sequence is presented to the next person to be used in a sentence. This same technique is used for *fourth-order* sentences, using three-word sequences; for *fifth-order* sentences, using four-word sequences; etc. *First-order* sentences are obtained by drawing words at random from all the higher-

TABLE 20.2. Samples of pseudo sentences constructed according to the statistical properties of English.

Zero order

Betwixt trumpeter pebbly complication vigorous tipple careen obscure attractive consequence expedition pene unpunished prominence chest sweetly basin awoke photographer ungrateful.

First order

Tea realizing most so the together home and for were wanted to concert I posted he her it the walked.

Second order

Sun was nice dormitory is I like chocolate cake but I think that book is he wants to school there.

Third order

Family was large dark animal came roaring down the middle of my friends love books passionately very kiss is fine.

Fourth order

Went to the movies with a man I used to go toward Harvard Square in Cambridge is mad fun for.

Fifth order

Road in the country was insane especially in dreary rooms where they have some books to buy for studying Greek.

Seventh order

Easy if you know how to crochet you can make a simple scarf if they knew the color that it.

Prose text

More attention has been paid to diet but mostly in relation to disease and to the growth of young children.

From Miller, G. A., & Selfridge, J. A. Verbal context and the recall of meaningful material. *Amer. J. Psychol.*, 1950, *63*, 176–185.

order sentences. The resulting sentences contain words occurring with about the same frequency with which they occur in common usage. The *zero-order* sentences can be obtained by choosing words at random from a dictionary. A small dictionary is best. Even better is a list of common words which has been compiled by Thorn-dike and Lorge.[10]

When sentences constructed in this way are examined, it is easy to see that from the low to higher orders the sentences gradually begin to convey what we ordinarily would accept as meaning. The higher-order sentences look meaningful in spite of the fact that they were not said by any one person intending to say something to somebody.

We should carefully notice here, how-ever, that the meaning of our language is not all carried by verbal context as defined by the sequence in which words occur. By using the method we have described, we could construct sentences out to the *fif-teenth order*, *twentieth order*, and beyond without ever producing sentences equivalent in real meaning to sentences taken from prose text. That is, sentences which are constructed by faithfully following the sta-tistical rules governing a language need not be good meaningful sentences. The reason is that, although we are accustomed to us-ing words in certain sequences, we still have a good deal of freedom in choosing a word even after lengthy sequences of previous words. This is a good thing, of course, since in order to communicate something new to another person we must be able to say something which he cannot predict with complete accuracy in advance.

■ DEFECTIVE LANGUAGE

The perceptions and skills involved in producing and understanding language are rather complex, and it takes an individual many years and an incalculable amount of learning to acquire them. It is therefore not surprising that such a delicate and complex function should at times develop trouble resulting in language defects. A person may be defective in one or in several of the as-pects of language we have described: ability

to comprehend it when it is spoken or to read it, ability to produce elementary pho-nemes or to combine them in the sequences necessary to be intelligible, or ability to use the language with a meaning that can be understood.

Some defects of language are the result of injury or disease in the brain. These are called *aphasias*, and we shall discuss them later in Chapter 21. Others are due to some kind of personal maladjustment. Stuttering and stammering, for example, have long been considered as stemming from emo-tional difficulties, although defects in func-tioning of the nervous system may play a part. Defects of language often appear in psychoneurotic disorders, and they are al-most always prominent in the psychoses (see Chapter 10). One can, in fact, use some of the indices and relations we have described above to help in the diagnoses of the psychoses. For in such forms of mental illness, there is usually a distortion in the way in which words are connected with each other and in the way in which they are used.

Consider, for example, the case of a fe-male schizophrenic patient presented with a block-sorting test. The examiner asked her the question, "What is the difference between this group and that?" She re-plied:[11]

Dividing by feeling your hand and calculating the rim. If I wrote on the blackboard by hand wouldn't give out anything at all, no chalk-mark. It's a certain light they leave careless with their work. It's light slatiness; and when I went out there to walk I found lots like that. Like those men working on the roof, keep slipping off. There's somebody copying that light all the time. How in God's name can a man keep spending money on a child and buy her clothes? And that's the way with Constance, and she going to school. They'll be going to fertilize her mind through our farm and get that light. My family took that up great. A woman in Missouri she worked on those children, boiled them and picked them and finished them. I like to do a work there.

This is an example of schizophrenic language. Such language is characteristically lacking in connectives and in precise meaning, it is filled with intrusive fragments of unrelated topics, and it is overinclusive. In brief, it does not follow very well the rules we use to understand each other. However, as in the case of all languages, there usually are some rules that the patient is following. If you understand them, you can understand the speech. What this patient was trying to say has, in fact, been understood.

SUMMARY

1. On the average, speech sounds contain more of the low frequencies than of the high ones.

2. Despite this fact, the high frequencies are more important than the low ones in the comprehension of speech. This is because consonantal sounds are high and vowel sounds are low, with the consonants being the more essential of the two to understanding speech.

3. The quality of a person's speech, as distinguished from its intelligibility, depends on such features as its intensity, dynamic range, fundamental pitch, and talking rate.

4. Although nearly 80 speech sounds can be distinguished by the skilled phonetician, only about 40 are necessary to understand speech.

5. Some of these sounds occur much more frequently than others, and some are more likely than others to follow a particular sound. The tendency of speech sounds to follow in a predictable sequence provides a context for understanding them.

6. The way in which people use language can be quantified in several ways. Size of vocabulary is one, but the vocabulary a person recognizes is usually much larger than the one he uses.

7. Verbal diversification is another measure. This may be represented by the ratio of the number of different words used to the total number used, or by such ratios as the number of verbs to the number of adjectives.

8. Another measure is the comprehensibility of a person, some people being more readily comprehended than others.

9. A final measure is fluency, which is the rate at which words can be produced.

10. Words have two kinds of meanings, extensional and intentional. Neither kind of meaning is very clear when words are considered one at a time.

11. Meanings are clarified by the context of words, that is, by the fact that some words occur more often than others and that words tend to come in expected sequences.

12. Language, being a very complex sort of learned behavior, often becomes defective. We see such defective language in some cases of brain damage and also in people suffering from emotional disturbances or mental illness.

SUGGESTIONS FOR FURTHER READING

Bloomfield, L. *Language*. New York: Holt, 1933.
> *A classical text in linguistics.*

Flesch, R. *The art of plain talk*. New York: Harper, 1946.
> *An interesting discussion of ways of making language easier to read and to understand.*

Fletcher, H. *Speech and hearing in communication*. New York: Van Nostrand, 1953.
> *An authoritative summary of the field of speech and hearing from the standpoint of communication.*

Korzybski, A. *Science and sanity*. Lancaster, Pa.: Science Press, 1933.
> *A pioneering book on the importance of understanding the meaning of words.*

Licklider, J. C. R., and Miller, G. A. The perception of speech. In S. S. Stevens (Ed.), *Handbook of experimental psychology*. New York: Wiley, 1951.
> *A summary of modern research on the factors involved in the perception of speech.*

Miller, G. A. *Language and communication*. New York: McGraw-Hill, 1951.
> *A text covering in detail topics discussed in this chapter.*

Ogden, C. K., and Richards, I. A. *The meaning of meaning* (Rev. Ed.). New York: Harcourt, Brace, 1947.
> *The revision of a classical analysis of meaning conveyed by language.*

Thorndike, E. L., and Lorge, I. *The teacher's word book of 30,000 words*. New York: Bureau of Publications, Teachers College, Columbia University, 1944.
> *A reference book for the frequency of occurrence of English words.*

Woodworth, R. S., and Schlosberg, H. *Experimental psychology* (Rev. Ed.). New York: Holt, 1954. Chaps. 23–26.
> *A summary of experiments on language, verbal behavior, and verbal learning.*

Zipf, G. K. *Human behavior and the principle of least effort*. Cambridge, Mass.: Addison-Wesley, 1949.
> *An interesting discussion of the statistical characteristics of language and communication.*

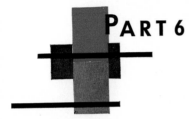

PART 6

Biological Background

Chapter 21 THE BRAIN AND NERVOUS SYSTEM

THE GENERAL ANATOMY of the nervous system has been known for hundreds of years, but the methods of modern science have permitted us to scrutinize it ever more closely. The neurologist, physiologist, psychologist, and other specialists—each has brought his methods to bear on the study of the nervous system. It is difficult to tell where the work of one leaves off and that of the other begins. We shall not try to make a distinction, but as students of psychology our principal purpose will be to understand how the nervous system participates in such activities as *motivation, learning, thinking,* and *perception.*

This chapter was drafted by Clifford T. Morgan of The Johns Hopkins University.

NEURONS

We have already explained how each individual begins life as a single cell (Chapter 2). This original cell divides and multiplies over and over again until the various organs of the body take form. In the multiplication, cells differentiate in structure and function, each coming to play a particular role in the body's activities. Although each organ of the body eventually consists of many kinds of cells, there is usually one kind that serves the principal function of the organ. In the case of the nervous system, this cell is the *neuron,* and its function is to conduct messages called *nervous impulses.*

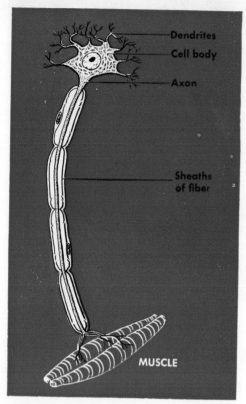

Fig. 21.1. A schematic drawing of a neuron.

Labels on figure: Dendrites, Cell body, Axon, Sheaths of fiber, MUSCLE

Structure of neurons. In Figure 21.1 is a schematic drawing of a neuron. Neurons actually vary a great deal in size and shape, but the illustration brings out all their essential features. They have two general parts: *fibers* and *cell bodies*. Within the cell body are structures that keep it alive and functioning normally, but they need not concern us here. For all practical purposes, we can think of the *neuron as a fiber with branches at each end and an enlargement, the cell body, in the middle.* The fiber leading to the cell body and the one leading away from it may be relatively long or short, depending on the distance it must traverse. A fiber may also have many branches or none at all.

Nervous impulses. *The neuron's principal function is to conduct nervous impulses.* These are very brief pulses traveling along the fiber at a relatively fast speed—from about 1 to 100 meters a second. Such a pulse undoubtedly represents some chemical reaction within the fiber, but it also consists of an electrical change. This change can be recorded on a voltmeter if electrodes are placed on the neuron and led into a suitable amplifier. In Figure 21.2 is an electrical record of such an impulse. As it passes one of the two electrodes, a voltage deflection is registered in one direction; then as it passes the second electrode, the voltmeter deflects in the opposite direction. It takes about a thousandth of a second, more or less, to pass any particular point on the fiber.

In attempting to account for this voltage deflection that represents the nervous impulse, physiologists have carefully examined the nerve fiber in a variety of ways. From chemical studies they have learned that the *membrane of the fiber is normally polarized;* it has an excess of positive ions on the outside and an excess of negative ions on the inside (see Figure 21.3). From electrical studies they have found that this polarization of the membrane is represented by a *resting potential* (voltage) across the membrane. This may be registered by placing one electrode on the outside of the membrane and a second electrode inside the fiber or at the end of a cut fiber (see Figure 21.3). What apparently happens, then, in a nervous impulse, is that the polarization of the membrane breaks down, which causes the resting potential to drop to zero.

▪ *All-or-none law.* Although many of the events in the membrane of the fiber are still obscure, some of them are known. When a stimulus is applied to the membrane, it disturbs the balance of ions across the mem-

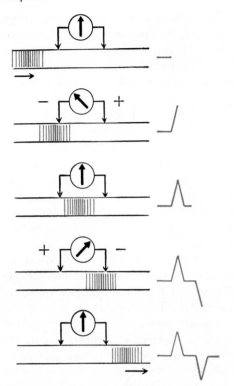

Fig. 21.2. The electrical record of a nervous impulse. The arrow in the circle represents the needle of a voltmeter whose terminals are placed on the membrane of the fiber. On the right is a drawing of the position of the needle as the impulse passes first one terminal, then the other. [*After Gardner, E. Fundamentals of neurology (2d Ed.). Philadelphia: Saunders, 1952, p. 94.*]

obeys an *all-or-none law*, which is to say, *it either occurs or it does not, and there are no shades in between.**

■ *Impulse size and speed.* One should not take this last statement to mean that all impulses are of the same size, for they are not. The resting potential, being generated by ions adjacent to the membrane, varies with the size of the fiber in which it is found. It is large in large fibers, small in small fibers. Consequently the nervous impulse varies with the size of fiber. In fact, it follows a rough rule of being proportional to the square of the fiber's diameter. The size of the nervous impulse also depends upon the condition of the fiber. If it is drugged, deprived of oxygen, fatigued, or otherwise in an abnormal state, its impulses will be altered accordingly. But in whatever condition, a fiber responds according to the all-or-none law. It gives its all or nothing at all. It might also be pointed out that the speed at which an impulse travels depends

* In some experiments, the voltage change in the nervous impulse is greater than the resting potential. The reason for this is not yet clear. The resting potential, however, accounts for nearly all the nervous impulse.

Fig. 21.3. The resting potential of a nerve fiber. Positive ions are in excess on the outside of the nerve membrane and negative ions are in excess on the inside. As a consequence, there is a resting potential that may be measured by placing one electrode on the outside of the fiber and the other at the cut end of the fiber.

brane, causing the resting potential to drop. If the stimulus is weak, the drop is small, and it is short-lived, for the membrane is restored rather quickly to its normal resting level. If the stimulus, on the other hand, is relatively strong, the drop in potential (1) is complete and (2) travels along the membrane to the very end of the fiber. It is this *potential change moving along a fiber that we call the nervous impulse.* Because such a propagated impulse represents a complete drop in resting potential, we say that it

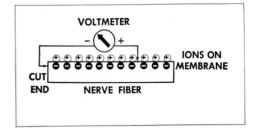

on the condition of the fiber in much the same way as does impulse size. Large impulses travel faster than small ones.

▪ *Impulse rates.* In some way that we do not yet fully understand, a fiber quickly recovers its balance once it has been discharged. Within a few thousandths of a second, it has restored its resting potential and is ready for any new stimulus that may come along. Even as it is recovering, it can be discharged if the stimulus is sufficiently

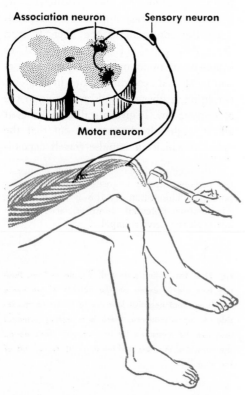

Fig. 21.4. The sensory-motor reflex arc. A sensory neuron (in this case, in the knee tendon) conducts impulses into the spinal cord. These may go directly to a motor cell in the cord or relay through an intervening association neuron (as indicated in the drawing). Impulses travel out over motor neurons to muscles to cause a reflex response. (After Krieg, W. J. S. *Functional neuroanatomy.* Philadelphia: Blakiston, 1942.)

strong. During this time, however, a stimulus must be considerably stronger than when the fiber is rested if it is to be effective. *This period of recovery, requiring unusually strong stimuli, is known as the refractory period.*

It is probably obvious that the length of this refractory period limits the rate of firing of a neuron. Just as the rifleman who can reload his gun faster can fire more often, so the neuron that recovers more quickly than another can deliver nervous impulses at a more rapid rate. The recovery rate of neurons varies with the same conditions that affect impulse size. The larger ones recover in about a millisecond and can fire as often as 1,000 times a second. Some of the smaller fibers can deliver impulses at the rate of only a few each second.

Synaptic connections. Knowing that nervous impulses travel along fibers, it is natural to ask where they come from and where they go to. This question has several answers. One is that impulses originate in the receptors of the various senses. Some receptors, like the *rods and cones* of the retina, the *hair cells of the olfactory sense,* and the *free nerve endings of the skin and deep senses, are themselves specialized neurons.* In them an external stimulus directly evokes an impulse. The receptors of some other senses are not neurons, but they are connected to neurons. When a stimulus disturbs them, they somehow trip off impulses in these neurons. In either case, whether the action is direct or indirect, the neuron conducting the impulse is called a *sensory neuron.*

At the end of each sensory neuron, the impulse comes to a gap which it cannot cross. *This gap, marking the end of one neuron and the beginning of another, is called a synapse.* But even though an impulse cannot cross this synapse, its electrical field traverses the gap well enough to stimulate the adjacent neuron and to start a new impulse in its fiber. Thus a new impulse is tripped off at the synapse where the ends of two neurons are adjacent to each other.

Most sensory neurons extend all the way from a sense organ—no matter how far away this may be—to the central nervous system, which is contained within the bony case of the skull or spinal column. They therefore make their synapses within the central nervous system. In some instances, for example, the eye, there are several synapses within the sense organ itself, and the neuron that enters the central nervous system is the third or fourth in a chain.

Within the central nervous system several arrangements of synapses are possible. In a few atypical cases, the sensory neuron synapses directly with a *motor* neuron which sends a fiber out to muscles or glands. More often, however, there are one or more intervening neurons called *association* neurons. We therefore think of the *simplest complete arrangement for a behavioral response to a stimulus as consisting of a sensory neuron, an association neuron, and a motor neuron.* This arrangement is called the *reflex arc* (see Figure 21.4) and is responsible for some of the more elementary reflexes.

The reflex arc, however, is only an idealized case. Synaptic connections are almost always more complicated than that (see Figure 21.5). Often a number of sensory neurons make synapse with one association neuron; we saw examples of this in the ending of many rods and cones on bipolar cells of the retina (Chapter 18). This means that association neurons in the central nervous system often have relatively large *receptive fields*, receiving impulses from many receptors in a sense organ. Association neurons, moreover, may loop back on each other to form *recurrent nervous circuits*. In such an arrangement, impulses keep themselves going with little or no aid from incoming sensory impulses. In this way nervous activity that is once started in the nervous system can continue indefinitely. This arrangement accounts for a considerable amount of nervous activity.

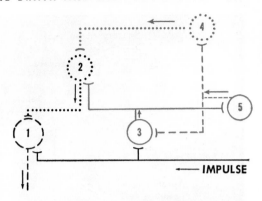

Fig. 21.5. Neurons are almost always connected in a complex way. They are connected in many arrangements. This diagram shows how neurons may form recurrent circuits that can maintain activity for some time after being activated by an impulse.

Reflexes. Of the synaptic arrangements we have mentioned, the reflex arc is of special interest to the psychologist because reflexes play a role in much of everyday behavior, both learned and unlearned. Reflex arcs are found in many parts of the nervous system. They are responsible for such reactions as the blink of the eyelid when the cornea of the eye is touched, the dilation of the pupil in bright light, the watering of the mouth in chewing food, the pricking of a dog's ears when it hears an unfamiliar sound, and a host of other automatic reactions.

The reflexes just mentioned all involve reflex arcs in the brain. Other reflexes involve only the spinal cord, and these can be classified into two general classes: the *flexion reflexes* and the *extension reflexes*. We have all observed our own flexion reflexes

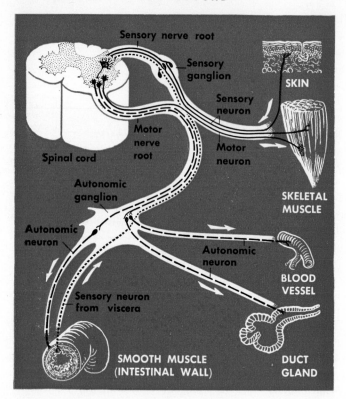

Fig. 21.6. Pathways of the peripheral nervous system. Sensory neurons from the various receptors have their cell bodies in the dorsal spinal ganglia. The motor nerve roots send fibers out to skeletal muscles and to autonomic ganglia. From the autonomic ganglia, fibers go to smooth muscles (e.g., intestine and blood vessels) and to various glands (both duct and ductless).

when we have inadvertently touched a hot stove or stepped on a sharp object. The reaction in each case is to flex (bend) quickly the limb concerned to withdraw it from the painful stimulus. Extension reflexes are even more common than flexion reflexes, but we are less aware of them because they are so "automatic." For example, when one's leg touches the ground, pressure on the foot reflexly extends and stiffens the leg to support one's weight. And when one lifts his foot off the ground, the opposite leg reflexly stiffens to support the body. The reflex in this latter case has its stimulus in the kinesthetic receptors of the flexed leg (see Chapter 19). Both are examples of extension reflexes. They aid us in standing, walking, and running, and they occur so regularly that we seldom notice them.

These are just a few examples of reflexes involving reflex arcs. More complex arcs involving several association neurons whose fibers extend some distance in the nervous system participate in other reflexes, such as the scratch reflex which we observe in our household pets or even in ourselves. The scratch reflex happens to be a nicely timed alternation of flexion and extension reflexes. It is not necessary for our purposes to consider reflexes in any more detail. All we need understand is that reflex arcs, consisting of sensory, association, and motor neurons, are responsible for relatively specific automatic responses.

THE NERVOUS SYSTEM

We have already indicated that the *central nervous system lies within the bony case of the skull and spine. The neurons, or parts of neurons, that lie outside this bony case constitute the peripheral nervous system.*

Peripheral nervous system. The peripheral nervous system consists in part of fibers of sensory and motor neurons. These fibers are always collected together in bundles called *nerves*. For most of the journey to and from the central nervous system, these nerves are both sensory and motor. Some of the nerves entering and leaving the skull, however, are only sensory or only motor. All nerves, moreover, usually divide just outside the central nervous system into two roots, a sensory root and a motor root (see Figure 21.6). They do this because they have different points of origin and departure within the central nervous system.

All that we have just said applies to *fibers* of the peripheral nervous system. This system, however, has two main divisions: the autonomic and the somatic systems. The *autonomic system* was already discussed briefly in connection with emotion (Chapter 4). It is a motor system serving the blood vessels, heart, glands, and other internal organs of the body. It is stirred up in emotion. The *somatic system,*

on the other hand, is both sensory and motor; it serves the various senses we have described and the skeletal muscles of the body involved in standing, walking, writing, and instrumental behavior in general.

Both the autonomic and somatic systems contain cell bodies as well as fibers. The cell bodies are collected together in groups called *ganglia*. Arranged along the spinal column are two series of these ganglia; one consists of the *autonomic ganglia*, containing cell bodies of the autonomic motor fibers, and the other consists of the *sensory ganglia* of the somatic system (see Figure 21.6). There are no motor ganglia of the somatic system, because the cell bodies of motor-nerve fibers are found inside the central nervous system.

Central nervous system. The neurons within the central nervous system are more or less segregated into centers and pathways. The pathways consist of bundles of fibers, and the centers are made up of cell bodies. Very frequently, however, the cell bodies in centers have very short fibers that make synapse with neighboring neurons within the center. Fibers in the pathways also usually synapse with other neurons in these centers. The center, therefore, is

DESCENDING TRACTS   **ASCENDING TRACTS**

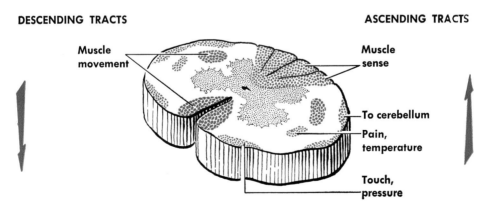

Fig. 21.7. A cross section of the spinal cord.

something of a mixture of cell bodies and fibers. Centers have specific names depending on where they are and how they are arranged. Sometimes they are called *nuclei*, in other cases *ganglia*, and in still others simply *areas*. We shall have occasion to use all three terms, but it should be remembered that *they refer to centers, or collections of cell bodies, where synapses are usually made*.

■ *White and Gray Matter.* A coincidence of nature makes it relatively easy to distinguish centers and pathways as one looks at the nervous system either with the naked eye or under a microscope. The normal color of a neuron is gray. It happens, however, that most of the fibers in the nervous system have a sheath around them and this is *white*. The cell bodies, however, do not have this sheath. Consequently, to the observer, pathways appear white and centers of cell bodies appear gray. For this reason we often refer to pathways as *white matter* and to centers as *gray matter*.

■ *The Spinal Cord.* The central nervous system is organized into two principal parts; the *spinal cord* within the spinal column and the *brain* within the skull. In Figure 21.7 is a cross section of a spinal cord. Notice that its center is gray and its outside is white. The *central gray* thus consists of cell bodies of neurons, while conducting pathways are in the outside white. Notice that motor pathways bringing impulses down from the brain are toward the front of the body. The sensory, or ascending pathways, on the other hand, are in several bundles in the white matter: pathways for the deep senses are toward the back of the body, while those for the skin senses are in two bundles on the side.

The spinal cord, generally speaking, has two functions: as a conduction path to and from the brain, and as an organ for effecting reflex action. Hardly any reflex is unaffected by impulses descending from the brain, yet many can be seen as purely spinal affairs when the brain is disconnected from the cord. In fact the extension, flexion, and scratch reflexes that we mentioned above, as well as the basic pattern of alternating steps in walking, are organized at the spinal level.

The brain. Of the two principal parts of the nervous system, the spinal cord and the brain, the brain is the more interesting because it plays the central role in all complex behavior: motivation, learning, thinking, perception, etc. Its part in these processes will be the subject of study in the remainder of this chapter. In order to understand it, however, we must first take time to outline the general structure of the brain.

The principal divisions of the brain are diagramed and labeled in Figure 21.8. They may be considered in three main groups; the *forebrain, midbrain,* and *hindbrain.* Within the hindbrain are the *cerebellum* and the *medulla.* The medulla contains vital centers for breathing and heart rate, but it also includes centers that relay sensory impulses upward to the midbrain and forebrain. The cerebellum is a center, but not the only center, for motor coordination; it helps make our movements smooth and accurate. By making use of vestibular and kinesthetic impulses, it also is an essential organ for maintaining posture and balance.

The *midbrain* is a sort of bridge connecting the forebrain and the hindbrain and therefore contains a number of tracts conveying impulses upward and downward, but it also has important centers in it for vision and hearing, and these will be mentioned again below.

The *forebrain* is the "highest" part of the brain. Though slow to develop in the animal kingdom, it eventually became the most highly developed part of the brain in man and the higher animals. As you can see in the diagram of the brain (Figure 21.8),

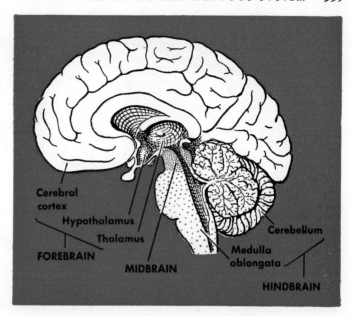

Fig. 21.8. The principal parts of the human brain.

its mass is considerably greater than that of the midbrain or hindbrain. Many parts of the forebrain are known to be involved in psychological phenomena, but the three parts of greatest interest to us are the *cerebral cortex*, the *thalamus*, and the *hypothalamus*.

As its name implies, the hypothalamus lies underneath the thalamus in a position that a surgeon can reach most easily by going through the roof of the mouth. The thalamus, lying just above it, is best thought of as a relay station. Sensory impulses coming in the spinal cord, hindbrain, and midbrain make their way, after intervening synapses, to centers in the thalamus. These centers then relay the impulses through fibers whose cell bodies are in the thalamus to various parts of the cerebral cortex.

A photograph of the human brain, such as you see in Figure 21.9, is more a picture of the *cerebral cortex* than of anything else because the cortex encloses almost all the forebrain and midbrain. The cortex, as the picture shows, is like a rumpled piece of cloth that has many ridges and valleys.

Anatomists call one of these ridges a *gyrus*; a valley or crevice is sometimes called a *sulcus* and sometimes a *fissure*.

The large sulci or fissures can be used to mark off the cerebral cortex. Along the midline dividing the brain into two symmetrical halves, called *cerebral hemispheres*, is the *longitudinal fissure*. Running from this fissure across the top and down the sides of the two hemispheres is the *central sulcus*. All the cortex in front of this fissure is called the *frontal lobe*, and this lobe may be considered the expressive part of the brain because it contains motor centers for controlling movements and actions. The cortex behind the central sulcus has been called the receptive part of the cortex, because it contains the centers at which incoming sensory impulses arrive. (There are certain exceptions to these statements, but they serve as a reasonably good way of dividing the functions of the cerebral cortex.) Finally, along the side of each hemisphere is a crevice known as the *lateral fissure*. The cortex below it and to the side of it makes up the *temporal lobe*. There are still two

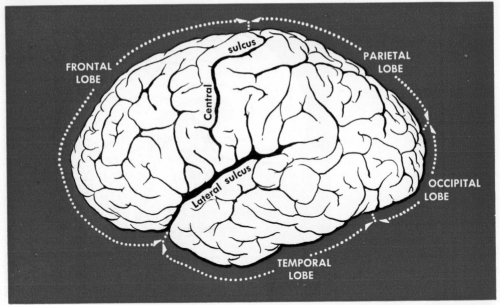

Fig. 21.9. The lobes of the cerebral cortex. Opposite is an actual photograph of a cerebral cortex. [*Photograph from Gardner E. Fundamentals of neurology (2d Ed.). Philadelphia: Saunders, 1952, p. 10.*]

other lobes of the cerebral cortex, making four lobes in all, that are not set off by any major fissures. These are the *parietal lobe* and *occipital lobe*. The parietal lobe lies immediately behind the central sulcus, and the occipital lobe is the cortex lying under the back of the skull. The functions of these various lobes will be described in the sections that follow.

▮ MOTIVATION AND EMOTION

We have drawn a sketchy picture of the nervous system, but it should suffice for our purposes. Our main task is to understand the nervous system's role in behavior. Additional details of brain structure can be supplied as they are needed. Our approach is to consider broad categories of psychological functioning and to see in each case what is known about their neural basis. We shall begin with motivation and emotion.

Sleep. Sleep has already been described as one of the physiological needs (Chapter 3). Most animals must sleep in order to stay alive as well as to retain their normal capacities for doing other things. Many animals, including man, the birds, and some domestic animals, take one long period of sleep each day. Other animals, such as the rat, cat, and human babies, sleep more often, alternating a few hours of sleep with a few hours of waking. In any case, whether the periods of sleep be long or short, they always fall into some kind of *rhythm or cycle of sleep and waking.*

The question that has long puzzled scientists is, What accounts for these cycles of sleep and waking? One possibility, namely, that there are chemical substances in the blood and brain that bring on sleep, has already been discussed (Chapter 3), but we still know practically nothing about them. Two other possibilities, however, are

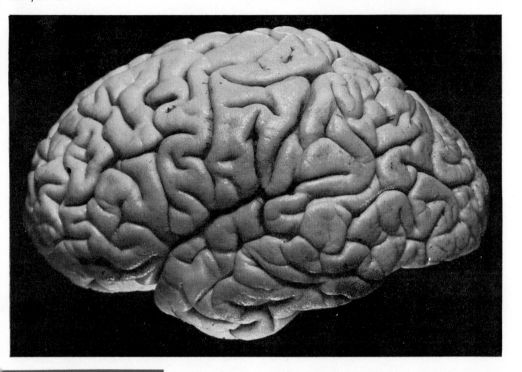

more firmly established. One is that there may be centers in the brain for sleep and waking; and the other is that sensory stimulation from the environment and sense organs in the body may control or influence sleep.

That there may be centers for sleep in the brain was first suggested many years ago when patients were encountered who had abnormal tendencies to sleep (somnolence). In some of these patients, tumors or disease were found in the *hypothalamus*. Following this lead, experimental scientists paid particular attention to the hypothalamus, making controlled lesions (injuries) in various parts of the hypothalamus of animals. Their efforts were rewarded, for they found one relatively small center whose destruction caused pronounced somnolence. Monkeys, for example, sleep almost continuously for 4 to 8 days after destruction of this center and are extremely drowsy for

many months afterward.[1] Such monkeys can be aroused briefly by noises or other strong sensory stimulation, but when left alone, they quickly fall asleep again. Similar results have been obtained with other animals, so there can be no doubt but that there is such a center in most animals.[2] Because the destruction of this center causes somnolence, it is presumed to keep the animal awake when it is functioning normally. Therefore it is called a *waking center*.

Once the waking center had been established, one investigator asked whether there might not also be a *sleep center*.[2] By exploring the hypothalamus with lesions placed in different spots, he located such a center some distance away from the waking center. Destruction of the sleep center, he found, keeps an animal (rat) from sleeping. Animals without this center eat, drink, and are otherwise normal but they have never been observed to sleep. Instead they stay awake and active until they are exhausted, then fall into a coma and eventually die. In other experiments, this investigator destroyed both the waking center and the sleep center; he found that the result was somnolence, just as when he destroyed the waking center alone. From this we may conclude that the waking center tends to be the dominant center and that sleep is probably produced by the sleep center's temporarily inhibiting the waking center.

These hypothalamic centers for sleep and waking, although important and basic, are not the only parts of the brain concerned with sleep. Cats deprived of their entire *forebrain*, including the hypothalamus, have been reported to sleep and wake, so there must be other influences of the midbrain and hindbrain upon sleep.[3] On the other hand, the cerebral cortex, though not necessary for sleep, has something to do with it, because *patients with injuries in the cortex sometimes have periods of drowsiness and somnolence.*[4] So far, however, the hypothalamic centers are the ones most clearly established.

We mentioned the possibility that sensory influences might control sleep. In fact, it is rather obvious that they do.[5] Many of the birds sleep only when it is dark and awake immediately when it is light; and people generally have difficulty sleeping in the midst of noise, light, or other strong stimulation. We know too that impulses from the skin and muscles influence sleep, for we usually must take pains to be completely relaxed, thereby reducing skin and muscle sensations, in order to get to sleep. From this fact we may conclude that *impulses pouring into the waking center help keep it active*; opposing these are influences of the sleep center. Whether we sleep or not, then, must depend largely on the balance of these influences.

Emotion. The *hypothalamus* is a relatively small area, but it is much more influential than its size would indicate. When we turn to emotion, or indeed to any other aspects of motivated behavior, we find again and again that it plays an important part.

▪ *Hypothalamus.* The role of the hypothalamus in emotion was first well established by the now classic experiments of Cannon and Bard.[6] Using cats as their experimental animals, they made a series of sections through the forebrain, each time slicing off a little more until they severed the entire forebrain from its connections with the midbrain and hindbrain. Usually only one level of section was used in any one subject and experiment. Each animal was tested before and after operation for angry behavior by such procedures as pinching its tail, presenting a dog, blowing a bugle, etc. Angry cats, as you probably have observed, have some characteristic behavior which includes growling, hissing, spitting, biting, lashing the tail, thrashing the forelegs, protruding the claws, urinating, and breathing rapidly. Cannon and Bard found that *the essential pattern of angry behavior was always present as long as the hypothalamus was intact.* When this was excluded by the operation, leaving only the midbrain and hindbrain, the pattern of rage response was broken up. Such subjects sometimes displayed *fragments of emotion,* such as meowing, hissing, or fur-ruffling, but without the hypothalamus they lost their characteristic pattern of anger. The investigators concluded, then, that the *hypothalamus is the area in which the various elements of hostile emotional behavior are organized into a pattern.*

This conclusion, however, has been modified by more recent research in which lesions have been made in the hypothalamus alone, leaving the rest of the forebrain intact.[7] From what we have just said, one would expect such lesions to abolish patterns of angry behavior, but this is only partly true. Such animals are more stolid, more somnolent, and generally more difficult to arouse than normal animals. The important fact, however, is that rage responses can sometimes be elicited from these animals lacking the crucial hypothalamic centers. Apparently, then, the hypothalamus is not the only organizing center for emotion. Without the cortex it is the "organizer," but higher centers of the brain can perform the same task.

▪ *Cerebral cortex*. This kind of result is probably as confusing to the student as it was to early investigators of the nervous system, but it is something one must become accustomed to. As we shall see later in this chapter, it very often happens that there are two or more parts of the brain which can perform essentially the same functions. When one is destroyed, the other one can take over. In rather recent experiments[7] we have learned what some of these alternative centers of emotion are; there are centers in the cortex that modify the activity of the hypothalamus. In some of these experiments, a considerable part of the cerebral cortex was removed, leaving only certain areas thought to be involved in emotion. The cortical areas left intact are rather complex anatomically, but they can be described as occupying part of the floor of the brain and part of the wall of the longitudinal fissure (see Figure 21.9). The interesting thing about cats prepared in this way is that they are extremely placid. They are so placid, in fact, that it is almost impossible to elicit a rage response from them. All the irritations that usually provoke rage in the normal cat leave these animals peaceful and friendly. In these areas, then, we have found *cortical centers that tend to restrain or inhibit the hypothalamus and lower centers for emotion.*

Having located these areas for "placidity," investigators could be expected to go on and do the reverse experiment of removing these areas while leaving the rest of the cortex intact. They did, and the expected result occurred.[7] Cats were made extremely ferocious by this operation. Almost anything, including a threatening gesture or even the appearance of the experimenter, brought forth angry behavior. From this fact, they conclude that areas elsewhere in the cortex, so far undetermined, normally excite the emotional mechanisms of the hypothalamus and lower centers but that these centers are normally counterbalanced by the "placid" areas.

That, briefly, is the picture we have at the present time of the brain mechanisms of the emotion of anger. We have said nothing about other emotions such as fear and pleasure, because we know so little about them. What evidence there is indicates that fear involves many of the same mechanisms as anger does. Pleasure, as we have seen elsewhere (Chapter 4), probably is not a unitary emotion but rather the result of many forms of need satisfaction. Hence we do not expect it to have any particular locus in the nervous system.

Needs. When we discussed the physiological needs in the chapter "Motivation," we explained that they arose from chemical conditions in the body, but we did not say how these conditions expressed themselves in motivated behavior. That question, which we shall now take up briefly, leads us once again to the *hypothalamus*, for this center proves to be important in the physiological needs, as well as in sleep and emotion. The three needs for which we know this to be true are *sex*, *hunger*, and *thirst*. We shall consider them in order.

▪ *Sexual behavior*. Investigators interested in finding out how the nervous system functions in sexual behavior have carried out experiments much like those we described above for emotional behavior. Sections were made at different levels through the forebrain and midbrain of female animals, and attempts were then made to induce typical mating behavior in the animals.[8] The experimenters found that mating behavior was normal so long as the back part of the *hypothalamus and a region behind the hypothalamus* (called mammillary bodies) were left intact. If, on the other hand, the section passed through the midbrain behind these structures, the experimenters could no longer observe full-fledged mating behavior.

Following this kind of experiment, the next logical step is to make restricted lesions in the hypothalamus. This has been done in several different animals, both male and female. In one fairly clear-cut experiment,[9] lesions in the hypothalamus abolished sexual behavior in both male and female animals, and no amount of the hormones which normally induce sexual behavior (see Chapter 3) could reinstate it. From experiments like these, physiologists have been led to believe that *hormones, excite the hypothalamus and associated structures* and that it is from this point that sexual responses are organized.

▪ *Hunger and thirst.* We have excellent evidence that the physiological needs of hunger and thirst are also mediated by the hypothalamus. The problem of thirst is still so complicated and obscure that we cannot go into it here. Suffice it to say that there is a *region in the hypothalamus whose destruction makes animals extremely thirsty.* This region sends fibers down to the pituitary gland (see next chapter) from which hormones involving thirst are secreted.

Fortunately modern experiments cast more light on the centers for hunger. The technique in these experiments has been to make relatively small lesions in the hypo-

thalamus and to measure the effect of these lesions on eating. *One center, located near the midline of the hypothalamus, restrains hunger and eating; when it is destroyed, animals develop voracious appetites.*[10] Such animals, even before they recover from the operation, usually attack food ravenously and eat large quantities of it. Their immense appetites continue day after day, while they gain weight rapidly, until they become so obese that they are about three times their normal weight. Then they slacken off somewhat and maintain their weight in this state. In Figure 21.10, you see the picture of a rat in which obesity was produced by a small lesion in the hypothalamus. Experimenters have studied such animals to see just what has gone wrong with them. Their metabolism is normal, and so is just about everything else in the machinery of the body. Apparently the main thing wrong is that their appetites have gotten out of hand. It is probably this hypothalamic center that is deficient in some human beings who eat themselves into obesity. On the other hand, it is very likely that most obesity in human beings is more a matter of bad eating habits and personality difficulties than of a deranged hypothalamus.

It is interesting that there is a second center in the hypothalamus that has quite the opposite function. When experimenters make their lesions just a fraction of an inch to the side of the lesion that produces ravenous appetite, the result is an animal that has no appetite at all. Such animals, unless given special care, never touch food again and if left alone eventually die of "voluntary" starvation. By maintaining the animals by artificial means (stomach tubes) and offering them especially desirable food, such as chocolate bars, it has been possible to teach some of them to start eating again. The important point, though, is that in the case of hunger, as in that of sleep, there are *two pairs of centers, one exercising a restraining influence, the other an exciting influence.*

SENSATION AND PERCEPTION

Now let us turn to the senses and see what events in the brain have to do with sensory experiences. In considering this topic, the reader should have in mind the ways in which we can classify the senses (see Chapter 19). For our purposes here, the most convenient classification is into four main groups: *vision, hearing, somesthesis,* and *chemical senses.* Somesthesis includes the skin senses of *pressure, pain, warmth,* and *cold* and the *kinesthetic pressure sense.* The chemical senses include *taste* and *smell.* Much that we have to say is true of all the senses within a group and sometimes of two or more of the groups.*

* In Chap. 20 it was pointed out that we probably have no direct experience of events in the vestibular sense organs. For that reason, the vestibular sense is not considered here.

Centers and pathways. Three of these groups, namely, vision, hearing, and the chemical senses, are located in the head. It is to be expected, therefore, that their nerves, centers, and pathways are found in the head and the brain and have nothing to do with the spinal cord (see Figure 21.11). The olfactory nerve leads off the olfactory organ behind the bridge of the nose and runs directly into the base of the cerebral cortex. The optic nerve emerges from the blind spot of the retina, proceeds through an opening in the eye socket, and ends in the thalamus. The auditory nerve and the taste nerves enter the hindbrain; from there impulses course upward to the midbrain and forebrain.

What is true of these groups of senses, however, does not apply entirely to the somesthetic senses that are located all over the body. Since these senses serve the head and face, they have nerves which, like those of hearing and taste, enter the hindbrain, but they also have nerves entering the spinal cord throughout its whole length from the base of the spine to the base of

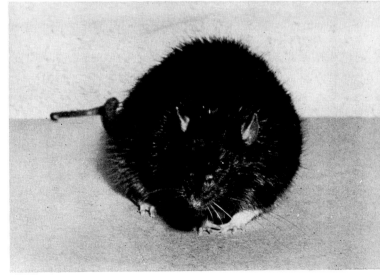

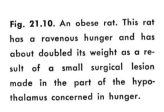

Fig. 21.10. An obese rat. This rat has a ravenous hunger and has about doubled its weight as a result of a small surgical lesion made in the part of the hypothalamus concerned in hunger.

the skull. These serve the sense organs of the body exclusive of the head. As we have already seen, the spinal sensory nerves feed into reflex arcs and take part in many spinal reflexes. In addition, however, they send branches coursing upward to the hindbrain where they join fibers from the somesthetic sense organs of the head. As a consequence, *pathways for all the senses are found in the brain*, whether they enter directly or come up from the spinal cord.

When we examine the sensory centers and pathways in the brain, we must distinguish between the two chemical senses of smell and taste. Smell, as we have said, is represented in the cerebral cortex on the floor of the brain. Taste, on the other hand, takes the route of the somesthetic senses. Joining them in the hindbrain, taste fibers are thereafter so intermixed that one cannot distinguish the centers and pathways

for taste and somesthesis. After making synapses in centers in the *hindbrain*, they all course upward to a single center in the *thalamus*.

All the senses except smell have relay centers in the thalamus. One center is for *vision*, another for *hearing*, and another for *somesthesis and taste.* These centers are called relay centers because they do not seem to have any special functions other than to relay impulses on to the cerebral cortex. There again we see three main areas for the respective senses. Just *behind the central sulcus is an area for somesthesis and taste*; in the very back of the cortex *in the occipital lobe is an area for vision*; and in the wall of the lateral fissure *in the temporal lobe is the area for hearing.* You can see all these areas depicted in Figure 21.12. We call these areas of the cerebral cortex the *primary sensory areas* because they re-

Fig. 21.11. A diagram of the brain as seen from below, showing the cranial nerves, their names and numbers.

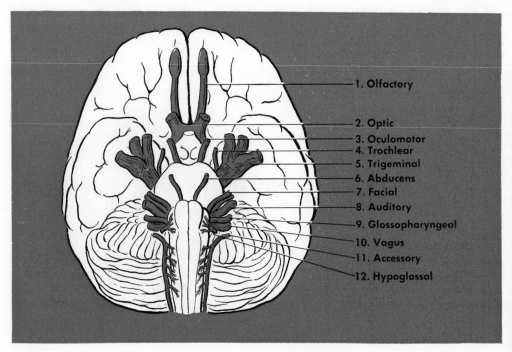

1. Olfactory
2. Optic
3. Oculomotor
4. Trochlear
5. Trigeminal
6. Abducens
7. Facial
8. Auditory
9. Glossopharyngeal
10. Vagus
11. Accessory
12. Hypoglossal

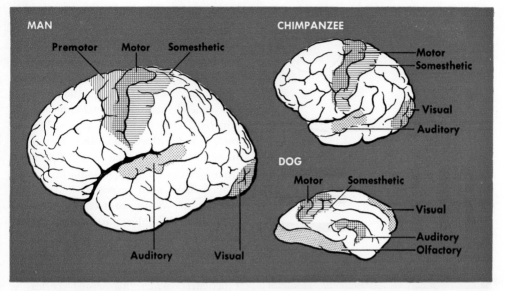

Fig. 21.12. The cerebral cortex of the dog, the chimpanzee, and man. Note the size and positions of the visual, auditory, and somesthetic areas. The diagram also shows the motor areas of all three species and the large olfactory areas of the dog. Note, too, how much larger the brain of man is compared with those of the chimpanzee and the dog.

ceive fibers in direct pathways from the respective sense organs. As we shall see in the next section, there are also some indirect pathways to other areas of the cortex.

Vision and hearing are different from the other senses in that they have additional centers in the midbrain. (Somesthetic fibers send some branches to the midbrain, but have no centers there.) On the roof of the *midbrain* are two pairs of bodies. The front pair is concerned in *vision* and the back pair in *hearing*. In lower animals such as the fish, which have no cerebral cortex to speak of, these midbrain centers are the principal centers for vision and hearing. In the mammalian animals, such as the rat, monkey, and man, these are alternative centers to those found in the cerebral cortex.

Topographical arrangement. From this point on, we shall have nothing to say about smell because we as yet know so little about

it and the statements we make about the other senses are generally not applicable to smell. It is characteristic of the other senses, however, that their centers have an orderly *topographical arrangement*—much like maps. In vision, for example, both the thalamic center and the primary cortical area are arranged so that different points on them represent different points on the retina. By recording with electrodes or using other anatomical techniques, one can show that *for every point on the retina there is a corresponding point in the thalamus and cortical area.* We often speak of this arrangement as *point-to-point projection.*

There is a similar, though perhaps not so accurate, projection in hearing and somesthesis. We have already seen that *different frequencies of sound waves stimulate different places in the cochlea.* This *tonotopic* organization is preserved in the auditory system so that it holds for the auditory

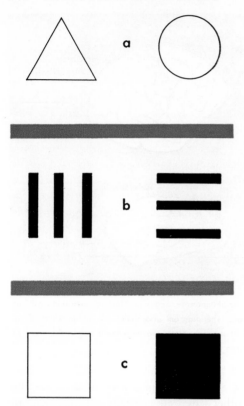

Fig. 21.13. Visual perception in animals lacking the primary visual cortex. In the absence of the visual cortex, rats cannot distinguish pairs **a** and **b**. They can, however, distinguish pair **c**, for they are able to perceive the difference between black and white.

cortex *via the thalamus are represented in a topographical way.*

Sensory experience. Knowing the centers and pathways of the various senses, we may go on to ask how they participate in sensory experience. To study this question we have two general methods: *stimulation* and *destruction.* One is used to excite different centers and pathways and the other to remove them. The method of stimulation has been used with human subjects whose brains have been exposed under local anesthesia.* While an electrical stimulus is applied, the subject is asked to report whatever he experiences.[11] The subject reports sensations of warmth or pressure when his somesthetic cortex is stimulated, visual experiences when his visual cortex is stimulated, and various sounds when his auditory cortex is the site of stimulation. It is interesting, however, that he never reports *pain* when his somesthetic areas are stimulated. Pain is obtained only when the thalamus is somehow involved. It therefore appears that the pain fibers of the somesthetic system go only as far as the thalamus and do not reach the cortex.

A second method of studying the sensory functions of the brain is to remove some particular center, testing the subject's sensory capacity both before and after the removal. This method, of course, is used ordinarily only with animals. It occasionally is used with human beings when injury or disease requires brain surgery. In general, experiments of this kind show that the cerebral cortex is concerned with the *spatial aspects* of perception while subcortical centers are more important in the *intensity* of experience. This, however, is only a general statement, and therefore is not true in every detail.

* Surgeons sometimes use this method to determine how they can best perform a necessary operation with the least damage to a person's sensory capacities.

cortex as well as for the cochlea. When electrodes are placed on this cortex while different tones are sounded, the electrical recordings show an orderly arrangement of places on the cortex corresponding to those in the cochlea. A similar order prevails in the somesthetic cortex, only in this case it is parts of the body that are represented. The upper part of the somesthetic cortex outlined in Figure 21.12 represents the legs and lower parts of the body, the middle part the arms and trunk, and the lower part the head, face, mouth, tongue, etc. In summary, then, *all the senses projected to the*

Vision is probably the best example of this general rule. In all the animals that have been studied, the *primary visual cortex is necessary to perceive patterns and visual detail.*[12] Remove this cortical area, and an animal cannot distinguish a triangle from a circle or vertical stripes from horizontal ones (see Figure 21.13). The same animal, however, can react to a light going on or off and can distinguish which of two panels is lighted. The *ability to experience intensity, as distinguished from spatial details, is therefore a property of subcortical centers* —presumably in the midbrain—rather than of the visual cortex. We should hasten to add, however, that in human beings the cortex seems to have taken over some of these subcortical functions, for when people lose their visual cortex they are reported to be completely blind.

In both hearing and the somesthetic senses matters are not so clear. These senses do not play so great a part in space perception as vision does, and it has proved more difficult to tell just how much their cortical areas are involved in it. We do know, though, that removal of the appropriate cortical areas reduces sensitivity to stimuli. The loss, however, is not great. In fact, removal of all the forebrain and midbrain centers for these senses still leaves the animal with capacity to react to fairly strong stimuli. It therefore appears that *all parts of these sensory systems, including those in the hindbrain, contribute something to sensory experience.*

■ LEARNING AND THINKING

Perhaps the most interesting property of the nervous system is that it enables us to learn and to think. For that reason a great deal of research has been devoted to the neural mechanisms of learning and thinking. Such research has been pointed at two general questions, one pertaining to the microscopic level and the other to the macroscopic one. The first question is, What changes take place in neurons or their synaptic connections to make learning possible? Although it has been studied diligently, the question is still without a firm answer. The consensus of opinion without any direct proof, however, is that *learning involves some sort of change in synapses that makes the passage of impulses easier than it was before.* This change might be a growing together of fibers at their juncture. But this is only a surmise. The other question concerns the centers and pathways of the nervous system: What parts of the nervous system are involved in any particular kind of learning? For this question we have some answers, and this section will deal with them.

Conditioning. Conditioning is usually regarded as the simplest form of learning (see Chapter 5). Certainly it is fair to assume that an organism, if it can learn at all, can learn a conditioned response. For this reason, investigators have used the conditioning method in attempting to discover what parts of the nervous system are capable of learning. Their method, typically, has been to remove some part of the nervous system —or at least to cut it off from the rest of the nervous system—and then to test the animal's capability of learning a conditioned reaction.

For many years it was thought that the highest part of the nervous system, the cerebral cortex, was necessary for even the most elementary conditioning to take place. Now we know that this is not so. Human beings born without a cerebral cortex and animals from whom it has been experimentally removed have both been conditioned. But there are limits to this conditioning. The normal animal learns to lift its paw promptly and smoothly when a signal warns him of impending shock. The decorticate animal, on the other hand, typically learns to squeal and squirm but does not acquire the smooth "adaptive" response.[13] *The decorticate animal has therefore lost some of the skill one normally sees in conditioning, even though it can learn to respond to the conditioning stimulus.*

There are many other experiments designed to determine whether certain sensory centers are necessary for a particular kind of conditioning. Is the visual cortex, for example, necessary for a visual conditioned reaction? In vision as well as the other senses, the answer seems to be "no." In the absence of the visual cortex, a dog may be conditioned to wink its eye when a light is flashed. (In this case, the unconditioned stimulus is a puff of air to the eyeball.) Nor is memory for the conditioned reaction disturbed when the visual cortex is removed. From these facts it seems evident that some *conditioning normally takes place in subcortical centers.*

Discriminative learning. This statement is not true, however, of more complex learning. Suppose, for example, that the task for the animal is one of discrimination rather than conditioning. It may be required to choose between two windows, one lighted and the other unlighted, being rewarded for correct responses and punished for incorrect ones. An animal that is taught such a discrimination and then has its visual cortex removed "forgets" what it has learned. Yet, if given the opportunity to relearn the discrimination, it will do so in just about the same number of trials and errors as it required before operation.[14] It would seem, consequently, that the sensory cortex is *not* necessary for *learning* a discrimination but is necessary for *remembering* it if it has been learned before injury

to the brain. Apparently subcortical centers can take over learning functions normally carried on cortically.

We have used vision as our example to illustrate the point, but there are numerous experiments with other senses giving about the same results. We do not yet understand just why one part of the nervous system can take over when another fails. The phenomenon nonetheless is important in understanding nervous function. It means that, within certain limits, there is an *equivalence of function*—a sort of built-in insurance—that offsets the handicap of injury to a particular center or area.[15]

This capacity of the nervous system, however, does not extend to every sort of learning. If we teach a rat to discriminate different patterns, such as a triangle versus a circle, and then destroy its cortex, it will never be able to relearn this discrimination. In this case the visual cortex is absolutely necessary for the ability to discriminate patterns, and no part of the visual system can take over this capacity.

Besides the primary sensory areas there are other areas of the cerebral cortex that are involved in the learning of discriminations (see Figure 21.14). Just in front of and more or less surrounding the visual cortex is an area sometimes called the *visual association area* or (by anatomists) the *prestriate area*. Just behind the somesthetic area and occupying the principal part of the parietal lobe is the *parietal association area*, which is concerned in somesthetic learning. And an area near the primary auditory area of the temporal lobe serves as an *auditory association area*. Each sense, therefore, has an area near its primary cortical area that functions as an association area.

We still have much to learn about these association areas, and it is not yet possible

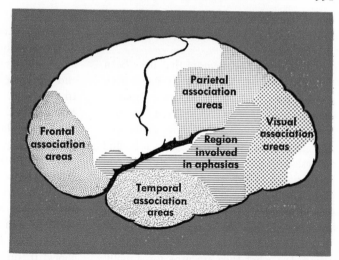

Fig. 21.14. The association areas of the cerebral cortex. Aphasias, which are disorders of linguistic functions, are discussed on p. 552. For further explanation, see text.

to ascribe to them really definite functions. There are, however, two general statements we can make about them. The first is that they sometimes have an equivalence of function with primary areas. One experimenter, for example, taught monkeys to make discriminations of size, color, and form.[16] Then he removed their prestriate areas on both sides. After allowing sufficient time for surgical recovery, he tested them on the discrimination habits. He found that they had complete amnesia—loss of memory—for the habits. Upon extensive retraining, however, he found that they could relearn the habits about as quickly as they had learned them preoperatively. Thus he showed that the prestriate association areas were important in the original learning of the habit, but that the remainder of the visual system could take over this capacity in their absence. Similar results have been obtained for other association areas and the respective discriminations that depend upon them.

The second general statement we can make about sensory association areas of the cortex is that they are involved in the more complex sensory discriminations. One in-

vestigator, for example, taught a chimpanzee to discriminate a cone from a pyramid by touch alone. The animal could not see the objects and had to discriminate them by handling them.[17] He also taught the chimpanzee the more difficult discrimination of a wedge from a pyramid. Then he removed the posterior parietal association area. After the operation, the animal lost both habits but upon retraining was able to learn again the discrimination of the pyramid and cone. With no amount of retraining, however, could he teach the animal again to discriminate the wedge and pyramid—the more complex discrimination. From this kind of experiment we are led to believe that the *association areas are necessary for learning the more difficult discriminations.*

Memory disorders. Although more definitive experiments on brain functions can be performed with animals than with man, human subjects naturally acquire a great many complex habits that can be taught to animals only with great labor or not at all. They can also be tested fairly extensively and easily once it is known that they have an injury. For that reason, much of our information about memory and brain functions has come from people who have suffered brain injury.

The disorders of memory that have been observed in the brain-injured have been divided into three general classes: *aphasia*, *agnosia*, and *apraxia*. An *aphasia* concerns language functions, including arithmetic and mathematics as well as words and names. Any loss of linguistic abilities and memories is called an aphasia. An *agnosia*, on the other hand, is nonlinguistic; it is a loss of memory for the meaning of objects, for example, loss of recognition of a fork or an automobile or a pencil—not their names but what they are used for. Finally, *apraxia* concerns movement; it is loss of memory for how to do things, such as how to throw a ball, open a door, dress oneself, or drive a car. Each of these memory disorders can be subdivided into a number of varieties. Aphasia, for example, can be divided into sensory aphasia, which is the inability to understand language, and motor aphasia, which is the inability to produce language through speech or writ-ing. Most of these distinctions, however, will not concern us here.

The memory disorders can alternatively be classified into the *expressive* disorders and *receptive* disorders (see Figure 21.15). In general, the expressive disorders (apraxias and motor aphasia) depend upon the frontal lobes, while the receptive disorders (agnosias and sensory aphasia) depend upon other lobes. When, for example, we encounter a person who can no longer speak or write words, though he understands them and is quite capable in other ways, we can be rather certain that he has sustained an injury or lesion in the frontal lobes. If, on the other hand, he does not recognize speech when he hears it or reads it, or does not recognize the names of familiar objects and people, the chances are high that his injury is farther back in the brain.

There is considerable disagreement among neurologists about how much farther we can carry the assignment of memory disorders to particular areas of the cortex. It seems fairly certain, however, that there

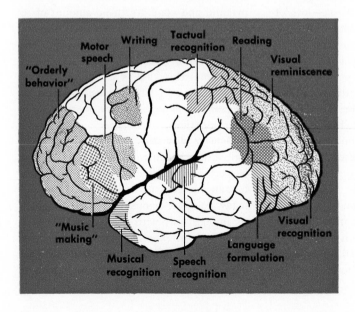

Fig. 21.15. A composite diagram of possible association areas of the cerebral cortex. Localization of memories is undoubtedly not so precise as this diagram would indicate. It gives a general idea, however, of the way in which various areas are more concerned in one memory function than in another.

is an *area for speech* in the lateral frontal part of the cortex, as you see it diagramed in Figure 21.15. When this area is obliterated, a person has speech aphasia; he no longer can remember how to make the sounds that are necessary to talk. It is probably also true that farther up in the frontal lobe is an *area for writing*. This must be intact for a person to remember how to make the highly coordinated movements involved in writing language and in drawing.

The localization of *sensory aphasia* and of the *agnosias* is more debatable, but some neurologists believe from their observations of a great many cases that it is reasonably good. The prestriate areas, they have concluded, are essential to complex visual memories, such as reading written language and recognizing the meaning and uses of objects. These areas are also considered necessary for visual reminiscence—visualizing and imagining things we have seen in the past. Near the auditory area in the temporal lobe, they believe, is an area for speech recognition; for without it, we are unable to understand what people say, even though we may hear perfectly well the sounds they make. There may also be other specific areas for complex memories such as recognizing musical melodies, being able to play music, and formulating linguistic expressions. In any case these complex memories are somehow dependent on the parts of the cerebral cortex that we label association areas. How specifically they may be assigned to these areas remains uncertain at the present time.

The localization of memory functions in man, however, cannot be extremely specific because it is usually possible for a person to relearn what he has "forgotten." Just as in the case of sensory learning, there is some equivalence of the parts lost and those remaining. A person simply must start the long laborious process of learning what took him months or years to learn in childhood. If he can no longer read, then like a child, he starts to learn his alphabet again, then simple words, then phrases and more complex sentences. Unless the damage has been very great or unless he suffers another injury, as often happens to older people with cerebral hemorrhage, he has a good chance of at least partial recovery of the memory functions he has lost.

Frontal association areas. In Figure 21.15, there are relatively large areas of the frontal lobe that are not concerned with specific memories but are nevertheless involved in intellectual processes. These have been called the *prefrontal areas* or the *frontal association areas* (see Figure 21.14). Their removal in man or animals is followed by a number of important changes in ability and in personality.

An inability to attend well to a task is one of the symptoms that follows destruction of the prefrontal areas. This fact has often been demonstrated in experiments with monkeys that have been taught a delayed reaction.[18] In such experiments, the monkey is shown that food is under one of two cans (see Figure 21.16). Then a screen is lowered between him and the cans so that he cannot stare at the correct can. After an interval of time, the screen is raised and the monkey's task is to select the correct can. Normal monkeys can do this after delays of several minutes (see Chapter 6). Prefrontal monkeys—those lacking the prefrontal areas—usually fail if the delay is more than a few seconds. By shutting lights out during the delay or doing other things to keep the animals from being distracted during the delay, it is possible to get them to solve the problem after some delay. Hence we cannot say that this problem can never be solved without the frontal lobes. Nevertheless it is much

Fig. 21.16. A monkey solving the delayed-reaction problem. At left, the monkey is shown the correct stimulus (tobacco can) and allowed to find food under it. After a delay, the monkey (*right*) is then presented with stimuli (oil can and tobacco can). He shows that he remembers which is correct by pushing aside the tobacco can. (*Courtesy of Dr. H. F. Harlow.*)

more difficult without them. From this fact and other things we know about prefrontal animals, it appears that *they have difficulty attending to which is the correct can.*

Human beings with injury to their prefrontal areas are able to solve the delayed-reaction problem, apparently because this is much less difficult for them than it is for monkeys. In many other little ways, however, they exhibit similar difficulties in attending, planning, and keeping their minds on what they should be doing. They are more likely to shirk responsibility, not to worry about the future, to be inconsiderate of people, and to react impulsively to their present inclinations than are normal people. Some observers of such individuals summarize all these changes by saying that the prefrontal areas have to do with a person's planning and regard for the future and that the person suffering damage to them loses much of his concern for the future.[19]

In recent years, this conception of the function of the prefrontal areas has been applied in an operation called *prefrontal lobotomy* or, more generally, *psychosurgery.* In this operation the prefrontal areas,

or rather the pathways leading to them from the thalamus, are destroyed. The operation is now frequently used with individuals who are so worried, depressed, and anxious about the future that they have become mentally ill. Often prefrontal lobotomy affords these people a good deal of relief, making them at least happier individuals, if not improving them enough to let them return to a normal life. Because the operation is rather drastic, however, neurologists ordinarily do not resort to it until all other methods of therapy have failed (Chapter 11). The operation is not a certain cure. It helps some more than others. Even those it helps may suffer some loss of the abilities that depend on the prefrontal areas.

■ SKILLED MOVEMENTS

In our account of brain functions, there are two areas of the cerebral cortex that we have not mentioned. These are the *motor* and *premotor* areas lying just in front of the central sulcus (see Figure 21.12). We need to consider them briefly just to round out our picture. They are both concerned, directly or indirectly, in the producing of skilled movements.

Various experiments show that the motor area is the "executive" area of the cortex. Through it an individual is able to execute different patterns of movement. In this area are neurons that send fibers downward to the motor neurons of the hindbrain and spinal cord that activate skeletal muscles. This fact can be demonstrated by electrically stimulating the motor area; such electrical stimulation evokes all sorts of specific movements of the face, arm, fingers, legs, etc., depending on where the electrode is put. Notice in Figure 21.17 that the motor area has a topographical arrangement much like that in the somesthetic cortex. The fact that the motor area is an area for movement is also demonstrated by the effects of destruction in the area. If, through surgery, cerebral hemorrhage, or other injury, some of this area is destroyed, a paralysis results. If the whole area on one side is damaged, then one sees a relatively complete paralysis of one side of the body—the opposite side, because fibers from the motor area cross over from one side to the other in their descending paths.

The premotor area is part of a complex system in the brain, involving the cerebellum and subcortical centers of the forebrain. Its functions are therefore difficult to describe. Generally speaking, it regulates tension and posture in different parts of the body and facilitates specific movements under the control of the motor area. If the premotor area is removed or damaged, the individual's *movements become awkward.*

Fig. 21.17. A homunculus showing the topographical organization of the motor area. Both the motor area in front of the central sulcus and the somesthetic area behind it are so arranged that the legs are represented near the top of the area, the arms in the middle, and the face and mouth near the bottom. The drawing is a way of representing the relative size of the subareas of the motor area serving different parts of the body. (*After Penfield, W., and Rasmussen, T. The cerebral cortex of man. New York: Macmillan, 1950.*)

He seems to know what he wants to do but has difficulty in doing it very well. Continuous tension in his extensor muscles prevents his making smooth, accurate movements.

Many centers outside the cerebral cortex are concerned in movement, but their function is no special concern of the psychologist. We have described briefly the role of the motor and premotor area only to account for the principal areas of the cortex and to give the student a bird's-eye view of the mechanism of movement.

Summary

1. The basic unit of the nervous system is the neuron. Stimulation of the fibers of neurons generates nervous impulses, which are conducted from one end of the neuron to the other.

2. The nervous impulse obeys an all-or-none law. It either reaches full size or it does not propagate at all.

3. At the end of one fiber and the beginning of another is a gap called the *synapse*. At this gap a new impulse is evoked as the old one dies out.

4. Neurons form many different kinds of synaptical connections. One arrangement is the reflex arc, consisting of a sensory neuron, an association neuron, and a motor neuron. Reflex arcs are involved in such reflexes as the flexion and extension reflexes.

5. The nervous system has two main divisions: (*a*) a peripheral nervous system, which consists in turn of the autonomic and somatic nervous systems; and (*b*) the central nervous system contained within the bony cavities of the skull and spine.

6. The peripheral nervous system conveys impulses to and from the central nervous system. This latter consists of centers and pathways in the brain and spinal cord. The spinal cord, in turn, conveys impulses to and from the brain, but it also is responsible for spinal reflexes.

7. The brain has three principal divisions: forebrain, midbrain, and hindbrain.

8. The forebrain contains the cerebral cortex, the thalamus, and the hypothalamus. The cerebral cortex consists of four lobes: the frontal, parietal, temporal, and occipital lobes.

9. The hypothalamus is the part of the brain of most interest in motivation and emotion. It contains a waking center and a sleep center for regulating sleep cycles, and centers for emotion, sexual behavior, hunger, and thirst.

10. Except for smell, pathways for all other senses proceed to the thalamus and are relayed to the cerebral cortex. Vision and hearing, in addition, have centers in the midbrain.

11. Each of these senses has an orderly topographical arrangement in the cortex, representing a point-to-point projection of the sense organs.

12. If a sensory area of a person's cortex is electrically stimulated, he reports the corresponding sensory experience. If, on the other hand, it is removed, his ability to use the sense in space perception is usually lost. Intensity of experience, however, depends primarily on subcortical centers.

13. Conditioning can take place without the cerebral cortex. Many kinds of discrimination can also be learned without the relevant cortical areas.

14. On the other hand, memory for a discrimination is frequently lost when the relevant area is destroyed. After such destruction, however, memories often may be reestablished by further training. Thus subcortical centers can take over cortical functions in memory.

15. Fairly complex discriminative learning involves other areas of the cortex called sensory association areas. There are one or more such association areas for each sense.

16. Memory disorders in man are also related to damage to these areas. In general, expressive disorders depend upon the frontal lobes and receptive disorders on other lobes of the cerebral cortex.

SUGGESTIONS FOR FURTHER READING

Fulton, J. F. *Frontal lobotomy and affective behavior: a neurophysiological analysis.* New York: Norton, 1951.

> *A readable summary and interpretation of animal and human research on the functions of the frontal lobes.*

Gardner, E. *Fundamentals of neurology* (Rev. Ed.). Philadelphia: Saunders, 1952.

> *An introductory text on the structure and function of the nervous system.*

Hathaway, S. R. *Physiological psychology.* New York: Appleton-Century-Crofts, 1942.

> *A text covering most of the topics considered in this chapter.*

Hebb, D. O. *The organization of behavior.* New York: Wiley, 1949.

> *A book presenting new theories, as well as many interesting experiments, concerning the functions of the brain in behavior.*

Marquis, D. G. The neurology of learning. In C. P. Stone (Ed.), *Comparative psychology* (3d Ed.). New York: Prentice-Hall, 1951. Chap. 9.

> *A chapter on the function of the brain in learning.*

Morgan, C. T., and Stellar, E. *Physiological psychology* (2d Ed.). New York: McGraw-Hill, 1950.

> *A standard text on the physiological mechanisms of perception, motivation, and learning.*

Nielson, J. M. *Agnosia, apraxia and aphasia* (Rev. Ed.). New York: Hoeber, 1946.

> *A description of memory disorders in human individuals with brain injuries.*

Penfield, W., and Rasmussen, T. *The cerebral cortex of man.* New York: Macmillan, 1950.

> *Descriptions of experiments in which the human cerebral cortex was electrically stimulated in conscious patients.*

Stevens, S. S. (Ed.). *Handbook of experimental psychology.* New York: Wiley, 1951. Chaps. 2–5, 14, 20, 24, and 28.

> *Compact, authoritative chapters on physiology of the nervous system and on the physiological mechanisms of emotion, learning, and perception.*

Chapter 22 THE INTERNAL ENVIRONMENT

THE PSYCHOLOGIST is interested in certain organs of the body—the sense organs, nervous system, and muscles—because they are the *organs of behavior*. Anything that affects them also affects the way in which people behave. This is why we considered the structure and function of the nervous system in some detail in the last chapter. There you saw that such psychological functions as perceiving, learning, remembering, and using language depend upon the normal functioning of the nervous system. When the nervous system is damaged by injury or disease, there are usually some important losses in psychological abilities.

To understand fully the biological background of behavior, however, we must consider also the *internal environment* in which the nervous system performs its functions. This environment is complex and delicately balanced (see discussion of homeostasis in Chapter 3). It usually maintains itself at a certain temperature, and even a small deviation from this normal value can make a difference in nervous function. The internal environment also supplies food, water, oxygen, and other chemical substances. Changes in the supply of these materials or in the chemical reactions through which they are utilized alter activity in the nervous system. Thus, strange as it may seem at first, the internal environment is of considerable importance in psychology. In order to see how it affects behavior, however, we must first devote a few pages to describing what it is and what it does.

This chapter was drafted by Eliot Stellar of the University of Pennsylvania.

METABOLIC MACHINERY

The internal environment is important, first of all, because it supplies energy. Muscles, quite obviously, must have energy supplied to them if they are to do their work. So also must the cells of the nervous system and of the sense organs. These organs, in fact, are somewhat like fuel-burning engines. They receive and store the food that is brought to them in the blood. Then they use the oxygen, transported by the hemoglobin in the blood, to burn this fuel, much as an engine burns its fuel. Only thus are the muscles able to contract and the nervous system to generate nervous impulses.

The body is always burning fuel, even when it is quiet as in sleep. At times, however, a relatively greater supply of cellular fuel must be on hand so that it can be available for immediate use. The cells of several tissues in the body therefore store it as well as burn it. Thus the *two processes, of building up and breaking down energy stores, go hand in hand and constitute what the physiologist calls metabolism.*

Metabolism is no simple matter. Since the food we eat is not in a form that we can use, it must be broken down—digested—into simple chemical packets that can pass through the walls of the intestines into the blood. Once there, it must be converted into other forms and transported to convenient places for storage. Some is stored in the liver, some in the muscles, and some in other tissues of the body. This storing involves several chemical steps. Then, when it is needed, it must be gotten out of storage—more chemical steps—and transported to its place of use. At that point, still more chemical steps are necessary to put it in a usable form.

So metabolism involves numerous chemical reactions and many different chemical materials. *Food materials* and the *oxygen* that is ultimately used to burn them are, of course, essentials in metabolism. A number of other substances enter into the process. These are the *hormones, vitamins,* and *enzymes.* Without these substances, metabolism could never run its course and our organs could not function. They are therefore of special interest to us.

Hormones. A *hormone is a chemical substance secreted by an endocrine gland* (page 35). This type of gland pours its secretion directly into the blood. There are a great many hormones, and physiologists have not yet identified all of them. Physiologists do know, however, what glands produce hormones and, in many instances,

Fig. 22.1. The names and positions in the body of the ductless (endocrine) glands that secrete hormones.

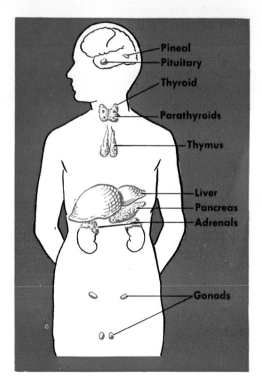

Pineal
Pituitary
Thyroid
Parathyroids
Thymus
Liver
Pancreas
Adrenals
Gonads

the chemical constitution of the most important hormones. They also know what many of the hormones do in metabolism. In the accompanying illustration (Figure 22.1), you see the names and positions in the body of the principal glands that produce hormones. We shall describe only those that have an important bearing on behavior.

▪ *Thyroid gland.* The thyroid gland, located in the tissue of the neck around the windpipe, produces a hormone known as *thyroxin.* This hormone controls the general rate at which energy is produced in the body. If the amount of thyroxin is low, energy is burned slowly, even though the body may have ample food resources. The individual is sluggish and shows many medical signs of low metabolism. If there is too much thyroxin, the individual is usually extremely active and shows signs of high metabolism. *Thyroxin, then, regulates metabolic rate.*

▪ *Parathyroid glands.* In the vicinity of the thyroid gland are two pairs of small glands, collectively called the *parathyroid glands. Their hormone regulates the level of calcium and phosphorus*—two chemical elements important in nerve activity. Parathyroid hormone keeps the supply of calcium in the blood high and that of phosphorus relatively low. If there is a deficiency in parathyroid hormone, calcium levels are lowered and those of phosphorus are raised.

▪ *Pancreatic gland.* The pancreas is located along the lower wall of the stomach. It secretes the hormone *insulin,* a substance primarily responsible for the *control of blood-sugar level.* If insulin is deficient, blood sugar rises above normal amounts; if it is in excess, blood sugar falls below normal. The blood-sugar level, in turn, indicates how much sugar the tissues are able to get for fuel. When blood sugar is high,

it means that not enough is getting out of the blood to the brain; as a result, the brain is "starving" for food. The converse is true when blood sugar falls because there is an excess of the hormone insulin. Thus insulin can affect how much sugar the brain gets for fuel and, in turn, for carrying out its functions.

▪ *Adrenal glands.* We have already mentioned the adrenal glands in describing bodily changes in emotion (Chapter 4). These glands are located in the back of the body above the kidney. One part of them secretes a hormone called *adrenalin.* It is this hormone that is released in strong emotion. Another part, the cortical part, secretes a number of hormones, collectively known as *cortin, which govern the level of sodium and the amount of water in the internal environment.*

▪ *Gonads.* The technical name for the sex glands of the male and female is gonads. In the male the gonads are called the *testes;* in the female, the *ovaries.* In each case they occur in pairs. They secrete several related hormones, but as you might expect, those of the male are somewhat different from those of the female. The sex hormones are not very active in young children. They come into play at puberty (about twelve years of age) and are responsible for the marked physical changes that take place in girls and boys at that time: *growth of the breasts, the beginning of menstruation, growth of the beard,* and *changes of the voice*—all the so-called secondary sex characteristics that distinguish between girls and boys.

▪ *Pituitary gland.* The sex hormones lie dormant for the first eleven or twelve years of life under the control of the *pituitary gland.* It is not until then that the pituitary gland stimulates gonads to secrete actively. The pituitary gland, in fact, *secretes a number of hormones that stimulate or inhibit secretion in other glands of the body.* It is for this reason that it is sometimes called the "master gland." In addition, the pituitary secretes other hormones that play a direct role in metabolism. One of these, the *growth hormone*, controls the general rate of growth in a child. If there is too little of it, he becomes a dwarf; if too much, a giant.

Enzymes, vitamins, and genes. It may be seen from this brief survey that the hormones take part in many aspects of the body's metabolism. Biochemists have been conducting intensive research in recent years to find out precisely how hormones participate in the chemical steps of metabolism. They have discovered that rather small amounts of them are required to maintain normal metabolism and that little of them is burned up in the course of metabolism. They conclude, therefore, that *hormones are agents that help or hinder certain chemical steps without directly supplying the energy for them.*[1]

▪ *Enzymes.* The hormones, however, are not alone in the job of regulating metabolic reactions. In fact, they probably work by increasing or decreasing the supply of other agents known as *enzymes*. Enzymes result from chemical reactions taking place in various cells of the body. These enzymes are the immediate agents, or *catalysts*, that *regulate particular chemical steps in metabolism*. There are many known enzymes, and each takes part in a particular reaction. For example, in the chemical reactions required to get sugar to the brain or to make use of the by-products of the burning of sugar, there are several specific enzymes, each involved in some one step. If one of these enzymes should be deficient, the chemical reactions with which it is concerned are blocked. We shall see in a moment how such blocking may produce feeble-mindedness.

▪ *Vitamins.* Vitamins are a class of substances closely related to the enzymes. The public is now fully indoctrinated about the importance of vitamins and is consuming vast quantities of them annually—usually without knowing exactly why. Unlike the hormones and enzymes, vitamins are *not* produced in the body. Instead they must be imported in the foods that are normally eaten or in the capsules available at drugstores. Although the body needs only small traces of them, the vitamins *control certain vital chemical reactions in the body*. Indeed, modern biochemical research seems to show that vitamins probably join with other products in the body to make enzymes. In any event enzymes and vitamins are closely related.

▪ *Genes.* You can see now that three kinds of chemicals—the *hormones, vitamins,* and *enzymes*—are the agents that control the complex chemical machinery of the body. This hierarchy of controlling agents, in turn, is the product of genetic factors.[2] We have already seen (Chapter 2) that the genes are the agents of heredity—the means by which physical characteristics are handed down from one generation to another. This transmission of hereditary characteristics has to be done by chemical reactions. The individual starts out as one cell, which multiplies and divides in various ways through many chemical reactions until eventually the various tissues and organs of our body are formed. Hence genes determine the ultimate form of the body by working through the hormones, enzymes, and vitamins.

This concludes a thumbnail sketch of the internal environment. We have made it brief because it itself is not our principal concern. All that is necessary is to have the

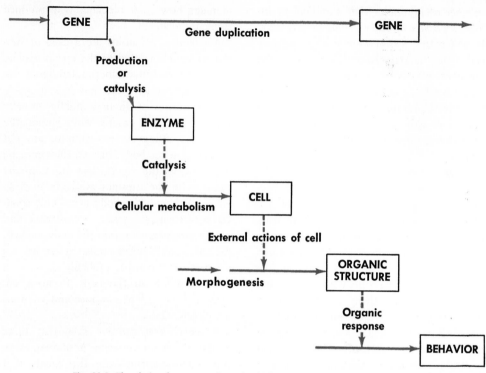

Fig. 22.2. The chain of processes through which genes and enzymes are related to behavior. For explanation, see text. (*After Zubek, J. P., & Solberg, P. A. Human development. New York: McGraw-Hill, 1954, p. 21.*)

bare essentials in mind so that we may understand the role of the internal environment in behavior.

Motivated behavior. In the chapter "Motivation" (Chapter 3), we told the story of a boy who died because the hospital diet did not give him the great quantities of salt that he craved. On autopsy, hospital physicians learned that he had a tumor of the adrenal gland; this had made him deficient in the output of the *cortin* hormone. Consequently his internal environment was lacking in salt, and his need for it was great. This is an example of the way in which the internal environment may govern our physiological needs.

We could cite many other examples. Organisms have specific appetites and aversions for such things as sugar, calcium,

phosphorus, and vitamins. Even thirst may be regarded as a specific appetite for water. In each case, the hormones of glands regulate the amounts of these materials in the body and thus the body's need for them. It follows, then, that damage to a gland or an excess in glandular output changes the appetite for the particular material concerned. There are many experiments that demonstrate clearly that these changes do take place as expected. They all point to the conclusion that the internal environment regulates our physiological needs.

■ INTELLIGENCE

Since we have covered motivation in some detail in Chapter 3, we shall not dwell on it here. It is more instructive to turn to other forms of behavior—those that involve learning and intelligence. These too are affected by the internal environment, because anything that is involved in the complex chemical reactions through which energy is stored and burned in the brain must necessarily be reflected in learning and intelligence.

Feeble-mindedness. There are some four million people in the United States whose intelligence is so low that they can be considered feeble-minded (see Chapter 15). Some cases of feeble-mindedness are caused by injury to the brain at birth. The great majority of cases, however, are not so readily explained. Because low intelligence tends to run in families, many of the feeble-minded probably inherit a defective nervous system. In such instances, we may suppose that the genes make something go wrong in the developing structure of the nervous system and in the internal environment on which it depends. So far, however, we are unable to say specifically in most cases just what has gone wrong.

There is one kind of feeble-mindedness, however, which is inherited and is known to be due to a defect in the internal environment. This is *phenylpyruvic oligophrenia*.[3] It is relatively rare, but its genetic mechanism is reasonably clear. It seems to be caused by a *single defective gene* which is responsible for an *enzyme* necessary to utilize phenylpyruvic acid. This acid is a product in the brain's burning of fuel. Ordinarily it is disposed of by a chemical reaction controlled by a specific enzyme. If this reaction is blocked and the acid accumulates in the brain, the result is a feeble-minded person. The diagnostic sign of such feeble-mindedness is excretion of phenylpyruvic acid, for some accumulated acid finds its way to the kidney, and individuals who excrete it are without exception feeble-minded.

The internal environment is also clearly involved in another type of feeble-mindedness, *cretinism*. In this case, the deficiency is in thyroid hormone. As we have already pointed out, the thyroid hormone regulates the rate of metabolism— the utilization of energy—and when it is deficient the brain and other tissues of the body cannot grow or function normally. The child suffering this deficiency becomes a cretin—a feeble-minded dwarf with a potbelly and thick, rough skin. Fortunately, we are able to recognize this disease reasonably early and to administer thyroid hormones to offset it. If treated early enough, the cretin develops normally and has normal intelligence.

Lack of oxygen known as *anoxia* is another important cause of feeble-mindedness. This is understandable, because the brain must have oxygen to get its energy and to maintain its normal function. If a person is deprived of adequate oxygen for long periods of time (or of all oxygen for a few minutes) and is still able to live, the chances are that he will suffer a serious loss in intelligence. Such cases occasionally occur in clinical practice, as when a person has nearly died of asphyxiation or has had the blood supply to his brain shut off too long while undergoing surgery.

Oxygen lack is most serious in the infant before it is born or at birth, because the brain is still being formed. It is during this time, too, that the chances of oxygen lack are high. Sometimes the blood supply to the fetus is inadequate, causing oxygen lack. The *mongoloids,* one large class of the feeble-minded, are probably produced in this way.[4] In some instances, the mother may be given drugs that reduce the oxygen that reaches the fetus. In other cases, the baby may be temporarily suffocated during delivery because the umbilical cord carrying oxygen from the mother is closed off before he starts breathing. In any event, lack of oxygen before or during birth can play havoc with the nervous system, and the result can be feeble-mindedness.

We might say in passing that we have considerable evidence on this point from experiments with animals.[5] Rats and guinea pigs that are partially asphyxiated at birth fail to grow normally. They are unable to learn mazes or other problems at a normal rate. They show other neurological defects such as partial paralysis, blindness, and deafness, as well as generally poor intelligence.

Improving intelligence. Perhaps the reader has wondered whether some drug or chemical substance might be used to improve intelligence. After all, we now have wonder drugs for almost "anything that ails you"; why not one for intelligence? Scientists have asked this question and have tried to find such a wonder drug. In the case of the cretin, we know that the trouble is a lack of thyroxin and that giving the cretin thyroxin early enough really does wonders. This is a special case, however, and the matter is not so simple when we come to other forms of feeble-mindedness or to the problem of improving the intelligence of normal people.

▪ *Glutamic acid.* Glutamic acid is a substance that only recently was thought to be useful in improving intelligence. Research employing this acid at first seemed to show that it could improve the intelligence of children and the learning ability of rats. In two experiments, one with feeble-minded children and the other with rats, glutamic acid seemed to have beneficial effects. These studies were not altogether convincing, however, for they were not completely controlled. Several subsequent studies have failed to confirm them.[6] Some people still hope and believe that glutamic acid can help the feeble-minded, and even that it

can improve normal intelligence. The weight of evidence, however, is against such a hope.

▪ *Thiamin.* Biochemists know that thiamin (otherwise known as vitamin B_1) is necessary in one of the essential chemical reactions of the brain. It is therefore another candidate for improving intelligence. It has been given to children in institutions for the feeble-minded. In some instances it seemed to improve intelligence a little. The best conclusions from such studies, however, are that it does no good after a child has reached the age of five or six years.[7] The results of experiments with rats suggest that it might be helpful if it is given early enough. Extra thiamin given through the mother during pregnancy and then after birth until weaning appears to improve greatly the ability of rats to learn mazes.[8] We do not yet know, however, whether these results can be applied to man.

As matters now stand, there is no wonder drug for feeble-mindedness or for improving intelligence. Such a drug, however, is not out of the question. It may be discovered in the near future.

■ PERSONALITY DISORDERS

You have learned in previous chapters that personality is largely formed by the experiences a person has and by the way he deals with motivational conflicts. You also saw that major personality disorders—the psychoneuroses and psychoses—develop when a person cannot cope effectively with motivational conflict. This approach, however, is only a part of the story. Motives, habits, and ways of dealing with conflict are also affected by the chemistry of the body— the internal environment. This very often disposes one person, more than another, to develop a personality disorder. Let us see how this can be.

Drugs and personality. Consider first how some drugs affect us.[9] Alcohol, if taken in sufficient quantity, frequently produces the incoherence and hallucinations that are also observed in psychoses. Nitrous oxide, or "laughing gas," can cause fits of uncontrollable emotions of the sort that occur only in the most severe mental disorders. Many of the narcotics put the drug addict into a trancelike state in which he "lives out" his dreams and is completely out of touch with reality. In this respect he is not unlike some patients one can see in the schizophrenic ward. Even the simple lack of oxygen, such as one experiences at high altitude, causes a person to become confused, display poor judgment, and lose emotional control much as these symptoms occur in personality disorders. There are, in fact, a long list of drugs, narcotics, and chemical conditions that can produce striking mental symptoms. This makes it seem plausible that *personal maladjustments may be caused, in part, by some maladjustment in the internal environment.*

On the other side of the picture is the fact that certain drugs seem to help mental disease. Injections of Metrazol, for example, produce violent convulsions, which sometimes help to cure psychoses. Similarly insulin (the hormone of the pancreas) given in heavy doses produces convulsions and a deep coma, which psychiatrists have found effective in dealing with some cases of psychoses.

Perhaps the most striking example of all is sodium Amytal.[10] It affects metabolism in the brain. It is sometimes given to patients who have completely withdrawn from the world of reality. Patients may be so severely disordered that they do not move or speak, do not eat, and have to be tube-fed. Yet when given sodium Amytal, they often show remarkable improvement. They get up briskly, talk eagerly and often coher-

ently, and eat ravenously. Unfortunately, the effect of sodium Amytal wears off after a short while, and the patient lapses back into his stuporous existence. The drug, however, at least gives the doctor a chance to contact the patient, to talk to him, and to get a better idea of what may be wrong (see Chapter 11).

We are still far from understanding how such drugs work. Moreover, we are continually discovering new drugs that have temporary or permanent benefits in mental disorder. As research continues, however, we can expect to make increasing progress on this front.

Alcoholism. There are more people in the United States suffering from alcoholism than from the various psychoses. Probably two million individuals are so handicapped by the excessive use of alcohol as to be called alcoholics. So alcoholism is one of the major personality disorders of our times.

In a large proportion of cases, alcoholism, like other forms of disorder, is plainly a reaction to motivational conflict (see Chapter 10). Alcohol is a way of solving temporarily the emotional problems a person cannot deal with when he is sober. Yet many people who are emotionally maladjusted never take to drink; and there are others who can develop a craving for alcohol without being in grave emotional trouble. This leads us to suspect that a person's general make-up—something in the chemistry of his body—may predispose him to alcoholism.

To study this possibility, biochemists have made chemical tests on normal and alcoholic people. They have concluded that each person has distinctive biochemical characteristics, just as they have unique physical features, such as facial features, eye color, hair color, etc. (see Figure 22.3).[11] They find, moreover, that alcoholics as a group are chemically different from non-

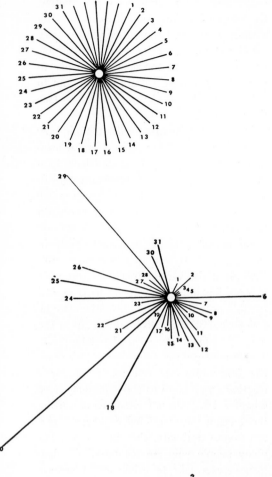

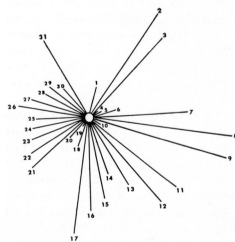

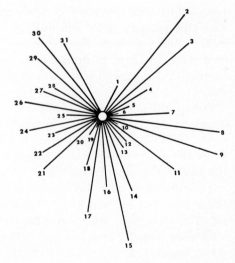

Fig. 22.3. Diagrams representing the biochemical make-up of individuals. The length of each spoke represents the relative amount of one biochemical characteristic. A hypothetical average individual has all spokes of equal length (*top drawing*). Spokes 1 through 5 represent measurements of taste sensitivity. For example, spoke 2 depicts a person's threshold for sugar, spoke 4 his threshold for salt. Spokes 6 through 17 represent measurements of the constituents of a person's saliva. Spokes 18 through 31 denote different measurements of substances in the urine. Each individual displays a unique pattern of biochemical characteristics. Note, however, the similarity of the two lower diagrams; they are for identical twins. (*From Woods, R. Nutrition and alcoholism: a genetotrophic approach. Borden's Rev. nutrit. Res., 1952, 13, 29–48.*)

alcoholics. In one study of four compulsive drinkers and eight normal individuals the alcoholics had more sodium and uric acid in the saliva, they had more of certain acids and less of certain hormones in the urine; and finally, they had greater sensitivity to salt than normal people. Apparently, the *internal environment of alcoholics is distinctively different.*

The B vitamins, particularly thiamin (vitamin B_1), may be especially important in alcoholism.[12] Rats, like people, will drink alcohol, sometimes in excessive quantities. One investigator gave large quantities of B vitamins to rats that had access to alcohol, and he found that this treatment abolished their excessive appetites for alcohol. On the other hand, when he put the rats on a vitamin-B-deficient diet, their "drinking" increased considerably. Hence in rats the craving for alcohol depends in part on how much vitamin B they are getting.

The body chemistry underlying alcoholism is undoubtedly too complex to be corrected in every case with sufficient quantities of vitamin B. We do, however, have some cases in which vitamins have helped human alcoholics. One man, a typical alcoholic, could never stop drinking once he had started until he fell into a stupor. When he was sober he always craved a drink; as soon as he had one drink he wanted a second even more, and so on. For a period of four months, this man took tremendous doses of 15 vitamins while managing to stay sober. By the end of this period, the craving was gone. Moreover, he could do what most alcoholics cannot do: he could take one or two drinks without craving more. Although few alcoholics are so easily cured, this is an example of treating personality disorders by treating the internal environment.

Reactions to stress. In a moment we shall treat other problems in personality dis-

order, but we must stop briefly to introduce a new concept—the concept of reaction to stress—because it is now apparent that psychological stress as well as physical stress can produce persistent changes in the internal environment. These changes are important in the production of personality disorder.

Most of us are sometimes exposed to unusual stresses. When we must go too long without sleep, when we suffer severe burns or protracted pain, when we are exposed to extreme cold or extreme heat, or when we work much too long at tiring and exacting tasks, we are stressing our bodies because such extreme conditions demand more of our bodies than they must normally bear. Harrowing emotional experiences, and indeed severe frustrations and motivational conflict, are also stresses, for they produce the physiological changes in emotion that we have previously described (see Chapter 4). Any situation that makes the body mobilize its resources and burn more energy than it normally does may be considered such a stress.

▪ *General adaptation syndrome.* As you see in the accompanying illustration (Figure 22.4), the way the body reacts to such stresses may be described in three stages.[13] The first stage, called the *alarm reaction*, consists of the typical bodily changes in emotion that we reviewed in an earlier chapter. If the stress continues for some time, however, a person enters a second stage called *resistance to stress*. In this, the person recovers from his first burst of emotion and tries to endure the situation as best he can. Such endurance, however, puts considerable strain on his resources. Then he may eventually reach a third stage, the stage of *exhaustion*. When he has arrived at this point, he has exhausted his internal resources for dealing with continued stress. We do not see this stage too frequently in emotional

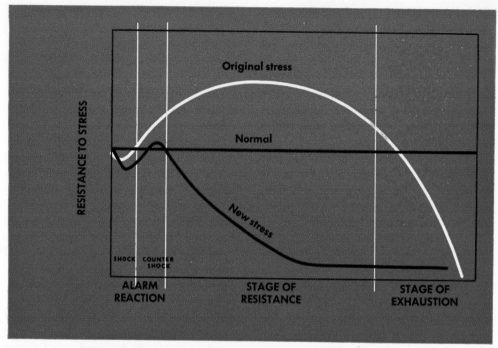

Fig. 22.4. Selye's concept of the general adaptation syndrome. Responses to stress are divided into three stages: the alarm reaction, resistance, and exhaustion. The lines represent relative resistance to stress: the white line represents resistance to the continuation of the original stress, the black line resistance to a new kind of stress imposed in different stages of the adaptation syndrome.

stresses, but in cases of reaction to severe heat or cold, he may finally weaken and die. These three stages together have been called the *general adaptation syndrome*.

This syndrome represents an attempt on the part of our bodies to protect us against stress. Unfortunately, however, an individual often pays a great price for this adaptation. It may result in such diseases as hypertension, rheumatism, arthritis, ulcers, allergies, and a host of related physical disorders. Such disorders are seldom caused by psychological stress alone, yet such stress may be crucial; it may so aggravate ordinary physical causes of disorder as to produce it when it would not otherwise occur. As you have already learned, when physical diseases are caused in large part by psychologi-

cal stresses, we call them *psychosomatic diseases*.

▪ *Adrenal reactions*. The particular diseases, whether mental or physical, that develop in reaction to stress depend upon the individual's predispositions—his weak spots —and also upon the kind of stress he suffers. In any case, they seem to result from changes in the metabolism of the body that are produced by stress. There are many such changes, but they are not yet fully understood. The most general one is a reaction of the *adrenal gland*. This appears to be the organ that participates most promptly and most vigorously in reactions to stress.

The adrenal gland, as you already know, secretes two kinds of hormones, adrenalin and cortin. Adrenalin mimics the action of the sympathetic nervous system by increasing heart rate and blood pressure and by making sugar available to the brain and muscles. Cortin includes many hormones that control sodium, water, and other chemical steps in the internal environment. One of the components of cortin is *cortisone,* of which you may already have heard through popular magazine articles. This drug, as well as another called ACTH, has received wide publicity in the treatment of rheumatism, arthritis, and kindred disorders. ACTH *is the pituitary hormone that stimulates the adrenal gland to secrete cortin.*

To understand how these facts relate to the general adaptation syndrome of reaction to stress refer again to Figure 22.4. Note that in the second stage of the adaptation syndrome, resistance to continued stress is increased. This means that *too much* adrenal secretion is being produced. In this stage, therefore, such diseases as hypertension (high blood pressure) and heart disease are prevalent. We can, in fact, duplicate the symptoms of these diseases in animals by injecting an excess of adrenal hormones. On the other hand, in the later stages of adaptation to prolonged stress, the person's resources become exhausted. This is accompanied by—in part, caused by—an exhaustion of adrenal hormones. Then such diseases as rheumatism and arthritis result. It is for this reason that such drugs as ACTH (which gives added stimulation to the adrenal cortex) and cortisone (which takes the place of insufficient cortical hormone) have been successful in the treatment of these diseases. These drugs make up for the exhaustion of adrenal activity resulting from prolonged stress.

Metabolism in mental disorder. The body's reactions to stress are important not only in the psychoneuroses and psychosomatic disorders but also in the psychoses. Schizophrenics, who make up the major proportion of psychotics, are persons who are not well equipped to deal with environmental stress. Scientists have been able to establish this fact by making chemical tests on the blood and urine. We do not need to go into the details of such chemical tests. Suffice it to say that characteristic changes take place in the blood and urine of *normal people* when they are exposed to stressful

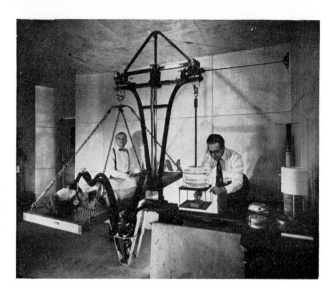

Fig. 22.5. Metabolic tests in mental disorder. The patient is undergoing a series of metabolic measurements. For further explanation, see text. (*Courtesy Life Magazine* © *Time Inc.*)

conditions. When *schizophrenics* are exposed to the same stresses, however, they fail to show these changes in the blood or urine. Schizophrenics, therefore, seem to be people whose biological equipment for reacting to stress is not functioning as it should.[14]

Simply knowing that schizophrenics have deficient metabolic reactions to stress does not tell us *why* they have them. Their reactions might have been acquired through learning and experience with their environment, or they might be constitutional. In other words, they might be inherited or acquired. Fortunately, we now have some fairly convincing answers to this question. They come from genetic studies of schizophrenia.[15]

The general incidence of schizophrenia in the United States population is less than 1 in 100. If a parent has the disease, however, the odds move up to 10 in 100 that his child will have it. If one child in a family develops it, the odds increase further to 15 in 100 that his brother or sister will have it. In fraternal twins, which differ as much in heredity as ordinary brothers and sisters, the odds are still about 15 in 100 that one twin will have schizophrenia if the other one does. When we come to identical twins, however, the odds jump up to 85 in 100 that both twins will have schizophrenia if one does.

Such figures argue strongly for the inheritance of a predisposition to schizophrenia. Members of the same family, of course, have a somewhat similar environment, but this cannot account for the different odds in fraternal twins and identical twins—15 as compared with 85 in 100. Moreover, it has been possible to study cases of identical twins who have been reared apart in different environments. Here again the odds are about the same as for identical twins reared together. We may conclude therefore that schizophrenics are persons who have inherited a deficient biological equipment that predisposes them to the disorder. Of course, the fact that the odds for identical twins are 85 and not 100 leaves some room for the effects of environment.

At present we do not know exactly how such predisposition is inherited. The genes, of course, govern the structure of the nervous system and of various organs of the body. They do this, as we have already pointed out, through their close relatives, the enzymes; and they indirectly influence the chemical functions of the body by the same means. Some day perhaps we shall understand this problem in greater detail. At present we have only a general picture of the relations among genes, enzymes, hormones, and reactions of the nervous system to stress.

TABLE 22.1.   The incidence of mental disease in the general population and among blood relatives of mental patients.

Type of mental disease	Incidence in general population, per cent	Incidence among relatives, per cent				
		Parents	Half siblings	Full siblings	Fraternal twins	Identical twins
Schizophrenia	0.9	9.3	7.1	14.2	14.5	86.2
Manic-depressive psychosis	0.4	23.4	16.7	23.0	26.3	95.7
Involutional melancholia	1.0	6.4	4.5	6.0	6.0	60.9

From Kallmann, F. J. Twin studies in relation to adjustive problems of man. *Trans. N.Y. Acad. Sci.*, 1951, **13**, 270–275

We should not leave the impression that schizophrenia is the only disorder in which there are deficient reactions to stress or an inherited predisposition. Metabolism may be disturbed in other disorders, and as you see in Table 22.1, others also have a genetic basis. Since we could not take up all the mental disorders, we have used schizophrenia as an example because we know the most about it.

SUMMARY

1. The internal environment consists of the chemical conditions in the blood and tissues that affect nervous functions. It is regulated by hormones, enzymes, and vitamins.

2. Hormones are produced by such endocrine glands as the pituitary, adrenal, thyroid, parathyroid, pancreatic and gonadal. These control levels in the blood of such materials as water, sugar, salt, calcium, phosphorus, and other minerals.

3. Hormones probably do their work by regulating the supply of *enzymes*, which are catalysts manufactured in the body that aid or hinder particular chemical reactions.

4. Helping the enzymes in this function are the vitamins that are obtained by eating food in which they occur. Relatively small quantities of the hormones, enzymes, and vitamins are required to carry on the regulation of the internal environment.

5. The internal environment is known to be important in several aspects of behavior. One is the physiological needs. Appetites and aversions for different dietary components are greatly affected by hormone and vitamin levels.

6. Another is learning and intelligent behavior. Deficiencies in hormones and enzymes, as well as of oxygen, can produce feeble-mindedness. On the other hand, we have not yet found substances that can improve intelligence, although we may some day be successful.

7. Drugs are not normally a part of the internal environment, but they have their effects on the individual through this environment. Some drugs, such as alcohol, anesthetics, and narcotics can produce personality disorders similar to those we see in the psychoses. Some drugs, on the other hand, can be used to alleviate psychotic disorders or to relieve their symptoms temporarily.

8. Alcoholism, though often caused partly by motivational conflicts, can sometimes be alleviated by drug or vitamin therapy.

9. Severe or prolonged emotional stress may produce a general adaptation syndrome consisting of three stages: the alarm reaction, resistance to stress, and exhaustion. This adaptation syndrome often leads to psychoso-

matic disorders or aggravates such disorders as hypertension, rheumatism, arthritis, ulcers, and allergies.

10. The adrenal gland is especially involved in severe stress reactions. For this reason, ACTH, which normally stimulates the adrenal gland, and cortisone, which takes the place of insufficient adrenal hormone, are often used to treat disorders resulting from stress.

11. Personality disorders are produced both by motivational difficulties and by conditions in the internal environment. Schizophrenics, for example, do not show the same reactions of the internal environment to stress as do normal people.

12. Several kinds of psychosis occur much more frequently in people with a biological predisposition to them than in other individuals. This fact is demonstrated by extensive studies of the genetics of personality disorders.

SUGGESTIONS FOR FURTHER READING

Beach, F. A. *Hormones and behavior.* New York: Hoeber, 1948.
　A summary of experiments on the effects of hormones on behavior.
Dempsey, E. W. Homeostasis. In S. S. Stevens (Ed.), *Handbook of experimental psychology.* New York: Wiley, 1951. Chap. 6.
　A compact summary of the physiology of the internal environment.
Hoskins, R. G. *The biology of schizophrenia.* New York: Norton, 1946.
　A discussion of the biological factors in schizophrenia.
Hunt, J. McV. (Ed.). *Personality and the behavior disorders.* Vol. I. Locust Valley, N.Y.: Ronald, 1944. Part IV.
　Several chapters covering physiological processes associated with personality disorders.
Kallmann, F. *The genetics of schizophrenia.* New York: Augustin, 1938.
　A survey of work on the genetic predisposition to schizophrenia.
Morgan, C. T., and Stellar, E. *Physiological psychology* (2d Ed.). New York: McGraw-Hill, 1950. Chap. 25.
　A chapter like this one, only somewhat more detailed and technical.
Selye, H. *The physiology and pathology of exposure to stress.* Montreal: Acta, Inc., 1950.
　Descriptions of the adaptation syndrome and of various physiological reactions to stress.
Stone, C. P. (Ed.). *Comparative psychology* (3d Ed.). New York: Prentice-Hall, 1951. Chap. 5.
　A chapter on the relation between internal secretions and animal behavior.
Williams, R. J. *Nutrition and alcoholism.* Norman, Okla.: Univ. of Oklahoma Press, 1951.
　Nutritional factors in alcoholism.

Chapter 23 ANIMAL BEHAVIOR

IN MANY PLACES in this book we have described animal experiments and have drawn conclusions from them. Because this is an introductory book, however, we have not stressed animal behavior, nor have we always made it plain how much we have relied upon animal experiments. However, as we explained in Chapter 1, animal behavior is part of the field of psychology. First we shall comment on the reasons for studying animal behavior, then proceed to a review of the important facts and concepts pertaining to animal behavior.

Why study animal psychology? When Faraday announced his discoveries in the field of electricity, someone asked him "Of what use are they?" His reply was,

"What is the use of a newborn child?" Scientific discoveries are often made, as children are born, with no specific purpose. They are the product of the scientist's curiosity. Just as the proud parent enjoys his child, so the scientist enjoys his research. Then, when he has told others about it, they may also find it a source of interest and enjoyment. Research on animal behavior, as you will see, is a particularly fascinating subject.

When the child that is born for no specific purpose has grown mature and skillful, he eventually becomes a useful member of society. So does much of pure science. Faraday's discoveries in electricity are today the basis of countless benefits in modern society. There are similar benefits of research on animal behavior. A German scientist named Von Frisch, for example, dis-

This chapter was drafted by Eckhard H. Hess of the University of Chicago.

covered that bees have a language, and he spent many years studying it. When he learned what it was, it became possible to guide bees to certain crops, thereby promoting their pollinization and increasing the yield by 30 or 40 per cent. This is just one example of the application of knowledge about animal behavior. At the end of this chapter we shall cite others.

Animal behavior, of course, is especially useful to the psychologist who is interested in human behavior. People are sometimes unavailable or unwilling to participate in an experiment, so he turns to the use of animals. In other instances, he may wish to avoid or eliminate uncontrollable influences on human behavior. For example, he cannot very well rear a child in isolation for the first two years of its life, nor can he control the mating of human beings. Yet measures of this sort are necessary in the study of such factors as heredity, maturation, and environmental influences on behavior. In still other kinds of research, it may be necessary to operate on the brain or to remove some gland in order to carry out an experiment (see Chapters 21 and 22). Obviously people prefer not to be subjects in this kind of experiment, so the research psychologist, like the medical research worker, must turn to animals.

These are some of the reasons why animal behavior, as well as human behavior, is part of the subject of psychology. In a moment, we shall present a picture of some of the more interesting and useful facts that have been collected in the study of animal behavior. As you read, however, it would be well to keep in mind a few basic points about the biologist's classification of animals.

Kinds of animals.   All animals in the world may be divided into two main groups, the *vertebrates* and the *invertebrates*. If an animal has a segmented backbone, composed of vertebrae, it is a vertebrate; if not, it is invertebrate. Actually the vertebrates are only one of 17 major groups (phyla) of animals, and the invertebrates comprise all the other phyla (see Table 23.1 and Figure 23.1). Included in the vertebrates are five main classes: *fishes, amphibia, reptiles, birds,* and *mammals.* The mammals include most of our four-footed animals such as the cat, dog, rabbit, rat, bear, cow, pig, horse, and monkey. Man, though not strictly four-footed, is also a mammal. Of the various invertebrate groups, the one that includes the insects is the most important to us, not only because it is the most highly evolved of the invertebrates but also because it affects human affairs the most. So psychologists and zoologists have given considerable attention to insect behavior.

TABLE 23.1.   Some of the phyla, classes, and orders of the animal kingdom.

Phylum, Class, Order	Examples
Protozoa	Amoeba, paramecium
Porifera	Sponge
Coelenterata	Hydra, jellyfish, corals
Echinodermata	Starfish, sea urchins
Annelida	Earthworm
Mollusca	Clam, oyster, scallop
Arthropoda	
Crustacea	Lobster, crayfish, shrimp
Arachnida	Spiders, scorpions
Insecta	Insects
Chordata (subphylum Vertebrata)	
Pisces	Fish
Amphibia	Salamander, frog, toad
Reptilia	Turtle, lizard, snake
Aves	Birds
Mammalia	
Marsupialia	Kangaroo, opossum
Eutheria	
Insectivora	Mole, hedgehog
Rodentia	Rabbit, rat, mouse, squirrel
Ungulata	Cattle, deer, horse
Carnivora	Cat, dog, bear
Cetacea	Whale, dolphin, porpoise
Primates	Lemur, monkey, ape, man

■ PERCEPTION

The senses that we have described for man are typical of all the vertebrates. Although there are scattered exceptions, almost all of them have eyes, ears, chemical senses, skin senses, and deep senses of the same type that man has. The situation is somewhat different in the invertebrates. Single-celled animals, such as the *amoeba* and *paramecium*, do not, of course, have specialized receptors, although some of them may have part of the cell more sensitive to one kind of stimulus than another. The multicellular invertebrates, in general, have receptors with some of the same capacities as the human senses, but they usually are of rather different structure. The hearing organs of insects, for example, may be membranes on the legs or wings, and the eyes are complex affairs consisting of many individual "eyes" called *ommatidia*. Despite these structural variations, many of the facts of perception, as we have described them in previous chapters, are just as true of insects as they are of vertebrates and man. Let us consider these comparisons in a little more detail.

Vision. Ability to perceive light and dark is the most elementary of visual perceptions since it is to be found in almost every animal from the single-celled animals to the vertebrates. It is easy to tell this in insects because so many of them innately avoid or are attracted to light. In the case of animals that do not have these innate reactions, it

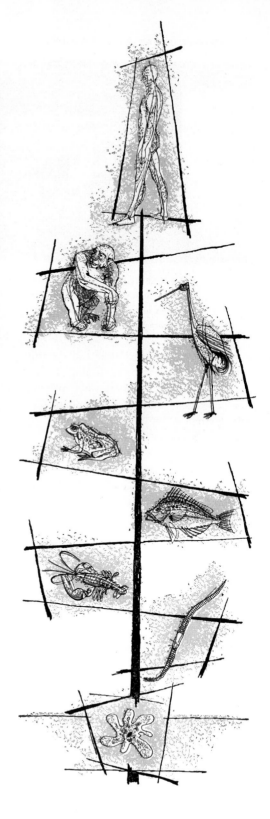

Fig. 23.1. Some branchings of the evolutionary tree. At the bottom is amoeba, a singled-celled animal. Above that are two examples of invertebrates, a worm and a crayfish. Then, in ascending order, are examples of vertebrates: fish, frog, bird, ape, and man.

Fig. 23.2. Testing visual discrimination in animals. This rat is jumping across a gap at an ink blot, behind which it will find food. Had it jumped to the other card, it would have found the door locked and would have fallen into a net below. The apparatus was devised by Dr. P. E. Fields. (*Science Service.*)

is possible to show that they can discriminate light from dark by rewarding them or punishing them in some way. Although some species of animals discriminate more acutely than others, no one *group* of animals seems more acute than another.

■ *Visual acuity.* Visual acuity— the ability to perceive patterns of lines and figures (see Chapter 18)—is generally poorer in the invertebrates than in the vertebrates and, in the typical case, is about one-tenth as good as ours. It varies somewhat among the vertebrates, but it usually is on a par with human visual acuity. Most birds have vision that is two or three times as acute as ours. We should probably expect theirs to be superior, because they must see at greater distances and rely on visual details more than we do. The primates, which include the monkeys, apes, and man, all seem to have about the same visual acuity.[1]

■ *Color vision.* The subject of color vision in animals has interested a good many people because we often use color in trying to lure or influence animals. The bullfighter with his red cape and the fisherman with his assortment of colored lures are examples.

It is very easy to be misled, however, about the reactions of animals to colors, because we cannot tell whether an animal is reacting to color or to the brightness of an object we show it.[6] It is very doubtful, for example, that a bull sees color. In all probability waving any kind of cape in front of it would serve to excite it. It takes rather careful tests, in which we can be sure animals are not reacting to brightness, to tell whether they have color vision. We have not yet been able to carry out such careful tests on very many animals.

From what we do know, however, we can say that some animals do have color vision and some do not, and that some have a very rudimentary color vision that is not nearly so good as ours. The rat, for example, can probably discriminate "red" and "not red," but no more.[2] Most of the common animals—horses, cows, dogs, cats, and mice—have either such imperfect color vision or no color vision at all. On the other hand, many invertebrates, including some insects, have well-developed color vision. Moreover, there seems to be no systematic trend from lower to higher animals. Color vision is well developed in many fishes, seems to be lacking in amphibia, is good in at least some reptiles, reaches a high level in birds, is lacking in some of the lower mammals that we mentioned above, and then reappears again in the monkeys, apes, and man. Thus it is difficult to draw generalizations about color vision on the basis of an animal's position in the evolutionary hierarchy. If we want to know about any particular animal, we have to test it to find out.

It is interesting to note that some animals can see parts of the electromagnetic spectrum that are invisible to us. You will remember (Chapter 18) that human beings are most sensitive at about 500 millimicrons in twilight and at 550 millimicrons in daylight. Most animals seem to have their best sensitivity in this range, and like man, they are able to see from about 400 to 760 millimicrons. Some of the insects, however, can see well down into the ultraviolet region* below 400 millimicrons.[3] We have no real notion of what *color* they perceive in this region, but we do know that it is the complementary of a yellow-green—a part of the spectrum for which we can find no complementary without mixing the two ends of the spectrum.

Hearing. Invertebrates and vertebrates have rather different auditory organs. Instead of an ear, for example, invertebrates have developed several different kinds of membranes that serve as microphones. Among insects, the legs and wings are the usual location for these membranes. Some insects can hear a wide range of sounds running up to several thousand cycles above the frequencies that man can hear. In many

* Man's vision in the ultraviolet would be much better than it is if it were not for the fact that the lens and other structures in his eyes absorb the ultraviolet and prevent it from stimulating his visual receptors.

insects—for example, the cricket—sound plays an important role in their behavior. It is difficult to state any general rule, however, about what frequencies insects hear and about how they use their hearing. When it is important for us to know such facts about any particular insect—and it sometimes is—we must conduct specific experiments to learn.[4]

Among the vertebrates, hearing contrasts with vision because it improves as we progress from fishes to man.[5] In fishes and amphibia, we find only a primitive organ of hearing. A large part of their "hearing" is not hearing at all but is a perception of mechanical vibration which is felt through the skin senses. Some of them, however, hear up to a few hundred or few thousand cycles per second. The range seems to be somewhat larger in reptiles and birds, but it is only when we get to mammals that we find frequency ranges that compare with

Fig. 23.3. The evolution of the inner ear in vertebrates. The vestibular apparatus does not change appreciably, but the cochlea begins to appear in the amphibian and is fully developed in the mammal.

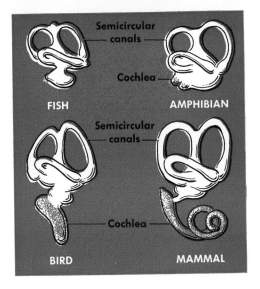

Fig. 23.4. A bat in flight. Bats emit very high frequency sounds which are reflected back from solid objects. By discriminating the direction of these reflected sounds, the bat can navigate around, finding food and nest. (*Courtesy H. E. Edgerton.*)

ours. In many mammals, moreover, the ranges are wider than ours (see Chapter 19). Dogs, for example, can hear sounds above 25,000 cycles per second, whereas we hear only up to 15,000 or 20,000 cycles per second. This makes it possible to train dogs to respond to the so-called "silent" whistle whose frequency they can hear and we cannot. Rats and monkeys both seem to hear higher frequencies than we do, and bats are able to hear and produce sounds as high as 40,000 or 50,000 cycles per second. By responding to the echoes of these extremely high frequencies when reflected from solid objects,[7] the bat is able both to navigate and to locate its food in a manner that has been called "bat radar."

Other senses. We do not know so much about the other senses of various animals as

we do about their vision and hearing. We do know that the acuity of these other senses is sometimes excellent and sometimes quite poor, according to the particular habits and needs of animals. Fishes, for example, live in an environment of water, which makes a good chemical medium, and they have highly developed chemical senses, especially of taste. Some, in fact, have taste buds all over their bodies, and it is interesting that many have greatly enlarged taste centers in their brains (see page 546). Birds, on the other hand, have almost no sense of smell and only a rudimentary sense of taste. They have very little occasion to use these senses, relying much more on their extremely acute vision.

We know very little about the skin senses in various animals, but we may infer that they are developed according to the degree to which animals make use of them. The deep senses of kinesthesis and of equilibrium (see page 505) seem to be highly developed in such animals as fishes and birds, which depend upon them to a high degree, and are about the same in most mammals as they are in man.

ORIENTATION

A dog or cat usually stands on its four feet so that its back is up and its belly downward. A fish, similarly, swims in the water with its belly downward. In fact, when you see one floating belly up, it is probably dead, because the "belly-down" orientation is a response to stimulation of the vestibular sense organs (see Chapter 19) and can take place only so long as the fish is alive. Lower animals also have a sense of equilibrium and orient with respect to gravity. They may also use other senses for such orientation. The common housefly, for example, responds to contact with a surface and is equally at home on the floor, wall, or ceiling. During flight, however, it moves with its dorsal surface upward, as do most flying animals.

Man and animals are alike in having this primary orientation to the earth and to the surfaces on which they stand. Unlike man, however, many animals have other kinds of orientation to different stimuli and situations. These other orientation reactions are "built in" to the organism and are displayed in the appropriate situation independent of learning.

Tropism, kinesis, and taxis. You must have observed examples of such orientation reactions, since they abound in common experience. The sunflower bends toward the sun by day and droops toward the ground by night. Fish tend to swim against a strong current. Night moths, mosquitoes, and many other insects are attracted to light—much to our annoyance when we want to read outside on a hot summer evening.

For many years students of animal behavior called such reactions as these *tropisms*, because *tropism* means "a turning movement." Now that we know much more about them, we find that the term tropism is better used in a more specific sense *to apply to bending or turning reactions in which the organism does not move from place to place.* Thus the bending of the sunflower toward the sun is a heliotropism—*helio* meaning "sun" and *tropism* meaning "turning." For reactions in which the animal *moves*, we use two other terms, *kinesis* and *taxis*.

A *kinesis is an undirected reaction* that is proportional to the intensity of a stimulus. A paramecium, for example, turns more frequently when it is in the light than when it is in the dark, but it does not necessarily move *toward* the light. Each time it turns, it may move toward or away from the light, but since it turns less frequently in the dark, it is less likely to turn from dark to

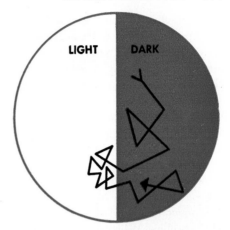

Fig. 23.5. Path of a single-celled animal having an undirected reaction (kinesis) to light. The animal turns more frequently in the light than in the dark. For this reason, it spends more time in the dark than in the light and appears to avoid light.

light than it is from light to dark. For this reason the animal spends more time in the dark than it does in the light, and thus it seems to avoid light (see Figure 23.5). A taxis, on the other hand, is a *directed reaction* to a stimulus in which the animal moves toward or away from a stimulus. A fish swimming against the current displays rheotaxis—*rheo* meaning "streaming movement" and *taxis* meaning "directed movement." A very common type of taxis is *tropotaxis*. In this kind of orientation the animal lines up its body in such a way that two sets of receptors—the eyes, for example—are stimulated with equal intensity. Then it moves forward. By making little adjustments when it gets off the path, it is able to go directly toward some source of stimulation. Thus the animal comes in "on a beam" just as a pilot does in following a radio beam into an airport. A good example of such tropotaxis is an insect flying toward some source of light.

One kind of taxis, *telotaxis*, is found only in response to light. To make this response, the animal has to have an eye which is made up of a number of elements—as bees do, for example—all pointed in different directions. By keeping a small source of light always in such a position that it stimulates one of the elements, the animal is able to steer a straight course to some point. This kind of navigation is sometimes called the light-compass reaction because it uses the sun as a compass point to steer by.

Transverse orientation. Bees use the light-compass reaction to maintain a *transverse orientation* toward sources of food and the beehive. When they move out from the hive in search of food, they keep the sun in a certain element of one of their faceted eyes. On the return trip, from food to home, they keep the sun in the corresponding element of the other eye. Thus they automatically end up in home territory —if they have not stayed away too long. In a classical experiment with ants,[15] which use the same method of orientation, ants were picked up on their way home and kept in a small dark box for about two and one-half hours. When subsequently released, they started off but missed their home by about the same number of degrees as the sun had moved during the intervening hours (Figure 23.6).

Among fishes we see another kind of transverse orientation to light. Fishes usu-

Fig. 23.6. The light-compass reaction in the homing ant. In its trek homeward toward N, an ant was kept in the dark for 2½ hours at a spot just above that marked with the cross. When released at the end of that time, it started homeward again but missed its home by the same number of degrees as the sun had moved in the intervening time. (*After Tinbergen, N. The study of instinct. London: Oxford Univ. Press, 1951.*)

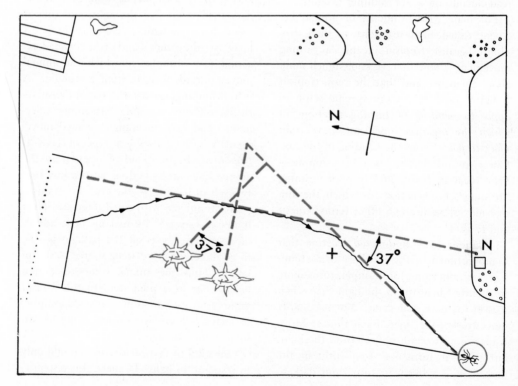

ally swim right side up because their vestibular organs respond to the pull of gravity. If, however, someone destroys a fish's vestibular system, it must fall back on the direction of light to keep its proper orientation. Light usually comes from above, so its response is merely to keep its back to the light. If you had such a fish in an aquarium, you could test its dependence on light simply by darkening the room and placing a light bulb *under* the aquarium (see Figure 23.7). Then you would see it nonchalantly swimming around upside down, always keeping the light "above" its back. The normal fish, however, does not behave this way because, even when the direction of light is inverted, its vestibular system keeps it orienting to gravity.

The language of bees. We explained above that bees can use the sun as a kind of "north pole" in a compass reaction. By keeping the sun in a certain element of their eyes, they can navigate back home from their feeding place. This in itself is a rather remarkable feat, but it is by no means the most wonderful of the bees' accomplishments. Bees not only can keep their orientation, *they communicate this orientation to other bees.* Indeed, they can tell other bees in the hive both the direction and the distance away from the hive where they found food. This "language of bees" was discovered by the German zoologist Von Frisch.[3] How he discovered it and learned what it is makes an interesting story.

Von Frisch once noticed that bees which had found a plentiful source of food would return to the hive and go through a particular kind of dance. This dance, he observed, was repeated a greater number of times per minute if the food source were near than if it were farther away. By making a great number of such observations, he was able to make a graph (see Figure 23.8) of the relationship between distance of food source

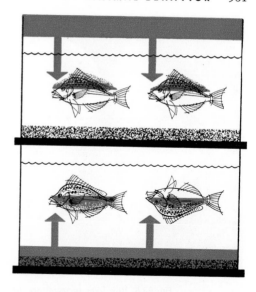

Fig. 23.7. Dorsal light reactions in the fish *Crenilabrus.* The colored arrows indicate the direction of light. On the left, top and bottom, is a normal fish. On the right is a fish whose vestibular organs have been removed. In light coming from below, it swims upside down.

and number of dances per minute. Thus he showed how bees communicate the *distance* of a food source.

But this was only part of the story. As he watched the bees, he noticed that their dances had a part in which they flew a straight course, all the time waggling their bodies. The direction of the straight course appeared to vary with the direction of the food. They seemed in this way to designate to other bees the *direction* of food. As in the light-compass reaction, they used the sun as a reference point. If the straight part of their dance led upward toward the sun, food was in the direction of the sun. If the direction of the straight "waggle" dance deviated 30 degrees to the right of the sun (see Figure 23.8), then food was to be found 30 degrees to the right. All other directions of the compass could be similarly indicated.

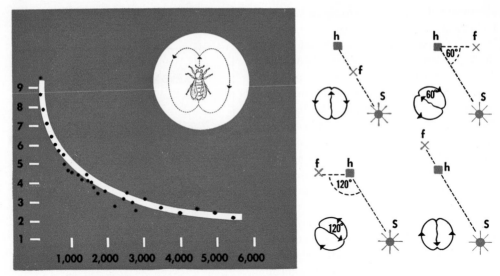

Fig. 23.8. How bees communicate the place in which they have found food. On returning to the hive, they execute a waggle dance diagramed in the inset. The speed of the dance (*graph*) communicates distance of food. Along the bottom of the graph is distance in thousands of meters; on the ordinate is number of turns in a 15-second period. The direction of food (*diagrams on right*) is communicated by varying the angle of the dance. The sun's bearing, straight up, is used as the reference point. If, for example, food (*f*) and the sun (*S*) make an angle of 60° with the hive (*h*), the angle of the dance is 60° off the vertical. (*Data of Von Frisch, K. Bees: their vision, chemical senses, and language. Ithaca, N.Y.: Cornell Univ. Press, 1950.*)

When Von Frisch had found this key to the language of bees, he decided to see whether he could really understand what the bees were saying. He had an assistant place a food source of sugar-water some distance from the hive, the distance and direction being unknown to Von Frisch. The assistant then marked the bees that located the sugar with a little colored shellac so that Von Frisch could know them as they returned to dance in the hive. By using a stop watch to time the number of dances per minute and a protractor to get the direction of the straight part of the dance, he was able to say, "The food has been placed so many yards from the hive and in such a direction." The assistant confirmed the fact that this was indeed the location of the food. Thus Von Frisch was able to show that bees not only can maintain their orien-

tation but can *communicate both orientation and distance to other bees.*

■ INSTINCTIVE BEHAVIOR

We have told the story of the language of bees as an example of orientation in animals. It is also an example of instinctive behavior—which raises another complex and fascinating subject.

Although laymen use the words *instinct* and *instinctive* rather loosely to describe almost any behavior that is habitual or "comes naturally," psychologists try to be careful how they bandy these words about (see discussion in Chapter 3). Since *instinctive* means "innate" or "built-in," they reserve the term for the kinds of behavior that, beyond reasonable doubt, are really innate and unlearned and are developed in the course of the maturation of an animal. It is not always easy to be sure on this point, for some habits are learned so universally by all animals of a species or all people in a culture that it takes very careful research to discover that they are not instinctive. We know, nevertheless, that some behavior is instinctive. We have already given examples in this chapter and in the chapter "Motivation," and we shall shortly give more.

We owe our modern conception of instinctive behavior to a European zoologist named Lorenz.[8] Instinctive behavior, he suggests, is really three kinds of behavior fitted into a pattern: *reflexes, taxes,* and *instinctive movements.* Reflexes are movements of specific limbs or muscles in response to stimulation. The various taxes, as you have just seen, are directed movements of the whole animal away from or toward some source of stimulation. Instinctive movements, however, differ from reflex and taxic movements in several important ways.

Species characteristics. Instinctive movements, first of all, are *species-specific.* Widely different animals in different phyla or groups may have similar reflex and taxic movements in common, but instinctive movements characterize particular species of animals. Many years ago, for example, a zoologist[9] noted that *all* pigeons drink in the same manner. They drink by lowering their heads into the water and then pumping it into their gullets. You can tell pigeons from other birds by this instinctive movement without the aid of structural differences.

The song that birds sing may also be a way of distinguishing species. One investigator[10] raised many different species of birds from the egg, giving them no chance to learn anything from their parents. In this way he could tell which items of behavior were learned and which ones developed innately. He found some species, for example,

which, when reared in isolation, were able to sing their characteristic song without ever having heard it before. In other species, this was possible only after the bird heard its song a few times.

The drinking of pigeons and the singing of birds are just two examples of instinctive movements that are specific to certain species of animals. This kind of evidence led Lorenz to believe that instinctive movements can be used as the basis of classification of different species of animals. By this means, in fact, Lorenz has been able to help reclassify various species within the group Anatinae (ducks) on the basis of similarities and differences in instinctive movements.

Releasers. Besides being species-specific, instinctive movements are *triggered* movements. Reflex and taxic movements are responses to stimulation; when the stimulus stops, they stop. Hence one can say that they are *steered* by a stimulus. Instinctive movements, however, need only to be started by a stimulus situation. Once started they can continue on without the original stimulus.

Let us take an example. Flies ordinarily clean their wings by passing their hind legs over and under the wings, meanwhile making small scrubbing movements. The gross movements of the legs back and forth are instinctive movements; the finer scrubbing movements are taxes. To demonstrate this, we need merely to remove the wings from the fly. When this is done, it still attempts to clean its wings periodically and moves its legs in the direction of the wings that are no longer there. Its smaller taxic responses, the scrubbing movements, however, are now missing. So the taxic movements drop out when the stimulus (wings) is no longer there, but instinctive movements continue.

From this triggering of instinctive movements we have developed the concept of the *releaser*. In the life of most animals, there are some kinds of unlearned behavior that are set off by extremely simple stimulus situations. In the male stickleback fish, for example, the color red releases an attack response. During the breeding season all male fish of this species develop bright red bellies, and at that time each of them drives away any other male that intrudes into its nesting area. It is the simple stimulus of color that seems to be the key to the attack response. For, by making different models and presenting them to male sticklebacks, we can show that little else matters except the red belly of the model (see Figure 23.10). (We might point out incidentally that the method of making models is one way of ferreting out the particular stimulus that sets off instinctive movements.)

The releaser is not always something as

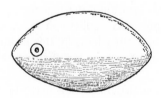

Fig. 23.9. The stickleback fish. The male stickleback is seen in its typical threat posture beside a mirror. (*Courtesy Dr. N. Tinbergen.*)

Fig. 23.10. Models used to test attack responses in male sticklebacks. The four models with red bellies release attack responses. The much more accurate model without coloring does not. (*After Tinbergen, N. The study of instinct. London: Oxford Univ. Press, 1951.*)

simple as a color. It may involve fairly complex relationships in the stimulus or environment. Figure 23.11, for example,
shows the silhouette of a bird. If someone
moves it overhead in the direction marked
plus, most game birds respond with fright
reactions. Moved in the opposite direction,
however, it does not bother them. Apparently when moved one way, it is perceived
as a short-necked bird of prey (hawk), but
moved in the other direction, it resembles
a long-necked waterfowl and is therefore
ignored. The response, in this case, has been
shown to be unlearned and may therefore
be regarded as an instinctive movement.

Thresholds for instinctive movements.
One other aspect of instinctive movements
is of importance. It, too, distinguishes them
from the taxes and reflexes. *The longer the
interval between instinctive responses, the
easier it is to set them off.* If, for example,
we use models to set off the attack response
in the stickleback and have left the fish
undisturbed for some time, then a model
with only the suggestion of red color is
enough to trigger off the attack. If, on the
other hand, we evoke the response several
times in succession, a more adequate coloring is necessary to elicit it. This example is
typical of the situations in which releasers
set off instinctive movements. The longer
the interval between responses, the more
readily the response comes; and vice versa.

You will probably recognize that this relation is also typical of motivated behavior.
It is as though there were some "need" for
making instinctive movements. When you
are very hungry, almost any kind of food is
acceptable. When you are moderately hungry, you are somewhat more particular
about your food, and you have to have
something *really special* to tempt you when
you are not hungry. In the case of instinctive movements, it appears that the movements satisfy some need or impulse to make

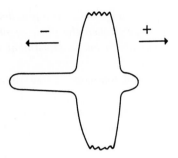

Fig. 23.11. Silhouette used to study the release of
fright reactions in game birds. For explanation, see
text. (*After Tinbergen, N. The study of instinct. London: Oxford Univ. Press, 1951.*)

them and that the stimulus must be more
adequate when the need is low than when it
is high.

◼ LEARNING

Most animals have a repertoire of instinctive movements. Such animals as the
insects, fish, and birds have a rather large
number of them; most mammals have somewhat fewer. But what about human beings?
Do people make instinctive movements?
Think hard for a moment and see whether
you can recall any human behavior that can
rightly be called instinctive. Remember that
instinctive movements must (1) be characteristic of the species, (2) be released by
external stimuli, and (3) wax and wane
with how much they have been exercised.
The chances are that you will not be able to
think of any, for instinctive movements are
apparently missing from man's patterns of
behavior. Some of the responses of young
infants—sucking, for example—are undoubtedly instinctive movements, but we
do not know too much about the early development of most of these processes. In
the place of instinctive behavior, you find
an ability to learn and think that is far
superior to that of the animals. Indeed, it

is fair to conclude that *learning and thinking have largely taken the place of instinctive movements in man's adjustment to his environment.*

Precursors of learning. From the study of animals, however, we can also tell something about the beginnings of learning— what it is like under the most primitive of conditions. In our account of learning in Chapter 5 and elsewhere, we have indicated that reinforcement is necessary for conditioning or instrumental learning to take place. Such reinforcement might be a shock, a piece of food, a grade, a compliment, or even the "feeling of a job well done." In certain situations with animals, however, we can see something akin to learning taking place without such a reinforcement. Here, it seems, we can observe the *precursors of learning.*

▪ *Habituation.* Suppose you have an animal in a cage—a dog, cat, rabbit, or rat— and suddenly sound a loud siren hidden in the floor of the cage. The chances are that the animal will respond with a sort of fright reaction, such as crouching or dashing about the cage. If, however, you sound the siren at regular intervals, the animal slowly becomes accustomed to it and acts less and less frightened. This change in the

animal's behavior is *habituation* and is a simple kind of learning. It is merely learning *not* to respond to a situation that proves harmless. You can sometimes see this habituation in a child, but it is more commonly seen in animals, especially in the process of taming.

▪ *Sensitization.* Closely related to habituation—in fact, almost its opposite—is a simple kind of learning called *sensitization.* To illustrate it, suppose that we have gotten our animal subject (see below) habituated to the sound of a siren. When the siren comes on, the animal no longer responds to it but goes about his business in the cage. Now suppose that through a grid in the floor of the cage we give the animal a few electric shocks. After that, if we sound the siren again, we will find that the animal again shows its original fright reaction. The shock has made the animal more "sensitive" and thus has reinstated responses that had died out.

This process is probably the most elementary precursor of learning, for we find it in the simplest one-celled animal. In a now classic experiment,[16] a zoologist placed a single paramecium in a small enclosure, about five millimeters in diameter, so arranged that half of it was in darkness and

Fig. 23.12. The sensitization of a paramecium to light. Before training, the paramecium swims in both light and dark parts of the container (*left*). During training, it avoids the lighted and hot part (*middle diagram.*) After training, it continues to avoid light even though entire container is again at a uniform temperature (*right diagram*).

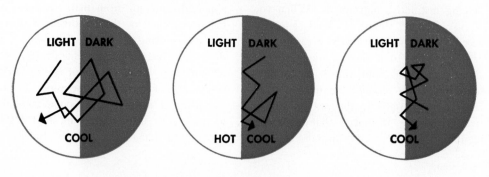

Fig. 23.13. Imprinting of goslings. The goslings have been imprinted on the experimenter, Dr. Konrad Lorenz. Though he carries a food bucket, his rhythmic sounds, not hunger, keep them with him. (*Courtesy Life Magazine* © *Time Inc.*)

the other half in the light (see Figure 23.12). The paramecium would swim about in the drop of water, spending some of the time in the light and some in the dark. Then the experimenter transferred the animal with a pipette to another drop of water, but one in which the light half was too warm while the dark half was at normal temperature. He observed that the paramecium soon came to avoid the light-warm part of the container. Then he transferred the animal back to its original container, which was of uniform temperature but still half dark, half light. He noticed that now the animal continued to avoid the lighted half of the environment. Thus it looked as though the paramecium had formed a conditioned response to light.

This result, however, troubled psychologists, for they had reason to believe that a nervous system, possessed only by more complex multicellular animals, is necessary for true learning. Subsequent experimentation proved them right, for when the attempt was made to condition the paramecium to the dark as it had been to the light, it failed. It became clear, in fact, that the warm water had sensitized the paramecium so that it avoided light, but it could not learn to associate warm water with either light or dark. Higher animals that possess a nervous system, however, can be conditioned to do this. Sensitization is thus a primitive precursor of learning that can take place in single-celled animals which are otherwise not capable of learning. (Sensitization is sometimes called pseudo conditioning, because it is not true conditioning but may easily be confused with it.)

▪ *Imprinting.* Another precursor of learning, closely linked with instinctive behavior, has only recently been given detailed study.[11] One investigator hatched out some goose eggs in an incubator and happened to be present when the eggs hatched. For this reason he was the first large moving object that the goslings saw. Much to his surprise, the goslings began following him about and acted as though he, rather than the mother goose, were their parent. The young goslings, in fact, would have nothing to do with their mother and insisted on having his constant company. *This learning, which takes place very rapidly and without any specific reward, is called imprinting.*

We have not yet fully explored the phenomenon of imprinting. We already know, though, that it is fairly widespread among birds. We know too that it can take place only *during a short interval* (a few hours or a day or two) and *at a certain time* (usually shortly following birth) in the life of an animal.[12] It also seems to be *irreversible;* once it has taken place, it is difficult to alter through subsequent learning. There may, however, be some **true** learning connected with it. Young goslings, for example, at first follow any person if a human being has been the first object with which they have contact after hatching. A few days later, however, they learn the individual characteristics of the person who ordinarily leads them to food and shelter, and then they will follow no one else. Thus imprinting may be a natural stage in the maturation of an animal.

Precursors of thinking. Man is better able than animals to *form concepts, to recall previous experiences, to imagine* relations in the external world, and *to represent the world with the symbols in language.* In a word, *man is better able to think.* When he has no opportunity to use his thinking abilities, he is no better than animals at trial-and-error learning or conditioning; when he has, he excels the animals.

As we indicated in Chapter 6, however, animals have some of these abilities. In fact, we can find each of the abilities involved in thinking present in some measure in some animal. The very fact that these abilities are considerably more rudimentary in animals is an advantage to the psychologist, for it allows him to experiment more easily with what otherwise are very difficult problems. Thus he can get at the precursors of thinking. Let us consider some of them briefly.

▪ *Delayed response.* Of the many aspects of thinking, one is an ability to *recall* at will, without any specific cue or stimulus, the time, place, or name of an event. We can test this kind of ability in animals with the delayed-response experiment (see Chapter 6). An animal may be shown where some food is hidden; then, after an interval in which it has had no cues, it may be allowed to go find the food. Most animals are able to do this. For rats, the interval after which they can respond correctly may be only a few seconds, for a dog a few minutes, for an ape several hours. In Chapter 6, we discussed experiments of this kind in some detail.[13]

▪ *Orderliness.* Another aspect of thinking is a matter of recalling the order in which things should be done. In giving a motorist directions, for example, you may be able to say, "Go three blocks, turn left; then two blocks, turn right. . . ." You can do this without remembering exactly what the corners look like or having any signs to guide your thinking. This kind of ability to do things in the correct order without specific objective cues is better in monkeys and apes than in lower animals and better in man than in monkeys and apes.

There have been several experiments to test this capacity in animals, but one of the clearest employs the "three-pedal box." This box has three platforms in it, arranged

TABLE 23.2. Limits reached by various mammals tested on the three-pedal-problem apparatus. The scores represent the length of a sequence of responses that can be learned.

Type of animal	Number of animals tested	Range of steps	Median	Average
Guinea pig	16	0– 1	1	0.5
Rat	24	0– 2	1	0.9
Kitten	62	3– 7	3	3.6
Rhesus monkey	17	2–22	5	7.4
Cebus monkey	6	5–15	9½	9.8

Modified from Munn, N. L. *The evolution and growth of human behavior.* Boston: Houghton Mifflin, 1955. P. 125.

as you see them in Figure 23.14. The experimenter can so arrange things that the animal must push these pedals *a particular number of times in a required order* to secure a food reward. He may require the animal to push simply 1, 2, and 3, in that order, or to push them 1, 3, 1, 2, 3, 2, . . ." He can then determine the longest order that an animal can correctly master. In Table 23.2, you see the results of experiments with different animals. Guinea pigs and rats are not very good at it, for they can, on the average, master a series only one or two pushes long. The kitten is somewhat better, with three. The monkey is still better, with five to ten. And children can master much longer series than that. So you can see that the ability to remember the order in which things should be done increases markedly from lower mammals to man.

▪ *Counting.* The ability to count develops slowly in children, usually two years or so after they have acquired the rudiments of language. It may be regarded as one of the more complex mental processes. Actually, there are not one but rather three ways of counting. One is *subitizing,* which is *perceiving a number of objects at a glance* without saying "one, two, three. . . ." A second

is *estimating,* which is *guessing a number without counting.* And thirdly, there is *true counting.*

You have probably heard about or seen "talking and counting" horses and dogs. They are often featured in vaudeville, motion pictures, or television. These animals, however, cannot count; they merely respond to cues from the trainer. Birds, however, can subitize. To see what they can do, please read the instructions at the bottom of page 590 (Figure 23.15). Which has the more dots, the pattern on the right or the one on the left? Birds that have been used in experiments can do just as well as

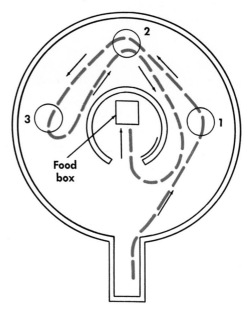

Fig. 23.14. The three-pedal box. Problems may be arranged to require pushing of the pedals in different orders. A relatively simple problem is 1-2-3, but a more complex one is 1-2-3-2-1-2-1-3-2-1. Comparing the performance of different animals in the box gives an idea of the development of abilities in the animal kingdom. (After Fjeld, H. A. *The limits of learning ability in Rhesus monkeys. Genet. Psychol. Monogr.,* 1934, 15, 403.)

you or I at this sort of counting, provided that the total number does not exceed six or seven. It is interesting, indeed, that both birds and people can subitize only about six or seven items. Above that number, people must estimate or take time to count, whereas birds are unable to arrive at the correct answer. Birds, however, can master other difficult problems involving numbers.

For one thing, they can match from sample. In Figure 23.16, you see a number of circles each of which has a number of dots. On the boxes are patterns of irregularly shaped blotches. A trained bird can pick out the proper box from the total group when shown any one of the circles and open only the lid of the box that has the matching number of spots. Again, however, the total number of spots cannot exceed seven.

A bird can also learn to leave a certain number of food objects and to eat no more than that number—say four. To train him to do this, the experimenter must shoo him away from a small pile of seeds when he has eaten all but four. After sufficient training, the bird stops eating when four grains are left. Similarly, the bird can learn to leave the number of grains shown him on a cardboard. If it has three or four or five spots,

the bird will leave the corresponding number of grains. This takes a little more elaborate training than the other tasks, but the bird can learn to do it.

THE USES OF ANIMAL BEHAVIOR

We opened this chapter with the question, Why study animal behavior? Perhaps you will agree now that it is both interesting and helpful in understanding human behavior. Besides that, however, animal behavior has some immediate uses in human affairs. You are already familiar with some of these, but there are others you probably do not know about.

In many instances, animals have better sensory acuity than man, and this fact has long been put to advantage. Watchdogs are employed to protect homes and property because they have keen hearing and smell. Bloodhounds can track down criminals and people who are lost, because they excel in olfactory sensitivity. Similar abilities in other dogs have made them useful in hunting. The Seeing Eye dog can be trained to take the place of a person's vision. These and many other instances are well known to everybody.

Fig. 23.15. Take a brief glance at the two blotches, then turn to the footnote on page 592.

Not so well known, however, are some special uses of animals as "detectors." Canaries are very sensitive to noxious gases and have been used in coal mines and tunnels to detect such gases. In Europe, the "weather frog" is often used as a prophet of rain. When kept in an aquarium partly filled with water, it will climb up a ladder to signal rain. Such behavior is a reasonably good predictor of rain because the frog climbs the ladder only when the humidity is high, which is usually before or during a rain.

Recently minnows have come into use to detect the pollution of streams—a problem of increasing technological importance. To use them as pollution detectors, minnows are first trained in an aquarium to avoid the side in which traces of polluting material are added.[14] The training follows standard conditioning procedures (see Chapter 5) in which an electric shock is paired with approaching the polluted side. In this way, they quickly learn to avoid polluted water. Once they have been trained in the laboratory, they can be taken into field situations. If water is suspected of pollution, a little of it may be introduced into the minnows' tank. By observing their responses, it is possible to tell whether even extremely small amounts of polluted material are present—because the minnow is extremely sensitive to dissolved material.

In our society, some animals are desirable and profitable, while others are a nuisance or a harm. Exterminating unwanted animals is a big job. Doing it by poison or traps is often expensive and/or ineffective. The mosquito, which is both a personal nuisance and a health hazard, is a good case in point. It happens, however, that male mosquitoes are attracted by the "mating call" or buzz of the female mosquito. This noise can easily be simulated. Electrified traps which sound the simulated

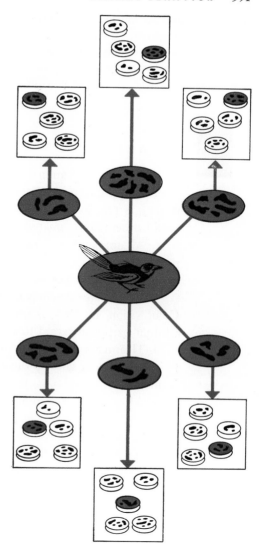

Fig. 23.16. Matching-from-sample problems used with birds. Six different problems are shown. In red are the sample and the correct one of a group of stimuli. The bird is shown the sample and a group of irregularly shaped blotches. A trained bird can pick out the stimulus having the same number of blotches as the sample. (*Based on the work of Koehler, O. Zahl-versuche an einem Kolkraben und Vergleichsversuche an Menschen. Z. f. Tierpsychol., 1943, 5, 575–712.*)

call of the mosquito can lure thousands of males to electrocution.[17]

These are a few examples of ways in which animal behavior may be used for man's benefit. Others are in common use, and still others are yet to be discovered. It is possible that specialists in animal behavior may some day be among those who play an important role in agriculture and public health.

SUMMARY

1. The study of animal behavior is interesting in its own right; it has practical applications in entertainment, agriculture, and public health; and it permits psychologists to answer questions about human behavior that would otherwise be unanswerable.

2. All animals from the lowly amoeba to man have sensory capacities permitting them to respond to stimuli, but the higher animals usually have more highly developed sense organs and better perceptual abilities.

3. Vertebrates generally have better visual acuity than the invertebrates. Color vision, however, is present in many animals and absent in others without particular regard to status in the animal kingdom.

4. Hearing is present in many invertebrates, but in vertebrates it tends to improve as one goes up the evolutionary scale. It is best, on the average, in mammals.

5. Most plants and animals orient themselves with respect to the earth and light. Many insects and lower vertebrates, however, exhibit specific bending or turning movements, called *tropisms*.

6. They may also make undirected movements called *kineses* or directed movements called *taxes*. All these reactions are in response to stimulation.

7. Some insects can navigate with great accuracy to and away from home by taking account of the position of the sun. Bees even are able to communicate to each other the place in which they have found food by performing a dance oriented with respect to the sun.

8. Instinctive movements have three important characteristics: (*a*) They are species-specific; each species of animal makes its instinctive movements in a distinctive way. (*b*) They are released by external stimuli; once they are triggered off by a stimulus, they continue in the absence of the stimulus. (*c*) They have thresholds that depend on the interval of time since they were last released; a relatively stronger stimulus is required if the interval has been short than if it has been long.

How many blotches were on the left side of Figure 23.15? How many on the right? When you have decided on your answer, turn back to determine whether you are correct. This is a demonstration of subitizing.

9. The precursors of learning can be seen in experiments with animals. Lower animals, for example, are readily habituated; if a stimulus, such as a loud sound, that normally alarms the animal, is presented a number of times, it comes to have no effect. Animals also show sensitization; a shock or other strong stimulus can make the animal more sensitive to other stimuli. Even single-celled animals exhibit this precursor of learning.

10. In animals, too, we see the phenomenon of imprinting—a kind of learning that takes place rapidly without any specific reward and during a relatively short period in the animal's infancy.

11. Animals also show some of the rudiments or precursors of thinking because they are able in many instances (*a*) to make delayed responses, (*b*) to learn a certain order of making responses, and (*c*) to count.

12. Animal behavior has many uses. Among them are (*a*) the employment of animals as "detectors," and (*b*) methods for catching and eliminating animals.

SUGGESTIONS FOR FURTHER READING

Köhler, W. *The mentality of apes.* New York: Harcourt, Brace, 1925.
> *An account of experiments on learning and thinking in apes.*

Maier, N. R. F., and Schneirla, T. C. *Principles of animal psychology.* New York: McGraw-Hill, 1935.
> *A text tracing the development of behavior from single-celled animals to man.*

Munn, N. L. *A handbook of psychological research on the rat.* Boston: Houghton Mifflin, 1950.
> *A comprehensive summary of over 2,500 experiments on the behavior of the rat.*

Munn, N. L. *The evolution and growth of human behavior.* Boston: Houghton Mifflin, 1955. Chaps. 2–5.
> *A compact summary of the evolution of behavior.*

Stone, C. P. (Ed.). *Comparative psychology* (3d Ed.). New York: Prentice-Hall, 1951.
> *A standard text on animal behavior, emphasizing mammalian behavior.*

Tinbergen, N. *The study of instinct.* London: Oxford Univ. Press, 1951.
> *An interesting account of experimental studies of instinct, especially in birds.*

Von Frisch, K. *Bees: their vision, chemical senses, and language.* Ithaca, N.Y.: Cornell Univ. Press, 1950.
> *A fascinating little book describing years of experimental work and of field studies with bees.*

Yerkes, R. M. *Chimpanzees: a laboratory colony.* New Haven, Conn.: Yale Univ. Press, 1943.
> *A summary of many observations and experiments on chimpanzees.*

TECHNIQUES OF STUDY

IN MANY PLACES throughout this book, we have described the applications of psychology to practical problems. To learn more about these applications, the student may enroll in other courses in psychology that cover his particular field of interest or study some of the books listed under "Suggestions for Further Reading" at the end of each chapter. One particular phase of applied psychology, however, is of importance to all students, regardless of their special interests. This is the improvement of study techniques. Considerable psychological research has been carried out on this subject. The practical benefits of this research can be used by the student here and now. Indeed, the sooner he makes use of them, the better. For that reason, we have included in

This chapter was drafted by James Deese of The Johns Hopkins University.

the book this brief chapter, which summarizes our present knowledge of techniques of study, as well as of some closely related problems. We have put the chapter at the end of the book because it is a "how to" chapter, somewhat different in character from the others. We recommend, however, that the student read it at the earliest opportunity.

Improving study habits. Almost every college student feels at one time or another that he should improve his study habits. If you are a typical student, you have probably worried about this yourself. The chances are, though, that you have done little about it, or if you have, your attempts probably have been haphazard and unsystematic. At least this is true of most students.

The fact is that most students do not know the best ways to improve their study habits, though there are some tried and proven ways of doing it. In this chapter are some principles which, if you understand and apply them, will make it easier for you to do good work, not only in this course but in all your studies.

But there is no magic in these techniques. Here, as everywhere else, there is no easy road to success. You will find it hard work to apply them—at least most of them. If you try them seriously, though, you should be well rewarded by learning more with less effort, by enjoying your studies more, and by making higher grades.

You might think that hints on how to study are only for the students who are hanging precariously on the edge of a C average. Actually they help good students as well as poor ones. In fact, several surveys[1] show that students who are already doing well profit the most from instructions in how to study. But whatever your grade average may be, there is reasonable possibility of raising it by practicing the most efficient techniques of study described below.

Being motivated. The hardest problem of all is to be motivated to study. One's motivation may be strong enough to read a book or chapter on "how to study" but not strong enough to follow its precepts. It requires some effort to study, and some amount of motivation is necessary before you will expend the needed effort. Without motivation no set of rules will do much good. It is hard to change one's motivation, but it can be done and is worth a try.

What are your motives and how strong are they? Could you make a list of your major motives and interests? More specifically, why did you come to college, what do you expect to gain from study, and what do you expect to do after college?

Perhaps the answer is simply that you would like to get a good job, become a distinguished member of the community, and

"make a lot of money." Certainly that is why some people go to college. If this is true of you, look carefully at the following facts: Those who make the best grades in college, are, on the average, those who make the best incomes later on.[2] The member of Phi Beta Kappa, for example, typically earns considerably more than college graduates in general.[3] And those who enjoy the distinction of being in *Who's Who* had, on the average, higher college grades than those who do not. Walter Gifford, former president of the American Telephone and Telegraph Company, wrote an article for *Harper's Magazine* in which he pointed out that the earning capacity of employees in his company showed a very close relation to their grades in college.[2]

There are probably several reasons for this correlation between grades and success in later life. If other things are equal, the person of the greatest ability should make both the best grades in college and the greatest success in employment. Undoubtedly, too, employers are often impressed by good grades and offer better employment opportunities to those who have them. Finally, learning to study effectively and thus to make good grades probably carries over into doing a good job and becoming a success. Whatever the explanation, the fact argues for doing the best one can in his college work.

Perhaps your main goal is to go on to professional school or graduate school to get a law degree, a medical degree, or a master's or doctor's degree. Here grades are especially important—perhaps too important—in being admitted to study. And if it is a scholarship you need to go on for such study, or even to stay in college, the competition is severe, and grades are all the more important.

But grades are only incidental. Your ultimate purpose in college should be to

TABLE 1. A sample schedule for a college student. This schedule is for a typical student carrying a moderately heavy load. Notice that the times set aside for study are labeled for specific subjects. Study time is about 25 hours per week; the student is also employed for 10 hours a week.

	Monday	Tuesday	Wednesday	Thursday	Friday	Saturday
7–8 a.m.	Dress, breakfast	Dress, breakfast	Dress, breakfast	Dress, breakfast	Dress, breakfast	
8–9 a.m.	Economics lecture	**Study economics**	Economics lecture	**Study psychology**	Economics lecture	Dress, breakfast
9–10 a.m.	**Study German**	English literature class	**Study German**	English literature class	**Study German**	Organic chem. lab.
10–11 a.m.	German class	**Study German**	German class	**Study German**	German class	Organic chem. lab.
11–12 a.m.	Psychology lecture	**Study German or psychology**	Psychology lecture	**Study German or psychology**	Psychology lecture	Organic chem. lab.
12–1 p.m.	Lunch	Lunch	Lunch	Lunch	Lunch	Lab. cont'd or lunch
1–2 p.m.	Organic chem. lecture	Study or recreation	Organic chem. lecture	Study or recreation	Organic chem. lecture	Lunch or recreation
2–3 p.m.	**Study organic chem.**	**Study psychology**	**Study organic chem.**	**Study psychology**	**Study organic chem.**	Recreation or study
3–4 p.m.	**Study economics**	ROTC or athletics	**Study economics**	ROTC or athletics	**Study organic chem.**	Recreation or study
4–5 p.m.	Employed	Employed	Employed	Employed	Employed	Recreation
5–6 p.m.	Employed	Employed	Employed	Employed	Employed	Recreation
6–7 p.m.	Dinner	Dinner	Dinner	Dinner	Dinner	Dinner
7–8 p.m.	**Study English**	**Study organic chem.**	**Study English**	**Study for subject that needs "catching up," library time**	Recreation, make-up study, or library	Recreation
8–9 p.m.	**Study English**	**Study organic chem.**	**Study English**			Recreation
9–10 p.m.						Recreation

learn facts and principles that will be of value later on in both work and play. Most of that learning will come from formal study in courses. Mastering the art of study will lead to better understanding, make you more at home with books and ideas, and provide a good deal more intrinsic satisfaction to the learning process in college. This alone is worth considerable effort.

Perhaps you are not clear about your goals in college. Perhaps you can't seem to find what interests you. Or perhaps, try as you may with all the best techniques of study, you just do not seem to succeed. In that case you may need the help of an adviser—a counselor or professional psychologist. He may be able to help you straighten out your motivations. He will have, among other things, some methods for finding out something about your vocational interests and abilities and for guiding you to the best program of study.

In any event, the point of this whole section is that you must be motivated to study in order to succeed at studying. The best of study techniques will be of no value to you unless you really want to reap the full benefits of your opportunities to learn.

ORGANIZING A STUDY ROUTINE

Surveys[1] of the study habits of college students show that they report three major difficulties in trying to study. One is that *they do not get as much studying done as they should.* Another is that *they waste time going from one thing to another.* The third is that *they have difficulty settling down to work.* These ills have remedies, and it may be of some help to you to look at them.

Setting up a schedule. The first thing to do is to *set up a schedule for studying.* A well-planned schedule makes time, and if you think that you do not study enough, a schedule that outlines definite times for study will help. It need not deprive you of time for other activities; it simply will see to it that each gets its fair share. It is a fact that students who work at outside jobs or have extracurricular activities, on the average, make better grades than those who do not.[4] Students who work outside are forced to schedule their time and in so doing are more likely to provide definite times for study. And if you plan your daily life well, you will find more time to study and to do other things than you had thought possible.

Table 1 shows one way to arrange a schedule. It is for a typical, though mythical, student. Notice that the time is blocked off in one-hour periods and that each period is earmarked for a specific subject. The time from seven to nine in the evening, for example, is not just blocked off for "study," it is set aside for specific subjects.

Two or three pointers may help you decide just when to schedule different subjects for study. In general, *a study period for a particular subject should come close to its class period.* If the class is mostly lecture, it is better to have the study period come shortly afterward so that you can review your lecture notes—but you should read assignments in the text *before* the lecture. If the class is recitation, then the study period is best put before the class so that the subject will be fresh in mind when you go to class.

How much time? The amount of time you allot to any particular subject depends on individual circumstances. Knowing that a particular course is difficult for you, or likely to be so, you will schedule more time to study for it. Moreover, even though you should have a schedule at the beginning of the term, you will want to modify it as the term goes along, in the light of your experience with how much time it takes you to meet the demands of the various courses.

Of course, in order to make out a schedule you need to know not only how to distribute your study time but how much you should study altogether. This too turns out to be a highly individual matter. Figure 1 shows the distribution of study time for a large number of college students, based on an actual survey. There you can see that some students study as much as 53 hours a week, while some get by on less than 10. Intellectual ability has something to do with the hours of study required, but so do study habits—as we are emphasizing here. Studying many hours does not necessarily mean higher grades, for one research worker[5] found that those who studied more than 35 hours a week made poorer grades than those who studied less.

To find out how much time to give to study, you must *evaluate your own abilities and study habits*. In doing this, it is best to be on the safe side, for most students tend to overestimate their own intelligence, speed of reading, ability to work, etc. It will therefore pay to be critical of how much you can accomplish in an allotted time, especially if your ambition is high. On the other hand, leave plenty of time for eating, sleeping, and leisure. Do not count too much on "grinding" unless you are sure you can do it, for trying to do too much often leads one to give up altogether. After you have made out a schedule, check yourself from time to time to see whether you have planned too much or too little time for various activities.

Getting down to work. Many students set up a schedule for themselves only to find that it does not help much because they never seem to be able to settle down to work. One student, for example, may make a determined effort to study French.

Promptly at seven o'clock and according to schedule, he sits down at his desk. In a moment he discovers that his pencil needs sharpening, and he runs across the hall to the room of a friend who has a sharpener. There he finds an interesting discussion in progress on the merits of Fords versus Chevrolets. Becoming absorbed in this, it is some time before he remembers that he is supposed to be studying French. Starting back to his room again with good intentions, he remembers that there is a good radio program on, and he convinces himself that it is just as easy to study French with the radio on as off. Next, our student, with his attention divided between the radio and the French text, finds himself gazing absently at a picture on his desk which conjures up fond memories of the last week end. And so it goes. Ten o'clock comes—time to go out for a hamburger—and he still has no work done.

This dribbling away of time is the major stumbling block to effective study. If this is your problem, try to solve it slowly and carefully. Start out by making your study periods short and interspersed with periods of rest. Then make sure to work during the study period, for it is much more *important to work effectively for short periods* than to schedule long periods and fritter them away in aimless procrastination. Once you have gotten into the swing of an easy schedule of work and rest, you can gradually change to working over longer and longer periods of time.

Where to study? The college library is probably the best place to work. At least there is good evidence that students who habitually study in the library make better grades than other students.[6] This is probably because the library keeps distractions at a minimum. It provides less opportunity to talk, it has no radio that one can turn on, and it makes one somewhat more

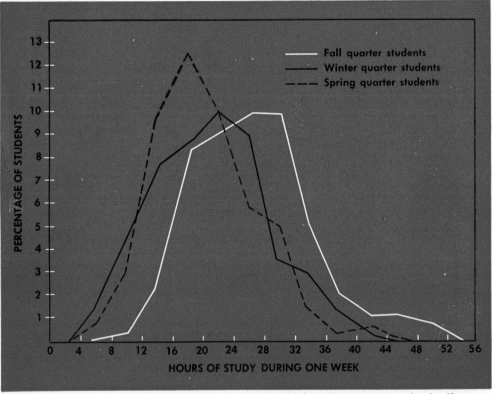

Fig. 1. Distribution of time spent in study each week by students in a state university. The curves show hours of study during one week for 108 fall-quarter students, 57 winter-quarter students, and 53 spring-quarter students enrolled in how-to-study classes. Notice the very great variation in amount of study. Also note the somewhat greater efforts of students in the fall quarter. (*After Bird, C., & Bird, D. M. Learning more by effective study. New York: Appleton-Century-Crofts, 1945, p. 56.*)

embarrassed to be seen daydreaming. Many students, however, claim that they feel uncomfortable in the library. Perhaps that is because they are not really motivated to study or are afraid that they are missing out on a good time at the dormitory or fraternity. But if you make up your mind to study in the library and go there only when you really intend to study, you should find it a good place to get some work done.

Although libraries on the whole are good places to study, some people can and do study effectively in their rooms or even on park benches. If you study in your room,

make sure that your room is equipped for it. The best place to study is at a desk, not on the bed. And a clean desk is a better place than a desk cluttered with mementos and pictures. Also a desk that faces the wall offers a little better protection against distraction than does one that faces a window or door (see Figure 2).

THE TECHNIQUE OF STUDY

Having stressed the importance of motivation and work schedule, we can now say more specifically how to improve study

Fig. 2. Study is best done at a desk, uncluttered and free of distractions.

habits. Every student, of course, has his own techniques, and this to a certain extent is a good thing. Different techniques are suited to different people. Nevertheless, there are some general rules, and it is worthwhile to see what they are.

Perhaps the best set of rules is to be found in the *Survey Q3R Method*.[1] This grew out of an elaborate program at The Ohio State University that was designed to analyze and treat students' academic problems. We can rely on it as being a soundly tested system. It consists of five specific steps, labeled *Survey, Question, Read, Recite*, and *Review*, and this is why it is called the Survey Q3R Method.

Survey. When most authors write textbooks, they go to some pains to organize their words under various headings so that the headings tell readers what they may expect to find in each section. If you leaf through this book, for example, you find scarcely a page without such a heading. Many students, however, ignore the headings and try to read textbooks in the same way they read novels. When they do that, they ignore much of the author's careful work and flounder in a morass of information they are not prepared to assimilate.

One important precept, then, is *use the headings*. They give the author's organization, they tell you how the material is put together, and they make it clear how topics go together and follow each other. Most important, they make it clear what the main subject of each section is going to be.

When you finish reading a section, you should have located a few points that bear on the heading. Anything else in the section will be secondary or relatively unimportant. The student should also pay attention to the order of headings. Most textbooks use two or three orders of headings. This one, for example, has three: center headings, main side headings, and side subheadings. To assist the reader in recognizing easily the main side headings, we have used a color bar to the left of each such heading.

At this point, the student who has noticed the heading of this section will realize that we have not yet come to the main idea, for that heading reads "Survey." We told you about headings in order to lead up to that point, and now we come to it. The first thing in picking up a textbook is to run through the headings of the various chapters, for this is a way of *surveying* the book in general. In starting on a chapter, begin by surveying the various headings of sections of the chapter. In this way, you learn generally what the chapter is about and know what to expect. It is also a good idea to skim some of the sentences here and there in the chapter and to look at some of the pictures and graphs. In addition, if there is a summary, read it as part of your survey, for it will give you the most important points of the chapter before details begin to clutter up the picture. All this is good advice, for several research studies[7] have shown that the *survey* technique greatly increases a student's ability to comprehend and learn new material.

Question. Some textbooks contain lists of review questions at the end of each chapter. (We have provided such questions in a separate workbook designed to accompany the text). These questions are usually the most neglected parts of the book, for students do not realize their value in studying. If a book has them, read them and try to answer them. It is also valuable for the student to *ask his own questions.* Try to turn the headings of sections into questions and read the sections with the idea of finding the answers to your questions.

Questions have several benefits. For one thing, they maintain interest in what is being read. For another, they make you actively participate in the learning process, rather than read passively. Psychological research clearly shows active participation to be a great aid in learning. Finally, questions are ways of testing yourself to see what you are learning or have learned. If you test yourself before the instructor does, you do much better when faced with a formal examination.

Read. The next step, of course, is to read—and to read carefully. Read to answer the questions you have asked yourself. Do not read passively, as you would a novel, but continually challenge yourself as you go along to make sure that you understand what you read. And, of course, *read to remember.* Every once in a while, remind yourself of your task—to understand and remember what you read. If you do, you will no longer voice the familiar complaint, "I forget what I read as soon as I am through." Notice especially any words or phrases that are italicized. Authors use italics to emphasize important terms, concepts, and principles.

Also, make sure to read everything, and that means tables, graphs, and other illustrations, as well as the main text. Illustrations are used to emphasize important points in the text and to clarify them. Sometimes, in fact, a mere glance at an illustration will tell vividly what a whole page of the book is about. In other cases, illustrations convey information that cannot be expressed easily in words. In this book, for example, we occasionally tell a story with pictures that are not specifically mentioned in the text. These are just as important in the reading of the book as are the headings, paragraphs, and sentences of the text.

Recite. Recitation is one of the most important techniques of effective study, yet it is very much neglected—because it takes effort. When one just reads, he has the comfort of thinking that what is read is understood and remembered, which is generally not true. To make certain that one understands and remembers, he should stop periodically and try to recall to himself what he has read. In other words, he should recite. At this point, for example, you might ask yourself what you have read so far in this chapter. Try to recall the main headings and the principal ideas under each heading. Can you give a synopsis of your reading without looking at the pages? Try to do it, then check yourself. See whether you have covered everything. If not, note your omissions and errors. Then a little later, recite again. As you read, stop at intervals to recite the substance of each major section of a chapter. When you review for examinations, again make recitation a substantial part of your study procedure.

Attesting to the importance of recitation in learning are many laboratory studies[8] on the relation between self-recall and forgetting. We mentioned some in Chapter 5. These studies show that recitation is a great help in preventing forgetting and thus increasing remembering. It is actually worthwhile to take time away from studying and to spend it on recitation, for learning is better when part of the study time is spent on recitation than when all of it is given to reading. In one research,[9] for example, people who spent up to 80 per cent of their study time on recitation did better than people who spent no time on recitation.

There are at least two good reasons for these findings. One is that recitation serves to keep your *attention* on the task, for you obviously cannot daydream while you are trying to recall something. Another is that it lets you *correct mistakes*; it shows you where you are weakest and where, in a second reading, you can profitably spend the most time.

Recitation is more useful for some subjects than it is for others. In general, it helps most when what you have to learn is disconnected and not too meaningful. If, for example, you have to learn a number of rules, items, names, laws, or formulas, then recitation is of great help. On the other hand, for meaningful, storylike material, such as one finds in history or philosophy, recitation is somewhat less useful—though never useless. Hence you should vary how much you use recitation according to the subject you are studying. Because this book contains considerable factual information, probably one-third to one-half the time spent in studying it should be spent in recitation.

Review. The fifth precept in the Survey Q3R technique is "review." To support this rule we have numerous psychological experiments,[1] all of which show review to be essential to remembering most efficiently. If, for example, you learn something perfectly but do not review it, you will find that a few days or even hours later you will remember only a small part of it.

Here are some pointers for the best way of reviewing. *The best times for review are immediately after first studying and again just before an examination,* but it will also pay to have one or two reviews in between. The first review may be fairly brief, because there has been little time for forgetting, and it should be mainly one of recitation. The review just before the examination should also emphasize recitation, but it should be much more intensive—and usually is. Intervening reviews that are relatively brief help, and these may emphasize rereading somewhat more than recitation. Perhaps it should go without saying that reviewing should not be crammed into the last few hours before an examination. This practice makes the final task too hard, and it does not give you, at the time of examination, the mastery that you could have with a few well-spaced reviews.

TAKING LECTURE NOTES

The Survey Q3R Method applies to lectures as well as to textbooks, but not in every detail. Obviously, it is difficult or impossible to survey a lecture in advance unless the instructor does it for you—and few do that. The student must therefore provide his own organization and headings as he goes. It is important, however, to *organize*. Do this by trying to identify the lecturer's main points. *Condense his paragraphs into simple phrases or sentences, and do this in words of your own phrasing.* But sometimes this is difficult to do, and you are forced to take copious, unorganized notes to keep up with the lecture. In such circumstances, do not spend so much time trying to take neat, well-organized notes that you lose the point of the lecture; almost any kind of notes is better than none at all. Still, the more organized your notes are, the better they will be.

It is hard to say how many notes you should take. This will vary with the lecture, the lecturer, and the temperament of the student. Some students do their best by taking many notes, and others do best by taking relatively few. If you write easily, it is probably best to *err on the side of taking too many.*

Review is even more important for lecture notes than it is for reading. Because lecture notes are incomplete, a brief review after class usually is necessary to fill in omitted essentials and correct minor errors. Waiting too long to do that makes one forget, and he may easily wind up saying, "My lecture notes just don't make sense." It will often pay to completely rewrite lecture notes shortly after each lecture, both to provide a good review with recitation and to make it possible to understand your notes later.

Finally, let us remind you that it is important to keep lecture notes in a well-organized state. It is well to use the same kind of paper for all notes in one subject, to keep them in a notebook and not lying around in various places, and to number the pages to keep them in order. In any event, make sure to have a system that is good enough to let you find all your material quickly and to study it easily.

TAKING EXAMINATIONS

Having read this heading, you may say, "Ah, that's what I want to know—how to take an examination." Many of us would like to know how to pass examinations without studying, but that is a bit of magic no psychologist has yet produced. In fact, the only good general rule for taking examinations is "Be prepared." And in preparation, do not bank too much on guessing what the instructor will ask. Sometimes this works, but sometimes it fails. It is a far better policy to be prepared for any reasonable question that the instructor might possibly ask.

Examinations divide themselves roughly into two classes, the *objective* and the *essay*, though there are several shades in between. You will probably want to prepare for the two types somewhat differently, and you should take them with somewhat different attitudes.

Objective examinations are usually *recognition* tests. They simply require that you recognize the right answer when you see it. It is important, however, to read and answer each question carefully. Sometimes the correct answer may hang on an all-important "not" or "always," and you may miss it if you read carelessly. It is best first to go straight through the examination, answering all the questions you are sure of and checking those you cannot answer immediately. When you are through, go back to the harder questions. Remember that in an objective examination it is a mistake to concentrate too much on a few difficult questions, for they usually count no more than the others. If you do that, you will not have time to finish, or you will have to rattle through the other questions so rapidly you will make needless mistakes. If you have time at the end, carefully review your answers and correct your mistakes where you think necessary.

Essay examinations emphasize the ability to understand, organize, and *recall* information. To prepare well for them, you should especially emphasize the active parts of studying—surveying and recitation. In taking the examination, remember that the instructor usually will think better of a paper if the information in it is well organized rather than rambling and discursive. So take time to organize your thoughts before you begin to write. Make sure to answer the question that the instructor asks, not a slightly different one on which you may be better prepared. Keep your answers to the point, and avoid digressions and irrelevant information—for they do not impress most instructors. Try to leave time to reread your answers at the end of the examination so that you can add important points you forgot or correct any mistakes.

CORRECTING COLLEGE DEFICIENCIES

All that we have said so far assumes normal skills in reading, writing, and arithmetic. Many American college students, however, have not mastered these skills well enough to use them as they should in study. Many of them have trouble with fractions, do not know the difference between a subject and predicate, and cannot read with the speed and comprehension they should. Many colleges, which recognize that substantial numbers of students come to them deficient in the basic skills, have set up remedial courses.

At the college level these deficiencies have little to do with intelligence. Students who are enrolled in reading clinics are usually about as bright as those who are not.[10] In one large state university system that enrolls students in two categories, "regular" and "deficient," there is no difference in intelligence between the two groups. The trouble lies elsewhere, somewhere in the earlier education of the students. But the main point is that some students, while as bright as others, are simply deficient in the basic skills. One of them is reading.

Reading. To get along in college these days, reading is more important than writing. Therefore, any serious *deficiency in reading ability impairs scholastic progress.* Yet it is surprising how poorly some students read. Some students read word by word, and this really produces trouble. People who read this way will read a fourth-grade geography book at the same rate at which they read an advanced treatise in economics. Word-by-word readers are frequently lip movers, so lip movements can often be used to reveal this kind of trouble. If you have any tendency to whisper or to

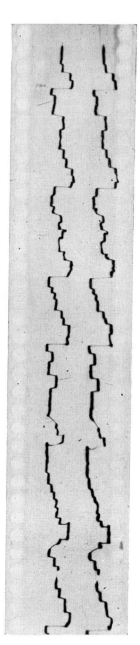

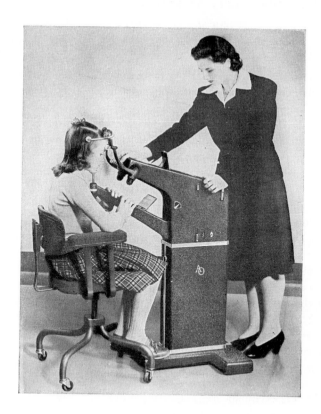

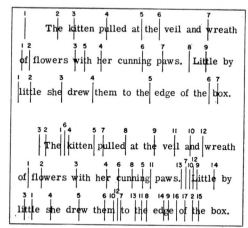

Fig. 3. Eye movements in reading. In the picture is an ophthalmograph used for photographing the movement of the eyes in reading. (*Courtesy American Optical Co.*) The film shows a record of eye movements made with such an instrument. (*Courtesy New York University Testing and Advisement Center.*) The lines of print show the difference between a good reader and a poor one. Each vertical bar accompanied by a number represents a fixation. The good reader makes relatively few fixations and does not retrace a line.

pronounce to yourself the words that you are reading, you are very likely to read too slowly.

Even if you are not a slower-than-average reader, the chances are that a little practice will improve your reading speed enormously. Take an inventory of your reading habits. For example, notice your eye movements and fixations during reading. As you probably know, your eyes do not move continuously while you are reading. Rather they move in quick jumps and rest for a fraction of a second at some point on the line you are reading (see Figure 3). It is during the rest period that you perceive what you are reading. There is no way to speed up the movements, and the duration of the rests can be speeded very little.

Your reading speed, however, can be greatly improved by decreasing the number of rests per line. To accomplish this, it is necessary to *expand the number of words perceived in one glance*. By reading as fast as you can without losing the sense of what is read, you can gradually increase the words comprehended in a glance and thereby reduce the number of glances per line. The best way to practice fast reading is on easy material—magazine articles, fiction, newspapers, etc. If you practice rapid reading, keep a record of your reading rate. Count the number of words you can read in a one-minute period each day, and draw a chart that shows your rate of reading on successive days of practice. You must be careful to check your comprehension to make sure that you are not sacrificing understanding for increased speed. If you practice reading *carefully*, you can actually *increase your comprehension* at the same time you are increasing your reading speed.

It is not possible to state precisely the standards for fast reading, for they depend on the nature of the material being read. On nontechnical material, fast readers can

do about 400 words a minute, while poor readers do only 100 words a minute. Technical material must, of course, be read more slowly. For a book like this one, a standard of 150 to 250 words a minute is not unreasonable.

Perhaps a word of caution is necessary. Reading is a complicated business, and a haphazard approach to improving it may do you no good at all and possibly some harm. There are individuals who are especially trained in the techniques of teaching people how to read better, and many colleges have them on their staffs. If you feel that you seriously need to improve your reading, it is best to get in touch with someone who knows something about the techniques of improving reading or with a reading clinic. If there is no one to whom you can go, the best thing you can do is to obtain one of the books listed at the end of this chapter and spend some time finding out how you may improve your reading by your own effort.

If your *vocabulary* is deficient, there are ways to go about improving it. One is to get the habit of checking definitions of unfamiliar words. Another is to make notes of unfamiliar words as they turn up in reading and then to look at them in the context in which they appeared. This often helps establish their meanings as well as their preferred usage.

The purpose of reading, of course, is to comprehend, but among college students there are wide individual differences in the ability to comprehend. Fortunately, it is possible for nearly every college student, within limits, to increase his comprehension. Improving one's vocabulary is one approach. Gearing rate of reading to the difficulty of the material is another. Still another is to practice on easy material. If you have trouble comprehending a rather difficult book, it may help to find a much simpler book on the same subject and read it before tackling the hard one.

Other skills. Writing and elementary mathematics are also skills in which students are frequently deficient. These skills are necessary in this course, in most courses in college, and in almost every position in the world in which a college student may find himself. It will therefore pay to develop them and to correct them if they are weak. Many colleges, recognizing this fact, have standard courses to meet this need. Don't avoid these courses or try to get along without these basic skills. They are essential to effective study now and will be essential in almost anything you do later in life.

SUMMARY

1. Most college students need to improve their study habits, but the biggest obstacle to improvement lies in not being properly motivated to study. If students only realized how important good study habits and good performance in college are to success in later life, most would try harder than they do.

2. Organizing a study routine is usually the first step in improving study habits. The routine should include a rather definite schedule for study— a schedule that may be changed if necessary, but nevertheless a schedule.

3. Experience indicates that students may carry rather heavy loads of academic work and outside work too if they organize their time on a schedule.

4. The best place to study is the library or some similar place that is free of distractions.

5. A proven technique for effective study is known as Survey Q3R. It consists of five parts: (*a*) a survey of headings, summaries, and topic sentences before detailed study; (*b*) the formulation of questions to be answered in studying, taking advantage of questions the author of the book may have posed; (*c*) reading carefully everything in the assignment, including tables and graphs, and doing this with an intent to remember; (*d*) reciting to oneself or other students what has been read; and then (*e*) reviewing carefully both after studying and just before an examination.

6. Lecture notes should be taken by attempting to select the lecturer's main points and organizing them in the student's own words.

7. It is important to review these notes very soon after the lecture to make sure they can be understood. Often it is profitable to rewrite and to reorganize them.

8. It is also important to keep notes in their proper order and in one place so that they may be found quickly and studied easily.

9. In taking objective examinations, questions should be read with extreme care and the easier ones answered first. In taking essay examinations, the student should carefully organize his answer, and allow time to reread and revise it if necessary.

10. Many students are deficient in reading skill or in vocabulary. With practice, both reading speed and comprehension may be improved. Where serious deficiencies exist, it is advisable for the student to take courses or to seek professional help toward correcting them.

SUGGESTIONS FOR FURTHER READING

Bennett, M. E. *College and life* (4th Ed.). New York: McGraw-Hill, 1952.
  A book designed to orient students to all aspects of college life, containing several chapters on learning and effective study.

Bird, C., & Bird, D. M. *Learning more by effective study.* New York: Appleton-Century-Crofts, 1945.
  Established principles and procedures for effective study, presented at the adult level.

Cole, L., & Ferguson, J. M. *Students' guide to efficient study* (3d Ed.). New York: Rinehart, 1946.
  An inexpensive manual giving rules pertaining to efficient study.

Gerken, C. d'A. *Study your way through school.* Chicago: Science Research Associates, 1953.
  A pamphlet designed to help students develop effective study habits.

McKown, H. C. *How to pass a written examination.* New York: McGraw-Hill, 1943.
  A book offering practical advice on how to study for different types of examinations.

Mursell, J. L. *Using your mind effectively.* New York: McGraw-Hill, 1951.
  A discussion of ways to improve mental effectiveness, with emphasis on problems of study.

Robinson, F. P. *Effective study* (Rev. Ed.). New York: Harper, 1946.
  A book based on results of a research program, describing methods of effective study and also the diagnosis of deficiencies.

Wrenn, C. G. *Studying effectively.* Stanford, Calif.: Stanford Univ. Press, 1950.
  Methods of effective study.

BIBLIOGRAPHY

The following lists of books and articles are references for statements made in the book. In most cases, they contain a detailed report of experiments or researches, but in some cases they supply additional information concerning a conclusion or point of view expressed in the text. The number preceding each reference is the superscript number used where the reference is relevant in the corresponding chapter of the book.

Chapter 1: The Science of Psychology

1. Keller, F. S. *The definition of psychology.* New York: Appleton-Century-Crofts, 1937.
2. Hunter, W. S. *Human behavior.* Chicago: Univ. of Chicago Press, 1928.
3. Warden, C. J. The development of modern comparative psychology. *Quart. Rev. Biol.,* 1928, **3**, 486–522.
4. Mees, C. E. Scientific thought and social reconstruction. *Electrical Engng.,* 1934, **53**, 383–384.
5. Stevens, S. S. Psychology and the science of science. *Psychol. Bull.,* 1939, **36**, 221–263.
6. Boring, E. G. A history of introspectionism. *Psychol. Bull.,* 1953, **50**, 169–189.
7. Watson, J. B. *Behaviorism.* New York: Norton, 1925.
8. Köhler, W. *Gestalt psychology.* New York: Liveright, 1947.
9. Freud, S. *The basic writings of Sigmund Freud* (Ed. by A. A. Brill). New York: Modern Library, 1938.
10. Dollard, J., & Miller, N. E. *Personality and psychotherapy.* New York: McGraw-Hill, 1950.
11. Terman, L. M. *Psychological factors in marital happiness.* New York: McGraw-Hill, 1938.

Chapter 2: Maturation and Development

1. Carmichael, L. The onset and early development of behavior. In L. Carmichael (Ed.), *Manual of child psychology.* New York: Wiley, 1946.
2. Munn, N. L. *Psychological development.* Boston: Houghton Mifflin, 1938.

3. Sherman, M. C., Sherman, I. C., & Flory, C. D. Infant behavior. *Comp. Psychol. Monogr.*, 1936, **12**, No. 4.

4. Smith, J. R. The frequency growth of the human alpha rhythms during normal infancy and childhood. *J. Psychol.*, 1941, **11**, 177–198.

5. Beach, F. A. Sexual behavior of prepuberal male and female rats treated with gonadal hormones. *J. comp. Psychol.*, 1942, **34**, 285–292.

6. Carmichael, L. A further study of the development of behavior in vertebrates experimentally removed from the influence of environmental stimulation. *Psychol. Rev.*, 1927, **34**, 34–47.

7. Dennis, W. Spalding's experiment on the flight of birds repeated with another species. *J. comp. Psychol.*, 1941, **31**, 337–348.

8. Cruze, W. W. Maturation and learning in chicks. *J. comp. Psychol.*, 1935, **19**, 371–409.

9. Lashley, K. S., & Russell, J. T. The mechanism of vision. XI. A preliminary test of innate organization. *J. genet. Psychol.*, 1934, **45**, 136–144.

10. Hebb, D. O. The innate organization of visual activity. I. Perception of figures by rats reared in total darkness. *J. genet. Psychol.*, 1937, **51**, 101–126.

11. Riesen, A. H. The development of visual perception in man and chimpanzee. *Science*, 1947, **106**, 107–108.

12. Hebb, D. O. *The organization of behavior.* New York: Wiley, 1949.

13. Dennis, W. The effect of cradling practices upon the onset of walking in Hopi children. *J. genet. Psychol.*, 1940, **56**, 77–86.

14. Davis, K. Final note on a case of extreme isolation. *Amer. J. Sociol.*, 1947, **52**, 432–437.

15. McGraw, Myrtle B. *Growth: a study of Johnny and Jimmy.* New York: Appleton-Century-Crofts, 1935.

16. Gesell, A., & Thompson, H. Learning and growth in identical infant twins: an experimental study by the method of co-twin control. *Genet. Psychol. Monogr.*, 1929, **6**, 1–124.

17. Kellogg, W. N., & Kellogg, L. A. *The ape and the child.* New York: McGraw-Hill, 1933.

18. Warden, C. J., Jenkins, T. N., & Warner, L. H. *Comparative psychology.* Vol. III. New York: Ronald, 1936. Pp. 391–392.

19. Hayes, K. J., & Hayes, C. The intellectual development of a home-raised chimpanzee. *Proc. Amer. phil. Soc.*, 1951, **95**, 105–109.

20. Anastasi, Anne. Practice and variability: a study in psychological method. *Psychol. Monogr.*, 1934, **45**, No. 5.

21. Thorpe, W. H. The concepts of learning and their relation to those of instinct. In *Physiological mechanisms in animal behavior.* New York: Academic Press, 1950.

22. Ramsay, A. O. Familial recognition in domestic birds. *Auk*, 1951, **68**, 1–16.

23. Hymovitch, B. The effects of experimental variations on problem solving in the rat. *J. comp. physiol. Psychol.*, 1952, **45**, 313–321.

24. Shirley, M. M. *The first two years, a study of twenty-five babies.* Vol. I. *Postural and locomotor development.* Minneapolis: Univ. of Minnesota Press, 1931.

25. Shirley, M. M. *The first two years, a study of twenty-five babies.* Vol. II. *Intellectual development.* Minneapolis: Univ. of Minnesota Press, 1933.

26. Halverson, H. M. An experimental study of prehension in infants by means of systematic cinema records. *Genet. Psychol. Monogr.*, 1931, **10**, 107–286.

27. McGraw, Myrtle B. Maturation of behavior. In L. Carmichael (Ed.), *Manual of child psychology.* New York: Wiley, 1946. Pp. 332–369.

28. Lewis, M. M. *Infant speech: a study of the beginnings of language.* New York: Harcourt, Brace, 1936.

29. McCarthy, Dorothea A. *The language development of the preschool child.* Minneapolis: Univ. of Minnesota Press, 1930.

30. Terman, L. M., et al. *Genetic studies of genius.* Vol. I. *Mental and physical traits of a thousand gifted children.* Stanford, Calif.: Stanford Univ. Press, 1925.

31. McCarthy, Dorothea A. Language development in children. In L. Carmichael (Ed.), *Manual of child psychology.* New York: Wiley, 1946. Pp. 476–581.

32. Jersild, A. T., & Ritzman, R. Aspects of language development: the growth of loquacity and vocabulary. *Child Develpm.*, 1938, **9**, 243–259.

33. Day, E. J. The development of language in twins. I. A comparison of twins and single children. *Child Develpm.*, 1932, **3**, 179–199.

34. Davis, E. A. *The development of linguistic skill in twins, singletons with siblings, and only children from age five to ten years.* Minneapolis: Univ. of Minnesota Press, 1932.
35. Smith, M. E. A study of the speech of eight bilingual children of the same family. *Child Develpm.*, 1935, **6**, 19–25.
36. Young, F. M. An analysis of certain variables in a developmental study of language. *Genet. Psychol. Monogr.*, 1941, **23**, 3–141.

Chapter 3: Motivation

1. Wilkins, L., & Richter, C. P. A great craving for salt by a child with cortico-adrenal insufficiency. *J. Amer. med. Ass.*, 1940, **114**, 866–868.
2. Cannon, W. B. *The wisdom of the body.* New York: Norton, 1932.
3. Richter, C. P. Total self-regulatory functions in animals and human beings. *Harvey Lect.*, 1942–1943, **38**, 63–103.
4. Cannon, W. B. Hunger and thirst. In C. Murchison (Ed.), *A handbook of general experimental psychology.* Worcester, Mass.: Clark Univ. Press, 1934. Pp. 247–263.
5. Steggerda, F. R. Observations on the water intake in an adult man with dysfunctioning salivary glands. *Amer. J. Physiol.*, 1941, **132**, 517–521.
6. Adolph, E. F. The internal environment and behavior. Part III. Water content. *Amer. J. Psychiat.*, 1941, **97**, 1365–1373.
7. Verney, E. B. The antidiuretic hormone and the factors which determine its release. *Proc. roy. Soc.*, 1947, **135**, 24–106.
8. Wangensteen, O. H., & Carlson, A. J. Hunger sensations in a patient after total gastrectomy. *Proc. Soc. exp. Biol., N.Y.*, 1931, **28**, 545–547.
9. Tsang, Y. C. Hunger motivation in gastrectomized rats. *J. comp. Psychol.*, 1938, **26**, 1–17.
10. Davis, C. M. Self-selection of diet by newly weaned infants. *Amer. J. Dis. Child.*, 1928, **36**, 651–679.
11. Pilgrim, F. J., & Patton, R. A. Patterns of self-selection of purified dietary components by the rat. *J. comp. physiol. Psychol.*, 1947, **40**, 343–348.
12. Richter, C. P. Increased salt appetite in adrenalectomized rats. *Amer. J. Physiol.*, 1936, **115**, 155–161.

13. Scott, E. M., & Verney, Ethel L. Self-selection of diet. IX. The appetite for thiamine. *J. Nutrition*, 1949, **37**, 81–92.
14. Young, P. T. Studies of food preference, appetite, and dietary habit. I. Running activity and dietary habit of the rat in relation to food preference. *J. comp. Psychol.*, 1944, **37**, 327–370.
15. Weiner, I. H. & Stellar, E. Salt preference of the rat determined by a single-stimulus method. *J. comp. physiol. Psychol.*, 1951, **44**, 394–401.
16. Mayer-Gross, W., & Walker, J. W. Taste and selection of food in hypoglycemia. *Brit. J. exp. Path.*, 1946, **27**, 297–305.
17. Katz, S. E., & Landis, C. Psychologic and physiologic phenomena during a prolonged vigil. *Arch. Neurol. Psychiat., Chicago*, 1935, **34**, 307–316.
18. Kleitman, N. *Sleep and wakefulness.* Chicago: Univ. of Chicago Press, 1939.
19. Beach, F. A. *Hormones and behavior.* New York: Hoeber, 1949.
20. Beach, F. A. Evolutionary changes in the physiological control of mating behavior in mammals. *Psychol. Rev.*, 1947, **54**, 297–315
21. Beach, F. A. A review of physiological and psychological studies of sexual behavior in mammals. *Physiol. Rev.*, 1947, **27**, 240–307.
22. Yerkes, R. M. *Chimpanzees.* New Haven, Conn.: Yale Univ. Press, 1943. P. 84.
23. Kinsey, A. C., Pomeroy, W. B., & Martin, C. E. *Sexual behavior in the human male.* Philadelphia: Saunders, 1948.
24. Ford, C. S., & Beach, F. A. *Patterns of sexual behavior.* New York: Hoeber, 1951.
25. Riddle, O., Bates, R. W., & Lahr, E. L. Maternal behavior in rats induced by prolactin. *Proc. Soc. exp. Biol., N.Y.*, 1935, **32**, 730–734.
26. Richter, C. P. A behavioristic study of the activity of the rat. *Comp. Psychol. Monogr.*, 1922, 1, 1–55.
27. Miller, N. E. Learnable drives and rewards. In S. S. Stevens (Ed.), *Handbook of experimental psychology.* New York: Wiley, 1951. Pp. 435–472.
28. Saltzman, I. J. Maze learning in the absence of primary reinforcement: a study of secondary reinforcement. *J. comp. physiol. Psychol.*, 1949, **42**, 161–173.
29. Wolfe, J. B. Effectiveness of token rewards for chimpanzees. *Comp. Psychol. Monogr.*, 1936, **12**, No. 60.

30. Miller, N. E. Studies of fear as an acquirable drive. I. Fear as motivation and fear-reduction as reinforcement in the learning of new responses. *J. exp. Psychol.*, 1948, **38**, 89–101.
31. Langer, W. C. *Psychology and human living.* New York: Appleton-Century-Crofts, 1943.
32. Schjelderup-Ebbe, T. Social behavior of birds. In C. Murchison (Ed.), *Handbook of social psychology.* Worcester, Mass.: Clark Univ. Press, 1935.
33. Bekhterev. Cited in J. F. Dashiell, *Fundamentals of general psychology* (3d Ed.). Boston: Houghton Mifflin, 1949. P. 509.
34. Mowrer, O. H. Social modification of organically motivated behavior. Pennsylvania State College, Psychological Cinema Register, Film No. PCR-24.
35. Crawford, M. P. The cooperative solving of problems by young chimpanzees. *Comp. Psychol. Monogr.*, 1937, **14**, No. 2.
36. Mead, M. *Cooperation and competition among primitive peoples.* New York: McGraw-Hill, 1937.
37. Allport, G. W. *Personality: a psychological interpretation.* New York: Holt, 1937. Chap. 7.
38. Gould, Rosalind. An experimental analysis of "level of aspiration." *Genet. Psychol. Monogr.*, 1939, **21**, 3–115.

Chapter 4: Feeling and Emotion

1. Bridges, K. M. B. Emotional development in early infancy. *Child Develpm.*, 1932, **3**, 324–341.
2. Watson, J. B., & Rayner, R. Conditioned emotional reactions. *J. exp. Psychol.*, 1920, **3**, 1–14.
3. Shaffer, L. F. Fear and courage in aerial combat. *J. consult. Psychol.*, 1947, **11**, 137–143.
4. Cannon, W. B. *Bodily changes in pain, hunger, fear, and rage* (2d Ed.). New York: Appleton-Century-Crofts, 1929.
5. Inbau, F. E. *Lie detection and criminal investigation.* Baltimore: Williams & Wilkins, 1942.
6. Lund, F. H. *Emotions.* New York: Ronald, 1939.
7. Landis, C., & Hunt, W. A. *The startle pattern.* New York: Rinehart, 1939.
8. Ruckmick, C. A. Preliminary study of the emotions. *Psychol. Monogr.*, 1931, **30**, 30–35.
9. Kline, L. W., & Johannsen, D. E. Comparative role of the face and of the face-body-hands as aids in identifying emotions. *J. abnorm. soc. Psychol.*, 1935, **29**, 415–426.
10. Klineberg, O. Emotional expression in Chinese literature. *J. abnorm. soc. Psychol.*, 1938, **33**, 517–520.
11. Munn, N. L. The effect of a knowledge of the situation upon judgment of emotion from facial expressions. *J. abnorm. soc. Psychol.*, 1940, **35**, 324–338.
12. Jersild, A. T., Markey, F. V., & Jersild, C. L. Children's fears, dreams, wishes, daydreams, dislikes, pleasant and unpleasant memories. *Child Develpm. Monogr.*, 1933, No. 12.
13. Anastasi, Anne, Cohen, N., & Spatz, D. A study of fear and anger in college students through the controlled diary method. *J. genet. Psychol.*, 1948, **73**, 243–249.
14. Washburn, R. W. A study of smiling and laughing of infants in the first year of life. *Genet. Psychol. Monogr.*, 1929, **6**, 397–539.
15. Britt, S. H. Social psychology of modern life (Rev. Ed.). New York: Rinehart, 1949.
16. Miller, N. E. Fear as an acquired drive. *J. exp. Psychol.*, 1948, **38**, 89–101.
17. Leonard, W. E. *The locomotive god.* New York: Appleton-Century-Crofts, 1927.
18. Dollard, J., Doob, L. W., Miller, N. E., Mowrer, O. H., Sears, R. R., Ford C. S., Hovland, C. I., & Sollenberger, R. T. *Frustration and aggression.* New Haven, Conn.: Yale Univ. Press, 1939.
19. Dunbar, H. F. *Emotions and bodily changes* (3d Ed.). New York: Columbia Univ. Press, 1946.
20. Cason, H. Common annoyances: a psychological study of everyday aversions and irritations. *Psychol. Monogr.*, 1930, No. 182.
21. Moore, J. E. Analysing habits of college professors. *J. abnorm. soc. Psychol.*, 1935, **30**, 43–46.
22. Kryter, K. D. Effects of noise on man. *J. Speech Hearing Disorders*, 1950, Suppl. No. 1, p. 18.
23. Guilford, J. P. *Psychometric methods* (2d Ed.). New York: McGraw-Hill, 1954.

Chapter 5: Learning and Remembering

1. Pavlov, I. P. *Conditioned reflexes* (Trans. by G. V. Anrep). London: Oxford Univ. Press, 1927.

2. Hovland, C. I. The generalization of conditioned responses. I. The sensory generalization of conditioned responses with varying frequencies of tone. *J. gen. Psychol.*, 1937, **17**, 125–148.

3. Skinner, B. F. *The behavior of organisms.* New York: Appleton-Century-Crofts, 1938.

4. Berch, P. J. The influence of two variables upon the establishment of a secondary reinforcer for operant responses. *J. exp. Psychol.*, 1951, **41**, 62–73.

5. Keller, F. S., & Schoenfeld, W. N. *Principles of psychology.* New York: Appleton-Century-Crofts, 1950.

6. Jenkins, W. O., & Stanley, J. C. Partial reinforcement: a review and critique. *Psychol. Bull.*, 1950, **47**, 193–234.

7. Estes, W. K. Experimental study of punishment. *Psychol. Monogr.*, 1944, **57**, No. 263.

8. Deese, J. *The psychology of learning.* New York: McGraw-Hill, 1952.

9. Postman, L. The history and present status of the law of effect. *Psychol. Bull.*, 1947, **44**, 489–563.

10. Bryan, W. L., & Harter, N. Studies on the telegraphic language: the acquisition of a hierarchy of habits. *Psychol. Rev.*, 1899, **6**, 345–375.

11. McGeoch, J. A., & Irion, A. L. *The psychology of human learning.* New York: Longmans, 1952.

12. Swift, E. J. *Psychology and the day's work.* New York: Scribner, 1918.

13. Cook, T. W. Massed and distributed practice in puzzle solving. *Psychol. Rev.*, 1934, **41**, 330–355. Also Ericksen, S. C. Variability of attack in massed and distributed practice. *J. exp. Psychol.*, 1942, **31**, 339–358.

14. Lorge, I. Influence of regularly interpolated time intervals upon subsequent learning. *Teach. Coll. Contr. Educ.*, 1930, No. 438. Also Kientzle, M. J. Properties of learning curves under varied distribution of practice. *J. exp. Psychol.*, 1946, **36**, 187–211.

15. Jost, A. Die Assoziationfestigkeit in ihrer Abhängigkeit von der Verteilung der Wiederholungen. *Z. Psychol.*, 1897, **14**, 436–472. Also Kimble, G. A., & Bilodeau, E. A. Work and rest as variables in cyclical motor learning. *J. exp. Psychol.*, 1949, **39**, 150–157.

16. Cook, B. S., & Hilgard, E. R. Distributed practice in motor learning: progressively increasing and decreasing rests. *J. exp. Psychol.*, 1949, **39**, 169–172.

17. Gates, A. I. Recitation as a factor in memorizing. *Arch. Psychol. N.Y.*, 1917, **6**, No. 40.

18. Miller, G. A., & Selfridge, J. A. Verbal context and the recall of meaningful material. *Amer. J. Psychol.*, 1950, **63**, 176–185.

19. Stroud, J. B. Experiments on learning in school situations. *Psychol. Bull.*, 1940, **37**, 777–807.

20. Kingsley, H. R. *The nature and conditions of learning.* New York: Prentice-Hall, 1944.

21. Burtt, H. E. An experimental study of early childhood memory. *J. genet. Psychol.*, 1941, **58**, 435–439.

22. Reich, E. The game of "Gossip" analyzed by the theory of information. *Bull. mathematical Biophysics*, 1951, **13**, 313–318.

23. Bartlett, F. C. *Remembering.* London: Cambridge Univ. Press, 1932.

24. Jenkins, J. G., & Dallenbach, K. M. Oblivescence during sleep and waking. *Amer. J. Psychol.*, 1924, **35**, 605–612.

25. Gibb, J. R. The relative effects of sleeping and waking upon the retention of nonsense syllables. *Psychol. Bull.*, 1941, **38**, 734.

26. Sharp, Agnes A. An experimental test of Freud's doctrine of the relation of hedonic tone to memory revival. *J. exp. Psychol.*, 1938, **22**, 395–418.

27. Edwards, A. L. Retention of affective experiences; a criticism and restatement of the problem. *Psychol. Rev.*, 1942, **49**, 43–53.

28. Zeller, A. F. An experimental analogue of repression. II. The effect of individual failure and success on memory measured by relearning. *J. exp. Psychol.*, 1950, **40**, 411–422.

29. Morgan, C. T. Studies in vision. I. A technique for the study of visual discrimination in the rat. *J. comp. Psychol.*, 1939, **28**, 73–79.

30. Munn, N. L. *Handbook of psychological research on the rat.* Boston: Houghton Mifflin, 1950.

31. Fields, P. E. Studies in concept formation. I. The development of the concept of triangularity in the rat. *Comp. Psychol. Monogr.*, 1932, No. 9.

32. Tolman, E. C., & Honzik, C. H. Introduction and removal of reward and maze performance in rats. *Univ. Calif. Publ. Psychol.*, 1930, **4**, 257–275.

33. Hull, C. L. *Principles of behavior.* New York: Appleton-Century-Crofts, 1943.

34. Chapanis, A., Garner, W. R., & Morgan, C. T. *Applied experimental psychology.* New York: Wiley, 1949. Chap. 11.

Chapter 6: Imagination and Thinking

1. Galton, F. *Inquiries into human faculty and its development* (2d Ed.). New York: Dutton, 1907.
2. Davis, F. C. The functional significance of imagery differences. *J. exp. Psychol.*, 1932, **15**, 630–661. Also Effect of maze rotation upon subjects reporting different methods of learning and retention. *Univ. Calif. Los Angeles Publ. Educ., Phil., Psychol.*, 1933, **1**, 47–63.
3. Humphrey, G. *Thinking; an introduction to its experimental psychology.* New York: Wiley, 1951. Chaps. 2, 3, and 4.
4. Allport, G. W. Eidetic imagery. *Brit. J. Psychol.*, 1924, **15**, 99–120.
5. Watson, J. B. *Psychology from the standpoint of a behaviorist* (2d Ed.). Philadelphia: Lippincott, 1924.
6. Jacobson, L. E. The electrophysiology of mental activities. *Amer. J. Psychol.*, 1932, **44**, 677–694.
7. Max, L. W. Experimental study of the motor theory of consciousness. IV. Action-current responses in the deaf during awakening, kinaesthetic imagery and abstract thinking. *J. comp. Psychol.*, 1937, **24**, 301–344.
8. Hunter, W. S. The delayed reaction in animals and children. *Behavior Monogr.*, 1913, Vol. 2.
9. For a summary of experiments on this topic, see Munn, N. L. *Handbook of psychological research on the rat.* Boston: Houghton Mifflin, 1950.
10. Hunter, W. S., & Nagge, J. W. The white rat and the double alternation temporal maze. *J. genet. Psychol.*, 1931, **39**, 303–319.
11. Fields, P. E. Studies in concept formation. I. The development of the concept of triangularity in the rat. *Comp. Psychol. Monogr.*, 1932, No. 9.
12. Hull, C. L. Quantitative aspects of the evolution of concepts. *Psychol. Monogr.*, 1920, No. 123.
13. Heidbreder, Edna. The attainment of concepts. *J. gen. Psychol.*, 1946, **35**, 173–223. Also *J. Psychol.*, 1947, **24**, 93–138; 1948, **25**, 299–329, **26**, 45–69, 193–216; 1949, **27**, 3–39, 263–309.
14. Harlow, H. F. Thinking. In H. Helson, *Theoretical foundations of psychology.* New York: Van Nostrand, 1951. P. 469.
15. Wertheimer, M. *Productive thinking.* New York: Harper, 1945.
16. Luchins, A. Mechanization in problem solving: the effect of Einstellung. *Psychol. Monogr.*, 1954, **54**, No. 6.
17. Poincaré, H. Mathematical creation. In *The foundations of science* (Trans. by G. H. Halsted). New York: Science Press, 1913. Pp. 383–394.
18. Köhler, W. *The mentality of apes.* New York: Harcourt, Brace, 1925.
19. Jackson, T. A. Use of the stick as a tool by young chimpanzees. *J. comp. Psychol.*, 1942, **34**, 223–235.
20. Richardson, H. M. The adaptive behavior of infants in the utilization of the lever as a tool: a developmental and experimental study. *J. genet. Psychol.*, 1934, **44**, 352–377.
21. Sells, S. B. The atmosphere effect: an experimental study of reasoning. *Arch. Psychol. N.Y.*, 1936, No. 200.
22. Morgan, J. J. B., & Morton, J. T. The distortion of syllogistic reasoning produced by personal convictions. *J. soc. Psychol.*, 1944, **20**, 39–59.
23. Hall, C. S. What people dream about. *Sci. Amer.*, 1951, **184**, 60–63.

Chapter 7: Attention and Perception

1. See Boring, E. G. *A history of experimental psychology* (Rev. Ed.). New York: Appleton-Century-Crofts, 1950. Chap. 5.
2. Wapner, S., Werner, H., & Chandler, K. A. Experiments on sensory-tonic field theory of perception. I. Effect of extraneous stimulation on the visual perception of verticality. *J. exp. Psychol.*, 1951, **42**, 341–346.
3. Ewert, P. H. Study of effect of inverted retinal stimulation upon spatially coordinated behavior. *Genet. Psychol. Monogr.*, 1930, **7**, 177–361.
4. Senden, M. v. *Raum- und Gestaltauffassung bei operierten Blindgeborenen vor und nach der Operation.* Leipzig: Barth, 1932.
5. Bogoras, W. *The Chukchee.* New York: Hafner, 1909.
6. Allport, G. W., & Kramer, B. M. Some roots of prejudice. *J. Psychol.*, 1946, **22**, 9–39.

7. Seeleman, V. The influence of attitude upon the remembering of pictorial material. *Arch. Psychol. N.Y.*, 1940, **36**, No. 258.

8. Bruner, J. S., & Goodman, C. C. Value and need as organizing factors in perception. *J. abnorm. soc. Psychol.*, 1947, **42**, 33–44.

9. Lambert, W. W., Solomon, R. L., & Watson, P. D. Reinforcement and extinction as factors in size estimation. *J. exper. Psychol.*, 1949, **39**, 637–641.

Chapter 8: Psychological Measurement

1. Dantzig, T. *Number: the language of science.* New York: Macmillan, 1939.

2. Stevens, S. S. On the theory of scales of measurement. *Science*, 1946, **103**, 677–680.

3. Thurstone, L. L., & Chave, E. J. *The measurement of attitudes.* Chicago: Univ. of Chicago Press, 1929.

4. Gulliksen, H. Paired comparisons and the logic measurement. *Psychol. Rev.*, 1946, **53**, 199–213.

5. Terman, L. M., & Merrill, M. A. *Measuring intelligence.* Boston: Houghton Mifflin, 1937.

6. Likert, R. The sample interview survey. In W. Dennis (Ed.), *Current trends in psychology.* Pittsburgh: Univ. of Pittsburgh Press, 1947.

7. Buros, O. K. (Ed.). *The nineteen-forty mental measurements yearbook.* Highland Park, N.J.: The Mental Measurements Yearbook, 1941.

8. Boring, E. G. (Ed.). *Psychology for the armed services.* Washington, D.C.: Combat, 1945.

9. Taylor, H. C., & Russell, J. R. The relationship of validity coefficients to practical effectiveness in test selection. *J. appl. Psychol.*, 1939, **23**, 565–578.

Chapter 9: Personality

1. Barker, R. G., & Wright, H. F. *One boy's day.* New York: Harper, 1951.

2. Allport, G. W., & Odbert, H. S. Trait-names, a psycholexical study. *Psychol. Monogr.*, 1936, **47**, 1–171.

3. Guilford, J. P. *Psychometric methods* (2d Ed.). New York: McGraw-Hill, 1954. Chap. 16.

4. Cattell, R. B. *Description and measurement of personality.* Yonkers, N.Y.: World, 1946. Pp. 293–340.

5. Murray, H. A. *Explorations in personality.* New York: Oxford Univ. Press, 1938.

6. Ferguson, L. *Personality measurement.* New York: McGraw-Hill, 1952.

7. Hathaway, S. R., & McKinley, J. C. *The Minnesota Multiphasic Personality Inventory* (Rev. Ed.). Minneapolis: Univ. of Minnesota Press, 1943.

8. Allport, G. W., & Vernon, P. E. *A study of values: a scale for measuring the dominant interests in personality.* Boston: Houghton Mifflin, 1931.

9. Hartshorne, H., & May, M. A. *Studies in deceit.* New York: Macmillan, 1928.

10. Office of Strategic Services, Assessment Staff. *Assessment of men: selection of personnel for the Office of Strategic Services.* New York: Rinehart, 1948.

11. Postman, L., Bruner, J. S., & McGinnies, E. Personal values as selective factors in perception. *J. abnorm. soc. Psychol.*, 1948, **43**, 142–154.

12. Witkin, H. A. Individual differences in ease of perception of embedded figures. *J. Pers.*, 1950, **19**, 1–15.

13. Block, J., & Block, Jeanne. An investigation of the relationship between intolerance of ambiguity and ethnocentrism. *J. Pers.*, 1951, **19**, 303–311.

14. Eysenck, H. J. *Dimensions of personality.* London: Routledge, 1947.

15. White, R. W. In J. McV. Hunt, *Personality and the behavior disorders.* New York: Ronald, 1944. Pp. 227–235.

16. Kallmann, F. J. *The genetics of schizophrenia.* Locust Valley, N.Y.: Augustin, 1938.

17. Sheldon, W. H., Stevens, S. S., & Tucker, W. B. *The varieties of human physique.* New York: Harper, 1940.

18. Sheldon, W. H., & Stevens, S. S. *The varieties of temperament.* New York: Harper, 1942.

19. Terman, L. M. *Genetic studies of genius.* Vol. I. *Mental and physical traits of a thousand gifted children.* Stanford, Calif.: Stanford Univ. Press, 1925.

20. Linton, R. *The cultural background of personality.* New York: Appleton-Century-Crofts, 1945.

21. Goldfarb, W. Variations in adolescent adjustment of institutionally reared children. *Amer. J. Orthopsychiat.*, 1947, **17**, 449–457.

22. Hilgard, Josephine R. Anniversary reactions in parents precipitated by children. *Psychiatry*, 1953, **16**, 73–80.
23. Adorno, T. W., Frenkel-Brunswik, E., Levinson, D. J., and Sanford, R. N. *The authoritarian personality*. New York: Harper, 1950.
24. Sears, R. R. Experimental studies of projection. I. Attribution of traits. *J. soc. Psychol.*, 1936, 7, 151–163. Also *Survey of objective studies of psychoanalytic concepts*. New York: Social Science Research Council, 1943.

Chapter 10: Frustration and Conflict

1. Lewin, K. *A dynamic theory of personality*. New York: McGraw-Hill, 1935. Chap. 3.
2. Brown, J. S. Gradients of approach and avoidance responses and their relation to motivation. *J. comp. physiol. Psychol.*, 1948, **41**, 450–465.
3. Dunbar, H. F. *Emotions and bodily changes*. New York: Columbia Univ. Press, 1946.
4. Maier, N. R. F. *Frustration*. New York: McGraw-Hill, 1949.
5. Mowrer, O. H. A stimulus-response analysis of anxiety and its role as a reinforcing agent. *Psychol. Rev.*, 1939, **46**, 553–566.
6. Sears, R. R. Experimental studies of projection. I. Attribution of traits. *J. soc. Psychol.*, 1936, 7, 151–163.
7. Miller, N. E. Theory and experiment relating psychoanalytic displacement to stimulus-response generalization. *J. abnorm. soc. Psychol.*, 1948, **43**, 155–178.
8. Barker, R. G., Dembo, T., & Lewin, K. Frustration and regression: an experiment with young children. *Univ. Ia. Stud. Child Welf.*, 1941, **18**, No. 386.
9. Masserman, J. B. *Behavior and neurosis*. Chicago: Univ. of Chicago Press, 1943.
10. Landis, C., & Page, J. D. *Modern society and mental disease*. New York: Farrar & Rinehart, 1938.

Chapter 11: Mental Health and Psychotherapy

1. Thorne, F. C. *Principles of personality counseling*. Brandon, Vt.: Journal of Clinical Psychology, 1950.

2. Alexander, F., & French, T. M. (Eds.). *Psychoanalytic therapy*. New York: Ronald, 1946.
3. Kubie, L. S. *Practical and theoretical aspects of psychoanalysis*. New York: International Universities Press, 1950.
4. Riggs, A. F. *Intelligent living*. New York: Doubleday, 1929.
5. Rogers, C. R. *Client-centered therapy*. Boston: Houghton Mifflin, 1939.
6. Moreno, J. L. *Psychodrama*. New York: Beacon House, 1946.
7. Rogerson, C. H. *Play therapy in childhood*. New York: Oxford Univ. Press, 1939.
8. Klapman, J. W. *Group psychotherapy*. New York: Grune & Stratton, 1946.
9. Hobbs, N. Nondirective group therapy. *J. nat. Ass. Deans Women*, 1949, **12**, 114–121.
10. McKinney, F. *Psychology of personal adjustment* (2d Ed.). New York: Wiley, 1949.
11. Fisher, G. C. Some psychological aspects of pain. *J. prosthetic Dentistry*, 1955, **5**, 15–19.

Chapter 12: Social Influences on Behavior

1. Benedict, R. *Patterns of culture*. Boston: Houghton Mifflin, 1934.
2. Linton, R. *The cultural background of personality*. New York: Appleton-Century-Crofts, 1945. Pp. 78–79.
3. Warner, W. L., & Lunt, P. S. *The social life of a modern community*. New Haven, Conn.: Yale Univ. Press, 1941.
4. Centers, R. *The psychology of social classes*. Princeton. Princeton Univ. Press, 1949.
5. Newcomb, T. M. *Social psychology*. New York: Dryden, 1950. Pp. 555–571.
6. Heberle, R. *Social movements*. New York: Appleton-Century-Crofts, 1951.
7. Browne, C. G. The concentric organization chart. *J. appl. Psychol.*, 1950, **34**, 375–377.
8. Moreno, J. L. *Who shall survive?* Washington: Nervous and Mental Disorders Publishing Company, 1934.
9. Jenkins, J. G. Nominating technique as a method of evaluating air group morale. *J. aviat. Med.*, 1948, **19**, 12–19.
10. Lewin, K., Lippitt, R., & White, R. K. Patterns of aggressive behavior in experimentally created social climates. *J. soc. Psychol.*, 1939, **10**, 271–299.

11. Jenness, A. Social influences in the change of opinion. *J. abnorm. soc. Psychol.*, 1932, 27, 29–34. Also The role of discussion in changing opinion regarding a matter of fact. *J. abnorm. soc. Psychol.*, 1932, 27, 279–296.

12. Harlow, H. F. Social facilitation of feeding in the albino rat. *J. genet. Psychol.*, 1932, 41, 211–221.

13. Allport, F. H. *Social psychology.* Boston: Houghton Mifflin, 1924.

14. Boring, E. G. *A history of experimental psychology* (2d Ed.). New York: Appleton-Century-Crofts, 1950. See especially the notes of Chap. 1.

15. Krech, D., & Crutchfield, R. *Theory and problems of social psychology.* New York: McGraw-Hill, 1948.

16. Hemphill, J. K. Situational factors in leadership. *Ohio State Univ. Stud., Bur. Educ. Res. Monogr.*, 1949, No. 32.

17. Stogdill, R. M. Personal factors associated with leadership: a survey of the literature. *J. Psychol.*, 1948, 25, 35–71.

18. Guetzkow, H. (Ed.). *Groups, leadership and men.* Pittsburgh: Carnegie Univ. Press, 1951.

19. Office of Strategic Services, Assessment Staff. *Assessment of men: selection of personnel for the Office of Strategic Services.* New York: Rinehart, 1948.

20. Warner, W. L., et al., Democracy in Jonesville, a study in quality and inequality. New York: Harper, 1949, p. 22.

Chapter 13: Attitudes and Beliefs

1. Social Science Research Council. *Public reaction to the atomic bomb and world affairs.* Ithaca, N.Y.: Cornell Univ., 1947.

2. Murphy, G., Murphy, L. B., & Newcomb, T. M. *Experimental social psychology.* New York: Harper, 1937.

3. Hirschberg, G., & Gilliland, A. R. Parent-child relationships in attitudes. *J. abnorm. soc. Psychol.*, 1942, 37, 125–130.

4. Morgan, C. L., & Remmers, H. H. Liberalism and conservatism of college students as affected by depression. *Sch. & Soc.*, 1935, 41, 780–784.

5. Horowitz, E. L. The development of attitudes toward the Negro. *Arch. Psychol. N.Y.*, 1936, 28, No. 194.

6. Dexter, E. S. Personality traits related to conservatism and radicalism. *Character & Pers.*, 1939, 7, 230–237.

7. Levine, J. M., & Murphy, G. The learning and forgetting of controversial material. *J. abnorm. soc. Psychol.*, 1943, 38, 507–517.

8. For a fuller discussion of this point, see Krech, D., & Crutchfield, R. S. *Theory and problems of social psychology.* New York: McGraw-Hill, 1948. Pp. 190–194.

9. Thurstone, L. L., & Chave, E. J. *The measurement of attitudes.* Chicago: Univ. of Chicago Press, 1929.

10. Likert, R. A technique for the measurement of attitudes. *Arch. Psychol. N.Y.*, 1932, No. 140.

11. Likert, R. The sample interview survey. In W. Dennis (Ed.), *Current trends in psychology.* Pittsburgh, Pa.: Univ. of Pittsburgh Press, 1947.

12. Newcomb, T. M. *Social psychology.* New York: Dryden, 1950. Pp. 183–184.

13. Hilgard, E. R., & Payne, S. L. Those not at home: riddle for pollsters. *Publ. Opin. Quart.*, 1944, 8, 254–261.

14. Dubois, C. How many readers? In A. B. Blankenship (Ed.), *How to conduct consumer and opinion research.* New York: Harper, 1946.

15. Hooper, C. E. The coincidental method of measuring radio audience size. In A. B. Blankenship (Ed.), *How to conduct consumer and opinion research.* New York: Harper, 1946.

16. Sargent, S. S. Emotional stereotypes in The Chicago Tribune. *Sociometry*, 1939, 2, 69–75.

17. The psychologist was Thorndike, but the analysis of the social significance of the arithmetic problems was made by Freeman. See Freeman, E. *Social psychology.* New York: Holt, 1936.

18. Asch, S. E., Block, H., & Hertzman, M. Studies in the principles of judgments and attitudes. II. Determination of judgments by group and by ego standards. *J. soc. Psychol.*, 1940, 12, 433–465.

19. Luchins, A. S. Social influence on perception of complex drawings. *J. soc. Psychol.*, 1945, 21, 257–273.

Chapter 14: Prejudice and Social Conflict

1. Klineberg, O. *Social psychology* (Rev. Ed.). New York: Holt, 1954.
2. Horowitz, E. L., & Horowitz, R. E. Development of social attitudes in children. *Sociometry*, 1938, 1, 301–338.
3. Newcomb, T. M., & Svehla, G. Intra-family relationships in attitudes. *Sociometry*, 1938, 1, 180–205.
4. Blake, R., & Dennis, W. The development of stereotypes concerning the Negro. *J. abnorm. soc. Psychol.*, 1943, 38, 525–531.
5. Rose, A. M. Army policies toward Negro soldiers. *Ann. Amer. Acad. political soc. Sci.*, 1946, 244, 90–94.
6. Sears, R. R., Hovland, C. I., & Miller, N. E. Minor studies in aggression. I. Measurement of aggressive behavior. *J. Psychol.*, 1940, 9, 277–281.
7. Miller, N. E., & Bugelski, R. Minor studies of aggression. II. The influence of frustration imposed by the in-group on attitudes expressed toward out-groups. *J. Psychol.*, 1948, 25, 437–452.
8. Frenkel-Brunswick, E., & Sanford, R. N. Some personality factors in anti-semitism. *J. Psychol.*, 1945, 20, 271–291.
9. Allport, G. W., & Kramer, B. M. Some roots of prejudice. *J. Psychol.*, 1946, 22, 9–39.
10. Levine, J. M., & Murphy, G. The learning and forgetting of controversial material. *J. abnorm. soc. Psychol.*, 1943, 38, 507–517.
11. Cooper, E., & Jahoda, M. The evasion of propaganda: how prejudiced people respond to anti-prejudice propaganda. *J. Psychol.*, 1947, 23, 15–25.
12. Hartley, E. *Problems in prejudice.* New York: King's Crown, 1946.
13. Katz, D., & Braly, K. Racial stereotypes of one hundred college students. *J. abnorm. soc. Psychol.*, 1933, 28, 280–290.
14. Bayton, J. A. The racial stereotypes of Negro college students. *J. abnorm, soc. Psychol.*, 1941, 36, 97–102.
15. Roethlisberger, F. J., & Dickson, W. J. *Management and the worker.* Cambridge, Mass.: Harvard Univ. Press, 1939.
16. Leighton, A. H. *The governing of men; general principles and recommendations based on experience at a Japanese relocation camp.* Princeton, N.J.: Princeton Univ. Press, 1945.
17. Mintz, A. Nonadaptive group behavior. *J. abnorm. soc. Psychol.*, 1951, 46, 150–159.
18. Sherif, M., & Sherif, C. W. *Groups in harmony and tension; an integration of studies of intergroup relations.* New York: Harper, 1953.
19. Stouffer, S. A., et al. *The American soldier.* Vol. II. *Combat and its aftermath.* Princeton, N. J.: Princeton Univ. Press, 1949.

Chapter 15: Intellectual Abilities

1. Terman, L. M., & Merrill, M. A. *Measuring intelligence.* Boston: Houghton Mifflin, 1937.
2. Wechsler, D. *The measurement of adult intelligence* (3d Ed.). Baltimore: Williams & Wilkins, 1944.
3. Wechsler, D. *Wechsler Intelligence Scale for children.* New York: Psychological Corp., 1949.
4. Thurstone, L. L. Primary mental abilities. *Psychometr. Monogr.*, 1938, No. 1. Also Thurstone, L. L., & Thurstone, T. G. Factorial studies of intelligence. *Psychometr. Monogr.*, 1941, No. 2.
5. Doll, E. A. *The Vineland Social Maturity Scale, revised condensed manual of instructions.* Vineland, N.J.: Smith Printing House, 1936.
6. Goodenough, F. *Mental testing; its history, principles, and applications.* New York: Rinehart, 1949.
7. Terman, L. M. Psychological approaches to the biography of genius. *Science*, 1940, 92, 293–301.
8. See a series of volumes by L. M. Terman and his associates entitled *Studies of Genius* and published by Stanford University Press.
9. Anastasi, A., & Foley, J. P., Jr. *Differential psychology* (Rev. Ed.). New York: Macmillan, 1949.
10. Johnson, W. B., & Terman, L. M. Some highlights in the literature of psychological sex differences. *J. Psychol.*, 1940, 9, 327–336. Also Terman, L. M. Psychological sex differences. In Carmichael, L. (Ed.), *Manual of child psychology.* New York: Wiley, 1946. Chap. 19.
11. U.S. Department of Commerce. *Statistical abstract of the United States* (72d Ed.). Washington: U.S. Government Printing Office, 1951. Pp. 1–54.

12. Jones, H. E., & Conrad, H. S. The growth and decline of intelligence: a study of a homogeneous group between the ages of ten and sixty. *Genet. Psychol. Monogr.*, 1933, **13**, 223–298.

13. Harrell, T. W., & Harrell, M. S. Army General Classification Test scores for civilian occupations. *Educ. psychol. Measmt.*, 1945, **5**, 229–239.

14. McNemar, Q. *The revision of the Stanford-Binet Scale.* Boston: Houghton Mifflin, 1942.

15. Hilgard, E. R. *Introduction to psychology.* New York: Harcourt, Brace, 1953. P. 403. Hilgard computed these correlations from data given by Skodak and Skeels, cited in reference 16 below.

16. Skodak, M., & Skeels, H. M. A final follow-up of one hundred adopted children. *J. genet. Psychol.*, 1949, **75**, 3–19.

17. Burks, B. S. The relative influence of nature and nurture upon mental development: a comparative study of foster parent–child resemblance and true parent–child resemblance. *Yearb. nat. Soc. Stud. Educ.*, 1928, **27**, 219–316. Also Leahy, A. M. Nature-nurture and intelligence. *Genet. Psychol. Monogr.*, 1935, **17**, 235–308.

18. Klineberg, O. *Negro intelligence and selective migration.* New York: Columbia Univ. Press, 1935.

Chapter 16: Aptitudes and Vocational Adjustment

1. Dorcus, R. M., & Jones, M. H. *Handbook of employee selection.* New York: McGraw-Hill, 1950.

2. Tiffin, J. *Industrial psychology* (3d Ed.). New York: Prentice-Hall, 1952.

3. Ferguson, L. W. *Personality measurement.* New York: McGraw-Hill, 1952.

4. Charters, W. W., & Whitley, I. B. *Analysis of secretarial duties and traits.* Baltimore: Williams & Wilkins, 1924.

5. Flanagan, J. C. Defining the requirements of the executive's job. *Personnel*, 1951, **28**, 28–35.

6. U.S. Department of Labor. *Dictionary of occupational titles.* Washington: U.S. Government Printing Office, 1939.

7. Spriegel, W. R., & Wallace, R. F. Recent trends in personnel selection and induction. *Personnel*, 1948, **25**, 77–88.

8. Hollingworth, H. L. *Vocational psychology and character analysis.* New York: Appleton-Century-Crofts, 1929. Pp. 115–119.

9. Hovland, H. C., & Wonderlic, J. T. Prediction of industrial success from a standardized interview. *J. appl. Psychol.*, 1939, **23**, 537–546.

10. Stead, W. H., et al. *Occupational counseling techniques.* New York: American Book, 1940.

11. Viteles, M. S. *Industrial psychology.* New York: Norton, 1932. P. 150.

12. Lindahl, L. G. Movement analysis as an industrial training method. *J. appl. Psychol.*, 1945, **29**, 420–436.

13. Bellows, R. M. *Psychology of personnel in business and industry.* New York: Prentice-Hall, 1949.

14. Sisson, E. D. Forced choice—the new Army rating. *Personnel Psychol.*, 1948, **1**, 365–381.

15. Roethlisberger, F. J., & Dickson, W. J. *Management and the worker.* Cambridge, Mass.: Harvard Univ. Press, 1939.

16. Harrell, T. W. *Industrial psychology.* New York: Rinehart, 1949. P. 319.

Chapter 17: Work and Efficiency

1. Mackworth, N. H. *Researches on the measurement of human performance.* Medical Research Council Report No. 268, 1950.

2. Robinson, E. S., & Bills, A. G. Two factors in the work decrement. *J. exp. Psychol.*, 1926, **9**, 415–443.

3. Muscio, B. *Lectures on industrial psychology* (2d Ed.). London: Routledge, 1920.

4. Poffenberger, A. T. *Principles of applied psychology.* New York: Appleton-Century-Crofts, 1942.

5. Mackworth, N. H. The breakdown of vigilance during prolonged visual search. *Quart. J. exp. Psychol.*, 1948, **1**, 6–21.

6. Manzer, C. W. Experimental investigation of rest pauses. *Arch. Psychol. N.Y.*, 1927, No. 90.

7. McGehee, W., & Owen, E. B. Authorized and unauthorized rest pauses in clerical work. *J. appl. Psychol.*, 1940, **24**, 605–614.

8. Miles, G. H., & Angles, A. The influence of short time on speed of production. *J. nat. Inst. industr. Psychol.*, 1925, **2**, 300–302.

9. Berrien, F. K. The effects of noise. *Psychol. Bull.*, 1946, **43**, 143–158.

10. Humes, J. F. Effects of occupational music on scrappage in the manufacture of radio tubes. *J. appl. Psychol.*, 1942, **25**, 573–587.
11. Roethlisberger, F. J., & Dickson, W. J. Management and the worker. Cambridge, Mass.: Harvard Univ. Press, 1939.
12. *IES lighting handbook: the standard lighting guide.* New York: Illuminating Engineering Society, 1948.
13. *Heating, ventilating, air conditioning guide.* New York: American Society of Heating and Ventilating Engineers, 1948.
14. Armstrong, H. G. Principles and practice of aviation medicine. Boston: Houghton Mifflin, 1946.
15. Edwards, A. S. Effects of the loss of one hundred hours of sleep. *Amer. J. Psychol.*, 1941, **54**, 80–91.
16. Marshall, H. Alcohol: a critical review of the literature. *Psychol. Bull.*, 1941, **38**, 193–217.
17. Hull, C. L. The influence of tobacco smoking on mental and motor efficiency. *Psychol. Monogr.*, 1924, **33**, No. 150.

Chapter 18: Vision

1. This work was not published in full until Newton brought forth his *Opticks* in 1704.
2. Oesterberg, G. Topography of the layer of rods and cones in the human retina. *Acta ophthal., Kbh.*, Suppl., 1935, **61**, 1–102.
3. Polyak, S. L. *The retina.* Chicago: Univ. of Chicago Press, 1941.
4. Dimmick, F. L., & Hubbard, M. R. The spectral location of psychologically unique yellow, green, and blue. *Amer. J. Psychol.*, 1939, **52**, 242–254. Also the spectral components of psychologically unique red. *Amer. J. Psychol.*, 1939, **52**, 348–353.
5. Helmholtz, H. L. F. von. *Physiological optics* (Trans. J. P. C. Southall). Vol. II. Rochester, N.Y.: Optical Society of America, 1924.
6. For additional information on Dalton's report of color deficiency, see Boring, E. G. *Sensation and perception in the history of experimental psychology.* New York: Appleton-Century-Crofts, 1942. Pp. 184, 196.
7. Geldard, F. A. *The human senses.* New York: Wiley, 1953. Chap. 4.
8. Gibson, K. S., & Tyndall, E. P. T. Visibility of radiant energy. *Sci. Papers Bureau Standards*, 1923, **19**, No. 475.

9. Hecht, S., & Williams, R. E. The visibility of monochromatic radiation and the absorption spectrum of visual purple. *J. gen. Physiol.*, 1922, **5**, 1–33.
10. Wertheim, T. Ueber die indirekte Sehschaerfe. *Z. Psychol.*, 1894, **7**, 172–187.
11. Moon, P., & Spencer, D. E. Visual data applied to lighting design. *J. opt. Soc. Amer.*, 1944, **34**, 605–617.
12. Connor, J. P., & Ganoung, R. E. An experimental determination of the visual thresholds at low levels of illumination. *J. opt. Soc. Amer.*, 1935, **25**, 287–294. Also Cobb, P. W., & Moss, F. K. The four variables of the visual threshold. *J. Franklin Inst.*, 1928, **205**, 831–884.
13. Luckiesh, M. *Light, vision and seeing.* New York: Van Nostrand, 1944.

Chapter 19: Hearing and Lower Senses

1. Stevens, S. S. (Ed.). *Handbook of experimental psychology.* New York: Wiley, 1951. Chaps. 25–28.
2. Geldard, F. A. *The human senses.* New York: Wiley, 1953. Pp. 131–132.
3. Crocker, E. C. *Flavor.* New York: McGraw-Hill, 1945.
4. Ross, S., & Harriman, A. E. A preliminary study of the Crocker-Henderson odor-classification system. *Amer. J. Psychol.*, 1949, **62**, 399–404.
5. Osgood, C. E. *Method and theory in experimental psychology.* New York: Oxford Univ. Press, 1953.
6. See reference 2 or 5, above.
7. Wolff, H. G., & Wolf, S. *Pain.* Springfield, Ill.: Charles C Thomas, 1948.
8. Boyd, D. A., Jr., & Nie, L. W. Congenital universal indifference to pain. *Arch. Neurol. Psychiat., Chicago*, 1949, **61**, 402–412.
9. Hardy, J. D., Goodell, H., & Wolff, H. G. The influence of skin temperature upon the pain threshold as evoked by thermal radiation. *Science*, 1951, **114**, 149–150.
10. Wendt, G. R. *Vestibular function.* In Stevens, S. S. (Ed.), *Handbook of experimental psychology.* New York: Wiley, 1951. Chap. 31.

Chapter 20: Language and Speech

1. Stevens, S. S. Introduction: a definition of communication. *J. acoust. Soc. Amer.*, 1950, **22**, 689–690.

2. Howes, D. H., & Solomon, R. L. Visual duration threshold as a function of word-probability. *J. exp. Psychol.*, 1951, **41**, 401–410.

3. Data of R. L. Solomon, discussed in Miller, G. A. *Language and communication.* New York: McGraw-Hill, 1951.

4. This experiment, performed by Miller, Bruner, and Postman, is described in Miller, G. A. *Language and communication.* New York: McGraw-Hill, 1951.

5. Johnson, W. *Language and speech hygiene* (2d Ed.). Chicago: Institute of General Semantics, Monogr. No. 1, 1941.

6. Boder, D. P. The adjective-verb quotient; a contribution to the psychology of language. *Psychol. Rec.*, 1940, **3**, 309–343.

7. Flesch, R. *The art of plain talk.* New York: Harper, 1946.

8. Reference 7, pp. 170 and 171.

9. Johnson, W. Studies in language behavior. I. A program of research. *Psychol. Monogr.*, 1944, **56**, 1–15.

10. Thorndike, E. L., & Lorge, I. *The teacher's word book of 30,000 words.* New York: Bureau of Publications, Teachers College, Columbia University, 1944.

11. Cameron, N., & Magaret, A. *Behavior pathology.* Boston: Houghton Mifflin, 1951. P. 510.

Chapter 21: The Brain and Nervous System

1. Ranson, S. W. Somnolence caused by hypothalamic lesions in the monkey. *Arch. Neurol. Psychiat., Chicago*, 1939, **41**, 1–23.

2. Nauta, W. J. H. Hypothalamic regulation of sleep in rats; an experimental study. *J. Neurophysiol.*, 1946, **9**, 285–316.

3. Keller, A. D. Autonomic discharges elicited by physiological stimuli in midbrain preparations. *Amer. J. Physiol.*, 1932, **100**, 576–586.

4. Davison, C., & Demuth, E. L. Disturbances in sleep mechanisms: a clinicopathologic study. *Arch. Neurol. Psychiat., Chicago*, 1945, **53**, 399–406; 1946, **55**, 126–133, 364–381.

5. Kleitman, N. *Sleep and wakefulness.* Chicago: Univ. of Chicago Press, 1939.

6. Bard, P. A diencephalic mechanism for the expression of rage with special reference to the sympathetic nervous system. *Amer. J. Physiol.*, 1928, **84**, 490–515. Also Cannon, W. B. The James-Lange theory of emotions: a critical examination and an alternative theory. *Amer. J. Psychol.*, 1927, **39**, 106–124.

7. Bard, P., & Mountcastle, V. B. Some forebrain mechanisms involved in the expression of rage with special reference to suppression of angry behavior. *Res. Publ. Ass. nerv. ment. Dis.*, 1947, **27**, 362–404.

8. Dempsey, E. W., & Rioch, D. McK. The localization in the brain stem of the oestrous responses of the female guinea pig. *J. Neurophysiol.*, 1939, **2**, 9–18.

9. Brookhart, J. M., & Dey, F. L. Reduction of sexual behavior in male guinea pigs by hypothalamic lesions. *Amer. J. Physiol.*, 1941, **133**, 551–554. Also Dey, F. L., Fisher, C., Berry, C. M., & Ranson, S. W. Disturbances in reproductive functions caused by hypothalamic lesions in female guinea pigs. *Amer. J. Physiol.*, 1940, **129**, 39–46.

10. Brobeck, J. R. Mechanism of the development of obesity in animals with hypothalamic lesions. *Physiol. Rev.*, 1946, **26**, 541–559.

11. Penfield, W. G., & Boldrey, E. Somatic motor and sensory representation in the cerebral cortex of man as studied by electrical stimulation. *Brain*, 1937, **60**, 389–443.

12. Kluever, H. Visual mechanisms. In *Biological Symposia.* Vol. VII. New York: Ronald, 1942.

13. Culler, E. A. Recent advances in some concepts of conditioning. *Psychol. Rev.*, 1938, **45**, 134–153.

14. Lashley, K. S. The mechanism of vision. XII. Nervous structures concerned in the acquisition and retention of habits based on reactions to light. *Comp. Psychol. Monogr.*, 1935, **11**, 43–79.

15. Lashley, K. S. *Brain mechanisms and intelligence.* Chicago: Univ. of Chicago Press, 1929.

16. Ades, H. W. Effect of extirpation of parastriate cortex on learned visual discrimination in monkeys. *J. Neuropath. exp. Neurol.*, 1946, **5**, 60–65.

17. Ruch, T. C., Fulton, J. F., & German, W. J. Sensory discrimination in the monkey,

chimpanzee, and man after lesions of the parietal lobe. *Arch. Neurol. Psychiat., Chicago,* 1938, **39,** 919–937.

18. Early studies of this problem were made by Jacobsen; see Jacobsen, C. F. Functions of the frontal association areas in primates. *Arch. Neurol. Psychiat., Chicago,* 1935, **33,** 558–569. For a more recent study of the factor of attention, see Harlow, H. F., & Johnson, T. Problem solution by monkeys following bilateral removal of the prefrontal areas. III. Test of initiation of behavior. *J. exp. Psychol.,* 1943, **32,** 495–500.

19. Freeman, W., & Watts, J. W. *Psychosurgery.* Springfield, Ill.: Charles C Thomas, 1942.

Chapter 22: The Internal Environment

1. Dempsey, E. W. Metabolic function of the endocrine glands. *Annu. Rev. Physiol.,* 1946, 8, 451–466.

2. Beadle, G. E. Genetics and metabolism in Neurospora. *Physiol. Rev.,* 1945, **25,** 643–663.

3. Jervis, G. A. A contribution to the study of the influence of heredity on mental deficiency. The genetics of phenylpyruvic oligophrenia. *Proc. Amer. Ass. Stud. ment. Def.,* 1939, **44,** 13–24.

4. Ingalls, T. H. Biologic implications of mongolism. In Milbank Memorial Fund, *The biology of mental health and disease.* New York: Hoeber, 1952. Also Ingalls, T. H. Mongolism. *Sci. Amer.,* 1952, **186,** 60–66.

5. See summary by Morgan, C. T., & Stellar, E. *Physiological psychology* (2d Ed.). New York: McGraw-Hill, 1950. Pp. 533–535.

6. Stellar, E., & McElroy, W. D. Does glutamic acid have any effect on learning? *Science,* 1948, **108,** 281–283.

7. Harrell, R. F. Further effects of added thiamine on learning and other processes. *Teach. Coll. Contr. Educ.,* 1947, No. 928.

8. O'Neill, P. H. The effect of subsequent maze-learning ability of graded amounts of vitamin B₁ in the diet of very young rats. *J. genet. Psychol.,* 1949, **74,** 85–95.

9. Shock, N. W. Some psychophysiological relations. *Psychol. Bull.,* 1939, **36,** 447–476.

10. Palmer, H. D., & Braceland, F. J. Six years experience with narcosis therapy in psychiatry. *Amer. J. Psychiat.,* 1937, **94,** 37–57.

11. Boerstecher, E., Jr., Sutton, H. E., Berry, H. K., Brown, W. D., Reed, J., Rich, G. B., Berry, L. J., & Williams, R. J. Biochemical individuality. V. Exploration with respect to the metabolic patterns of compulsive drinkers. *Arch. Biochem.,* 1950, **29,** 27–40.

12. Williams, R. J. *Nutrition and alcoholism.* Norman, Okla.: Univ. of Oklahoma Press, 1951.

13. Selye, H. *The physiology and pathology of exposure to stress.* Montreal: Acta, Inc., 1950.

14. Hoskins, R. G. *The biology of schizophrenia.* New York: Norton, 1946.

15. Kallman, F. J. The genetic theory of schizophrenia: an analysis of 691 schizophrenic twin index families. *Amer. J. Psychiat.,* 1946, **103,** 309–322.

Chapter 23: Animal Behavior

1. Grether, W. F. Comparative visual acuity thresholds in terms of retinal image widths. *J. comp. Psychol.,* 1941, **31,** 23–33. Also Warkentin, J. The visual acuity of some vertebrates. *Psychol. Bull.,* 1937, **34,** 793.

2. Walton, W. E., & Bornemeier, R. T. Color discrimination in rats. *J. comp. Psychol.,* 1939, **28,** 417–436.

3. Von Frisch, K. *Bees: their vision, chemical senses, and language.* Ithaca, N.Y.: Cornell Univ. Press, 1950.

4. Wever, E. G., & Bray, C. W. Auditory sensitivity of katydids and crickets. *Psychol. Bull.,* 1933, **30,** 548.

5. Munn, N. L. *The evolution and growth of human behavior.* Boston: Houghton Mifflin, 1955. Pp. 95–98.

6. Ash, P. The sensory capacities of infrahuman mammals: vision, audition, gustation. *Psychol. Bull.,* 1951, **48,** 289–326.

7. Griffin, D. R., & Galambos, R. The sensory basis of obstacle avoidance by flying bats. *J. exp. Zool.,* 1941, **86,** 481–506.

8. Lorenz, K. Z. King Solomon's Ring. New York: Crowell, 1952. Also see reference 15 below.

9. Whitman, C. O. *Animal behaviour.* Woods Hole, Mass.: Marine Biological Laboratory, 1899.

10. Eliot, H. H. *An introduction to the study of bird behaviour.* London: Cambridge Univ. Press, 1929.

11. Lorenz, K. The companion in the bird's world. *Auk*, 1937, **54**, 245–273.
12. Ramsay, A. O., & Hess, E. H. A laboratory approach to the study of imprinting. *Wilson Bull.*, 1954, **66**, 196–206.
13. For a summary of research on this topic, see reference 5 above, Chap. 5.
14. Hasler, A. D., & Wisby, W. J. Experiments described in Stone, C. P. (Ed.), *Comparative psychology* (3d Ed.). New York: Prentice-Hall, 1951. Pp. 325–326.
15. Tinbergen, N. *The study of instinct.* London: Oxford Univ. Press, 1951.
16. For summary of research on learning in paramecium, see reference 5 above, pp. 114–116.
17. *Time*, Oct. 11, 1948, p. 71.

Techniques of Study

1. Robinson, F. P. *Effective study* (Rev. Ed.). New York: Harper, 1946.
2. Gifford, W. S. Does business want scholars? *Harper's Magazine*, 1928, **156**, 669–674.
3. Gambrill, B. L. *College achievement and vocational efficiency.* New York: Columbia Univ. Press, 1922.
4. Remmlein, M. K. Scholastic accomplishment as affected by intelligence and participation in extra-curricular activities. *J. appl. Psychol.*, 1939, **23**, 602–607.
5. Bird, C., & Bird, D. M. *Learning more by effective study.* New York: Appleton-Century-Crofts, 1945.
6. Eruick, A. The significance of library reading among college students. *Sch. & Soc.*, 1932, **36**, 92–96.
7. McClusky, H. Y. An experiment on the influence of preliminary skimming on reading. *J. educ. Psychol.*, 1934, **25**, 521–529.
8. Deese, J. *The psychology of learning.* New York: McGraw-Hill, 1952.
9. Gates, A. I. Recitation as a factor in memorizing. *Arch. Psychol. N.Y.*, 1917, **6**, No. 40.
10. Robinson, F. P., & Hall, Prudence. Studies of higher level reading abilities. *J. educ. Psychol.*, 1941, **32**, 241–252.

GLOSSARY

This glossary defines all important terms and phrases used in the book. It includes both technical terms and common words used in a special or restricted sense in psychology. In each case, the meaning given is that used in the book. For other meanings or more complete definitions, one of the standard psychological dictionaries should be consulted.

Ability. A general term referring to any knowledge, skill, or capacity that can be demonstrated by appropriate measurements.

Absolute threshold. The minimum intensity of a stimulus that can be perceived or, in the case of nerve fibers, that can elicit a nervous impulse.

Abstraction. A learning process in which an individual learns to disregard some properties of objects and to respond only to certain properties that the objects have in common. It is the process through which concepts (*q.v.*) are formed.

Accommodation. A change in the shape of the lens of the eye that focuses the image of an object on the retina. It compensates for the distance of the object from the observer.

Acquired fear. A learned fear.

Acquired motive. A learned motive.

Activity. A general term covering restlessness, running, exploration, and miscellaneous responses to environmental stimuli.

Adaptation. A change in the sensitivity of a sense organ due to stimulation or lack of stimulation. In general, all senses become less sensitive as they are stimulated and more sensitive in the absence of stimulation. For an example, *see* Dark adaptation.

Adjustment. The relationship that exists between an individual and his environment, especially his social environment, in the satisfaction of his motives.

Adrenal glands. A pair of endocrine glands located on the top of the kidneys. They secrete the hormones adrenalin and cortin.

Adrenalin. A hormone secreted by the adrenal glands. It mimics the action of the sympathetic system, and it is secreted in strong emotion.

Affiliative needs. Needs to affiliate with other people. They include several specific needs, such as those for companionship and for sexual affiliation.

Aggression. A general term applying to feelings of anger or hostility. Aggression functions as a motive, which is often frustrated.

Agnosia. Inability to recognize objects and their meaning, usually due to damage in the brain.

Alarm reaction. The first stage of the general adaptation syndrome, in which a person reacts vigorously to a stressful situation.

Albedo. The percentage of light falling on a surface that is reflected by the surface. It is the important factor in brightness constancy.

Alcoholic psychosis. A psychosis developing as a result of prolonged alcoholism. It is characterized by defects of memory, disorientation, delusions, and other symptoms similar to those seen in senile psychosis.

All-or-none law. The principle that a nervous impulse is either evoked at full strength or not evoked at all.

Alternation. An experimental method in which the subject is required to alternate responses in a pattern such as left-right-left-right or left-left-right-right. The method has been used in the study of thinking in animals and children. *See also* Delayed alternation, Delayed reaction.

Amoeba. One kind of a single-celled animal.

Amphibia. A class of vertebrates that includes frogs, toads, and salamanders.

Animistic reasoning. Reasoning based on coincidences of nature. For example, if there is a thunderstorm on the day a boy plays hooky from school, then according to animistic reasoning, the boy's truancy caused the thunderstorm.

Anomalous color defect. Color weakness in which a person is able to discriminate colors when they are vivid but is color-blind when they are poorly saturated. There are the same varieties of anomalous color defect as there are of color blindness (*q.v.*).

Anoxia. Lack of sufficient oxygen to maintain normal metabolism.

Anxiety. A vague fear, acquired through learning and through stimulus generalization, often a consequence of frustration.

Anxiety reactions. One of the major classes of psychoneurosis, characterized by excessive, chronic anxiety.

Apes. A group of animals resembling man and including monkeys, gorillas, chimpanzees, and baboons.

Aphasia. A language defect ordinarily due to damage or disease in the brain. It may be a sensory disorder consisting of some impairment in reading or understanding of speech, or it may be a motor disorder consisting of an impairment in the writing or speaking of language.

Apparent movement. Movement that is perceived because the observer sees an object in successively different positions rather than because the object is seen to move. For example, motion pictures are really rapidly presented stationary pictures but are perceived as moving.

Approach-approach conflict. Conflict in which a person is motivated to approach two different goals that are incompatible.

Approach-avoidance conflict. Conflict in which a person is both attracted and repelled by the same goal.

Apraxia. A memory disorder, due to brain injury, characterized by inability to remember the performance of skilled movements, such as driving a car, dressing oneself, or playing baseball. *See also* Agnosia, Aphasia.

Aptitude. Ability to profit by training. *See* Scholastic aptitude, Vocational aptitude.

Area and block sampling. A sampling procedure, used in surveys and public-opinion polls, in which the interviewer is sent to specific addresses previously selected from a detailed map. *See also* Sampling, Survey methods.

Arithmetic mean. One measure of central tendency, commonly called the average; computed by summing all the scores in a frequency distribution, then dividing by the number of scores. *Cf.* Median.

Association area. A general term for an area of the cerebral cortex concerned in learning and memory.

Association neuron. A neuron, usually within the central nervous system, which occupies a position between sensory and motor neurons.

Astigmatism. Irregularities in the shape of the cornea or other structures of the eye transmitting light to the retina, which irregularities cause parts of an image projected on the retina to be out of focus.

Attention. Focusing on certain aspects of current experience and neglecting others. Attention has a focus in which events are clearly perceived and a margin in which they are less clearly perceived.

Attitude. A tendency to respond either positively (favorably) or negatively (unfavorably) toward certain persons, objects, or situations.

Attitude scale. A method of measuring attitudes, which typically consists of a set of items, each having a pre-established scale value, to be checked with favor or disfavor by the testee.

Audience measurement. Measurement of the characteristics of the people who read a periodical or listen to radio and television programs; designed to assist advertisers in determining what and how to advertise in a particular medium.

Audiogram. A graph representing the absolute threshold of hearing at different frequencies.

Audiometer. A device for measuring the audiogram, used to detect deafness.

Auditory canal. The canal leading from the outside of the head to the eardrum; also called the external auditory meatus.

Auditory nerve. The nerve leading from the cochlea and conducting auditory impulses to the brain. The term is often used loosely to refer to the eighth cranial nerve, which contains nerve fibers for the vestibular sense as well as for hearing.

Autonomic changes. Changes in heart rate, blood pressure, breathing, etc., controlled by impulses in the autonomic system.

Autonomic system. A division of the nervous system serving the endocrine glands and the smooth muscles. It controls internal changes in the body during emotion as well as other functions essential to homeostasis.

Avoidance-avoidance conflict. Conflict in which a person is caught between two negative goals. As he tries to avoid one goal, he is brought closer to the other, and vice versa.

B

Basic motives. A set of motives that can be used generally to describe and compare the motives of different people.

Basket nerve ending. A specialized structure at the root of hairs on the body. It is regarded as a sense organ for pressure or touch.

Basilar membrane. The membrane in the cochlea on which the organ of Corti is located. Its motion is important in hearing.

Beginning spurt. The tendency for the work curve to be elevated briefly at the beginning of a period of work; opposite to warming up.

Behavioral sciences. The sciences most concerned with human and animal behavior. The principal behavioral sciences are psychology, sociology, and social anthropology, but they also include certain aspects of history, economics, political science, physiology, zoology, and physics.

Behaviorism. A viewpoint held early in the twentieth century by some experimental psychologists opposed to the method of introspection, who proposed that psychology be limited to the study of observable behavior.

Belief. The acceptance of a statement or proposition. It does not necessarily involve an attitude, although it frequently does.

Binaural. Pertaining to the simultaneous use of the two ears.

Binocular. Pertaining to the simultaneous use of the two eyes.

Bizarre images. Images that are distortions or peculiar combinations of past experience. They occur in dreams and in hallucinations.

Blind spot. The point on the retina where fibers leave the eyeball to form the optic nerve. There are no photosensitive receptors at this point. However, the blind spots of the two retinas are not on corresponding points; hence a person can see with one eye what he cannot see with the other.

Brain. The part of the nervous system encased in the skull. It is the site of centers for sensory experience, motivation, learning, and thinking.

Brightness. A dimension of color that refers to the relative degree of whiteness, grayness, or blackness of the color, as distinguished from hue and saturation. The term is also used in a slightly different sense to refer to the perceived intensity of a light.

Brightness constancy. A phenomenon of perception in which a person perceives an object as having the same brightness whether it be in bright or in dim illumination. For example, snow looks white in moonlight, and coal appears black in sunlight, even though, under these circumstances, coal reflects more light than snow.

Cafeteria feeding. A method used to study specific hungers. Different kinds of food are offered to a subject, and he chooses the ones he wants.

Castration. Operative removal of the male gonads, used experimentally to study the effects of reducing sex hormones. *Cf.* Ovariectomy.

Catatonia. A state of muscular rigidity, seen in certain cases of schizophrenia. In the catatonic state, a person may remain fixed in an absurd position for minutes or hours.

Cathode-ray oscilloscope. An electrical device which translates a sound wave into a picture that may be viewed on a screen.

Centile score. The percentage of the scores in a distribution that are equal to or less than the obtained score; sometimes called percentile score. The centile score is a convenient method of expressing a score so that its relative meaning can be understood without knowing the original units of measurement.

Central nervous system. The part of the nervous system enclosed in the bony case of the skull and backbone. *Cf.* Peripheral nervous system.

Central sulcus. A sulcus (*q.v.*) or fissure in the cerebral cortex dividing the frontal lobe from the parietal lobe.

Cerebral cortex. A large mass of gray matter, which is part of the forebrain, lying in folds near the interior surface of the skull.

Cerebral hemispheres. Two symmetrical halves of the cerebral cortex and their associated structures.

Chemical senses. The senses of taste and smell.

Chimpanzee. One of the higher apes; a primate.

Choroid coat. The middle layer of the wall of the eyeball, dark in color and opaque. It reduces stray light which might otherwise enter the eyeball from the side and blur vision.

Chromosomes. Colored bodies seen under the microscope in the nucleus of the cells of the body. They contain genes.

Ciliary muscle. A muscle attached to the lens of the eye which thickens the lens when it contracts and flattens the lens when it relaxes. It controls accommodation.

Classical conditioning. Learning that takes place when a conditioning stimulus is paired with an unconditioned stimulus.

Client-centered therapy. A nondirective therapy developed by Carl Rogers, which typically is not so intensive or prolonged as psychoanalysis.

Clinical methods. Methods of collecting data in which information is obtained about people who come to physicians and psychologists for assistance with their problems.

Clinical psychology. A branch of psychology concerned with psychological methods of recognizing and treating mental disorders and problems of adjustment.

Closure. The tendency for gaps to be perceived as filled in. For example, the dotted outline of an object may be recognized almost as easily as a continued outline of it.

Cochlea. A bony cavity, coiled like a snail shell, containing receptor organs for hearing. It contains three canals: vestibular, tympanic, and cochlear.

Cochlear canal. One of the canals in the cochlea.

Coefficient of correlation. A number between +1.00 and −1.00 expressing the degree of relationship between two sets of measurements arranged in pairs. A coefficient of +1.00 (or −1.00) represents perfect correlation, and a coefficient of .00 represents no correlation at all. Symbol: r.

Color blindness. A defect that makes a person unable to tell the difference between two or more colors that most other people can easily distinguish. Total color blindness is very rare, but two-color vision occurs in one out of fifteen men. There are three kinds of color-blind: protanopes, deuteranopes, and tritanopes (*q.v.*).

Color solid. A three-dimensional diagram representing the relationships of hue, saturation, and brightness in the perception of color.

Compensation. A defense mechanism in which an individual substitutes one activity for another in an attempt to satisfy frustrated motives. It usually implies failure or loss of self-esteem in one activity and the compensation of this loss by efforts in some other realm of endeavor.

Complementary colors. Pairs of hues that, when mixed in proper portions, are seen as gray.

Compulsion. An irrational, useless act that constantly intrudes into a person's behavior; seen in psychasthenia.

Concept. The name of a class of objects or of some property that objects have in common.

Conditioning. A general term referring to the learning of some particular response. *See also* Classical conditioning.

Conditioning stimulus. The stimulus that is originally ineffective but that, after pairing with an unconditioned stimulus, evokes the conditioned response. *See also* Classical conditioning.

Conduction deafness. Deafness due to an impairment of the conduction of sounds to the cochlea.

Cone. A photosensitive receptor in the retina, shaped like a cone and most sensitive under daytime conditions of seeing. Cones are closely packed in the fovea and are the important receptors in color vision.

Conflict of motives. *See* motivational conflict.

Continuation. The tendency to perceive objects as forming a line, curve, or other continuous pattern. *See also* grouping.

Contour. The line of demarcation perceived by an observer whenever there is a marked difference between the brightness or color in one place and that in an adjoining region.

Contrast. A marked difference in stimulation, as between light and dark, silence and noise, and hot and cold; also, more specifically, the difference in brightness between an object and its immediate surround.

Control. The group or condition in an experiment that is similar in all respects to the experimental group or condition except that it does not include the experimental variable. For example, in an experiment on the effects of caffeine, the experimental group receives caffeine pills, while the control group is given a similar pill containing no caffeine.

Controlled sampling. Selecting a sample according to some plan that provides for certain numbers of people in each category according to their incidence in the population sampled.

Convergence. Turning the eyes inward toward the nose as objects are brought closer to the eyes.

Cornea. The outermost, transparent layer of the front of the eye.

Correlation. *See* Coefficient of correlation.

Cortex. A rind or covering. *See* Cerebral cortex, Cortical, Cortin.

Cortical. Pertaining to a cortex; usually refers to the cerebral cortex but can also refer to the cortex of other structures, e.g., the adrenal gland.

Cortin. A general term for the hormones secreted by the cortical part of the adrenal glands. It governs, among other things, levels of sodium and water in the internal environment.

Counseling. The giving of advice and assistance to individuals with vocational or personal problems. It often involves some psychotherapy.

Cranial nerves. The nerves serving the brain. There are twelve cranial nerves, some sensory, some motor, and some of mixed function.

Cretinism. A physical disorder caused by insufficient thyroxin in infancy and childhood. It results in dwarfism and feeble-mindedness, but it can be alleviated or cured by feeding thyroxin.

Criterion. In the evaluation of tests, the job or performance that a test is supposed to predict; in learning, the level of performance considered to represent relatively complete learning.

Critical incidents. A technique of making a job analysis by compiling instances that are critical for doing the job satisfactorily, as distinguished from those representing work that can be done by almost anybody and are not important in determining whether a job is done satisfactorily.

Cue-producing response. A response which serves as a kinesthetic stimulus for another response. It may be either an observable response or an implicit response.

Culture. The customs, habits, and traditions that characterize a people or a social group. It includes the attitudes and beliefs that the group has about important aspects of its life.

Dark adaptation. The increase in sensitivity of the eye that takes place when the eye is allowed to remain in the dark.

Deaf mute. A person who is completely deaf and consequently unable to talk. Such a person, however, ordinarily can be taught how to talk.

Decibel. The unit of measurement used to express the intensity of a sound. It is a relative measure which has meaning only when some reference level is given. It is one tenth of a bel, which is the logarithm of the ratio of two sounds having intensities of 10 to 1. The reference level ordinarily employed in hearing is 0.0002 dyne per square centimeter.

Decorticate. Lacking the cerebral cortex.

Deep senses. The kinesthetic sense, vestibular sense, and organic sense.

Defense mechanism. A reaction to frustration that defends the person against anxiety and serves to disguise his motives, so that he deceives himself about his real motives and goals. For examples, *see* Reaction formation, Displacement, Repression.

Delayed alternation. A variation on the alternation method in which a subject is required to wait for an interval between each response in a series of alternations. *See also* Alternation, Delayed reaction.

Delayed reaction. A type of experiment in which a subject is shown the correct stimulus along with incorrect stimuli but must wait for an interval before having an opportunity to make the correct choice. This kind of experiment has been used to study thinking in animals and children.

Delusion. A groundless, irrational belief or thought, usually of grandeur or of persecution. It is characteristic of paranoia.

Dependency need. The need to depend on other people for advice, counsel, and moral support.

Dependent variable. The variable that changes as a result of changes in the independent variable. For example, if the number of errors made in typing increases as the environmental temperature becomes hotter, errors in typing are the dependent variable.

Depth perception. Perception of the relative distance of objects from the observer.

Descriptive statistics. Statistical measures that summarize the characteristics of a frequency distribution or the relationship between two or more distributions. *Cf.* Interpretative statistics.

Desensitization. A method used in psychotherapy to enable a person to be comfortable in situations in which he has previously been highly anxious. It consists of having the person deliberately face anxiety-arousing situations and thereby gradually extinguish his emotional response to them.

Deuteranope. A partially color-blind person who is unable to distinguish red and green. *Cf.* Protanope.

Deviation score. The difference between the score obtained and the mean of the distribution that includes the obtained score. Symbol: x.

Differential reinforcement. Reinforcement of one stimulus but not of another. Such reinforcement is used experimentally to establish a discrimination. *See also* Discriminative learning.

Differential threshold. The smallest difference in a stimulus that can be perceived.

Directive therapy. Therapy in which the therapist prescribes remedies and courses of action much as a physician prescribes medicine. It was used extensively in the early history of psychotherapy but is not so common at present.

Discriminative learning. Learning to respond positively to one stimulus and negatively to another.

Displacement. The disguising of the goal of a motive by substituting another in place of it.

Distribution. *See* Frequency distribution.

Dominant gene. A gene whose hereditary characteristics are observable in the individual who has the gene. *Cf.* Recessive gene.

Drive. A term implying an impetus to behavior or active striving; often used synonymously with need.

Dynamic range. In sound and hearing, the total range of intensities of sound emitted by a loudspeaker or a human voice.

Educational psychology. A field of specialization concerned with psychological aspects of teaching and of formal learning processes in school.

Ego. In psychoanalysis, a term referring to the self and to ways of behaving and thinking realistically. The ego delays the satisfaction of motives, when necessary, and directs motives into socially acceptable channels.

Eidetic imagery. Extremely detailed imagery; a sort of projection of an image on a mental screen. Such imagery is more common in children than in adults and is found in some individuals more than others.

Electromagnetic radiation. A general term referring to a variety of physical changes in the environment, including light, radio waves, X rays, and cosmic rays. It travels at approximately 186,000 miles per second and can be specified in terms of either wavelength or frequency of vibrations.

Embryo. A young organism in the early stages of development. In man, it refers to the period from shortly after conception until two months later. *Cf.* Fetus.

Empirical. Founded on experiments, surveys, and proven facts, as distinguished from that which is asserted by argument, reasoning, or opinion.

Endocrine glands. Glands that secrete substances called hormones directly into the blood. The thyroid gland is an example. *Cf.* Exocrine glands.

End spurt. A tendency to give a final spurt of effort at the end of a period of work. It is a factor in the shape of the work curve.

Engineering psychology. *See* Human engineering.

Enzyme. An organic catalyst regulating particular chemical steps in metabolism.

Exhaustion. The third stage of the general adaptation syndrome, in which a person is no longer able to endure stress.

Exocrine glands. Glands that secrete through ducts into cavities of the body. The salivary glands are an example.

Experimental method. A scientific method in which conditions that are likely to affect a result are controlled by the experimenter. It involves dependent and independent variables.

Expressive disorder. A general term for any disorder, usually caused by brain damage, in which a person does not know how to do things, including talking, that were once familiar to him. *Cf.* Receptive disorder.

Extension reflex. A reflex in which a limb is straightened. *Cf.* Flexion reflex.

Extensional meaning. Meaning that can be established by pointing to objects or events; sometimes called ostensive meaning; distinguished from intentional meaning.

External auditory meatus. *See* Auditory canal.

Extinction. The procedure of presenting the conditioning stimulus without reinforcement to an organism previously conditioned; also the diminution of a conditioned response resulting from this procedure. *See also* Primary reinforcement.

Extinction curve. A graph of the diminution of previously learned responses during the course of extinction (*q.v.*).

Face validity. The appearance of validity (*q.v.*) in a test because of the similarity of the test to the job to be performed. Face validity is not, however, necessarily true validity. Tests should always be examined with validating procedures to determine whether they are, in fact, valid.

Factor analysis. A general statistical method, involving coefficients of correlation, that isolates a few common factors in a large number of tests, ratings, or other measurements.

Familial feeble-mindedness. *See* Primary feeble-mindedness.

Fantasy. Daydreaming and imagining a world of one's own, often used as a defense mechanism. Carried to the extreme, fantasy is characteristic of schizophrenia.

Fatigue. A general term referring to the effects of prolonged work or lack of sleep, probably best defined as a feeling of being tired. Fatigue, however, is often reflected in a decrement in performance.

Feeble-mindedness. A general term applying to the condition of individuals who are both mentally deficient and retarded in social and occupational skills. *See also* Mental deficiency.

Fetus. A young organism in the later stages of prenatal development. In man, it refers to the period from two months after conception until birth. *Cf.* Embryo.

Figure-ground perception. Perception of objects or events as standing out clearly from a background. For example, pictures hang *on* walls, words are *on* a page, and an automobile travels *on* a road.

Fissure. *See* Sulcus.

Flexion reflex. A reflex in which a limb is bent. *Cf.* Extension reflex.

Fluency. The amount of language or the number of words that a person can produce in any given time. It is one of the factors measured in intelligence tests.

Folkways. Conventions and habitual behavior that serve to perpetuate social values.

Forced choice. A method developed relatively recently for evaluating the effectiveness of a worker by forcing an informed judge to choose one phrase as more or less descriptive of the worker than another phrase.

Forebrain. The most forward of three divisions of the brain. In man and higher animals, it is the most highly developed part of the brain. It includes the cerebral cortex, thalamus, and hypothalamus.

Forgetting. A partial or total loss of retention of material previously learned.

Formal-discipline theory. *See* Mental-faculty theory.

Formal group. A social group that has a relatively permanent structure of positions, jobs, and roles.

Fourier analysis. The analysis of a complex tone into sine-wave components, each specified in terms of frequency and intensity.

Fovea. A central region of the retina where cones are closely packed together and visual acuity is at its best. The fovea is the part of the retina that is used when one looks directly at an object.

Fraternal twins. Twins who develop from two different fertilized eggs (ova) and who consequently may be as different in hereditary characteristics as ordinary brothers and sisters. *Cf.* Identical twins.

Free association. The technique of requiring a patient in psychotherapy to say whatever comes to his mind regardless of how irrelevant or objectionable it may seem.

Free nerve endings. Nerve endings that are not associated with any special structures. They are found in the skin, blood vessels, and many parts of the body. They are regarded as sense organs for pain and probably also for pressure.

Frequency. One of the dimensions of vibrational stimuli, such as light or sound. It is most often used with sound and is stated in number of cycles per second, which is the number of alternations in air pressure per second. It is a physical measure of a sound wave as distinguished from the psychological attribute pitch.

Frequency composition. The composition of complex tones as specified by Fourier analysis.

Frequency distribution. A set of measurements arranged from lowest to highest (or highest to lowest) and accompanied by a count (frequency) of the number of times each measurement or class of measurements occurs.

Frequency polygon. A frequency distribution represented by plotting a point on a graph for each frequency of each score, or class of scores, and connecting the points with straight lines.

Frontal association area. Part of the frontal lobe lying in front of the motor and premotor areas; also called prefrontal area. It functions in attention, planning, and expressive aspects of memory.

Frontal lobe. The part of the cerebral cortex lying in front of the central sulcus. It contains areas involved in motor functions, attention, and planning behavior.

Frustration. The thwarting of motivated behavior directed at a goal.

Frustration tolerance. Ability to tolerate frustration and its accompanying anxiety. It is characteristic of well-adjusted people and is something to be learned in achieving mental health.

Functional autonomy. The ability of certain motives to continue functioning without further reinforcement of the conditions under which they were learned. *See also* Learned goal.

Functionalism. A viewpoint taking the middle course among introspectionism, behaviorism, and gestalt psychology. Functionalists proposed that all activities serving some function, including both behavior and experience, be studied by psychologists.

Functional psychosis. A psychosis that has no known organic basis in damage or disease of the brain. *Cf.* Organic psychosis.

Fundamental. In hearing, the lowest frequency in a complex tone.

Galvanic skin response. A change in the electrical resistance of the skin, occurring in emotion and in certain other conditions.

Ganglion. A collection of the cell bodies of neurons.

General adaptation syndrome. A sequence of physiological reactions to prolonged physical or emotional stress; consists of three stages: the alarm reaction, resistance to stress, and exhaustion.

Generalization. The phenomenon of an organism's responding to all situations similar to one in which it has been conditioned, for example, giving a galvanic skin response to high-pitched tones when one has been conditioned with electric shocks to respond to low-pitched tones. *See also* Stimulus generalization.

Genes. The essential elements in the transmission of hereditary characteristics, carried in chromosomes. *See also* Dominant gene, Recessive gene.

Gestalt psychology. A viewpoint, developed by German psychologists, that considered introspectionism and behaviorism too atomistic and emphasized the importance of configuration and insight in perception.

Gland. An organ that secretes. There are two general types: endocrine and exocrine glands.

Glutamic acid. An acid believed to be concerned in metabolism of the nervous system. It has been used without success to improve intelligence.

Goal. The place, condition, or object that satisfies a motive.

Golgi tendon organs. Receptors located in tendons that are activated when the muscle to which the tendon is attached contracts, thereby putting tension on the tendon.

Gonads. The sex glands, which are the testicles in the male and the ovaries in the female. They determine secondary sex characteristics such as growth of the breasts, beginning of menstruation, growth of the beard, and change of the voice. They are also involved in sexual motivation.

Gradient. In the study of motivational conflict, the increasing strength of a goal, the nearer one is to the goal. Other things being equal, the avoidance gradient for negative goals is steeper than the approach gradient for positive goals.

Gray matter. Nervous tissue without any covering. It usually consists of cell bodies of neurons. Cf. White matter.

Grouping. The tendency to perceive objects in groups rather than as isolated elements. Grouping is determined by such factors as nearness, similarity, symmetry, and continuation of objects.

Group test. A test that may be administered to a group of people at one time.

Group therapy. A specialized technique of psychotherapy, consisting of a group of patients discussing their personal problems under the guidance of a therapist.

Growth hormone. A hormone secreted by the pituitary gland and controlling the general rate of growth of the body.

Gyrus. A ridge in the cerebral cortex of the brain. Cf. Sulcus.

Hallucination. An image that is regarded by the person as real sensory experience. Hallucinations are diagnostic of certain mental disorders such as schizophrenia.

Harmonics. Components of complex tones that are multiples of the fundamental frequency.

Hebephrenia. A state characterized by childishness and regressive behavior, seen in some cases of schizophrenia. The hebephrenic person may behave in almost every way as though he were a small child.

Hindbrain. The third of three divisions of the brain. It includes the medulla, which is a vital center for breathing, heartbeat, etc., and the cerebellum, which is a center for motor coordination. It also contains pathways passing between the spinal cord and other parts of the brain. Cf. Forebrain, Midbrain.

Histogram. A frequency distribution represented by erecting bars whose heights vary with the frequencies of the scores or classes of scores.

Homeostasis. The tendency of the body to maintain a balance among internal physiological conditions such as temperature, sugar, air, and salt.

Hormones. Secretions of endocrine glands that help or hinder certain chemical steps in the body without directly supplying the energy for them.

Hostility. See Aggression.

Hue. The aspect of a color that is determined by the dominant wavelength and that enables us to discriminate blue from red, red from yellow, and so on, as distinguished from brightness and saturation.

Human engineering. In psychological usage, the field of specialization concerned with the design of equipment and of tasks individuals perform in the operation of equipment. It is sometimes called engineering psychology.

Hunger. A drive stemming from a physiological need for food.

Hypnosis. A trancelike state resembling sleep in which a person is extremely susceptible to the suggestion of the hypnotist.

Hypochondriasis. A neurotic reaction in which a person is excessively concerned with his physical welfare or constantly complaining of minor ailments, seen in anxiety reactions.

Hypomania. A disturbance characterized by elation and excitement without any clear reason for them. See also Manic-depressive psychosis.

Hypothalamus. A region in the floor of the brain just above the throat that is part of the forebrain. It contains centers for the regulation of sleep, temperature, thirst, hunger, and emotion.

Hysteria. Neurotic behavior in which motivational conflict has been converted into physical symptoms. The hysterical person appears to have various ailments, such as headaches or paralysis, that have no physical basis.

Id. In psychoanalytic theory, the aspect of personality concerned with instinctual reactions for satisfying motives. The id seeks immediate gratification of motives with little regard for the consequences or for the realities of life.

Identical twins. Twins who develop from the same fertilized egg (ovum). They have exactly the same kinds of chromosomes and genes and hence have the same hereditary characteristics. *Cf.* Fraternal twins.

Ideological group. A group whose principal purpose is to effect some social change.

Idiot. A person with an intelligence quotient of 20 or less.

Illusion. A perception that does not agree with other, more trustworthy perceptions.

Image. A representation in the brain of sensory experience. Images are involved in thinking.

Imageless thought. Thought occurring without the presence of images. The phrase refers particularly to a theory of the nature of thinking entertained by a group of German psychologists about 1900.

Imbecile. A person with an intelligence quotient between 20 and 50.

Imitation. Copying the behavior of another.

Implicit response. A minute muscle movement ordinarily detectable only by special electrical or mechanical recording methods. Implicit responses are miniatures of large, observable movements, acquired in previous learning and involved in thinking.

Imprinting. Very rapid learning that takes place in some animals, notably birds, at a certain early stage of development.

Impulse. Sometimes used in psychoanalysis to refer to motive, but usually refers to the nervous impulse.

Incentive. A term approximately synonymous with goal, but implying the manipulation of a goal to motivate the individual. Money, for example, is used as an incentive to motivate people to work.

Incidental learning. Learning without an incentive and without reinforcement. *See also* Latent learning.

Independent variable. The variable that may be selected or changed by the experimenter and is responsible for changes in the dependent variable. For example, if errors made in typing depend on environmental temperature, temperature is the independent variable.

Individual psychograph. A profile of an individual's traits and abilities. It may be compared with a job psychograph to determine whether the individual is fitted for a particular job.

Individual test. A test that can be given to only one individual at a time, e.g., the Stanford-Binet intelligence test.

Industrial psychology. A field of specialization concerned with methods of selecting, training, counseling, and supervising personnel in business and industry. It sometimes includes problems of increasing efficiency in work and of redesigning machines to suit better the capacities of the worker. *See also* Human engineering.

Informal group. A social group having no formal or permanent structure and consisting of people who happen to be assembled together at a particular time. Sometimes, however, the members of a formal group (e.g., the employees of a company) may constitute an informal group that is different from the one prescribed by the formal structure of the organization.

Inner ear. *See* Cochlea, Vestibular sense.

Insight. In learning and problem solving, the relatively sudden solution of a problem; in psychotherapy, the understanding of one's own motives and their origins.

Insight therapy. Treatment of a personality disorder by attempting to uncover the deep causes of the patient's difficulty and to help him rid himself of his defense mechanisms. It represents an attempt to guide the patient in self-understanding of his motives and his resources for satisfying them. Sometimes it is called uncovering therapy.

Instinctive. Pertaining to complex, unlearned patterns of behavior motivated by a physiological drive.

Instinctive behavior. A complex pattern consisting of reflexes, taxes, and instinctive movements.

Institutional ways. The laws of a society used to enforce social values considered essential to the society's way of life.

Instrumental behavior. Behavior that typically accomplishes a purpose, usually the satisfaction of a need, e.g., working for a living.

Instrumental learning. Learning to make a response that is instrumental in satisfying a need. It is sometimes referred to as instrumental conditioning.

Intelligence. A general term covering a person's abilities on a wide range of tasks involving vocabulary, numbers, problem solving, concepts, and so on. As measured by a standardized intelligence test, it generally involves several specific abilities, with special emphasis on verbal abilities.

Intelligence quotient. A number obtained by dividing chronological age into mental age and multiplying by 100. This rule applies only to children; more complex methods are used to compute the intelligence quotient for teenagers and adults. Abbreviation: IQ.

Intensity. A general term referring to the amount of physical energy stimulating a sense organ. It is expressed in physical units appropriate to the kind of energy involved.

Intentional meaning. Meaning of a word derived by using other words, e.g., its dictionary meaning.

Internal environment. The environment of the nervous system, including the temperature of the body, oxygen, food supplies, minerals, hormones, and related substances that are important in the functioning of the nervous system.

Interpretative statistics. Statistical measures that permit inferences about the population from which a particular sample of measurements is drawn. *Cf.* Descriptive statistics.

Interval scale. A scale in which differences between numbers may be regarded as equal, e.g., $3 - 1 = 4 - 2$.

Introspection. A method of psychological experimentation in which a subject is presented with some stimulus, such as a colored light, and asked to give a detailed report of his sensations; seldom used at the present time.

Introspectionism. A viewpoint, held early in the twentieth century, of one group of experimental psychologists who employed the method of introspection. It regarded sensation as the important psychological element in consciousness and attempted to analyze mental content.

Inventory. A detailed questionnaire that provides specific information about a person's likes, dislikes, habits, preferences, and so on. It usually refers to a personality or interest test.

Invertebrates. In general, animals that are not vertebrates, such as worms, shellfish, insects, and other animals without segmented backbones.

Involutional melancholia. An organic psychosis, often transitory, whose chief symptoms are depression, a frivolous regression to the clothes and manners of younger days, and somewhat paranoid accusations against one's friends and even oneself. It is seen most frequently in women undergoing menopause.

IQ. *See* Intelligence quotient.

Iris. The set of muscles, controlled by the autonomic system, that varies the amount of light admitted to the eye by narrowing or enlarging the pupil. It gives the eye its distinctive color, such as blue or brown.

Job. A set of activities performed by an individual worker. Several individuals, however, may do the same kind of work and be said to have the same job. *Cf.* Position.

Job analysis. The process of finding out what constitutes a particular job. It is carried out with a variety of different methods according to the type of job being analyzed.

Job description. A statement of the significant characteristics of a job and of the worker characteristics necessary to perform the job satisfactorily.

Job evaluation. The assessment of the remuneration to be offered or paid for a particular job.

Job psychograph. A profile of the traits and abilities required in a job or a family of jobs. *Cf.* Individual psychograph.

Job specification. A detailed account of all the facts pertinent to a particular job. It should be based on information secured in a job analysis.

Kinesis. An undirected, unlearned reaction to a stimulus. *Cf.* Taxis, Tropism.

Kinesthetic receptors. Sense organs located in the muscles, tendons, and joints that convey impulses to the brain when muscles are contracted or stretched.

Knowledge of results. A person's knowledge of how he is progressing in training or in the performance of his job. It is usually necessary for the most rapid learning and for the best performance of the job.

Kymograph. A device which makes a record of movement. It may be used to measure heartbeat, body sway, breathing, finger tremor, etc.

Landolt ring. A test object used in measurements of visual acuity, consisting of a circle interrupted by a space.

Latent learning. Learning that becomes evident only when the occasion arises for using it. *See also* Incidental learning.

Lateral fissure. A crevice in the cerebral cortex dividing the temporal lobe from the frontal and parietal lobes.

Learned goal. A goal that has been acquired through learning, as distinguished from a physiological goal.

Learning. A general term referring to a relatively permanent change in behavior that is the result of past experience. It includes conditioning, instrumental learning, and perceptual learning.

Learning curve. Any graphical representation of progress in learning.

Learning set. A kind of transfer of training (*q.v.*), in which a subject becomes increasingly adept at learning problems of the same general type.

Level of aspiration. The level at which a person sets certain goals.

Level of performance. The achievement of a person as distinguished from his level of aspiration.

Lie detector. A popular name for a device designed to detect guilt. It usually involves measures of breathing, heart rate, blood pressure, and galvanic skin response.

Light. The portion of the visible spectrum (*q.v.*) of electromagnetic radiation. It may be specified by wavelength and intensity.

Light-compass reaction. An unlearned reaction in which an animal uses some source, such as the sun, as a compass for maintaining transverse orientation. The reaction is seen in bees and enables them to navigate between a food source and the hive.

Linear perspective. The perception of faraway objects as close together and of nearby objects as far apart. It is an important factor in depth perception.

Loaded words. Words having an emotional tone, used by propagandists and advertisers for creating and maintaining attitudes.

Logical thinking. Reasoning carried out according to the formal rules of logic; not very common in human thinking.

Loudness. A psychological attribute of tones, related to intensity but not directly proportional to it.

Luminosity. The perceived brightness of a visual stimulus. *See also* Luminosity curve.

Luminosity curve. A curve depicting the threshold at different wavelengths. The luminosity curve for daylight vision has its greatest sensitivity at about 555 millimicrons; the comparable curve for night vision has its greatest sensitivity at about 505 millimicrons. *See also* Cone, Rod.

Maladjustment. A broad term covering not only the psychoneuroses and psychoses but also mild disturbances in which a person is anxious or peculiar.

Mammals. The class of vertebrates that nourish their young with milk.

Manic-depressive psychosis. A psychosis characterized by extremes of mood. In the manic state, the person may be extremely active, elated, aggressive, and/or obstreperous; in the depressed state, he may feel melancholy, worthless, guilty, and hopeless.

Man-to-man rating. A method of evaluating workers by having informed judges compare individuals two at a time and rate one as better than the other. It is a specific case of the method of paired comparisons (*q.v.*).

Market research. Research consisting of surveys conducted in much the same manner as public-opinion polls but with the purpose of measuring attitudes concerning specific products, the effectiveness of advertising, and the relative preferences of consumers for different brands.

Masking. The deleterious effect of one sound on a person's ability to hear other sounds simultaneously.

Maternal behavior. Behavior concerned with giving birth to young, nursing them, and caring for them. Maternal behavior in animals presents many examples of truly instinctive behavior.

Maturation. The completion of developmental processes in the body. Maturation is governed both by heredity and by environmental conditions.

Maze. A device used in animal and human learning experiments that has blind alleys and a correct path. It presents the subject with the task of taking a path through it without entering any blind alleys.

Mean. *See* Arithmetic mean.

Mechanical-ability test. A vocational-aptitude test for predicting success in jobs requiring mechanical ability.

Median. The middle score in a frequency distribution when all scores are ranked from highest to lowest (or lowest to highest). It is one measure of central tendency.

Meissner corpuscle. A specialized structure in the skin regarded as a sense organ for pressure or touch.

Mental age. The age at which the average child passes tests equivalent in difficulty to those passed by a child to which a mental age is assigned. It is a relative measure of mental growth. For example, if a child with a chronological age of 5 does as well on an intelligence test as the average child of 7, his mental age is 7. *See also* Intelligence quotient.

Mental deficiency. The condition of individuals who have an IQ of less than 70. There are three grades of mental deficiency: morons, imbeciles, and idiots (*q.v.*).

Mental disorder. A general term referring to the more severe personality disorders, usually implying a psychosis, rather than a neurosis, though its usage is not hard and fast. It means about the same thing as mental illness.

Mental-faculty theory. The theory that formal education generally develops mental faculties so that a person is better able to solve all sorts of problems. The theory is sometimes called formal-discipline theory or the doctrine of formal discipline.

Mental health. A general term referring to personal adjustments that are satisfying and relatively free of neurotic and psychotic symptoms.

Mental hygiene. A general term, similar in meaning to mental health, which refers to the maintenance of satisfying personal adjustments.

Mental illness. *See* Mental disorder.

Metabolism. A general term referring to chemical processes in the cells of the body. It includes the assimilation of food, the storing of energy, the utilization of energy, the repairing of tissues, and the disposition of cellular wastes.

Meter. A unit of length in the metric system; 39.37 inches.

Method of rating. A method that requires a person to assign numbers on a scale, or adjectives, to indicate preferences, judgments, or opinions. *See also* Rating.

Midbrain. The middle of three divisions of the brain. It contains reflex centers for hearing and vision, pathways to and from the forebrain, and several other centers.

Middle ear. A bony cavity containing ossicles which link the eardrum to the cochlea.

Millimicron. A unit of measurement used with light and other electromagnetic radiations. It is usually abbreviated mμ. Milli- means one thousandth, and micron means one millionth of a meter.

Mode of adjustment. The characteristic way in which an individual attempts to satisfy his motives.

Mongoloid. A type of feeble-minded individual characterized by mongolian facial features; not hereditary. Mongolism is believed to be due to insufficient oxygen or to a similar condition affecting metabolism in the early stages of prenatal development.

Monocular. Pertaining to the use of only one eye. *Cf.* Binocular.

Mores. Customs that enforce social values having ethical or moral significance. Violation of mores brings strong social disapproval.

Moron. A feeble-minded person with an intelligence quotient of 50 to 70.

Motivation. A general term referring to behavior instigated by needs and directed toward goals.

Motivational conflict. A conflict between two or more motives resulting in the frustration of a motive. Most motivational conflict involves acquired motives.

Motive. A term implying a need and the direction of behavior toward a goal; often used synonymously with need or drive.

Motor area. An area of the cerebral cortex lying just in front of the central sulcus. It is concerned in the execution of skilled movements. Damage to the area, if sufficiently great, produces paralysis.

Motor neuron. A neuron conveying impulses away from the central nervous system toward a muscle or gland.

Munsell system. A system of denoting colors in steps of hue, saturation, and brightness that are equidistant in terms of ability to discriminate them.

Nationalism. A set of attitudes, held by numbers of people, that are prejudicial to foreigners and other countries. It includes a feeling that one's own country is superior in manners, morals, and way of life to other countries.

Natural observation. The observation of events as they occur in nature or in the course of human affairs without exercising experimental controls and without using methods of systematic sampling.

Need. *See* Physiological needs, Social needs.

Negative acceleration. The characteristic of a curve that is steep at its beginning but becomes increasingly flatter as it approaches its end. Learning curves are typically of this shape.

Negative transfer. Slower learning in one situation because of previous learning in another situation. It is due to incompatible responses being required in the two situations.

Nerve. A bundle of nerve fibers.

Nerve deafness. Deafness due to an impairment of the sense organs or of the nerves concerned in hearing. It is also called perception deafness or perceptual deafness.

Nerve fiber. An axon or a dendrite of a neuron. It conducts nervous impulses.

Nervous impulse. An electrical change in the membrane of a nerve fiber that is propagated along the length of the fiber. It is the basic message unit of the nervous system and obeys an all-or-none law.

Nervous system. The brain, spinal cord, and nerves serving the various sense organs, endocrine glands, and muscles of the body.

Neurasthenia. A neurotic reaction in which the person complains of general nervousness, fatigue and insomnia; often accompanied by depression, feelings of inadequacy, and inability to work.

Neuron. The cell that is the basic unit of the nervous system. It conducts nervous impulses and consists of dendrite(s), cell body, and axon.

Neurosis. *See* Psychoneurosis.

Nominal scale. A scale in which numbers are assigned to objects or persons only to distinguish those that are alike from those that are different, e.g., postal zone numbers. The numbers of a nominal scale may not be used additively.

Nondirective therapy. Psychotherapy in which the patient is dominant and given the greatest possible opportunity to express himself. The method is based on the principle that the patient must learn how to solve his own problems and cannot have them solved for him by the therapist.

Nonsense syllable. A syllable, usually of three letters, constructed so as to resemble meaningful English as little as possible. Nonsense syllables are used in learning experiments as material that is unfamiliar to the subject.

Normal curve. A bell-shaped frequency distribution, also called the normal probability curve, which is an ideal approximated by many distributions obtained in psychology and biological sciences. It can be derived mathematically from the laws of chance.

Norms. An average or standard, or a distribution of measurements, obtained from a large number of people. It permits the comparison of an individual score with the scores of comparable individuals.

Nucleus. A collection of cell bodies of neurons within the central nervous system; also a structure within the neuron containing chromosomes. Plural: nuclei.

Obsession. A foolish or groundless idea that constantly intrudes into a person's thoughts; seen in psychasthenia. *Cf.* Compulsion.

Occipital lobe. The part of the cerebral cortex lying at the back of the head. It contains the highest centers for vision.

Olfactorium. A specially designed room free of all odors except those introduced in measured quantities by an experimenter. It is used in the study of smell.

Ommatidia. Elements of the complex eye of the insect and certain other invertebrates. Each element is a complete structure capable of responding to light, even when other elements are destroyed or covered.

Open-end question. The type of question that allows a respondent to answer in his own words

Opinion. The acceptance of a statement accompanied by an attitude pro or con. It has characterstics of both attitudes and beliefs.

Optic nerve. The nerve formed by axons of the ganglion cells of the retina. It leaves the eye at the blind spot and ends in relay centers in the thalamus.

Order of skill. A type of motor ability, such as control of neck muscles, control of trunk and upper limb muscles, etc., observed in the development of infants.

Ordinal scale. A scale in which numbers are assigned to objects or persons so as to rank them in order according to some quality or magnitude, e.g., ranking students 1, 2, 3, etc., according to their grades.

Organ of Corti. The organ containing receptors for hearing, located on the basilar membrane which separates the vestibular and tympanic canals of the cochlea.

Organic psychosis. A psychosis known to be caused or aggravated by some damage or disease in the brain. *Cf.* Functional psychosis.

Organic senses. Sense organs located in the internal organs of the body, such as receptors for cold and warmth in the stomach.

Ossicles. Three bones in the middle ear, through which sound is conducted from the eardrum to the oval window of the cochlea.

Otolith organs. Sense organs found in chambers near the cochlea. They are sensitive to gravity and to the position of the head; they are part of the vestibular sense.

Oval window. The entrance to the cochlea through which sound vibrations pass from the ossicles of the middle ear to the canals of the cochlea.

Ovariectomy. Operative removal of the female ovaries, used experimentally to study the effect on behavior of a reduction in sex hormones. *Cf.* Castration.

Ovum. The cell formed in the ovary of the female which, when fertilized by the sperm of the male, may develop into a new individual. Plural: ova.

Pacinian corpuscle. A specialized structure serving as a receptor for pressure, located below the skin, in joints, and other deep parts of the body.

Paired-associate learning. Learning in which the subject must respond with one word or syllable when presented with another word or syllable.

Paired comparisons. A method of measurement in which things or people are taken two at a time and a judgment is made as to which is greater than the other, better than the other, etc.

Pancreas. An endocrine gland, located along the lower wall of the stomach, which secretes the hormone insulin. This hormone is concerned in the control of blood-sugar level.

Parallel bars. A test object used in measurements of visual acuity in place of the letters of the familiar eye chart.

Paramecium. A single-celled animal shaped like a slipper.

Paranoia. A personality disorder marked by extreme suspiciousness of the motives of others, often taking the form of elaborate beliefs that they are plotting against the person.

Parasympathetic system. A subdivision of the autonomic system that generally functions to conserve the resources of the body. It acts antagonistically to the sympathetic system.

Parathyroid glands. Two pairs of endocrine glands located on the thyroid glands of the neck. They secrete hormones concerned in the regulation of calcium and phosphorus levels in the body.

Parietal lobe. The part of the cerebral cortex lying immediately behind the central sulcus. It contains areas involved in somesthesis and somesthetic memory.

Partial reinforcement. Reinforcement of some proportion of unconditioned responses (in conditioning) or of instrumental responses (in instrumental learning).

Perception. A general term referring to the awareness of objects, qualities, or events stimulating the sense organs.

Perceptual constancy. A general term referring to the tendency of objects to be perceived in the same way despite wide variations in the manner of viewing them. For examples, see Brightness constancy, Shape constancy, Size constancy.

Peripheral nervous system. The part of the nervous system lying outside the skull and the backbone. *Cf.* Central nervous system.

Personality. The traits, modes of adjustment, and ways of behaving that characterize the individual and his relation to others in his environment.

Personality disorder. A general term referring to a neurosis or psychosis. *See also* Mental disorder.

Personality structure. In general, the unique organization of traits, motives, and ways of behaving that characterizes a particular person; in psychoanalysis, the conception of the personality in terms of id, ego, and superego.

Phase difference. The difference in pressure (negative or positive) between two tones at any particular instant. A tone coming from a person's left, for example, and heard simultaneously by the two ears, is in a different part of its cycle of vibration when it strikes the left ear than when it strikes the right ear. Consequently, there is a phase difference between the two ears.

Phenylpyruvic oligophrenia. A type of feeble-mindedness that is inherited and that is caused by a lack of an enzyme for utilizing phenylpyruvic acid, a product of brain metabolism. It is recognized by the presence of phenylpyruvic acid in the urine.

Philology. The study of the history and development of languages.

Phobia. An intense, irrational fear, usually acquired through conditioning to an unpleasant object or situation.

Phoneme. A speech sound that is distinguishable from other speech sounds used in a particular language.

Phonetics. The study of the sounds made in speech.

Physiological needs. Needs arising from some lack or deficit in the body; distinguished from acquired and social needs.

Pinna. The part of the external ear that protrudes from the head; the structure which in common parlance is called simply the ear.

Pitch. A psychological attribute of tones, related to frequency but not directly proportional to it.

Pitch scale. A curve depicting the relationship between physical frequency and perceived pitch.

Pituitary gland. A gland located beneath the hypothalamus that secretes a number of hormones which stimulate or inhibit other glands of the body. It also secretes a growth hormone that controls general rate of growth of the body.

Plateau. A flat portion in a learning curve (*q.v.*) representing a temporary slowing of progress in learning.

Play therapy. A technique for the study of personality and for the treatment of personality problems in children. It permits the child to express his conflicts in play with toys, dolls, etc.

Polarized membrane. The membrane of a nerve fiber that has an excess of positive ions on its outside and an excess of negative ions on its inside. In the passage of the nervous impulse, this polarized membrane is temporarily depolarized.

Poll question. The type of question, used in public-opinion polls, that gives the respondent a fixed number of alternatives.

Positive transfer. More rapid learning in one situation because of previous learning in another situation. It is due to a similarity of the stimuli and/or responses required in the two situations.

Posthypnotic suggestion. Suggestion made by the hypnotist while a person is in a hypnotic trance but carried out after his awakening from the trance.

Power. In psychological usage, the ability to control or influence the behavior of others; a social need.

Power structure. In social groups, the disposition of ability to control. An autocratic power structure is one in which this ability is concentrated at the top of the organization; a democratic power structure is one in which the ability resides in the collective action of its members, even if control is delegated to the leaders of the organization.

Predisposition. In the study of personal adjustment, a tendency that is inherited or has a biological basis to develop certain personality disorders. Some individuals, for example, seem to have a biological predisposition for schizophrenia.

Prefrontal areas. *See* Frontal association area.

Prefrontal lobotomy. The surgical interruption of pathways from the frontal association areas, often performed in extreme cases of mental disorder after other forms of therapy have failed. The operation, sometimes called psychosurgery, tends to allay anxiety and worry.

Prehension. The grasping of objects with the hands, the fingers, or (in the case of some monkeys) the tail.

Prejudice. Literally, a prejudgment; more generally, an emotionally toned attitude for or against an object, person, or group of persons. Typically, it is a hostile attitude that places a person or group at a disadvantage.

Premotor area. An area of the cerebral cortex lying just in front of the motor area. It is concerned with posture and the execution of skilled movements.

Prenatal. Before birth.

Prestige. The feeling of being better than other persons with whom one compares himself. The prestige need is a social need to achieve prestige. The need is frequently exploited with propaganda and social techniques.

Prestriate area. An area of the cerebral cortex lying near the primary visual area, concerned in visual memory.

Primary feeble-mindedness. Feeble-mindedness having no known organic basis. Usually it is correlated with feeble-mindedness in other members of the family and is therefore considered to have a hereditary basis. Sometimes it is called familial feeble-mindedness.

Primary reinforcement. In conditioning, the presentation of the unconditioned stimulus immediately following the conditioning stimulus; in instrumental learning, the presentation of an incentive satisfying a physiological motive immediately following the instrumental response.

Primary sensory area. An area of the cerebral cortex to which fibers transmit impulses from the receptors of a particular sense. There are primary sensory areas for each of the senses except pain, the vestibular sense, and smell.

Primates. Monkeys, man, and closely related species of animals.

Projection. The disguising of a source of conflict by ascribing one's own motives to someone else; prominent in paranoia.

Projective methods. Methods used in the study of personality, in which a subject is presented with a relatively ambiguous stimulus and asked to describe it in a meaningful way or to tell a story about it.

Prolactin. A hormone secreted by the pituitary gland. It stimulates the development of the breasts and is concerned in maternal behavior.

Propaganda. The deliberate attempt to influence attitudes and beliefs in a direction desired by the propagandist.

Protanope. A partially color-blind person who is unable to distinguish red and green and who is also weak in sensitivity to the red end of the spectrum. *Cf.* Deuteranope.

Pseudo-isochromatic plates. Plates consisting of colored dots so arranged that the color-blind person sees either no pattern at all or a different pattern of dots from the normal person. They are used as a test for color blindness.

Pseudophone. A device used in experiments on perception to reverse the reception of sound by the two ears. It carries sound normally reaching the right ear to the left ear, and vice versa.

Pseudo words. Words constructed by choosing letters at random according to the frequency with which these letters are used in language and to the probability of one particular letter following another.

Psychasthenia. An emotional disturbance characterized by irrational thoughts and/or strong compulsions (*q.v.*) to repeat seemingly meaningless acts.

Psychiatry. A branch of medicine specializing in the diagnosis and treatment of mental illness.

Psychoanalysis. Primarily a method of psychotherapy developed by Sigmund Freud, but also a theory of the development and structure of personality. As a psychotherapy, it is rather nondirective in approach and emphasizes the techniques of free association and the phenomenon of transference.

Psychodrama. A specialized technique of psychotherapy in which patients act out the roles, situations, and fantasies relevant to their personal problems. Psychodrama is usually conducted in front of a small audience of patients.

Psychograph. A profile of traits and abilities involved in the performance of a job. *See also* Individual psychograph, Job psychograph.

Psychology. The science that studies the behavior of animals and human beings.

Psychomotor test. A test involving movement and coordination; usually a vocational-aptitude test.

Psychoneurosis. A personality disorder, less severe than a psychosis, in which a person is unusually anxious, miserable, troublesome, or incapacitated in his work and relations with other people. It results from an inability to cope with frustration and anxiety.

Psychopathic deviate. An individual with a personality disorder characterized by antisocial, amoral conduct.

Psychosis. A mental or personality disorder, more severe than a psychoneurosis, characterized by bizarre, unrealistic behavior that is often so incompetent and dangerous that the person must be given custodial care.

Psychosomatic illness. A bodily disorder precipitated or aggravated by emotional disturbance.

Psychosurgery. *See* Prefrontal lobotomy.

Psychotherapy. The treatment of mental disorder and mild adjustment problems with psychological techniques.

Public-opinion poll. A method of surveying opinions on certain issues by selecting a sample of the population and interviewing personally each member of the sample.

Punctate sensitivity. In the study of the skin senses, greater sensitivity in certain spots of the skin than in others. It is a phenomenon that distinguishes four primary senses among the skin senses.

Punishment. The application of an unpleasant stimulus for the purpose of eliminating undesirable behavior.

Pupil. The aperture through which light is admitted to the eye; altered in size by the action of the iris muscles.

Purkinje effect. A change in the perception of color as the eye shifts from daylight to twilight levels of adaptation.

Quota sampling. A method of sampling in which the polling agency sets quotas for certain categories, such as age, sex, and socioeconomic status, and then permits the interviewer to select the particular individuals who satisfy the quota requirements.

R

Race. A group of human beings having common and distinctive innate physical characteristics.

Random noise. A noise consisting of a random mixture of many different frequencies that are not multiples or harmonics of each other.

Random sampling. Selecting samples of individuals, objects, or measurements solely by chance.

Range. The difference between the highest score and the lowest score in a frequency distribution. It is a measure of the variability of a distribution, but a very crude one.

Rating. A general term for the method in which a judge or observer rates the amount of aptitude, interest, ability, or other characteristic that an individual is considered to have.

Rationalization. The interpretation of one's own behavior so as to conceal the motive it expresses and to assign the behavior to some other motive.

Ratio scale. A scale in which equal ratios may be regarded as equal, e.g., $4:2 = 10:5$.

Reaction formation. The disguising of a motive so completely that it is expressed in a form that is directly opposite to its original intent.

Reality principle. In personal adjustments, the principle of setting attainable goals and of finding practicable ways of eliminating motivational conflicts and hence of satisfying motives; in psychoanalysis, a function served by the ego.

Reasoning. Thinking in which one attempts to solve a problem by combining two or more elements from past experience.

Recall. A method of measuring retention, in which the subject must reproduce with a minimum of cues something that he has previously learned.

Receptive disorder. A general term for a disorder, usually caused by brain damage, in which a person cannot recognize or remember the meaning of sensory stimuli, such as words or familiar objects. *Cf.* Expressive disorder.

Receptive field. The area from which a neuron receives impulses. Because many sensory neurons often make synapse with a single association neuron, the latter may have a relatively large field from which it receives impulses.

Recessive gene. A gene whose hereditary characteristics are not expressed when it is paired with a dominant gene.

Recognition. A method of measuring retention in which the subject is required only to recognize the correct answer when it is presented to him along with incorrect answers, e.g., in a true-false or multiple-choice examination.

Recollection. A general term meaning about the same thing as recall, i.e., remembering past events and their related circumstances.

Recurrent nervous circuit. An endless loop made by the synapses of neurons, permitting nervous impulses to circle back to the point from which they originate.

Reflex. A relatively rapid and consistent unlearned response to a stimulus. It is ordinarily not conscious or subject to voluntary control.

Reflex reserve. The total number of learned responses that can be expected to occur during a prolonged extinction.

Refractory period. A brief period during and after the discharge of a nervous impulse when unusually strong stimuli are required to evoke another impulse.

Regression. A retreat to earlier or more primitive forms of behavior, frequently encountered in children and adults faced with frustration.

Regulatory behavior. Behavior that aids in maintaining a homeostatic balance by leading to the satisfaction of physiological needs.

Reinforcement. *See* Primary reinforcement, Secondary reinforcement.

Release therapy. Similar to play therapy, but useful with older children and adults. It may consist of finger painting, games, or other unstructured activities. Its general purpose is to permit the expression of deep-seated motivational conflicts.

Releasers. Stimulus situations that trigger instinctive (*q.v.*) movements.

Reliability. The self-consistency of a method of measurement, or the degree to which separate, independent measurements of the same thing agree with each other. Reliability is usually expressed by a coefficient of correlation representing the relationship between two sets of measurements of the same thing.

Representative sampling. Sampling so as to obtain a fair cross section of a population without introducing biases that make the sample unrepresentative of the population.

Repression. A psychological process in which memories and motives are not permitted to enter consciousness but are operative at an unconscious level. Repression is one of several reactions to frustration and anxiety. It serves as a means of altering conscious motives and goals.

Resistance. A phenomenon observed in psychotherapy, exhibited as an inability to remember important events in one's past or to talk about certain anxiety-charged subjects. Resistance may be indicated by a blocking of free associations or by a person's steering away from certain subjects during free association.

Resistance to stress. The second stage of the general adaptation syndrome in which a person endures stress without showing any observable impairment.

Resting potential. An electrical difference, found in the inactive nerve fiber, between the outside and the inside of the polarized membrane. It is temporarily abolished during the passage of a nervous impulse.

Retention. The amount correctly remembered. The principal methods of measuring retention are savings, recognition, and recall.

Retina. The photosensitive layer of the eye on which images of objects are projected. It contains receptors known as rods and cones, and nerve cells that convey impulses to the brain.

Retinal disparity. A slight difference in the images of an object projected on the retinas of the two eyes. It arises from the fact that the two eyes view the object from slightly different angles.

Retroactive inhibition. The harmful effect of learning or activity on the retention of previous learning. Such inhibition is a special case of negative transfer, and it is the most important factor in forgetting.

Rod. A photosensitive receptor in the retina, long and cylindrical like a rod, and most sensitive in nighttime conditions of seeing. It is probably not involved in color vision.

Role. A pattern of behavior that a person in a particular social status is expected to exhibit.

Rotary pursuitmeter. A device used in human learning experiments that requires the subject to keep a stylus on a moving spot while the spot rotates on a circular platform.

Rotation nystagmus. Movement of the eyes, slowly in one direction and quickly in the other, caused by rotation of the head.

Sampling. The process of selecting a set of individuals or measurements from a large population of possible individuals or measurements. Almost all frequency distributions in psychology are samples. *See also* Controlled sampling, Random sampling, Representative sampling, Quota sampling.

Saturation. A dimension of color that refers to the amount or richness of a hue, as distinguished from brightness or hue. A red, for example, that is barely distinguishable from a gray is low in saturation.

Savings. A method of measuring retention in which the subject learns again what he previously learned. Savings are measured by the difference between the number of trials or errors originally required to learn and the number required in relearning.

Scale of measurement. In general, a set of numbers assigned to some aspect of objects or events according to some rule. The term is also used in a more limited sense to refer to a well-standardized test, such as the Wechsler-Bellevue Intelligence Scale.

Scale value. In the measurement of attitudes, a number assigned to a statement representing the degree to which approval or disapproval of the statement indicates a favorable or unfavorable attitude toward the subject of the statement.

Scapegoating. The displacement of aggression to a convenient group or class. It is a defense mechanism that operates as a prejudice against racial, religious, or other groups.

Schizophrenia. One of the psychoses, characterized by fantasy, regression, hallucinations, delusions, and general withdrawal from contact with the person's environment.

Scholastic aptitude. Ability to succeed in some specified type of formal schooling. For example, college aptitude refers to aptitude for doing college work.

Sclerotic coat. The white outermost coat of the eyeball. It gives way in the front of the eye to the transparent cornea.

Secondary feeble-mindedness. Feeble-mindedness due to birth injury, to disease, or to damage in the brain.

Secondary reinforcement. The reinforcing effect of a stimulus that has been paired with a primary reinforcement.

Security. The feeling of being safe against loss of status, friends, loved ones, income, etc. The need to feel secure is an important social need.

Self-selection. Selection of specific foods when offered in a cafeteria-feeding situation.

Semantics. The study of the meaning of words and sounds.

Semicircular canals. Three canals found near the cochlea in each ear. They are sensitive to rotation and to changes in the position of the head; they are part of the vestibular sense.

Senile psychosis. An organic psychosis that tends to appear in some individuals with advancing age; characterized by defects of memory, general disorientation, and delusions. *See also* Alcoholic psychosis.

Sensitization. A phenomenon similar to learning in which a response is facilitated by an intense or unpleasant stimulus. For example, an animal that has become habituated to a loud sound may again show fright if the sound is preceded by an electric shock.

Sensory area. An area of the brain concerned in sensory functions. It is usually an area of the cerebral cortex. *See also* Primary sensory area.

Sensory neuron. A neuron that conveys nervous impulses away from sense organs into the central nervous system. It usually has its cell body in a ganglion just outside the central nervous system.

Set. A readiness to react in a certain way when confronted with a problem or stimulus situation.

Sex differences. Differences between men and women in interests, abilities, etc.

Sex hormones. Hormones secreted by the gonads and responsible for secondary sex characteristics such as the male's beard and the female's breasts. They are involved in sexual motivation.

Sex-linked characteristic. A hereditary characteristic controlled by a gene carried on the chromosome that determines sex. For an example, *see* Color blindness.

Shape constancy. The tendency to perceive the "true" shape of an object even when the image on the retina is distorted. For example, a circle is seen as a circle even when viewed at an acute angle.

Sine wave. The simplest kind of sound wave, generated by a vibrating object moving back and forth freely like a pendulum.

Situational therapy. The treatment of a personality problem by changing the person's situation—his work, his way of life, or his relationships with family and associates.

Situation test. A test in which a person is observed in some real-life situation, e.g., in managing a group of men in the building of a small bridge.

Size constancy. The tendency to perceive the size of familiar objects as constant even when viewed at a distance that makes the image of them on the retina very small. For example, a man 100 feet away is perceived as being as large as the same man nearby.

Skewness. The degree to which a frequency distribution departs from a symmetrical shape. The curve of a distribution that has its longer tail on the right is said to be skewed to the right.

Skin senses. The senses of pain, warmth, cold, and pressure located in the skin.

Sleep center. A center in the hypothalamus whose destruction results in chronic insomnia. Animals in which the sleep center has been destroyed stay awake until they die of exhaustion.

Smell prism. A three-dimensional diagram representing six primary odors and their mixture.

Smooth muscle. Muscle that under the microscope exhibits no stripes. It is found in blood vessels, intestines, and certain other organs. *Cf.* Striped muscle.

Social attitude. An attitude held in common with a number of other persons as distinguished from personal attitudes, which may be unique to a single individual.

Social class. A grouping of people on a scale of prestige in a society according to their social status. It is determined by many factors such as nature of occupation, kind of income, moral standing, family genealogy, social relationships and organizations, and area of residence.

Social facilitation. Increased motivation and effort arising from the stimulus provided by other people.

Social group. Any group of people, formal or informal, assembled or dispersed, who are related to each other by some common interest or attachment. When a social group is defined in a more limited sense as people in a face-to-face relationship, other dispersed groups such as unions are defined as social organizations or institutions.

Social institution. A collection of objects, customary methods of behavior, and techniques of enforcing such behavior on individuals, e.g., a union, an army, or a political party.

Socialization. Learning to behave in a manner prescribed by one's family and culture and to adjust in relationships with other people.

Social maturity. The degree of development of social and vocational abilities. It may be measured by the Vineland Social Maturity Scale, from which a social-maturity quotient can be computed in much the same way as an intelligence quotient is obtained.

Social needs. Needs, usually learned, that require the presence or reaction of other people for their satisfaction. *See also* Affiliative needs, Status needs.

Social psychology. A field of specialization concerned with attitudes, beliefs, and psychological factors in group behavior.

Social structure. A general term referring to the fact that each society typically assigns ranks to its members, expects them to do certain kinds of work and to have certain attitudes and beliefs.

Social technique. Behavior that makes use of other people to achieve satisfaction of a need.

Social value. A learned goal involving one's relationship to society and other people.

Social worker. A person with advanced training in sociology, abnormal psychology, and social science, who investigates the family and social background of persons with personality problems and who assists the psychotherapist by maintaining contact with a patient and his family. The social worker is often a member of a psychiatric team, consisting also of psychiatrists and clinical psychologists.

Society. A group of individuals, as large as several countries or as small as a portion of a community, that have a distinguishable culture.

Sociogram. A diagram showing preferences and aversions among members of a group; a way of depicting the structure of an informal group.

Sociometric test. A set of ratings made by members of a group, from which a sociogram may be constructed.

Sodium Amytal. A drug that, given in light doses, tends to make a person talk more freely. It is sometimes used as a "truth drug" and as a means, in psychotherapy, of making withdrawn patients temporarily more communicative.

Somatic system. The part of the nervous system serving the sense organs and the skeletal muscles.

Somesthesis. The senses of the skin and of kinesthesis.

Somnolence. A tendency to sleep all the time.

Sound pressure level. The intensity of a tone expressed in decibels (*q.v.*) above a reference level.

Sound wave. Alternating increases and decreases in pressure propagated through a medium, usually air. It may be regarded as a vibration having a certain frequency (or its inverse, wavelength) and a certain intensity.

Spaying. *See* Ovariectomy.

Specific hunger. A hunger for a specific kind of food. *See also* Cafeteria feeding.

Sphincter. Smooth muscle whose action controls elimination from such organs as the stomach, bladder, and bowels.

Spinal cord. The part of the nervous system encased in the backbone. It is a reflex center and a pathway for impulses to and from the brain.

Standard deviation. A precise measure of the variability of a frequency distribution, computed by squaring the deviation of each score from the arithmetic mean, summing the resulting squares, dividing by the number of scores, and finally taking the square root of the resulting quantity. In other words, it is the root-mean-square of the deviations from the mean. Its symbol is the Greek letter σ.

Standard score. In the strict sense, a score equivalent to a z score, but often a score obtained by multiplying a z score by an arbitrary constant (e.g., 10 or 20) and adding the result to an arbitrary mean (e.g., 50 or 100). It permits a direct comparison with scores made by a standardization group.

Standardization. The establishment of uniform conditions for administering a test and uniform methods of interpreting test results. A large number of individuals is tested in the same way to provide norms with which to compare any particular test score.

Standardization group. The group of people on which a test is standardized. To interpret individual scores on a test, one should know the characteristics of the standardization group.

Startle pattern. An extremely rapid reaction to a sudden, unexpected stimulus (e.g., a gunshot), relatively consistent from person to person. It consists in part of a closing of the eyes, a widening of the mouth, and a thrusting forward of the head and neck.

Static senses. The part of the vestibular senses responding to gravity and to position of the head.

Status. In motivation, a social motive; in a social structure, a position representing differences that are important in the exchange of goods and services and in the satisfaction of needs in a society. *See also* Role.

Status needs. Needs to achieve a status with respect to other people in a group. They include more specific needs, such as needs for prestige, power, and security.

Stereotype. A fixed set of beliefs that is greatly oversimplified and held generally by members of a group.

Stimulus. Any energy or energy change in the physical environment that excites a sense organ.

Stimulus generalization. The tendency to react to stimuli that are different from, but somewhat similar to, the stimulus used as a conditioning stimulus.

Striped muscle. Muscle that, under the microscope, appears to be striped. It is found in the muscles of the skeleton, such as those that move the trunk and limbs. *Cf.* Smooth muscle.

Subcortical centers. Centers of the brain below the cerebral cortex.

Subitizing. Perceiving at a glance the number of objects present. Many animals and people can subitize objects up to approximately seven.

Sublimation. The use of a substitute activity to gratify a frustrated motive. Freud believed, for example, that a frustrated sex drive could be partially gratified by channeling it into art, religion, music, or aesthetic activity.

Subvocal speech. Talking that is inaudible to others, but sufficiently stimulating (kinesthetically) to oneself to permit an internal conversation. It is one kind of implicit response involved in thinking.

Suggestion. The uncritical acceptance of an idea. Suggestion is used in psychotherapy to effect temporary relief of neurotic symptoms, particularly hysterical symptoms. It is also used generally by propagandists and advertisers to change or maintain attitudes and beliefs.

Sulcus. A crevice in the cerebral cortex; sometimes called a fissure.

Superego. In psychoanalytic theory, that which restrains the activity of the ego and the id. The superego corresponds closely to what is commonly called conscience; it keeps a person working toward ideals acquired in childhood.

Superstition. A belief concerning natural phenomena that is widely held by members of a group or society but is demonstrably false.

Supportive therapy. Treatment of a personality problem by listening to a person's problems, suggesting courses of action, and reassuring him about what he has done or proposes to do. Such therapy may be effective in mild or temporary disturbances.

Survey methods. Methods of collecting data by sampling a cross section of people, e.g., questioning a large number of married couples about factors in marital happiness, or conducting a public-opinion poll; distinguished from experimental methods.

Symbol. That which suggests something else by reason of relationship, association, convention, etc. A symbol may be an external stimulus (e.g., a traffic signal), or it may be an internal process (e.g., images involved in thinking).

Symbolic process. Same as representative process; a process within the individual representing previous experience. It is the essential process in thinking.

Sympathetic system. A subdivision of the autonomic system most concerned in emotional states. It mobilizes the body for action and acts antagonistically to the parasympathetic system.

Synapse. The juncture of two neurons. It is not a direct connection, but rather a place where the fibers of the two neurons come into close proximity with one another.

Syndrome. A pattern of personality characteristics and its underlying causes in the life history of the person.

Tabes dorsalis. One type of syphilitic infection of the central nervous system, principally of the spinal cord, in which pathways of the kinesthetic senses degenerate.

Taboos. The do's and don't's of a particular society, strongly inculcated into most members of that society.

Taxis. An unlearned, directed reaction to a stimulus in which the animal moves toward or away from the stimulus. *Cf.* Kinesis, Tropism.

Temperament. The aspect of personality pertaining to mood, activity, general level of energy, interest in food, exercise, and intellectual activities.

Temporal lobe. The part of the cerebral cortex lying on the side of the head beneath the lateral fissure. It contains centers for hearing, speech perception, and related memories.

Temporal maze. A maze so constructed that the subject keeps returning to the same choice point but must turn left or right each time according to some sequence established by the experimenter. Such a maze has been used in conjunction with the alternation method, in which a sequence of simple or double alternation (*q.v.*) is required.

Test. A sample of the performance of a person on a task or set of tasks.

Thalamus. An area in the forebrain concerned with relaying nervous impulses to the cerebral cortex.

Theory. In science, a principle or set of principles that explains a number of facts and predicts future events and outcomes of experiments.

Therapy. The treatment of an illness. *See also* Psychotherapy.

Thiamin. Vitamin B_1. It is concerned in the utilization of sugars by the brain.

Thinking. Processes that are representative of previous experience; consisting of images, minute muscle movements, and other activities in the central nervous system. *See also* Image, Implicit response.

Thirst. A drive stemming from a physiological need for water.

Thought experiment. A type of experiment employed by early experimental psychologists in an attempt to discover the nature of thought. *See also* imageless thought.

Threshold. The smallest amount of a stimulus, or the smallest difference in a stimulus, that can be detected or that can elicit a response. *See also* Absolute threshold, Differential threshold.

Thyroid gland. An endocrine gland in the neck, which produces the hormone thyroxin.

Thyroxin. The hormone secreted by the thyroid gland. It controls the general rate at which energy is produced in the body; it is a regulator of metabolism.

Timbre. The tonal quality that enables us to distinguish different musical instruments and voices having the same fundamental frequency. It is determined by the frequencies comprising a sound, especially the harmonics.

Tonotopic organization. A topographical arrangement of auditory areas of the brain corresponding to different parts of the cochlea and consequently to different frequencies of stimulation.

Topographical arrangement. A spatial arrangement of the nervous system that corresponds to a similar arrangement of the sense organs or of the muscles of the body. Cortical areas for the various senses and for motor functions are topographically arranged.

Trade test. An achievement test that measures a person's knowledge of important elements in his trade.

Trait. An aspect of personality that is reasonably characteristic of a person and distinguishes him from many other people.

Transfer of training. More rapid learning in one situation because of previous learning in another situation (positive transfer, *q.v.*); or slower learning in one situation because of previous learning in another situation (negative transfer, *q.v.*). *See also* Stimulus generalization.

Transference. In psychotherapy and especially psychoanalysis, the reenactment of previous relationships with people and principally of the parent-child relationship. In psychoanalysis, the therapist becomes the object of transference; the transference aids in the analysis because it permits the patient to express toward the therapist attitudes and feelings he has held toward other people.

Trial and error. A phrase describing attempts to learn, or to solve a problem, by trying alternative possibilities and eliminating those that prove to be incorrect. Such behavior is characteristic of instrumental learning and is involved in some thinking.

Tritanope. A partially color-blind person who appears to be unable to see blue.

Tropism. An unlearned bending or turning movement in which the organism does not move from place to place. *Cf.* Kinesis, Taxis.

Tympanic membrane. Another name for eardrum.

Type. A class of individuals alleged to have a particular trait; but a concept not accepted as valid by psychologists because individuals cannot be grouped together into a few discrete classes.

Type-token ratio. The ratio of the number of different words a person uses to the total number of words in a sample of his speech or writing. It is one index of verbal diversification.

Unconscious motivation. Motivation that can be discerned in a person's behavior but that he cannot report and does not perceive.

Unconscious processes. Psychological processes or events of which a person is unaware.

Valence. A term proposed by Lewin to refer to the attraction or repulsion of a goal. It is indicated by a plus or minus sign. Goals with negative valences are those a person fears or tries to avoid; those with positive valences are those he seeks to attain.

Validity. The extent to which a method of measurement measures what it is supposed to measure. Validity is expressed in terms of a coefficient of correlation representing the relationship of a set of measurements to some criterion.

Value. A learned goal.

Variable. One of the conditions measured in an experiment. *See also* Dependent variable, Independent variable.

Vector. A term proposed by Lewin, for use in psychology analogous to its use in physics, meaning the resultant of motivational forces when a person is attracted and/or repelled by different goals.

Verb-adjective ratio. The ratio of the number of verbs used to the number of adjectives used in a sample of speech or writing. It varies with conditions of measurements and with personality characteristics. It is one index of verbal diversification.

Verbal diversification. The degree to which different words and different constructions of words are employed in a person's language.

Vertebrates. Animals with segmented backbones. The group includes fishes, amphibia, reptiles, birds, and mammals.

Vestibular sense. The sense of balance and movement, consisting of two groups of sense organs: the semicircular canals and the otolith organs.

Visible spectrum. Those electromagnetic radiations that are visible, extending from less than 400 to nearly 800 millimicrons.

Visual acuity. Ability to discriminate fine differences in visual detail. It may be measured with the physician's eye chart or by more precise tests, such as the Landolt ring or parallel bars.

Vitamin. A substance essential to metabolism but not manufactured in the body, so that it must be obtained in food.

Vocabulary. A general and somewhat vague term referring to the words a person knows. However, the words he can recognize are more numerous than those he uses; and those he uses in writing are more numerous than those he uses in everyday speech. Hence, size of vocabulary varies greatly with the circumstances under which it is measured.

Vocational aptitude. Aptitude for learning a specified vocation. For example, clerical aptitude is the ability to learn a clerical vocation.

Waking center. A center in the hypothalamus whose destruction results in somnolence. *Cf.* Sleep center.

Warming up. The tendency for the work curve to rise at the beginning of a period of work; opposite in effect to the beginning spurt. It is a factor in the shape of the work curve.

White matter. Nerve fibers covered with a white sheath. The peripheral part of the spinal cord is white matter; so are several different regions of the brain. Its presence indicates tracts of nerve fibers, as distinguished from cell bodies. *Cf.* Gray matter.

Work curve. A line representing some measure of work for some given period of time.

Worker characteristics. The physical and psychological characteristics required of a person in a particular job. They are best stated in terms of the proportion of the population having the required degree of the characteristic.

Work-sample performance test. A test consisting of a sample of the work for which a person is being evaluated.

z score. A score obtained by dividing the standard deviation into the deviation of an obtained score from the mean of the frequency distribution. It is convenient for the comparison of scores without regard to the units of measurement employed.

NAME INDEX

SUBJECT INDEX